ONE T...

Bilingual ...

English-Arabic
Arabic-English
Dictionary

Compiled by
Rania-al-Qass

STAR Foreign Language BOOKS

© Publishers

ISBN : 978 1 908357 72 4

First Edition	:	2011
Second	:	2013
Third Edition	:	2015
Fourth Edition	:	2017
Fifth Edition	:	2018

Published by

STAR Foreign Language BOOKS

a unit of
ibs BOOKS (UK)
56, Langland Crescent
Stanmore HA7 1NG, U.K.
info@starbooksuk.com
www.starbooksuk.com

Printed in India at
Star Print-O-Bind, New Delhi-110 020

About this Dictionary.

Developments in science and technology today have narrowed down distances between countries, and have made the world a small place. A person living thousands of miles away can learn and understand the culture and lifestyle of another country with ease and without travelling to that country. Languages play an important role as facilitators of communication in this respect.

To promote such an understanding, **STAR Foreign Language BOOKS** has planned to bring out a series of bilingual dictionaries in which important English words have been translated into other languages, with Roman transliteration in case of languages that have different scripts. This is a humble attempt to bring people of the word closer through the medium of language, thus making communication easy and convenient.

Under this series of *one-to-one dictionaries*, we have published over 35 languages, the list of which has been given in the opening pages. These have all been compiled and edited by teachers and scholars of the relative languages.

Publishers.

Bilingual Dictionaries in this Series

English-Afrikaans / Afrikaans-English	Abraham Venter
English-Albanian / Albanian-English	Theodhora Blushi
English-Amharic / Amharic-English	Girun Asanke
English-Arabic / Arabic-English	Rania-al-Qass
English-Bengali / Bengali-English	Amit Majumdar
English-Bosnian / Bosnian-English	Boris Kazanegra
English-Bulgarian / Bulgarian-English	Vladka Kocheshkova
English-Cantonese / Cantonese-English	Nisa Yang
English-Chinese (Mandarin) / Chinese (Mandarin)-Eng	Y. Shang & R. Yao
English-Croatian / Croatain-English	Vesna Kazanegra
English-Czech / Czech-English	Jindriska Poulova
English-Dari / Dari-English	Amir Khan
English-Dutch / Dutch-English	Lisanne Vogel
English-Estonian / Estonian-English	Lana Haleta
English-Farsi / Farsi-English	Maryam Zaman Khani
English-French / French-English	Aurélie Colin
English-Gujarati / Gujarati-English	Sujata Basaria
English-German / German-English	Bicskei Hedwig
English-Greek / Greek-English	Lina Stergiou
English-Hindi / Hindi-English	Sudhakar Chaturvedi
English-Hungarian / Hungarian-English	Lucy Mallows
English-Italian / Italian-English	Eni Lamllari
English-Korean / Korean-English	Mihee Song
English-Latvian / Latvian-English	Julija Baranovska
English-Levantine Arabic / Levantine Arabic-English	Ayman Khalaf
English-Lithuanian / Lithuanian-English	Regina Kazakeviciute
English-Nepali / Nepali-English	Anil Mandal
English-Norwegian / Norwegian-English	Samuele Narcisi
English-Pashto / Pashto-English	Amir Khan
English-Polish / Polish-English	Magdalena Herok
English-Portuguese / Portuguese-English	Dina Teresa
English-Punjabi / Punjabi-English	Teja Singh Chatwal
English-Romanian / Romanian-English	Georgeta Laura Dutulescu
English-Russian / Russian-English	Katerina Volobuyeva
English-Serbian / Serbian-English	Vesna Kazanegra
English-Sinhalese / Sinhalese-English	Naseer Salahudeen
English-Slovak / Slovak-English	Zuzana Horvathova
English-Slovenian / Slovenian-English	Tanja Turk
English-Somali / Somali-English	Ali Mohamud Omer
English-Spanish / Spanish-English	Cristina Rodriguez
English-Swedish / Swedish-English	Madelene Axelsson
English-Tagalog / Tagalog-English	Jefferson Bantayan
English-Tamil / Tamil-English	Sandhya Mahadevan
English-Thai / Thai-English	Suwan Kaewkongpan
English-Turkish / Turkish-English	Nagme Yazgin
English-Ukrainian / Ukrainian-English	Katerina Volobuyeva
English-Urdu / Urdu-English	S. A. Rahman
English-Vietnamese / Vietnamese-English	Hoa Hoang
English-Yoruba / Yoruba-English	O. A. Temitope

More languages in print

STAR Foreign Language BOOKS

ENGLISH-ARABIC

A

aback *adv.* متراجع mutaraaji'

abaction *n.* سرقةالماشية sariqat almashiyah

abactor *n.* سارقالماشية sariq almashiyah

abandon *v.* يتخلى yatakhalla

abase *v.* يحتقر yahtaqir

abasement *n.* إحتقار ehtiqaar

abash *v.* خجّل khajjala

abate *v.* يتراجع yataraaja'

abatement *n.* تراجع taraajo'

abbey *n.* دير dayr

abbreviate *v.* يختصر yakhtasir

abbreviation *n.* اختصار ekhtisaar

abdicate *v.t,* يعتزل ya'tazil

abdication *n.* إعتزال e'tizaal

abdomen *n.* بطن batn

abdominal *adj.* بطني batniy

abduct *v.* يختطف yakhtatif

abduction *n.* اختطاف ekhtitaaf

aberrance *n.* انحراف enhiraaf

abet *v.* يحث yahoth

abetment *n.* حث hath

abeyance *n.* تعليق ta'leeq

abeyant *adj.* معلّق mo'allaq

abhor *v.* يمقت yamqot

abhorrence *n.* مقت maqt

abide *v.* يلتزم yaltazim

abiding *adj.* إلتزام eltizaam

ability *n.* مقدرة maqdirah

abject *adj.* يائس yaauis

ablaze *adv.* يشتعل yashta'il

ablactate *v.* يفطم yaftim

ablactation *n.* فطم fatm

able *adj.* قادر qaadir

ablepsy *n.* عمى ama

ablush *adv.* محمر mohmar

ablution *n.* وضوء wodoou

abnegate *v.* ينكر yankor

abnegation *n.* نكرانالذات nokraano dhdhaat

abnormal *adj.* غيرعادي ghayr 'aadiy

aboard *adv.* علىمتن ala matn

abode *n.* مسكن maskan

abolish *v.* يبطل yobtil

abolition *v.* إلغاء elghaau

abominable *adj.* بغيض bagheed

aboriginal *adj.* أصلي asliy

aborigines *n.* pl مواطنونأصليون mowaatinoon asliyyoon

abort *v.* يحبط yohbit

abortion *n.* إجهاض ejhaad

abortive *adv.* فاشل faashil

abound *v.* يزدهر yazdahir

about *adv.* موجود mawjood

about *prep.* عن an

above *adv.* أعلى a'laa

above *prep.* فوق fawq

abreast *adv.* بجانب bijaanib

abridge *v.* يختصر yakhtasir

abridgement *n.* إختصار ekhtisaar

abroad *adv.* فيالخارج fil khaarij

abrogate *v.* يلغي yalghi

abrupt *adj.* مفاجئ mofaajiu

abruption *n.* إنفصالمفاجئ enfisaal

abscess *n.* ملتهب moltahib

absonant *adj.* غير طبيعي ghayr tabee'iy

abscond *v.* يهرب yahrob

absence *n.* غياب ghiyaab

absent *adj.* غائب ghaauib

absent *v.* يستغيب yastagheeb

absolute *adj.* مطلق motlaq

absolutely *adv.* إطلاقاً etlaaqan

absolve *v.* يعفي ya'fee

absorb *v.* يمتص yamtas

abstain *v.* يمتنع yamna'

abstract *adj.* تجريدي tajreediy

abstract *n.* ملخص molakhas

abstract *v.* يستخلص yastakhlis

abstraction *n.* 1 تجريد tajreed

abstraction *n.* 2 إستخلاص estikhlaas

absurd *adj.* سخيف sakheef

absurdity *n.* سخف sokhf

abundance *n.* وفرة wafra

abundant *adj.* فائض faauid

abuse *v.* يعتدي ya'tadi

abuse *n.* إعتداء e'tidaau

abusive *adj.* مسيء moseeu

abut *v.* يرافق yoraafiq

abutment *n.* دعم da'm

abyss *n.* هاوية haawiyah

academic *adj.* أكاديمي akaadeemiy

academy *n.* أكاديمية akaadeemiyah

acarpous *adj.* غير مثمر ghayr mothmir

accede *v.* يقبل yaqbal

accelerate *v.* يتسارع yatasaara'

acceleration *n.* تسارع tasaaro'

accent *n.* لهجة lahjah

accent *v.* يبرز yabroz

accept *v.* يقبل yaqbal

acceptable *adj.* مقبول maqbool

acceptance *n.* قبول qobool

access *n.* مدخل madkhal

accession *n.* معاهدة mo'aahadah

accessory *n.* ملحق molhaq

accident *n.* حادث haadith

accidental *adj.* عرضي aradiy

accipitral *adj.* جارح jaarih

acclaim *v.* يمدح yamdah

acclaim *n.* استقبال حميم estiqbaal hameem

acclamation *n.* 1 تزكية tazkiyah

acclamation *n.* 2 مديح madeeh

acclimatise *v.* يتأقلم yatauaqlam

accommodate *v.* 1 يأوي yauwi

accommodate *v.* 2 يستوعب yastaw'ib

accommodation *n.* إقامة eqaamah

accompaniment *n.* مرافقة moraafaqah

accompany *v.* يرافق yoraafiq

accomplice *n.* مرافق في الجريمة moraafiq fil jareemah

accomplish *v.* ينجز yonjiz

accomplished *adj.* منجز monjaz

accomplishment *n.* إنجاز enjaaz

accord *v.* يعهد إليه ya'hado elayhi

accord *n.* معاهدة mo'aahadah

accordingly *adv.* بناءً عليه binaauan 'alayhi

account *n.* حساب hisaab

account *v.* يحسب yahsib

accountable *adj.* مسؤول masuool

accountancy *n.* محاسبة mohaasabah

accountant *n.* محاسب mohaasib

accredit *v.* يمنح yamnah

accrementition *n.* تجدّدالخلايا tajaddod ual khalaaya

accrete *v.* يكبر yakbor

accrue *v.* يزيد yazeed

accumulate *v.* يتراكم yataraakam

accumulation *n.* تراكم taraakom

accuracy *n.* دقّة diqqah

accurate *adj.* دقيق daqeeq

accursed *adj.* ملعون mal'oon

accusation *n.* إتهام ettihaam

accuse *v.* يتّهم yattahim

accused *n.* متهم mottaham

accustom *v.* يتعوّد yata'awwad

accustomed *adj.* متعوّد mota'awwid

ace *n.* محترف mohtarif

acentric *adj.* بلامركز bila markiz

acephalous *adj.* بلازعيم bila za'eem

acephalus *n.* بلازعامة bila za'aamah

acetify *v.* يخلّل yokhallil

ache *n.* ألم ualam

ache *v.* يؤلم youlim

achieve *v.* ينجز yonjiz

achievement *n.* إنجاز enjaaz

achromatic *adj.* بلالون bila lawn

acid *adj.* حمضي himdiy

acid *n.* حامض haamid

acidity *n.* حموضة homoodah

acknowledge *v.* يعترف ya'tarif

acknowledgement *n.* اعتراف e'tiraaf

acne *n.* حبّشباب hab shabaab

acorn *n.* بلوط balloot

acoustic *adj.* صوتي sawtiy

acoustics *n.* صوتيّات sawtiyyaat

acquaint *v.* يعرّف yo'arrif

acquaintance *n.* زميل zameel

acquest *n.* ممتلكات momtalakaat

acquiesce *v.* يتقبّل yataqabbal

acquiescence *n.* تقبّل taqabbol

acquire *v.* يكتسب yaktasib

acquirement *n.* إكتساب ektisaab

acquisition *n.* إكتساب ektisaab

acquit *v.* يبرئ yobarriu

acquittal *n.* تبرئة tabriua

acre *n.* فدان faddaan

acreage *n.* مساحة masaahah

acrimony *n.* حدّة hiddah

acrobat *n.* بهلوان bahlawaan

across *adv.* بالعرض bil'ard

across *prep.* عبر abr

act *n.* مشهد mashhad

act *v.* يمثّل yomaththil

acting *n.* تمثيل tamtheel

action *n.* حركة harakah

activate *v.* يحرّك yoharrik

active *adj.* متحرّك motaharrik

activity *n.* حركة harakah

actor *n.* ممثّل momaththil

actress *n.* ممثّلة momaththilah

actual *adj.* فعليّ fi'liy

actually *adv.* بالفعل bil fi'l

acumen *n.* فطنة fitnah

acute *adj.* حاد haad

adage *n.* قول مأثور qawl mauthoor

adamant *adj.* عنيد aneed

adamant *n.* عنادة anaadah

adapt *v.* يتأقلم yatauaqlam

adaptation *n.* تأقلم tauaqlom

adays *adv.* يومي yawmiy

add *v.* يضيف yodeef

addict *v.* يدمن yodmin

addict *n.* مدمن modmin

addiction *n.* إدمان edmaan

addition *n.* إضافة edaafah

additional *adj.* إضافي edaafiy

addle *adj.* مشوّش moshawwash

address *v.* يخاطب yokhaatib

address *n.* عنوان onwaan

addressee *n.* مخاطب mokhaatab

adduce *v.* يدلّل yodallil

adept *n.* ماهر maahir

adept *adj.* ماهر maahir

adequacy *n.* كفاية kifaayah

adequate *adj.* كافي kaafi

adhere *v.* يلتزم yaltazim

adherence *n.* إلتزام eltizaam

adhesion *n.* إلصاق elsaaq

adhesive *n.* لاصق laasiq

adhesive *adj.* لاصق laasiq

adhibit *v.* يطبق yotabbiq

adieu *n.* وداع wadaa'

adieu *interj.* وداعاً wadaa'an

adjacent *adj.* متاخم motaakhim

adjective *n.* نعت na't

adjoin *v.* يجاور yojaawir

adjourn *v.* يأجَل youajjil

adjournment *n.* تأجيل taujeel

adjudge *v.* يحكم yahkom

adjunct *n.* محلّف mohallaf

adjure *v.* يستحلف yastahlif

adjuration *n.* استحلاف estihlaaf

adjust *v.* يضبط yadbit

adjustment *n.* تسوية taswiyah

administer *v.* يدير yodeer

administration *n.* إدارة edaarah

administrative *adj.* إداري edaariy

administrator *n.* مدير modeer

admirable *adj.* بديع badee'

admiral *n.* أميرال uameeraal

admiration *n.* إعجاب e'jaab

admire *v.* يعجب yo'jib

admissible *adj.* مقبول maqbool

admission *n.* 1 اعتراف e'tiraaf

admission *n.* 2 ادخال edkhaal

admit *v.* يعترف ya'tarif

admittance *n.* إعتراف e'tiraaf

admonish *v.* يعاتب yo'atib

admonition *n.* معاتبة mo'aatabah

adnascent *adj.* ينموعلى غيره yanmo 'ala ghayrih

ado *n.* ضجة dajjah

adobe *n.* طوب صلصالي toobon silsaaliy

adolescence *n.* مراهقة moraahaqah

adolescent *adj.* مراهق moraahiq

adopt *v.* يتبنّى yatabanna

adoption *n.* تبنّي tabanni

adorable *adj.* بديع badee'

adoration *n.* عشق ishq

adore *v.* يعشق ya'shaq

adorn *v.* يزين yozayyin

adscititious *adj.* اضافي edaafiy

adscript *adj.* معهود مع الأملاك ma'hoodon ma'al uamlaak

adulation *n.* تملَق tamalloq

adult *adj.* بالغ baaligh

adult *n.* ناضج nadij
adulterate *v.* يغش yaghosh
adulteration *n.* غش ghosh
adultery *n.* زنا zinaa
advance *v.* يتقدم yataqaddam
advance *n.* دفعة dof'ah
advancement *n.* تقدم taqaddom
advantage *n.* فائدة faauidah
advantage *v.* يفيد yafeed
advantageous *adj.* مفيد mofeed
advent *n.* الحضور ualhodoor
adventure *n.* مغامرة moghaamarah
adventurous *adj.* مغامر moghaamir
adverb *n.* ظرف ddarf
adverbial *adj.* ظرفي ddarfiy
adversary *n.* خصم khasm
adverse *adj.* سلبية salbiyyah
adversity *n.* محنة mihnah
advert *v.* ينوه إلى yonawwiho ela
advertise *v.* يعلن yo'lin
advertisement *n.* إعلان e'laan
advice *n.* نصيحة naseehah
advisable *adj.* ينصح به yonsaho bih
advisability *n.* نصح nos h
advise *v.* ينصح yansah
advocacy *n.* 1 دعم da'm
advocacy *n.* 2 محاماة mohaamaah
advocate n. داعية daa'iyah
advocate *v.* يدعو إلى yad'o ela
aerial *adj.* هوائي hawaauiy
aerial *n.* الهوائي ual hawaauiy
aeriform *adj.* غازي ghaaziy
aerify *v.* يبخر yobakhkhir

aerodrome *n.* حول إلى غاز hawwala ela ghaaz
aeronautics *n.pl.* علم الهوائيات ilmol hawaauiyyaat
aeroplane *n.* طائرة هوائية taauirah hawaauiyyah
aesthetic *adj.* جميل jameel
aesthetics *n.pl.* علم الجماليات uilmol jamaaliyyaat
aestival *adj.* صيفي sayfiy
afar *adv.* بعيد ba'eed
affable *adj.* حميم hameem
affair *n.* علاقة alaaqah
affect *v.* يؤثر youaththir
affectation *n.* تكلّف takallof
affection *n.* مودّة mawaddah
affectionate *adj.* حنون hanoon
affidavit *n.* شهادة shahaadah
affiliation *n.* انتماء entimaau
affinity *n.* ألفة uolfah
affirm *v.* يؤكّد youakkid
affirmation *n.* تأكيد taukeed
affirmative *adj.* 1 إيجابي ueejaabiy
affirmative *adj.* 2 مؤكّد mouakkad
affix *v.* يلصق yolsiq
afflict *v.* يبتلي yabtali
affliction *n.* إبتلاء ebtilaau
affluence *n.* تأثير tautheer
affluent *adj.* مؤثّر mouaththir
afford *v.* قادر qadir
afforest *v.* يشجّر yoshajjir
affray *n.* عراك iraak
affront *v.* يهين yoheen
affront *n.* إهانة ehaanah
afield *adv.* خارج النطاق khaarij uannitaaq

aflame *adv.* ملتهب moltahib

afloat *adv.* عائم aauim

afoot *adv.* يحدث yahdoth

afore *prep.* سالف saalif

afraid *adj.* خائف khaauif

afresh *adv.* جاذط taadhaj

after *prep.* خلف khalf

after *prep.* بعد ba'd

after *adv.* فيمابعد feema ba'd

after *conj.* عند ind

after *adj.* خلفية khalfiyyah

after *adj.* متقدّم motataqaddim

afterwards *adv.* بعدذلك ba'da dhaalik

again *adv.* مجدّداً mojaddadan

against *prep.* ضد did

against *adj.* بجانب bijaanib

agamist *n.* أعزك ua'zab

agape *adv.,* فاغرالفم faghirol fam

agape *n.* المحبةالإلهية ual mahabbal elaahiyyah

agaze *adv.* بحلقة bahlaqah

age *n.* عمر omr

aged *adj.* معمّر mo'ammir

agency *n.* وكالة wakaalah

agenda *n.* مذكرة modhakkirah

agent *n.* وكيل wakeel

aggravate *v.* يزيدسوءاً yazeedo soouan

aggravation *n.* إغضاب eghdaab

aggregate *v.* يجمع yajma'

aggression *n.* عدوان odwaan

aggressive *adj.* عدواني odwaaniy

aggressor *n.* معتدي mo'tadi

aggrieve *v.* يضطهد yadtahid

aghast *adj.* مذعور madh'oor

agile *adj.* رشيق rasheeq

agility *n.* رشاقة rashaaqah

agitate *v.* يزعج yoz'ij

agitation *n.* إزعاج ez'aaj

agist *v.* يرعىالماشية yar'al maashiyah

aglow *adv.* يتوهج yotawajjah

agnus *n.* عفيف feef

ago *adv.* قبل qabl

ago *adv.* منذ mondho

agog *adj.* مشوّق moshawwiq

agonist *n.* متباري motabaari

agonize *v.* يعذّب yo'adhdhib

agony *n.* عذاب adhaab

agronomy *n.* هندسةزراعية handasah ziraa'iyyah

agoraphobia *n.* خوفمنالأماكن المفتوحة khawf mina uamaakinil maftoohah

agrarian *adj.* زراعي ziraa'iy

agree *v.* يوافق yowaafiq

agreeable *adj.* متوافق motawaafiq

agreement *n.* إتفاقية ettifaaq

agricultural *adj.* زراعي ziraa'iy

agriculture *n.* زراعة ziraa'ah

agriculturist *n.* مزارع mozaari'

ague *n.* قشعريرة qash'areerah

ahead *adv.* مسبق mosbaqan

aheap *adv.* مكوم mokawwam

aid *n.* مساعدة mosaa'adah

aid *v.* يساعد yosaa'id

aigrette *n.* زينةمنريشالبلشون zeenaton min reeshil balshoon

ail *v.* يؤلم youlim

ailment *n.* ألم ualam

aim *n.* هدف hadaf	alike *adv.* سواء sawaau
aim *v.* يهدف yahdif	aliment *n.* غذاء ghidhaau
air *n.* هواء hawaau	alimony *n.* نفقة nafaqah
aircraft *n.* طائرةهوائية taauirah hawaauiyyah	aliquot *n.* قسمةصحيحة qismaton saheehah
airy *adj.* هوائي hawaauiy	alive *adj.* حي hai
ajar *adv.* مفتوح maftooh	alkali *n.* قلوي qalawiy
akin *adj.* قريب qareeb	all *adj.* كامل kaamil
alacrious *adj.* هوائي hayawiy	all *n.* الكل ual kol
alacrity *n.* نشيط nasheet	all *adv.* بالكامل bil kaamil
alamort *adj.* مميت momeet	all *pron* كل kol
alarm *n.* منبه monabbih	allay *v.* يهدئ yohaddiu
alarm *v.* ينبه yonabbih	allegation *n.* ادعاء eddi'au
alas *interj.* للأسف lil uasaf	allege *v.* يزعم yaz'am
albeit *conj.* رغم roghma	allegiance *n.* ولاء walaau
album *n.* ألبوم ualboom	allegorical *adj.* استعاري esti'aariy
albumen *n.* زلال zolaal	allegory *n.* استعارة esti'aarah
alchemy *n.* الخيمياء ual kheemyaau	allergy *n.* حساسية hasaasiyyah
alcohol *n.* كحول kohool	alleviate *v.* تخفيف takhfeef
ale *n.* جعة ji"ah	alleviation *n.* يخفف yokhaffif
alegar *n.* خلّالجعة khallol jji"ah	alley *n.* زقاق zoqaaq
alert *adj.* متنبه motanabbih	alliance *n.* تحالف tahaalof
alertness *n.* تنبه tanabboh	alligator *n.* تمساح timsaah
algebra *n.* الجبر ual jabr	alliterate *v.* استخدمالجناس estakhdamal jinaas
alias *n.* اسممستعار esmon mosta'aar	alliteration *n.* جناس jinaas
alias *adv.* معروفب ma'roofon bi-	allocate *v.* يخصص yokhassis
alibi *n.* عذرالغيبة odhrol ghaybah	allocation *n.* تخصيص takhsees
alien *adj.* غريب ghareeb	allot *v.* يخصص yokhassis
alienate *v.* يغرب yogharrib	allotment *n.* مخصص mokhassas
aliferous *adj.* مجنح mojannah	allow *v.* يسمح yasmah
alight *v.* يحط yahot	allowance *n.* سماح samaah
align *v.* يحاذي yohaadhi	alloy *n.* معدنمخلوط ma'dan makhloot
alignment *n.* محاذاة mohaadhaah	allude *v.* يلمح yolammih
alike *adj.* متشابه motashaabih	allure *v.* يجذب yajdhib

allurement *n.* إغراء eghraau

allusion *n.* تلميح talmeeh

allusive *adj.* ملمّح molammih

ally *v.* يتحالف yatahaalaf

ally *n.* حليف haleef

almanac *n.* تقويم taqweem

almighty *adj.* القادر ualqaadir

almond *n.* لوز lawz

almost *adv.* بالكاد bil kaad

alms *n.* صدقة sadaqah

aloft *adv.* عاليا aaliyan

alone *adj.* وحيد waheed

along *adv.* بقرب biqorb

along *prep.* مع ma'

aloof *adv.* بمعزل bima'zal

aloud *adv.* مرتفع mortafi'

alp *n.* جبل شاهق jabalon shaahiq

alpha *n.* الألف ual ualif

alphabet *n.* الأبجدية ual uabjadiyyah

alphabetical *adj.* أبجديّ uab jadiy

alpinist *n.* متسلق الجبال motasalliqol jibaal

already *adv.* سابقاً saabiqan

also *adv.* أيضاً uaydan

altar *n.* مذبح madhbah

alter *v.* يغيّر yoghayyir

alteration *n.* تغيير taghyeer

altercation *n.* مشادة moshaadaah

alternate *adj.* متناوب motanaawib

alternate *v.* يبدّل yobaddil

alternative *n.* بديل badeel

alternative *adj.* بديل badeel

although *conj.* بالرغم birraghm

altimeter *n.* جهاز لقياس الإرتفاع jihaazon liqiyaasil ertifaa'

altitude *n.* إرتفاع ertifaa'

alto *n.* أوسط uawsat

altogether *adv.* بالأكمل bil uakmal

aluminate *v.* ألومينات ualoomeenaat

aluminium *n.* الألومنيوم ual ualominyom

alumna *n.* خرّيج khirreej

always *adv.* دائماً daauiman

alveary *n.* خلية khaliyyah

am أكون uakoon

amalgam *n.* مزيج mazeej

amalgamate *v.* يدمج yadmij

amalgamation *n.* دمج damj

amass *v.* يجمع yajma'

amateur *n.* هاوي haawi

amatory *adj.* غرامي gharaamiy

amaurosis *n.* فقد البصر faqdol basar

amaze *v.* يذهل yozhil

amazement *n.* ذهول zohool

ambassador *n.* قنصل qonsol

amberite *n.* مسحوق متفجر mashooqon motafajjir

ambient *adj.* محيط moheet

ambiguity *n.* غموض ghomood

ambiguous *adj.* غامض ghaamid

ambition *n.* طموح tomooh

ambitious *adj.* طموح tamooh

ambry *n.* خزانة المؤونة khazaanatol mauoonah

ambulance *n.* إسعاف es'aaf

ambulant *adj.* متنقل motanaqqil

ambulate *v.* يتنقل yatanaqqal

ambush *n.* كمين kameen

ameliorate *v.* يتحسّن yatahassan

amelioration *n.* تحسّن tahasson

amen *interj.* آمين uaameen

amenable *adj.* قابل qabil

amend *v.* يعدّل yo'addil

amendment *n.* تعديل ta'deel

amends *n.pl.* تعويض ta'weed

amenorrhoea *n.* انقطاع الطمث enqitaa' uattamath

amiability *n.* ظرافة ddaraafah

amiable *adj.* ظريف ddareef

amicable *adj.* ظريف ddareef

amid *prep.* وسط wasat

amiss *adv.* خاطئ khaadiu

amity *n.* تفاهم tafaahom

ammunition *n.* ذخيرة dhakheerah

amnesia *n.* فقدان الذاكرة foqdaano dhaakirah

amnesty *n.* العفو ual'afo

among *prep.* بين bayn

amongst *prep.* بين bayn

amoral *adj.* غير أخلاقي ghayr uakhlaaqi

amount *n.* كمية kammiyyah

amount *v.* يعادل yo'aadil

amorous *adj.* غرامي gharaamiy

amour *n.* غرام gharaam

ampere *n.* أمبير uambeer

amphibious *adj.* برمائي barmaauiy

amphitheatre *n.* مدرّج modarraj

ample *adj.* وافر waafir

amplification *n.* تضخيم tadkheem

amplifier *n.* مضخّم modakhkhim

amplify *v.* يضخّم yodakhkhim

amuck *adv.* باهتياج bihtiyaaj

amulet *n.* تميمة tameemah

amuse *v.* يسلّي yosalli

amusement *n.* تسلية tasliyah

an *art.* ذا dha

anabaptism *n.* المعمودية في الرشد ualma'moodiyyah firroshd

anachronism *n.* مفارقة تاريخية mofaaraqa taareekhiyyah

anaclisis *n.* الاعتماد على الآخرين uali'timaado 'alal uaakhareen

anaemia *n.* فقر الدم faqroddam

anaesthesia *n.* تخدير takhdeer

anaesthetic *n.* مخدّر mokhaddir

anal *adj.* شرجي sharjiy

analogous *adj.* مماثل momaathil

analogy *n.* تماثل tamaathol

analyse *v.* يحلّل yohallil

analysis *n.* تحليل tahleel

analyst *n.* محلّل mohallil

analytical *adj.* تحليلي tahleeliy

anamnesis *n.* 1 تذكّر tadhakkor

anamnesis *n.* 2 سجلّ المريض sijillol mareed

anamorphosis *adj.* تحوّل tahawwol

anarchism *n.* فوضوية fawdawiyyah

anarchist *n.* فوضوي fawdawiy

anarchy *n.* فوضى fawda

anatomy *n.* تشريح tashreeh

ancestor *n.* سلف salaf

ancestral *adj.* سلفي salafiy

ancestry *n.* أصل uasl

anchor *n.* مرساة mirsaah

anchorage *n.* مرسى marsa

ancient *adj.* قديم qadeem

ancon *n.* دعامة da"aamah

and *conj.* و wa

androphagi *n.* آكل لحوم البشر
uaakilo lohoomil bashar

anecdote *n.* حكاية hikaayah

anemometer *n.* مقياس الريح
miqyaas uarreeh

anew *adv.* متجدّد motajaddid

anfractuous *adj.* متعرج mota'arrij

angel *n.* ملاك malaak

anger *n.* غضب ghadab

angina *n.* ذبحة صدرية dhabhaton
sadriyyah

angle *n.* 1 زاوية zaawiyah

angle *n.* 2 صنارة sonnaarah

angry *adj.* غاضب ghaadib

anguish *n.* كرب karb

angular *adj.* زاوي zaawiy

animal *n.* حيوان hayawaan

animate *v.* يحرّك yoharrik

animate *adj.* متحرك motaharrik

animation *n.* حركة harakah

animosity *n.* عداء idaau

animus *n.* نية niyyah

aniseed *n.* اليانسون ual yaansoon

ankle *n.* كاحل kaahil

anklet *n.* خلخال kholkhaal

annalist *n.* حولي hawliy

annals *n.pl.* الحوليات ual
hawliyyaat

annectent *adj.* ملحق molhiq

annex *v.* يرفق yorfiq

annexation *n.* إرفاق erfaaq

annihilate *v.* يبيد yabeed

annihilation *n.* إبادة ebaadah

anniversary *n.* ذكرى dhikra

announce *v.* يعلن yo'lin

announcement *n.* إعلان e'laan

annoy *v.* يزعج yoz'ij

annoyance *n.* إزعاج ez'aaj

annual *adj.* سنوي sanawiy

annuitant *n.* الحاصل على راتب سنوي
ualhaasilo 'ala raatibin
sanawiy

annuity *n.* راتب سنوي raatibon
sanawiy

annul *v.* يفسخ yafsakh

annulet *n.* خويتم khowaytim

anoint *v.* يمسح بالزيت yamsaho
bizzayt

anomalous *adj.* شاذ shaadh

anomaly *n.* شذوذ shodhoodh

anon *adv.* حالاً haalan

anonymity *n.* إخفاء الهوية ekhfaau
ualhowiyyah

anonymous *adj.* مجهول majhool

another *adj.* آخر uaakhar

answer *n.* جواب jawaab

answer *v.* يجيب yojeeb

answerable *adj.* مسؤول masuool

ant *n.* نملة namlah

antacid *adj.* مضاد للحموضة
modaad lil homoodah

antagonism *n.* خصام khisaam

antagonist *n.* خصم khasm

antagonize *v.* يعادي yo'aadi

antarctic *adj.* الأنتاركتيك ual
uantaarktik

antecardium *n.* جزء من البطن
jozuon minalbatn

antecede *v.* يسبق yasbiq

antecedent *n.* سابق saabiq

antecedent *adj.* الأسبق ual uasbaq

antedate *n.* مؤرَّخ mouarrakh

antelope *n.* بقرٍ وحشيّ baqar wahshiy

antenatal *adj.* سابق للولادة saabiq lil wilaadah

antennae *n.* هوائيات hawaauiyyaat

antenuptial *adj.* مستشعر mostash'ir

anthem *n.* نشيد nasheed

anthology *n.* مقتطفات أدبية moqtatafaaton uadabiyyah

anthropoid *adj.* شبيه بالانسان shabeehon bil ensaan

anti *pref.* ضد did

anti-aircraft *adj.* مضاد للطائرات modaad littaauiraat

antic *n.* سلوك غريب solookon ghareeb

anticipate *v.* يتوقع yatawaqqa'

anticipation *n.* توقع tawaqqo'

antidote *n.* ترياق tiryaaq

antinomy *n.* تناقض tanaaqod

antipathy *n.* كراهية karaahiyah

antiphony *n.* مجاوبة صوتية mojaawabah sawtiyyah

antipodes *n.* الأقطاب ualuaqtaab

antiquarian *adj.* أثري uathariy

antiquarian *n.* محل أثار mahal uaathaar

antiquary *n.* جامع الآثار jamiuol uaathaar

antiquated *adj.* أثريّ uathariy

antique *adj.* أثريّ uathariy

antiquity *n.* قدم qidam

antiseptic *n.* مطهِّر motahhir

antiseptic *adj.* مطهِّر motahhir

antithesis *n.* نقيض naqeed

antitheism *n.* مناهضة الدين monaahadato ddeen

antitheist *n.* مناهض للدين monaahidon liddeen

antler *n.* قرن qarn

antonym *n.* مضاد modaad

anus *n.* شرج sharj

anvil *n.* سندان sindaan

anxiety *adj.* قلق qalaq

anxious *adj.* قلق qaliq

any *adj.* أي uay

any *adv.* أي uay

anyhow *adv.* على أيّ حال ala uayyi haal

apace *adv.* على قدم وساق ala qadamin wa saaq

apart *adv.* بعيداً ba'eedan

apartment *n.* شقة shaqqah

apathy *n.* لامبالاة laamobaalaah

ape *n.* قرد qird

ape *v.* يقلّد yoqallid

aperture *n.* فتحة fathah

apex *n.* قمة qimmah

aphorism *n.* قول مأثور qawl mauthoor

apiary *n.* منحل manhal

apiculture *n.* نحالة nahaalah

apish *adj.* كالقرد kal qird

apnoea *n.* انقطاع النفس enqitaa'o nnafas

apologize *v.* يعتذر ya'tadhir

apologue *n.* خرافة أخلاقية المغزى khoraafah uakhlaaqiyyatol maghza

apology *n.* اعتذار e'tidhaar

apostle *n.* رسول rasool

apostrophe *n.* الفاصلةالعليا ual faasilal 'olya

apotheosis *n.* 1 تأليه tauleeh

apotheosis *n.* 2 رقي roqiy

apparatus *n.* جهاز jihaaz

apparel *n.* ملابس malaabis

apparel *v.* يكسو yakso

apparent *adj.* واضح waadih

appeal *n.* استئناف estiunaaf

appeal *v.* يستأنف yastaunif

appear *v.* يظهر yaddhar

appearance *n.* مظهر maddhar

appease *v.* يسترضي yastardi

appellant *n.* مستأنف mostaunaf

append *v.* يلحق yolhiq

appendage *n.* ملحق molhaq

appendicitis *n.* التهاب الزائدةالدودية eltihaabo zzaauida ddoodiyyah

appendix *n.* ملحق molhaq

appendix *n.* الزائدة uazzauidah

appetence *n.* شهوة shahwah

appetent *adj.* مشتهي moshtahi

appetite *n.* شهية shahiyyah

appetizer *n.* مقبلات moqabbilaat

applaud *v.* يصفق yosaffiq

applause *n.* تصفيق tasfeeq

apple *n.* تفاحة toffaahah

appliance *n.* جهاز jihaaz

applicable *adj.* منطبق montabiq

applicant *n.* مقدمالطلب moqaddimo ttalab

application *n.* 1 تطبيق tatbeeq

application *n.* 2 طلب talab

apply *v.* 1 يطبق yotabbiq

apply *v.* 2 يقدمطلب yoqaddimo ttalab

appoint *v.* يعين yo'ayyin

appointment *n.* موعد maw'id

apportion *v.* يقسم yoqassim

apposite *adj.* مناسب monaasib

appositely *adv.* بصورةمناسبة bisoora monaasibah

appraise *v.* يقيم yoqayyim

appreciable *adj.* مقدّر moqaddar

appreciate *v.* يقدّر yoqaddir

appreciation *n.* تقدير taqdeer

apprehend *v.* يعتقل ya'taqil

apprehension *n.* اعتقال e'tiqaal

apprehensive *adj.* 1 مفهوم mafhoom

apprehensive *adj.* 2 قلق qaliq

apprentice *n.* مبتدئ mobtadiu

apprise *v.* يطلع yotli'

approach *v.* ينهج yanhaj

approach *n.* نهج nahj

approbate *v.* يخوّل yokhawwil

approbation *n.* 1 تخويل takhweel

approbation *n.* 2 إستحسان estihsaan

appropriate *v.* يجعله مناسباً yaj'aloho monaasiban

appropriate *adj.* مناسب monasib

appropriation *n.* 1 تخصيص takhsees

appropriation *n.* 2 إعتماد e'timaad

approval *n.* موافقة mowaafaqah

approve *v.* يوافق yowaafiq

approximate *adj.* تقريبي taqreebiy

appurtenance *n.* التبعية uattaba'iyyah

apricot *n.* مشمش mishmish

April *n.* نيسان neesaan

apron *n.* مئزر miuzar

apt *adj.* 1 مناسب monaasib

apt *adj.* 2 عرضة ordah

apt *adj.* 3 سريع التعلّم saree'o tta'allom

aptitude *n.* أهلية uohliyyah

aquarium *n.* حوض السمك hawdo ssamak

aquarius *n.* برج الدلو borjo ddalw

acuatic *adj.* مائي mauiy

aqueduct *n.* قناة qanah

Arab *n.* عربي arabiy

Arabic *n.* اللغة العربية ualloghal 'arabiyyah

Arabic *adj.* عربي arabiy

arable *adj.* صالحة للزراعة saliha lizziraa'a

arbiter *n.* حكم hakam

arbitrary *adj.* تعسفي ta'assofiy

arbitrate *v.* يحكّم yahkom

arbitration *n.* تحكيم tahkeem

arbitrator *n.* محكّم mohakkim

arc *n.* قوس qaws

arcade *n.* رواق riwaaq

arch *n.* قوس qaws

arch *v.* تقوّس taqawwos

arch *adj.* متقوّس motaqawwis

archaeology *n.* علم الآثر ilmol uaathaar

archaic *adj.* قديم qadeem

archangel *n.* رئيس الملائكة raueesol malaauikah

archbishop *n.* مطران matraan

alphabet *n.* رام القوس raamel qaws

architect *n.* مهندس معماري mohandis mi'maari

architecture *n.* الهندسة المعمارية ual handasal mi'maariyyah

archives *n.pl.* أرشيف uarsheef

Arctic *n.* القطب الشمالي ualqotbo shshamaaliy

ardent *adj.* متحمس motahammis

ardour *n.* حماس hamaas

arduous *adj.* شاق shaaq

area *n.* منطقة mantiqah

areca *n.* نخيل nakheel

arefaction *n.* تجفيف tajfeef

arena *n.* حلبة halabah

argil *n.* صلصال silsaal

argue *v.* يجادل yojaadil

argument *n.* 1 حجة hijjah

argument *n.* 2 جدال jidaal

argute *adj.* مجادل mojaadil

arid *adj.* جاف jaaf

aries *n.* برج الحمل borjol hamal

aright *adv.* صحيح saheeh

arise *v.* ينشأ yanshau

aristocracy *n.* أرستقراطية uaristoqraatiyyah

aristocrat *n.* أرستقراطي uaristoqraatiy

arithmetic *n.* حسابي hisaabiy

arithmetical *adj.* حسابي hisaabiy

ark *n.* 1 قارب qaarib

ark *n.* 2 خزانة khizaanah

arm *n.* ذراع dhiraa'

arm *v.* يسلّح yosallih

armada *n.* أسطول حربي uostool harbiy

armament *n.* تسلح tasalloh

armature *n.* 1 قطعةمن مولدمغناطيسئ qit'aton min mowallidin mighnaadeesiy

armature *n.* 2 إطارمعدنئ edaaron ma'daniy

armature *n.* 3 غطاءواقي ghidaauon waaqi

armistice *n.* هدنة hodnah

armlet *adj.* 1 سوارللذراع siwaaron lidhiraa'

armlet *adj.* 2 لسانمائي lisaanon maauiy

armour *n.* درع dir'

armoury *n.* مستودعالأسلحة mostawda'ol uaslihah

army *n.* جيش jaysh

around *prep.* حول hawl

around *adv.* حول hawl

arouse *v.* يثير yotheer

arraign *v.* يستدعيالىالمحكمة yastad'i elal mahkamah

arrange *v.* يرتب yorattib

arrangement *n.* ترتيب tarteeb

arrant *n.* بكلمعنىالكلمة bikolli ma'nal kalimah

array *v.* يصفَف yosaffif

array *n.* صفيف safeef

arrears *n.pl.* متأخرات motauakhkhiraat

arrest *v.* يعتقل ya'taqil

arrest *n.* اعتقال e'tiqaal

arrival *n.* وصول wosool

arrive *v.* يصل yasil

arrogance *n.* غطرسة ghatrasah

arrogant *adj.* متغطرس motaghatris

arrow *n.* سهم sahm

arrowroot *n.* الأروروت ual uaroroot

arsenal *n.* الترسانة uattarsaanah

arsenic *n.* زرنيخ zarneekh

arson *n.* حريقمتعمَد hareeqon mota'ammad

art *n.* فن fan

artery *n.* شريان shiryaan

artful *adj.* داهية daahiyah

arthritis *n.* التهابالمفاصل eltihaabol mafaasil

artichoke *n.* أرضيشوكي uardi shawki

article *n.* مقالة maqaalah

articulate *adj.* موضح mowaddah

articulate *v.* يوضح yowaddih

artifice *n.* حيلة heelah

artificial *adj.* اصطناعي estinaa'iy

artillery *n.* مدفعية madfa'iyyah

artisan *n.* حرفي hirafiy

artist *n.* فنان fannaan

artistic *adj.* فني fanniy

artless *adj.* ساذج saadaj

as *adv.* كما kama

as *conj.* 1 عندما indama

as *conj.* 2 لأنَ liuanna

as *pron.* 1 كـ ka-

as *pron.* 2 عندما indama

asafoetida *n.* خلاصةجذرالبقدونس kholasato jadhril baqdoonis

asbestos *n.* أسبستوس uasbistos

ascend *v.* يصعد yas'ad

ascent *n.* صعود so'ood

ascertain *v.* يتأكد yatauakkad

ascetic *n.* زاهد zaahid

ascetic *adj.* زاهد zaahid

ascribe *v.* يعزو ya'zo

ash *n.* رماد ramaad

ashamed *adj.* مخجل mokhjal

ashore *adv.* الى الشاطئ elashshaatiu

aside *adv.* جانباً jaaniban

aside *n.* حديث جاني hadeethon jaanibiy

asinine *adj.* أبله uablah

ask *v.* يطلب yatlob

asleep *adv.* نائم nauim

aspect *n.* جانب jaanib

asperse *v.* يذم yadhim

aspirant *n.* طموح tamooh

aspiration *n.* طموح tumooh

aspire *v.* يطمح yatmah

ass *n.* حمار himaar

assail *v.* هاجم بعنف haajama bi'onf

assassin *n.* قاتل qaatil

assassinate *v.* يغتال yaghtaal

assassination *n.* اغتيال eghtiyaal

assault *n.* اعتداء e'tidaau

assault *v.* يعتدي ya'tadi

assemble *v.* يجمع yajma'

assembly *n.* جمعية jam'iyyah

assent *v.* يوافق yowaafiq

assent *n.* موافقة mowaafiq

assert *v.* يأكد youakkid

assess *v.* يقيم yoqayyim

assessment *n.* تقييم taqyeem

asset *n.* ممتلك momtalak

assibilate *v.* يصفر yosaffir

assign *v.* يعين yo'ayyin

assignee *n.* المعين ual mo'ayyan

assimilate *v.* يستوعب yastaw'ib

assimilation *n.* استيعاب estee'aab

assist *v.* يساعد yosaa'id

assistance *n.* مساعدة mosaa'adah

assistant *n.* مساعد mosaa'id

associate *v.* يربط yarbit

associate *adj.* تساهمي tasaahomiy

associate *n.* شريك shareek

association *n.* رابطة raabitah

assoil *v.* يعف ya'fi

assort *v.* يجانس yojaanis

assuage *v.* يهدئ yohaddiu

assume *v.* يفترض yaftarid

assumption *n.* افتراض eftiraad

assurance *n.* تأكيد taukeed

assure *v.* يؤكّد youakkid

astatic *adj.* متقلّب motaqallib

asterisk *n.* نجمة najmah

asterism *n.* مجموعة نجوم majmoo'at nojoom

asteroid *adj.* كويكب kawaykab

asthma *n.* الربو uarrabo

astir *adv.* هرج ومرج haraj wa maraj

astonish *v.* يذهل yodhhil

astonishment *n.* ذهول dhohool

astound *v.* يذهل yodhhil

astray *adv.*, ضال daal

astrologer *n.* منجم monajjim

astrology *n.* علم التنجيم ilmo ttanjeem

astronaut *n.* رائد فضاء raauido fadaau

astronomer *n.* عالم الفلك alimol falak

astronomy *n.* علم الفلك ilmol falak

asunder *adv.* ارباً eraban

asylum *n.* لجوء lojoou

at *prep.* في fi

atheism *n.* إلحاد elhaad

atheist *n.* ملحد molhid

athirst *adj.* عطشان atshaan

athlete *n.* رياضي riyaadiy

athletic *adj.* رياضي riyaadiy

athletics *n.* ألعاب القوى ual'aabol qiwa

athwart *prep.* بالعرض bil 'ard

atlas *n.* أطلس uatlas

atmosphere *n.* جو jaw

atoll *n.* جزيرة مرجانية jazeeraton morjaaniyyah

atom *n.* ذرة dharrah

atomic *adj.* ذري dharriy

atone *v.* يكفر yakfor

atonement *n.* كفر kofr

atrocious *adj.* فظيع faddee'

atrocity *n.* فظاعة faddaa'ah

attach *v.* 1 يتعلّق yata'allaq

attach *v.* 2 يلحق yolhiq

attache *n.* ملحق molhaq

attachment *n.* ملحق molhaq

attack *n.* هجوم hojoom

attack *v.* يهجم yahjim

attain *v.* يحقق yohaqiq

attainment *n.* نيل nayl

attaint *v.* يعدي yo'di

attempt *v.* يحاول yohaawil

attempt *n.* محاولة mohaawalah

attend *v.* يحضر yahdor

attendance *n.* حضور hodoor

attendant *n.* حاضر haadir

attention *n.* اهتمام ehtimaam

attentive *adj.* منتبه montabih

attest *v.* يشهد yashhad

attire *n.* ملابس malaabis

attire *v.* يكسو yakso

attitude *n.* موقف mawqif

attorney *n.* محام mohaami

attract *v.* يجذب yajdhib

attraction *n.* جاذبية jaadhibiyyah

attractive *adj.* جذاب jadhdhaab

attribute *v.* يربط yarbit

attribute *n.* سمة simah

auction *n.* مزاد mazaad

auction *v.* يزاود yozaawid

audible *adj.* مسموع masmoo'

audience *n.* جمهور jomhoor

audit *n.* مراجعة الحسابات moraaja'atol hisaabaat

audit *v.* يراجع الحسابات yoraaji'ol hisaabaat

auditive *adj.* سمعية sama'iyyah

auditor *n.* مدقق الحسابات modaqqiqol hisaabaat

auditorium *n.* قاعة qaa'ah

auger *n.* مثقب mithqab

aught *n.* بأية حال biuayyati haal

augment *v.* يزيد yazeed

augmentation *n.* زيادة ziyaadah

August *n.* آب uaab

august *adj.* محترم mohtaram

aunt *n.* عمة amma

auriform *adj.* أذني uodhoniy

aurilave *n.* منظف الأذن monaddddifol uodhon

aurora *n.* فجر fajr

auspicate *v.* يتكهن yatakahhan

auspice *n.* تكهن takahhon

auspicious *adj.* ميمون maymoon

austere *adj.* متقشف motaqashshif

authentic *adj.* حقيقي haqeeqiy

author *n.* كاتب kaatib

authoritative *adj.* موثوق mawthooq

authority *n.* سلطة soltah

authorize *v.* يأذن yaudhan

autobiography *n.* سيرةذاتية seeraton dhaatiyyah

autocracy *n.* استبداد estibdaad

autocrat *n.* مستبد mostabid

autocratic *adj.* استبدادي estibdaadiy

autograph *n.* توقيع خطيّ tawqee'on khattiy

automatic *adj.* آلية uaaliyyah

automobile *n.* سيارة sayyarah

autonomous *adj.* مستقل mostaqil

autumn *n.* خريف khareef

auxiliary *adj.* مساعد mosaa'id

auxiliary *n.* مساعد mosaa'id

avale *v.* يحط yahot

avail *v.* يفيد yofeed

available *adj.* متاح motaah

avarice *n.* جشع jasha'

avenge *v.* يثأر yathuar

avenue *n.* سبيل sabeel

average *n.* متوسط motawassit

average *adj.* متوسط motawassit

average *v.* 1 يحسب المتوسط yahsibol motawassit

average *v.* 2 يتوسط yatawassat

averse *adj.* مكره mokrah

aversion *n.* نفور nofoor

avert *v.* يتجنب yatajannab

aviary *n.* مطير matyar

aviation *n.* طيران tayaraan

aviator *n.* طيار tayyar

avid *adj.* طماع tammaa'

avidity *adv.* طمع tama'

avidly *adv.* بطمع bitama'

avoid *v.* يتجنب yatajannab

avoidance *n.* تجنب tajannob

avow *v.* يعترف ya'tarif

avulsion *n.* وقوع الإصابة woqaa'ol esaabah

await *v.* ينتظر yantaddir

awake *v.* يوقظ yooqidd

awake *adj.* مستيقظ mostayqidd

awakening *n.* يقظة yaqaddah

award *v.* يمنح yamnah

award *n.* جائزة jaauizah

aware *adj.* واع waa'in

awareness *n.* وعي wa'y

away *adv.* بعيداً ba'eedan

awe *n.* رعب ro'b

awful *adj.* مروع morawwi'

awhile *adv.* لحظة lahddah

awkward *adj.* غير ملائم ghayro molaauim

axe *n.* فأس faus

axis *n.* محور mihwar

axle *n.* محور العجلة mihwarol 'ajalah

B

babble *n.* ثرثرة thartharah

babble *v.* يثرثر yotharthir

babe *n.* 1 صديقة sadeeqah

babe *n.* 2 طفل رضيع tiflon radee'

babel *n.* بابل baabil
baboon *n.* قرد qird
baby *n.* طفل tifl
0bachelor *n.* أعزب ua'zab
back *n.* ظهر ddhr
back *adv.* خلف khalf
back *adj.* خلفي khalfiy
back *v.* يسند yasnid
backbite *v.* يستغيب yastaghyib
backbone *n.* عمودفقري amoodon fiqariy
background *n.* خلفية khalfiyyah
backhand *n.* ضربةبقفاالید darbaton biqafal yad
backslide *v.* يعودللعصيان ya'oodo lil 'isyaan
backward *a.* رجعي raj'iy
backward *adv.* الىالوراء elal waraau
bacon *n.* لحمخنزيرمقدد lahmo khanzeerin moqaddad
bacteria *n.* بكتيريا bakteerya
bad *adj.* سيئ sayyiu
badge *n.* شارة shaarah
badger *n.* غرير ghorayr
badly *adv.* 1 بشكلسيء bishaklin sayyiu
badly *adv.* 2 بشدة bishiddah
badminton *n.* رياضةالريشة riyaadato rreeshah
baffle *v.* يحير yohayyir
bag *n.* حقيبة haqeebah
bag *v.* 1 يضعفيحقيبة yada'o fil haqeebah
bag *v.* 2 ينتفخ yantafikh
baggage *n.* أمتعة uamti'ah

bagpipe *n.* مزمارالقربة mizmaarol qirbah
bail *n.* كفالة kafaalah
bail *v.* يكفل yakfal
bailable *adj.* ممكنكفله momkino kafloh
bailiff *n.* حاجبمحكمة hajibol mahkamah
bait *n.* طعم to'm
bait *v.* يغري yoghri
bake *v.* يخبز yakhbiz
baker *n.* خباز khabbaaz
bakery *n.* مخبز makhbaz
balance *n.* توازن tawaazon
balance *v.* يوازن yowaazin
balcony *n.* شرفة shorfah
bald *adj.* أصلع uasla'
bale *n.* حزمة hozmah
bale *v.* يحزم yahzim
baleful *adj.* مؤذ moudhi
baleen *n.* عظمالحوت addmol hoot
ball *n.* كرة korah
ballad *n.* أغنيةراقصة uoghniyaton raaqisah
ballet *sn.* رقصالباليه raqsol baalih
balloon *n.* بالون baaloon
ballot *n.* اقتراع eqtiraa'
ballot *v.* يقترع yaqtari'
balm *n.* مرهم mirham
balsam *n.* بلسم balsam
bam *n.* صوتمفاجئ sawton mofaajiu
bamboo *n.* خيزران khayzoraan
ban *n.* حظر haddr
ban *v.* يمنع yamna'
banal *adj.* تافه tafih

banana *n.* موزة mawzah	**barbarian** *n.* همجي hamajiy
band *n.* فرقة firqah	**barbarism** *n.* همجية hamajiyyah
bandage ~*n.* ضمادة dammaadah	**barbarity** *n.* همجية hamajiyyah
bandage *v.* يضمّد yodammid	**barbarous** *adj.* همجي hamajiy
bandit *n.* قاطع طريق qaati'o tareeq	**barbed** *adj.* شائك shaauik
bang *v.* يخبط yakhbit	**barber** *n.* حلاق hallaaq
bang *n.* فرقعة farqa'ah	**bard** *n.* شاعر shaa'ir
bangle *n.* سوار siwaar	**bare** *a.* مجرد mojarrad
banish *v.* يبعد yob'id	**bare** *v.* يجرد yojarrid
banishment *n.* نفي nafy	**barely** *adv.* بالكاد bilkaad
banjo *n.* البانجو ual banjo	**bargain** *n.* صفقة safqah
bank *n.* 1 مصرف masrif	**bargain** *v.* يعقدصفقة ya'qido safqah
bank *n.* 2 ضفّة diffah	**barge** *n.* زورق البارجة zawraqol baarijah
bank *v.* 1 يودع yoodi'	
bank *v.* 2 يتراكم yataraakam	**bark** *n.* نباح nobaah
banker *n.* مصرفي masrifiy	**bark** *v.* 1 يصرخ yasrokh
bankrupt *n.* مفلس moflis	**bark** *v.* 2 ينبح yanbah
bankruptcy *n.* إفلاس eflaas	**barley** *n.* شعير sha'eer
banner *n.* راية raayah	**barn** *n.* إسطبل establ
banquet *n.* مأدبة maudobah	**barnacles** *n.* نظارات naddddaaraat
banquet *v.* يقيم مأدبة yoqeemo maudobah	**barometer** *n.* بارومتر baaroomitr
bantam *n.* قزم qazam	**barouche** *n.* عربة arabah
banter *v.* يداعب yodaa'ib	**barrack** *n.* ثكنة thaknah
banter *n.* مزاح mozaah	**barrage** *n.* سد sad
bantling *n.* 1 لقيط laqeet	**barrel** *n.* برميل barmeel
bantling *n.* 2 طفل صغير tiflon sagheer	**barren** *n.* قاحل qaahil
banyan *n.* تين هندي teenon hindiy	**barricade** *n.* متراس mitraas
baptism *n.* معمودية ma'moodiyyah	**barrier** *n.* حاجز haajiz
baptize +*v.t.* يعمد yo'ammid	**barrister** *n.* محام mohaami
bar *n.* 1 قضيب qadeeb	**barter** *v.* يقايض yoqaayid
bar *n.* 2 حانة haanah	**barter** *n.* مقايدة moqaayadah
bar *v.* يعترض ya'tarid	**basal** *adj.* قاعدي qaa'idiy
barb *n.* شوكة shawkah	**base** *n.* قاعدة qaa'idah
barbarian *adj.* همجي hamajiy	**base** *adj.* قاعدئ qaa'idiy

base v. يستند yastanid

baseless adj. لا أساس له la usaasa lah

basement n. طابق أرضي taabiqon uardiy

bashful adj. محتشم mohtashim

basic adj. أساسي usaasiy

basil n. ريحان reehaan

basin n. حوض hawd

basis n. أساس uasaas

bask v. يتشمس yatashammas

basket n. سلة sallah

bass n. جهور jahoor

bastard n. ولد غير شرعي waladon ghayro shar'iy

bastard adj. زائف zaauif

bat n. خفاش khaffaash

bat n. مضرب midrab

bat v. يضرب yadrib

batch n. دفعة dof'ah

bath n. حمام hammaam

bathe v. يستحم yastahim

baton n. عصا asa

batsman n. ضارب الكرة daaribol korah

battalion n. كتيبة kateebah

battery n. بطارية battaariyyah

battle n. معركة ma'rakah

battle v. يعارك yo'aarik

bawd n. مومس moomas

bawl n.i. زعق za'q

bawn n. حظيرة محصنة haddeeraton mohassanah

bay n. خليج khaleej

bayonet n. حربة hirbah

be v. يكون yakoon

be pref. أن uan

beach n. شاطئ shaatiu

beacon n. منارة manaarah

bead n. خرزة kharazah

beadle n. شماس الكنيسة shammasol kaneesah

beak n. منقار minqaar

beaker n. فنجان finjaan

beam n. شعاع sho'aa'

beam v. يشع yashi'

bean n. فاصوليا faasoolyaau

bear n. دب dob

bear v. 1 يحمل yahmil

bear v. 2 يتحمل yatahammal

beard n. لحية lihyah

bearing n. تحمل tahammol

beast n. بهيمة baheemah

beastly adj. بغيض bagheed

beat v. 1 يهزم yahzim

beat v. 2 يضرب yadrib

beat n. إيقاع ueeqaa'

beautiful adj. جميل jameel

beautify v. يجمل yojammil

beauty n. جمال jamaal

beaver n. سمور sammoor

because conj. لأن liuannah

beck n. غدير ghadeer

beckon v. 1 يؤشر youashshir

beckon v. 2 يغري yoghri

become v. يصبح yosbih

becoming adj. لائق laauiq

bed n. سرير sareer

bedevil v. يشوش yoshawwish

bedding n. فراش firaash

bedight v. يجمل yojammil

bed-time *n.* وقت النوم waqto nnawm

bee *n.* نحلة nahlah

beech *n.* خشب الزان khashabo zzaan

beef *n.* لحم البقر lahmol baqar

beehive n. خلية نحل khaliyyato nahl

beer *n.* بيرة beerah

beet *n.* بنجر banjar

beetle *n.* خنفساء khonfosaau

befall *v.* يصيب yaseeb

before *prep.* 1 أمام umaam

before *prep.* 2 قبل qabl

before *adv.* من قبل min qabl

before *conj.* قبل qabl

beforehand *adv.* سلفاً salafan

befriend *v.* يصاحب yosaahib

beg *v.* يتوسل yatawassal

beget *v.* ينجب yonjib

beggar *n.* متسول motasawwil

begin *v.* يبدأ yabdau

beginning *n.* بداية bidaayah

begird *v.* يأسر yausir

beguile *v.* 1 يخدع yakhda'

beguile *v.* 2 يسحر yashar

behalf *n.* باسم biuism

behave *v.* يتصرف yatasarraf

behaviour *n.* سلوك solook

behead *v.* يقطع رأس yaqta'o raus

behind *n.* مؤخرة mouakhkharah

behind *adv.* خلف khalf

behind *adj.* متأخر motauakhkhir

behind *prep.* وراء waraau

behold *v.* يتأمّل yatauammal

being *n.* وجود wojood

belabour *v.* يناقش yonaaqish

belated *adj.* متأخر motauakhkhir

belch *v.* يجشأ yajshou

belch *n.* تجشّؤ tajashshou

belief *n.* 1 إيمان ueeman

belief *n.* 2 إعتقاد e'tiqaad

believe *v.* 1 يؤمن youmin

believe *v.* 2 يعتقد ya'taqid

bell *n.* جرس jaras

belle *n.* حسناء hasnaau

bellicose *adj.* معاد mo'aadi

belligerency *n.* عداء adaau

belligerent *adj.* متحارب motahaarib

belligerent *n.* محارب mohaarib

bellow *v.* يخور yakhoor

bellows *n.* منفاخ minfaakh

belly *n.* بطن batn

belong *v.* ينتمي yantami

belongings *n.* ممتلكات momtalakaat

beloved *adj.* محبوب mahboob

beloved *n.* محبوب mahboob

below *adv.* 1 أسفل uasfal

below *adv.* 2 تحت taht

below *prep.* 1 أسفل uasfal

below *prep.* 2 أقل uaqal

belt *n.* حزام hizaam

belvedere *n.* مصيف بفرجة masyafon biforjah

bemask *v.* يخفي yokhfi

bemire *v.* يوحّل yowahhil

bemuse *v.* يذهل yodhhil

bench *n.* مقعد maq'ad

bend *n.* انحناء enhinaau

bend *v.* ينحني yanhani

beneath *adv.* 1 تحت taht	**betel** *n.* التنبول uattanbool
beneath *adv.* 2 أسفل uasfal	**betray** *v.* يخون yakhoon
beneath *prep.* 1 تحت taht	**betrayal** *n.* خيانة khiyaanah
beneath *prep.* 2 أسفل uasfal	**betroth** *v.* يخطب yakhtib
benefaction *n.* إحسان ehsaan	**betrothal** *n.* خطبة khitbah
benefice *n.* إقطاع eqtaa'	**better** *adj.* أفضل uafdal
beneficial *adj.* مفيد mofeed	**better** *adv.* أفضل uafdal
benefit *n.* مصلحة maslahah	**better** *v.* يحسّن yohassin
benefit *v.* يستفيد yastafeed	**betterment** *n.* تحسين tahseen
benevolence *n.* إحسان ehsaan	**between** *prep.* بين bayn
benevolent *adj.* محسن mohsin	**beverage** *n.* شراب sharaab
benight *v.* يضلّل yodallil	**bewail** *v.* ينوح yanooh
benign *adj.* حميد hameed	**beware** *v.* يحترس yahtaris
benignly *adv.* بحمد bihimd	**bewilder** *v.* يحيّر yohayyir
benison *n.* نعمة ni'mah	**bewitch** *v.* يفتن yaftin
bent *n.* 1 عزم azm	**beyond** *prep.* مابعد ma ba'd
bent *n.* 2 ميل mayl	**beyond** *adv.* مابعد ma ba'd
bent *adj.* 1 ملتوي moltawi	**bi pref** ثنائي thonaauiy
bent *adj.* 2 مقوّس moqawwas	**biangular** *adj.* ثنائي الزاوية thonaauiyo zzaawiyah
bequeath *v.* يورث yawrith	**bias** *n.* انحياز enhiyaaz
bereave *v.* يثكل yathkol	**bias** *v.* ينحاز yanhaaz
bereavement *n.* 1 ثكل thakl	**biaxial** *adj.* ذومحورين dho mihwarayn
bereavement *n.* 2 حرمان hirmaan	
berth *n.* مرسى marsa	**bibber** *n.* سكير sakeer
beside *prep.* بجانب bijaanib	**bible** *n.* الكتاب المقدس ualkitaabol moqaddas
besides *prep.* بالإضافةإلى biluidaafati ela	**bibliography** *n.* قائمةالمراجع qaauimatol maraaji'
besides *adv.* بالإضافةإلى biluidaafati ela	**bibliographer** *n.* مجمَعالمراجع mojammi'ol majaami'
beslaver *v.* ساللعابه saala lo'aaboh	**bicentenary** *adj.* ذكرىمئويةثانية dikra miuawiyyaton thaaniyah
besiege *v.* يحاصر yahaasir	
bestow *v.* يمنح yamnah	**biceps** *n.* عضلةذاترأسين adalaton dhaato rausayn
bestrew *v.* يغط yaghot	
bet *v.* يرهن yarhin	
bet *n.* رهان rahaan	

bicker v. يتشاحن yatashaahan

bicycle n. دراجة darraajah

bid v. 1 يأمر yaumor

bid v. 2 يزاود yozaawid

bid n. مزاودة mozaawadah

bidder n. مزاود mozaawid

bide v. ينتظر yantaddir

biennial adj. مرةكل سنتين marraton kolla sanatayn

bier n. نعش na'sh

big adj. كبير kabeer

bigamy n. مضارة modaarrah

bight n. غرور ghoroor

bigot n. متعصب mota'asib

bigotry n. تعصب ta'assob

bile n. 1 نكد makad

bile n. 2 فرازةالكبد foraazatol kabid

bilingual adj. ثنائياللغة thonaauiyo lloghah

bill n. فاتورة faatoora

billion n. مليونمليون malyoono malyoon

billow n. موجة mawjah

billow v. 1 يتدفق yatadaffaq

billow v. 2 ينتفخ yantafikh

biliteral adj. ثنائيالحروف thonaauiyol horoof

bilk v. يحتال yahtaal

bimonthly adj. 1 نصفشهري nisfo shahriy

bimonthly adj. 2 مرةكلشهرين marraton kolla shahrayn

binary adj. ثنائي thonaauiy

bind v. يربط yarbit

binding adj. ملزم molzim

binocular n. مجهر mijhar

biographer n. كاتبسيرة kaatibo seerah

biography n. سيرة seerah

biologist n. أحيائي uahyaauiy

biology n. علمالاحياء ilmol uahyaau

bioscope n. عارضللصور aridom lissowar

biped n. ذواتالقدمين dhawaatol qadamayn

birch v. يجلد yajlid

birch n. البتولا albatoola

bird n. طائر tauir

birdlime n. مادةلاصقة maaddaton laasiqah

birth n. ولادة wilaadah

biscuit n. بسكويت biskweet

bisect v. يشطر yashtir

bisexual adj. 1 يستهويكلاالجنسين yastahwi kilal jinsayn

bisexual adj. 2 ثنائيالجنس thonaauiyol jins

bishop n. أسقف uosqof

bison n. ثورالبيسون thawr albaysoon

bisque n. حساءسمكدسم hasaauo samakin dasim

bit n. بت bit

bitch n. كلبة kalbah

bite v. يعض ya'od

bite n. عضة addah

bitter adj. مرير mareer

bi-weekly adj. كلأسبوعين kollo usboo'ayn

bizarre adj. غريب ghareeb

blab v. يثرثر yotharthir

blab *n.* ثرثار thirthaar

black *adj.* أسود uosood

blacken *v.* يسود yasood

blackmail *n.* ابتزاز ebtizaaz

blackmail *v.* يبتز yabtaz

blacksmith *n.* حدّاد haddaad

bladder *n.* مثانة mathaanah

blade *n.* شفرة shafrah

blain *n.* التهاب جلدي eltihaabon jildiy

blame *v.* يلوم yaloom

blame *n.* لوم lawm

blanch *v.* يشحب yashhob

bland *adj.* 1 فاتر faatir

bland *adj.* 2 طعم بلا bila ta'm

blank *adj.* 1 فارغ faarigh

blank *adj.* 2 خال من التعبير khalin mina tta'beer

blank *n.* 1 فراغ faarigh

blank *n.* 2 خرطوش faarigh

blanket *n.* بطانية bataaniyyah

blare *v.* 1 يدوي yodawwi

blare *v.* 2 يعلن yo'lin

blast *n.* انفجار enfijaar

blast *v.* يفجّر yofajjir

blaze *n.* حريق hareeq

blaze *v.* يحترق yahtariq

bleach *v.* يبيّض yobayyid

blear *v.* يغشي yaghshi

bleat *n.* ثغاء thoghaau

bleat *v.* يثغي yathghi

bleb *n.* بثرة bathrah

bleed *v.* ينزف yanzif

blemish *n.* عيب ayb

blemish *v.* يعيب yo'eeb

blend *v.* يمزج yamzij

blend *n.* مزيج mazeej

bless *v.* بارك baaraka

blether *v.* يثرثر yotharthir

blether *n.* ثرثرة thartharah

blight *n.* آفة uaafah

blind *adj.* أعمى ua'ma

blindage *n.* درع dir'

blindfold *v.* يعصب العينين ya'sibol 'oyoon

blindfold *n.* عصابة osaabah

blindness *n.* عمى ama

blink *v.* يرمش yarmosh

bliss *n.* نعمة ni'mah

blister *n.* بثرة bathrah

blizzard *n.* عاصفة ثلجية aasifaton thaljiyyah

bloc *n.* حزب hizb

block *n.* كتلة kotlah

block *v.* يعرقل yo'arqil

blockade *n.* حصار hisaar

blockhead *n.* أبله uablah

blood *n.* دم dam

bloodshed *n.* سفك الدماء safko ddimaau

bloody *adj.* دموي damawiy

bloom *n.* إزدهار ezdihaar

bloom *v.* يزدهر yazdahir

blossom *n.* زهرة zahrah

blossom *v.* يزهر yozhir

blot *n.* لطخة latkhah

blot *v.* يلطّخ yolattikh

blotted *adj.* ملطّخ molattikh

blouse *n.* قميص qamees

blow *v.* يضرب yadrib

blow *n.* ضربة darbah

blue *n.* أزرق uazraq

blue *adj.* حزين hazeen	boil *v.* يسلق yasliq
bluff *v.* يخدع yakhda'	boiler *n.* مرجل mirjal
bluff *n.* خداع khidaa'	bold *adj.* جريء jareeu
blunder *n.* حماقة hamaaqah	boldness *n.* جرأة joruah
blunder *v.* تخبّط takhabbot	bolt *n.* برغي borghiy
blunt *adj.* 1 صريح sareeh	bolt *v.* يثبّت yothabbit
blunt *adj.* 2 غير حاد ghayro haad	bomb *n.* قنبلة qonbolah
blur *n.* 1 تشويش tashweesh	bomb *v.* يفجّر yofajjir
blur *n.* 2 لطخة latkhah	bombard *v.* يقصف yaqsif
blur *v.* يشوّش yoshawwish	bombardment *n.* قصف qasf
blurt *v.* أفشى ufsha	bomber *n.* مفجّر mofajjir
blush *n.* خجل khajal	bonafide *adv.* بخلاص biuikhlaas
blush *v.* يخجل yakhjal	bonafide *adj.* مخلص mokhlis
boar *n.* خنزير khanzeer	bond *n.* رباط ribaat
board *n.* 1 مجلس majlis	bondage *n.* عبودية obodiyyah
board *n.* 2 وجبة wajbah	bone *n.* عظم addm
board *n.* 3 لوح lawh	bonfire *n.* موقد mawqid
board *v.* 1 يركب yarkab	bonnet *n.* قلنسوة qolonsowah
board *v.* 2 يقيم yoqeem	bonus *n.* علاوة alaawah
boast *v.* يتباهى yatabaaha	book *n.* كتاب kitaab
boast *n.* تباهي tabaahi	book *v.* يحجز yahjiz
boat *n.* قارب qaarib	book-keeper *n.* مدوّن modawwin
boat *v.* تنقّل بالقارب tanaqqala bilqaarib	book-keeping *n.* تدوين tadween
bodice *n.* سترة sotrah	book-mark *n.* مؤشر mouashshir
bodily *adv.* جسدي jasadiy	book-seller *n.* بائع الكتب baaui'ol kotob
body *n.* 1 هيئة hayuah	book-worm *n.* عثة الكتب aththatol kotob
body *n.* 2 جسد jasad	
bodyguard *n.* حارس haaris	bookish *n.* شديد الاطلاع shadeedol ettilaa'
bog *n.* 1 حمّام hammaam	bookish *n.* كتابي kitaabiy
bog *n.* 2 مستنقع mostanqa'	booklet *n.* كتيب kotayyib
bog *v.* يعلق yo'alliq	boon *n.* نعمة ni'mah
bogle *n.* فزّاعة fazzaa'ah	boor *n.* غليظ ghaleedd
bogus *adj.* زائف zaauif	boost *n.* زيادة ziyaadah
boil *n.* سلق salq	boost *v.* 1 يرفع yazeed

boost v. 2	يزيد yarfa'
boot n.	جزمة jizmah
booth n.	كشك koshk
booty n.	غنيمة ghaneemah
booze v.	خمر khamr
border n.	حد had
border v.	يحد yahid
bore v.	يحمل yahmil
bore n.	حمل haml
born v.	يولد yoolad
born rich adj.	ولدغنياً wolida ghaniyyan
borne adj.	مدرك modrak
borrow v.	يقترض yaqtarid
bosom n.	حضن hodn
boss n.	رئيس rauees
botany n.	علمالنبات ilmo nnabaat
botch v.	يفسد yafsid
both adj.	كلا kila
both pron.	كلا kila
both adv.	سواء sawaau
both conj.	كلا kila
bother v.	يزعج yoz'ij
botheration n.	إزعاج ez'aaj
bottle n.	زجاجة zojaajah
bottle v.	يعلّب yo'allib
bottler n. 1	بارز baariz
bottler n. 2	معلّب mo'allib
bottler n. 3	صانع saani'
bottom n. 1	مؤخرة mouakhkhirah
bottom n. 2	أسفل uasfal
bough n.	غصن ghosn
boulder n.	جلمود jalmood
bouncer n.	حافظالنظام haafiddo nniddaam
bound n.	ملزم molzam

boundary n.	حد had
bountiful adj.	وافر waafir
bounty n.	هبة hibah
bouquet n.	باقةأزهار baaqato uazhaar
bout n.	نوبة nawbah
bow v.	ينحني yanhany
bow n.	انحناء enhinaau
bow n.	قوس qaws
bowel n.	معيّ ma'iy
bower n.	مصيف masyaf
bowl n.	زبدية zibdiyyah
bowl v.	يدحرج yodahrij
box n.	صندوق sandooq
boxing n.	ملاكمة lolaakamah
boy n.	صبي sabiy
boycott v.	يقاطع yoqaati'
boycott n.	مقاطعة moqaata'ah
boyhood n.	الصبا uassiba
brace n.	دعامة da'aamah
bracelet n.	سوار siwaar
brag v.	يتبجح yatabajjah
brag n.	متبجح motabajjih
braille n.	بريل breel
brain n.	دماغ dimaagh
brake n.	فرامل faraamil
brake v.	يوقف yowqif
branch n.	فرع fir'
brand n. 1	علامةتجارية alaamaton tijaariyyah
brand n. 2	نوع naw'
brandy n.	البراندي albraandi
brangle v.	جدالحاد jidaalon haad
brass n.	نحاس nahhaas
brave adj.	شجاع shojaa'
bravery n.	شجاعة shajaa'ah

brawl v. يشاجر yoshaajir

brawl n. شجار shijaar

bray n. نهيق naheeq

bray v. ينهق yanhaq

breach n. خرق kharq

breach v. يخرق yakhriq

bread n. خبز khobz

breaden v. يصنع من الخبز yasna'o minal khobz

breadth n. اتساع ettisaa'

break v. 1 يستريح yastareeh

break v. 2 يكسر yaksir

break n. استراحة estiraahah

breakage n. كسر kasr

breakdown n. انهيار enhiyaar

breakfast n. إفطار eftaar

breakneck n. جد الخطورة jiddol khodoorah

breast n. ثدي thady

breath n. نفس nafas

breathe v. يتنفس yatanaffas

breeches n. بنطال bintaal

breed v. يتكاثر yatakaathar

breed n. نوع naw'

breed n. نسل nasl

breeze n. نسيم naseem

breviary n. كتاب الادعيه kitaabol uad'iyah

brevity n. إيجاز ueejaaz

brew v. 1 يصنع الشاي yasna'o shshaay

brew v. 2 يخمّر yokhammir

brew n. 1 شاي shaay

brew n. 2 خمر khamr

brewery n. مخمرة mokhmarah

bribe n. رشوة rashwah

bribe v. يرشي yarshi

brick n. قرميد qarmeed

bride n. عروس aroos

bridegroom n. عريس arees

bridge n. جسر jisr

bridge v. يقلّص yoqallis

bridle n. لجام lijaam

brief adj. موجز mojaz

brigade n. لواء liwaau

brigadier n. عميد ameed

bright adj. مشرق moshriq

brighten v. يفتّح yofattih

brilliance n. تألق taualloq

brilliant adj. رائع raaui'

brim n. حافة haaffah

brine n. محلول ملحي mahloolon milhiy

bring v. يجلب yajlib

brinjal n. باذنجان baadhinjaan

brink n. حافة haaffah

brisk adj. منعش mon'ish

bristle n. شعر الفرشاة sha'rol forshaah

british adj. بريطاني bareetaaniy

brittle adj. هش hash

broad adj. واسع waasi'

broadcast n. بث bath

broadcast v. يبث yabith

brocade n. حرير مطرّز hareeron motarraz

brocade v. يطرّز yotarriz

broccoli n. قرنبيط qarnabeet

brochure n. كراسة korraasah

brochure n. نشرة nashrah

broker n. وسيط waseet

brood n. نوع naw'

brood *n.* فراخ firaakh	**buffalo** *n.* جاموس jaamoos
brood *v.* يتأمل yatauammal	**buffoon** *n.* مهرج moharrij
brood *v.* يفقس yafqis	**bug** *n.* حشرة hasharah
brood *adj.* مفرخ mofarrikh	**bugle** *n.* بوق booq
broom *n.* مكنسة miknasah	**build** *v.* يبني yabni
bronze *n.* برونز bronz	**build** *n.* بناء binaau
bronze *adj.* برونزي bronziy	**building** *n.* بناء binaau
broth *n.* مرق maraq	**bulb** *n.* 1 بصيلة bosaylah
brothel *n.* بيت دعارة bayt da'aarah	**bulb** *n.* 2 مصباح misbaah
brother *n.* شقيق shaqeeq	**bulk** *n.* كتلة kotlah
brotherhood *n.* أخوة uokhowwah	**bulky** *adj.* ضخم dakhm
brow *n.* جبين jabeen	**bull** *n.* ثور thawr
brown *adj.* بني bonniy	**bulldog** *n.* كلب البلدغ Kalbol boldogh
brown *n.* بني bonniy	**bull's eye** *n.* هدف hadaf
browse *n.* تصفح tasaffoh	**bullet** *n.* رصاصة rasaasah
browse *v.* يتصفح yatasaffah	**bulletin** *n.* نشرة nashrah
bruise *n.* كدمة kadmah	**bullock** *n.* عجل ijl
bruit *v.* يشيع yasheeu	**bully** *n.* متغطرس motaghatris
bruit *n.* وشوشة washwashah	**bully** *v.* يتغطرس yataghatras
brush *n.* فرشاة forshaah	**bulwark** *n.* متراس mitraas
brush *v.* يفرك yafrik	**bumper** *n.* ممتص الصدمات momtason lisadamaat
brustle *v.* يطقطق yotaqtiq	
brutal *adj.* وحشي wahshiy	**bumpy** *adj.* وعر wa'ir
brute *n.* وحش wahsh	**bunch** *n.* باقة baaqah
bubble *n.* فقاعة foqaa'ah	**bundle** *n.* حزمة hozmah
bucket *n.* دلو dalw	**bungalow** *n.* جناح صغير janaahon sagheer
buckle *n.* إبزيم ebzeem	
buckle *v.* يربط yarbit	**bungalwo** *v.* يعمل بغير اتقان ya'malo bighayri etqaan
bud *n.* برعم bor'om	
budge *v.* يتزحزح yatazahzah	**bungle** *n.* عمل غير متقن amalon ghayro motqanin
budge *n.* تزحزح tazahzoh	
budget *n.* ميزانية meezaaniyyah	**bunk** *n.* 1 سرير مزدوج sareeron mozdawaj
buff *n.* 1 جلد الجاموس jildol jaamoos	
buff *n.* 2 برتقالي مصفر bortoqaaliyon mosfar	**bunk** *n.* 2 كلام فارغ kalaamon faarigh

bunker *n.* القبو ualqabw
buoy *n.* عوامة awwaamah
buoyancy *n.* طفو tafw
burden *n.* عبء ibu
burden *v.* يثقل yothqil
burdensome *adj.* مثقل mothqil
bureau *n.* مكتب maktab
Bureacuracy *n.* بيروقراطية beeroqraatiyyah
bureaucrat *n.* بيروقراطي beeroqraatiy
burglar *n.* لص lis
burglary *n.* سطو satw
burial *n.* دفن dafn
burk *v.* غابي ghabiy
burn *v.* يحرق yahriq
burn *n.* حرق harq
burrow *n.* ملجأ maljau
burst *v.* ينفجر yanfajir
burst *n.* انفجار enfijaar
bury *v.* يدفن yadfin
bus *n.* حافلة haaffah
bush *n.* شجيرة shojayrah
business *n.* عمل amal
businessman *n.* رجل اعمال rajolol ua'maal
bustle *v.* ينشط yanshat
busy *adj.* مشغول mashghool
but *prep.* إلى ella
but *conj.* لكن laakin
butcher *n.* جزار jazzaar
butcher *v.* يذبح yadhbah
butter *n.* زبدة zobdah
butter *v.* يدهن بالزبد yadhano bizzobdah
butterfly *n.* فراشة faraashah

buttermilk *n.* مخيض اللبن makheedo llaban
buttock *n.* ردف rodf
button *n.* زر zir
button *v.* يزرر yozarrir
buy *v.* يشتري yashtari
buy *n.* شروة sharwah
buyer *n.* مشتر moshtari
buzz *v.* يطن yatin
buzz *n.* طنين taneen
by *prep.* قرب qorb
by *prep.* عبر abr
by *prep.* بواسطة biwaasitat
by *adv.* بجانب bijaanib
bye-bye *interj.* وداعا wadaa'an
by-election *n.* الانتخابات الفرعية ualuintikhaabaatol fir'iyyah
bylaw, bye-law *n.* قانون qaanoon
bypass *n.* ممر جانبي mamarron jaanibiy
by-product *n.* نتيجة ثانوية nateejah thaanawiyyah
byre *n.* حظيرة أبقار haddeerato uabqaar
byword *n.* قول مأثور qawlon mauthoor

C

cab *n.* سيارة أجرة sayyarato ujrah
cabaret *n.* ملهى malha
cabbage *n.* ملفوف malfoof
cabin *n.* قمرة qomrah
cabinet *n.* 1 خزانة khizaanah

cabinet *n.* 2 مجلس‌الوزراء majlisol wozaraau

cable *n.* كابل kaabil

cable *v.* يبرق yabriq

cache *n.* مخبأ makhbau

cachet *n.* دمغة damghah

cackle *v.* قهقرة qahqarah

cactus *n.* صبار sabbaar

cad *n.* نذل nadhl

cadet *n.* طالب كلية‌حربية taalibo kolliyatin harbiyyah

cadge *v.* يتطفل yatataffal

cadmium *n.* الكادميوم ualkadmiyom

cafe *n.* مقهى maqha

cage *n.* قفص qafas

cake *n.* كعكة ka'kah

calamity *n.* مصيبة moseebah

calcium *n.* الكلسيوم ualkaalsyom

calculate *v.* يحسب bahsib

calculator *n.* آلة‌حاسبة uaalaton haasibah

calculation *n.* حساب hisaab

calendar *n.* تقويم taqweem

calf *n.* عجل ijl

call *v.* يتصل yattasil

call *v.* يدعو yad'o

call *n.* قرار qaraar

call *n.* دعوة da'wah

caller *n.* مستدعي mostad'i

calligraphy *n.* تخطيط takhteet

calling *n.* استدعاء estid'aau

callow *adj.* قليل‌الخبرة qaleelol khibrah

callous *adj.* قاسي‌القلب qaasil qalb

calm *n.* هدوء hodoou

calm *v.* يهدأ yahdau

calmative *adj.* مهدئ mohaddiu

calorie *n.* سعرة‌حرارية so'raton haraariyyah

calumniate *v.* يفتري yaftari

camel *n.* جمل jamal

camera *n.* آلة‌تصوير uaalato tasweer

camlet *n.* قماش‌من‌شعر‌الجمل qimaashon min sha'ril jamal

camp *n.* مخيم mokhayyam

camp *v.* يخيم yokhayyim

campaign *n.* حملة hamlah

camphor *n.* كافور kaafoor

can *n.* علبة ilbah

can *v.* يستطيع yastatee'

can *v.* يعلّب yo'allib

canal *n.* قناة qanah

canard *n.* إشاعة‌كاذبة eshaa'aton kaadhibah

cancel *v.* يلغي yalghi

cancellation *n.* إلغاء elghaau

cancer *n.* سرطان sarataan

candid *adj.* صريح sareeh

candidate *n.* مرشح morashshah

candle *n.* شمعة sham'ah

candour *n.* صراحة saraahah

candy *n.* حلوى halwa

candy *v.* حلوى halwa

cane *n.* قصب qasab

cane *v.* يستنفز yastanfiz

canister *n.* عليبة olaybah

cannon *n.* مدفع madfa'

cannonade *v.* يهاجم‌بالمدفعية haajama bilmadfa'iyyah

canon *n.* شريعة sharee'ah

canopy *n.* مظلّة middallah	captivate *v.* يأسر yausor
canteen *n.* مقصف maqsaf	captive *n.* أسير uaseer
canter *n.* تخبّب takhabbob	captive *adj.* مأسور mausoor
canton *n.* إقليم eqleem	captivity *n.* أسر uasr
cantonment *n.* مقرمؤقت maqaron mouaqqat	capture *v.* يأسر yausor
	capture *n.* أسر uasr
canvas *n.* قماش qimaash	car *n.* سيارة sayyarah
canvass *v.* يستطلع yastatli'	carat *n.* قيراط qeeraat
cap *n.* قبعة qobba'ah	caravan *n.* قافلة qaafilah
cap *v.* يغطّي yoghatti	carbide *n.* كربيد karbeed
capability *n.* قدرة qodrah	carbon *n.* كربون karboon
capable *adj.* قادرعلى qaadiron 'ala	card *n.* بطاقة bitaaqah
capacious *adj.* فسيح faseeh	cardamom *n.* هال haal
capacity *n.* قدرة qodrah	cardboard *n.* ورقمقوّى waraqon moqawwa
cape *n.* رداءبلاأكمام ridaauon bila uakmaam	cardiac *adj.* قلبي qalbiy
cape *n.* رأس raus	cardinal *adj.* كاردينالي kaardinaaliy
capital *n.* 1 رأسالمال rausol maal	cardinal *n.* كاردينال kaardinaal
capital *n.* 2 عاصمة aasimah	care *n.* رعاية ri'aayah
capital *n.* 3 حرفكبير harfon kabeer	care *v.* يرعى yar'a
capital *adj.* 1 ممتاز momtaaz	career *n.* مهنة mihnah
capital *adj.* 2 عاصمي aasimiy	careful *adj.* حريص harees
capitalist *n.* رأسمالي rausomaaliy	careless *adj.* مهمل mohmil
capitulate *v.* يستسلم yastaslim	caress *v.* يعانق yo'aaniq
caprice *n.* نزوة nazwah	cargo *n.* حمولة hamoolah
capricious *adj.* نزوي nazwah	caricature *n.* رسمهزلي rasmon hazaliy
Capricorn *n.* برجالجدي borjol jadi	carious *adj.* نخر nakhr
capsicum *n.* فلفلحلو filfilon holw	carl *n.* غليظ ghaleedd
capsize *v.* ينقلب yanqalib	carnage *n.* مجزرة majzarah
capsular *adj.* كبسولي kabsooliy	carnival *n.* مهرجان mahrajaan
capsule *n.* كبسولة kabsoolah	carol *n.* أغنيةمرحة uoghniyaton mariha
captain *n.* قبطان qobtaan	carpal *adj.* رسغي rosghiy
captaincy *n.* قبطنة qabtanah	carpenter *n.* نجّار najjaar
caption *n.* تعليق ta'leeq	

carpentry *n.* نجارة nijaarah

carpet *n.* سجادة sijjaadah

carriage *n.* 1 حمل haml

carriage *n.* 2 نقل naql

carrier *n.* 1 حامل haamil

carrier *n.* 2 ناقل naaqil

carrot *n.* جزرة jazarah

carry *v.* يحمل yahmil

cart *n.* 1 عربة arabah

cart *n.* 2 سلّة sallah

cartage *n.* نقل naql

carton *n.* علبة olbah

cartoon *n.* رسوم متحركة rosoomon motaharrikah

cartridge *n.* خرطوشة khartooshah

carve *v.* 1 يحفر yahfir

carve *v.* 2 ينقش yanqosh

cascade *n.* تتالي tataali

case *n.* 1 حالة haalah

case *n.* 2 وضع wad'

case *n.* 3 قضية qadiyyah

case *n.* 4 صندوق sondooq

cash *n.* نقد naqd

cash *v.* يصرف yasrif

cashier *n.* أمين الصندوق umeeno ssandooq

casing *n.* غلاف ghilaaf

cask *n.* برميل خشبي barmeelon khashabiy

casket *n.* نعش na'sh

cassette *n.* شريط shareet

cast *v.* 1 يلقي yolqi

cast *v.* 2 يلقي yosabbik

cast *v.* 3 يلقي يختار yakhtaaro momathilan

cast *n.* 1 رمية ramyah

cast *n.* 2 قالب qaalib

cast *n.* 3 ممثل momathil

caste *n.* طبقة tabaqah

castigate *v.* يوبّخ yowabbikh

casting *n.* صب sab

cast-iron *adj.* صلب salb

castle *n.* قلعة qal'ah

castor oil *n.* زيت الخروع zaytol kharwa'

casual *adj.* عرضي aradiy

casualty *n.* مصاب mosaab

cat *n.* هر hir

catalogue *n.* فهرس fahras

cataract *n.* شلال shallaal

catch *v.* يقبض yaqbid

catch *n.* حيلة heelah

categorical *adj.* قاطع qaati'

category *n.* فئة fiuah

cater *v.* يلبّي yolabbi

caterpillar *n.* يرقة yaraqah

cathedral *n.* كاتدرائية kaatidraauiyyah

catholic *adj.* كاثوليكي kaathooleeki

catholicism *n.* الكاثوليكية ualkaathooleekiyyah

cattle *n.* ماشية mashiyah

cauliflower *n.* زهر zahr

causal *adj.* سببي sababiy

causality *n.* سببية sababiyyah

cause *n.* 1 هدف hadaf

cause *n.* 2 سبب sabab

cause *v.* يسبّب yosabbib

causeway *n.* ممر مرتفع mamarron mortafi'

caustic *adj.* كاوي kaawi

caution *n.* 1 إحتراس ehtiraas
caution *n.* 2 إنذار endhaar
caution *v.* يحذِر yohadhdhir
cautious *adj.* حذر hadhir
cavalry *n.* سلاح الفرسان silaahol forsaan
cave *n.* كهف kahf
cavern *n.* كهف كبير kahfon kabeer
cavil *v.* يعترض ya'tarid
cavity *n.* تجويف tajweef
caw *n.* نعيق na'eeq
caw *v.* ينعق yan'aq
cease *v.* يوقف yoqif
ceaseless *adj.* متواصل motawaasil
cedar *n.* أرز uarz
ceiling *n.* سقف saqf
celebrate *v.* يحتفل yahtafil
celebration *n.* احتفال ehtifaal
celebrity *n.* شهرة shohrah
celebrity *n.* شخص مشهور shakhson mashhoor
celestial *adj.* سماوي samaawiy
celibacy *n.* 1 تبتل tabattol
celibacy *n.* 2 عذوبة ozoobah
celibate *adj.* أعزب ua'zab
cell *n.* 1 زنزانة zinzaanah
cell *n.* 2 خانة khaanah
cell *n.* 3 خلية khaliyyah
cellar *n.* قبو qabw
cellular *adj.* خلوي khalawiy
cement *n.* أسمنت esmant
cement *v.* يغطي بالأسمنت yaghaddi bilesmant
cemetery *n.* مقبرة maqbarah
cense *v.* يبخر yobakhkhir
censer *n.* مبخرة mabkhara

censor *n.* رقيب raqeeb
censor *v.* يراقب yoraaqib
censorious *adj.* ناقد naaqid
censorship *n.* رقابة raqaabah
censure *n.* توبيخ tawbeekh
censure *v.* يوبِّخ yowabbikh
census *n.* تعداد السكان ti'daado ssokkaan
cent *n.* سنت sint
centenarian *n.* مئوي miuawiy
centenary *n.* ذكرى مئوية dhikra miuawiyyah
centennial *n.* ذكرى مئوية dhikra miuawiyyah
center *n.* مركز markiz
centigrade *adj.* درجة مئوية darajah miuawiyyah
centipede *n.* حريش hareesh
central *adj.* مركزي markaziy
centre *n.* مركز markiz
centrifugal *adj.* طرد مركزي tardon markaziy
centuple *n. & adj.* مئة ضعف miuato di'f
century *n.* قرن qarn
ceramics *n.* خزف khazaf
cerated *adj.* مغطى بالشمع moghatta bishsham'
cereal *n.* حبوب hboob
cereal *adj.* حبيبي hobaybiy
cerebral *adj.* دماغي dimaaghiy
ceremonial *adj.* إحتفالي ehtifaaliy
ceremonious *adj.* رسمي rasmiy
ceremony *n.* مراسم احتفال maraasimo hhtifaal
certain *adj.* 1 متأكّد motauakkad

certain *adj.* 2 معيّن mo'ayyan

certainly *adv.* بالتأكيد bittaukeed

certainty *n.* يقين yaqeen

certificate *n.* شهادة shahaadah

certify *v.* تصديق tasdeeq

cerumen *n.* خ صملا simaagh

cesspool *n.* بالوعة baaloo'ah

chain *n.* سلسلة silsilah

chair *n.* كرسي korsiy

chairman *n.* رئيس مجلس raueeso majlis

chaise *n.* عربة arabah

chalice *n.* 1 كأس القربان kausol qorbaan

chalice *n.* 2 ميسم maysam

challenge *n.* تحد tahaddi

challenge *v.* يتحدّى yatahadda

chamber *n.* غرفة ghorfah

chamberlain *n.* حاجب haajib

champion *n.* بطل batal

champion *v.* يحامي yohaami

chance *n.* فرصة forsah

chancellor *n.* مستشار mostashaar

chancery *n.* مكتب المحفوظات maktabol mahfooddaat

change *v.* يغيّر yoghayyir

change *n.* تغيير taghyeer

channel *n.* قناة qanaah

chant *n.* ترنيمة tarneemah

chant *v.* يرنّم yorannim

chaos *n.* فوضى fawda

chaotic *adv.* فوضوي fawdaawiy

chapel *n.* كنيسة kaneesah

chapter *n.* فصل fasl

character *n.* شخصية shakhsiyyah

charge *v.* يتهم yattahim

charge *n.* تهمة tohmah

chariot *n.* عربة arabah

charitable *adj.* خيري khayriy

charity *n.* صدقة sadaqah

charm *n.* سحر sihr

charm *v.* يسحر yashar

chart *n.* 1 رسم توضيحي rasmon tawdeehiy

chart *n.* 2 خريطة khareetah

charter *n.* ميثاق meethaaq

chase *v.* يطارد yotaarid

chase *n.* مطاردة motaaradah

chaste *adj.* عفيف afeef

chastity *n.* عفة iffa

chat *n.* دردشة dardashah

chat *v.* يدردش yodardish

chatter *v.* يثرثر yotharthir

chauffeur *n.* سائق saauiq

cheap *adj.* رخيص rakhees

cheapen *v.* يرخّص yorakhkhis

cheat *v.* يخدع yakhda'

cheat *n.* مخادع mokhaadi'

cheat *n.* خدعة khid'ah

check *v.* يتفحص yatafahhas

check *n.* تفحّص tafahhos

checkmate *n.* كش ملك kish malik

cheek *n.* خد khad

cheek *n.* وقاحة waqaahah

cheep *v.* يزقزق yozaqziq

cheer *n.* ابتهاج ebtihaaj

cheer *v.* يبهج yobhij

cheerful *adj.* مرح marah

cheerless *adj.* كئيب kaueeb

cheese *n.* جبن jibn

chemical *adj.* كيميائي kimyaauiy

chemical *n.* مادة كيميائية maadaton keemyaauiyyah

chemise *n.* قميص qamees

chemist *n.* صيدلي saydaliyyah

chemistry *n.* كيمياء keemyaau

cheque *n.* صك sak

cherish *v.* يعتز ya'taz

cheroot *n.* سيجار مربّع seejaar morabba'

chess *n.* شطرنج shitaranj

chest *n.* صدر sadr

chestnut *n.* كستناء kastanaau

chew *v.* يمضغ yamdogh

chevalier *n.* نبيل nabeel

chicken *n.* دجاجة dajaajah

chicken *adj.* جبان jabaan

chide *v.* يوبّخ yowabbikh

chief *adj.* رئيس rauees

chieftain *n.* شيخ القبيلة shaykhol qabeelah

child *n.* طفل tifl

childhood *n.* طفولة tofoolah

childish *adj.* طفولي tofooliy

chiliad *n.* مجموعة ألفيّة majmoo'aton ualfiyyah

chill *n.* قشعريرة qash'areerah

chilli *n.* فلفل حار filfilon haar

chilly *adj.* بارد baarid

chimney *n.* مدخنة madkhanah

chimpanzee *n.* الشمبانزي uashimbaanziy

chin *n.* ذقن dhaqn

China *n.* الصين uasseen

china *n.* فخّار fakhkhaar

chirp *v.* يغرّد yogharrid

chirp *n.* تغريد taghreed

chisel *n.* إزميل ezmeel

chisel *v.* ينحت بالإزميل yanhato bil ezmeel

chit *n.* 1 مذكرة modhakkirah

chit *n.* 2 فتاة وقحة fataaton waqihah

chivalrous *adj.* شهم shahm

chivalry *n.* شهامة shahaamah

chlorine *n.* كلور kloor

chloroform *n.* كلوروفورم kloorofoorm

choice *n.* خيار khayaar

choir *n.* جوقة jawqah

choke *v.* يختنق yakhtaniq

cholera *n.* كوليرا kolira

chocolate *n.* حلوى الكاكاو halwal kaakaaw

choose *v.* يختار yakhtaar

chop *v.* يقطّع yoqta'

chord *n.* وتر watar

choroid *n.* غلاف العين المشيمي ghilaafol 'aynil masheemiy

chorus *n.* جوقة jawqah

Christ *n.* المسيح ualmaseeh

Christendom *n.* المسيحية ualmaseehiyyah

Christian *n.* مسيحي maseehiy

Christian *adj.* مسيحي maseehiy

Christianity *n.* الديانة المسيحية uaddiyanah ualmaseehiyyah

Christmas *n.* عيد الميلاد eedol meelaad

chrome *n.* كروم kroom

chronic *adj.* مزمن mozmin

chronicle *n.* وقائع waqaaui'

chronological *n.* متسلسل motasalsil

chronology *n.* تسلسل زمني tasalsolon zamaniy

chronograph *n.* جدول زمني jadwalon zamaniy

chuckle *v.* يضحك yad hak

chum *n.* صديق sadeeq

church *n.* كنيسة kaneesah

churchyard *n.* فناء الكنيسة finaauol kaneesah

churl *n.* بخيل bakheel

churn *v.* يخض yakhod

churn *n.* ممخضة الزبدة mimkhadato zzibdah

cigar *n.* سيجار seejaar

cigarette *n.* سيجارة seejaarah

cinema *n.* قاعة العرض qaa'atol 'ard

cinnabar *n.* الزنجفر uazzanjafr

cinnamon *n.* قرفة qirfah

cipher *n.* شيفرة sheefrah

cipher *v.* يفك الشيفرة yafokko shsheefrah

circle *n.* دائرة daauirah

circle *v.* يدور yadoor

circuit *n.* 1 وصلة waslah

circuit *n.* 2 حلبة halabah

circumfluence *n.* تطويق مائي tatweeqon maauiy

circumspect *adj.* متعقّل mota'aqqil

circular *adj.* دائري daauiriy

circular *n.* دورية dawriyyah

circulate *v.* يعمّم yo'ammim

circulation *n.* تعميم ta'meem

circumference *n.* محيط moheet

circumstance *n.* ظرف ddarf

circus *n.* سيرك sirk

cist *n.* تابوت taaboot

citadel *n.* قلعة qal'ah

cite *v.* يستشهد yastashhid

citizen *n.* مواطن mowaatin

citizenship *n.* مواطنة mowaatanah

citric *adj.* حامضي haamidiy

citrus *n.* حامض haamid

city *n.* مدينة madeenah

civic *adj.* مدني madaniy

civics *n.* التربية المدنية uattarbiyatol madaniyyah

civil *adj.* مدني madaniy

civilian *n.* مدني madaniy

civilization *n.* حضارة hadaarah

civilize *v.* يحضر yohaddir

clack *v.* يثرثر yotharthir

clack *n.* ثرثرة thartharah

claim *n.* مطالبة motaalabah

claim *v.* يطالب yotaalib

claimant *n.* مطالب motaalib

clamber *v.* يتسلّق yatasallaq

clamour *n.* صخب sakhb

clamour *v.* يصخب yaskhab

clamp *n.* مشبك mashbak

clandestine *adj.* سري sirriy

clap *v.* يصفّق yosaffiq

clap *n.* تصفيق tasfeeq

clarify *v.* يوضّح yowaddih

clarification *n.* توضيح tawdeeh

clarion *n.* بوق booq

clarity *n.* وضوح wodooh

clash *n.* اشتباك eshtibaak

clash *v.* يشتبك yashtabik

clasp *n.* مشبك mashbak

class *n.* 1 صف saf

class *n.* 2 فئة fiuah

classic *adj.* كلاسيكي Klaaseekiy

classic *n.* كلاسيكي Klaaseekiy

classical *adj.* تقليدي taqleediy

classification *n.* تصنيف tasneef

classify *v.* يصنّف yosannif

clause *n.* جملة jomlah

claw *n.* مخلب mikhlab

clay *n.* صلصال silsaal

clean *adv.* نظيف naddeef

clean *adj.* نظيف naddeef

clean *v.* ينظّف yonaddddif

cleanliness *n.* نظافة naddaafah

cleanse *v.* يطهّر yotahhir

clear *adj.* واضح waadih

clear *v.* 1 يفرّغ yofarrigh

clear *v.* 2 يوضّح yowaddih

clearance *n.* تخليص takhlees

clearly *adv.* بوضوح biwodooh

cleft *n.* شق shiq

clergy *n.* رجل دين rajolo deen

clerical *adj.* كتبة katabah

clerk *n.* كاتب kaatib

clever *adj.* ذكي dhakiy

clew *n.* كرة خيوط korato khoyoot

click *n.* نقرة naqrah

click *v.* ينقر yanqor

client *n.* عميل ameel

cliff *n.* جرف jorf

climate *n.* مناخ manaakh

climax *n.* ذروة dhorwah

climb *n.* تسلّق tasalloq

climb *v.* يتسلّق yatasallaq

cling *v.* يتشبّث yatashabbath

clinic *n.* عيادة iyaadah

clink *n.* صلصلة salsalah

cloak *n.* عباءة abaauah

clock *n.* ساعة saa'ah

clod *n.* كتلة تراب kotlato toraab

cloister *n.* دير dayr

close *n.* قريب qareeb

close *adj.* مغلق moghlaq

close *v.* يغلق yoghliq

closet *n.* خزانة khizaanah

closure *n.* إغلاق eghlaaq

clot *n.* جلطة jaltah

clot *v.* يتجلط yatajallat

cloth *n.* قماش qimaash

clothe *v.* يكسي yaksi

clothes *n.* ملابس malaabis

clothing *n.* ملبس malbas

cloud *n.* سحابة sahaabah

cloudy *adj.* غائم ghaauim

clove *n.* كبش قرنفل kabsho qronfol

clown *n.* مهرج moharrij

club *n.* ناد nadi

clue *n.* دليل daleel

clumsy *adj.* أخرق uakhraq

cluster *n.* كتلة kotlah

cluster *v.* يتكتل yatakattal

clutch *n.* قابض qaabid

clutch *v.* يقبض yaqbid

clutter *v.* ضوضاء dawdaau

coach *n.* مدرب modarrib

coachman *n.* حوذي hoodhiy

coal *n.* فحم fahm

coalition *n.* تحالف tahaalof

coarse *adj.* خشن khashin

coast *n.* ساحل saahil

coat *n.* معطف mi'taf

coating *n.* طلاء tilaau

coax *v.* يتملّق yatamallaq

cobalt *n.* الكوبالت ualkoobalt

cobbler *n.* إسكافي eskaafiy

cobra *n.* أفعى الكوبرا uf'al kobra

cobweb *n.* بيت العنكبوت baytol 'ankaboot

cocaine *n.* كوكايين kokaayeen

cock *n.* ديك deek

cocker *v.* يدلل yodallil

cockle *v.* يجعّد yoja"id

cock-pit *n.* حجيرة الطيّار hojayrato ttayyaar

cockroach *n.* صرصور sarsoor

coconut *n.* جوزة الهند jawzatol hind

code *n.* رمز ramz

co-education *n.* التعليم المختلط uatta'leemol mokhtalat

coefficient *n.* معامل الضرب mo'aamilo ddaeb

co-exist *v.* يتعايش yata'aayash

co-existence *n.* تعايش ta'aayosh

coffee *n.* قهوة qahwah

coffin *n.* نعش na'sh

cog *n.* دولاب مسنّن doolaabon mosannan

cogent *adj.* مقنع moqni'

cognate *adj.* من أصل واحد min uaslin waahid

cognizance *n.* إدراك edraak

cohabit *v.* يتعايش yata'aayash

coherent *adj.* 1 مفهوم mafhoom

coherent *adj.* 2 متماسك motmaasik

cohesive *adj.* 1 مفهوم mafhoom

cohesive *adj.* 2 متماسك motmaasik

coif *n.* 1 تسريحة tasreehah

coif *n.* 2 قلنسوة qolonsowah

coin *n.* نقد قطعة qit'ato naqd

coinage *n.* عملة imlah

coincide *v.* يتزامن yatazaaman

coir *n.* ألياف جوز الهند ualyaafo jawzil hind

coke *v.* فحم الكوك fahmol kook

cold *adj.* بارد baarid

cold *n.* 1 زكام zokaam

cold *n.* 2 برد bard

collaborate *v.* يتعاون yata'aawan

collaboration *n.* تعاون ta'aawon

collapse *v.* ينهار yanhaar

collar *n.* قلادة qilaadah

colleague *n.* زميل zameel

collect *v.* يجمع yajma'

collection *n* مجموعة majmoo'ah

collective *adj.* جماعي jamaa'iy

collector *n.* جامع jaami'

college *n.* كلية kolliyyah

collide *v.* يتصادم yatasaadam

collision *n.* تصادم tasaadom

collusion *n.* تواطؤ tawaatou

colon *n.* القولون ualqooloon

colonel *n.* كولونيل koloneel

colonial *adj.* استعماري esti'maariy

colony *n.* مستعمرة mosta'marah

colour *n.* لون lawn

colour *v.* يلوّن yolawwin

colter *n.* سكة المحراث sikkatol mihraath

column *n.* عمود amood

coma *n.* غيبوبة ghayboobah

comb *n.* مشط misht

combat *n.* قتال qitaal

combat *v.* يقاتل yoqaatil

combatant *n.* مقاتل moqaatil

combatant *adj.* قتالي qitaaliy

combination *n.* مجموعة majmoo'ah

combine *v.* يدمج yadmij

come *v.* يأتي yauti

comedian *n.* ممثل هزلي momaththilon hazaliy

comedy *n.* الكوميديا lkoomeedyah

comet *n.* مذنّب modhannab

comfit *n.* حلوى محشوّة halwaa mahshowwah

comfort *n.* راحة raahah

comfort *v.* 1 يطمئن yotamuin

comfort *v.* 2 يريح yoreeh

comfortable *adj.* مريح moreeh

comic *adj.* فكاهي fokaahiy

comic *n.* مجلّة هزلية majallaton hazaliyyah

comical *adj.* هزلي hazaliy

comma *n.* فاصلة faasilah

command *n.* 1 أمر uamr

command *n.* 2 قيادة qiyaadah

command *v.* يقود yaqood

commandant *n.* قائد qaauid

commander *n.* قائد qaauid

commandment *n.* وصيّة wasiyyah

commemorate *v.* يحيي ذكرى yohyi dhikra

commemoration *n.* إحياء ذكرى ehyaauo dhikra

commence *v.* يباشر yobaashir

commencement *n.* بدء bidu

commend *v.* يثني yathni

commendable *adj.* جدير بالثناء jadeeron biththanaau

commendation *n.* ثناء thanaau

comment *v.* يعلّق yo'alliq

comment *n.* تعليق ta'leeq

commentary *n.* تعليق ta'leeq

commentator *n.* معلّق mo'allaq

commerce *n.* تجارة tijaarah

commercial *adj.* تجاري tijaariy

commiserate *v.* يرثي yarthi

commission *n.* 1 مفوضيّة mofawwadiyyah

commission *n.* 2 عمولة omoolah

commissioner *n.* مفوض mofawwad

commissure *n.* منطقة رابطة mantiqaton raabitah

commit *v.* 1 يلتزم yaltazim

commit *v.* 2 يرتكب yartakib

commitment *n.* إلتزام eltizaam

committee *n.* لجنة lajnah

commodity *n.* سلعة sil'ah

common *adj.* مشترك moshtarak

commoner *n.* من العامّة minal 'aamah

commonplace *adj.* مألوف mauloof

commonwealth *n.* الكومنولث ualkomonwilth

commotion *n.* هياج hayaaj

commove *v.* يهيّج yaheej

communal *adj.* اشتراكي eshtiraakiy

commune *n.* بلدية baladiyyah

commune *v.* 1 يندمج yandamij

commune *v.* 2 يتناول yatanaawal

communicate *v.* يتواصل yatawaasal

communication *n.* تواصل tawaasol

communiqué *n.* بيان bayaan

communism *n.* شيوعية shoyoo'iyyah

communist *n.* شيوعي shoyoo'iy

community *n.* مجتمع mojtama'

commute *v.* 1 خفف العقوبة khaffafal 'oqoobah

commute *v.* 2 يتنقّل yatanaqqal

compact *adj.* مدمج modmaj

compact *n.* 1 علبة الزينة olbato zzeenah

compact *n.* 2 عقد aqd

companion *n.* رفيق rafeeq

company *n.* شركة sharikah

comparative *adj.* مقارن moqaarin

compare *v.* يقارن yoqaarin

comparison *n.* مقارنة moqaaranah

compartment *n.* مقصورة maqsoorah

compass *n.* بوصلة boosalah

compassion *n.* شفقة shafaqah

compel *v.* يجبر yajbir

compensate *v.* يعوّض yo'awwid

compensation *n.* تعويض ta'weed

compete *v.* يتنافس yatanaafas

competence *n.* اختصاص ekhtisaas

competent *adj.* مختص mokhtas

competition *n.* منافسة monaafasah

competitive *adj.* تنافسي tanaafosiy

compile *v.* يجمع yajma'

complacent *adj.* مرضي mardiy

complain *v.* يشكو yashko

complaint *n.* شكوى shakwa

complaisance *n.* لطف lotf

complaisant *adj.* لطيف lateef

complement *n.* تكملة takmilah

complementary *adj.* مكمل mokammil

complete *adj.* كامل kaamil

complete *v.* يتمَم yotammim

completion *n.* إتمام etmaam

complex *adj.* معقّد mo'aqqad

complex *n.* مجمع majma'

complexion *n.* بشرة basharah

compliance *n.* إمتثال emtithaal

compliant *adj.* متوافق motawaafiq

complicate *v.* يعقّد yo'aqqid

complication *n.* تعقيد ta'qeed

compliment *n.* إطراء etraau

compliment *v.* يطري yotri

comply *v.* يمتثل yamtathil

component *adj.* مكون mokawwin

compose *v.* 1 يشكّل yoshakkil

compose *v.* 2 يؤلّف youallif

composition *n.* تركيب tarkeebah

compositor *n.* طابعة taabi'ah

compost *n.* سماد samaad

composure *n.* صفاء safaau

compound *n.* 1 مادَة مركَّبة maaddaton morakkabah

compound *adj.* مركب morakkab

compound *n.* 2 مجمَع mojamma'

compound *v.* يركّب yorakkib

compounder *n.* مركّب morakkib

comprehend *v.* يفهم yafham

comprehension *n.* فهم fahm

comprehensive *adj.* شامل shaamil

compress *v.* يضغط yadghat

compromise *n.* حل وسط hallon wasat

compromise *v.* يضحّي yodahhi

compulsion *n.* إكراه ekraah

compulsory *adj.* إلزامي elzaamiy

compunction *n.* ندم nadam

computation *n.* حساب hisaab

compute *v.* يحسب yahsib

comrade *n.* رفيق rafeeq

concave *adj.* مقعر moqa"ar

conceal *v.* يخفي yakhfi

concede *v.* يتنازل yatanaazal

conceit *n.* غرور ghoroor

conceive *v.* 1 يتصوَّر yatasawwar

conceive *v.* 2 تحمل tahmil

concentrate *v.* يركّز yorakkiz

concentration *n.* تركيز tarkeez

concept *n.* مفهوم mafhoom

conception *n.* تصور tasawwor

concern *v.* يقلق yoqliq

concern *n.* قلق qalaq

concert *n.* حفلة موسيقية haflaton mooseeqiyyah

concert *v.* يخطّط yokhattit

concession *n.* امتياز emtiyaaz

conch *n.* محار mahaar

conciliate *v.* يوفّق yowaffiq

concise *adj.* موجز moojaz

conclude *v.* يستخلص yastakhlis

conclusion *n.* استنتاج estintaaj

conclusive *adj.* قطعي qat'iy

concoct *v.* يخترع yakhtari'

concoction *n.* خلطة khaltah

concord *n.* توافق tawaafoq

concrescence *n.* أنسجة نامية uansijaton namiyah

concrete *n.* إسمنت esmant

concrete *adj.* ملموس malmoos

concrete *v.* يضع الإسمنت yada'ol esmant

concubinage *n.* معاشرة خليلية mo'aasharaton khaleeliyyah

concubine *n.* خليلة khaleelah

conculcate *v.* يدوس yadoos

condemn *v.* يدين yodeen

condemnation *n.* إدانة edaanah

condense *v.* يكثّف yokaththif

condite *v.* يوخلّل yokhallil

condition *n.* 1 شرط shart

condition *n.* 2 وضع wad'

conditional *adj.* مشروط mashroot

condole *v.* يعزّي yo'azzi

condolence *n.* تعزية ta'ziyah

condonation *n.* إعفاء دين e'faauo dayn

conduct *n.* سلوك solook

conduct *v.* 1 يقود yaqood

conduct *v.* 2 يوصّل yowasil

conductor *n.* 1 موصل mowasil

conductor *n.* 2 قائد الأوركسترا qaauido uoorkistra

conductor *n.* 3 لاقط البرق laaqitol barq

cone *n.* مخروط makhloot

confectioner *n.* حلواني halawaaniy

confectionery *n.* صناعة الحلويات sinaa'atol halawiyyaat

confer *v.* 1 يمنح yamnah	conjecture *n.* حدس hads
confer *v.* 2 يتحاور yatahaawar	conjecture *v.* يستشعر yastash'ir
conference *v* مؤتمر moutamar	conjugal *adj.* زوجية zawjiyyah
confess *v.* يعترف ya'tarif	conjugate *v.* يصرّف yosarrif
confession *n.* اعتراف e'tiraaf	conjunct *adj.* إقتراني eqtiraaniy
confidant *n.* مؤتمن moutaman	conjunctiva *n.* الملتحمة
confide *v.* يثق yathiqo	ualmoltahimah
confidence *n.* ثقة thiqah	conjuncture *n.* توليفة tawleefah
confident *adj.* واثق waathiq	conjure *v.* يسحر yashar
confidential *adj.* سري sirriy	connect *v.* يربط yarbit
confine *v.* يحصر yahsor	connection *n.* صلة silah
confinement *n.* حبس habs	connivance *n.* تواطؤ tawaatou
confirm *v.* يؤكّد youakkid	conquer *v.* 1 يقهر yaqhar
confirmation *n.* تأكيد taukeed	conquer *v.* 2 يحتل yahtal
confiscate *v.* يصادر yosaadir	conquest *n.* فتح fath
confiscation *n.* مصادرة	conscience *n.* ضمير dameer
mosaadarah	conscious *adj.* واع wa'i
conflict *n.* صراع siraa'	consecrate *v.* يكرّس yokarris
conflict *v.* يتضارب yatadaarab	consecutive *adj.* متوالي motawaali
confluence *n.* حشد hashd	consecutively *adv.* على التوالي ala
confluent *adj.* رافد raafid	ttawaali
conformity *n.* مطابقة motaabaqah	consensus *n.* إجماع ejmaa'
confraternity *n.* أخوة uokhwah	consent *n.* موافقة mowaafaqah
confrontation *n.* مواجهة	consent *v.* يوافق yowaafiq
mowaajahah	consequence *n.* نتيجة nateejah
confuse *v.* 1 يخلط yakhlit	consequent *adj.* مترتّب عليه
confuse *v.* 2 يربك yorbik	motarattibon 'alayh
confusion *n.* ارتباك ertibaak	conservative *adj.* محافظ
confute *v.* يفنّد yofannid	mohaafidd
conge *n.* تغيّب taghayyob	conservative *n.* محافظ mohaafidd
congenial *adj.* متجانسة	conserve *v.* يحفظ yahfadd
motajaanisah	consider *v.* يعتبر ya'tabir
conglutinate *v.* يعلّق ya'laq	considerable *adj.* معتبر mo'tabar
congratulate *v.* يهنّئ yohanniu	considerate *adj.* بمراعاة
congratulation *n.* تهنئة tahniuah	bimoraa'aat
congress *n.* مؤتمر moutamar	consideration *n.* إعتبار e'tibaar

considering *prep.* الإعتبار الأخذبعين
ualuakhdho bi'ayni e'tibaar

consign *v.* يودّع yowaddi'

consignment *n.* شحنة shahnah

consist *v.* يتألّف Yatauallaf

consistence *n.* تناسق tanaasoq

consistency *n.* 1 تناسق tanaasoq

consistency *n.* 2 كثافة Kathaafah

consistent *adj.* متسق mottasiq

consolation *n.* عزاء azaau

console *v.* يعزي yo'azzi

consolidate *v.* يدمج yadmij

consolidation *n.* توحيد tawheed

consonance *n.* تدفق tadaffoq

consonant *n.* متدفق motadaffiq

consort *n.* انسجام ensijaam

conspectus *n.* موجز moojaz

conspicuous *adj.* بادئ baadi

conspiracy *n.* مؤامرة
mouaamarah

conspirator *n.* متآمر motauaamir

conspire *v.* يتآمر yatauaamar

constable *n.* شرطي shortiy

constant *adj.* ثابت thaabit

constellation *n.* كوكبة kawkabah

constipation *n.* إمساك emsaak

constituency *n.* دائرةانتخابية
dauiraton uintikhaabiyyah

constituent *n.* مقوّم moqawwim

constituent *adj.* تأسيسي
tauseesiy

constitute *v.* يشكل yoshakkil

constitution *n.* دستور dostoor

constrict *v.* يقلّص yoqallis

construct *v.* يبني yabni

construction *n.* مبنى mabna

consult *v.* يتشاور yatashaawar

consultation *n.* تشاور tashaawor

consume *v.* يستهلك yastahlik

consumption *n.* استهلاك estihlaak

contact *n.* تلامس talaamos

contact *v.* يتصل yattasil

contagious *adj.* معد mo'di

contain *v.* يحوي yahwi

contaminate *v.* يلوّث yolawwith

contemplate *v.* يتأمل yatauammal

contemplation *n.* تأمل tauammol

contemporary *adj.* معاصر
mo'aasir

contempt *n.* احتقار ehtiqaar

contemptuous *adj.* محقر mohqir

contend *v.* يجادل yojaadel

content *adj.* مسرور masroor

content *v.* يرضي yordi

content *n.* محتوى mohtawa

content *n.* رضى rida

contention *n.* خلاف khilaaf

contentment i اطمئنان etmiunaan

contest *v.* ينافس yonaafis

contest *n.* مسابقة mosaabaqah

context *n.* سياق siyaaq

continent *n.* قارة qaarah

continental *adj.* قاري qaariy

contingency *n.* طوارئ tawaariu

continual *adj.* مستمر mostamir

continuation *n.* استمرار estimraar

continue *v.* يواصل yowaasil

continuity *n.* إستمرارية
estimraariyyah

continuous *adj.* متواصل
motawaasil

contour *n.* محيط moheet

contra *pref.* مضاد modaad

contraception *n.* منع الحمل man'ol haml

contraceptive *adj.* مانع للحمل maani'on lilhaml

contract *n.* عقد aqd

contract *v.* يتقلّص yataqallas

contractor *n.* مقاول moqaawil

contradict *v.* يعارض yo'aarid

contradiction *n.* تناقض tanaaqod

contrary *adj.* عكس aks

contrast *v.* يفزق yofarriq

contrast *n.* تباين tabaayon

contribute *v.* يساهم yosaahim

contribution *n.* مساهمة mosaahamah

control *n.* تحكّم tahakkom

control *v.* يتحكّم yatahakkam

controller *n.* ضابط daabit

controversy *n.* جدال jidaal

contuse *v.* يكدم yakdim

conundrum *n.* لغز loghz

convene *v.* يعقد ya'qid

convener *n.* إجتماع ejtimaa'

convenience *n.* ملاءمة molaauamah

convenient *adj.* ملائم molaauim

convent *n.* دير dayr

convention *n.* اتفاقية ettifaaqiyyah

conversant *adj.* ملم molim

conversation *n.* محادثة mohaadathah

converse *v.* يحادث yohaadith

conversion *n.* تحويل tahweel

convert *v.* يحوّل yohawwil

convert *n.* محوّل mohawwil

convey *v.* ينقل yanqol

conveyance *n.* وسيلة نقل waseelato naql

convict *v.* يدين yodeen

convict *n.* مدان modaan

conviction *n.* إدانة edaanah

convince *v.* يقنع yoqni'

convivial *adj.* بهيج baheej

convocation *n.* دعوة da'wah

convoke *v.* يعقد ya'qid

convolve *v.* يلف yalof

coo *n.* هديل hadeel

coo *v.* يهدل yahdol

cook *v.* يطبخ yatbokh

cook *n.* طبّاخ tabbaakh

cooker *n.* فرن forn

cool *adj.* بارد baarid

cool *v.* يبرّد yobarrid

cooler *n.* بزّاد barraad

co-operate *v.* يتعاون yat'aawan

co-operation *n.* تعاون ta'aawon

co-operative *adj.* تعاوني ta'aawoniy

co-ordinate *adj.* منسّق monassaq

co-ordinate *v.* ينسّق yonassiq

co-ordination *n.* تنسيق tanseeq

coot *n.* أبله uablah

co-partner *n.* شريك shareek

cope *v.* يتحمّل yatahammal

coper *n.* تاجر خيول taajiro khoyool

copper *n.* نحاس nohaas

coppice *n.* حرج horj

coprology *n.* دراسة البراز dirasatol boraaz

copulate *v.* يجمع yajma'

copy *n.* نسخة noskhah

copy *v.* ينسخ yansakh

coral *n.* مرجان morjaan

cord *n.* حبل habl

cordial *adj.* ودي woddiy

corbel *n.* طوق جداري tawqon jidaariy

cordate *adj.* قلبي الشكل qalbiyo shshakl

core *n.* جوهر jawhar

coriander *n.* كزبرة kozbarah

cork *n.* 1 فلين falleen

cork *n.* 2 سدادة saddaadah

cormorant *n.* شره sharah

corn *n.* ذرة dhorah

cornea *n.* قرنية qarniyyah

corner *n.* ركن rokn

cornet *n.* بوق booq

cornicle *n.* عضو أنبوبي odwon uonboobiy

coronation *n.* تتويج tatweej

coronet *n.* إكليل ekleel

corporal *adj.* بدني badaniy

corporate *adj.* شراكي sharaakiy

corporation *n.* شركة sharikah

corps *n.* فيلق faylaq

corpse *n.* جثة joththah

correct *adj.* صحيح saheeh

correct *v.* يصحح yosahhih

correction *n.* تصحيح tasheeh

correlate *v.* يربط yarbit

correlation *n.* ارتباط ertiBaat

correspond *v.* يتطابق yatataabaq

correspondence *n.* مراسلة moraasalah

correspondent *n.* مراسل moraasil

corridor *n.* رواق rowaaq

corroborate *v.* يثبت yothbit

corroborative *adj.* مثبت mothbat

corrosive *adj.* تآكل tauaakol

corrupt *v.* يفسد yofsid

corrupt *adj.* فاسد faasid

corruption *n.* فساد fasaad

cosmetic *adj.* تجميلي tajmeeliy

cosmetic *n.* مستحضر التجميل mostahdaro ttajmeel

cosmic *adj.* كوني kawniy

cost *v.* يكلّف yokallif

cost *n.* تكلفة taklifah

costal *adj.* ضلعي dil'iy

cote *n.* زريبة zareebah

costly *adj.* مكلف moklif

costume *n.* زي ziy

cosy *adj.* دافئ daafiu

cot *n.* طفل سرير sareerotifl

cottage *n.* كوخ kookh

cotton *n.* قطن qotn

couch *n.* أريكة areekah

cough *n.* سعال so'aal

cough *v.* يسعل yas'ol

council *n.* مجلس majlis

councillor *n.* عضو مجلس odwo majlis

counsel *n.* مشورة mashoorah

counsel *v.* ينصح yansah

counsellor *n.* مستشار mostashaar

count *n.* عد ad

count *n.* الكونت ualkoont

count *v.* يعد ya'od

countenance *n.* سيماء saymaau

counter *n.* عداد addaad

counter *v.* يعكس ya'kis
counteract *v.* يواجه yowaajih
countercharge *n.* تهمةمضادة tohmaton modaaddah
counterfeit *adj.* تزوير tazweer
counterfeiter *n.* مزور mozawwir
countermand *v.* يبطل yobtil
counterpart *n.* نظير naddeer
countersign *v.* يوقّع yowaqqi'
countess *n.* سيدةنبيلة sayyidaton nabeelah
countless *adj.* لايحصى laa yohsa
country *n.* بلد balad
county *n.* مقاطعة moqaata'ah
coup *n.* انقلاب enqilaab
couple *n.* زوج zawj
couple *v.* يزاوج yozaawij
couplet *n.* زوج zawj
coupon *n.* قسيمة qaseemah
courage *n.* شجاعة shajaa'ah
courageous *adj.* شجاع shojaa'
courier *n.* ساعي saa'i
course *n.* مسار masaar
court *n.* محكمة mahkamah
court *v.* يتودَد yatawaddad
courteous *adj.* مهذب mohazzab
courtesan *n.* مومس moomis
courtesy *n.* مجاملة mojaamalah
courtier *n.* متودد motawaddid
courtship *n.* تودد tawaddod
courtyard *n.* فناء fanaau
cousin *n.* ابن عم ibno 'am
covenant *n.* عهد ahd
cover *v.* يغطّي yaghatti
cover *n.* غطاء ghitaau
coverlet *n.* غطاءالسرير ghitaauo ssareer

covet *v.* يشتهي yashtahi
cow *n.* بقرة baqarah
cow *v.* يرعب yor'ib
coward *n.* جبان jabaan
cowardice *n.* جبن jobn
cower *v.* ينكمش yankamish
cozy *adj.* دافئ daafiu
crab *n.* سلطعون saltaa'oon
crack *n.* تصدّع tasaddo'
crack *v.* يشق yashiq
cracker *n.* 1 بسكويت baskaweet
cracker *n.* 2 كسّارة kassaarah
cracker *n.* 3 مفرقعة mofarqa'ah
crackle *v.* يفرقع yofarqi'
cradle *n.* مهد mahd
craft *n.* حرفة hirfah
craftsman *n.* حرفي hirafiy
crafty *adj.* مخادع mokhaadi'
cram *v.* يحشر yahshor
crambo *n.* مسابقةكلامية mosaabaqaton kalaamiyyah
crane *n.* لقلق laqlaq
crane *n.* مرفاع mirfaa'
crankle *v.* يجعّد yoja"id
crash *v.* يتحطم yatahattam
crash *n.* تحطم tahattom
crass *adj.* تام taam
crate *n.* صندوق sondooq
crave *v.* يحن yahin
craw *n.* معدةالحيوان ma'idatol hayawaan
crawl *v.* يزحف yazhaf
crawl *n.* زحف zahf
craze *n.* جنون jonoon
crazy *adj.* مجنون majnoon

creak v. يصر yosarri	cripple n. مشلول mashlool
creak n. صرير sareer	crisis n. أزمة uazmah
cream n. معجون ma'joon	crisp adj. 1 هش hash
crease n. تجعد taja"od	crisp adj. 2 هش naadir
create v. يخلق yakhliq	criterion n. معيار mi'yaariy
creation n. خلق khalq	critic n. ناقد naaqid
creative adj. خلّاق khallaq	critical adj. حاسم haasim
creator n. مبدع mobdi'	criticism n. نقد naqd
creature n. مخلوق makhlooq	criticize v. ينقد yanqod
credible adj. موثوق mawthooq	croak n. تشاءم tashaauom
credit n. ائتمان eutimaan	crockery n. آنيةفخارية uaaniyaton fakhkhaariyah
creditable adj. جديربالتصديق jadeeron bittasdeeq	crocodile n. تمساح timsaah
creditor n. دائن daauin	croesus n. غني ghaniy
credulity adj. سذاجة sadhaajah	crook adj. محتال mohtaal
creed n. عقيدة aqeedah	crop n. محصول mahsool
creek n. جدول jadwal	cross v. يعبر ya'bor
creep v. يزحف yazhaf	cross n. صليب saleeb
creeper n. زاحف zaahif	cross adj. 1 متقاطع motaqaati'
cremate v. يحرقجثة yahriqo joththah	cross adj. 2 منزعج monza'ij
cremation n. إحراقالجثة ehraaqol joththah	crossing n. نقطةعبور noqtatol 'oboor
crest n. قمة qimmah	crotchet n. نزوةغريبة nazwaton gharebah
crevet n. إناءالصهر enaauo ssahr	crouch v. يربض yarbid
crew n. طاقم taaqam	crow n. غراب ghoraab
crib n. مهد mahd	crow v. يصيح yaseeh
cricket n. 1 صرصور sarsoor	crowd n. حشد hashd
cricket n. 2 كريكيت krikit	crown n. تاج taaj
crime n. جريمة jareemah	crown v. يتوّج yotawwij
crimp n. تجعيد taj'eed	crucial adj. حاسم haasim
crimple v. يجعّد yoja"id	crude adj. خام khaam
criminal n. مجرم mojrim	cruel adj. قاس qaasi
criminal adj. جنائي jinaauiy	cruelty n. قسوة qaswah
crimson n. قرمزي qormoziy	cruise v. يبحر yobhir
cringe v. ينكمش yankamish	cruiser n. باخرة baakhirah

crumb *n.* كسرة kisrah

crumble *v.* يفتّت yofattit

crump *v.* يطحن yat han

crusade *n.* حرب صليبية harbon saleebiyyah

crush *v.* يسحق yashaq

crust *n.* قشرة qishrah

crutch *n.* عكاز okkaaz

cry *n.* صرخة sarkhah

cry *v.* 1 يبكي yabki

cry *v.* 2 يطلب yatlob

cryptography *n.* علم الشيفرة ilmo shsheefrah

crystal *n.* بلور balloor

cub *n.* شبل shibl

cube *n.* مكعب moka"ab

cubical *adj.* تكعيبي tak'eebi

cubiform *adj.* مكعب moka"ab

cuckold *n.* مكعباني شبيه بالمكعب makabani shabih bilmakab

cuckoo *n.* أبله uablah

cucumber *n.* خيار khiyaar

cudgel *n.* هراوة hiraawah

cue *n.* جديلة jadeelah

cuff *n.* صفعة saf'ah

cuff *v.* يصفع yasfa'

cuisine *n.* مطبخ matbakh

cullet *n.* قطع زجاج qita'o zojaaj

culminate *v.* يتوّج yotawwaj

culpable *adj.* ملام molaam

culprit *n.* مذنب modhnib

cult *n.* عبادة abaauah

cultivate *v.* يزرع yazra'

cultrate *adj.* حاد haad

cultural *adj.* ثقافي thaqaafiy

culture *n.* ثقافة thaqaafah

culvert *n.* قناة qanaah

cunning *adj.* ماكر maakir

cunning *n.* مكر makr

cup *n.* كوب koob

cupboard *n.* خزانة khizaanah

Cupid *n.* ملاك الحب malaakol hob

cupidity *n.* طمع tama'

curable *adj.* معالج mo'aalaj

curative *adj.* علاجي ilaajiy

curb *n.* كابح kaabih

curb *v.* يكبح yakbah

curcuma *n.* كركم korkom

curd *n.* تخثر takhaththor

cure *n.* علاج ilaaj

cure *v.* يشفي yoshfi

curfew *n.* حظر التجول haddro ttajawwol

curiosity *n.* فضول fodool

curious *adj.* فضولي fodooliy

curl *n.* حليقة holayqah

curly *adj.* مجعّد moja"ad

currant *n.* زبيب zabeeb

currency *n.* عملة imlah

current *n.* تيار tayyaar

current *adj.* حالي haaliy

curriculum *n.* منهاج minhaaj

curse *n.* لعنة la'nah

curse *v.* يلعن yal'an

cursory *adj.* خاطف khaadif

curt *adj.* جاف jaaf

curtail *v.* يقلّص yoqallis

curtain *n.* ستارة sitaarah

curve *n.* منحنى monhana

curve *v.* ينحني yanhani

cushion *n.* وسادة wisaadah

cushion v. يوسد yowassid

custard n. كاسترد kaastard

custodian n. ولي waliy

custody n. 1 حبس habs

custody n. 2 وصاية wisaayah

custom n. عرف orf

customary adj. عرفي orfiy

customer n. زبون zaboon

cut v. يقطع yaqta'

cut n. جرح jorh

cutis n. ترهل tarahhol

cuvette n. إناءمخبري enaauon makhbariy

cycle n. دورة dawrah

cyclic adj. دوري dawriy

cyclist n. دراج darraaj

cyclone n. إعصار e'saar

cyclostyle n. مثقابللإستنساخ mithqaabon lil uistinsaakh

cyclostyle v. يستنسخبالمثقاب yastansikho bilmithqaab

cylinder n. أسطوانة uostowaanah

cynic n. ساخر saakhir

cypher n. صفر sifr

cypress n. سرو sarw

D

dabble v. يشتغل yashtaghil

dacoit n. عضوعصابة odwo 'isaabah

dacoity n. سرقةمسلّحة sariqaton mosallahah

dad n. أب uab

daddy n. أب uab

daffodil n. نرجس narjis

daft adj. معتوه ma'tooh

dagger n. خنجر khinjar

daily adj. يومي yawmiy

daily adv. يوميا yawmiyyan

daily n. يومي yawmiy

dainty adj. أنيق uaneeq

dainty n. لذيذ ladheedh

dairy n. ألبان lbaan

dais n. منصة minassah

daisy n. زهرة zahrah

dale n. واد wadi

dam n. سد sad

damage n. ضرر darar

damage v. يخرب yokharrib

dame n. سيدة sayyidah

damn v. يلعن yal'an

damnation n. لعن la'n

damp adj. رطب ratib

damp n. رطوبة rotoobah

damp v. يرطّب yorattib

dampen v. يرطّب yorattib

damsel n. آنسة uaanisah

dance n. رقصة raqsah

dance v. يرقص yarqos

dandelion n. هندباء hindibaau

dandle v. يدلّل yodallil

dandruff n. هبرية habriyyah

dandy n. مدهش modhish

danger n. خطر khatar

dangerous adj. خطير khateer

dangle v. يدل yodalli

dank adj. رطب ratb

dap v. يصطاد yastaad

dare *v.* يجرؤ yajrou	deal *v.* يتعامل yata'aamal
daring *n.* جرأة joruah	dealer *n.* تاجر taajir
daring *adj.* جريء jareeu	dealing *n.* تعامل ta'aamol
dark *adj.* غامق ghaamiq	dean *n.* عميد ameed
dark *n.* ظلام ddalaam	dear *adj.* عزيز azeez
darkle *v.* يختفي yakhtafi	dearth *n.* قلة qillah
darling *n.* حبيب habeeb	death *n.* موت mawt
darling *adj.* محبوب mahboob	debar *v.* يحرم yahrim
dart *n.* سهم sahm	debase *v.* يهين yoheen
dash *v.* يندفع yandafi'	debate *n.* مناقشة monaaqashah
dash *n.* اندفاع endifaa'	debate *v.* يحاور yohaawir
date *n.* بلح balah	debauch *v.* يفسق yafsoq
date *n.* موعد maw'id	debauch *n.* فسق fosq
date *n.* تاريخ taareekh	debauchee *n.* منغمس monghamis
date *v.* يؤرّخ youarrikh	debauchery *n.* فسوق fosooq
daub *n.* لوحةغيرمتقنة lawhaton ghayro motqanah	debility *n.* ضعف da'f
daub *v.* يطلي yatli	debit *n.* مدين madeen
daughter *n.* ابنة ebnah	debit *v.* يدين yadeen
daunt *v.* يرغب yarghab	debris *n.* حطام hotaam
dauntless *adj.* شجاع shojaa'	debt *n.* دين dayn
dawdle *v.* يتوان yatawaanah	debtor *n.* مدين madeen
dawn *n.* فجر fajr	decade *n.* عقد aqd
dawn *v.* يبزغ yabzogh	decadent *adj.* منحط monhat
day *n.* يوم yawm	decamp *v.* يفر yafor
daze *n.* ذهول dhohool	decay *n.* 1 إضمحلال edmihlaal
daze *v.* يدوخ yadookh	decay *n.* 2 تحلّل tahallol
dazzle *n.* ميهر mobhir	decay *v.* يتحلّل yatahallal
dazzle *v.* ينبهر yanbahir	decease *n.* ميت mawt
deacon *n.* شمّاس shammaas	decease *v.* يموت yamoot
dead *adj.* ميت mayyit	deceit *n.* خداع khidaa'
deadlock *n.* مأزق mauziq	deceive *v.* يخدع yakhda'
deadly *adj.* قاتل qaatil	december *n.* كانون الأول kaanoonol uawwal
deaf *adj.* أصم uasam	decency *n.* إحترام ehtiraam
deal *n.* اتفاق ettifaaq	decennary *n.* عقد aqd

decent *adj.* لائق laauiq

deception *n.* خداع khidaa'

decide *v.* يقرّر yoqarrir

decillion *n.* مليون عقد mallioono 'aqd

decimal *adj.* عشري ashriy

decimate *v.* يهلك yahlik

decision *n.* قرار qaraar

decisive *adj.* حاسم haasim

deck *n.* سطح sat h

deck *v.* يزين yozayyin

declaration *n.* إعلان e'laan

declare *v.* يعلن yo'lin

decline *n.* هبوط hoboot

decline *v.* يتراجع yataraaja'

declinous *adj.* متراجع motaraaji'

decompose *v.* يتحلّل yatahallal

decomposition *n.* تحلل tahallol

decontrol *v.* يحرز yohriz

decorate *v.* يزيّن yozayyin

decoration *n.* زخرفة zakhrafah

decorum *n.* لياقة layaaqah

decrease *v.* ينقص yanqos

decrease *n.* نقصان noqsaan

decree *n.* مرسوم marsoom

decree *v.* يصدر مرسوم yosdiro marsooman

decrement إنقاص i enqaas

dedicate *v.* يهدي yahdi

dedication *n.* تفان tafaani

deduct *v.* يخصم yakhsom

deed *n.* عمل amal

deem *v.* يرى yara

deep *adj.* عميق ameeq

deer *n.* أيل uayl

defamation *n.* قذف qadhf

defame *v.* يقذف yaqdhif

default *n.* إفتراضي eftiraadhiy

defeat *n.* هزيمة hazeemah

defeat *v.* يهزم yahzim

defect *n.* خلل khalal

defence *n.* دفاع difaa'

defend *v.* يدافع yodaafi'

defendant *n.* مدّعى عليه modda'a 'alayh

defensive *adv.* دفاعي difaa'iy

deference *n.* إذعان edh'aan

defiance *n.* تحد tahaddi

deficit *n.* عجز ajz

deficient *adj.* ناقص naaqis

defile *n.* دنس danas

define *v.* يعرّف yo'arrif

definite *adj.* واضح waadih

definition *n.* تعريف ta'reef

deflation *n.* إنكماش enkimaash

deflect *v.* يصرف yasrif

deft *adj.* ماهر maahir

degrade *v.* يتحلّل yatahallal

degree *n.* درجة darajah

dehort *v.* يثن yothni

deism *n.* الربوبية uarroobiyyah

deist *n.* الربوبي uarrooboobiy

deity *n.* إله elaah

deject *v.* يغتنم yaghtanim

dejection *n.* كآبة kauaabah

delay *v.* يؤخّر youakhkhir

delibate *v.* يتذوّق yatadhawwaq

deligate *v.* يضمد yodammid

delegate *n.* مندوب mandoob

delegate *v.* يفوّض yofawwid

delegation *n.* وفد wafd

delete v. يحذف yahdhif	denial n. إنكار enkaar
deliberate v. يتعمّد yata'ammad	denote v. يدلّل yodallil
deliberate adj. متعمد mota'ammid	denounce v. يشجب yashjob
deliberation n. تداول tadaawol	dense adj. كثيف katheef
delicate adj. دقيق daqeeq	density n. كثافة kathaafah
delicious adj. لذيذ ladheedh	dentist n. طبيب أسنان tabeebo usnaan
delight n. بهجة bahjah	
delight v. يبهج yobhij	denude v. يعرّ yo'arri
deliver v. ينقل yanqil	denunciation n. استنكار estinkaar
delivery n. تسليم tasleem	deny v. ينكر yonkir
delta n. دلتا dilta	depart v. يغادر yoghaadir
delude n.t. إيهام ueehaam	department n. قسم qasam
delusion n. وهم wahm	departure n. رحيل raheel
demand n. مطلب matlab	depauperate v. يحن yohin
demand v. يطلب yatlob	depend v. يعتمد ya'tamid
demarcation n. تعيين الحدود ta'yeenol hodood	dependant n. معتمد mo'tamid
dement v. يجنن yojannin	dependence n. اعتماد e'timaad
demerit n. نقيصة naqeesah	dependent adj. معتمد mo'tamid
democracy n. ديمقراطية deemoqraatiyyah	depict v. يصوّر yosawwir
	deplorable adj. مرثي marthi
democratic adj. ديمقراطي deemoqraatiy	deploy v. ينشر yanshor
demolish v. يهدم yahdim	deponent n. 1 الفعل الغيبي ualfi'lol ghaybiy
demon n. شيطان shaytaan	
demonetize v. يلغي قيمة المعدن yalghi qeematal ma'din	deponent n. 2 محلّف mohallaf
	deport v. يرحّل yorahhil
demonstrate v. يعرض ya'rid	depose v. يعزل ya'zil
demonstration n. مظاهرة moddaaharah	deposit n. وديعة wadee'ah
	deposit v. يودع yoodi'
demoralize v. يثبت yothbit	depot n. مستودع mostawda'
demur n. اعتراض e'tiraad	depreciate v. يخفض yokhfid
demur v. يعترض ya'tarid	depredate v. يسلب yaslib
demurrage n. غرامة gharaamah	depress v. 1 يكأب yokuib
den n. عرين areen	depress v. 2 يخفض yokhfid
dengue n. حمى الضنك homma ddank	depression n. 1 إنخفاض enkhifaad
	depression n. 2 إكتآب ektiuaab

depression *n.* 3 ركود rokood	detach *v.* يفصل yafsil
depression *n.* 4 غور ghawr	detachment *n.* انفصال enfisaal
deprive *v.* يحرم yahrim	detail *n.* تفصيل tafseel
depth *n.* عمق omq	detail *v.* يفصّل yofassil
deputation *n.* انتداب entidaab	detain *v.* يعتقل ya'taqil
depute *v.* ينتدب yantadib	detect *v.* يشعر yash'or
deputy *n.* نائب nauib	detective i استشعاري estish'aariy
derail *v.* يعطّل yo'attil	detective *n.* مخبر mokhbir
derive *v.* يستمد yastamid	determination *n.* 1 قرار qaraar
descend *v.* يهبط yahbit	determination *n.* 2 إصرار esraar
descendant *n.* سليل saleel	determine *v.* يحدّد yohaddid
descent *n.* أصل uasl	dethrone *v.* يخلع yakhla'
describe *v.* يوصف yoosif	develop *v.* يطوّر yotawwir
description *n.* وصف wasf	development *n.* تنمية tanmiyah
descriptive *adj.* وصفي wasfiy	deviate *v.* يتحيّد yatahayyad
desert *v.* يتخلّى yatakhalla	deviation *n.* إنحراف enhiraaf
desert *n.* صحراء sahraau	device *n.* جهاز jihaaz
deserve *v.* يستحق yastahiq	devil *n.* شيطان shaytaan
design *v.* يصمّم yosammim	devise *v.* يستنبط yastanbit
design *n.* تصميم tasmeem	devoid *adj.* يخلو yakhlo
desirable *adj.* مرغوب marghoob	devote *v.* يكرّس yokarris
desire i رغبة raghbah	devotee *n.* مخلص mokhlis
desire *v.* يرغب yarghab	devotion *n.* إخلاص ekhlaas
desirous *adj.* مرغوب marghoob	devour *v.* يفترس yaftaris
desk *n.* مكتب maktab	dew *n.* ندى nada
despair *n.* يأس yaus	diabetes *n.* سكري sakeer
despair *v.* ييأس yayuas	diagnose i يشخّص yoshakhis
desperate *adj.* يائس yaauis	diagnosis *n.* تشخيص tashkhees
despicable *adj.* حقير haqeer	diagram *n.* رسم بياني rasmon bayaaniy
despise *v.* يحتقر yahtaqir	
despot *n.* مستبد mostabid	dial *n.* اتصال ettisaal
destination *n.* وجهة wijhah	dialect *n.* لهجة lahjah
destiny *n.* مصير maseer	dialogue *n.* حوار hiwaar
destroy *v.* يهدم yahdim	diameter *n.* قطر qotr
destruction *n.* تدمير tadmeer	diamond *n.* الماس ualmaas

diarrhoea *n.* إسهال eshaal	**dim** *v.* يخفت yakhfit
diary *n.* مذكّرة modhakkarah	**dimension** *n.* بعد bo'd
dice *n.* نرد nard	**diminish** *v.* يخفت yakhfit
dice *v.* يشرّح yosharrih	**din** *n.* ضج daj
dictate *v.* يملي yomli	**dine** *v.* يتعشّى yata'ashsha
dictation *n.* إملاء emlaau	**dinner** *n.* عشاء ashaau
dictator *n.* دكتاتور diktaatoor	**dip** *n.* تجويف tajweef
diction *n.* أسلوب uosloob	**dip** *v.* يغمس yaghmis
dictionary *n.* قاموس qaamoos	**diploma** *n.* دبلوم dibloom
dictum *n.* قول مأثور qawlon mauthoor	**diplomacy** *n.* دبلوماسية diblomaasiyyah
didactic *adj.* تعليمي ta'leemiy	**diplomat** *n.* دبلوماسي diblomaasiy
die *v.* يموت yamoot	**diplomatic** *adj.* دبلوماسي diblomaasiy
die *n.* 1 نرد nard	**dire** *adj.* خيمة khaymah
die *n.* 2 ختم khitm	**direct** *adj.* مباشر mobaashir
diet *n.* حمية himyah	**direct** *v.* يوجّه yowajjih
differ *v.* يختلف yakhtalif	**direction** *n.* اتجاه ettijaah
difference *n.* فرق farq	**director** *n.* مدير modeer
different *adj.* مختلف mokhtalif	**directory** *n.* دليل daleel
difficult *adj.* صعب sa'b	**dirt** *n.* قذارة qadhaarah
difficulty *n.* صعوبة so'oobah	**dirty** *adj.* قذر qadhir
dig *n.* وخزة wakhzah	**disability** *n.* عجز ajz
dig *v.* يحفر yahfir	**disable** *v.* يعطّل yo'attil
digest *v.* يهضم yahdim	**disabled** *adj.* عاجز aajiz
digest *n.* ملخّص molakhkhas	**disadvantage** *n.* سيئة sayyiuah
digestion *n.* هضم hadm	**disagree** *v.* يخالف yokhaalif
digit *n.* رقم raqam	**disagreeable** *adj.* كريه kareeh
dignify *v.* يبجّل yobajjil	**disagreement** *n.* خلاف khilaaf
dignity *n.* كرامة karaamah	**disappear** *v.* يختفي yakhtafi
dilemma *n.* معضلة mo'dilah	**disappearance** *n.* اختفاء ekhtifaau
diligence *n.* اجتهاد ejtihaad	**disappoint** *v.* يخيب yokhayyib
diligent *adj.* مجتهد mojtahid	**disapproval** *n.* استنكار estinkaar
dilute *v.* يميّع yomayyi'	**disapprove** *v.* يرفض yarfid
dilute *adj.* مميّع momayyi'	
dim *adj.* خافت khaafit	

disarm v. ينزع yanza'

disarmament n. نزع naz'

disaster n. كارثة kaarithah

disastrous adj. كارثي kaarithiy

disc n. قرص qors

discard v. ينبذ yanbidh

discharge v. 1 يسرّح yosarrih

discharge v. 2 يأدالواجب youaddil waajib

discharge n. إعفاء e'faau

discharge n. إفرازات efraazaat

disciple n. تلميذ tilmeedh

discipline انضباط endibaat

disclose v. يكشف yakshif

discomfort n. إزعاج ez'aaz

disconnect v. يقطع yaqta'

discontent n. استياء estiyauu

discontinue v. يوقف yooqif

discord n. خلاف khilaaf

discount n. خصم khasm

discourage v. يثبط yothbit

discourse n. خطاب khitaab

discourteous adj. فظ fadd

discover i يكتشف yaktashif

discovery n. اكتشاف ektishaaf

discretion n. تعقّل ta'aqqol

discriminate v. يميّز yomayyiz

discrimination n. تمييز tamyeez

discuss v. يباحث yobaahith

disdain v. ازدراء ezdiraau

disdain v. يزدري yazdari

disease n. مرض marad

disguise n. تمويه tamweeh

disguise v. يموّه yomawwih

dish n. طبق tabaq

dishearten v. يثبط yothabbit

dishonest adj. غيرأمين ghayro uameen

dishonesty n. عدمالأمانة adamol uamaanah

dishonour v. يخزي yokhzi

dishonour n. عار aar

dislike v. يكره yakrah

dislike n. كره korh

disloyal adj. خائن khaauin

dismiss v. 1 يصرف yasrif

dismiss v. 2 يقيل yoqeel

dismissal n. إقالة eqaalah

disobey v. يعصي ya'si

disorder n. اضطراب edtiraab

disparity n. تفاوت tafaawot

dispensary n. مستوصف mostawsaf

disperse v. يفرّق yofarriq

displace v. يهجّر yohajjir

display v. يعرض ya'rid

display n. عرض ard

displease v. يغضب yoghdib

displeasure n. استياء estiyauu

disposal n. تصريف tasreef

dispose v. يتخلّص yatakhallas

disprove v. يدحض yadhad

dispute v. نزاع nizaa'

dispute v. يناقش yonaaqish

disqualification n. تنحية tanhiyah

disqualify v. ينحي yanhani

disquiet n. قلق qalaq

disregard n. تجاهل tajaahol

disregard v. يتجاهل yatajaahal

disrepute n. مذموم madhmoom

disrespect *n.* ازدراء ezdiraau

disrupt *v.* يعطّل yo'attil

dissatisfaction *n.* استياء estiyaau

dissatisfy *v.* يخيّب yokhayyib

dissect *v.* يشرّح yosharrih

dissection *n.* تشريح tashreeh

dissimilar *adj.* متباين motabaayin

dissolve *v.* 1 يذوب yadhoob

dissolve *v.* 2 يفضّ yafod

dissuade *v.* يثني yathni

distance *n.* مسافة masaafah

distant *adj.* بعيد ba'eed

distil *v.* يقطّر yoqattir

distillery *n.* مقطرة maqtarah

distinct *adj.* متميز motamayyiz

distinction *n.* تميز tamayyoz

distinguish *v.* يميّز yomayyiz

distort *v.* يشوّه yoshawwih

distress i محنة mihnah

distress *v.* يقلق yoqliq

distribute i يوزّع yowazzi'

distribution *n.* توزيع tawzee'

district *n.* حي hay

distrust *n.* ثقة عدم adamo thiqah

distrust *v.* يثق لا laa yathiq

disturb *v.* يزعج yoz'ij

ditch *n.* خندق khandaq

ditto *n.* الشيءنفسه uashshayuo nafsoh

dive *v.* يغطس yaghtos

dive *n.* غطس ghats

diverse *adj.* متنوع motanawwi'

divert *v.* يحوّل yohawwil

divide *v.* يقسم yaqsim

divine *adj.* إلهي elaahiy

divinity *n.* ألوهية uloohiyyah

division *n.* تقسيم taqseem

divorce *n.* طلاق talaaq

divorce *v.* يطلّق yotalliq

divulge *v.* يكشف yakshif

do *v.* يفعل yaf'al

docile *adj.* منصاع monsaal

dock *n.* 1 قفص الاتهام qafaso ettihaam

dock *n.* 2 حوض السفينة hawdo ssafeenah

doctor *n.* طبيب tabeeb

doctorate *n.* دكتوراه doktooraah

doctrine *n.* مذهب madhhab

document *n.* وثيقة watheeqah

dodge *n.* مراوغة moraawaghah

dodge *v.* يراوغ yoraawigh

doe *n.* ظبية ddabyah

dog *n.* كلب kalb

dog *v.* يلاحق yolaahiq

dogma *n.* عقيدة aqeedah

dogmatic *adj.* عقائدي aqaauidiy

doll *n.* دمية domyah

dollar *n.* دولار doolaar

domain *n.* نطاق nitaaq

dome *n.* قبة qobbah

domestic *adj.* محلي mahalliy

domestic *n.* أليف ualeef

domicile *n.* منزل manzil

dominant *adj.* مهيمن mohaymin

dominate *v.* يهيمن yohaymin

domination *n.* هيمنة haymanah

dominion *n.* سلطان soltaan

donate *v.* يتبرّع yatabarra'

donation *n.* هبة hibah

donkey *n.* حمار himaar

donor *n.* مانح maanih	**draftsman** *adj.* رسام rassaam
doom i موت mawt	**drag** *n.* عائق aauiq
doom *v.* يميت yomeet	**drag** *v.* يجر yajor
door i باب baab	**dragon** *n.* تنين tinneen
dose *n.* جرعة jor'ah	**drain** *n.* استنزاف estinzaaf
dot *n.* نقطة noqtah	**drain** *v.* يستنزف yastanzif
dot *v.* ينقّط yonaqqit	**drainage** *n.* صرف sarf
double *adj.* مزدوج mozdawaj	**dram** *n.* درهم dirham
double *v.* يضاعف yodaa'if	**drama** *n.* دراما draama
double *v.1* مزدوج mozdawaj	**dramatic** *adj.* درامي draamiy
double *n. 2* مثيل matheel	**dramatist** *n.* كاتب دراما kaatibo draama
doubt *v.* يشك yashok	**draper** *n.* تاجر الأجواخ taajirol uajwaakh
doubt *n.* شك shak	
dough *n.* عجين ajeen	**drastic** *adj.* جذري jadhriy
dove *n.* حمامة hamaamah	**draught** *n. 1* مسودة miswaddah
down *adv.* إلى الأسفل elal uasfal	**draught** *n. 2* تيار tayyaar
down *prep.* أسفل uasfal	**draw** *v. 1* يتعادل yata'aadal
down *v.* ينهي yonhi	**draw** *v. 2* يرسم yarsom
downfall *n.* سقوط soqoot	**draw** *v. 3* يسحب yashab
downpour *n.* هطول hotool	**draw** *v. 4* يجذب yajdhib
downright *adv.* بصراحة bisaraahah	**draw** *n. 1* تعادل ta'aadol
downright *adj.* صريح sareeh	**draw** *n. 2* سحب sahb
downward *adj.* هابط haabit	**draw** *n. 3* جاذبية jaadhibiyyah
downward *adv.* هبوطاً hobootan	**drawback** *n.* عقبة aqabah
downwards *adv.* نزولا nozoolan	**drawer** *n.* جرّار jarraar
dowry *n.* مهر mahr	**drawing** *n.* رسمة rasmah
doze *n.* غفوة ghafwah	**drawing-room** *n.* قاعة استقبال qaa'ato sstiqbaal
doze *v.* يغفو yaghfo	
dozen *n.* دزينة dazzeenah	**dread** *n.* فزع faza'
draft *v. 1* يسوّد yosawwid	**dread** *v.* يخاف yakhaaf
draft *v. 2* يجنّد yojannid	**dread** *adj.* مخيف mokheef
draft *n. 1* مسودة miswaddah	**dreadfull** *adj.* مفزع mofzi'
draft *n. 2* كمبيالة kimbyaalah	**dream** *n.* حلم holm
draft *n. 3* تجنيد tajneed	**dream** *v.* يحلم yahlam
	drench *v.* يجرع yajra'

dress *n.* ثوب thawb	**duke** *n.* دوق dooq
dress *v.* يلبس yalbis	**dull** *adj.* ممل momil
dressing *n.* ضمادة dammaadah	**dull** *v.* يثبت yothabbit
drill *n.* حفّار haffaar	**duly** *adv.* كماينبغي kama yanbaghi
drill *v.* يحفر yahfir	**dumb** *adj.* أبكم uabkam
drink *n.* شرب shorb	**dunce** *n.* مغفل moghaffal
drink *v.* يشرب yashrab	**dung** *n.* روث rawath
drip *n.* قطّارة qattaarah	**duplicate** *adj.* مكرر mokarrar
drip *v.* يقطر yaqtor	**duplicate** *n.* نسخة noskhah
drive *v.* يقود yaqood	**duplicate** *v.* يكرّر yokarrir
drive *n.* 1 حافظ haafiz	**duplicity** *n.* نفاق nifaaq
drive *n.* 2 جولة jawlah	**durable** *adj.* دائم daauim
drive *n.* 3 ممر mamar	**duration** *n.* مدة moddah
driver *n.* سائق saauiq	**during** *prep.* خلال khilaal
drizzle *n.* رذاذ radhaadh	**dusk** *n.* غسق ghasaq
drizzle *v.* يقطر yaqtor	**dust** *n.* غبار ghobaar
drop *n.* قطرة qatrah	**dust** *v.* يمسح yamsah
drop *v.* يسقط yasqot	**duster** *n.* منفضة minfadah
drought *n.* جفاف jafaaf	**dutiful** *adj.* مطيع motee'
drown *v.* يغرق yaghraq	**duty** *n.* واجب waajib
drug *n.* عقار oqaar	**dwarf** *n.* قزم qazam
druggist *n.* عطار attaar	**dwell** *v.* يسكن yaskon
drum *n.* طبل tabl	**dwelling** *n.* سكن sakan
drum *v.* يطبل yotabbil	**dwindle** *v.* يقلّص yoqallis
drunkard *n.* سكير sakeer	**dye** *v.* يصبغ yasbigh
dry *adj.* جاف jaaf	**dye** *n.* صبغة sabghah
dry *v.* يجفّف yojaffif	**dynamic** *adj.* حيوي hayawiy
dual *adj.* مزدوج mozdawaj	**dynamics** *n.* علم الحركة ilmol harakah
duck *n.* بط bat	
duck *v.* ينبطح yanbatih	**dynamite** *n.* ديناميت deenaameet
due *adj.* مستحق mostahaq	**dynamo** *n.* مولّد mowallid
due *n.* استحقاق estihqaaq	**dynasty** *n.* سلالة solaalah
due *adv.* كالمتوقّع kalmotawaqa'	**dysentery** *n.* زحار zohaar
duel *n.* مبارزة mobaarazah	
duel *v.* يبارز yobaariz	

E

each *adj.* كل kol
each *adv.* لكل likol
each *pron.* كل kol
eager *adj.* حريص harees
eagle *n.* نسر nisr
ear *n.* أذن uodhon
early *adv.* مبكّراً mobakkiran
early *adj.* مبكر mobakkir
earn *v.* يكسب yaksab
earnest *adj.* جاد jaad
earth *n.* أرض uard
earthen *adj.* ترابي toraabiy
earthly *adj.* أرضي rdiy
earthquake *n.* زلزال zilzaal
ease *n.* سهولة sohoolah
ease *v.* يرخي yorkhi
east *n.* شرق sharq
east *adv.* شرقاً sharqan
east *adj.* شرقي sharqiy
easter *n.* الفصح ualfish
eastern *adj.* شرقي sharqiy
easy *adj.* سهل sahl
eat *v.* يأكل yaukol
eatable *n.* مأكول maukool
eatable *adj.* مأكول maukool
ebb *n.* جزر jazar
ebb *v.* ينحصر yanhassir
ebony *n.* أبنوس uabnoos
echo *n.* صدى sada
echo *v.* يدوي yodwi
eclipse *n.* كسوف kosoof
economic *adj.* اقتصادي eqtisaadiy

economical *adj.* اقتصادي eqtisaadiy
economics *n.* علم الاقتصاد ilmo liqtisaad
economy *n.* اقتصاد eqtisaad
edge *n.* حافة haafah
edible *adj.* مأكول maukool
edifice *n.* صرح sarh
edit *v.* يعدّل yo'addil
edition *n.* طبعة tab'ah
editor *n.* محرر moharrir
editorial *adj.* تحريري tahreeriy
editorial *n.* إفتتاحية eftitaahiyyah
educate *v.* يثقّف yothaqqif
education *n.* تعليم ta'leem
efface *v.* يطمس yatmos
effect *n.* أثر uathar
effect *v.* يحدث yohdith
effective *adj.* فعال fa"aal
effeminate *adj.* مخنث mokhannath
efficacy *n.* فعالية fa'aaliyyah
efficiency *n.* كفاءة kafaauah
efficient *n.* كفؤ kafou
effigy *n.* تمثال timthaal
effort *n.* جهد johd
egg *n.* بيضة baydah
ego *n.* غرور ghoroor
egotism *n.* غرور ghoroor
eight *n.* ثمانية thamaaniyah
eighteen *adj.* ثمانيةعشر thamaaniyato 'ashar
eighty *n.* ثمانون thamaanoon
either *a.* إما emma
either *adv.* أيضاً uaydan
eject *v.* يطرد yatrod

elaborate *v.* يفصّل yofassil	**elusion** *n.* مراوغة moraawaghah
elaborate *adj.* تفصيلي tafseeliy	**elusive** *adj.* مراوغ moraawigh
elapse *v.* ينقضي yanqadi	**emancipation** *n.* تحرير tahreer
elastic *adj.* مطاط mattaat	**embalm** *v.* يحنّط yohannit
elbow *n.* كوع koo'	**embankment** *n.* جسر jisr
elder *adj.* أكبر uakbar	**embark** *v.* يشرع yashra'
elder *n.* زعيم za'eem	**embarrass** *v.* يحرج yohrij
elderly *adj.* عجوز jooz	**embassy** *n.* سفارة safaarah
elect *v.* ينتخب yantakhib	**embitter** *v.* يمرر yomarrir
election *n.* انتخابات entikhaabaat	**emblem** *n.* شعار shi'aar
electorate *n.* ناخبون naakhiboon	**embodiment** *n.* تجسيد tajseed
electric *adj.* كهربائي kahrobaauiy	**embody** *v.* يجسّد yojassid
electricity *n.* كهرباء kahrobaau	**embolden** *v.* يجرئ yajrou
electrify *v.* يكهرب yokahrib	**embrace** *v.* يحتضن yahtadin
elegance *n.* أناقة uanaaqah	**embrace** *n.* احتضان ehtidaan
elegant *adj.* أنيق uaneeq	**embroidery** *n.* تطريز tatreez
elegy *n.* مرثاة morthaah	**embryo** *n.* جنين janeen
element *n.* عنصر onsor	**emerald** *n.* زمرد zomorrod
elementary *adj.* إبتدائي ebtidaauiy	**emerge** *v.* يخرج yakhroj
elephant *n.* فيل feel	**emergency** *n.* طارئ taariu
elevate *v.* يرفع yarfa'	**eminence** *n.* سمو somow
elevation *n.* ارتفاع uirtifaa'	**eminent** *adj.* بارز baariz
eleven *n.* أحدعشر uahada 'ashar	**emissary** *n.* مبعوث mab'ooth
elf *n.* قزم qazam	**emit** *v.* ينبعث yanba'ith
eligible *adj.* مؤهل mouahhal	**emolument** *n.* مكافأة mokaafauah
eliminate *v.* يقضي yaqdi	**emotion** *n.* عاطفة aatifah
elimination *n.* قضاء qadaau	**emotional** *adj.* عاطفي aatifiy
elope *v.* يهرب yahrob	**emperor** *n.* إمبراطور embraatoor
eloquence *n.* بلاغة balaaghah	**emphasis** *n.* تشديد tashdeed
eloquent *adj.* بليغ baleegh	**emphasize** *v.* يشدّد yoshaddid
else *adj.* آخر uaakhar	**emphatic** *adj.* مؤكد mouayyid
else *adv.* آخر uaakhar	**empire** *n.* إمبراطورية embraatootiyyah
elucidate *v.* يشرح yashrah	**employ** *v.* يوظّف yowadddif
elude *v.* يتملّص yatamallas	**employee** *n.* موظّف mowaddddaf

employer *n.* موظِّف mowaddddif
employment *n.* توظيف tawddeef
empower *v.* يمكّن yomakkin
empress *n.* إمبراطورة embraatoorah
empty *adj.* فارغ faarigh
empty *v.* يفرّغ yofarrigh
emulate *v.* يضاه yodaahi
enable *v.* يمكّن yomakkin
enact *v.* يسن yasin
enamel *n.* مينا meena
enamour *v.* يسحر yashar
encase *v.* يكسو yakso
enchant *v.* يسحر yashar
encircle *v.* يطوّق yotawwiq
enclose *v.* يضمن yadman
enclosure *n.* سياج siyaaj
encompass *v.* يشمل yashmal
encounter *n.* لقاء liqaau
encounter *v.* يلاقي yolaaqi
encourage *v.* يشجّع yoshajji'
encroach *v.* يتجاوز yatajaawaz
encumber *v.* يعيق yo'eeq
encyclopaedia *n.* موسوعة mawsoo'ah
end *v.* ينهي yonhi
end *n.* نهاية nihaayah
endanger *v.* يعرض للخطر yo'arrido lilkhatar
endear *v.* يحب yohib
endearment *n.* تحبب tahabbob
endeavour *n.* مسعى mas'a
endeavour *v.* يسعى yas'a
endorse *v.* يؤيّد youayyid
endow *v.* يمنح yamnah
endurable *adj.* يطاق yotaaq

endurance *n.* احتمال ehtimaal
endure *v.* يتحمّل yatahammal
enemy *n.* عدو adow
energetic *adj.* نشيط nasheet
energy *n.* طاقة taaqah
enfeeble *v.* يضعف yod'if
enforce *v.* يفرض yafrid
enfranchise *v.* يعتق yo'tiq
engage *v.* يشتبك yashtabik
engagement *n.* اشتباك eshtibaak
engine *n.* محرك moharrik
engineer *n.* مهندس mohandis
English *n.* اللغةالإنجليزية ualloghatol enjleeziyyah
engrave *v.* ينقش yanqosh
engross *v.* يستغرق yastaghriq
engulf *v.* يعم ya'im
enigma *n.* لغز loghz
enjoy *v.* يستمتع yastamti'
enjoyment *n.* متعة mot'ah
enlarge *v.* يكبّر yokabbir
enlighten *v.* ينوّر yonawwir
enlist *v.* يجنّد yojannid
enliven *v.* يحيي yohyi
enmity *n.* عداوة adaawah
ennoble *v.* يعظم yo'addim
enormous *adj.* هائل haauil
enough *adj.* كاف kaafi
enough *adv.* كفاية kifaayah
enrage *v.* يغيظ yogheedd
enrapture *v.* يبهج yobhij
enrich *v.* يثري yothri
enrol *v.* يسجّل yosajjil
enshrine *v.* يكرّس yokarris
enslave *v.* يستعبد yasta'bid

ensue v. يترتب yatarattab

ensure v. يضمن yadman

entangle v. يشبك yashbik

enter v. يدخل yadkhol

enterprise n. مشروع mashroo'

entertain v. يسلّي yosalli

entertainment n. تسلية tasliyah

enthrone v. يمجّد yomajjid

enthusiasm n. حماس hamaas

enthusiastic adj. متحمس motahammis

entice v. يجذب yajdhib

entire adj. كامل kaamil

entirely adv. تماما tamaaman

entitle v. يخول yokhawwil

entity n. كيان kayaan

entomology n. علم الحشرات ilmol hasharaat

entrails n. أحشاء uahshaau

entrance n. مدخل madkhal

entrap v. يصطاد yastaad

entreat v. يتوسل yatawassal

entreaty n. توسل tawassol

entrust v. يعهد ya'had

entry n. دخول dokhool

enumerate v. يسرد yasrid

envelop v. يغلّف yoghallif

envelope n. مغلف moghallaf

enviable adj. محسود mahsood

envious adj. حسود hasood

environment n. بيئة beeuah

envy v. حسد hasad

envy v. يحسد yahsid

epic n. ملحمي malhamiy

epidemic n. وباء wabaau

epigram n. ساخر saakhir

epilepsy n. صرع sara'

epilogue n. خاتمة khaatimah

episode n. حادثة haadithah

epitaph n. نقش على ضريح naqshon 'ala dareeh

epoch n. عهد ahd

equal adj. متساو motasaawi

equal v. يساو yosaawi

equal n. مماثل momaathil

equality n. مساواة mosaawaah

equalize v. يعادل yo'aadil

equate v. يساوي yosaawi

equation n. معادلة mo'aadalah

equator n. خط الاستواء khadol estiwaau

equilateral adj. متساوي الاضلاع motasaawil uadlaa'

equip v. يجهّز yojahhiz

equipment n. عدّة oddah

equitable adj. منصف monsif

equivalent adj. معادل mo'aadil

equivocal adj. مريب moreeb

era n. عصر asr

eradicate v. يقضي yaqdi

erase v. يمحو yamho

erect v. ينصب yansib

erect adj. منتصب montasib

erection n. انتصاب entisaab

erode v. يحت yahhit

erosion n. تآكل tauaakol

erotic adj. جنسي jinsiy

err v. يضل yadol

errand n. مأمورية maumooriyyah

erroneous adj. خاطئ khaatiu

error n. خطأ khatau

erupt v. يندلع yandali'

eruption *n.* ثوران thawaraan

escape *n.* فرار firaar

escape *v.* يهرب yahrob

escort *n.* مرافق moraafiq

escort *v.* يرافق yoraafiq

especial *adj.* خاص khaas

essay *n.* مقال maqaal

essay *v.* يمتحن yamtahin

essayist *n.* كاتب المقال kaatibol maqaal

essence *n.* جوهر jawhar

essential *adj.* أساسي usaasiy

establish *v.* ينشئ yonshiu

establishment *n.* تأسيس tausees

estate *n.* عقار iqaar

esteem *n.* احترام ehtiraam

esteem *v.* يحترم yahtarim

estimate *n.* مقدّر moqaddar

estimate *v.* يقدّر yoqaddir

estimation *n.* تقدير taqdeer

etcetera *adv.* إلى آخره ela uaakhirihi

eternal *adj.* أبدي uabadiy

eternity *n.* أبدية uabadiyyah

ether *n.* أثير uathariy

ethical *adj.* أخلاقي uakhlaaqiy

ethics *n.* أخلاق uakhlaaq

etiquette *n.* منهج التصرف manhajo ttasarrof

etymology *n.* منشأ الكلمة manshauol kalimah

eunuch *n.* مخصي makhsiy

evacuate *v.* يخلي yokhli

evacuation *n.* إخلاء ekhlaau

evade *v.* يهرب yahrob

evaluate *v.* يقدّر yoqaddir

evaporate *v.* يتبخّر yatabakhkhar

evasion *n.* تهزب taharrob

even *adj.* 1 متساو motasaawi

even *adj.* 2 مستو mostawi

even *adj.* 3 زوجي zawjiy

even *v.* يسوّي yasawwi

even *adv.* حتى hatta

evening *n.* مساء masaau

event *n.* حدث hadath

eventually *adv.* أخيرا uakheeran

ever *adv.* أبدا uabadan

evergreen *adj.* دائم الخضرة daauimol khodrah

evergreen *n.* دائم الخضرة daauimol khodrah

everlasting *adj.* أبدي uabadiy

every *adj.* كل kol

evict *v.* يطرد yatrod

eviction *n.* طرد tard

evidence *n.* دليل daleel

evident *adj.* واضح waadih

evil *n.* شر shar

evil *a* شرير shirreer

evoke *v.* يستحضر yastahdir

evolution *n.* تطور tatawwor

evolve *v.* يتطور yatatawwar

ewe *n.* نعجة na'jah

exact *adj.* دقيق daqeeq

exaggerate *v.* يبالغ yobaaligh

exaggeration *n.* مبالغة mobaalaghah

exalt *v.* يكثف yokaththif

examination *n.* فحص fahs

examine *v.* يفحص yafhas

examinee *n.* ممتحَن momtahan

examiner *n.* ممتحِن momtahin

example *n.* مثال mithaal
excavate *v.* ينقب yonaqqib
excavation *n.* تنقيب tanqeeb
exceed *v.* يتجاوز yatajaawaz
excel *v.* يفوق yafooq
excellence *n.* امتياز emtiyaaz
excellency *n.* سعادة sa'aadah
excellent *adj.* ممتاز momtaaz
except *v.* يستثني yastathni
except *prep.* إلا ela
exception *n.* استثناء estithnaau
excess *n.* تجاوز tajaawoz
excess *adj.* فائض faauid
exchange *n.* تبادل tbaadol
exchange *v.* يتبادل yatabaadal
excise *n.* ضريبة dareebah
excite *v.* يثير yotheer
exclaim *v.* يتعجب yata'ajjab
exclamation *n.* تعجب ta'ajjob
exclude *v.* يستبعد yastab'id
exclusive *adj.* حصري hasriy
excommunicate *v.* يعزل ya'zil
excursion *n.* نزهة nozhah
excuse *v.* يعذر ya'dhor
excuse *n.* عذر odhr
execute *v.* ينفّذ yonaffidh
execution *n.* إعدام e'daam
executioner *n.* جلّاد jallaad
exempt *v.* يعفي ya'fi
exempt *adj.* معفى mo'fah
exercise *n.* ممارسة momaarasah
exercise *v.* يمارس yomaaris
exhaust *v.* يتعب yat'ab
exhibit *n.* معرض ma'rad
exhibit *v.* يعرض ya'rid

exhibition *n.* معرض ma'rad
exile *n.* منفى manfa
exile *v.* ينفي yanfi
exist *v.* يوجد yojad
existence *n.* وجود wojood
exit *n.* مخرج makhraj
exit *v.* يخرج yakhroj
expand *v.* يوسع yoosi'
expansion *n.* توسع tawasso'
ex-parte *adj.* متحيّز motahayyiz
ex-parte *adv.* متحيّز motahayyiz
expect *v.* يتوقّع yatawaqqa'
expectation *n.* توقع tawaqqo'
expedient *adj.* وسيلة waseelah
expedite *v.* يعجّل yo'ajjil
expedition *n.* بعثة bi'thah
expel *v.* يطرد yatrod
expend *v.* ينفق yonfiq
expenditure *n.* إنفاق enfaaq
expense *n.* نفقة nafaqah
expensive *adj.* غالي ghaali
experience *n.* تجربة tajribah
experience *v.* يجرّب yojarrib
experiment *n.* تجربة tajribah
expert *adj.* خبير khabeer
expert *n.* خبير khabeer
expire *v.* ينقضي yanqadi
expiry *n.* انقضاء enqidaau
explain *v.* يشرح yashrah
explanation *n.* تفسير tafseer
explicit *adj.* صريح sareeh
explode *v.* ينفجر yanfajir
exploit *n.* استغلال estighlaal
exploit *v.* يستغل yastaghil
exploration *n.* استكشاف estikshaaf

explore v. يستكشف yastakshif

explosion n. انفجار enfijaar

explosive n. متفجر motafajjir

explosive adj. متفجر motafajjir

exponent n. مؤَيد mouayyid

export n. تصدير tasdeer

export v. يصدَر yosaddir

expose v. 1 يعزض ya'rid

expose v. 2 يفضح yafdah

express v. يعرب yo'rib

express adj. سريع saree'

express n. خدمة سريعة khidmaton saree'ah

expression n. تعبير ta'beer

expressive a. معبر mo'abbir

expulsion n. طرد tard

extend v. يمد yamid

extent n. مدى mada

external adj. خارجي khaarijiy

extinct adj. منقرض monqarid

extinguish v. يطفئ yotfiu

extol v. يمجَد yomajjid

extra adj. إضافي edaafiy

extra adv. غير عادي ghayr 'aadiy

extract n. مقتطف moqtataf

extract v. يستخلص yastakhlis

extraordinary adj. استثنائي estithnaauiy

extravagance n. إسراف esraaf

extravagant adj. مسرف mosrif

extreme adj. أقصى uaqsa

extreme n. حد أقصى hadon uaqsa

extremist n. متطرف motatarrif

exult v. يهلل yohallil

eye n. عين ayn

eyeball n. مقلة moqlah

eyelash n. رمش romsh

eyelet n. عيينة oyaynah

eyewash n. غسول للعين ghasoolon lil'a

F

fable n. أسطورة ustoorah

fabric n. قماش qiraash

fabricate v. يصنع yasna'

fabrication n. تلفيق talfeeq

fabulous adj. رائع raaui'

facade n. واجهة waajihah

face n. وجه wajh

face v. يواجه yowaajih

facet n. 1 وجيه wojayh

facet n. 2 صفة sifah

facial adj. وجهي wajhiy

facile adj. سطحي sathiy

facilitate v. ييسَر yoyassir

facility n. تسهيل tasheel

fac-simile n. صورة طبق الأصل sooraton tibqol uasl

fact n. حقيقة haqeeqiy

faction n. فصيل faseel

factious adj. مثير للشقاق motheeron lishshiqaaq

factor n. عامل aamil

factory n. مصنع masna'

faculty n. هيئة تدريسية hayuaton tadreesiyyah

fad n. بدعة bid'ah

fade v. يتلاشى yatalaasha

faggot *n.*	لوطي	lootiy
fail *v.*	يفشل	yafshal
failure *n.*	فشل	fashal
faint *adj.*	خافت	khaafit
faint *v.*	يغشو	yaghsho
fair *adj.*	عادل	aadil
fair *n.*	إحتفال	ehtifaal
fairly *adv.*	بإنصاف	biuinsaaf
fairy *n.*	جنية	jinniyyah
faith *n.*	إيمان	ueeman
faithful *adj.*	مخلص	mokhlis
falcon *n.*	صقر	saqr
fall *v.*	يقع	yaqa'
fall *n.*	خريف	khareef
fallacy *n.*	مغالطة	moghaalatah
fallow *n.*	اراحةالأرض	eraahatol 'ard
false *adj.*	زائف	zaauif
falter *v.*	يتداع	yatadaa'a
fame *n.*	شهرة	shohrah
familiar *adj.*	مألوف	mauloof
family *n.*	عائلة	aauilah
famine *n.*	مجاعة	majaauah
famous *adj.*	مشهور	mashhoor
fan *n.* 1	مروحة	mirqahah
fan *n.* 2	معجب	mo'jab
fanatic *adj.*	متعصب	mota'assib
fanatic *n.*	متعصب	mota'assib
fancy *n.*	نزوة	nazwah
fancy *v.*	يرغب	yarghab
fantastic *adj.*	خيالي	khayaaliy
far *adv.*	بعيدا	ba'eedan
far *adj.*	بعيد	ba'eed
farce *n.*	مهزلة	mahzalah
fare *n.*	أجرة	uojrah
farewell *n.*	وداع	wadaa'
farewell *interj.*	وداعاً	wadaa'an
farm *n.*	مزرعة	mazra'ah
farmer *n.*	مزارع	mozaari'
fascinate *v.*	يفتن	yaftin
fascination *n.*	استهواء	estihwaau
fashion *n.*	موضة	moodah
fashionable *adj.*	مألوف	mauloof
fast *adj.* 1	سريع	saree'
fast *adj.* 2	محكم	mohkam
fast *adv.*	بسرعة	bisor'ah
fast *n.*	صيام	siyaam
fast *v.*	يصوم	yasoom
fasten *v.*	يربط	yarbit
fat *adj.*	بدين	badeen
fat *n.*	دهن	dohn
fatal *adj.*	مميت	momeet
fate *n.*	مصير	maseer
father *n.*	أب	uab
fathom *v.*	يقيس	yaqees
fathom *n.*	مقياس	miqyaas
fatigue *n.*	تعب	ta'ab
fatigue *v.*	يتعب	yat'ab
fault *n.*	خطأ	khatau
faulty *adj.*	خاطئ	khaatiu
fauna *n.*	علمالحيوانات	ilmol hayawaanaat
favour *n.*	مَعروف	ma'roof
favour *n.*	صالح	saalih
favour *v.*	يحبذ	yohabbidh
favourable *adj.*	مؤات	mouaati
favourite *adj.*	مفضل	mofaddal
favourite *n.*	مفضل	mofaddal
fax *n.*	فاكس	faaks
fear *n.*	خوف	khawf

fear *v.* يخاف yakhaaf	**fertile** *adj.* خصب khisb
fearful *adj.* مخيف mokheef	**fertility** *n.* خصوبة khosoobah
feasible *adj.* ممكن‌تحقيقه momkinon tahqeeqoh	**fertilize** *v.* يخصب yokhsib
	fertilizer *n.* سماد samaad
feast *n.* وليمة waleemah	**fervent** *adj.* متحمس motahammis
feast *v.* يتغذى yataghadhdha	**fervour** *n.* حماسة hamaasah
feat *n.* عمل amal	**festival** *n.* مهرجان mihrajaan
feather *n.* ريشة reeshah	**festive** *adj.* احتفالي ehtifaaliy
feature *n.* ميزة mayyizah	**festivity** *n.* إحتفال ehtifaal
February *n.* شباط shbaat	**festoon** *n.* إكليل‌معلّق ekleelon mo'allaq
federal *adj.* اتحادي ettihaadiy	
federation *n.* اتحاد ettihaad	**fetch** *v.* يجلب yajlib
fee *n.* رسم rasm	**fetter** *n.* غل ghol
feeble *adj.* ضعيف da'eef	**fetter** *v.* يكبّل yokabbil
feed *v.* يأكل yaukol	**feud** *n.* عداء idaau
feed *n.* علف alaf	**feudal** *adj.* إقطاعي eqtaa'iy
feel *v.* يشعر yash'or	**fever** *n.* حمى hamma
feeling *n.* إحساس ehsaas	**few** *adj.* قليل qaleel
feign *v.* يختلق yakhtaliq	**fiasco** *n.* فشل fashal
felicitate *v.* يهنئ yohanniu	**fibre** *n.* ليف leef
felicity *n.* سعادة sa'aadah	**fickle** *adj.* متقلب motaqallib
fell *v.* يقطع yaqta'	**fiction** *n.* خيال khayaal
fellow *n.* زميل zameel	**fictitious** *adj.* خيالي khayaaliy
female *adj.* أنثى uontha	**fiddle** *n.* كمان kamaan
female *n.* أنثى uontha	**fiddle** *v.* يعبث ya'bath
feminine *adj.* مؤنّث mouannath	**fidelity** *n.* إخلاص ekhlaas
fence *n.* سياج siyaaj	**fie** *interj* التعبيرعن‌عدم‌الرضا uatta'beero 'an 'adami rrida
fence *v.* يسيّج yosayyij	
fend *v.* يصد yasod	**field** *n.* حقل haql
ferment *n.* خمر khamr	**fiend** *n.* مدمن modmin
ferment *v.* يتخمّر yatakhammar	**fierce** *adj.* عنيف aneef
fermentation *n.* تخمير takhmeer	**fiery** *adj.* ناري naariy
ferocious *adj.* شرس sharis	**fifteen** *n.* خمسة‌عشر khamsato 'ashar
ferry *n.* عبّارة abbaarah	
ferry *v.* ينقل yanqil	**fifty** *n.* خمسون khamsoon
	fig *n.* تين teen

fight *n.* قتال qitaal	finite *adj.* محدود mahdood
fight *v.* يقاتل yoqaatil	fir *n.* التنوب uattannoob
figment *n.* ملفق molaffaq	fire *n.* حريق hareeq
figurative *adj.* رمزي ramziy	fire *v.* يطرد yatrod
figure *n.* 1 شخصية shakhsiyyah	firm *adj.* متماسك motamaasik
figure *n.* 2 مجسم mojassam	firm *n.* شركة sharikah
figure *v.* يستنتج yastantij	first *adj.* أول uawwal
file *n.* 1 ملف malaf	first *n.* أول uawwal
file *n.* 2 طابور taaboor	first *adv.* أولاً uawwalan
file *n.* 3 مبرد mibrad	fiscal *adj.* مالي maliy
file *v.* 1 يضع في ملف yada'o fi malaf	fish *n.* سمك samak
file *v.* 2 يسير في طابور yaseero fi taaboor	fish *v.* يصطاد yastaad
	fisherman *n.* صياد sayyad
file *v.* 3 يبرد yabrod	fissure *n.* فجوة fajwah
fill *v.* يملأ yamlau	fist *n.* قبضة qabdhah
film *n.* فيلم film	fistula *n.* ناسور naasoor
film *v.* يصور yosawwir	fit *v.* يناسب yonaasib
filter *n.* مرشح marshah	fit *adj.* جيد jayyid
filter *v.* يرشح yorshih	fit *n.* 1 مناسب monaasib
filth *n.* قذارة qadhaarah	fit *n.* 2 نوبة nawbah
filthy *adj.* قذر qadhir	fitful *adj.* متقطع motaqatti'
fin *n.* زعنفة zo'nofah	fitter *n.* مُرَكِّب morakkib
final *adj.* نهائي nihaauiy	five *n.* خمسة khamsah
finance *n.* تمويل tamweel	fix *v.* يحل yahil
finance *v.* يمول yomawwel	fix *n.* حل hal
financial *adj.* مالي maaliy	flabby *adj.* مترهل motarahhil
financier *n.* ممول momawwil	flag *n.* علم alam
find *v.* يعثر ya'thor	flagrant *adj.* فاضح faadih
fine *n.* غرامة gharaamah	flame *n.* لهب lahab
fine *v.* يغرم yogharrim	flame *v.* يهب yahib
fine *adj.* حسن hasan	flannel *n.* فانلّة faanillah
finger *n.* إصبع esba'	flare *v.* يتوهَج yatawahhaj
finger *v.* يَلمس بالإضبَع yalmiso biluisba'	flare *n.* توهج tawahhoj
	flash *n.* وميض wameed
finish *v.* ينهي yonhi	flash *v.* يومض yoomid
finish *n.* نهاية nihaayah	

flask *n.* قارورة qaaroorah	**flourish** *v.* يزدهر yazdahir
flat *adj.* مسطّح mosatah	**flow** *n.* تدفق tadaffoq
flat *n.* شقة shaqah	**flow** *v.* يتدفّق yatadaffaq
flatter *v.* يطري yotri	**flower** *n.* زهرة zahrah
flattery *n.* إطراء etraau	**flowery** *adj.* منمق monammaq
flavour *n.* نكهة nakhah	**fluent** *adj.* طليق taleeq
flaw *n.* عيب ayb	**fluid** *adj.* مائع maaui'
flea *n.* برغوث barghooth	**fluid** *n.* سائل saauil
flee *v.* يهرب yahrob	**flush** *v.* يتورد yatawarrad
fleece *n.* صوف soof	**flush** *v.* يتدفّق yatadaffaq
fleece *v.* يجز yajiz	**flush** *n.* تورّد tawarrod
fleet *n.* أسطول uostool	**flush** *n.* تدفّق tadaffoq
flesh *n.* لحم lahm	**flute** *n.* ناي naay
flexible *adj.* مرن marin	**flute** *v.* يعزف الناي ya'zifo nnaay
flicker *n.* رمشة ramshah	**flutter** *n.* رفرفة rafrafah
flicker *v.* يرمش yarmosh	**flutter** *v.* يرفرف yorafrif
flight *n.* طيران tayaraan	**fly** *n.* ذبابة dhobaabah
flimsy *adj.* مهلهل mohalhal	**fly** *v.* يطير yateer
fling *v.* يقذف yaqdhif	**foam** *n.* رغوة raghwah
flippancy *n.* تهكم tahakkom	**foam** *v.* يزبد yozaddid
flirt *n.* مغازلة moghaazalah	**focal** *adj.* مركزي markaziy
flirt *v.* يغازل yoghaazil	**focus** *n.* تركيز tarkeez
float *v.* يعوم ya'oom	**focus** *v.* يركّز yorakkiz
flock *n.* قطيع qatee'	**fodder** *n.* علف alaf
flock *v.* يتوفّق yatawaafad	**foe** *n.* عدو adow
flog *v.* يجلد yajlid	**fog** *n.* ضباب dabaab
flood *n.* فيضان fayadaan	**foil** *v.* يحبط yohbit
flood *v.* يفيض yafeed	**fold** *n.* طية tayyah
floor *n.* 1 طابق taabiq	**fold** *v.* يطوي yatwi
floor *n.* 2 أرضيّة uardiyyah	**foliage** *n.* أوراق الشجر uawraaqo shshajar
floor *v.* يصرع yasra'	**follow** *v.* يتبع yatba'
flora *n.* نبات nabaat	**follower** I تابع taabi'
florist *n.* بائع الزهور baaui'o zzohoor	**folly** *n.* حماقة hamaaqah
flour *n.* طحين taheen	**foment** *v.* يثير yotheer

fond adj. مغرم moghram

fondle v. يربت yorabbit

food n. غذاء ghidhaau

fool v. يخدع yakhda'

fool v. يتسكع yatasakka'

fool n. مغفل moghaffal

foolish adj. أحمق uahmaq

foolscap n. قبعة qobba'ah

foot n. قدم qadam

for prep. إلى ela

for conj. لأن liuanna

forbid v. يمنع yamna'

force n. قوة qowwah

force v. يجبر yojbir

forceful adj. قوي qawiy

forcible adj. قسري qasriy

forearm n. ساعد saa'id

forearm v. يتحضر لنزال yatahaddaro linizaal

forecast n. توقع tawaqqo'

forecast v. يتوقع yatawaqqa'

forefather n. جد jad

forefinger n. سبابة sabbaabah

forehead n. جبين jabaan

foreign adj. أجنبي uajnabiy

foreigner n. أجنبي uajnabiy

foreknowledge n. معرفة مسبقة ma'rifaton mosbaqah

foreleg n. رجل أمامية rijlon uamaamiyyah

forelock n. ناصية naasiyah

foreman n. رئيس العمال raueesol 'ommaal

foremost adj. بارز baariz

forenoon n. صدر النهار sadro nnahaar

forerunner n. رائد raauid

foresee v. يتوقع yatawaqqa'

foresight n. بصيرة baseerah

forest n. غابة ghaabah

forestall v. يحبط yohbit

forester n. حراجي hiraajiy

forestry n. حراجة hiraajah

foretell v. يتنبأ yatanabbau

forethought n. مدروس madroos

forever adv. الأبد إلى elal uabad

forewarn v. يحذر yohadhdhir

foreword n. مقدمة moqaddimah

forfeit v. يصادر yosaadir

forfeit n. مصادرة mosaadarah

forfeiture n. مصادرة mosaadarah

forge n. أتون uaatoon

forge v. 1 يزور yozawwir

forge v. 2 يتقدم yataqaddam

forge v. 3 يصهر yashar

forgery n. تزوير tazweer

forget v. ينسى yansa

forgetful adj. كثير النسيان katheero nnasayaan

forgive v. يغفر yaghfor

forgo v. يتخلى عن yatakhalla 'an

forlorn adj. بائس baauis

form n. 1 شكل shakl

form n. 2 طلب talab

form v. يشكل yoshakkil

formal adj. رسمي rasmiy

format n. شكل shakl

formation n. تشكيل tashkeel

former adj. سابق saabiq

former pron. السابق uassaabiq

formerly adv. سابقاً saabiqan

formidable *adj.* هائل haauil

formula *n.* صيغة seeghah

formulate *v.* يصيغ yaseegh

forsake *v.* يهجر yahjor

forswear *v.* يبتعد yabta'id

fort *n.* حصن hisn

forte *n.* موطن قوة mawtino qowwah

forth *adv.* 1 إلى آخره ela uaakhirih

forth *adv.* 2 قدماً qodoman

forthcoming *a.* قريبا qareeban

forthwith *adv.* فوري fawriy

fortify *v.* يحصّن yohasin

fortitude *n.* جلد jalad

fort-night *n.* أسبوعين uosboo'ayn

fortress *n.* حصن hisn

fortunate *a.* محظوظ mahddoodd

fortune *n.* ثروة tharwah

forty *n.* أربعون uarba'oon

forum *n.* منتدى montada

forward *a.* متقدّم motaqaddim

forward *adv.* إلى الأمام elal uamaam

forward *v.* يرسل yorsil

fossil *n.* أحفورة uohfoorah

foster *v.* يعزّز yo'azziz

foster *v.* يربّي yorabbi

foul *n.* مخلّفات mokhaalafah

foul *a.* فاسد faasid

foul *v.* يوسخ yowassikh

found *v.* يؤسس youassis

foundation *n.* مؤسسة mouassasah

founder *n.* مؤسس mouassis

foundry *n.* مسبك masbak

fountain *n.* نافورة naafoorah

four *n.* أربعة uarba'ah

fourteen *n.* أربعة عشرة uarba'ato 'ashrah

fowl *n.* طير tayr

fowler *n.* صيّاد sayyaad

fox *n.* ثعلب tha'lab

fraction *n.* كسر kasr

fracture *n.* كسر kasr

fracture *v.* يكسر yaksir

fragile *a.* هش hash

fragment *n.* شظية shaddiyyah

fragrance *n.* رائحة raauihah

fragrant *a.* عبق abaq

frail *a.* ضعيف da'eef

frame *v.* 1 يلفّق تهمة yolaffiqo tohmah

frame *v.* 2 يؤطّر youattir

frame *n.* إطار etaar

franchise *n.* شركة sharikah

frank *a.* صريح sareeh

frantic *a.* مسعور mas'oor

fraternal *a.* أخوي uakhawiy

fraternity *n.* أخوية uakhawiyyah

fratricide *n.* قتل الإخوة qatlol ekhwah

fraud *n.* احتيال ehtiyaal

fraudulent *a.* إحتيالي ehtiyaaliy

fraught *a.* مشحون mashhoon

fray *n.* نزاع nizaa'

free *a.* حر hor

free *v.* يحرّر yoharrir

freedom *n.* حرية horriyyah

freeze *v.* يجمّد yojammid

freight *n.* شحن shahn

French *a.* فرنسي faransiy

French *n.* اللغة الفرنسية ualloghatol faransiyyah

frenzy *n.* نوبة nawbah	**fry** *v.* يقلي yaqli
frequency *n.* تردد taraddod	**fry** *n.* مقلاة miqlah
frequent *n.* متكرر motakarrir	**fuel** *n.* وقود waqood
fresh *a.* طازج taazaj	**fugitive** *a.* هارب haarib
fret *n.* غيظ ghaydd	**fugitive** *n.* مشرّد mosharrad
fret *v.* يغتاظ yaghtaadd	**fulfil** *v.* يوفي yoofi
friction *n.* احتكاك ehtikaak	**fulfilment** *n.* تحقيق tahqeeq
Friday *n.* الجمعة ualjomo'ah	**full** *a.* كامل kaamil
fridge *n.* ثلاجة thallaajah	**full** *adv.* بالأكمل biluakmal
friend *n.* صديق sadeeq	**fullness** *n.* إمتلاء emtilaau
fright *n.* رعب ro'b	**fully** *adv.* تماماً tamaaman
frighten *v.* يخيف yokheef	**fumble** *v.* يتلعثم yatala'tham
frigid *a.* فاتر faatir	**fun** *n.* مرح marah
frill *n.* هدب hodb	**function** *n.* وظيفة waddeefah
fringe *n.* 1 حافة haaffah	**function** *v.* يعمل ya'mal
fringe *n.* 2 تسريحة tasreehah	**functionary** *n.* موظّف mowadddaf
fringe *v.* يحد yahod	
frivolous *a.* تافه taafih	**fund** *n.* منحة minhah
frock *n.* فستان fostaan	**fundamental** *a.* أساسي usaasiy
frog *n.* ضفدع difda'	**funeral** *n.* دفن dafn
frolic *n.* مرح marah	**fungus** *n.* فطر fitr
frolic *v.* يمرح yamrah	**funny** *n.* مضحك mod hik
from *prep.* من min	**fur** *n.* فرو farw
front *n.* جبهة jabhah	**furious** *a.* غاضب ghaadib
front *adj.* أمام uamaam	**furl** *v.* يلف yalof
front *v.* يوجه yowaajih	**furlong** *n.* وحدةقياس wihdato qiyaas
frontier *n.* حدود hodood	**furnace** *n.* فرن forn
frost *n.* صقيع saqee'	**furnish** *v.* يؤثّث youaththith
frown *n.* عبوس oboos	**furniture** *n.* أثاث uathaath
frown *v.* يعبس ya'bis	**furrow** *n.* ثلم thalm
frugal *a.* مقتصد moqtasid	**further** *adv.* أكثر uakthar
fruit *n.* فاكهة faakihah	**further** *adj.* مزيد mazeed
fruitful *a.* مثمر mothmir	**further** *v.* يزيد yazeed
frustrate *v.* يحبط yohbit	**fury** *n.* ضراوة daraawah
frustration *n.* إحباط ehbaat	

fuse *v.* يلحم yolhim	gallows *n.* . مشنقة mishnaqah
fuse *n.* فتيل fateel	galore *adv.* وافر waafir
fusion *n.* انصهار ensihaar	galvanize *v.* يدفع yadfa'
fuss *n.* جلبة jalabah	gamble *v.* يقامر yoqaamir
fuss *v.* يضج yadoj	gamble *n.* مغامرة moghaamarah
futile *a.* عقيم aqeem	gambler *n.* مقامر moqaamir
futility *n.* عبث abath	game *n.* لعبة lo'bah
future *a.* مستقبلي mostaqbaliy	game *n.* صيد sayd
future *n.* مستقبل mostaqbal	game *v.* يقامر yoqaamir
	gander *n.* إوزة ewazzah
	gang *n.* عصابة isaabah
G	gangster *n.* رجل عصابة rajolo 'isaabah
	gap *n.* فجوة fajwah
gabble *v.* يهذر yahdhor	gape *v.* يتثاءب yatathaauab
gadfly *n.* ذبابة الخيل dhobaabatol khayl	garage *n.* كراج karaaj
gag *v.* 1 يسكت yoskit	garb *n.* زي ziy
gag *v.* 2 يمزح yamzah	garb *v.* يكسو yakso
gag *n.* 1 كمّامة kammaamah	garbage *n.* قمامة qomaamah
gag *n.* 2 مزحة mozhah	garden *n.* حديقة hadeeqah
gaiety *n.* مسرة masarrah	gardener *n.* بستاني bostaaniy
gain *v.* يكسب yaksab	gargle *v.* يتغرغر yatagharghar
gain *n.* كسب kasb	garland *n.* زينة zeenah
gainsay *v.* ينكر yonkir	garland *v.* يزيّن yozayyen
gait *n.* مشية mashyah	garlic *n.* ثوم thawm
galaxy *n.* مجرة majarrah	garment *n.* ثوب thawb
gale *n.* عاصفة aasifah	garter *n.* وسام wisaam
gallant *a.* شجاع shojaa'	gas *n.* غاز ghaaz
gallant *n.* شيك sheek	gasket *n.* سدّادة saddaadah
gallantry *n.* بسالة basaalah	gasp *n.* لهاث lohaath
gallery *n.* معرض ma'rad	gasp *v.* يلهث yalhath
gallon *n.* غالون ghaalon	gassy *a.* غازي ghaaziy
gallop *n.* رماحة rimaahah	gastric *a.* معدي ma'idiy
gallop *v.* يرمح yarmoh	gate *n.* بوابة bawaabah
	gather *v.* يجمع yajma'

gaudy *a.* مبهرج mobahraj	germicide *n.* مبيدللجراثيم mobeedonliljaraatheem
gauge *n.* قياس qiyaas	germinate*v* يتبرعم yatabar'am
gauntlet *n.* تحد tahaddi	germination *n.* تبرعم tabar'om
gay *a.* لواطي lowaatiy	gerund *n.* صيغةالفعل seeghatol fi'l
gay *n.* لواطي lowaatiy	gesture *n.* إيماءة ueemauah
gaze *v.* ينظر yanddor	get *v.* يحصل yahsol
gaze *n.* نظرة naddrah	ghastly *a.* مروع morawwi'
gazette *n.* جريدة jareedah	ghost *n.* شبح shabah
gear *n.* معدات mo'iddaat	giant *n.* عملاق imlaaq
geld *v.* يهذّب yohadhdhib	gibbon *n.* قرد qird
gem *n.* جوهرة jawharah	gibe *v.* يهزأ yahzau
gender *n.* جنس jins	gibe *n.* هزء hazau
general *a.* عام aam	giddy *a.* دائخ daauikh
generally *adv.* عموما omooman	gift *n.* هدية hadiyyah
generate *v.* يولّد yowallid	gifted *a.* موهوب mawhoob
generation *n.* جيل jeel	gigantic *a.* ضخم dakhm
generator *n.* مولد mowallid	giggle *v.* يضحك yad hak
generosity *n.* كرم karam	gild *v.* يموّه yomawwih
generous *a.* سخي sakhiy	gilt *a.* مذهّب madhhab
genius *n.* عبقري abqariy	ginger *n.* زنجبيل zangabeel
gentle *a.* لطيف lateef	giraffe *n.* زرافة zaraafah
gentleman *n.* نبيل nabeel	gird *v.* يكسو yakso
gentry *n.* الطبقةالعليا uattabaqatol 'olya	girder *n.* عارضة aaridah
genuine *a.* حقيقي haqeeqiy	girdle *n.* حزام hizaam
geographer *n.* جغرافي joghraafiy	girdle *v.* يحازم yohazzim
geographical *a.* جغرافي joghraafiy	girl *n.* فتاة fataah
geography *n.* جغرافيا joghraafya	girlish *a.* بناتي bannaatiy
geological *a.* جيولوجي jiyooloogiy	gist *n.* جوهر jawhar
geologist *n.* جيولوجي jiyooloogiy	give *v.* يمنح yamnah
geology *n.* جيولوجيا jiyooloogya	glacier *n.* جليد jaleed
geometrical *a.* هندسي handasiy	glad *a.* سعيد sa'eed
geometry *n.* هندسة handasah	gladden *v.* يسعد yos'id
germ *n.* جرثومة jorthoomah	glamour *n.* سحر sihr
	glance *n.* لمحة lamhah

81

glance *v.* يلمح yalmah
gland *n.* غدة ghoddah
glare *n.* تحديق tahdeeq
glare *v.* يحدّق yohaddiq
glass *n.* زجاج zojaajah
glaucoma *n.* زرق zorraq
glaze *v.* يزجّج yozajjij
glaze *n.* زجاج zojaaj
glazier *n.* زجّاج zajjaaj
glee *n.* طرب tarab
glide *v.* يتزحلق yatazahlaq
glider *n.* طائرة شراعية taauiraton shiraa'iyyah
glimpse *n.* لمحة lamhah
glitter *v.* يلمع yalma'
glitter *n.* لمعان lama'aan
global *a.* عالمي aalamiy
globe *n.* عالم aalam
gloom *n.* ظلام ddlaam
gloomy *a.* كئيب kaueeb
glorification *n.* تمجيد tamjeed
glorify *v.* يمجّد yomajjid
glorious *a.* مجيد majeed
glory *n.* مجد majd
gloss *n.* لمعان lama'aan
glossary *n.* مسرد masrad
glossy *a.* لامع laami'
glove *n.* قفاز qoffaaz
glow *v.* يتوهّج yatawahhaj
glow *n.* توهّج tawahhoj
glucose *n.* جلوكوز jlookooz
glue *n.* غراء ghiraau
glut *v.* يتخم yotkhim
glut *n.* تخمة tokhmah
glutton *n.* شره sharah

gluttony *n.* نهم naham
glycerine *n.* غليسيرين ghleesireen
go *v.* يذهب yadhhab
goad *n.* منخس minkhas
goad *v.* يستحث yastahith
goal *n.* هدف hadaf
goat *n.* ماعز maa'iz
gobble *n.* كركرة karkarah
goblet *n.* كأس kaus
god *n.* إله elaah
goddess *n.* إلهة elaahah
godhead *n.* ألوهية uoloohiyyah
godly *adj.* إلهي elaahiy
godown *n.* مستودع بضائع mostawda'o badaaui'
godsend *n.* مصادفة سعيدة mosaadafaton sa'eedah
goggles *n.* نظارات واقية naddddaaraaton waaqiyah
gold *n.* ذهب dhahab
golden *a.* ذهبي dhahabiy
goldsmith *n.* صائغ saauigh
golf *n.* غولف ghoolf
gong *n.* جرس jaras
good *a.* جيد jayyid
good *a.* طيب tayyib
good *n.* خير khayr
good *n.* فائدة faauidah
good-bye *interj.* وداعا wadaa'an
goodness *n.* صلاح salaah
goodwill *n.* نية حسنة niyyaton hasanah
goose *n.* إوزّة ewazzah
gooseberry *n.* عنب uinab
gorgeous *a.* رائع raaui'
gorilla *n.* غوريلا ghoorillaa

gospel *n.* إنجيل enjeel	graph *n.* رسم بياني rasmon bayaaniy
gossip *n.* نميمة nameemah	graphic *adj.* بياني bayaaniy
gourd *n.* قرع qar'	grapple *n.* صراع siraa'
gout *n.* نقرس noqros	grapple *v.* يتصارع yatasaara'
govern *v.* يحكم yahkom	grasp *v.* يفهم yafham
governance *n.* حكم hokm	grasp *n.* فهم fahm
governess *n.* حاكمة haakimah	grass *n.* عشب oshb
government *n.* حكومة hokoomah	grate *n.* حاجز الموقد haajizol mawqid
governor *n.* محافظ mohaafidd	grate *v.* يبشر yabshor
gown *n.* ثوب thawb	grateful *adj.* ممتن momtan
grab *v.* ينتزع yantazzi'	grater *n.* مبشرة mibsharah
grace *n.* نعمة ni'mah	gratification *n.* مسرة masarrah
grace *v.* ينعم yan'am	gratis *adv.* بلاش bibalaash
gracious *a.* رؤوف rauoof	gratitude *n.* إمتنان emtinaan
gradation *n.* تدرج tadarroj	gratuity *n.* عطية atiyyah
grade *n.* 1 درجة darajah	grave *n.* قبر qabr
grade *n.* 2 منحدر monhadar	grave *a.* محتّم mohattam
grade *v.* يدرّج yodarrij	gravitate *v.* ينجذب yanjadhib
gradual *a.* تدريجي tadreejiy	gravitation *n.* جاذبية jaadhibiyyah
graduate *v.* يتخرّج yatakharraj	gravity *n.* خطورة khotoorah
graduate *n.* خريج khirreej	graze *v.* 1 يَكشُط yaqshot
graft *n.* 1 إبتزاز ebtizaaz	graze *v.* 2 يَرعَى yar'a
graft *n.* 2 رقعة roq'ah	graze *n.* كَشْط qasht
graft *v.* يرقع yoraqqi'	grease *n.* شحم shahm
grain *n.* حبوب hoboob	grease *v.* يدهن بالشحم yadhano bishshahm
grammar *n.* نحو nahw	greasy *a.* دهني dohniy
grammarian *n.* نحوي nahawiy	great *adj.* عظيم addeem
gramme *n.* غرام ğhraam	greed *n.* جشع jasha'
gramophone *n.* الحاكي ualhaaki	greedy *a.* جشع jashi'
granary *n.* هُزي hory	Greek *n.* اللغة اليونانية ualloghatol yoonaaniyyah
grand *a.* كبير kabeer	Greek *adj.* يوناني yoonaaniy
grandeur *n.* عظمة addamah	
grant *v.* يمنح yamnah	
grant *n.* منحة minhah	
grape *n.* عنب inab	

green *a.* أخضر uakhdar	**grower** *n.* مزارع mozaari'
green *n.* خضار khadaar	**growl** *v.* يزمجر yozamjir
greenery *n.* خضرة khodrah	**growl** *n.* دمدمة damdamah
greet *v.* يحيي yohayyi	**growth** *n.* نمو nomow
grenade *n.* قنبلة qonbolah	**grudge** *v.* يحقد yahqid
grey *a.* رمادي ramaadiy	**grudge** *n.* ضغينة dagheenah
greyhound *n.* كلب kalb	**grumble** *v.* يتذمّر yatadhammar
grief *n.* حزن hozn	**grunt** *n.* نخر nakhr
grievance *n.* شكوى shakwa	**grunt** *v.* ينخر yankhar
grieve *v.* يحزن yohzin	**guarantee** *n.* ضمان damaan
grievous *a.* موجع mooji'	**guarantee** *v.* يضمن yadman
grind *v.* يطحن yat han	**guard** *v.* يحرس yahros
grinder *n.* طاحونة taahoonah	**guard** *n.* حارس haaris
grip *v.* يقبض yaqbid	**guardian** *n.* وصي wasiy
grip *n.* قبضة qabdah	**guava** *n.* جوافة jawaafah
groan *v.* يتأوه yatauawwah	**guerilla** *n.* فدائي fidaauiy
groan *n.* تأوه tauawwoh	**guess** *n.* تخمين takhmeen
grocer *n.* بقّال baqqaal	**guess** *v.* يخمّن yokhammin
grocery *n.* بقالة baqqaalah	**guest** *n.* ضيف dayf
groom *n.* عريس arees	**guidance** *n.* توجيه tawjeeh
groom *v.* يُعِدّ yo'ad	**guide** *v.* يوجّه yowajjih
groove *n.* أخدود uokhdood	**guide** *n.* دليل daleel
groove *v.* يحتفل yahtafil	**guild** *n.* نقابة naqaabah
grope *v.* يَتَحَسَّس yatahassas	**guile** *n.* دهاء dahaau
gross *n.* مجمل mojmal	**guilt** *n.* ذنب dhanb
gross *adj.* 1 إجمالي ejmaaliy	**guilty** *a.* مذنب modhnib
gross *adj.* 2 فاحش faahish	**guise** *n.* مظهر maddhar
grotesque *a.* قبيح qabeeh	**guitar** *n.* قيثارة qeethaarah
ground *n.* 1 أساس uasaas	**gulf** *n.* خليج khaleej
ground *n.* 2 أرض uard	**gull** *n.* 1 نورس nawras
ground *v.* 1 يقوم على yaqoomo 'ala	**gull** *n.* 2 مخدوع makhdoo'
ground *v.* 2 يمنع yamna'	**gull** *v.* يخدع yakhda'
group *n.* مجموعة majmoo'ah	**gulp** *v.* يبلع yabla'
group *v.* يجمع yajma'	**gulp** *n.* إبتلاع ebtilaa'
grow *v.* ينمو yanmo	**gum** *n.* علكة ilkah

gun *n.* بندقية bondoqiyyah

gust *n.* عاصفة aasifah

gutter *n.* مزراب mizraab

guttural *a.* حلقي halqiy

gymnasium *n.* ستاداللعب staado lla'ib

gymnast *n.* لاعبرياضي laa'ibon riyaadiy

gymnastic *adj.* رياضي riyaadiy

gymnastics *n.* ألعابالحركة ual'aabol harakah

H

habeas corpus *n.* قراراستدعاء qaraaro estid'aau

habit *n.* عادة aadah

habitable *a.* صالحللسكن saalihon lissakan

habitat *n.* موطن mawtin

habitation *n.* سكن sakan

habituate *v.* يتعود yata'awwad

hack *v.* يخترق yakhtariq

hag *n.* مشعوذة mosha'widhah

haggard *a.* منهك monhak

haggle *v.* يساوم yosaawim

hail *n.* برد barad

hail *v.* يحيي yohayyi

hair *n.* شعر sha'ar

hale *a.* معافى mo'aafa

half *n.* نصف nisf

half *adj.* نصف nisf

hall *n.* قاعة qaa'ah

hallmark *n.* سمةمميزة simaton momayyizah

hallow *v.* يقدس yoqaddis

halt *v.* يقف yaqif

halt *n.* توقف tawaqqof

halve *v.* ينصف yanassif

hamlet *n.* قرية qaryah

hammer *n.* مطرقة mitraqah

hammer *v.* يطرق yatroq

hand *n.* يد yad

hand *v.* يسلم yosallim

handbill *n.* منشور manshoor

handbook *n.* كتيب kotayyib

handcuff *n.* كلبشة kalabshah

handcuff *v.* يكبل yokabbil

handful *n.* حفنة hafnah

handicap *v.* يعيق yo'eeq

handicap *n.* عائق aauiq

handicraft *n.* حرفة hirfah

handiwork *n.* عمليدوي amalon yadawiy

handkerchief *n.* منديل mindeel

handle *n.* مقبض maqbad

handle *v.* يتعامل yata'aamal

handsome *a.* وسيم waseem

handy *a.* مفيد mofeed

hang *v.* يعلق yo'alliq

hanker *v.* يتوق yatooq

haphazard *a.* مصادفة mosaadafah

happen *v.* يحدث yahdoth

happening *n.* حدث hadath

happiness *n.* سعادة sa'aadah

happy *a.* سعيد sa'eed

harass *v.* يضايق yodaayiq

harassment *n.* مضايقة modaayaqah

harbour *n.* ميناء meenaau

harbour *v.* يأوي yauwi	**havoc** *n.* خراب kharaab
hard *a.* صلب salb	**hawk** *n.* صقر saqr
hard *a.* صعب sa'b	**hawker** *n.* بائع متجول baaui'on motajawwil
hard *adv.* بشدّة bishiddah	
harden *v.* ييبس yoyabbis	**hawthorn** *n.* زعرور za'roor
hardihood *n.* وقاحة waqaahah	**hay** *n.* تبن tibn
hardly *adv.* بالكاد bilkaad	**hazard** *n.* خطر khatar
hardship *n.* معاناة mo'aanaah	**hazard** *v.* يخاطر yokhaatir
hardy *adj.* جسور jasoor	**haze** *n.* ضباب dhabaab
hare *n.* أرنب uarnab	**hazy** *a.* ضبابي dhabaabiy
harm *n.* ضرر darar	**he** *pron.* هو howah
harm *v.* يؤذي youdhi	**head** *n.* رأس raus
harmonious *a.* متناغم motanaaghim	**head** *v.* يترأس yatarauuas
	headache *n.* صداع sodaa'
harmonium *n.* أورغن هوائي uoorghon hawaauiy	**heading** *n.* عنوان onwaan
	headlong *adv.* بتهور bitahawwir
harmony *n.* إنسجام ensijaam	**headstrong** *a.* عنيد aneed
harness *n.* لجام lijaam	**heal** *v.* يشفي yashfi
harness *v.* يسخّر yosakhkhir	**health** *n.* صحة sihhah
harp *n.* قيثار qeethaar	**healthy** *a.* صحي sihhiy
harsh *a.* قاس qaasi	**heap** *n.* كومة kawmah
harvest *n.* حصاد hasaad	**heap** *v.* يكوّم yokawwim
harvest *v.* يحصد yahsid	**hear** *v.* يسمع yasma'
harvester *n.* حاصد hasaad	**hearsay** *n.* إشاعة eshaa'ah
haste *n.* تسرع tasarro'	**heart** *n.* قلب qalb
hasten *v.* يعجّل yo'ajjil	**hearth** *n.* موقد mawqid
hasty *a.* متسرع motasarri'	**heartily** *adv.* بإخلاص biuikhlaas
hat *n.* قبعة qobba'ah	**heat** *n.* حرارة haraarah
hatchet *n.* فأس faus	**heat** *v.* يسخّن yosakhkhin
hate *n.* كراهية karaahiya	**heave** *v.* يرفع yarfa'
hate *v.* يكره yakrah	**heaven** *n.* جنة jannah
haughty *a.* متغطرس motaghatris	**heavenly** *a.* سماوي smaawiy
haunt *v.* يتردّد yataraddad	**hedge** *n.* سياج من الشجيرات siyaajon mina shshojayraat
haunt *n.* متردّد motaraddad	
have *v.* يحوي yahwi	**hedge** *v.* 1 يحوّط yohawwit
haven *n.* ملاذ malaadh	**hedge** *v.* 2 يتملّص yatamallas

heed *v.* ينتبه yantabih	**herdsman** *n.* راعي raa'i
heed *n.* انتباه entibaah	**here** *adv.* هنا hona
heel *n.* كعب ka'b	**hereabouts** *adv.* في هذه الناحية fi hadhihi nnaahiyah
hefty *a.* ضخم dakhm	**hereafter** *n.* بعد الآن ba'dal uaan
height *n.* ارتفاع ertifaa'	**hereafter** *adv.* آخرة uaakhirah
heighten *v.* يرفع yarfa'	**hereditary** *n.* وراثي wiraathiy
heinous *a.* شنيع shanee'	**heredity** *n.* وراثة wiraathah
heir *n.* وريث wareeth	**heritable** *a.* موروث mawrooth
hell *a.* جحيم jaheem	**heritage** *n.* تراث toraath
helm *n.* دفة daffah	**hermit** *n.* ناسك naasik
helmet *n.* خوذة khoodhah	**hermitage** *n.* صومعة sawma'ah
help *v.* يساعد yosaa'id	**hernia** *n.* فتق fatq
help *n.* مساعدة mosaa'adah	**hero** *n.* بطل batal
helpful *a.* مفيد mofeed	**heroic** *a.* بطولي botooliy
helpless *a.* عاجز aajiz	**heroine** *n.* بطلة batalah
helpmate *n.* رفيق rafeeq	**heroism** *n.* بطولة botoolah
hemisphere *n.* نصف كرة nisfo korah	**herring** *n.* سمك مملح samakon momallah
hemp *n.* قنب qinnab	**hesitant** *a.* متردد motaraddid
hen *n.* دجاجة dajaajah	**hesitate** *v.* يتردّد yataraddad
hence *adv.* بالتالي bittali	**hesitation** *n.* تردد taraddod
henceforth *adv.* من الآن فصاعدا minal uaana fasaa'idan	**hew** *v.* يحطب yohattib
henceforward *adv.* من الآن فصاعدا minal uaana fasaa'idan	**heyday** *n.* ذروة dhorwah
henchman *n.* نصير naseer	**hibernation** *n.* سبات sobaat
henpeck *v.* يضايق بالنق yodaayiq binnaq	**hiccup** *n.* فواق fowaaq
her *pron.* ـها -ha	**hide** *n.* مخبأ makhbau
her *adj.* ـها -ha	**hide** *v.* يخفي yokhfi
herald *n.* رسول rasool	**hideous** *a.* بشع bashi'
herald *v.* ينبئ بمجيء yonabbiuo bimajeeu	**hierarchy** *n.* تسلسل tasalsol
herb *n.* عشبة oshbah	**high** *a.* مرتفع mortafi'
herculean *a.* هرقلي hiraqliy	**highly** *adv.* جداً jidan
herd *n.* قطيع qatee'	**Highness** *n.* سمو somow
	highway *n.* طريق سريع tareeqon saree'
	hilarious *a.* مضحك mod hik

hilarity *n.* مرح marah

hill *n.* تل tal

hillock *n.* أكمة uakimmah

him *pron.* ـه -ho

hinder *v.* يعوّق yo'awwiq

hindrance *n.* عائق aauiq

hint *n.* علامة laamah

hint *v.* يلمَح yolammih

hip *n.* ورك wirk

hire *n.* موظف mowaddddaf

hire *v.* يؤجَر youajjir

hireling *n.* ذليل dhaleel

his *pron.* ـه -ho

hiss *n.* همسة hamsah

hiss *v.* يهمس yahmis

historian *n.* مؤرخ mouarrikh

historic *a*. تاريخي taareekhiy

historical *a.* تاريخي taareekhiy

history *n.* تاريخ taareekh

hit *v.* يضرب yadrob

hit *n.* عصابة esaabah

hitch *n.* عقبة aqabah

hither *adv.* هنا hona

hitherto *adv.* حتى اليوم hattal yawm

hive *n.* خلية khaliyyah

hoarse *a.* أجش uajash

hoax *n.* خدعة khod'ah

hoax *v.* يخدع yakhda'

hobby *n.* هواية hiwaayah

hobbyhorse *n.* حصان متأرجح hisaanon motauarjih

hockey *n.* الهكي ualhokee

hoist *v.* يرفع yarfa'

hold *n.* 1 قبضة qabdah

hold *n.* 2 عنبر anbar

hold *v.* 1 يعقد ya'qid

hold *v.* 2 يحمل yahmil

hold *v.* 3 يستوعب yastaw'ib

hole *n.* ثقب thoqb

hole *v.* يثقب yathqob

holiday *n.* عطلة otlah

hollow *a.* أجوف uajwaf

hollow *n.* تجويف tajweef

hollow *v.* يجوّف yojawwif

holocaust *n.* محرقة mihraqah

holy *a.* مقدَس moqaddas

homage *n.* إجلال ejlaal

home *n.* منزل manzil

homicide *n.* قتل qatl

homeopath *n.* معالج mo'aalij

homeopathy *n.* معالجة mo'aalajah

homogeneous *a.* متجانس motajaanis

honest *a.* صادق saadiq

honesty *n.* أمانة uamaanah

honey *n.* عسل asal

honeycomb *n.* مستودع شمعي mostawda'on sham'iy

honeymoon *n.* شهر العسل shahrol 'asal

honorarium *n.* أتعاب uat'aab

honorary *a.* فخري fakhriy

honour *n.* شرف sharaf

honour *v.* يشرَف yosharrif

honourable *a.* مشرف mosharrif

hood *n.* قلنسوة qolonsowah

hoodwink *v.* يخدع yakhda'

hoof *n.* حافر haafir

hook *n.* كلاب kallaab

hooligan *n.* همجي hamajiy

hoot *n.* صياح siyaah

hoot *v.* يصيح yaseeh

hop *v.* يقفز yaqfiz

hop *n.* قفزة qafzah

hope *v.* يأمل yaumal

hope *n.* أمل uamal

hopeful *a.* متفائل motafaauil

hopeless *a.* ميئوس منه mayuooson minh

horde *n.* حشد hashd

horizon *n.* أفق uofoq

horn *n.* قرن qarn

hornet *n.* زنبور zonboor

horrible *a.* فظيع faddee'

horrify *v.* يرهب yorhib

horror *n.* رعب ro'b

horse *n.* حصان hisaan

horticulture *n.* بستنة bastanah

hose *n.* خرطوم khortoom

hosiery *n.* جورب jawrab

hospitable *a.* مضياف midyaaf

hospital *n.* مستشفى mostashfa

hospitality *n.* ضيافة diyaafah

host *n.* مضيف modeef

hostage *n.* رهينة raheenah

hostel *n.* نزل nozol

hostile *a.* معاد mo'adi

hostility *n.* عداء idaau

hot *a.* حار haar

hotchpotch *n.* يخنة yakhnah

hotel *n.* فندق fondoq

hound *n.* كلب kalb

hour *n.* ساعة saa'ah

house *n.* منزل manzil

house *v.* يأهل yauhol

how *adv.* كيف kayf

however *adv.* كيفما kayfama

however *conj.* لكن laakin

howl *v.* يعوي ya'wi

howl *n.* عواء iwaau

hub *n.* محور mihwar

hubbub *n.* هرج ومرج harajon wa maraj

huge *a.* ضخم dakhm

hum *v.* يهمهم yohamhim

hum *n.* همهمة hamhamah

human *a.* إنسان ensaan

humane *a.* إنساني ensaaniy

humanitarian *adj.* إنساني ensaaniy

humanity *n.* إنسانية ensaaniyyah

humanize *v.* يؤنس youannis

humble *a.* متواضع motawaadi'

humdrum *a.* رتيب rateeb

humid *a.* رطب ratib

humidity *n.* رطوبة rotoobah

humiliate *v.* يذل yadhil

humiliation *n.* إذلال edhlaal

humility *n.* تواضع tawaado'

humorist *n.* فكاهي fokaahiy

humorous *a.* مضحك mod hik

humour *n.* فكاهة fokaahah

hunch *n.* إحساس ehsaas

hundred *n.* مائة maauah

hunger *n.* جوع joo'

hungry *a.* جائع jaaui'

hunt *v.* يصطاد yastaad

hunt *n.* مطاردة motaaradah

hunter *n.* صياد sayyaad

huntsman *n.* قناص qannaas

hurdle *n.* حاجز haajiz

hurdle *v.* يَشتَرِك في سِباق حَواجِز yashtariko fi sibaaqi hawaajiz

hurl *v.* يدحرج yodahrij	
hurrah *interj.* مرحى marha	
hurricane *n.* إعصار e'saar	
hurry *v.* يعجّل yo'ajjil	**I** *pron.* أنا uana
hurry *n.* عجل ajal	**ice** *n.* جليد jaleed
hurt *v.* يؤذي youdhi	**iceberg** *n.* جبل جليدي jabalon
hurt *n.* آذى uadha	jaleediy
husband *n.* زوج zawj	**icicle** *n.* كتلة ثلجية مدلاة katlaton
husbandry *n.* زراعة ziraa'ah	thaljiyyaton modallaah
hush *n.* سكون sokoon	**icy** *a.* جليدي jaleediy
hush *v.* يسكت yoskit	**idea** *n.* فكرة fikrah
husk *n.* قشر qishr	**ideal** *a.* مثالي mithaaliy
husky *a.* أجش ujash	**ideal** *n.* مثالي mithaaliy
hut *n.* كوخ kookh	**idealism** *n.* مثالية mithaaliyyah
hyaena, hyena *n.* ضبع dab'	**idealist** *n.* مثالي mithaaliy
hybrid *a.* مهجّن mohajjan	**idealistic** *a.* مثالي mithaaliy
hybrid *n.* هجين hajeen	**idealize** *v.* يجعله مثالياً yaj'aloho
hydrogen *n.* هيدروجين	mithaaliyyan
haydroojeen	**identical** *a.* مطابق motaabiq
hygiene *n.* نظافة naddaafah	**indentification** *n.* تعريف ta'reef
hygienic *a.* صحي sihhiy	**identify** *v.* يتعرّف yata'arraf
hymn *n.* ترنيمة tarneemah	**identity** *n.* هوية howiyyah
hyperbole *n.* مبالغة mobaalaghah	**idiocy** *n.* بلاهة balaahah
hypnotism *n.* تنويم مغناطيسي	**idiom** *n.* مصطلح mostalah
tanweemon mighnaateesiy	**idiomatic** *a.* اصطلاحي estilaahiy
hypnotize *v.* ينوّم مغناطيسياً	**idiot** *n.* أبله uablah
yonawwimo	**idiotic** *a.* مخبل mikhlab
mighnaateesiyyan	**idle** *a.* راكد raakid
hypocrisy *n.* نفاق nifaaq	**idleness** *n.* ركود rokood
hypocrite *n.* منافق monaafiq	**idler** *n.* مهمل mohmal
hypocritical *a.* منافق monaafiq	**idol** *n.* معبود ma'bood
hypothesis *n.* فرضية faradiyyah	**idolater** *n.* وثني wathaniy
hypothetical *a.* افتراضي eftiraadiy	**if** *conj.* إذا edha
hysteria *n.* هستيريا histeerya	**ignoble** *a.* خسيس khasees
hysterical *a.* هستيري histeeriy	**ignorance** *n.* جهل jahl
	ignorant *a.* جاهل jaahil

ignore v. يتجاهل yatajaahal

ill a. سيئ siyyiu

ill adv. سوء soou

ill n. مريض mareed

illegal a. غيرشرعي ghayro shar'iy

illegibility n. تَعَذُّرقِراءة ta'adhdhoro qiraauat

illegible a. غيرمقروء ghayro maqroou

illegitimate a. غيرشرعي ghayro shar'iy

illicit a. غيرمشروع ghyro mashroo'

illiteracy n. أمية uommiyyah

illiterate a. أمي uommiy

illness n. مرض mareed

illogical a. غير منطقي ghayro mantiqiy

illuminate v. يضيء yodeeu

illumination n. إضاءة edaauah

illusion n. وهم wahm

illustrate v. يوضّح yowadih

illustration n. توضيح tawdeeh

image n. صورة soorah

imagery n. الصورية uassowariyyah

imaginary a. خيالي khayaaliy

imagination n. مخيلة mokhayyilah

imaginative a. خيالي khayaaliy

imagine v. يتخيّل yatakhayyal

imitate v. يقلّد yoqallid

imitation n. تقليد taqleed

imitator n. مقلد moqallid

immaterial a. اللامادية uallaamaadiyyah

immature a. غيرناضج ghayro naadij

immaturity n. قلّةالخبرة qillatol khibrah

immeasurable a. بلاحد bila had

immediate a فوري fawriy

immemorial a. سحيق saheeq

immense a. هائل haauil

immensity n. ضخامة dakhaamah

immerse v. يغمر yaghmir

immersion n. غمر ghamr

immigrant n. مهاجر mohaajir

immigrate v. يهاجر yohaajir

immigration n. هجرة hijrah

imminent a. وشيك washeek

immodest a. غيرمتواضع ghayro motawaadi'

immodesty n. بذاءة badhaauah

immoral a. غيرأخلاقي ghayro uakhlaaqiy

immorality n. فجور fojoor

immortal a. خالد khaalid

immortality n. خلود kholood

immortalize v. يخلّد yokhallid

immovable a. ثابت thaabit

immune a. مناعي manaa'iy

immunity n. حصانة hasaanah

immunize v. يحصّن yohassin

impact n. تأثير tautheer

impart v. يضفي على yodfi 'ala

impartial a. نزيه nazeeh

impartiality n. نزاهة nazaahah

impassable a. غيرسالك ghayro saalik

impasse n. طريقمسدود tareeqon masdood

impatience *n.* نفاذصبر nafaadho sabr

impatient *a.* غيرصبور ghayro saboor

impeach *v.* يتهم بالخيانة yattahimo bilkhiyaanah

impeachment *n.* لائحةاتهام laauihato ettihaam

impede *v.* يعوّق yo'awwiq

impediment *n.* عائق aauiq

impenetrable *a.* منيع manee'

imperative *a.* حتمي hatmiy

imperfect *a.* ناقص naaqis

imperfection *n.* نقص naqs

imperial *a.* إمبريالي embiryaaliy

imperialism *n.* الإمبريالية ualimmbiryaaliyyah

imperil *v.* يعرض للخطر yo'arrido lilkhatar

imperishable *a.* خالد khaalid

impersonal *a.* غيرشخصي ghayro shakhsiy

impersonate *v.* ينتحل yantahil

impersonation *n.* إنتحال entihaal

impertinence *n.* وقاحة waqaahah

impertinent *a.* وقح waqih

impetuosity *n.* طيش taysh

impetuous *a.* متهور motahawwir

implement *n.* أداة uadaah

implement *v.* ينفذ yonaffidh

implicate *v.* يورّط yowarrit

implication *n.* توريط tawreet

implicit *a.* ضمني dhimniy

implore *v.* يناشد yonaashid

imply *v.* يعني ya'ni

impolite *a.* غيرمهذب ghayro modhnib

import *v.* يستورد yastawrid

import *n.* استيراد esteeraad

importance *n.* أهمية uahammiyyah

important *a.* مهم mohim

impose *v.* يفرض yafrid

imposing *adj.* فارض faarid

imposition *n.* فرض fard

impossibility *n.* استحالة estihaalah

impossible *a.* مستحيل mostaheel

impostor *n.* محتال mohtaal

imposture *n.* دجل dajal

impotence *n.* عجز ajz

impotent *a.* عاجز aajiz

impoverish *v.* يفقر yofqir

impracticability *n.* اللاتطبيقية uallaatatbeeqiyyah

impracticable *a.* عملي غير ghayro 'amaliy

impress *v.* يعجب yo'jib

impression *n.* إنطباع entibaa'

impressive *a.* مؤثر mouaththir

imprint *v.* يبصم yabsim

imprint *n.* بصمة basmah

imprison *v.* يسجن yasjin

improper *a.* غيرلائق ghayro laauiq

impropriety *n.* عَدَملياقَه adamo lyaaqah

improve *v.* يحسّن yohassin

improvement *n.* تحسن tahasson

imprudence *n.* تهور tahawwor

imprudent *a.* متهوّر motahawwir

impulse *n.* دفعة daf'ah

impulsive *a.* مندفع mondafi'

impunity *n.* حسنة hasaanah

impure *a.* نجس najis

impurity *n.* نجاسة najaasah

impute *v.* يعزي yo'zi

in *prep.* في fi

inability *n.* عجز ajz

inaccurate *a.* غير دقيق ghayro daqeeq

inaction *n.* تقاعس taqaa'os

inactive *a.* غير فعال ghayro fa"aal

inadmissible *a.* غير مقبول ghayro maqbool

inanimate *a.* جامد jaamid

inapplicable *a.* غير مطبق ghayro motabbaq

inattentive *a.* غافل ghaafil

inaudible *a.* غير مسموع ghayro masmoo'

inaugural *a.* إفتتاحي eftitaahiy

inauguration *n.* افتتاح eftitaah

inauspicious *a.* منحوس manhoos

inborn *a.* وراثي wiraathiy

incalculable *a.* لا يحصى laa yohsa

incapable *a.* عاجز aajiz

incapacity *n.* عجز ajz

incarnate *a.* متجسد motajassid

incarnate *v.* يتجسد yojassid

incarnation *n.* تجسد tajassod

incense *v.* يحفّز yohaffiz

incense *n.* بخور bakhkhoor

incentive *n.* حافز haafiz

inception *n.* بداية bidaayah

inch *n.* بوصة boosah

incident *n.* حادث haadith

incidental *a.* عرضي aradiy

incite *v.* يحرّض yoharrid

inclination *n.* ميل mayl

incline *v.* يميل yameel

include *v.* يشمل yashmal

inclusion *n.* تضمين tadmeen

inclusive *a.* شامل shaamil

incoherent *a.* غير مفهوم ghayro mafhoom

income *n.* دخل dakhl

incomparable *a.* لا يقارن laa yoqaaran

incompetent *a.* غير كفؤ ghayro kafou

incomplete *a.* غير كامل ghayro kaamil

inconsiderate *a.* غير مبال ghayro mobaali

inconvenient *a.* غير مريح ghayro moreeh

incorporate *v.* يدرج yodrij

incorporate *a.* مدرج modraj

incorporation *n.* دمج damj

incorrect *a.* خاطئ khaatiu

incorrigible i عنيد aneed

incorruptible *a.* غير مفسد ghayro mofsad

increase *v.* يزيد yazeed

increase *n.* زيادة ziyaadah

incredible *a.* لا يصدق laa yosaddaq

increment *n.* زيادة ziyaadah

incriminate *v.* يجرم yojarrim

incubate *v.* يحتضن yahtadin

inculcate *v.* يغرس yaghris

incumbent *n.* محتل المنصب mohtalol mansib

incumbent *adj.* متوجب motawajjib

incur v. يتحمل yatahammal

incurable a. عضال odaal

indebted a. مثقل mothqal

indecency n. قِلَّةإحْتِشام qilato ehtishaam

indecent a. غَيرمُخَتَشِم ghayro mohtashim

indecision n. تردد taraddod

indeed adv. فعلاً fi'lan

indefensible a. غيرمدافع عنه ghayro modaafa'in 'anh

indefinite a. غير محدد ghayro mohaddad

indemnity n. تعويض ta'weed

independence n. استقلال estiqlaal

independent a. مستقل mostaqil

indescribable a. لايوصف laa yoosaf

index n. مؤشر mouashshir

Indian a. هندي hindiy

indicate v. يؤشر youashshir

indication n. إشارة eshaarah

indicative a. إرشادي ershaadiy

indicator n. مؤشر mouashshir

indict v. يتهم yattahim

indictment n. اتهام ettihaam

indifference n. لامبالاة laa mobaalaah

indifferent a. لامبالي laa mobaali

indigenous a. أصلي uasliy

indigestible a. عسير aseer

indigestion n. عسرالهضم osrol hadm

indignant a. ساخط saakhit

indignation n. سخط sakht

indigo n. نيلي neeliy

indirect a. غيرمباشر ghayro mobaashir

indiscipline n. اللاانضباط uallaauindibaat

indiscreet a. غَيرمُتَحَفِظ ghayro motahaffidd

indiscretion n. طيش taysh

indiscriminate a. عشوائي ashwaauiy

indispensable a. لاغنىعنه laa ghina 'anh

indisposed a. متوعك motawa'ik

indisputable a. غيرمجادل ghayro mojaadal

indistinct a. غامض ghaamid

individual a. فرد fard

individualism n. فردية fardiyyah

individuality n. شخصية shakhsiyyah

indivisible a. لايتجزأ laa yatajazzau

indolent a. كسلان kaslaan

indomitable a. لايقهر laa yoqhar

indoor a. داخلي daakhiliy

indoors adv. فيالداخل fi ddaakhil

induce v. يحث yahith

inducement n. حث hath

induct v. يقلدمنصباً yoqalido mansiban

induction n. 1 إستقراء estiqraau

induction n. 2 إحتفالقبول ehtifaalo qobool

indulge v. ينغمس yanghamis

indulgence n. تساهل tasaahol

indulgent a. متسامح motasaamih

industrial *a.* صناعي sinaa'iy	**infinity** *n.* أزلية uazaliyyah
industrious *a.* كادح kaadih	**infirm** *a.* عاجز aajiz
industry *n.* صناعة sinaa'ah	**infirmity** *n.* عجز ajz
ineffective *a.* غير فعّال ghayro fa"aal	**inflame** *v.* يشعل yosh'il
inert *a.* خامل khaamil	**inflammable** *a.* مشتعل moshta'il
inertia *n.* عطالة ataalah	**inflammation** *n.* التهاب eltihaab
inevitable *a.* محتّم mohattam	**inflammatory** *a.* ملتهب moltahib
inexact *a.* غير دقيق ghayro daqeeq	**inflation** *n.* تضخّم tadakhkhom
inexorable *a.* لا يرحم laa yarham	**inflexible** *adj.* غير مرن ghayro marin
inexpensive *a.* رخيص rakhees	**inflict** *v.* يلحق yolhiq
inexperience *n.* قلةخبرة qillato khibrah	**influence** *n.* نفوذ nofoodh
inexplicable *a.* غير مفسّر ghayro mofassar	**influence** *v.* يؤثّر youaththir
infallible *a.* معصوم ma'soom	**influential** *a.* مؤثّر mouaththir
infamous *a.* سيّءالسمعة sayyiuo ssom'ah	**influenza** *n.* حمّى homma
infamy *n.* عملشائن amalon shaauin	**influx** *n.* تدفق tadaffoq
infancy *n.* طفولة tofoolah	**inform** *v.* يعلم yo'lim
infant *n.* رضيع radee'	**informal** *a.* غير رسمي ghayro rasmiy
infanticide *n.* وأد waud	**information** *n.* معلومة ma'loomah
infantile *a.* صبياني sibyaaniy	**informative** *a.* إعلامي e'laamiy
infantry *n.* مشاة moshaah	**informer** *n.* مخبر mokhbir
infatuate *v.* يوله yoolih	**infringe** *v.* ينتهك yantahik
infatuation *n.* وله walah	**infringement** *n.* انتهاك entihaak
infect *v.* يعدي yo'di	**infuriate** *v.* يغضب yoghdib
infection *n.* عدوى adwa	**infuse** *v.* يخلط yakhlit
infectious *a.* معد mo'di	**infusion** *n.* خلطة khaltah
infer *v.* يستنتج yastantij	**ingrained** *a.* متأصل motauasil
inference *n.* استدلال estidlaal	**ingratitude** *n.* نكرانالجميل nokraanol jameel
inferior *a.* أدنى uadna	**ingredient** *n.* عنصر onsor
inferiority *n.* تدنّي tadanni	**inhabit** *v.* يسكن yaskon
infernal *a.* جهنمي jahannamiy	**inhabitable** *a.* مسكون maskoon
infinite *a.* أزلي uazaliy	**inhabitant** *n.* مواطن mowaatin
	inhale *v.* يستنشق yastanshiq
	inherent *a.* متأصل motauasil

inherit *v.* يورث yoorith

inheritance *n.* وراثة wiraathah

inhibit *v.* يكبح yakbah

inhibition *n.* كبت kabt

inhospitable *a.* غير مضياف ghayro midyaaf

inhuman *a.* لا إنساني laa uinsaaniy

inimical *a.* معاد mo'aad

inimitable *a.* غير مضاهي ghayro modaahi

initial *a.* أولي uawwaliy

initial *n.* بادئة baadiuah

initial *v.* يبدأ yabdau

initiate *v.* يبدأ yabdau

initiative *n.* مبادرة mobaadarah

inject *v.* يحقن yahqin

injection *n.* حقن haqn

injudicious *a.* غير حكيم ghayro hakeem

injunction *n.* إنذار قضائي endhaaron qadaauiy

injure *v.* يجرح yajrah

injurious *a.* جارح jaarih

injury *n.* جرح jorh

injustice *n.* ظلم ddalaam

ink *n.* حبر hibr

inkling *n.* معرفة محدودة ma'rifaton mahdoodah

inland *a.* داخلي daakhiliy

inland *adv.* داخلياً daakhiliyyan

in-laws *n.* الحمو ualhamo

inmate *n.* سجين sajeen

inmost *a.* أعمق ua'maq

inn *n.* خان khaan

innate *a.* فطري fitriy

inner *a.* داخلي daakhiliy

innermost *a.* مركزي markaziy

innings *n.* نوبات nawbaat

innocence *n.* براءة baraauah

innocent *a.* بريء bareeu

innovate *v.* يبتكر yabtakir

innovation *n.* ابتكار ebtikaar

innovator *n.* مبتدع mobtadiu

innumerable *a.* لا يُحصى laa yohsa

inoculate *v.* يلقّح yolaqqih

inoculation *n.* تلقيح talqeeh

inoperative *a.* غير فعال ghayro fa"aal

inopportune *a.* في غير محله fi ghayri mahallih

input *n.* مساهمة mosaahamah

inquest *n.* تحقيق tahqeeq

inquire *v.* يستفسر yastafsir

inquiry *n.* إستفسار estifsaar

inquisition *n.* محاكمة mohaakamah

inquisitive *a.* فضولي fodooliy

insane *a.* مجنون majnoon

insanity *n.* جنون jonoon

insatiable *a.* نهم naham

inscribe *v.* يسجّل yosajjil

inscription *n.* نقش naqsh

insect *n.* حشرة hasharah

insecticide *n.* مبيد الحشرات mobeedol hasharaat

insecure *a.* غير آمن ghayro uaamin

insecurity *n.* عدم أمان adamo uamaan

insensibility *n.* عدم إدراك adamo edraak

insensible *a.* غافل ghaafil	**install** *v.* يركَّب yorakkib
inseparable *a.* غير منفصل ghayro monfasil	**installation** *n.* تركيب tarkeeb
insert *v.* يدخل yodkhil	**instalment** *n.* قسط qast
insertion *n.* إدخال edkhaal	**instance** *n.* مثل mathal
inside *n.* داخل daakhil	**instant** *n.* لحظة lahdda
inside *prep.* داخل daakhil	**instant** *a.* لحظي lahddiy
inside *adj.* داخلي daakhiliy	**instantaneous** *a.* فوري fawriy
inside *adv.* نحو الداخل nahwa ddaakhil	**instantly** *adv.* فوراً fawran
insight *n.* تبصر tabassor	**instigate** *v.* يحرّض yoharrid
insignificance *n.* تفاهة tafaahah	**instigation** *n.* تحريض tahreed
insignificant *a.* تافه taafih	**instil** *v.* يغرس yaghris
insincere *a.* منافق monaafiq	**instinct** *n.* غريزة ghareezah
insincerity *n.* نفاق nifaaq	**instinctive** *a.* غريزي ghareeziy
insinuate *v.* يلمَح yolammih	**institute** *n.* معهد ma'had
insinuation *n.* تلميح talmeeh	**institution** *n.* مؤسسة mouassasah
insipid *a.* مشوق غير ghayro moshawwiq	**instruct** *v.* يعطي تعليمات yo'ti ta'leemaat
insipidity *n.* تفاهة tafaahah	**instruction** *n.* تعليمات ta'leemaat
insist *v.* يصر yasir	**instructor** *n.* معلَم mo'allim
insistence *n.* إصرار esraar	**instrument** *n.* ألة uaalah
insistent *a.* ملح molih	**instrumental** *a.* آلاتي uaalaatiy
insolence *n.* وقاحة waqaahah	**instrumentalist** *n.* عازف aazif
insolent *a.* وقح waqih	**insubordinate** *a.* متمرد motamarrid
insoluble *n.* غير مذاب ghayro modhaab	**insubordination** *n.* تمرد tamarrod
insolvency *n.* إعسار e'saar	**insufficient** *a.* غير كاف ghayro kaafi
insolvent *a.* معسر mo'assar	**insular** *a.* ضيق الأفق dayyiqol uofoq
inspect *v.* يفحص yafhas	**insularity** *n.* انفصال enfisaal
inspection *n.* تفتيش tafteesh	**insulate** *v.* يعزل ya'zil
inspector *n.* مفتش mofattish	**insulation** *n.* عزل azl
inspiration *n.* إلهام elhaam	**insulator** *n.* عازل aazil
inspire *v.* يلهم yolhim	**insult** *n.* إهانة ehaanah
instability *n.* عدم الاستقرار adamo lisstiqraar	**insult** *v.* يهين yoheen

insupportable *a.* غير محتمل ghayro mohtamal

insurance *n.* تأمين taumeen

insure *v.* يأمن youammin

insurgent *a.* متمرد motamarrid

insurgent *n.* متمرد motamarrid

insurmountable *a.* لا يقهر laa yoqhar

insurrection *n.* تمرد tamarrod

intact *a.* سليم saleem

intangible *a.* غير ملموس ghayro malmoos

integral *a.* متكامل motakaamil

integrity *n.* سلامة salaamah

intellect *n.* مفكّر mofakkir

intellectual *a.* فكري fikriy

intellectual *n.* مفكّر mofakkir

intelligence *n.* 1 ذكاء dhakaau

intelligence *n.* 2 استخبارات estikhbaaraat

intelligent *a.* ذكي dhakiy

intelligentsia *n.* مفكّرون mofakkiroon

intelligible *a.* واضح waadih

intend *v.* يعتزم ya'tazim

intense *a.* شديد shadeed

intensify *v.* يكثف yokaththif

intensity *n.* حدّة hiddah

intensity *n.* كثافة kthaafah

intensive *a.* مكثّف mokaththaf

intent *n.* نية niyyah

intent *a.* منوي manwiy

intention *n.* قصد qasd

intentional *a.* مقصود maqsood

intercept *v.* يعترض ya'tarid

interception *n.* اعتراض e'tiraad

interchange *n.* تبادل tbaadol

interchange *v.* يتبادل yatabaadal

intercourse *n.* جماع jimaa'

interdependence *n.* ترابط taraabot

interdependent *a.* مترابط motaraabit

interest *n.* مصلحة maslahah

interested *a.* مهتم mohtam

interesting *a.* مثير للاهتمام motheeron liluihtimaam

interfere *v.* يتدخّل yatadakhkhal

interference *n.* تدخل tadakhkhol

interim *n.* مؤقت mouaqqat

interior *a.* داخلي daakhiliy

interior *n.* داخل daakhil

interjection *n.* إقحام eqhaam

interlock *v.* يتشابك yatashaabak

interlude *n.* فاصل faasil

intermediary *n.* وسيط waseet

intermediate *a.* متوسط motawassit

interminable *a.* غير منتهي ghayro montahi

intermingle *v.* يتخالط yatakhaalat

intern *n.* متدرّب motadarrib

internal *a.* داخلي daakhiliy

international *a.* دولي dawliy

interplay *n.* تفاعل tafaa'ol

interpret *v.* يفسّر yofassir

interpreter *n.* مترجم motarjim

interrogate *v.* يستجوب yastajwib

interrogation *n.* استجواب estijwaab

interrogative *a.* استفهامي estifhaamiy

interrogative *n.* مستفحم mostafham	**introductory** *a.* استهلالي estihlaaliy
interrupt *v.* يقاطع yoqaati'	**introspect** *v.* يستبطن yastabtin
interruption *n.* انقطاع enqitaa'	**introspection** *n.* استبطان estibtaan
intersect *v.* يتقاطع yataqaata'	**intrude** *v.* يتطفل yatataffal
intersection *n.* تقاطع taqaato'	**intrusion** *n.* تطفل tataffol
interval *n.* فاصل faasil	**intuition** *n.* حدس hads
intervene *v.* يتدخل yatadakhkhal	**intuitive** *a.* حدسي hadsiy
intervention *n.* تدخل tadakhkhol	**invade** *v.* يغزو yaghzo
interview *n.* مقابلة moqaabalah	**invalid** *a.* باطل baatil
interview *v.* يقابل yoqaabil	**invalid** *n.* مُقعَد moq'ad
intestinal *a.* معوي ma'awiy	**invalidate** *v.* يبطل yobtil
intestine *n.* أمعاء uam'aam	**invaluable** *a.* لا تقدر بثمن laa toqaddaro bithaman
intimacy *n.* ألفة uolfah	**invasion** *n.* اجتياح ejtiyaah
intimate *a.* حميم hameem	**invective** *n.* ذم dham
intimate *v.* يوحي yoohi	**invent** *v.* يخترع yakhtari'
intimation *n.* إعلام e'laam	**invention** *n.* اختراع ekhtiraa'
intimidate *v.* يخيف yokheef	**inventive** *a.* مبتكر mobtakar
intimidation *n.* تخويف takhweef	**inventor** *n.* مخترع mokhtari'
into *prep.* إلى ela	**invert** *v.* يقلب yaqlib
intolerable *a.* لا يطاق laa yotaaq	**invest** *v.* يستثمر yastathmir
intolerance *n.* تعصب ta'assob	**investigate** *v.* يحقّق yohaqqiq
intolerant *a.* متعصب mota'assib	**investigation** *n.* تحقيق tahqeeq
intoxicant *n.* مسكر moskir	**investment** *n.* استثمار estithmaar
intoxicate *v.* يسمّم yosammim	**invigilate** *v.* يراقب yoraaqib
intoxication *n.* تسمم tasammom	**invigilation** *n.* مراقبة moraaqabah
intransitive *a.* (verb) غير متعدد ghayro mota'ammad	**invigilator** *n.* مراقب moraaqib
intrepid *a.* باسل baasil	**invincible** *a.* لا يقهر laa yoqhar
intrepidity *n.* بسالة basaalah	**inviolable** *a.* محرّم moharram
intricate *a.* معقد mo'aqqad	**invisible** *a.* خفي khafiy
intrigue *v.* يحفز yohaffiz	**invitation** *n.* دعوة da'wah
intrigue *n.* دسيسة daseesah	**invite** *v.* يدعو yad'o
intrinsic *a.* جوهري jawhariy	**invocation** *n.* احتجاج ehtijaaj
introduce *v.* يقدِم yoqaddim	**invoice** *n.* فاتورة faatoorah
introduction *n.* مقدمة moqaddimah	**invoke** *v.* يستدعي yastad'i

involve *v.* ينطوي yantawi

inward *a.* باطني baatiniy

inwards *adv.* نحوالداخل nahwa ddaakhil

irate *a.* غاضب ghaadib

ire *n.* غضب ghadab

Irish *a.* ايرلندي ueerlaandiy

Irish *n.* اللغةالايرلندية ualloghatol ueerlaandiyyah

irksome *a.* مضجر modjir

iron *n.* حديد hadeed

iron *v.* يكوي yakwi

ironical *a.* ساخر saakhir

irony *n.* سخرية sokhriyah

irradiate *v.* يشرق yoshriq

irrational *a.* غيرمنطقي ghayro mantiqiy

irreconcilable *a.* غيرمتوافق ghayro motawaafiq

irrecoverable *a.* متعذرإصلاحه mota'adhiron eslaahoh

irrefutable *a.* لايدحض laa yadhad

irregular *a.* غيرمنتظم ghayro montaddim

irregularity *n.* مخالفة mokhaalafah

irrelevant *a.* غيرمتعلّق ghayro mota'alliq

irrespective *a.* بغضالنظر bighadi nnaddar

irresponsible *a.* غيرمسؤول ghayro masuool

irrigate *v.* يروي yarwi

irrigation *n.* ري ray

irritable *a.* منزعج monza'ij

irritant *a.* مهيج mohayyij

irritant *n.* مهيج mohayyij

irritate *v.* يزعج yoz'ij

irritation *n.* 1 تهييج tahayyoj

irritation *n.* 2 إزعاج ez'aaj

irruption *n.* ثوران thawaraan

island *n.* جزيرة jazeerah

isle *n.* جزيرة jazeerah

isobar *n.* تساوي الضغط tasaawi ddaght

isolate *v.* يعزل ya'zil

isolation *n.* عزلة ozlah

issue *v.* يصدر yosdir

issue *n.* 1 قضية qadiyyah

issue *n.* 2 إصدار esdaar

it *pron.* هو howa

Italian *a.* إيطالي ueetaaliy

Italian *n.* اللغةالإيطالية ualloghatol ueetaaliyyah

italic *a.* مائل maauil

italics *n.* تمييل tamyeel

itch *n.* حكة hakkah

itch *v.* يحك yahik

item *n.* بند band

ivory *n.* عاج aaj

ivy *n.* لبلاب loblaab

J

jab *v.* ينخز yankhaz

jabber *v.* يثرثر yotharthir

jack *n.* رافعة raafi'ah

jack *v.* يرفع yarfa'

jackal *n.* ابن آوى ebno uaawa

jacket *n.* سترة sotrah	**jewel** *v.* يرصع بالمجوهرات yorasi'o bilmojawharaat
jade *n.* يشم yashm	**jeweller** *n.* صائغ saauigh
jail *n.* سجن sijn	**jewellery** *n.* مجوهرات mojawharaat
jail *v.* يسجن yasjon	**jingle** *n.* جلجل jaljal
jailer *n.* سجان sajjaan	**jingle** *v.* يجلجل yojaljil
jam *n.* مربى morabba	**job** *n.* وظيفة waddeefah
jam *v.* يحشر yahshor	**jobber** *n.* سمسار simsaar
January *n.* كانون الثاني kaanoon uaththaani	**jobbery** *n.* إستغلال الوظيفة estighlaalol waddeefah
jar *n.* جرة jarrah	**jocular** *a.* مزوح mazooh
jargon *n.* رطانة rataanah	**jog** *v.* يهرول yoharwil
jasmine, jessamine *n.* الياسمين ualyaasameen	**join** *v.* ينضم yandam
jaundice *n.* اليرقان ualyaraqaan	**joiner** *n.* نجار najjar
jaundice *v.* يشوش yoshawwish	**joint** *n.* مَفصَل mafsal
javelin *n.* رمي الرمح ramyo rromh	**joint** *adj.* مشترك moshtarak
jaw *n.* فك fak	**jointly** *adv.* معاً ma'an
jay *n.* أبوزرزق uabo zorraq	**joke** *n.* نكتة noktah
jealous *a.* غيور ghayoor	**joke** *v.* يمزح yamzah
jealousy *n.* غيرة ghayrah	**joker** *n.* مهرج moharrij
jean *n.* دنيم dinim	**jollity** *n.* بهجة bahjah
jeer *v.* يتهكّم yatakahhan	**jolly** *a.* مرح marah
jelly *n.* هلام holaam	**jolt** *n.* هزة hazzah
jeopardize *v.* يعرض للخطر yo'arrido lilkhatar	**jolt** *v.* يهز yahiz
jeopardy *n.* خطر khataar	**jostle** *n.* تصادم tasaadom
jerk *n.* رعشة ra'shah	**jostle** *v.* يتصادم yatasaadam
jerkin *n.* سترة بلا أكمام sotraton bila uakmaam	**jot** *n.* ذرة dharrah
jerky *a.* متشنج motashannij	**jot** *v.* يَدَوِّن بِسُرعَه yodawwino bisor'ah
jersey *n.* جرزة jarzah	**journal** *n.* صحيفة saheefah
jest *n.* مزاح mozaah	**journalism** *n.* صحافة sahaafah
jest *v.* يمزح yamzah	**journalist** *n.* صحافي sahafiy
jet *n.* طائرة taauirah	**journey** *n.* رحلة rihlah
Jew *n.* يهودي yahoodiy	**journey** *v.* يرحل yarhal
jewel *n.* جوهرة jawharah	**jovial** *a.* مرح marah

joviality *n.* مرح marah
joy *n.* فرح farah
joyful *n.* بهيج baheej
joyous *n.* سعيد sa'eed
jubilant *a.* متهلل motahalhil
jubilation *n.* ابتهاج ebtihaaj
jubilee *n.* يوبيل yoobeel
judge *n.* قاضي qaadi
judge *v.* يحكم yahkom
judgement *n.* حكم hokm
judicature *n.* قضاء qadaau
judicial *a.* قضائي qadaauiy
judiciary *n.* سلطةقضائية soltaton qadaauiyyah
judicious *a.* حكيم hakeem
jug *n.* إبريق ebreeq
juggle *v.* يتلاعب yatalaa'ab
juggler *n.* بهلوان bahlawaan
juice *n.* عصير aseer
juicy *adj.* 0 katheerol 'aseer
jumble *n.* مزيج mazeej
jumble *v.* يمزج yamjij
jump *n.* قفزة qafzah
jump *v.* يقفز yaqfiz
junction *n.* تقاطع taqaato'
juncture *n.* مرحلة marhalah
jungle *n.* أدغال uadghaal
junior *a.* مبتدئ mobtadiu
junior *n.* صَغيرالسِّن sagheero ssin
junk *n.* خردة khordah
jupiter *n.* المشتري ualmoshtari
jurisdiction *n.* إختصاص ekhtisaas
jurisprudence *n.* فقه fiqh
jurist *n.* فقيه fiqhiy
juror *n.* محلف mohallaf

jury *n.* هيئةالمحلفين hayuatol mohallafeen
juryman *n.* محلَف mohallaf
just *a.* عادل aadil
just *adv.* فقط faqat
justice *n.* عدالة adaalah
justifiable *a.* مبرر mobarrar
justification *n.* مبرر mobarrir
justify *v.* يبرّر yobarrir
justly *adv.* بالعدل bil'adl
jute *n.* قنب qinnab
juvenile *a.* صِبياني sibyaaniy

K

keen *a.* متشوّق motashawwiq
keenness *n.* تشوّق tashawwoq
keep *v.* يحفظ yahfadd
keeper *n.* حارس haaris
keepsake *n.* تذكار tidhkaar
kennel *n.* ملجأللحيوانات maljauon lìlhayawaanaat
kerchief *n.* منديل mindeel
kernel *n.* نواة nowaah
kerosene *n.* كيروسين keerooseen
ketchup *n.* ربالطماطم robbo ttamaatim
kettle *n.* إبريق ebreeq
key *n.* مفتاح miftaah
key *v.* يقفل yoqfil
kick *n.* ركلة raklah
kick *v.* يركل yarkil
kid *n.* طفل tifl

kidnap *v.* يخطف yakhtif

kidney *n.* كلية kilya

kill *v.* يقتل yaqtol

kill *n.* قتل qatl

kiln *n.* فرن forn

kin *n.* قريب qareeb

kind *n.* نوع naw'

kind *adj.* كريم kareem

kindergarten *n.* رياض الأطفال riyaadol uatfaal

kindle *v.* أضرم uadramah

kindly *adv.* يرجى yorja

kindness *n.* كرم karam

king *n.* ملك malik

kingdom *n.* مملكة mamlakah

kinship *n.* قرابة qaraabah

kiss *n.* قبلة qoblah

kiss *v.* يقبل yoqabbil

kit *n.* عدة oddah

kitchen *n.* مطبخ matbakh

kite *n.* طائرة ورقية taauiraton waraqiyyah

kith *n.* صحابة sahaabah

kitten *n.* هرير horayr

knave *n.* وغد waghd

knavery *n.* احتيال ehtiyaal

knee *n.* ركبة rokbah

kneel *v.* يركع yarka'

knife *n.* سكين sikkeen

knight *n.* فارس faaris

knight *v.* يوسم yawsim

knit *v.* يحبك yahbik

knock *v.* يخبط yakhbit

knot *n.* عقدة oqdah

knot *v.* يعقد ya'qid

know *v.* يعرف ya'rif

knowledge *n.* معرفة ma'rifah

L

label *n.* ملصق molsaq

label *v.* يعنون yo'anwin

labial *a.* شفوي shafawiy

laboratory *n.* مختبر mokhtabar

laborious *a.* شاق shaaq

labour *n.* عمل amal

labour *v.* يعمل ya'mal

laboured *a.* جاهد jaahid

labourer *n.* عامل aamil

labyrinth *n.* متاهة mataahah

lac, lakh *n.* ألف مئة miuato ualf

lace *n.* 1 رباط ribaat

lace *n.* 2 تخريم takhreem

lace *v.t.* يَشُد yashid

lacerate *v.* يمزّق yomazziq

lachrymose *a.* باكي baaki

lack *n.* نقص naqs

lack *v.* ينقص yanqos

lackey *n.* خادم khaadim

lacklustre *a.* باهت baahit

laconic *a.* مقتضب moqtadab

lactate *v.* ينتج الحليب yontijol haleeb

lactometer *n.* مقياس للحليب miqyaason lilhaleeb

lactose *n.* اللاكتوز uallaktooz

lacuna *n.* ثغرة thaghrah

lacy *a.* شريطي shareetiy

lad *n.* فتى fata

ladder *n.* سلم sollam	**languish** *v.* يرزح yarzah
lade *v.* يعتدي ya'tadi	**lank** *a.* ضامر daamir
ladle *n.* مغرفة mighrafah	**lantern** *n.* فانوس faanoos
ladle *v.* يغرف yaghrif	**lap** *n.* حضن hodn
lady *n.* سيدة sayyidah	**lapse** *v.* يهفو yahfo
lag *v.* يتأخر yatauakhkhar	**lapse** *n.* هفوة hafwah
laggard *n.* متقاعس motaqaa'is	**lard** *n.* شحم shahm
lagoon *n.* بحيرة bohayrah	**large** *a.* كبير kabeer
lair *n.* مخبأ makhbau	**largesse** *n.* سخاء sakhaau
lake *n.* بحيرة bohayrah	**lark** *n.* قبرة qobbarah
lama *n.* لاما laama	**lascivious** *a.* فاسق faasiq
lamb *n.* خاروف khaaroof	**lash** *a.* جلدة jaldah
lambaste *v.* يجلد yajlid	**lash** *n.* يجلد yajlid
lambkin *n.* حمل صغير hamalon sagheer	**lass** *n.* معشوقة ma'shooqah
lame *a.* أعرج ua'raj	**last** *a.* أخير uakheer
lame *v.* يعرج ya'roj	**last** *adv.* آخر uaakhir
lament *v.* يندب yandob	**last** *v.* يبقى yabqa
lament *n.* ندب nadb	**last** *n.* أخير uakheer
lamentable *a.* مؤسف mousif	**lastly** *adv.* أخيراً uakheeran
lamentation *n.* رثاء rithaau	**lasting** *a.* دائم daauim
laminate *v.* يصفح yosaffih	**latch** *n.* مزلاج mizlaaj
lamp *n.* مصباح misbaah	**late** *a.* متأخر motauakhkhir
lampoon *n.* سخرية sokhriyah	**late** *adv.* متأخر motauakhkhir
lampoon *v.* يسخر yaskhar	**lately** *adv.* مؤخراً mouakhkharan
lance *n.* رمح romh	**latent** *a.* كامن kaamin
lance *v.* يرمح yarmah	**lath** *n.* شرائح خشبية sharaauihon khashabiyyah
lancer *n.* رماح rammah	
lancet *a.* مشرط mishrat	**lathe** *n.* مخرطة makhratah
land *n.* أرض uard	**lather** *n.* خراط kharraat
land *v.* يهبط yahbit	**latitude** *n.* خط العرض khattol 'ard
landing *n.* مهبط mihbat	**latrine** *n.* مرحاض mirhaad
landscape *n.* منظر manddar	**latter** *a.* الأخير ualuakheer
lane *n.* ممر mamar	**lattice** *n.* شعرية sha'riyyah
language *n.* لغة loghah	**laud** *v.* يمدح yamdah
	laud *n.* مديح madeeh

laudable *a.* جدير بالثناء jadeeron biththanaau	**layer** *n.* طبقة tabaqah
laugh *n.* ضحكة dahikah	**layman** *n.* علماني ilmaaniy
laugh *v.* يضحك yad hak	**laze** *v.* يكسل yaksol
laughable *a.* مضحك mod hik	**laziness** *n.* كسل kasal
laughter *n.* ضحك dahik	**lazy** *n.* كسول kasool
launch *v.* يطلق yotliq	**lea** *n.* مرجة marjah
launch *n.* إطلاق etlaaq	**leach** *v.* يصفى yasfa
launder *v.* يغسل yaghsil	**lead** *n.* 1 رصاص rasaas
laundress *n.* غاسلة الملابس ghaasilatol malaabis	**lead** *v.* يقود yaqood
laundry *n.* غسيل ghaseel	**lead** *n.* 2 قيادة qiyaadah
laurel *n.* غار ghaar	**leaden** *a.* رصاصي rasaasiy
laureate *a.* حائز على جائزة haauizon 'ala jaauizah	**leader** *n.* زعيم za'eem
laureate *n.* حائز على جائزة haauizon 'ala jaauizah	**leadership** *n.* قيادة qiyaadah
lava *n.* حمم himam	**leaf** *n.* ورقة waraqah
lavatory *n.* مرحاض mirhaad	**leaflet** *n.* منشور manshoor
lavender *n.* خزامي khozaami	**leafy** *a.* مشجّر moshajjar
lavish *a.* مسرف mosrif	**league** *n.* دوري dawriy
lavish *v.* يسرف yosrif	**leak** *n.* تسرب tasarrob
law *n.* قانون qaanoon	**leak** *v.* يتسرب yatasarrab
lawful *a.* قانوني qaanooniy	**leakage** *n.* تسرب tasarrob
lawless *a.* خارج عن القانون khaarijon 'anil qaanoon	**lean** *n.* هزيل hazeel
lawn *n.* مَخضَره makhdarah	**lean** *v.* يميل yameel
lawyer *n.* محام mohaami	**leap** *v.* يقفز yaqfiz
lax *a.* متراخي motaraakhi	**leap** *n.* طفرة tafrah
laxative *n.* مادة ملينة maadaton molayyinah	**learn** *v.* يتعلّم yata'allam
laxative *adj.* ملين molayyin	**learned** *a.* متعلم mota'allam
laxity *n.* لين leen	**learner** *n.* متعلم mota'allim
lay *v.* يضع yada'	**learning** *n.* تعلم ta'allom
lay *a.* ممدود mamdood	**lease** *n.* إيجار ueejaar
lay *n.* مدة maddah	**lease** *v.* يؤجّر youajjir
	least *a.* الأقل ualuaqal
	least *adv.* الأقل ualuaqal
	leather *n.* جلد jild
	leave *v.* إجازة ejaazah
	leave *v.* يترك yatrok

lecture *n.* محاضرة mohaadarah	**lemon** *n.* ليمون laymoon
lecture *v.* يحاضر yohaadir	**lemonade** *n.* عصيرالليمون aseero llaymoon
lecturer *n.* محاضر mohaadir	**lend** *v.* يقرض yaqrid
ledger *n.* دفترالأستاذ daftarol uastaadh	**length** *n.* طول tool
lee *n.* جانب jaanib	**lengthen** *v.* يطيل yoteel
leech *n.* علقة alaqah	**lengthy** *a.* مطول motawwal
leek *n.* كرّاث korraath	**lenience** *n.* تساهل tasaahol
left *a.* متروك matrook	**leniency** *n.* تساهل tasaahol
left *n.* يسار yasaar	**lenient** *a.* متساهل motasaahil
leftist *n.* يساري yasaariy	**lens** *n.* عدسة adasah
leg *n.* ساق saaq	**lentil** *n.* عدس adas
legacy *n.* تراث toraath	**Leo** *n.* الأسد ualuasad
legal *a.* قانوني qaanooniy	**leonine** *adj.* أسدي uasadiy
legality *n.* شرعية shar'iyyah	**leopard** *n.* فهد fahd
legalize *v.* يشرّع yashra'	**leper** *n.* مجذوم majdhoom
legend *n.* أسطورة uostoorah	**leprosy** *n.* جذام jodhaam
legendary *a.* أسطوري uostooriy	**leprous** *a.* مجذوم majdhoom
leghorn *n.* قشّ إيطالي qashshon ueetaaliy	**less** *a.* أقل uaqal
	less *n.* أقل uaqal
legible *a.* مقروء maqroou	**less** *adv.* أقل uaqal
legibly *adv.* مقروء maqroou	**less** *prep.* أقل uaqal
legion *n.* فيلق faylaq	**lessee** *n.* مستأجر mostaujir
legionary *n.* فيلقي faylaqiy	**lessen** *v.* يخفض yokhaffid
legislate *v.* يشرّع yosharri'	**lesser** *a.* أهون uahwan
legislation *n.* تشريع tashree'	**lesson** *n.* درس dars
legislative *a.* تشريعي tashree'iy	**lest** *conj.* أن خشية khishyata uan
legislator *n.* مشرع mosharri'	**let** *v.* يسمح yasmah
legislature *n.* هيئةتشريعية hayuaton tashree'iyyah	**lethal** *a.* قاتل qaatil
	lethargic *a.* كسول kasool
legitimacy *n.* شرعية shar'iyyah	**lethargy** *n.* سبات sobaat
legitimate *adj.* شرعي shar'iy	**letter** *n.* رسالة risaalah
leisure *n.* وقتالفراغ waqtol faraagh	**level** *n.* مستوى mostawa
	level *adj.* مستوي mostawi
leisurely *a.* علىمهل ala mahl	**level** *v.* يسوّي yosawwi
leisurely *adv.* بتمهّل bitamahhol	

lever *n.* رافعة raafi'ah

lever *v.* يرفع yarfa'

leverage *n.* نفوذ nofoodh

levity *n.* خفة khiffah

levy *v.* يَفرِض ضريبة yafrido dareebah

levy *n.* ضريبة dareebah

lewd *a.* خليع khalee'

lexicography *n.* علم المعاجم ilmol ma'aajim

lexicon *n.* قاموس qaamoos

liability *n.* مسئولية masuooliyyah

liable *a.* عرضة irdah

liaison *n.* اتصال ettisaal

liar *n.* كذاب kadhaab

libel *n.* تشهير tashheer

libel *v.t.* يشهّر yoshahhir

liberal *adj.* ليبرالي leebraaliy

liberalism *n.* الليبرالية uallibraaliyyah

liberality *n.* تسامح tasaamoh

liberate *v.* يحرّر yoharrir

liberation *n.* تحرير tahreer

liberator *n.* محرر moharrir

libertine *n.* زنديق zindeeq

liberty *n.* حرية horriyyah

librarian *n.* أمين مكتبة umeeno maktabah

library *n.* مكتبة maktabah

licence *n.* ترخيص tarkhees

license *v.* يرخّص yorakhis

licensee *n.* مرخّص له morakhason lah

licentious *a.* فاجر faajir

lick *v.* يلعق yal'aq

lick *n.* لعقة la'qah

lid *n.* غطاء ghitaau

lie *v.* 1 يكذب yakdhib

lie *v.* 2 يتمدّد yatamaddad

lie *n.* كذبة kidhbah

lien *n.* امتياز emtiyaaz

lieu *n.* بدل badal

lieutenant *n.* ملازم molaazim

life *n.* حياة hayaah

lifeless *a.* ميت mayyit

lifelong *a.* مدى الحياة madal hayaat

lift *n.* مصعد mas'ad

lift *v.* يرفع yarfa'

light *n.* ضوء dawu

light *adj.* خفيف khafeef

light *v.* يضيء yodeeu

lighten *v.* يخفّف yokhaffif

lighter *n.* ولاعة walla'ah

lightly *adv.* برفق birifq

lightening *n.* برق barq

lignite *n.* فحم حجري fahmon hajariy

like *a.* مثل mithl

like *n.* شَبيه shabeeh

like *v.* يحب yohib

like *prep.* مُشابه moshaabih

likelihood *n.* احتمال ehtimaal

likely *a.* من المحتمل minal mohtamal

liken *v.* يشبّه yoshabbih

likeness *n.* شبه shabah

likewise *adv.* كذلك kadhaalikah

liking *n.* ميل mayl

lilac *n.* أرجواني uorjowaaniy

lily *n.* زنبق zanbaq

limb *n.* طرف taraf

limber v. يتنشّط yatanashshat

limber adj. رشيق rasheeq

limber n. عربةبعجلتين arabaton bi'ajalatayn

lime n. 1 كلس kils

lime v. يطليبالكلس yatli bilkils

lime n. 2 ليمون laymoon

limelight n. أضواء udwaau

limit n. حد had

limit v. يحد yahid

limitation n. تقييد taqyeed

limited a. محدود mahdood

limitless a. حدود بلا bila hodood

line n. خط khat

line v. يصفف yosaffif

lineage n. نسب nasab

linen n. كتان kittaan

linger v. يعيش ya'eesh

lingo n. لغة loghah

lingual a. لغوي laghawiy

linguist n. لغوي laghawiy

linguistic a. لغوي laghawiy

linguistics n. علماللغة ilmo lloghah

lining n. بطانة bitaanah

link n. رابط raabit

link v. يربط yarbit

linseed n. بذرالكتان bidhrol kittaan

lintel n. أسكفة uaskafah

lion n. أسد uasad

lioness n. لبؤة labouah

lip n. شفة shiffah

liquefy v. يميّع yomayyi'

liquid a. سائل saauil

liquid n. سائل saauil

liquidate v. يصفّي yosaffi

liquidation n. تصفية tasfiyah

liquor n. خمر khamr

lisp v. يلثغ yalthogh

lisp n. لثغة lathgha

list n. قائمة qaauimah

list v. يضععلىالقائمة yada'o 'alal qaauimah

listen v. يستمع yastami'

listener n. مستمع mostami'

listless a. فاتر faatir

literacy n. معرفة ma'rifah

literal a. حرفي harfiy

literary a. أدبي uadabiy

literate a. متعلم mota'allim

literature n. أدب uadab

litigant n. خصم khasm

litigate v. يرفعدعوى yarfa'o da'wa

litigation n. دعوى da'wa

litre n. لتر litir

litter n. نفايات nifaayaat

litter v. يغطّيبالنفايات yoghatti binnifaayaat

litterateur n. أديب uadeeb

little a. قليل qaleel

little adv. قليلاً qaleelan

little n. صغير sagheer

littoral a. ساحلي saahiliy

liturgical a. طقسي taqsiy

live v. 1 يحيى yahya

live v. 2 يعيش ya'eesh

live adj. حي hay

live adv. مباشر mobaashir

livelihood n. رزق rizq

lively a. حي hay

liver n. كبد kabid

livery *n.* كسوة kiswah

living *a.* حي hay

living *n.* الأحياء ualuahyaau

lizard *n.* سحلية sihliyyah

load *n.* حمل haml

load *v.* يحمَل yahmil

loadstar *n.* نجمةشمال najmato shshamaal

loadstone *n.* مغناطيس mighnaatees

loaf *n.* رغيف ragheef

loaf *v.* يَتَسَكَّع yatasakka'

loafer *n.* كسول kasool

loan *n.* قرض qard

loan *v.* يقرض yoqrid

loath *a.* مشمئز moshmauiz

loathe *v.* يكره yakrah

loathsome *a.* كريه kareeh

lobby *n.* ردهة rodhah

lobe *n.* شحمة shahmah

lobster *n.* سرطانالبحر sarataanol bahr

local *a.* محلي mahalliy

locale *n.* مكان makaan

locality *n.* مكان makaan

localize *v.* يوطن yowattin

locate *v.* يحدّد yohaddid

location *n.* موقع mawqi'

lock *n.* قفل qofl

lock *v.* يقفل yoqfil

locker *n.* خزانة khizaanah

locket *n.* مدلاة midlaah

locomotive *n.* قاطرة qaatirah

locus *n.* مكان makaan

locust *n.* جراد jaraad

locution *n.* عبارة ibaarah

lodge *n.* سكن sakan

lodge *v.* يسكن yaskon

lodging *n.* سكن sakan

loft *n.* علئة illiyyah

lofty *a.* نبيل nabeel

log *n.* 1 سجل sijil

log *n.* 2 خشبة khashabah

logarithim *n.* اللوغارثمات uallogharithmaat

loggerhead *n.* سلحفاةبحرية solhafaaton bahriyyah

logic *n.* منطق mantiq

logical *a.* منطقي mantiqiy

logician *n.* منطقي mantiqiy

loin *n.* عانة aanah

loiter *v.* يتلكأ yatalakkau

loll *v.* يسترخي yastarkhi

lollipop *n.* مصاصة massaasah

lone *a.* وحيد waheed

loneliness *n.* عزلة ozlah

lonely *a.* وحيد waheed

lonesome *adj.* وحيد waheed

long *a.* طويل taweel

long *adv* طويل taweel

long *v.* يطوق yatooq

longevity *n.* طولالعمر toolal 'omr

longing *n.* شوق shawq

longitude *n.* خطالطول khatto ttool

look *v.* ينظر yanddor

look *adj.* نظرة naddrah

loom *n.* نول nowl

loom *v.* يلوح yalooh

loop *n.* حلقة halaqah

loop-hole *n.* منفذ manfadh

loose *a.* فضفاض fadfaad

loosen *v.* يرخي yarkhi	**loyalist** *n.* موالي mowaali
loot *n.* مسروقات masrooqaat	**loyalty** *n.* ولاء walaau
loot *v.* ينهب yanhab	**lubricant** *n.* شحم shahm
lop *v.* يشذب yoshadhdhib	**lubricate** *v.* يزيّت yozayyit
lop *n.* يشذوب mashdhoob	**lubrication** *n.* تشحيم tashheem
lord *n.* سيّد sayyid	**lucent** *a.* مضيء modeeu
lordly *a.* وقور waqoor	**lucerne** *n.* فصفصة fasfasah
lordship *n.* سيادة siyaadah	**lucid** *a.* واضح waadih
lore *n.* تقاليد taqaaleed	**lucidity** *n.* صفاء safaau
lorry *n.* شاحنة shaahinah	**luck** *n.* حظ hadd
lose *v.* يفقد yafqid	**luckily** *adv.* لحسن الحظ lihosnil hadd
loss *n.* خسارة khasaarah	**luckless** *a.* منحوس manhoos
lot *n.* كميه kammiyyah	**lucky** *a* محظوظ mahddoodd
lot *n.* نَصيب naseeb	**lucrative** *a.* مربح morbih
lotion *n.* محلول mahlool	**lucre** *n.* ربح ribh
lottery *n.* يانصيب yaanaseeb	**luggage** *n.* أمتعة uamti'ah
lotus *n.* لوتس lootas	**lukewarm** *a.* فاتر faatir
loud *a.* عال aali	**lull** *v.* يركد yarkod
lounge *v.* يستريح yastareeh	**lull** *n.* ركود rokood
lounge *n.* استراحة estiraahah	**lullaby** *n.* تهويدة tahweedah
louse *n.* قملة qamlah	**luminary** *n.* جرم سماوي jormon samaawiy
lovable *a.* محبوب mahboob	
love *n.* حب hob	**luminous** *a.* مشرق moshriq
love *v.* يحب yohib	**lump** *n.* نتوء notoou
lovely *a.* جميل jameel	**lump** *v.* يتعامل yata'aamal
lover *n.* عاشق aashiq	**lunacy** *n.* جنون jonoon
loving *a.* محب mohib	**lunar** *a.* قمري qamariy
low *a.* منخفض monkhafid	**lunatic** *n.* مجنون majnoon
low *adv.* منخفضاً monkhafidan	**lunatic** *a.* جنوني jonooniy
low *v.* يخور yakhoor	**lunch** *n.* غداء ghadaau
low *n.* منخفض monkhafad	**lunch** *v.* يتغدّى yataghadda
lower *v.* يخفض yokhfid	**lung** *n.* رئة riuah
lowliness *n.* تواضع tawaado'	**lunge** *n.* إندفاع endifaa'
lowly *a.* متواضع motawaadi'	**lunge** *v.* يندفع yandafi'
loyal *a.* مخلص mokhlis	**lurch** *n.* تمايل tamaayol

lurch *v.* يتمايل yatamaayal
lure *n.* إغراء eghraau
lure *v.* يغري yoghri
lurk *v.* يستتر yastatir
luscious *a.* فاتن faatin
lush *a.* خصب khasb
lust *n.* شهوة shahwah
lustful *a.* شبق shabaq
lustre *n.* بريق bareeq
lustrous *a.* لامع laami'
lusty *a.* حيوي hayawiy
lute *n.* عود ood
luxuriance *n.* تزخرف tazakhrof
luxuriant *a.* مترف motraf
luxurious *a.* فاخر faakhir
luxury *n.* ترف taraf
lynch *v.* يعدم ya'dim
lyre *n.* قيثارة qeethaarah
lyric *a.* مغنى moghanna
lyric *n.* كلمات الأغنية kalimaatol uoghniyah
lyrical *a.* مغنى moghanna
lyricist *n.* شاعر غنائي shaa'iron ghinaauiy

M

magic *n.* سحر sihr
magical *a.* سحري sihriy
magician *n.* ساحر saahir
magisterial *a.* وقور waqoor
magistracy *n.* قضاء qadaau
magistrate *n.* قاض qaadi

magnanimity *n.* شهامة shahaamah
magnanimous *a.* رحب rahib
magnate *n.* قطب qotb
magnet *n.* مغناطيس mighnaatees
magnetic *a.* مغناطيسي mighnaateesiy
magnetism *n.* مغناطيسية mighnaateesiyyah
magnificent *a.* رائع raaui'
magnify *v.* يكبر yokabbir
magnitude *n.* حجم hajm
magpie *n.* عقعق oq'oq
mahogany *n.* ماهوغاني mahoghani
mahout *n.* فيال fayyaal
maid *n.* خادمة khaadimah
maiden *n.* عذراء adhraau
maiden *adj.* 1 عزباء azbaau
maiden *adj.* 2 أولى uoola
mail *n.* بريد bareed
mail *v.* يرسل yorsil
main *adj.* رئيسي raueesiy
main *n.* أساسي uasaasiy
mainly *adv.* بشكل رئيسي bishaklin raueesiy
mainstay *n.* عماد imaad
maintain *v.* يحافظ yohaafidd
maintenance *n.* صيانة siyaanah
maize *n.* ذرة dhorah
majestic *a.* مهيب moheeb
majesty *n.* عظمة addamah
major *a.* أساسي uasaasiy
major *n.* 1 رائد raauid
major *n.* 2 تخصص takhassos
majority *n.* أغلبية uaghlabiyyah

make v. 1 يصنع yasna'
make v. 2 يجعل yaj'al
make n. صنع son'
maker n. صانع saani'
mal adjustment n. سوءالتكيف soouo ttakayyof
mal administration n. سوءالإدارة soouol edaarah
malady n. داء daau
malaria n. ملاريا malaarya
maladroit a. أخرق uakhraq
malaise n. توعك tawa'ok
malcontent a. ساخط saakhit
malcontent n. سخط sakht
male a. ذكر dhakar
male n. ذكر dhakar
malediction n. لعنة la'nah
malefactor n. مجرم mojrim
maleficent a. مؤذ moudhi
malice n. خبث khobth
malicious a. خبيث khabeeth
malign v. يؤذ youdhi
malign adj. مؤذ moudhi
malignancy n. خبث khobth
malignant a. خبيث khabeeth
malignity n. خبث khobth
malleable a. طوعي taw'iy
malmsey n. نبيذحلو nabeedhon holw
malnutrition n. سوءالتغذية soouo ttaghdhiyah
malpractice n. ممارسةخاطئة momaarasaton khaatiuah
malt n. جعة ja'ah
mal-treatment n. سوءالمعاملة soouol mo'aamalah

mamma n. ثدي thady
mammal n. ثدييات thadiyyaat
mammary a. ثديئ thadiy
mammon n. ثروةمعبودة tharwaton ma'boodah
mammoth n. الماموث ualmaamooth
mammoth adj. ضخم dakhm
man n. رجل rajol
man v. يحرس yahros
manage v. يدير yodeer
manageable a. مدار madaar
management n. إدارة edaarah
manager n. مدير modeer
managerial a. إداري edaariy
mandate n. تفويض tafweed
mandatory a. إلزامي elzaamiy
mane n. عرف orf
manes n. أرواح uarwaah
manful a. رجولي rojooliy
manganese n. منغيز manghaneez
manger n. مذود midhwad
mangle v. يفسد yofsid
mango n. مانجو maanjo
manhandle v. يحرّكيدويّاً yoharriko yadawiyyan
manhole n. فتحة fathah
manhood n. رجولة rojoolah
mania n. هوس hawas
maniac n. مهووس mahwoos
manicure n. طلاءالأظافر tilaauol 'addaafir
manifest a. واضح waadih
manifest v. يظهر yoddhir
manifestation n. مظهر maddhar

manifesto *n.* بيان رسمي bayaanon rasmiy	**many** *adj.* كثير katheer
manifold *a.* متعدّد mota'addid	**map** *n.* خريطة khareetah
manipulate *v.* يتلاعب yatalaa'ab	**map** *v.* يرسم خريطة yarsomo khareetah
manipulation *n.* تلاعب talaa'ob	**mar** *v.* يشوّه yoshawwih
mankind *n.* الجنس البشري ualjinsol bashariy	**marathon** *n.* الماراثون ualmaaraathoon
manlike *a.* رجولي rojooliy	**maraud** *v.* يسلب yaslob
manliness *n.* رجولة rojoolah	**marauder** *n.* نهاب nahhaab
manly *a.* رجولي rojooliy	**marble** *n.* رخام rokhaam
manna *n.* المن ualman	**march** *n.* 1 مسيرة maseerah
mannequin *n.* عارضة أزياء aaridato uazyaau	**March** *n.* 2 آذار uaadhaar
manner *n.* أسلوب uosloob	**march** *v.* يسير yaseer
mannerism *n.* تصرّف tasarrof	**mare** *n.* فرس faras
mannerly *a.* مهذب mohadhdhab	**margarine** *n.* سمن samn
manoeuvre *n.* مناورة monaawarah	**margin** *n.* هامش haamish
manoeuvre *v.* يناور yonaawir	**marginal** *a.* هامشي haamishiy
manor *n.* عزبة izbah	**marigold** *n.* آذريون uaadhriyoon
manorial *a.* عزبوي izbawiy	**marine** *a.* بحري bahriy
mansion *n.* قصر qasr	**mariner** *n.* بحار bahhaar
mantel *n.* رف المستوقد raffol mostawqad	**marionette** *n.* دمية domyah
mantle *n.* عباءة abaauah	**marital** *a.* زوجي zawjiy
mantle *v.* يخفي yakhfi	**maritime** *a.* بحري bahriy
manual *a.* يدوي yadawiy	**mark** *n.* علامة alaamah
manual *n.* كتيب kotayyib	**mark** *v.* يضع علامة yada'o 'alaamah
manufacture *v.* يصنع yasna'	**marker** *n.* مؤشّر mouashshir
manufacture *n.* صناعة sinaa'ah	**market** *n.* سوق sooq
manufacturer *n.* صانع saani'	**market** *v.* يسوّق yosawwiq
manumission *n.* إعتاق ui'taaq	**marketable** *a.* مسوّق mosawwaq
manumit *v.* يعتق yo'tiq	**marksman** *n.* هداف haddaaf
manure *n.* سماد samaad	**marl** *n.* صلصالي سماد samaadon silsaaliy
manure *v.* يسمّد yosammid	**marmalade** *n.* مربّى morabba
manuscript *n.* مخطوطة makhtootah	**maroon** *n.* منبوذ manboodh
	maroon *adj.* كستنائي kastanaauiy
	maroon *v.* ينبذ yanbodh

marriage *n.* زواج zawaaj

marriageable *a.* مزوّج mozawwaj

marrow *n.* نخاع nokhaa'

marry *v.* يتزوّج yotajawwaj

Mars *n.* المرّيخ ualmarrikh

marsh *n.* مستنقع mostanqa'

marshal *n.* مارشال maarshal

marshal *v.t* ينظّم yonaddddim

marshy *a.* مستنقعي mostanqa'iy

marsupial *n.* جرابي joraabiy

mart *n.* سوق sooq

marten *n.* الدلق uaddolq

martial *a.* عسكري askarriy

martinet *n.* متشدّد ضابط daabiton motashaddid

martyr *n.* شهيد shaheed

martyrdom *n.* استشهاد estishhaadiy

marvel *n.* أعجوبة uo'joobah

marvel *v.* يتعجّب yata'ajjab

marvellous *a.* رائع raaui'

mascot *n.* جالب الحظ jaalibol hadd

masculine a. مذكر modhakkar

mash *n.* هَريس harees

mash *v.* يَهْرُس yahros

mask *n.* قناع qinaa'

mask *v.* يتقنّع yataqanna'

mason *v.* بناء bannaau

masonry *n.* بناء binaau

masquerade *n.* حفلةتنكرية haflaton tanakkoriyyah

mass *n.* كتلة kotlah

mass *v.* يَختَشِد yahtashid

massacre *n.* مجزرة majzarah

massacre *v.* يجزر yajzor

massage *n.* تدليك tadleek

massage *v.* يدلّك yodallik

masseur *n.* مدلك modallik

massive *a.* هائل haauil

massy *a.* هائل haauil

mast *n.* سارية saariyah

master *n.* سيّد sayyid

master *n.* رئيس rauees

master *n.* ماجستير maajisteer

master *v.* يُسَيطر على yosaytiro 'ala

masterly *a.* بارع baari'

masterpiece *n.* تحفة tohfah

mastery *n.* براعة baraa'ah

masticate *v.* يعجن ya'jin

masturbate *v.* يستمني yastamni

mat *n.* حصيرة haseerah

matador *n .* مصارعالثيران mosaari'o ththeeran

match *n.* 1 مباراة mobaaraah

match *v.* يطابق yotaabiq

match *n.* 2 عودثيقاب oodo theeqaab

match *n.* 3 نَظير naeerdd

matchless *a.* منقطعالنظير monqati'o nnaddeer

matchmaker *n.* خاطبة khaatibah

mate *n.* 1 رفيق rafeeq

mate *v.* 1 يتزاوج yatazaawaj

mate *n.* 2 إمائةالشّاه emaatato shshaah

mate *v.* 2 يميت الشاه yomeeto shshaah

material *a.* مادي maddiy

material *n.* مادة maaddah

materialism *n.* مادية maaddiyyah

materialize v. يتحقق yatahaqqaq

materialize v. يَتَجَسَّد yatajassad

maternal a. أمومي uomoomiy

maternity n. أمومة uomoomah

mathematical a. رياضي riyaadiy

mathematician n. رياضي riyaadiy

mathematics n. الرياضيات uarriyaadiyyat

matinee n. عرض مسرحي ardon masrahiy

matriarch n. حاكمة haakimah

matricidal adj. قاتل للأم qatilon liluom

matricide n. قتل الأم qatlol uom

matriculate v. يلتحق بالجامعة yaltahiqo biljaami'ah

matriculation n. الالتحاق بالجامعة ualuiltihaqo biljaami'ah

matrimonial a. زوجي zawjiy

matrimony n. زواج zawaaj

matrix n. مصفوفة masfoofah

matron n. سَيِّدَهُ مُتَزَوِّجَهُ مَهِيبَه sayyidaton motazawijaton maheebah

matter n. مسألة masualah

matter n. مادَه maaddah

matter v. يهم yahom

mattock n. معول mi'wal

mattress n. فراش firaash

mature a. ناضج naadij

mature v. ينضج yandoj

maturity n. نضج nodj

maudlin adj. جياش jayyaash

maul n. هراوة hiraawah

maul v. يَنْهَش yanhash

maulstick n. عصا الرسام asa rrassaam

maunder v. يهذي yahdhi

mausoleum n. ضريح dareeh

mawkish a. مثير للغثيان motheeron lilghathayaan

maxilla n. عظام الفك iddaamol fak

maxim n. حكمة hikmah

maximize v. يعظّم yo'addddim

maximum a. أقصى uaqsa

maximum n. الحدّ الأقصى ualhaddol uaqsa

May n. أيّار uayyaar

may v. يمكن yomkin

mayor n. عمدة omdah

maze n. متاهة mataahah

me pron. أنا uana

mead n. خمر العسل khamrol 'asal

meadow n. مرج marj

meagre a. هزيل hazeel

meal n. وجبة wajbah

mealy a. دقيقي daqeeqiy

mean a. لئيم laueem

mean n. متوسّط motawassit

mean v. يقصد yaqsid

meander v. يتسكّع yatasakka'

meaning n. معنى ma'nah

meaningful adj. مجدي mojdi

meaningless a. معنى بلا bila ma'na

meanness n. لؤم loum

means n. وسيلة waseelah

meanwhile adv. في الأثناء fil uathnaau

measles n. حصبة hasbah

measurable a. مقاس moqaas

measure *n.* مقياس miqyaas	**meek** *a.* وديع wadee'
measure *v.* يقيس yaqees	**meet** *n.* 1 تقاطع taqaato'
measureless *a.* لايقاس laa yoqaas	**meet** *n.* 2 لقاءرياضي liqauon riyaadiy
measurement *n.* قياس qiyaas	**meet** *v.* 1 يلتقي yaltaqi
meat *n.* لحم lahm	**meet** *v.* 2 يفي yafi
mechanic *n.* ميكانيكي meekaaneeki	**meeting** *n.* اجتماع ejtimaa'
mechanic *adj.* ميكانيكي meekaaneeki	**megalith** *n.* حجرضخم hajaron dakhm
mechanical *adj.* ميكانيكي meekaaneeki	**megalithic** *a.* مجاليثي mijaleethiy
mechanics *n.* ميكانيكا meekaaneeka	**megaphone** *n.* مكبرالصوت mokabbiro ssawt
mechanism *n.* آلية uaaliyyah	**melancholia** *n.* سواد sawaad
medal *n.* ميدالية meedaaliyah	**melancholic** *a.* كئيب kaueeb
medallist *n.* حامل ميدالية haamilo meedaaliyah	**melancholy** *n.* كآبة kauaabah
meddle *v.* يتطفل yatataffal	**melancholy** *adj.* حزن hozn
medieval *a.* من القرون الوسطى minal qoroonil wosta	**melee** *n.* شجار shijaar
median *a.* متوسط motawassit	**meliorate** *v.* يحسن yohassin
mediate *v.* يتواسط yatawaasat	**mellow** *a.* يانع yaani'
mediation *n.* وساطة wasaatah	**melodious** *a.* شجي shajiy
mediator *n.* وسيط waseet	**melodrama** *n.* مَشجاه mahjaah
medic *n.* مسعف mos'if	**melodramatic** *a.* مَسرَحي عاطِفي masrahiyyon 'aatifiy
medical *a.* طبي tibbiy	**melody** *n.* لحن lahn
medicament *n.* دواء dawaau	**melon** *n.* شمام shammaam
medicinal *a.* دوائي dawaauiy	**melt** *v.* يصهر yashar
medicine *n.* دواء dawaau	**member** *n.* عضو odw
mediocre *a.* متوسط motawassit	**membership** *n.* عضوية odwiyyah
mediocrity *n.* توسط tawassot	**membrane** *n.* غشاء ghishaau
meditate *v.* يتأمل yatauammal	**memento** *n.* تذكار tidhkaar
meditation *n.* تأمّل tauammol	**memoir** *n.* مذكرة modhakkirah
meditative *a.* تأملي tauammoliy	**memorable** *a.* لاينسى laa yansa
medium *n.* وسيط waseet	**memorandum** *n.* مذكرة modhakkirah
medium *adj.* متوسط motawassit	**memorial** *n.* نصب تذكاري nasb tidhkaariy

memorial *adj.* تذكاري tidhkaariy
memory *n.* ذاكرة dhaakirah
menace *n.* تهديد tahdeed
menace *v.* يهدّد yohaddid
mend *v.* يصلح yoslih
mendacious *a.* كذوب kadhoob
menial *a.* وضيع wadee'
menial *n.* خادم khaadim
meningitis *n.* التهاب السحايا uiltihaabo ssahaaya
menopause *n.* انقطاع الطمث enqitaa'o ttamath
menses *n.* حيض haydh
menstrual *a.* حيضي haydhiy
menstruation *n.* حيض haydh
mental *a.* عقلي aqliy
mentality *n.* عقلية aqliyyah
mention *n.* ذكر dhikr
mention *v.* يذكر yadhkor
mentor *n.* معلّم mo'allim
menu *n.* قائمة qaauimah
mercantile *a.* تجاري tijaariy
mercenary *a.* مرتزق mortazaqa
mercerise *v.* يعالج القماش yo'aalijol qimaash
merchandise *n.* بضاعة bidaa'ah
merchant *n.* تاجر taajir
merciful *a.* رحيم raheem
merciless *adj.* لا يرحم la yarham
mercurial *adj.* زئبقي ziubaqiy
mercury *n.* زئبق ziubaq
mercy *n.* رحمة rahmah
mere *a.* مجرد mojarrad
merge *v.* يدمج yadmij
merger *n.* مدمج modmaj
meridian *n.* خط الزوال khato zzawaal

merit *n.* جدارة jadaarah
merit *v.* يَسْتَحِق yastahiq
meritorious *a.* جدير jadeer
mermaid *n.* حورية hooriyyah
merman *n.* حوري hooriy
merriment *n.* مرح marah
merry *a* مرح marah
mesh *n.* شبكة shabakah
mesh *v.* يتشابك yatashaabak
mesmerism *n.* مسمرية mismaariyyah
mesmerize *v.* يمسمر yomasmir
mess *n.* فوضى fawda
mess *v.* يَعْبَث ya'bath
message *n.* رسالة risaalah
messenger *n.* رسول rasool
messiah *n.* مسيح maseeh
Messrs *n.* السادة uassaadah
metabolism *n.* أيض uayd
metal *n.* معدن ma'dan
metallic *a.* معدني ma'daniy
metallurgy *n.* علم المعادن ilmol ma'aadin
metamorphosis *n.* مسخ maskh
metaphor *n.* استعارة esti'aarah
metaphysical *a.* غيبي ghaybiy
metaphysics *n.* علم الغيبيات ilmol ghaybiyyaat
mete *v.* يعاقب yo'aaqib
meteor *n.* نيزك nayzak
meteoric *a.* نيزكي nayzakiy
meteorologist *n.* عالم الأرصاد الجوية aalimol uarsaadil jawwiyyah
meteorology *n.* علم الأرصاد الجوية ilmol uarsaadil jawwiyyah

meter *n.* متر mitr
method *n.* أسلوب usloob
methodical *a.* منهجي manhajiy
metre *n.* متر mitr
metric *a.* متري mitriy
metrical *a.* متري mitriy
metropolis *n.* مدينة madeenah
metropolitan *a.* مدني madaniy
metropolitan *n.* عاصمة aasimah
mettle *n.* مزاج mazaaj
mettlesome *adj.* شجاع shojaa'
mew *v.* يموي yamwi
mew *n.* مواء mowaau
mezzanine *n.* طابق متوسط
taabiqon motawassit
mica *n.* معدنية صفائح safaauihon
ma'daniyyah
microfilm *n.* فِلم مصغَر filmon
mosaghar
micrology *n.* علم المجهريات ilmol
mijhariyyaat
micrometer *n.* جهاز قياس Jihaazo
qiyaas
microphone *n.* ميكروفون
maykrofoon
microscope *n.* مجهر mijhar
microscopic *a.* مجهري mijhariy
microwave *n.* مايكروويف
maykroweef
mid *a.* منتصف montasaf
midday *n.* منتصف النهار montasafo
nnahaar
middle *a.* مُنتَصَف montasaf
middle *n.* وسط wasat
middleman *n.* وسيط waseet
middling *a.* متوسط motawassit

midget *n.* قزم qazam
midland *n.* داخل البلد daakhilol
balad
midnight *n.* منتصف الليل
montasafo llayl
mid-off *n.* قبالة المنتصف qobaalatol
montasaf
mid-on *n.* في منتصف fil mintasaf
midriff *n.* الحجاب الحاجز
ualhijaabol haajiz
midst *n.* وسط wasat
midsummer *n.* منتصف الصيف
montasafo ssayf
midwife *n.* قابلة qaabilah
might *n.* ربما robbama
mighty *adj.* عظيم addeem
migraine *n.* صداع نصفي sodaa'on
nisfiy
migrant *n.* مهاجر mohaajir
migrate *v.* يهاجر yohaajir
migration *n.* هجرة hijrah
milch *a.* حلوب haloob
mild *a.* معتدل mo'tabil
mildew *n.* عفن فطري afanon fitriy
mile *n.* ميل meel
mileage *n.* عدد الأميال adadol
uamyaal
milestone *n.* مؤشر حجري
mouashiron hajariy
milieu i بيئة beeuah
militant *a.* مسلَح mosallah
militant i مسلَح mosallah
military *a.* عسكري askarriy
military *n.* عسكر askar
militate *v.* يناضل yonaadil
militia *n.* الميليشا ualmileesha

milk *n.* حليب haleeb

milk *v.* يحلب yahlib

milky *a.* حليبي haleeb

mill *n.* طاحونة taahoonah

mill *v.* يطحن yat han

millennium *n.* ألفية ualfiyyah

miller *n.* طحان tahhaan

millet *n.* دخن dokhn

milliner *n.* قبعاتي qobba'aatiy

millinery *n.* محل قبعات mahallo qobba'aat

million *n.* مليون malyoon

millionaire *n.* مليونير malyooneer

millipede *n.* ام أربعة وأربعين uomo uarba'atin wa uarba'oon

mime *n.* تَمثيل إيمائي tamtheelon ueemaauiy

mime *v.* يُمثِّل إيمائيا yomaththilo ueemaauiyyan

mimesis *n.* تنكر بيئي tanakkoron beeuiy

mimic *a.* مقلَّد moqallad

mimic *n.* مقلَّد moqallad

mimic *v.* يقلّد yoqallid

mimicry *n.* تقليد taqleed

minaret *n.* مئذنة miudhanah

mince *v.* يفرم yafrom

mind *n.* عقل aql

mind *v.t.* يحرس yahris

mindful *a.* مُنتَبِه لواجباته montabihon liwaajibaatih

mindless *a.* طائش taauish

mine *pron.* لي lee

mine *n.* منجم manjam

miner *n.* عامل منجم aamilol manjam

mineral *n.* معدن ma'dan

mineral *adj.* معدني ma'daniy

mineralogist *n.* عالم المعادن aalimol ma'aadin

mineralogy *n.* علم المعادن ilmol ma'aadin

mingle *v.* يختلط yakhtalit

miniature *n.* مصغر mosaghghar

miniature *a.* مصغر mosaghghar

minim *n.* كمية ضئيلة kamiyyaton daueelah

minimal *a.* أدنى uadna

minimize *v.* يدنّي yodanni

minimum *n.* حدّ أدنى hadon uadna

minimum *adj.* أدنى uadna

minion *n.* تابع taabi'

minister *n.* وزير wazeer

minister *v.* يَرعى yar'a

ministrant *a.* كاهِن kaahin

ministry *n.* وزارة wizaarah

mink *n.* المنك mink

minor *a.* ثانوي thaanawiy

minor *n.* قاصر qaasir

minority *n.* أقلية qalliyyah

minster *n.* كنيسة kaneesah

mint *n.* 1 نعناع na'naa'

mint *n.* 2 دار سَك العُمْلَه daaro sakkil 'omlah

mint *v.t.* يَسُكّ العملَه yasokkol 'omlah

minus *prep.* ناقص naaqis

minus *adj.* سالب saalib

minus *n.* ناقص naaqis

minuscule *a.* صغير sagheer

minute *a.* دقيق daqeeq

minute *n.* دقيقة daqeeqah

minutely *adv.* بدقة bidiqqah

minx n. فتاةوقحة fataaton waqihah

miracle *n.* معجزة mo'jizah

miraculous *a.* معجزي mo'jaziy

mirage *n.* سراب saraab

mire *n.* مستنقع mostanqa'

mire *v.* يعيق yo'eeq

mirror *n.* مرآة miruaah

mirror *v.* يعكس ya'kis

mirth *n.* إبتهاج ebtihaaj

mirthful *a.* مبتهج mobtahij

misadventure *n.* حادِث مُؤسِف haadithon mousif

misalliance *n.* زواجغيرموفق zawaajon ghayro mowaffaq

misanthrope *n.* كارهالبشر kaarihon lilbashar

misapplication *n.* سوءاستعمال soouo esti'maal

misapprehend *v.* يخطئالفهم yakhtiuo ffahm

misapprehension *n.* سوءفَهُمsoouo fahm

misappropriate *v.* يختلس yakhtalis

misappropriation *n.* اختلاس ekhtilaas

misbehave *v.* يسيءالتصرف yoseeuo ttasarrof

misbehaviour iسوءتصرف soouo tasarrof

misbelief *n.* سوءالاعتقاد soouol e'tiqaad

miscalculate *v.* يخطئالتقدير yokhtiuo ttaqdeer

miscalculation *n.* خطأحسابي khatauon hisaabiy

miscall *v.* يخطئالاسم yokhtiuol esm

miscarriage *n.* إجهاض ejhaad

miscarry *v.* تجهض tojhid

miscellaneous *a.* متفرقات motafarriqaat

miscellany *n.* منوّعات monawwauaat

mischance *n.* سوءطالع soouo taali'

mischief *n.* أذية uadhiyyah

mischievous *a.* مؤذ moudhi

misconceive *v.* يخطئالفهم yokhtiuol fahm

misconception *n.* سوءفهم soouo fihm

misconduct *n.* سوءسلوك soouo solook

misconstrue *v.* يسيءالتفسير yoseeuo ttafseer

miscreant *n.* وغد waghd

misdeed *n.* إثم ethm

misdemeanour *n.* جنحة jonhah

misdirect *v.* يضلَل yodallil

misdirection *n.* توجّهخاطئ tawajjohon khaatiu

miser n. بخيل bakheel

miserable *a.* بائس baauis

miserly *a.* ببخل bibokhl

misery *n.* بؤس bous

misfire *v.* يَفشَل yafshal

misfit *n.* غيرمتكيَف ghayro motakayyif

misfortune *n.* سوءحظ soouo hadd

misgive v. يشك yashok

misgiving n. هاجِس haajis

misguide v. يضلَل yodallil

mishap n. حادث مؤسف haadithon mousif

misjudge v. يخطئ الحكم yokhtiuol hokm

mislead v. يضلَل yodallil

mismanagement n. سوء إدارة soouo uidaarah

mismatch v. يخطئ التطبيق yokhtiuo ttatbeeq

misnomer n. خطأ تسمية khatauo tasmiyah

misplace v. يخطئ الوضع yokhtiuol wad'

misprint n. خطأ مطبعي khatauon matba'iy

misprint v. يخطئ الطباعة yokhtiuo ttibaa'ah

misrepresent v. يحرَف yoharrif

misrule n. سوء حكم soouo hokm

miss n. 1 آنسة uaanisah

miss n. 2 فشل fashal

miss v. يفقد yafqid

missile n. صاروخ saarookh

mission n. بعثة bi'tha

missionary n. مبشر mobashshir

missis, missus n.. إمرأة متزوَجة emrauaton motazawwijah

missive n. رسالة رسمية risaalaton rasmiyyah

mist n. ضباب dabaab

mistake n. خطأ khatau

mistake v. يخطِئ yokhtiu

mister n. سيد sayyid

mistletoe n. الدبق uaddibq

mistreat v. يسيء المعاملة yoseeuol mo'aamalah

mistress n. عشيقة asheeqah

mistrust n. عدم ثقة adamo thiqah

mistrust v. لا يثق laa yathiq

misty a. ضبابي dabaabiy

misunderstand v. يسيء الفهم yoseeuo ffahm

misunderstanding n. سوء تفاهم soouo tafaahom

misuse v. إساءة esaauah

misuse v. يسيء الإستعمال yoseeuol uisti'maal

mite n. 1 كمية صغيرة kamiyyaton sagheerah

mite n. 2 حشرة صغيرة hasharaton sagheerah

mithridate n. مضاد للسم modaadon lissom

mitigate v. يخفَف yokhaffif

mitigation n. تخفيف takhfeef

mitre n. قلنسوة qolonsowah

mitten n. قفاز qoffaaz

mix v. يمزج yamzij

mixture n. خليط khaleet

moan v. يئن yauin

moan n. أنين uaneen

moat n. خندق khandaq

moat v. يخندق yokhandiq

mob n. غوغاء ghawghaau

mob v. يتجمهر yatajamhar

mobile a. نقَال naqqaal

mobility n. تنقَل tanaqqol

mobilize v. يحشد yahshid

mock v. يستهزئ yastahziu

mock adj. صوَري sowariy

mockery n. استهزاء estihzaau

modality n. شكل shakl

mode n. طريقة tareeqah

model n. نموذج namoodhaj

model v. يُشَكِّل yoshakkil

moderate a. معتدل mo'tadil

moderate v. يُعَدِّل yo'addil

moderation n. إعتدال u'tidaal

modern a. حديث hadeeth

modernity n. حداثة hadaathah

modernize v. يحدّث yohaddith

modernization n. تحديث tahdeeth

modest a. متواضع motawaadi'

modesty n. تواضع tawaado'

modicum n. قليل qaleel

modification n. تعديل ta'deel

modify v. يعدّل Yo'addil

module n. وحدة wihdah

modulate v. يُعَدِّل yo'addil

moil v. يكدح yakdah

moist a. رطب ratib

moisten v. يرطّب yorattib

moisture n. رطوبة rotoobah

molar n. ضرس dirs

molar adj. ضرسي dirsiy

molasses n. دبس السكر dibso ssokkar

mole n. خلد khold

molecular a. جزيئي jozayuiy

molecule n. جزيء jozayu

molest v. يَتَحَرَّش yataharrash

molestation n. مضايقة modaayaqah

molten a. مصهور mashoor

moment n. لحظة lahddah

momentary a. لحظي lahddiy

momentous a. جسيم jaseem

momentum n. زخم zakham

monarch n. عاهل aahil

monarchy n. ملكية malakiyyah

monastery n. دير dayr

monasticism n. رهبنة rahbanah

Monday n. الإثنين ualuithnayn

monetary a. نقدي naqdiy

money n. مال maal

monger n. تاجر taajir

mongoose n. نمس nims

mongrel adj. هجين hajeen

monitor n. شاشة shaashah

monitor v. يرصد yarsid

monitory a. رقابة raqaabah

monk n. راهب raahib

monkey n. قرد qird

monochromatic a. أحادي اللون uhaadiyo llawn

monocle n. نظارة لعين واحدة nadddaaraton li'aynin wahidah

monocular a. أحادي uhaadiy

monody n. قصيدة نادبة qaseedaton naadibah

monogamy n. زواج أحادي zawaajon uhaadiy

monogram n. رمز مطبوع ramzon matboo'

monograph n. كتاب بموضوع واحد kitaabon bimawdoo'in waahid

monogynous a. أحادي الزوجة uohaadiyo zzawjah

monolatry n. عبادة إله واحد ibaadato elaahin waahid

monolith n. حجر عمودي الشكل hajaron 'amoodiyo shshakl

monologue *n.* مناجاةذاتية
monaajaaton dhaatiyyah

monopolist *n.* محتكر mohtakir

monopolize *v.* يحتكر yahtakir

monopoly *n.* إحتكار ehtikaar

monosyllable *n.* أحاديةالمقطع
uhaadiyatol maqta'

monosyllabic *a.* أحاديالمقطع
uhaadiyol maqta'

monotheism *n.* الإيمانبإلهواحد
ualueemaano biuilaahin
waahid

monotheist *n.* المؤمنبإلهواحد
ualmoumino biuilaahin
waahid

monotonous *a.* رتيب rateeb

monotony *n.* رتابة rataabah

monsoon *n.* رياحموسمية rihaahon
mawsimiyyah

monster *n.* وحش wahsh

monstrous *a.* وحشي wahshiy

monoestrous *n.* أحاديالجماع
uohaadiyol jimaa'

month *n.* شهر shahr

monthly *a.* شهرياً shahriyyan

monthly *adv.* شهريا shahriyyan

monthly *n.* مجلةشهرية majallaton
shahriyyah

monument *n.* نصبتذكاري nasbon
todhkaariy

monumental *a.* تذكاري
tidhkaariy

moo *v.* يخور yakhor

mood *n.* مزاج mazaaj

moody *a.* مزاجي mazaajiy

moon *n.* قمر qamar

moor *n.* أرضبور uardon boor

moor *v.* يُرسيالسَفينَه yorsi
ssafeenah

moorings *n.* المراسي ualmaraasi

moot *n.* حالةفرضية haalaton
faradiyyah

mop *n.* ممسحة mamsahah

mop *v.* يمسح yamsah

mope *v.* يكتئب yaktauib

moral *a.* أخلاقي ukhlaaqiy

moral *n.* عِبره ibrah

morale *n.* معنويات ma'nawiyyaat

moralist *n.* فاضل faadil

morality *n.* أخلاقية ukhlaaqiyyah

moralize *v.* يستخلصالعبرة
yastakhlisol 'ibrah

morbid *a.* معتل mo'tal

morbidity *n.* اعتلال e'tilaal

more *adj.* أكثر uakthar

more *adv.* بِدَرَجَةأكْبر bidarajatin
uakbar

moreover *adv.* أيضاً uaydan

morganatic *a.* متكافئ motakaafiu

morgue *n.* مشرحة mashrahah

moribund *a.* محتضر mohtadir

morning *n.* صباح sabaah

moron *n.* مغفَل moghaffal

morose *a.* عابس aabis

morphia *n.* مُخَدِر mokhaddir

morrow *n.* غد ghad

morsel *n.* لقمة loqmah

mortal *a.* 1 مميت momeet

mortal *a.* 2 فان faani

mortal *n.* مَخلوقفان makhlooqon
faani

mortality *n.* 1 فَناء fanaau

mortality *n.* 2 معدلالوفيات

mo'addalol wafiyyaat

mortar v. هاون haawin

mortgage n. رهن عقاري rahnon 'aqaariy

mortgage v. يرهن عقار yarhano 'aqaar

mortgagee n. راهن عقار raahino 'aqaar

mortgagor n. صاحب عقار saahibo 'aqaar

mortify v. يُذِل yodhil

mortuary n. مستودع الجثث mostawda'ol jothath

mosaic n. فسيفساء fosayfisaau

mosque n. مسجد masjid

mosquito n. بعوض ba'ood

moss n. طحلب tohlob

most a. معظم mo'ddam

most adv. أقصى uaqsa

most n. أعظم مقدار miqdaaron ua'ddam

mote n. ذَرَه dharrah

motel n. فندق fondoq

moth n. عثّة athah

mother n. والدة waalidah

mother v. يرعى yar'a

motherhood n. أمومة umoomah

motherlike a. أمومي uomoomiy

motherly a. رؤوم rauoom

motif n. نمط namat

motion n. 1 حركة harakah

motion n. 2 اقتراح eqtiraah

motion v. يتحرّك yataharrak

motionless a. ثابت thaabit

motivate v. يحث yahith

motivation n. حافز haafiz

motive n. دافع daafi'

motley a. مشكل moshakkal

motor n. محرك moharrik

motor v. يَسوق السَيّارَه yasooqo ssayyaarah

motorist n. سائق saauiq

mottle n. رقش rashq

motto n. شعار shi'aar

mould n. 1 قالب qaalib

mould v. يَصوغ yasoogh

mould n. 2 عفن afan

mouldy a. متعفن mota'affin

moult v. يفقدشعره yafqido sha'rah

mound n. تل tal

mount n. 1 جبل jabal

mount v. يَمتَطي yamtati

mount n. 2 مَطِيّه madyah

mountain n. جبل jabal

mountaineer n. متسلّق motasalliq

mountainous a. جبلي jabaliy

mourn v. يحزن yahzan

mourner n. متفجع motafajji'

mournful n. حزين hazeen

mourning n. حداد hadaad

mouse n. فأر faur

moustache n. شارب shaarib

mouth n. فم fam

mouth v. ينطق yantoq

mouthful n. مِلءالفَم miluo ffam

movable a. متحرك motaharrik

movables n. منقولات manqoolaat

move n. حركة harakah

move v. يتحرّك yataharrak

movement n. حركة harakah

mover n. محرك moharrik

movies *n.* أفلام uflaam	mota'addido nnasl
mow *v.* يجز yajiz	**multiple** *a.* متعدد mota'addid
much *a* كثير katheer	**multiple** *n.* عددمُضاعَف adadon
much *adv.* كثيرا katheeran	modaa'af
mucilage *n.* هلامنباتي holaamon nabaatiy	**multiped** *n.* متعددالأرجل mota'addidol uarjol
muck *n.* ارضخصبة uardon khisbah	**multiplex** *a.* متعدد mota'addid
mucous *a.* مخاطي mokhaatiy	**multiplicand** *n.* مضروب madroob
mucus *n.* مخاط mokhaat	**multiplication** *n.* ضرب darb
mud *n.* طين teen	**multiplicity** *n.* تعددية ta'addodiyyah
muddle *n.* تشوش tashawwosh	**multiply** *v.* يضرب yadrib
muddle *v.* يشوّش yoshawwish	**multitude** *n.* تعدد ta'addod
muffle *v.* يدثر yadthor	**mum** *a.* صامت saamit
muffler *n.* كاتمصوت kaatimo sawt	**mum** *n.* ماما maama
mug *n.* قَدَح qadah	**mumble** *v.* يُتَمتِم yatamtim
muggy *a.* رطبوحار ratibon wa haar	**mummer** *n.* ممثلصامت momaththilon saamit
mulatto *n.* شخصذونسبمختلط shakhson dho nasabin mokhtalat	**mummy** *n.* مومياء moomyaau
	mummy *n.* ماما maama
mulberry *n.* توت toot	**mumps** *n.* نكاف nokaaf
mule *n.* بغل baghl	**munch** *v.* يقضم yaqdim
mulish *a.* عنيد aneed	**mundane** *a.* دنيوي donyawiy
mull *n.* نسيجقطني naseejon qotniy	**municipal** *a.* بلدي baladiy
mull *v.* يتفكر yatafakkar	**municipality** *n.* بلدية baladiyyah
mullah *n.* مَلّا mollaa	**munificent** *a.* سخي sakhiy
mullion *n.* قاطععمودي qaati'on 'amoodiy	**munitions** *n.* ذخيرة dhakheerah
	mural *a.* جداري jidaariy
multifarious *a.* متنوّع motanawwi'	**mural** *n.* جدارية jadaarah
multiform *n.* متعدّدالهيئة mota'addidol hayuah	**murder** *n.* جريمةقتل jareemato qatl
multilateral *a.* متعدّدالأطراف mota'addidol uatraaf	**murder** *v.* يقتل yaqtol
	murderer *n.* قاتل qaatil
multiparous *a.* متعدّدالنسل	**murderous** *a.* قاتل qaatil
	murmur *n.* تذمر tadhammor
	murmur *v.* يتذمَر yatadhammar

muscle *n.* عضلة adalah

muscovite *n.* سيليكات البوتاسيوم والألومنيوم silikaatol bootasyom wal ualaminyom

muscular *a.* عضلي adaliy

muse *v.* يوحي yowhi

muse *n.* وحي yahy

museum *n.* متحف mathaf

mush *n.* عصيدة aseedah

mushroom *n.* فطر fitr

music *n.* موسيقى mooseeqa

musical *a.* موسيقي mooseeqiy

musician *n.* موسيقي mooseeqiy

musk *n.* مسك misk

musket *n.* بندقية قديمة bondoqiyyaton qadeemah

musketeer *n.* جندي مشاه jondiyyon moshaah

muslim *adj.* مسلم moslim

muslin *n.* نسيج قطني naseejon qotniy

must *v.* يجب yajib

must *n.* واجب waajib

mustache *n.* شارب shaarib

mustang *n.* فرس faras

mustard *n.* خردل khardal

muster *v.* يجمع yajma'

muster *n.* تجمع tajammo'

musty *a.* عفن afan

mutation *n.* طفرة tafrah

mutative *a.* متحول motahawwil

mute *a.* صامت saamit

mute *n.* أبكم uabkam

mutilate *v.* يبتر yabtor

mutilation *n.* بتر batr

mutinous *a.* متمرد motamarrid

mutiny *n.* تمرد tamarrod

mutiny *v.* يتمرد yatamarrad

mutter *v.* يتمتم yotamtim

mutton *n.* لحم الضأن lahno ddaun

mutual *a.* متبادل motabaadal

muzzle *n.* كمامة kammaamah

muzzle *v.* يكمّم yokammim

my *a.* ي -i

myalgia *n.* ألم عضلي ualamon 'adaliy

myopia *n.* قصر البصر qosrol basar

myopic *a.* قصير البصر qaseerol basar

myosis *n.* انقباض عضلة العين enqibaado 'adalatil 'ayn

myriad *n.* عدد لا يحصى adadon laa yohsa

myriad *adj.* غير معدود ghayro ma'dood

myrrh *n.* المر ualmor

myrtle *n.* الآس ualuaas

myself *pron.* نفسي nafsi

mysterious *a.* غامض ghaamid

mystery *n.* غموض ghomood

mystic *a.* صوفي soofiy

mystic *n.* صوفي soofiy

mysticism *n.* تصوف tasawwof

mystify *v.* يحيّر yohayyir

myth *n.* أسطورة uostoorah

mythical *a.* أسطوري uostooriy

mythological *a.* أسطوري uostooriy

mythology *n.* علم الأساطير ilmol uasaateer

N

nab *v.* يعتقل ya'taqil

nabob *n.* شخص ذو ثروة shakhson dho tharwah

nadir *n.* 1 النظير uanaddeer

nadir *n.* 2 أدنى درجة uadnaa darajah

nag *n.* متذمر motadhammir

nag *v.* يتذمر yatadhammar

nail *n.* 1 إظفر eddfar

nail *n.* 2 مسمار mismaar

nail *v.* يدق بالمسمار yadoqo bilmismaar

naive *a.* ساذج saadhaj

naivete *n.* سذاجة sadhaajah

naivety *n.* سذاجة sadhaajah

naked *a.* عار aar

name *n.* اسم esm

name *v.* يسمي yosammi

namely *adv.* أي uay

namesake *n.* مسمّى mosamma

nap *v.* يأخذ قيلولة yaukhodho qayloolah

nap *n.* قيلولة qayloolah

nap *n.* قماش أزغب qimaashon uazghab

nape *n.* مؤخر العنق mouakharol 'onoq

napkin *n.* منديل mindeel

narcissism *n.* النرجسية uannarjisiyyah

narcissus *n.* نرجس narjis

narcosis *n.* تخدير takhdeer

narcotic *n.* مخدر mokhaddir

narrate *v.* يقص yaqos

narration *n.* قص qas

narrative *n.* قصة qissah

narrative *a.* سردي sardiy

narrator *n.* راوي raawi

narrow *a.* ضيق dayyiq

narrow *v.* يضيق yadeeq

nasal *a.* أنفي uanfiy

nasal *n.* أنفي uanfiy

nascent *a.* ناشئ naashiu

nasty *a.* رديء radeeu

natal *a.* إنجابي enjaabiy

natant *a.* عائم aauim

nation *n.* دولة dawlah

national *a.* وطني wataniy

nationalism *n.* قومية qawmiyyah

nationalist *n.* قومي qawmiy

nationality *n.* قومية qawniyyah

nationalization *n.* تأميم taumeem

nationalize *v.* يأمّم youammim

native *a.* أصلي uasliy

native *n.* أصلي uasliy

nativity *n.* مولد المسيح mawlidol maseeh

natural *a.* طبيعي tabee'iy

naturalist *n.* طبيعي tabee'iy

naturalize *v.* يؤقلم youaqlim

naturally *adv.* بالطبع bittab'

nature *n.* طبيعة tabee'ah

naughty *a.* غير مطيع ghayro motee'

nausea *n.* غثيان ghathayaan

nautic(al) *a.* مثير للغثيان motheeron lilghathayaan

naval *a.* بحري bahriy

nave *n.* صحن الكنيسة sahnol kaneesah

navigable *a.* صالح للملاحة saalihon lilmilaahah

navigate *v.* يُبحِر yobhir

navigation *n.* ملاحة milaahah

navigator *n.* ملاح mallaah

navy *n.* البحرية سلاح silaahol bahriyyah

nay *adv.* لا laa

neap *a.* مدّي maddiy

near *a.* قريب qareeb

near *prep.* قرب qorb

near *adv.* على مَقْرُبَه ala maqrobah

near *v.* يَقْتَرِب من yaqtaribo min

nearly *adv.* تقريبا taqreeban

neat *a.* أنيق uaneeq

nebula *n.* سديم sadeem

necessary *n.* ضروري darooriy

necessary *adj.* ضروري darooriy

necessitate *v.* يستلزم yastalzim

necessity *n.* ضرورة daroorah

neck *n.* عنق onoq

necklace *n.* قلادة qilaadah

necklet *n.* قلادة qilaadah

necromancer *n.* مستحضرالأرواح mostahdirol uarwaah

necropolis *n.* مقبرةكبيرة maqbaraton kabeerah

nectar *n.* رحيق raheeq

need *n.* حاجة haajah

need *v.* يحتاج yahtaaj

needful *a.* احتياجي ehtiyaajiy

needle *n.* إبرة ebrah

needless *a.* غيرضروري ghayro darooriy

needs *adv.* احتياجات ehtiyaajaat

needy *a.* محتاج mohtaaj

negate *v.* يجادل yojaadil

nefarious *a.* شائن shaauin

negation *n.* نفي nafy

negative *a.* سلبي salbiy

negative *n.* سلبي salbiy

negative *v.* يجادل yojaadil

neglect *v.* يهمل yohmil

neglect *n.* إهمال ehmaal

negligence *n.* إهمال ehmaal

negligent *a.* مهمل mohmil

negligible *a.* مهمل mohmal

negotiable *a.* قابل للتفاوض qabil littafaawod

negotiate *v.* يتفاوض yatafaawad

nagotiation *n.* تفاوض tafaawod

negotiator *n.* مفاوض mofaawid

negress *n.* زنجية zonjiyyah

negro *n.* زنجي zonjiy

neigh *v.* يصهل yashol

neigh *n.* صهيل saheel

neighbour *n.* جار jaar

neighbourhood *n.* حي hai

neighbourly *a.* جواري jiwaariy

neither *conj.* ليس كلاهما laysa kilaahoma

nemesis *n.* شؤم shoum

neolithic *a.* العصر الحجري الحديث ual'asrol hajariyol hadeeth

neon *n.* نيون niyon

nephew *n.* أخ ابن ebno uakh

nepotism *n.* محاباةالأقارب mohaabbaatol uaqaarib

Neptune *n.* نبتون nibtoon

nerve *n.* 1 جرأة joruah

nerve *n.* 2 عصب asab

nerveless *a.* واهن waahin

nervous *a.* متوتّر motawattir

nescience *n.* جهل jahl

nest *n.* عش osh

nest *v.* يعشّش yo'ashshish

nether *adj.* سفلي sofliy

nestle *v.* يحتضن yahtadin

nestling *n.* فرخ farkh

net *n.* 1 شبكة shabaka

net *n.* 2 صافي saafi

net *v.* يصطاد yastaad

net *adj.* صاف saafi

net *v.* يحرزربحأصافياً yohrizo ribhan saafi

nettle *n.* كتّان kittaan

nettle *v.* يلسع yalsa'

network *n.* شبكة shabaka

neurologist *n.* خبيرالأعصاب khabeerol ua'saab

neurology *n.* علمالأعصاب ilmol ua'saab

neurosis *n.* إضطراب عصبي edtiraabon 'asabiy

neuter *a.* محايد mohaadi

neuter *n.* محايد mohaadi

neutral *a.* حيادي hiyaadiy

neutralize *v.* يحيّد yohayyid

neutron *n.* نيوترون nyootroon

never *adv.* أبدًا uabadan

nevertheless *conj.* مع ذلك ma'a dhaalik

new *a.* جديد jadeed

news *n.* أخبار uakhbaar

next *a.* التالي uattaali

next *adv.* لاحقاً laahiqan

nib *n.* منقار minqaar

nibble *v.* يقضم yaqdom

nibble *n.* قضم qadm

nice *a.* لطيف lateef

nicely *adv.* بلطف bilotf

nicety *n.* دقة diqqah

niche *n.* مشكاه mishkaah

nick *n.* شق shiq

nickel *n.* نقد قطعة qit'ato naqd

nickname *n.* كنية kinyah

nickname *v.* يكنّي yokanni

nicotine *n.* النيكوتين uannikoteen

niece *n.* أخ ابنة ebnato uakh

niggard *n.* بخيل bakheel

niggardly *a.* ببخل bibokhl

nigger *n.* زنجي zonjiy

nigh *adv.* قريب qareeb

nigh *prep.* قريب qareeb

night *n.* ليل layl

nightingale *n.* عندليب andaleeb

nightly *adv.* ليلة كل kollo laylah

nightmare *n.* كابوس kaaboos

nightie *n.* قميص نوم نسائي qameeso nawmin nisaauiy

nihilism *n.* عدمية adamiyyah

nil *n.* صفر sifr

nimble *a.* رشيق rasheeq

nimbus *n.* هالة نورانية haalaton noraaniyyah

nine *n.* تسعة tis'ah

nineteen *n.* تسعةعشر tis'ato 'ashar

nineteenth *adj.* التاسع عشر uattasi'o 'ashar

ninetieth *adj.* التسعون uattis'oon

ninth *a.* التاسعة uattaasi'ah

ninety *n.* تسعون tis'oon

nip *v.* يرتشف yartashif

nipple *n.* حلمة halamah

nitrogen *n.* نتروجين nitroojeen
no *a.* لا laa
no *adv.* ليس laysa
no *n.* رفض rafd
nobility *n.* نبل nobl
noble *a.* نبيل nabeel
noble *n.* نبيل nabeel
nobleman *n.* نبيل nabeel
nobly *adv.* بنبالة nabaalah
nobody *pron.* نكره nakirah
nocturnal *a.* ليلي layliy
nod *v.* يومئ yomiu
nod *n.* إيماءة ueemaauah
node *n.* عقدة oqdah
noise *n.* ضجيج dajeej
noisy *adj.* صاخب saakhib
nomad *n.* بدوي badawiy
nomadic *a.* بدوي badawiy
nomenclature *n.* تسمية tasmiyah
nominal *a.* اسمي esmiy
nominate *v.* يرشح yorashih
nomination *n.* ترشيح tarsheeh
nominee *n.* مرشح morashshah
non-alignment *n.* عدم الإنحياز adamol enhiyaaz
nonchalance *n.* لا مبالاة laa mobaalaah
nonchalant *a.* غير مكترث ghayro moktarith
none *pron.* لا شيء laa shayu
none *adv.* أبداً uabadan
nonentity *n.* اللاوجود uallaawojood
nonetheless *adv.* مع ذلك ma'a dhaalik
nonpareil *a.* بلا شبيه bila shabeeh

nonpareil *n.* بلا شبيه bila shabeeh
nonplus *v.* يحير yohayyir
nonsense *n.* هراء horaau
nonsensical *a.* غير عقلاني ghayro 'aqlaaniy
nook *n.* زاوية zaawiyah
noon *n.* الظهر uaddddohr
noose *n.* أنشوطة uonshootah
noose *v.* يعلّق بالأنشوطة yo'alliqo biluonshootah
nor *conj.* ولا wala
norm *n.* معيار mi'yaar
normal *a.* عادي aadiy
normalcy *n.* الحياة الطبيعية ualhayaato ttabee'iyyah
normalize *v.* يطبّع yotabbi'
normalization *n.* تطبيع tatbee'
north *n.* شمال shamaal
north *adj.* شَمالي shamaaliy
north *adv.* شَمالاً shamaalan
northerly *a.* شَمالي shamaaliy
northerly *adv.* شَمالاً shamaalan
northern *a.* شمالي shamaaliy
nose *n.* أنف uanf
nose *v.* يحشر نفسه yahshoro nafsah
nosegay *n.* باقة زهر صغيرة baaqato zahrin sagheerah
nosey *a.* فضولي fodooliy
nosy *a.* فضولي fodooliy
nostalgia *n.* حنين haneen
nostril *n.* فتحة الأنف fathatol uanf
nostrum *n.* عقار محذّ oqaaron mohabbadh
not *adv.* ليس lays
notability *n.* شهرة shohrah
notable *a.* بارز baariz

notary *n.* كاتب العدل kaatibol 'adl

notation *n.* تدوين tadween

notch *n.* حز haz

note *n.* ملاحظة molaahadda

note *v.* يلاحظ yolaahidd

noteworthy *a.* جدير بالملاحظة jadeeron bilmolaahadda

nothing *n.* لا شيء laa shayu

nothing *adv.* لا شيء laa shayu

notice *n.* إشعار esh'aar

notice *v.* ينتبه yantabih

notification *n.* إعلام e'laam

notify *v.* يخطر yokhtir

notion *n.* فكرة fikrah

notional *a.* نظري naddariy

notoriety *n.* سوء السمعة soouo ssom'ah

notorious *a.* سيء السمعة sayyiuo ssom'ah

notwithstanding *prep.* بالرَغم من ذلك birraghmi min dhaalik

notwithstanding *adv.* مَع ذلك ma'a dhaalik

notwithstanding *conj.* بالرَغم من ذلك birraghmi min dhaalik

nought *n.* صفر sifr

noun *n.* اسم esm

nourish *v.* يغذّي yoghadhdhi

nourishment *n.* تغذية taghdhiyah

novel *a.* رواية riwaayah

novel *n.* رواية riwaayah

novelette *n.* رواية قصيرة riwaayaton qaseerah

novelist *n.* روائي riwaauiy

novelty *n.* حداثة hadaathah

November *n.* تشرين الثاني tishreeno ththaani

novice *n.* مبتدئ mobtadiu

now *adv.* الآن ualuaan

now *conj.* الآن ualuaan

nowhere *adv.* لا مكان laa makaan

noxious *a.* ضار daar

nozzle *n.* فوهة fowwaha

nuance *n.* فارق بسيط faariqon baseet

nubile *a.* صالح للزواج saalihon lizzawaaj

nuclear *a.* نووي nawawiy

nucleus *n.* نواة nowah

nude *a.* عاري aari

nude *n.* عاري aari

nudity *n.* عري oriy

nudge *v.* يدفع yadfa'

nugget *n.* كتلة kotlah

nuisance *n.* إزعاج ez'aaj

null *a.* لا غ laaghi

nullification *n.* إبطال ebtaal

nullify *v.* يبطل yobtil

numb *adj.* مخدّر mokhaddir

number *n.* عدد adad

number *v.* يُرَقِّم yoraqqim

numberless *a.* غير معدود ghayro ma'dood

numeral *a.* رقمي raqamiy

numerator *n.* عداد addaad

numerical *a.* عددي adadiy

numerous *a.* عديد adeed

nun *n.* راهبة raahibah

nunnery *n.* دير dayr

nuptial *a.* عرسي orsi

nuptials *n.* زفاف zifaaf

nurse *n.* ممرض momarrid

nurse v. يرعى yar'a

nursery n. 1 مشتل mashtal

nursery n. 2 حاضنة haadinah

nurture n. رعاية ri'aayah

nurture v. يرعى yar'a

nut n. بندق bondoq

nutrition n. تغذية taghdhiyah

nutritious a. مغذ moghadhi

nutritive a. مغذ moghadhi

nuzzle v. استكان estakaan

nylon n. نايلون naayloon

nymph n. حورية hooriyyah

oak n. بلوط balloot

oar n. مجذاف mijdaaf

oarsman n. مجذّف mojaddif

oasis n. واحة waahah

oat n. قمح qamh

oath n. قسم qasam

obduracy n. عناد inaad

obdurate a. عنيد aneed

obedience n. طاعة taa'ah

obedient a. مطيع motee'

obeisance n. إكبار ekbaar

obesity n. بدانة badaanah

obey v. يطيع yotee'

obituary a. نعي na'i

object n. موضوع mawdoo'

object v. يعترض ya'tarid

objection n. اعتراض e'tiraad

objectionable a. قابل للنقض qaabilon linnaqd

objective n. هدف hadaf

objective a. مَوضوعي mawdoo'iy

oblation n. قربان qorbaan

obligation n. التزام eltizaam

obligatory a. ملزم molzim

oblige v. يلزم yolzim

oblique a. منحرف monharif

obliterate v. يطمس yatmis

obliteration n. محو mahw

oblivion n. نسيان nisyaan

oblivious a. غافل ghaafil

oblong a. مستطيل mostateel

oblong n. مستطيل mostateel

obnoxious a. ذميم dhameem

obscene a. فاحش faahish

obscenity n. فحش fahsh

obscure a. غامض ghaamid

obscure v. يخفي yokhfi

obscurity n. غموض ghomood

observance n. مراعاة moraa'aah

observant a. يقظ yaqidd

observation n. مراقبة moraaqabah

observatory n. مرصد mirsad

observe v. يرصد yarsod

obsess v. يهجس yahjis

obsession n. هاجس haajis

obsolete a. عفاعليها الزمن afaa 'alayhi zzaman

obstacle n. عقبة aqabah

obstinacy n. عناد inaad

obstinate a. عنيد aneed

obstruct v. يعرقل yo'arqil

obstruction n. عرقلة arqalah

obstructive a. معوّق mo'awwiq

obtain v. يَكتَسِب yaktasib

obtainable a. مُمْكِن الحصول عَلَيْه momkinon lhosoolo 'alayh

obtuse a. بليد baleed

obvious i واضح waadih

occasion n. مناسبة monaasabah

occasion v. يسبِّب yosabbib

occasional a. عرضي aradiy

occasionally adv. أحيانًا uahyaanan

occident n. الغرب ualgharb

occidental a. غربي gharbiy

occult a. غامض ghaamid

occupancy n. إشغال eshghaal

occupant n. محتل mohtal

occupation n. 1 عمل amal

occupation n. 2 إحتلال ehtilaal

occupier n. محتل mohtal

occupy v. يحتل yahtal

occur v. يحدث yahdoth

occurrence n. ظاهرة ddaahirah

ocean n. محيط moheet

oceanic a. محيطي moheetiy

octagon n. مثمن mothamman

octangular a. ثماني thomaaniy

octave n. ثماني thomaaniy

October n.
تشرين الأول tishreenol uawwal

octogenarian n. في الثَمانين من عُمرِه fi ththamaaneen min 'omrih

octogenarian adj. في الثَمانين من عُمرِه fi ththamaaneen min 'omrih

octroi n. واردات الضريبة waaridaato ddareebah

ocular a. بصري basariy

oculist n. طبيب العيون tabeebol 'oyoon

odd a. 1 غريب ghareeb

odd a. 2 فردي fardiy

oddity n. حب إستطلاع hobo sstitlaa'

odds n. خلاف khilaaf

ode n. قصيدة غنائية qaseedaton ghinaauiyyah

odious a. بغيض bagheed

odium n. جحد johd

odorous a. عطر atir

odour i رائحة raauihah

offence n. جريمة jareemah

offend v. يسيء yoseeu

offender i مسيء moseeu

offensive a. 1 مسيء moseeu

offensive a. 2 هجومي hojoomiY

offensive n. هجوم hojoom

offer v. يعرض ya'rid

offer n. عرض ard

offering n. هبة hibah

office n. مكتب maktab

officer n. ضابط daabit

official a. رسمي rasmiy

official n. رسمي rasmiy

officially adv. رسمياً rasmiyyan

officiate v. يتولَى مهام منصبه yatawalla mahaamma mansibih

officious a. فضولي fodooliy

offing n. عرض البحر ardol bahr

offset v. يعوض yo'awwid

offset n. عوض iwad

offshoot n. فرع fir'

offspring n. نسل nasl

oft *adv.* غالباً ghaaliban

often *adv.* غالباً ghaaliban

ogle *v.* يغمز yaghmiz

ogle *n.* غمز ghamz

oil *n.* 1 نفط nift

oil *n.* 2 زيت zayt

oil *v.* يزيّت yozayyit

oily *adj.* زيتي zaytiy

ointment *n.* مرهم mirham

old *a.* قديم qadeem

oligarchy *n.* حكومةصغيرة hokoomaton sagheerah

olive *n.* زيتون zaytoon

olympiad *n.* الأولمبياد ualuolombyaad

omega *n.* أوميغا uomigha

omelette *n.* عجّة ijjah

omen *n.* فأل faul

ominous *a.* مشؤوم mashuoom

omission *n.* 1 إغفال eghfaal

omission *n.* 2 حذف hadhf

omit *v.* يحذف yahdhif

omnipotence *n.* المقدرةالكاملة ualmaqdiratol kaamilah

omnipotent *a.* كليّالمقدرة kolliyol maqdirah

omnipresence *n.* الوجودالكلّي ualwojoodol kolliy

omnipresent *a.* كليّالوجود kolliyol wojood

omniscience *n.* المعرفةالكلية ualma'rifatol kolliyyah

omniscient *a.* كليّالمعرفة kolliyol ma'rifah

on *prep.* على ala

on *adj* قائم qaauim

on *adv* فَوقَ fawq

once *adv.* مرة marrah

one *a.* واحد waahid

one *pron.* الواحَد ualwaahid

oneness *n.* الوحدانية ualwihdaaniyyah

onerous *a.* شاق shaaq

onion *n.* بصل basal

on-looker *n.* مُتَفَرِّج motafarrij

only *a.* وَحيد waheed

only *adv.* فقط faqat

only *conj.* لكن laakin

onomatopoeia *n.* المحاكاةالصوتية ualmohaakaato ssawtiyyah

onrush *n.* تدفق tadaffoq

onset *n.* بداية bidaayah

onslaught *n.* هجوم hojoom

onus *n.* عبء ibu

onward *a.* إلىالأمام elal uamaam

onwards *adv.* فصاعداً fasaa'idan

ooze *n.* طينَيّه رَواسِب rawaasibon teeniyyah

ooze *v.* يرشح yarshah

opacity *n.* غموض ghomood

opal *n.* حَجَرعَينِالشَّمس hajaro 'ayni shshams

opaque *a.* غيرشفاف ghayro shaffaaf

open *a.* فتح fath

open *v.* يفتح yaftah

opening *n.* افتتاح eftitaah

openly *adv.* علناً alanan

opera *n.* أوبرا uobra

operate *v.* يعمل ya'mal

operation *n.* عملية amaliy

operative *a.* فعال fa"aal

operator *n.* عامل aamil

opine *v.* يرتئي yartaui

opinion *n.* رأي rauy

opium *n.* أفيون uafyoon

opponent *n.* خصم khasm

opportune *a.* مناسب monaasib

opportunism *n.* انتهازية entihaaziyyah

opportunity *n.* فرصة forsah

oppose *v.* يعارض yo'aarid

opposite *a.* معاكس mo'aakis

opposition *n.* معارضة mo'aaradah

oppress *v.* يقمع yaqma'

oppression *n.* قمع qam'

oppressive *a.* قمعي qam'iy

oppressor *n.* مضطهد modtahad

opt *v.* يختار yakhtaar

optic *a.* بصري basariy

optician *n.* خبير النظارات khabeero nnaddddaaraat

optimism *n.* تفاؤل tafaauol

optimist *n.* متفائل motafaauil

optimistic *a.* متفائل motafaauil

optimum *n.* أمثل uamthal

optimum *adj.* أمثل uamthal

option *n.* خيار khayaar

optional *a.* اختياري ekhtiyaariy

opulence *n.* ترف taraf

opulent *a.* غني ghaniy

oracle *n.* نبوءة naboouah

oracular *a.* نبوئي naboouiy

oral *a.* 1 عن طريق الفم an tareeqil fam

oral *a.* 2 شفوي shafawiy

orally *adv.* شفوياً shafawiyyan

orange *n.* برتقال bortoqaal

orange *adj.* برتقالي bortoqaaliy

oration *n.* خطاب رسمي khitaabon rasmiy

orator *n.* خطيب khateeb

oratorical *a.* خطابي khitaabiy

oratory *n.* فن الخطابة fil khitaabah

orb *n.* فلك falak

orbit *n.* مدار madaar

orchard *n.* بستان bostaan

orchestra *n.* أوركسترا uorkistra

orchestral *a.* أوركستري uorkistriy

ordeal *n.* محنة mihnah

order *n.* نظام niddaam

order *v.* ينظم yonaddddim

orderly *a.* منظم monaddddam

orderly *n.* منظم monaddddam

ordinance *n.* مرسوم marsoom

ordinarily *adv.* عادة aadah

ordinary *a.* عادي aadiy

ordnance *n.* منفجر monfajir

ore *n.* ركاز rokaaz

organ *n.* عضو odw

organic *a.* عضوي odwiy

organism *n.* كائن حي kaauinon hay

organization *n.* منظمة monaddddamah

organize *v.* ينظّم yonaddddim

orient *n.* مشرق mashriq

orient *v.* يوجَه yowajjih

oriental *a.* شرقي sharqiy

oriental *n.* شرقي sharqiy

orientate *v.* يقود yaqood

origin *n.* أصل uasl

original *a.* أصلي uasliy

original *n.* أصلي uasliy	**outburst** *n.* فورة fawrah
originality *n.* أصالة uasaalah	**outcast** *n.* منبوذ manboodh
originate *v.* ينشأ yanshau	**outcast** *adj.* منبوذ manboodh
originator *n.* منشئ manshau	**outcome** *n.* نتيجة nateejah
ornament *n.* زخرفة zakhrafah	**outcry** *a.* احتجاج ehtijaaj
ornament *v.* يزخرف yozakhrif	**outdated** *a.* قديم qadeem
ornamental *a.* زخرفي zokhrofiy	**outdo** *v.* يتغلّب yataghallab
ornamentation *n.* زخرفة zakhrafah	**outdoor** *a.* خارجاً khaarijan
orphan *n.* يتيم yateem	**outer** *a.* خارجي khaarijiy
orphan *v.* ييتم yoyattim	**outfit** *n.* لباس libaas
orphanage *n.* دار الأيتام daarol uaytaam	**outfit** *v.* يجهّز yojahhiz
orthodox *adj.* ارثوذكسي uorthoodhoksiy	**outgrow** *v.* يتخلّص من yatakhallaso min
orthodoxy *n.* أرثوذكسية uorthoodhoksiyyah	**outhouse** *n.* مبنى خارجي mabna khaarijiy
oscillate *v.* يذبذب yodhabdhib	**outing** *n.* نزهة nozhah
oscillation *n.* ذبذبة dhabdhabah	**outlandish** *a.* غير تقليدي ghayro taqleediy
ossify *v.* يتحجر yatahajjar	**outlaw** *n.* خارج عن القانون khaarijon 'anil qaanoon
ostracize *v.* يُنبذ yanbidh	
ostrich *n.* نعامة na"aanah	**outlaw** *v.* يحظر yohddir
other *a.* آخر uaakhar	**outline** *n.* الخطوط العريضة ualkhotootol 'areedah
other *pron.* آخر uaakhar	
otherwise *adv.* عدا ذلك adaa dhaalik	**outline** *v.* يبرز yabroz
	outlive *v.* ينجو yanjo
otherwise *conj.* وإلا wa ellah	**outlook** *n.* توقّع tawaqo'
otter *n.* قضاعة qaddaa'ah	**outmoded** *a.* بال baali
ottoman *n.* عثماني othmaaniy	**outnumber** *v.* يتفوق بالعدد yatafawwaqo bil'adad
ounce *n.* أوقية uwqiyyah	
our *pron.* لنا lana	**outpatient** *n.* العيادات الخارجية ual'iyaadaatol khaalijiyyah
oust *v.* يطرد yatrod	
out *adv.* خارج khaarij	**outpost** *n.* مركز نقطة noqtato markiz
out-balance *v.* يرجّح yorajjih	
outbid *v.* يتفوّق yatafawwaq	**output** *n.* إنتاج entaaj
	outrage *n.* غضب ghadab
outbreak *n.* اندلاع endilaa'	**outrage** *v.* يغضب yoghdib

outright *adv.* صريح sareeh

outright *adj.* صريح sareeh

outrun *v.* يتجاوز yatajaawaz

outset *n.* بداية didaayah

outshine *v.* يتألق yatauallaq

outside *a.* خارجي khaarijiy

outside *n.* خارج khaarij

outside *adv.* خارجاً khaarijan

outside *prep.* خارج khaarij

outsider *n.* مَنبوذ manboodh

outsize *a.* أكبرمن العادي uakbaro minal 'aadiy

outskirts *n.pl.* ضواحي dawaahi

outspoken *a.* صريح sareeh

outstanding *a.* بارِز baariz

outward *a.* خارجي khaarijiy

outward *adv.* نحو الخارج nahwal khaarij

outwards *adv.* نحو الخارج nahwal khaarij

outwardly *adv.* ظاهريا ddaahiriyyan

outweigh *v.* يفوق yafooq

outwit *v.* يتغلَب yataghallab

oval *a.* بيضوي baydawiy

oval *n.* بيضوي baydawiy

ovary *n.* مبيض mobayyed

ovation *n.* تصفيق tasfeeq

oven *n.* فرن forn

over *prep.* فوق fawq

over *adv.* فوق fawq

over *n.* ضَرْبَةفيلُعْبَةالكريكيت darbaton fi lo'batil krikit

overact *v.* يبالغبالتمثيل yobaaligho bittamtheel

overall *n.* أوفرهول uoofirhool

overall *adj.* شامل shaamil

overawe *v.* يرهب yorhib

overboard *adv.* عن متن السفينة an matni ssafeenah

overburden *v.* يثقل كاهل yothqilo kaahil

overcast *a.* معتم mo'tim

overcharge *v.* يفرط الثمن yofrito ththaman

overcharge *n.* ثمن فاحش thamanon faahish

overcoat *n.* معطف mi'taf

overcome *v.* يتغلَب yataghallab

overdo *v.* يتطرّف yatatarraf

overdose *n.* جرعةمفرطة jor'aton mofritah

overdose *v.* يفرط الجرعة yofritol jor'ah

overdraft n. افراط السحب efraato ssahb

overdraw *v.* يبالغ yobaaligh

overdue *a.* متأخَر motauakhir

overhaul *v.* يعدِّل yo'addil

overhaul *n.* تعديل شامل ta'deelon shaamil

overhear *v.* يسمع مصادفة yosma'o mosaadafah

overjoyed *n.* بسعادةغامرة bisa'aadatin ghaarirah

overlap *v.* يتداخل yatadaakhal

overlap n. تداخل tadaakhol

overleaf *adv.* على ظهر ala ddahr

overload *v.* يخرج عن حد التحمل yakhrojo 'an haddi ttahammol

overload *n.* خارج حد التحمل khaarija haddi ttahammol

overlook *v.* يغفل yaghfal

overnight *adv.* بين‌عشيةوضحاها
bayna 'ashiyyatin wa dohaaha

overnight *adj.* خلال‌الليل khilaalal
llayyl

overpower *v.* يقهر yaqhar

overrate *v.* يبالغ‌في‌التقدير
yobaaligho fi ttaqdeer

overrule *v.* ينقض yanqad

overrun *v.t* يتجاوز yatajaawaz

oversee *v.* يشرف yosharrif

overseer *n.* مشرف mosharrif

overshadow *v.* يحجب yahjob

oversight *n.* مراقبة moraaqabah

overt *a.* علني alaniy

overtake *v.* يتجاوز yatajaawaz

overthrow *v.* يقلب yaqlib

overthrow *n.* قلب qalb

overtime *adv.* إضافي edaafiy

overtime *n.* إضافي edaafiy

overture *n.* مفاتحة mofaatahah

overwhelm *v.* يسحق yashaq

overwork *v.* يرهق yorhiq

overwork *n.* إرهاق erhaaq

owe *v.t* يدين yadeen

owl *n.* بوم boom

own *a.* خاص khaas

own *v.* يملك yamlik

owner *n.* مالك maalik

ownership *n.* ملكية molkiyyah

ox *n.* ثور thawr

oxygen *n.* الأوكسجين
ualuoksoojeen

oyster *n.* محار mahaar

P

pace *n.* 1 سرعة sor'ah

pace *n.* 2 خطى khota

pace *v.* 1 يسرع yosri'

pace *v.* 2 يخطو yakhto

pacific *a.* 1 هادئ haadiu

pacific *a.* 2 سلمي silmiy

pacify *v.* يهدئ yohaddiu

pack *n.* حزمة hozmah

pack i*p* يحزم yahzim

package *n.* طرد tard

package *a.* صفقة safqah

packet *n.* حزمة hozmah

packing *n.* حزم hazm

pact *n.* اتفاق ettifaaq

pad *n.* وسادة wisaadah

pad *v.* يحشو yahsho

padding *n.* حشوة hashwah

paddle *v.* يجدَف yojaddif

paddle *n.* مجداف mijdaaf

paddy *n* أرز حقل haqlo uaroz

page *n.* صفحة safhah

page *n.* خادم‌الفُنْدُق khaadimol
fondoq

page *v.* يُرقّم‌صفحات yoraqqimo
safahaat

page *v.* يُنادي yonaadi

pageant *n.* مَوْكِب‌تاريخي
mawkibon taareekhiy

pageantry *n.* أبهة uobbahah

pagoda *n.* معبد ma'bad

pail i دلو dalw

pain *n.* ألم ualam

pain *v.* يؤلم youlim

painful *a.* مؤلم moulim

painstaking *a.* مضني madniy

paint *n.* طلاء tilaau

paint *v.* يطلي yatli

painter n. رسام rassaam

painting *n.* 1 لوحة lawhah

painting *n.* 2 رسم rasm

pair *n.* زوج zawj

pair *v.* يزاوج yozaawij

pal *n.* صديق sadeeq

palace *n.* قصر qasr

palanquin *n.* مقطورةمحمولة maqtooraton mahmoolah

palatable *a.* سائغ saauigh

palatal *a.* حنكي hanakiy

palate n. حنك hanak

palatial *a.* فخم fakhm

pale *n.* عامودالسور aamoodo ssoor

pale *adj.* شاحب shaahib

pale *v.* يشحب yashhob

palette *n.* لوح lawh

palm *n.* 1 نخيل nakheel

palm *n.* 2 كف kaf

palm *v.* يتعامل yata'aamal

palmist *n.* قارئالكف qaariuol kaf

palmistry *n.* قراءةالكف qiraauatol kaf

palpable *a.* واضح waadih

palpitate *v.* يرتجف yartajif

palpitation *n.* خفقان khafaqaan

palsy *n.* شلل shalal

paltry *a.* تافه taafih

pamper *v.* يدلل yodallil

pamphlet *n.* كتيب kotayyib

pamphleteer *n.* موزعالكتيبات mowazzi'ol kotayyibaat

panacea *n.* ترياق tiryaaq

pandemonium *n.* هرج haraj

pane *n.* جزء jozu

panegyric *n.* مديح madeeh

panel *n.* لوحة lawhah

panel *v.* يغطيبالألواح yoghatti bilualwaah

pang *n.* ألممفاجئ ualamon mofaajiu

panic *n.* ذعر dho'r

panic *v.* يذعر yadh'ar

panorama *n.* بانوراما baanooraama

pant *v.* يلهث yalhath

pant *n.* لهاث lohaath

pantaloon *n.* سروال sorwaal

pantheism *n.* وحدةالوجود wihdatol wojood

pantheist *n.* الوحديوجودي ualwihdiwojoodi

panther *n.* نمر namir

pantomime *n.* إيماء ueemau

pantry *n.* المؤن حجرة hojratol mouan

papacy *n.* بابوية baabawiyyah

papal *a.* بابوي baabawiy

paper *n.* ورقة waraqah

par *n.* قدمالمساواة qadamol mosaawaah

parable *n.* مثل mathal

parachute *n.* مظلّة moddallah

parachutist *n.* مظلي middalliy

parade *n.* موكب mawkib

parade *v.* يستعرض yasta'rid

paradise *n.* جنة jannah

paradox *n.* مفارقة mofaaraqah

paradoxical *a.* متناقض motanaaqid

paraffin *n.* البارافين ualbaaraafeen

paragon *n.* نموذج مثالي namoodhajon mithaaliy

paragraph *n.* فقرة faqarah

parallel *a.* مواز mowaazi

parallel *v.* يوازي yowaazi

parallelism *n.* تواز tawaazi

parallelogram *n.* متوازي الاضلاع motawaazil uadlaa'

paralyse *v.* يشل yashil

paralysis *n.* شلل shalal

paralytic *a.* مشلول mashlool

paramount *n.* قصوى qoswa

paramour *n.* عشيق asheeq

paraphernalia *n.* pl أدوات uadawaat

paraphrase *n.* إعادة صياغة النص e'aadato siyaaghati nnas

paraphrase *v.* يعيد صياغة النص yo'eedo siyaaghata nnas

parasite *n.* طفيلي tofayliy

parcel *n.* طرد tard

parcel *v.* يَخزم yahzim

parch *v.* يظمأ yaddmau

pardon *v.* يعفو ya'fo

pardon *n.* عفو afw

pardonable *a.* مغفور maghfoor

parent *n.* أَحَدُ الوالِدَين uahadol waalidayn

parentage *n.* نسب nasab

parental *a.* أبوي uabawiy

parenthesis *n.* قوس qaws

parish *n.* أبرشية uabrashiyyah

parity *n.* تكافؤ takaafou

park *n.* متنزه motanazzah

park *v.* يتنزّه yatanazzah

parlance *n.* لغة loghah

parley *n.* مفاوضات mofaawadaat

parley *v.* يفاوض yofaawid

parliament *n.* برلمان barlamaan

parliamentarian *n.* برلماني barlamaaniy

parliamentary *a.* برلماني barlamaaniy

parlour *n.* دار daar

parody *n.* مُحاكاة تَهَكُّمِيَه mohaakaaton tahakkomiyyah

parody *v.* يُحاكي بصورة ساخِرَه yohaaki bisooratin saakhirah

parole *n.* إطلاق سراح مشروط etlaaqo saraahin mashroot

parole *v.* يطلق سراح yotliqo saraah

parricide *n.* قتل الأب أو الأم qatlol uabi wal uom

parrot *n.* بغاء babaghaau

parry *v.* يصد yasod

parry *n.* صد sad

parson *n.* كاهن kaahin

part *n.* جزء jozu

part *v.* يبعد yobuid

partake *v.* يشارك yoshaarik

partial *a.* متحيز motahayyiz

partial *a.* جزئي jozuiy

partiality *n.* تحيز tahayyoz

participate *v.* يشارك yoshaarik

participant *n.* مشارك moshaarik

participation *n.* مشاركة moshaarakah

particle *a.* جسيم josaym

particular *a.* محدد mohaddad

particular *n.* خاصة khaassah

particularly *adv.* بالأخص biluakhas

partisan *n.* حزبية hizbiyyah

partisan *a.* نَصير naseer

partition *n.* قسم qism

partition *v.* يقسّم yoqassim

partner *n.* شريك shareek

partnership *n.* شراكة sharaakah

party *n.* حزب hizb

pass *v.* يمر yamor

pass *n.* تصريح tasreeh

passage *n.* مرور moroor

passenger *n.* راكب raakib

passion *n.* عاطفة aatifah

passionate *a.* عاطفي aatifiy

passive *a.* سلبي salbiy

passport *n.* جوازسفر jawaazo safar

past *a.* ماضي maadi

past *n.* ماضي maadi

past *prep.* عَبَر abr

paste *n.* 1 عجينة ajeenatah

paste *n.* 2 غراء ghiraau

paste *v.* يلصق yolsiq

pastel *adj.* فاتح اللون faatiho llawn

pastel *n.* باستِل baastil

pastime *n.* تسلية tasliyah

pastoral *a.* رعوي ra'awiy

pasture *n.* مرعى mar'a

pasture *v.* يرعى yar'a

pat *v.t.* يربّت yorabbit

pat *n.* تربيت tarbeet

pat *adv.* جاهز jaahiz

patch *v.* يَرقَع yoraqqi'

patch *n.* رقعَه roq'ah

patent *a.* مفتوح للمعاينة maftoohon lilmo'ayanah

patent *n.* بَراءةالإختِراع braauatol ekhtiraa'

patent *v.* يَحصَل على بَراءةالإختِراع yahsolo 'ala braauatil ekhtiraa'

paternal *a.* أبوي uabawiy

path *n.* مسار masaar

pathetic *a.* مثير للشفقة motheeron lishafaqah

pathos *n.* رثاء rithaau

patience *n.* صبر sabr

patient *a.* صبور saboor

patient *n.* مريض mareed

patricide *n.* قتل الأب qatlol uab

patrimony *n.* إرث erth

patriot *n.* وطني wataniy

patriotic *a.* وطني wataniy

partiotism *n.* وطنية wataniyyah

patrol *v.* يَقوم بدَوريَه yaqoomo bidawriyyah

patrol *n.* دورية dawriyyah

patron *n.* راعي raa'i

patronage *n.* رعاية ri'aayah

patronize *v.* ينظر بازدراء yanddoro bizdiraau

pattern *n.* نمط namat

paucity *n.* ندرة nodrah

pauper *n.* فقير faqeer

pause *n.* وقفة waqfah

pause *v.* يقف yaqif

pave *v.* يمهّد yomahhid

pavement *n.* رصيف raseef

pavilion *n.* جناح janaah

paw *n.* مخلب mikhlab

paw v. ينبش yanbish

pay v. يدفع yadfa'

pay n. أجرة uojrah

payable a. مدفوع madfoo'

payee n. مستفيد mostafeed

payment n. دفع daf'

pea n. بازيلاء baazillaau

peace n. سلام salaam

peaceable a. مسالم mosaalim

peaceful a. سلمي silmiy

peach n. خوخ khawkh

peacock n. طاووس taawoos

peahen n. untha ttaawoos

peak n. قمة qimmah

pear n. كمثرى kommathra

pearl n. لؤلؤة loulouah

peasant n. فلاح fallaah

peasantry n. فلاحين fallaaheen

pebble n. حصاة hasaah

peck n. قلق qalaq

peck v. يقلق yoqliq

peculiar a. غريب ghareeb

peculiarity n. خصوصية khosoosiyyah

pecuniary a. مالي maaliy

pedagogue n. مرب morabi

pedagogy n. علم التربية ilmo ttarbiyah

pedal n. دواسة dawwaasah

pedal v. يدوس yadoos

pedant n. متحذلق motahadhliq

pedantic n. متحذلق motahadhliq

pedantry n. حذلقة hadhlaqah

pedestal n. قاعدة التمثال qaa'idato ttimthaal

pedestrian n. مشاة moshaah

pedigree n. نسب nasab

peel v. يقشر yoqashir

peel n. قشر qishr

peep v. يزقزق yozaqziq

peep n. زقزقة zaqzaqah

peer n. نظير naddeer

peerless a. منقطع النظير monqati'o nnaddeer

peg n. وتد watad

peg v. 1 يعلّق yo'alliq

peg v. 2 يدق بالوتد yadoqqo bilwatad

pelf n. مال maal

pell-mell adv. بتهور bitahawwor

pen n. 1 قلم حبر qalamo hibr

pen n. 2 حظيره haddeerah

pen v. يكتب yaktob

penal a. جزائي jazaauiy

penalize v. يعاقب yo'aaqib

penalty n. عقوبة oqoobah

pencil n. قلم رصاص qalamo rasaas

pencil v. يكتب yaktob

pending prep. ريثما raythama

pending adj. منتظر montaddar

pendulum n. رقاص الساعة raqqaaso ssaa'ah

penetrate v. يخترق yakhtariq

penetration n. اختراق ekhtiraaq

penis n. قضيب qadeeb

penniless a. مفلس mofallis

penny n. قرش qirsh

pension n. معاش ma'aash

pension v. يحيل إلى التّقاعد yoheelo ela ttaqaa'od

pensioner n. متقاعد motaqaauid

pensive a. متأمل motauammil

pentagon *n.* مخمّس mokhammas

peon *n.* كادح kaadih

people *n.* أناس uonaas

people *v.* يُعَمِّر yo'ammir

pepper *n.* فلفل filfil

pepper *v.* يضيف الفلفل yodeefol filfil

per *prep.* لكل likol

perambulator *n.* عَرَبَةُأطُفال arabato uatfaal

perceive *v.* 1 يدرك yodrik

perceive *v.* 2 يتصوّر yatasawwar

perceptible *adj.* ملموس malmoos

per cent *adv.* في المائة fil maauah

percentage *n.* نسبةمئوية nisbaton miuawiyyah

perception *n.* إدراك edraak

perceptive *a.* مدرك modrik

perch *n.* جثم jathm

perch *v.* يجثم yajthim

perennial *a.* معمّر mo'ammir

perennial *n.* معمّر mo'ammir

perfect *a.* مثالي mithaaliy

perfect *v.* يكمّل yokammil

perfection *n.* كمال kamaal

perfidy *n.* خيانة khiyaanah

perforate *v.* يخرم yakhrom

perforce *adv.* بحكم الضرورة bihokmi ddaroorah

perform *v.* يؤدّ youaddi

performance *n.* أداء uadaau

performer *n.* مؤد mouaddi

perfume *n.* عطر otr

perfume *v.* يعطّر yo'attir

perhaps *adv.* ربما robbama

peril *n.* خطر khattar

peril *v.* يعرّض للخطر yo'arrido lilkhatar

perilous *a.* محفوف بالمخاطر mahfoofon bilmakhaatir

period *n.* فترة fatrah

periodical *n.* دورية dawriyyah

periodical *a.* دوري dawriy

periphery *n.* محيط moheet

perish *v.* يهلك yahlak

perishable *a.* معرّض للتلف mo'arradon littalaf

perjure *v.* يحنث بقسمه yahnitho biqasamih

perjury *n.* شهادةزور shahaadato zoor

permanence *n.* دوام dawaam

permanent *a.* دائم daauim

permissible *a.* جائز jaauiz

permission *n.* إذن uidhn

permit *v.* 1 يسمح yasmah

permit *v.* 2 يصرّح yosarrih

permit *n.* تصريح tasreeh

permutation *n.* تبديل tabdeel

pernicious *a.* خبيث khabaath

perpendicular *a.* عمودي amoodiy

perpendicular *n.* قائم qaauim

perpetual *a.* دائم daauim

perpetuate *v.* يديم yodeem

perplex *v.* يحيّر yohayyir

perplexity *n.* حيرة heerah

persecute *v.* يضطهد yadtahid

persecution *n.* اضطهاد edtihaad

perseverance *n.* مثابرة mothaabarah

persevere *v.* يثابر yothaabir

persist *v.* يلح yolih
persist *n.* 1 مستمر mostamir
persist *n.* 2 ملح molih
persistence *n.* إصرار esraar
persistent *a.* 1 مستمر mostamir
persistent *a.* 2 ملح molih
person *n.* شخص shakhs
personage *n.* شخصية shakhsiyyah
personal *a.* شخصي shakhsiy
personality *n.* شخصية shakhsiyyah
personification *n.* تجسيد tajseed
personify *v.* يجسّد yojassid
personnel *n.* موظفون mowaddddafoon
perspective *n.* منظور manddoor
perspiration *n.* تعرّق ta'arroq
perspire *v.* يعرق ya'raq
persuade *v.* يقنع yoqni'
persuasion *n.* إقناع eqnaa'
pertain *v.* يتعلّق yata'allaq
pertinent *a.* متعلّق mota'alliq
perturb *v.* يشوّش yoshawwish
perusal *n.* مطالعة motaala'ah
peruse *v.* يتصفّح yatasaffah
pervade *v.* يعم ya'im
perverse *a.* منحرف monharif
perversion *n.* إنحراف enhiraaf
perversity *n.* فساد fasaad
pervert *v.* منحرف monharif
pessimism *n.* تشاؤم tashaauom
pessimist *n.* متشائم motashaauim
pessimistic *a.* متشائم motashaauim
pest *n.* آفة uaafah

pesticide *n.* مبيدالحشرات mobeedol hasharaat
pestilence *n.* وباء wabaau
pet *n.* حيوانأليف hayawaanon ualeef
pet *v.* يربّت yorabbit
petal *n.* بتلة batalah
petition *n.* عريضة areedah
petition *v.* يلتمس yaltamis
petitioner *n.* ملتمس moltamis
petrol *n.* البترول ualbitrool
petroleum *n.* البترول ualbitrool
petticoat *n.* ثوبنسائي thawbon nisaauiy
petty *a.* صغير sagheer
petulance *n.* نكد nakad
petulant *a.* شكس shakis
phantom *n.* شبح shabah
pharmacy *n.* صيدلية saydaliyyah
phase *n.* مرحلة marhalah
phenomenal *a.* هائل haauil
phenomenon *n.* ظاهرة ddaahirah
phial *n.* قارورة qaaroorah
philanthropic *a.* خيري khayriy
philanthropist *n.* محسن mohsim
philanthropy *n.* إحسان ehsaan
philological *a.* متعلقبفقهاللغة mota'alliqon bifiqhil loghah
philologist *n.* عالمبفقهاللغة aalimon bifiqhi lloghah
philology *n.* علمفقهاللغة ilmo fiqhi lloghah
philosopher *n.* فيلسوف faylasoof
philosophical *a.* فلسفي falsafiy
philosophy *n.* فلسفة falsafah

phone *n.* هاتف haatif	**pickle** *n.* مخلل mokhallal
phonetic *a.* صوتي sawtiy	**pickle** *v.* يخلّل yokhallil
phonetics *n.* علم الصوتيات ilmo ssawtiyyaat	**picnic** *n.* نزهة nozhah
phosphate *n.* فوسفات fosfaat	**picnic** *v.* يتنزّه yatanazzah
phosphorus *n.* فوسفور fosfoor	**pictorial** *a.* تَصويري tasweeriy
photo *n.* صورة soorah	**picture** *n.* صورة soorah
photograph *v.* يصَوّر yosawwir	**picture** *v.* يتصوّر yatasawwar
photograph *n.* صورة soorah	**picturesque** *a.* رائع raaui'
photographer *n.* مصوَّر mosawwir	**piece** *n.* قطعة qit'ah
photographic *a.* صوري sowariy	**piece** *v.* يقطّع yoqatti'
photography *n.* تصوير tasweer	**pierce** *v.* يثقب yathqob
phrase *n.* عبارة ibaarah	**piercing** *n.* ثقب thoqb
phrase *v.* يعبّر yo'abbir	**piercing** *adj.* حاد haad
phraseology *n.* علم التعبير ilmo tta'beer	**piety** *n.* تقوى taqwa
physic *n.* علاج ilaaj	**pig** *n.* خنزير khanzeer
physic *v.* يعالج yo'aalij	**pigeon** *n.* حمامة hamaamah
physical *a.* 1 جسدي jasadiy	**pigmy** *n.* قزم qazam
physical *a.* 2 مادي maadiy	**pile** *n.* كومة kawmah
physician *n.* طبيب tabeeb	**pile** *v.* يكوّم yokawwim
physicist *n.* فيزيائي feezyaauiy	**piles** *n.* بواسير bawaaseer
physics *n.* فيزياء feezyaau	**pilfer** *v.* يَسرق أشياء زهيدَه yasriqo uashyaauan zaheedah
physiognomy *n.* علم الفراسة ilmol fraasah	**pilgrim** *n.* حاج haaj
physique *n.* بنية الجسم bonyatol jism	**pilgrimage** *n.* حج haj
pianist *n.* عازف البيانو aazifol biyaano	**pill** *n.* دواء قرص qorso dawaau
	pillar *n.* عمود amood
piano *n.* بيانو biyaano	**pillow** *n.* وسادة wisaadah
pick *v.* يختار yakhtaar	**pillow** *v.* يُوَسِّد yowassid
pick *n.* اختيار ekhtiyaar	**pilot** *n.* طيار tyyaar
picket *n.* وتد watad	**pilot** *v.* يُرشد yorshid
picket *v.* يدق بالوتد yadoqqo bilwatad	**pimple** *n.* بثرة bothrah
	pin *n.* دبوس daboos
	pin *v.* يعلّق yo'alliq
	pinch *v.* يقرص yaqros
	pinch *v.* حفنة hafnah

pine *n.* صنوبر sanawbar

pine *v.* يَشتاق yashtaaq

pineapple *n.* أناناس uananaas

pink *n.* وردي wardiy

pink *adj.* وردي wardiy

pinkish *a.* مائل ألى الوردي maauilon elal wardiy

pinnacle *n.* قمة qimmah

pioneer *n.* رائد raauid

pioneer *v.* يرئد yaruad

pious *a.* تقي taqiy

pipe *n.* 1 غليون ghalyoon

pipe *n.* 2 أنبوب uonboob

pipe *n.* 3 مِزمار mizmaar

pipe *v.* ينقل بالأنبوب yanqilo biluonboob

piquant *a.* لاذع laadhi'

piracy *n.* قرصنة qarsanah

pirate *n.* قرصان qorsaan

pirate *v.* ينشر بدون تفويض yanshoro bidooni tafweed

pistol *n.* مسدس mosaddas

piston *n.* مكبس makbas

pit *n.* حفرة hofrah

pit *v.* يحرض yoharrid

pitch *n.* 1 حِدَّه hiddah

pitch *n.* 2 زِفت zift

pitch *v.* 1 يَرمي yarmi

pitch *v.* 2 يئعَين درجةالصوت yo'ayyino darajata ssawt

pitcher *n.* 1 رامٍ raami

pitcher *n.* 2 إبريق uibreeq

piteous *a.* بائس baauis

pitfall *n.* شرك shark

pitiable *a.* حقير haqeer

pitiful *a.* هزيل hazeel

pitiless *a.* عديم الرحمة adeemo rrahmah

pitman *n.* عامل منجم aamilo manjam

pittance *n.* مبلغ زهيد mablaghon zaheed

pity *n.* شفقة shafaqah

pity *v.* يشفق yashfaq

pivot *n.* محور mihwar

pivot *v.* يدور حول محور yadooro hawla mihwar

playcard *n.* ورق اللعب waraqo lla'ib

place *n.* مكان makaan

place *v.* يضع yada'

placid *a.* هادئ haadiu

plague *a.* طاعون taa'oon

plague *v.* يُزعِج yoz'ij

plain *a.* عادي aadiy

plain *n.* سهل sahl

plaintiff *n.* مدعي modda'i

plan *n.* خطة khittah

plan *v.* يخطّط yokhattit

plane *n.* 1 طائرة taauirah

plane *v.* يتَحَرَّك بنعومَه yataharrako bino'oomah

plane *a.* مستوي mostawi

plane *n.* 2 صِنار sinnar

planet *n.* كوكب kawkab

planetary *a.* كوكبي kawkabiy

plank *n.* لوح خشب lawho khashab

plank *v.* يغطي بالألواح yoghatti bilualwaah

plant *n.* نبتة nabtah

plant *v.* يزرع yazra'

plantain *n.* الجنة موز mawzol jannah

plantation *n.* مزرعة mazra'ah

plaster *n.* جص jis

plaster *v.* يغطي بالجص yoghatti biljis

plate *n.* 1 صَفيحَة safeehah

plate *n.* 2 صحن sahn

plate *v.* يغطي بالصفائح yoghattI bissafaauih

plateau *n.* هضبة hadabah

platform *n.* منصَة minassah

platonic *a.* أفلاطوني uaflaatooniy

platoon *n.* فصيلة faseelah

play *n.* لعب la'ib

play *v.* يلعب yal'ab

player *n.* لاعب laa'ib

plea *n.* حجة hijjah

plead *v.* يرافع yoraafi'

pleader *n.* مستأنف mostaunif

pleasant *a.* لطيف lateef

pleasantry *n.* هزل hazal

please *v.* يسعد yos'id

please *adv.* من فَضلَك min fadlik

pleasure *n.* متعة mot'ah

plebiscite *n.* استفتاء estiftaau

pledge *n.* تعهد ta'ahhod

pledge *v.* يتعهّد yata'ahhad

plenty *n.* كثير katheer

plight *n.* محنة mihnah

plod *v.* يتحدّ yatahaada

plot *n.* مؤامرة mouaamarah

plot *v.* يتآمر yatauaamar

plough *n.* محراث mihraath

plough *v.* يحرث yahroth

ploughman *n.* حزات harraath

pluck *v.* ينتف yantif

pluck *n.* إقدام eqdaam

plug *n.* سدَادة saddaadah

plug *v.* يسد yasid

plum *n.* برقوق barqooq

plumber *n.* سمكري samkariy

plunder *v.* ينهب yanhab

plunder *n.* نهب nahb

plunge *v.* يسقط yasqot

plunge *n.* سقوط soqoot

plural *a.* صيغة الجمع seeghatol jam'

plurality *n.* تعدّد ta'addod

plus *a.* زائد zaauid

plus *n.* زائد zaauid

ply *v.* يستمر yastamir

ply *n.* قرطاس qirtaas

pneumonia *n.* إلتهاب رئوي eltihaabon riuawwiy

pocket *n.* جيب jayb

pocket *v.* يحفظ yahfadd

pod *n.* جراب jiraab

poem *n.* قصيدة qaseedah

poesy *n.* شاعرية shaa'iriyyah

poet *n.* شاعر shaa'ir

poetaster *n.* متشاعر motashaa'ir

poetess *n.* شاعرة shaa'irah

poetic *a.* شاعري shaa'iriy

poetics *n.* شاعرية shaa'iriyyah

poetry *n.* شعر shi'r

poignacy *n.* تأثير tautheer

poignant *a.* مؤثر mouathir

point *n.* نقطة noqtah

point *v.t.* يشير yosheer

poise *v.* يتَزن yattazin

poise *n.* اتزان ettizaan

poison *n.* سم som

poison *v.* يسم yasom

poisonous *a.* سام saam

poke *v.* ينخز yankhaz

poke *n.* نخز nakhz

polar *n.* قطبي qotbiy

pole *n.* قطب qotb

police *n.* شرطة shortah

policeman *n.* شرطي shortiy

policy *n.* سياسة siyaasah

polish *v.* يلمَع yolammi'

polish *n.* طلاءلامع tilaauon laami'

polite *a.* مؤدب mouaddab

politeness *n.* أدب uadab

politic *a.* سياسي siyaasiy

political *a.* سياسي siyaasiy

politician *n.* سياسي siyaasiy

politics *n.* سياسة siyaasah

polity *n.* تنظيم tanddeem

poll *n.* استطلاع estitlaa'

poll *v.* أصواتاً ينال yanaalo uaswaatan

pollen *n.* لقاح loqaah

pollute *v.* يلوّث yolawwith

pollution *n.* تلوّث talawwoth

polo *n.* بولو boolo

polygamous *a.* متعددالزوجات mota'addido zzawjaat

polygamy *n.* تعددالزوجات ta'addodo zzawjaat

polyglot *n.* متعدداللغات mota'addido lloghaat

polyglot *a.* متعدداللغات mota'addido lloghaat

polytechnic *a.* متعددالفنون mota'addidol fonoon

polytechnic *n.* كليةمتعددةالفنون kolliyyaton mota'addidatol fonoon

polytheism *n.* الايمانبعدةآلهة ualueemano bi'iddati uaaliha

polytheist *n.* المؤمنبعدةآلهة ualmoumino bi'iddati uaaliha

polytheistic *a.* متعددالآلهة mota'addidol uaalihah

pomp *n.* متباه motabaahi

pomposity *n.* تباه tabaahi

pompous *a.* متباه motabaahi

pond *n.* بركة birkah

ponder *v.* يتأمَل yatauammal

pony *n.* 1 حصانالبوني hisaanol booni

pony *n.* 2 ترجمةحرفية tarjamaton harfiyyah

poor *a.* فقير faqeer

pop *v.* يفرقع yofarqi'

pop *n.* فرقعة farqa'ah

pope *n.* البابا ualbaaba

poplar *n.* حور howwar

poplin *n.* قماشالببلين qimaashol bobleen

populace *n.* جماهير jamaaheeriy

popular *a.* شعبي sha'biy

popularity *n.* شعبية sha'biyyah

popularize *v.* ينشر yanshor

populate *v.* 1 يسكن yasakkin

populate *v.* 2 يعبئ yo'abbiu

population *n.* سكان sokkaan

populous *a.* مأهولبكثافة mauhoolon bikathaafah

porcelain *n.* خزف khazaf

porch *n.* شرفة shorfah

pore *n.* سم sam

pork *n.* لحم خنزير lahmo khanzeer
porridge *n.* عصيدة aseedah
port *n.* منفذ manfadh
portable *a.* محمول mahmool
portage *n.* حمل haml
portal *n.* بوابة bawwaabah
portend *v.* يتنبأ yatanabbau
porter *n.* حمّال hammaal
portfolio *n.* محفظة mihfaddah
portico *n.* رواق بأعمدة riwaaqon biua'midah
portion *n.* جزء jozu
portion *v.* يجزئ yojazziu
portrait *n.* صورة شخصية sooraton shakhsiyyah
portraiture *n.* فن التصوير fanno ttasweer
portray *v.* يوصف yoosif
portrayal *n.* تصوير tasweer
pose *v.* 1 يستعرض yasta'rid
pose *v.* 2 يشكّل yoshakkil
pose *n.* وضعيّه wad'iyyah
position *n.* موقف mawqif
position *v.* يضع yada'
positive *a.* إيجابي ueejaabiy
possess *v.* يمتلك yamtalik
possession *n.* حيازة hiyaazah
possibility *n.* إمكانية emkaaniyyah
possible *a.* ممكن momkin
post *n.* 1 بريد bareed
post *v.* يرسل yorsil
post *n.* 2 عمود amood
post *n.* 3 مهنه mihnah
post *adv.* بسرعه bisor'ah
postage *n.* رسوم البريد rosoomol bareed

postal *a.* بريدي bareediy
post-date *v.* يحدث لاحقاً yahdotho laahiqan
poster *n.* ملصق molsaq
posterity *n.* أجيال قادِمَه uajyaalon qaadimah
posthumous *a.* بعد الوفاة ba'dal wafaah
postman *n.* ساعي البريد saa'il bareed
postmaster *n.* مدير مكتب البريد modeero maktabil bareed
post-mortem *a.* تشريحي tashreehiy
post-mortem *n.* تشريح tashreeh
post-office *n.* مكتب البريد maktabol bareed
postpone *v.* يؤجّل youajjil
postponement *n.* تأجيل taujeel
postscript *n.* حاشية haashiyah
posture *n.* وضع wad'
pot *n.* وعاء wi'aau
pot *v.* يضع في الوعاء yada'o fi wi'aau
potash *n.* بوتاس bootaas
potassium *n.* بوتاسيوم bootaasyom
potato *o.* بطاطس bataatis
potency *n.* فاعليّة faa'iliyyah
potent *a.* قوي qawiy
potential *a.* محتمل mohtamal
potential *n.* إمكانية emkaaniyyah
potentiality *n.* إحتمالية ehtimaaliyyah
potter *n.* خزاف khazzaaf
pottery *n.* فخار fakhkhaar
pouch *n.* جراب joraab
poultry *n.* دواجن dawaajin

pounce *v.* يَنْقَضُّ yanqad

pounce *n.* إنْقضاض enqidaad

pound *n.* جنيه jineeh

pound *v.* يَسْحَق yashaq

pour *v.* يصب yasob

poverty *n.* فقر faqr

powder *n.* مسحوق mashooq

powder *v.* يتبرّج yatabarraj

power *n.* قوة qowwah

powerful *a.* قوي qawwiy

practicability *n.* عملية amaliyyah

practicable *a.* عملي amaliy

practical *a.* عملي amaliy

practically *adv.* عملياً amaliyyan

practice *n.* ممارسة momaarasah

practise *v.* يمارس yomaaris

practitioner *n.* متمرّس motamarris

pragmatic *a.* عملي amaliy

pragmatism *n.* البراغماتية ualbraaghraatiyyah

praise *n.* مديح madeeh

praise *v.* يمدح yamdah

praiseworthy *a.* جدير بالثناء jadeeron bithanaau

prank *n.* مزحة mazhah

prattle *v.* يثرثر yotharthir

prattle *n.* ثرثرة thartharah

pray *v.* يصلّي yosalli

prayer *n.* صلاة salaah

preach *v.* يعظ ya'idd

preacher *n.* واعظ waa'idd

preamble *n.* مقدمة moqaddimah

precaution *n.* إحتياطات ehtiyaataat

precautionary *a.* وقائي wiqaauiy

precede *v.* يسبق yasbiq

precedence *n.* أسبقية usbaqiyyah

precedent *n.* سابقة saabiqah

precept *n.* مبدأ mabdau

preceptor *n.* مؤدب mouaddab

precious *a.* ثمين thameen

precis *n.* موجز moojaz

precise *n.* دقيق daqeeq

precision *n.* دقة diqqah

precursor *n.* نذير nadheer

predecessor *n.* سلف salaf

predestination *n.* مصير maseer

predetermine *v.* سلفاً يقرّر yoqarriro salafan

predicament *n.* مأزق mauziq

predicate *n.* مسند masnad

predict *v.* يتنبأ yatanabbau

prediction *n.* تنبؤ tanabbou

predominance *n.* هيمنة haymanah

predominant *a.* مهيمن mohaymin

predominate *v.* يهيمن yohaymin

pre-eminence *n.* تفوق tafawwoq

pre-eminent *a.* بارز baariz

preface *n.* مقدمة moqaddimah

preface *v.* يكتب مقدمة yaktobo moqaddimah

prefect *n.* حاكم haakim

prefer *v.* يفضّل yofaddil

preference *n.* تفضيل tafdeel

preferential *a.* تفضيلي tafdeeliy

prefix *n.* بادئة baadiuah

prefix *v.* يضيف بادئة yodeefo baadiuah

pregnancy *n.* حمل haml

pregnant *a.* حامل haamil

prehistoric *a.* قبل‌التاريخqabla ttaareekh

prejudice *n.* تحيز tahayyoz

prelate *n.* أسقف uosqof

preliminary *a.* تمهيدي tamheediy

preliminary *n.* تمهيد tamheed

prelude *n.* تمهيد tamheed

prelude *v.* يمهّد yomahhid

premarital *a.* قبل‌الزواجqabla zzawaaj

premature *a.* لأوانه سابق saabiqon liuawaanih

premeditate *v.* يصمم yosammim

premeditation *n.* مع‌سبق‌الاصرار ma'a sabqil esraar

premier *a.* أسبق uasbaq

premier *n.* رئيس‌الوزراءraueesol wozaraau

premiere *n.* عرض‌أولardon uawwal

premium *n.* علاوة alaawah

premonition *n.* هاجس haajis

preoccupation *n.* انهماك enhimaak

preoccupy *v.* ينهمك yanhamik

preparation *n.* إعداد e'daad

preparatory *a.* تحضيري tahdeeriy

prepare *v.* يعد yo'id

preponderance *n.* رجحان rojhaan

preponderate *v.* يرجّح yorajjih

preposition *n.* جر حرف harfo jar

prerequisite *a.* شرط‌أساسي sharton uasaasiy

prerequisite *n.* شرطي shartiy

prerogative *n.* امتياز emtiyaaz

prescience *n.* علم‌الغيبeilmol ghayb

prescribe *v.* يصف yasif

prescription *n.* وصفة‌طبية wasfaton tibbiyyah

presence *n.* وجود wojood

present *a.* حالي haaliy

present *n.* 1 حاضر haadir

present *n.* 2 هدية hadiyyah

present *v.* يقدّم yoqaddim

presentation *n.* عرض ard

presently *adv.* حالياً haliyyan

preservation *n.* حفظ hifdd

preservative *n.* مادة‌حافظة maadaton haafiddah

preservative *a.* حافظ haafidd

preserve *v.* يحفظ yahfadd

preserve *n.* مَخمِيَّة yahmiyyah

preside *v.* يترأس yatarauuas

president *n.* رئيس rauees

presidential *a.* رئاسي riuaasiy

press *v.* يضغط yadghat

press *n.* صحافة sahaafah

pressure *n.* ضغط daght

pressurize *v.* يضغط yadghat

prestige *n.* هيبة haybah

prestigious *a.* مرموق marmooq

presume *v.* يفترض yaftarid

presumption *n.* إفتِراض eftiraad

presuppose *v.* يفترض yaftarid

presupposition *n.* افتراض eftiraad

pretence *n.* زَعم za'm

pretend *v.* يتظاهر yataddaahar

pretension *n.* ادعاء eddi'aau

pretentious *a.* مُهَرَج mobahraj

pretext *n.* ذريعة dharee'ah

prettiness *n.* حسن hosn

pretty *adj.* جميل jameel

pretty *adv.* جميل jameel

prevail *v.* يسود yasood

prevalence *n.* إنتِشار entishaar

prevalent *a.* سائد saauid

prevent *v.* يمنع yamna'

prevention *n.* منع man'

preventive *a.* وقائي wiqaauiy

previous *a.* سابق saabiq

prey *n.* فريسة fareesah

prey *v.* يفترس yaftaris

price *n.* سعر si'r

price *v.* يسعَر yosa"ir

prick *n.* وخزة wakhzah

prick *v.* يخز yakhiz

pride *n.* كبرياء kibriyaau

pride *v.* يفتخر yaftakhir

priest *n.* كاهن kaahin

priestess *n.* كاهنة kaahinah

priesthood *n.* كهنوت kahanoot

prima facie *adv.* لأولوهلة liuawwali wahlah

primarily *adv.* بصورةأساسية bisooratin uasaasiyyah

primary *a.* أساسي uasaasiy

prime *v.* يُعِدُّ yo'id

prime *a.* رئيسي raueesiy

prime *n.* رَيعانالشَّباب ray'aano shshabaab

primer *n.* كتابتمهيدي kitaabon tamheediy

primeval *a.* فيأولالزمان fi uawali zamaan

primitive *a.* بدائي bidaauiy

prince *n.* أمير uameer

princely *a.* أميري uameeriy

princess *n.* أميرة uameerah

principal *n.* مُديرالمَدرَسه modeerol madrasah

principal *adj.* رئيسي raueesiy

principle *n.* مبدأ mabdau

print *v.* يطبع yatba'

print *n.* طباعة tibaa'ah

printer *n.* طابعة taabi'ah

prior *a.* مسبق mosbaq

prior *n.* رئيسالدير raueeso ddayr

prioress *n.* رئيسةالدير raueesato ddayr

priority *n.* أولوية uawlawiyyah

prison *n.* سجن sijn

prisoner *n.* سجين sajeen

privacy *n.* خصوصية khosoosiyyah

private *a.* خاص khaas

privation *n.* حرمان hirmaan

privilege *n.* امتياز emtiyaaz

prize *n.* جائزة jaauizah

prize *v.* يُقَدِّر yaqaddir

probability *n.* احتمال ehtimaal

probable *a.* محتمل mohtamal

probably *adv.* ربما robbama

probation *n.* امتحان emtihaan

probationer *n.* متمرن motamarrin

probe *v.* يَسْبُر yasbor

probe *n.* مسبار misbaar

problem *n.* مشكلة moshkilah

problematic *a.* إشكالية eshkaaliyah

procedure *n.* إجراء ejraau

proceed *v.* يمضي قدماً yamdi qodoman

proceeding *n.* إجراء ejraau

proceeds *n.* عائدات aauidaat

process *n.* عملية amaliyyah

procession *n.* موكب mawkib

proclaim *v.* يعلن yo'lin

proclamation *n.* إعلان e'laan

proclivity *n.* ميل mayl

procrastinate *v.* يماطل yomaatil

procrastination *n.* مماطلة momaatalah

proctor *n.* مراقب moraaqib

proctor *v.* يراقب yoraaqib

procure *v.* يشتري yashtari

procurement *n.* مشتريات moshtarayaat

prodigal *a.* مبذر mobadhdhir

prodigality *n.* إسراف esraaf

produce *v.* ينتج yontij

produce *n.* منتج montaj

product *n.* ناتج naatij

production *n.* إنتاج entaaj

productive *a.* مثمر mothmir

productivity *n.* إنتاجية entaajiyyah

profane *a.* مدنس modannas

profane *v.* يدنس yodannis

profess *v.* يصرح yosarrih

profession *n.* مهنة mihnah

professional *a.* محترف mohtarif

professor *n.* أستاذ uostaadh

proficiency *n.* إتقان etqaan

proficient *a.* متقن motqan

profile *n.* صورة جانبيّة sooraton jaanibiyyah

profile *v.* يرسم صورة جانبيّة yarsomo sooratan jaanibiyyah

profit *n.* ربح ribh

profit *v.* يربح yorbih

profitable *a.* مربح morbih

profiteer *n.* انتهازي entihaaziy

profiteer *v.* ينتهز yantahiz

profligacy *n.* إسراف esraaf

profligate *a.* مبذر mobadhdhir

profound *a.* عميق ameeq

profundity *n.* عمق omq

profuse *a.* مسرف mosrif

profusion *n.* إسراف esraaf

progeny *n.* ذرية dhoriyyah

programme *n.* برنامج barnaamaj

programme *v.* يبرمج yobarmij

progress *n.* تقدم toqaddom

progress *v.* يتقدّم yataqaddam

progressive *a.* تقدمي taqdeem

prohibit *v.* يحظر yohddir

prohibition *n.* حظر haddr

prohibitive *a.* محظور mahddoor

prohibitory *a.* مانع maani'

project *n.* مشروع mashroo'

project *v.* يسلّط yosallit

projectile *n.* قذيفة qadheefah

projectile *adj.* مقذوف maqdhoof

projection *n.* إسقاط esqaat

projector *n.* مسلاط mislaat

proliferate *v.* يتكاثر yatakaathar

proliferation *n.* تكاثر takaathor

prolific *a.* خصب khasb

prologue *n.* مقدمة moqaddimah

prolong *v.* يطيل yoteel

prolongation *n.* إطالة etaalah

prominence *n.* بروز borooz

prominent *a.* بارز baariz

promise *n.* وعد wa'd

promise *v.* يعد ya'id

promising *a.* واعد waa'id

promissory *a.* إذني edhniy

promote *v.* 1 يعزّز yo'azziz

promote *v.* 2 يروّج yorawwij

promotion *n.* 1 تَرقيه tarqiyah

promotion *n.* 2 ترويج tarweej

prompt *a.* عاجل aajil

prompt *v.* يُحَفِز yohaffiz

prompter *n.* مُلَقِن molaqqin

prone *a.* معرّض mo'arrad

pronoun *n.* ضمير dameer

pronounce *v.* ينطق yantoq

pronunciation *n.* لفظ lafdd

proof *n.* دليل daleel

proof *adj.* حصين haseen

prop *n.* دعامَه di'aamah

prop *v.* يدعم yad'am

propaganda *n.* دعاية di'aayah

propagandist *n.* داع daa'i

propagate *v.* ينشر yanshor

propagation *n.* نشر nashr

propel *v.* يدفع yadfa'

proper *a.* مناسب monaasib

property *n.* ممتلكات momtalakaat

prophecy *n.* نبوءة naboouah

prophesy *v.* يتنبأ yatanabbau

prophet *n.* نبي nabiy

prophetic *a.* نبوي nabawiy

proportion *n.* نسبة nisbah

proportion *v.* يناسب yonaasib

proportional *adj.* متناسب motanaasib

proportionate *a.* متناسب motanaasib

proposal *n.* اقتراح eqtiraah

propose *v.* يقترح yaqtarih

proposition *n.* إقتراح eqtiraah

propound *v.* يقترح yaqtarih

proprietary *a.* ملكية molkiyyah

proprietor *n.* مالك maalik

propriety *n.* لياقة layaaqah

prorogue *v.* يرجئ yorjiu

prosaic *a.* ركيك rakeek

prose *n.* نثر nathr

prosecute *v.* يقاضي yoqaadi

prosecution *n.* مقاضاة moqaadaah

prosecutor *n.* نائبعام naauibon 'aam

prosody *n.* علمالعروض ilmol 'arood

prospect *n.* احتمال ehtimaal

prospective *a.* محتمل mohtamal

prospectus *n.* نشرةدعائية nashraton di'aauiyyah

prosper *v.* يزدهر yazdahir

prosperity *n.* ازدهار ezdihaar

prosperous *adj.* مزدهر mozdahir

prostitute *n.* عاهر aahir

prostitute *v.* يعهر ya'har

prostitution *n.* بغاء baghaau

prostrate *a.* ساجد saajid

prostrate *v.* يسجد yasjod

prostration *n.* سجود sojood

protagonist *n.* بطل batal

protect *v.* يحمي yahmi

protection *n.* حماية himaayah

protective *a.* واقي Waaqi

protector *n.* حامي haami

protein *n.* بروتين brooteen

protest *n.* احتجاج ehtijaaj

protest *v.* يحتج yahtaj

protestation *n.* احتجاج ehtijaaj

prototype *n.* نموذج أولي namoodhajon uawwaliy

proud *a.* فخور fakhoor

prove *v.* يثبت yothbit

proverb *n.* مثل mathal

proverbial *a.* مثلي mathaliy

provide *v.* يقدم yoqaddim

providence *n.* الإلهية العناية ual'inaayatol elaahiyyah

provident *a.* حكيم hakeem

providential *a.* محظوظ mahddoodd

province *n.* مقاطعة moqaata'ah

provincial *a.* إقليمي eqleemiy

provincialism *n.* سذج sodhj

provision *n.* توفير tawfeer

provisional *a.* مؤقت mouaqqat

proviso *n.* فقرة شرطية faqaraton shartiyyah

provocation *n.* إستفزاز estifzaaz

provocative *a.* استفزازي estifzaaziy

provoke *v.* يستفز yastafiz

prowess *n.* شجاعة shajaa'ah

proximate *adj.* قريب qareeb

proximity *n.* قرب qorb

proxy *n.* وكيل wakeel

prude *n.* متحشم mohtashim

prudence *n.* تعقّل ta'aqqol

prudent *a.* متعقّل mota'aqqil

prudential *a.* حيطة haytah

prune *v.* يقلّم yoqallim

pry *v.* ينقب yonaqqib

psalm *n.* مزمور mazmoor

pseudonym *n.* مستعار mosta'aar

psyche *n.* نفس nafs

psychiatrist *n.* طبيب نفساني tabeebon nafsaaniy

psychiatry *n.* طب النفس tibbo nnafs

psychic *a.* نفسي nafsiy

psychological *a.* نفسي nafsiy

psychologist *n.* عالم نفس aalimo nnafs

psychology *n.* علم النفس ilmo nnafs

psychopath *n.* مضطرب modtarib

psychosis *n.* إضطراب ed tiraab

psychotherapy *n.* علاج نفسي ilaajon nafsiy

puberty *n.* سن البلوغ sinol boloogh

public *a.* عام aam

public *n.* جمهور jomhoor

publication *n.* منشور manshoor

publicity *n.* دعاية di'aayah

publicize *v.* ينشر yanshor

publish *v.* ينشر yanshor

publisher *n.* ناشر naashir

pudding *n.* حلوى الحليب halwal haleeb

puddle *n.* بركة birkah

puddle *v.* يوحّل yowahhil

puerile *a.* صبياني sibyaaniy

puff *n.* نفخة nafkhah

puff *v.* ينفخ yanfokh

pull *v.* يسحب yashab

pull *n.* سحب sahb

pulley *n.* بكرة bakarah

pullover *n.* كنزةصوفية kanzaton soofiyyah

pulp *n.* لب lob

pulp *v.* يلبِّب yolablib

pulpit *a.* منبرالوعظ minbaro wa'dd

pulpy *a.* لُبِي lobbiy

pulsate *v.* يخفق Yakhfiq

pulsation *n.* خفقان khafaqaan

pulse *n.* نبض nabd

pulse *v.* ينبض yanbid

pump *n.* مضخة madakhkhah

pump *v.* يضخ yadokh

pumpkin *n.* يقطين yaqteen

pun *n.* تَوْرِيه tawriyah

pun *v.* يَتلاعَبُبالألفاظ yatalaa'abo biluolfaadd

punch *n.* لكمة lakmah

punch *v.* يلكم yalkom

punctual *a.* دقيق daqeeq

punctuality *n.* دقة diqqah

punctuate *v.* ينقط yonaqqit

punctuation *n.* تنقيط tanqeet

puncture *n.* ثقب thoqb

puncture *v.* يثقب yathqob

pungency *n.* لذع ladh'

pungent *a.* لاذع laadhi'

punish *v.* يعاقب yo'aaqib

punishment *n.* عقاب iqaab

punitive *a.* عقابي iqaabiy

puny *a.* سقيم saqeem

pupil *n.* تلميذ tilmeedh

puppet *n.* دمية domyah

puppy *n.* جرو jarw

purblind *n.* أعمىجزئيا ua'ma jozuiyyan

purchase *n.* شراء shiraau

purchase *v.* يشتري yashtari

pure *a* نقي naqiy

purgation *n.* طهارة tahaarah

purgative *n.* مسهل moshil

purgative *adj.* مسهل moshil

purgatory *n.* مطهر mathar

purge *v.* يطهّر yotahhir

purification *n.* تنقية tanqiyah

purify *v.* ينقّ yonaqqi

purist *n.* مصف mosaffi

puritan *n.* بروتستانتي brootostantiy

puritan *n.* متزمّت motazammit

puritanical *a.* متزمّت motazammit

purity *n.* نقاء naqaau

purple *adj./n.* بنفسجي banafsajiy

purport *n.* مضمون madmoon

purport *v.* يضمن yadman

purpose *n.* غرض gharad

purpose *v.* يعتزمحل ya'tazimo hal

purposely *adv.* عمداً amdan

purr *n.* خرخرة kharkharah

purr *v.* يخرخر yokharkhir

purse *n.* محفظة mihfadda

purse *v.* يَزِمُشَفَتَيه yazimmo shafatayh

pursuance *n.* متابعة motaaba'ah

pursue *v.* يتابع yotaabi'

pursuit *n.* مطاردة motaaradah

purview *n.* اختصاص ekhtisaas

pus *n.* صديد sadeed

push *v.* يدفع yadfa'

push *n.* دفعة daf'ah

put *v.* يضع yada'

put *n.* رمية ramyah

puzzle *n.* لغز loghz

puzzle *v.* يُربك yorbik

pygmy *n.* قزم qazam

pyorrhoea *n.* إلتهاب اللثة eltihaabo lliththah

pyramid *n.* هرم haram

pyre *n.* محرقةالجثث mahraqatol jothath

python *n.* ثعبان tho'baan

Q

quack *v.* يُبطبط yobatbit

quack *n.* دجّال dajjal

quackery *n.* دجل dajal

quadrangle *n.* ذوأربعزوايا dho uarba'i zawaaya

quadrangular *a.* رباعيالزوايا robaa'iyyo zzawaaya

quadrilateral *n.* رباعيالأضلاع robaa'iyol uadlaa'

quadrilateral *adj.* رباعيالأضلاع robaa'iyol uadlaa'

quadruped *n.* رباعيالأرجل robaauiyol uarjol

quadruple *a.* أربعةأضعاف uarba'ato uad'aaf

quadruple *v.* يضاعفأربعةمرّات yodaa'ifo uarba'ata marraat

quail *n.* سمّان sammaan

quaint *a.* جذّابلقِدَمِه jadhaabon liqidamih

quake *v.* يزلزل yozalzil

quake *n.* زلزال zilzaal

qualification *n.* مؤهّل mouahhal

qualify *v.* يؤهّل youahhil

qualitative *a.* نوعي naw'iy

quality *n.* جودة joodah

quandary *n.* مأزق mauziq

quantitative *a.* كمّي kammi

quantity *n.* كمية kammiyyah

quantum *n.* كم kam

quarrel *n.* شجار shijaar

quarrel *v.* يشاجر yoshaajir

quarrelsome *a.* خصامي khisaamiy

quarry *n.* 1 مَحجَر mahjar

quarry *n.* 2 طَريدَه tareedah

quarry *v.* يقتلعالحجارة yaqtali'ol hijaarah

quarter *n.* ربع rob'

quarter *v.* يقسمإلىأرباع yoqassimo ela 'rbaa'

quarterly *a.* فصلي fasliy

queen *n.* ملكة malikah

queer *a.* شاذ shaadh

quell *v.* يُخمِد yakhmid

quench *v.* يظمأ yarwi ddamau

query *n.* استعلام esti'laam

query *v.* يستعلم yasta'lim

quest *n.* بحث bahth

quest *v.t.* يبحث yabhath

question *n.* سؤال souaal

question *v.* يشك yashok

questionable *a.* مشكوك فيه
mashkookon feeh

questionnaire *n.* استبيان
estibyaan

queue *n.* طابور taaboor

queue *v.* يقف في طابور yaqifo fi
ttaaboor

quibble *n.* مواربة mowaarabah

quibble *v.* يوارب yowaarib

quick *a.* سريع saree'

quick *n.* منطقة حساسة mantiqaton
hassaasah

quicksand *n.* رمل متحرك ramlon
motaharrik

quicksilver *n.* زئبقي ziubaqiy

quiet *a.* هادئ haadiu

quiet *n.* سكون sokoon

quiet *v.t.* يهدئ yohaddiu

quilt *n.* لحاف lihaaf

quinine *n.* كينين keeneen

quintessence *n.* جوهر jawhar

quit *v.* يستقيل yastaqeel

quite *adv.* تماماً tamaaman

quiver *n.* ارتجاف ertijaaf

quiver *v.* يرتجف yartajif

quixotic *a.* نزق naziq

quiz *n.* إمتحان emtihaan

quiz *v.* يمتحن yamtahin

quorum *n.* نصاب قانوني nisaabon
qaanooniy

quota *n.* نصيب naseeb

quotation *n.* اقتباس eqtibaas

quote *v.* يقتبس yaqtabis

quotient *n.* حاصل haasil

R

rabbit *n.* أرنب uarnab

rabies *n.* داء الكلب daauol kalab

race *n.* سباق sibaaq

race *v.* يسابق yosaabiq

racial *a.* عرقي irqiy

racialism *n.* عرقية irqiyyah

racism *n.* عنصرية onsoriyyah

racist *adj.* عنصري onsorriy

rack *v.* يعذّب yo'adhib

rack *n.* رف raf

racket *n.* 1 جلبة jalabah

racket *n.* 2 مضرب midrab

radiance *n.* إشعاع esh'aa'

radiant *a.* مشع moshi'

radiate *v.* يشع yoshi'

radiation *n.* إشعاع esh'aa'

radical *a.* جذري jadhriy

radio *n.* مذياع midhyaa'

radio *v.* يُرسِل لاسلكياً yorsilo
laasilkiyyan

radish *n.* فجلَ fijil

radium *n.* راديوم raadium

radius *n.* نصف القطر nisfol qotr

rag *n.* خرقة khirqah

rag *v.* يضايق yodaayiq

rage *n.* غضب ghadab

rage *v.* يغضب yoghdib

raid *n.* غارة ghaarah

raid *v.* يغير yogheer

rail *n.* سكة حديدية sikkaton
hadeediyyah

rail *v.* يُسَيِّج yosayyij

railing *n.* درابزين draabzeen

raillery *n.* مزاح mozaah	**rapier** *n.* سَيفٌ مُدَبَّب sayfon modabbab
railway *n.* سكّةحديديّة sikkaton hadeediyyah	**rapport** *n.* علاقة alaaqah
rain *v.* تمطر tomtir	**rapt** *a.* مُنتَشٍ montashi
rain *n.* مطر matar	**rapture** *n.* نشوة nashwah
rainy *a.* ممطر momtir	**rare** *a.* نادر naadir
raise *v.* يرفع yarfa'	**rascal** *n.* وغد waghd
raisin *n.* زبيب zabeeb	**rash** *a.* طفحجلدي tafahon jildiy
rally *v.* يجمع yajma'	**rat** *n.* فأر faur
rally *n.* تجمع tajammo'	**rate** *v.* يُقَيِّم yoqayyim
ram *n.* كبش kabsh	**rate** *n.* معدل mo'addal
ram *v.* يَضدِمبقوة yasdimo biqowwah	**rather** *adv.* بالأحرى biluahrah
ramble *v.* يتنزّه yatanazzah	**ratify** *v.* يصدّق yosaddiq
ramble *n.* نزهة nozhah	**ratio** *n.* نسبة nisbah
rampage *v.* يثور yathoor	**ration** *n.* حصة hissah
rampage *n.* ثورة thawrah	**rational** *a.* عقلاني aqlaaniy
rampant *a.* 1 هائج haauij	**rationale** *n.* منطق mantiq
rampant *a.* 2 متفشّي motafashshi	**rationality** *n.* عقلانيّة aqlaaniyyah
rampart *n.* متراس mitraas	**rationalize** *v.* يعقل ya'qil
rancour *n.* ضغينة dagheenah	**rattle** *v.* يحشرج yohashrij
random *a.* عشوائي ashwaauiy	**rattle** *n.* حشرجة hashrajah
range *v.* يَتَراوَح yataraawah	**ravage** *n.* نهب nahb
range *n.* نطاق nitaaq	**ravage** *v.* ينهب yanhab
ranger *n.* جوّال jawwaal	**rave** *v.* يهذي yahdhi
rank *n.* مرتبة martabah	**raven** *n.* غراب ghoraab
rank *v.* يتمركز yatamarkaz	**ravine** *n.* وهد wahd
rank *adj.* مُعَفِّن mo'affin	**raw** *a.* خام khaam
ransack *v.* ينهب yanhab	**ray** *n.* شعاع sho'aa'
ransom *n.* فدية fidyah	**raze** *v.* يقشط yaqshot
ransom *v.* يَفتَديبالمال yaftadi bilmaal	**razor** *n.* شفرة shafrah
rape *n.* اغتصاب eghtisaab	**reach** *v.* يصل yasil
rape *v.* يغتصب yaghtasib	**react** *v.* يتفاعل yatafaa'al
rapid *a.* سريع saree'	**reaction** *n.* تفاعل tafaa'ol
rapidity *n.* سرعة sor'ah	**reactionary** *a.* متفاعل motafaa'il
	read *v.t.* يقرأ yaqrau

reader *n.* قارئ qaariu	**recall** *n.* تذكر tadhakkor
readily *adv.* باستعداد biesti'daad	**recede** *v.* يتراجع yataraaja'
readiness *n.* استعداد esti'daad	**receipt** *n.* فاتورة faatoorah
ready *a.* مستعد mosta'id	**receive** *v.* يستلم yastalim
real *a.* حقيقي haqeeqiy	**receiver** *n.* مستلم mostalim
realism *n.* واقعية waaqi'iyyah	**recent** *a.* مؤخر mouakhkhar
realist *n.* واقعي waaqi'iy	**recently** *adv.* مؤخراً mouakhkharan
realistic *a.* واقعي waaqi'iy	
reality *n.* واقع waaqi'	**reception** *n.* استقبال estiqbaal
realization *n.* إدراك edraak	**receptive** *a.* متقبل motaqallib
realize *v.* يدرك yodrik	**recess** *n.* عطلة otlah
really *adv.* حقاً haqqan	**recession** *n.* ركود rokood
realm *a.* مملكة mamlakah	**recipe** *n.* وصفة wasfah
ream *n.* خداع khidaa'	**recipient** *n.* مستلم mostalim
reap *v.* يجني yajni	**reciprocal** *a.* متبادل motabaadal
reaper *n.* جاني jaani	**reciprocate** *v.* يتبادل yatabaadal
rear *n.* خلفية khalfiyyah	**recital** *n.* تلاوة tilaawah
rear *v.* يُرَبّي yorabbi	**recitation** *n.* تلاوة tilaawah
reason *n.* سبب sabab	**recite** *v.* يتلو yatlo
reason *v.* يجادل yojaadil	**reckless** *a.* متهور motahawwir
reasonable *a.* معقول ma'qool	**reckon** *v.* يحسب yahsab
reassure *v.* يطمئن yatmauin	**reclaim** *v.* يستعيد yasta'eed
rebate *n.* حَسْم hasm	**reclamation** *n.* 1 استصلاح estislaah
rebel *v.* يتمرد yatamarrad	
rebel *n.* متمرد motamarrid	**reclamation** *n.* 2 استعادة esti'aadah
rebellion *n.* تمرد tamarrod	**recluse** *n.* منعزل mon'azil
rebellious *a.* متمرد motamarrid	**recognition** *n.* اعتراف e'tiraaf
rebirth *n.* تجدّد tajaddod	**recognize** *v.* يتعرّف yata'arraf
rebound *v.* يرتد yartad	**recoil** *v.* ينكص yankos
rebound *n.* ارتداد ertidaad	**recoil** *adv.* نكص naks
rebuff *n.* رفض rafd	**recollect** *v.* يتذكر yatadhakkar
rebuff *v.* يرفض yarfod	**recollection** *n.* تذكر tadhakkor
rebuke *v.* يوبّخ yowabbikh	**recommend** *v.* يوصي yoosi
rebuke *n.* توبيخ tawbeekh	**recommendation** *n.* توصية tawsiyah
recall *v.* يتذكر yatadhakkar	**recompense** *v.* يجزي yajzi

recompense *n.* جزاء jazaau

reconcile *v.* يصالح yosaalih

reconciliation *n.* مصالحة mosaalahah

record *v.* يسجّل yosajjil

record *n.* سجل sijil

recorder *n.* مسجل mosajjil

recount *v.* يسرد yasrod

recoup *v.* يعوّض yo'awwid

recourse *n.* 1 لجوء lojoou

recourse *n.* 2 خيار khayaar

recover *v.* 1 يستعيد yasta'eed

recover *v.* 2 يشفى yashfa

recovery *n.* 1 إستعادة esti'aadah

recovery *n.* 2 شفاء shifaau

recreation *n.* استجمام estijmaam

recruit *n.* توظيف tawddeef

recruit *v.* يوظّف yowaddddif

rectangle *n.* مستطيل mostateel

rectangular *a.* مستطيلي mostateeliy

rectification *n.* تصحيح tas heeh

rectify *v.* يستدرك yastadrik

rectum *n.* المستقيم ualmostaqeem

recur *v.* يتكرّر yatakarrar

recurrence *n.* تكرار tikraar

recurrent *a.* متكرّر motakarrir

red *a.* أحمر uahmar

red *n.* أحمر uahmar

redden *v.* يخجل yakhjal

reddish *a.* مائل إلى الحمرة maauilom elal homrah

redeem *v.* يخلّص yokhallis

redemption *n.* فداء fidaau

redouble *v.* يضاعف yodaa'if

redress *v.* يصلح yoslih

redress *n.* إصلاح eslaah

reduce *v.* يخفض yokhfid

reduction *n.* تخفيض takhfeed

redundance *n.* إطناب etnaab

redundant *a.* مكرّر mokarrar

reel *n.* بكرة bakarah

reel *v.* 1 يتمايل yatamaayal

reel *v.* 2 يلف yalif

refer *v.* يرجع yarji'

referee *n.* حكم hakam

reference *n.* مرجع marji'

referendum *n.* استفتاء estiftaau

refine *v.* يصقل yasqol

refinement *n.* تحسين tahseen

refinery *n.* مصفاة misfaah

reflect *v.* يعكس ya'kis

reflection *n.* انعكاس en'ikaas

reflective *a.* عاكس aakis

reflector *n.* عاكس aakis

reflex *n.* ردة فعل raddato fi'l

reflex *adj.* لاإرادي laa uiraadiy

reflexive *adj.* انعكاسي en'ikaasiy

reform *v.* يصلح yoslih

reform *n.* إصلاح eslaah

reformation *n.* إصلاح eslaah

reformatory *n.* إصلاحية eslaahiyyah

reformatory *adj.* إصلاحي eslaahiy

reformer *n.* مصلح moslih

refrain *v.* يمتنع yamtani'

refrain *n.* إمتناع emtinaa'

refresh *v.* يحدّث yohaddith

refreshment *n.* مرطبات morattibaat

refrigerate *v.* يبرّد yobarrid

refrigeration *n.* تبريد tabreed

refrigerator *n.* ثلاجة thallaajah

refuge *n.* ملجأ maljau

refugee *n.* لاجئ laajiu

refulgence *n.* لمعان lama'aan

refulgent *a.* لامع laami'

refund *v.* يرّدالمال yaroddol maal

refund *n.* إعادةالمال e'aadatol maal

refusal *n.* رفض rafd

refuse *v.* يرفض yarfod

refuse *n.* قمامة qomaamah

refutation *n.* دحض dahd

refute *v.* يدحض yadhad

regal *a.* ملكي malakiy

regard *v.* يعتبر ya'tabir

regard *n.* صدد sadad

regenerate *v.* يتجدّد yatajaddad

regeneration *n.* تجدّد tajaddod

regicide *n.* قتلالملك qatlol malik

regime *n.* نظام niddaam

regiment *n.* فوج fawj

regiment *v.* ينظّم yonaddddim

region *n.* منطقة mantiqah

regional *a.* إقليمي eqleemiy

register *n.* سجل sijil

register *v.* يسجّل yosajjil

registrar *n.* مسجّل mosajjil

registration *n.* تسجيل tasjeel

registry *n.* سجل sijil

regret *v.* يأسف yausaf

regret *n.* أسف uasaf

regular *a.* منتظم montaddim

regularity *n.* إنتظام entiddaam

regulate *v.* يضبط yadbot

regulation *n.* نظام niddaam

regulator *n.* منظم monaddim

rehabilitate *v.* يعيدتأهيل yo'eedo tauheel

rehabilitation *n.* إعادةتأهيل e'aadato tauheel

rehearsal *n.* حلقةتدريب halaqato tadreeb

rehearse *v.* يتدرّب yatadarrab

reign *v.* يحكم yahkom

reign *n.* حكم hokm

reimburse *v.* يسدّد yosaddid

reimbursement *n.* تسديد tasdeed

rein *n.* كبح kabh

rein *v.* يكبح yakbah

reinforce *v.* يعزّز yo'azziz

reinforcement *n.* تعزيز ta'zeez

reinstate *v.* يعيد yo'eed

reinstatement *n.* إعادة e'aadah

reiterate *v.* يكرّر yokarrir

reiteration *n.* تكرار tikraar

reject *v.* يرفض yarfod

rejection *n.* رفض rafd

rejoice *v.* يبتهج yabtahij

rejoin *v.* 1 يعود ya'ood

rejoin *v.* 2 يجاوب yojaawib

rejoinder *n.* جواب jawaab

rejuvenate *v.* يجدّد yojaddid

rejuvenation *n.* تجديد tajdeed

relapse *v.* ينتكس yontakis

relapse *n.* انتكاس entikaas

relate *v.* يربط yarbit

relation *n.* رابط raabit

relative *a.* نسبي nisbiy

relative *n.* قريب qareeb

relax *v.* يسترخي yastarkhi

relaxation *n.* استرخاء estirkhaau	remedy *n.* علاج ilaaj
relay *n.* تتابع tataabo'	remedy *v.* يعالج yo'aalij
relay *v.* يتتابع yatataaba'	remember *v.* يتذكّر yatadhakkar
release *v.* يطلق yotliq	remembrance *n.* تذكّر tadhakkor
release *n.* إطلاق etlaaq	remind *v.* يذكّر yodhakkir
relent *v.* يلين yaleen	reminder *n.* تذكير tadhkeer
relentless *a.* بلاهوادةbila hawaadah	reminiscence *n.* تذكّر tadhakkor
relevance *n.* علاقة alaaqah	reminiscent *a.* مذكّر modhakkir
relevant *a.* متعلّق mota'alliq	remission *n.* غفران ghofraan
reliable *a.* معتمدعليهmo'tamad 'alayh	remit *v.* 1 يقلّل yoqallil
reliance *n.* اعتماد e'timaad	remit *v.* 2 يحوّل yohawwil
relic *n.* بقايا baqaaya	remittance *n.* تحويل الأموال tahweelol uamwaal
relief *n.* 1 إغاثة eghaathah	remorse *n.* ندم nadam
relief *n.* 2 راحة raahah	remote *a.* بعيد ba'eed
relieve *v.* يخفّف yokhaffif	removable *a.* مزال mozaal
religion *n.* ديانة diyaanah	removal *n.* إزالة ezaalah
religious *a.* ديني deeniy	remove *v.* يزيل yozeel
relinquish *v.* يتنازل yatanaazal	remunerate *v.* يجازي yojaazi
relish *v.* يستمتع yastamti'	remuneration *n.* مكافأة mokaafauah
relish *n.* استمتاع estimtaa'	remunerative *a.* مجزي mojzi
reluctance *n.* تردّد taraddod	renaissance *n.* نهضة nahdah
reluctant *a.* متردّد motaraddid	render *v.* يقدّم yoqaddim
rely *v.* يعتمد ya'tamid	rendezvous *n.* موعد maw'id
remain *v.* يبقى yabqa	renew *v.* يجدّد yojaddid
remainder *n.* باقي baaqi	renewal *n.* تجديد tajdeed
remains *n.* بقايا baqaaya	renounce *v.* ينبذ yanbidh
remand *v.* يعيدُإلىالسِّجنyo'eedo ela ssijn	renovate *v.* يجدّد yajaddid
remand *n.* إعادةالحبسe'aadatol habs	renovation *n.* تجديد tajdeed
remark *n.* ملاحظة molaahaddah	renown *n.* شهرة shohrah
remark *v.* يشير yosheer	renowned *a.* مشهور mashhoor
remarkable *a.* رائع raaui'	rent *n.* إيجار ueejaar
remedial *a.* علاجي ilaajiy	rent *v.* يؤجّر youajjir
	renunciation *n.* تنازل tanaazol
	repair *v.* يصلح yoslih

repair *n.* إصلاح eslaah

repairable *a.* مستصلح mostaslah

repartee *n.* البديهة حضور hodoorol badeehah

repatriate *v.* يعود ya'ood

repatriate *n.* عائد aauid

repatriation *n.* عودة awdah

repay *v.* يسدّد yosaddid

repayment *n.* سداد sadaad

repeal *v.* يلغ yalghi

repeal *n.* إلغاء elghaau

repeat *v.* يكرّر yokarrir

repel *v.* يطرد yatrod

repellent *a.* طارد taarid

repellent *n.* طاردللحشرات taaridol hasharaat

repent *v.* يتوب yatoob

repentance *n.* توبة tawbah

repentant *a.* تائب taauib

repercussion *n.* صدى sada

repetition *n.* تكرار tikraar

replace *v.* يستبدل yastabdil

replacement *n.* بديل badeel

replenish *v.* يجدّد yojaddid

replete *a.* مفعم mof'am

replica *n.* نسخةطبق الأصل noskhaton tibqol uasl

reply *v.* يرد yarod

reply *n.* ردّ rad

eport *v.* يقدّمتقريرا yoqaddimo taqreeran

report *n.* تقرير taqreer

reporter *n.* صحافي sahaafiy

repose *n.* راحة raahah

repose *v.* يرتاح yartaah

repository *n.* مستودع mostawda'

represent *v.* يمثّل yomaththil

representation *n.* تمثيل tamtheel

representative *n.* ممثل momathil

representative *a.* ممثل momathil

repress *v.* يقمع yaqma'

repression *n.* قمع qam'

reprimand *n.* تأنيب tauneeb

reprimand *v.* يؤنّب youannib

reprint *v.* يطبع yatba'

reprint *n.* طبع tab'

reproach *v.* يعاتب yo'aatib

reproach *n.* عتاب itaab

reproduce *v.* 1 ينجب yonjib

reproduce *v.* 2 ينسخ yansakh

reproduction *n.* 1 انجاب enjaab

reproduction *n.* 2 انتاج entaaj

reproductive *a.* إنجابي enjaabiy

reproof *n.* تأنيب tauneeb

reptile *n.* زاحف zaahif

republic *n.* جمهورية jomhooriyyah

republican *a.* جمهوري jomhooriy

republican *n.* جمهوري jomhooriy

repudiate *v.* يرفض yarfod

repudiation *n.* رفض rafd

repugnance *n.* اشمئزاز eshmiuzaaz

repugnant *a.* بغيض bagheed

repulse *v.* يصد yasod

repulse *n.* صد sad

repulsion *n.* تنافر tanaafor

repulsive *a.* منفّر monaffir

reputation *n.* سمعة som'ah

repute *v.* يفترض yaftarid	**resistant** *a.* مقاوم moqaawim
repute *n.* سمعة som'ah	**resolute** *a.* حازم haazim
request *v.* يطلب yatlob	**resolution** *n.* قرار qaraar
request *n.* طلب talab	**resolve** *v.* يحل yahol
requiem *n.* صلاةلراحةالميت salaaton liraahatil mayyit	**resonance** *n.* صدى sada
require *v.* يتطلب yatatallab	**resonant** *a.* رنّان rannan
requirement *n.* مطلب matlab	**resort** *v.* يلجأ إلى yaljauo ela
requisite *a.* مُتَطَلَّب motatallab	**resort** *n.* منتجع montaja'
requisite *n.* شرط shart	**resound** *v.* يضج yadoj
requisition *n.* رسالةطلب risaalato talab	**resource** *n.* مورد mawrid
requisition *v.* يُطَالِب yotaalib	**resourceful** *a.* داهية daahiyah
requite *v.* يجازي yojaazi	**respect** *v.* يحترم yahtarim
rescue *v.* ينقذ yonqidh	**respect** *n.* احترام ehtiraam
rescue *n.* إنقاذ enqaadh	**respectful** *a.* محترم mohtaram
research *v.* يبحث yabhath	**respective** *a.* مختص mokhtas
research *n.* بحث bahth	**respiration** *n.* تنفس tanaffos
resemblance *n.* تشابه tashaaboh	**respire** *v.* يتنفَّس yatanaffas
resemble *v.* يشابه yoshaabih	**resplendent** *a.* متألق motaualliq
resent *v.* يستاء yastaau	**respond** *v.* يرد yarod
resentment *n.* استياء estiyaau	**respondent** *n.* مدعىعليه modda'a 'alayh
reservation *n.* حجز hajz	**response** *n.* استجابة estijaabah
reserve *v.* يحجز yahjiz	**responsibility** *n.* مسؤولية masuooliyyah
reservoir *n.* خَزَّان khazzaan	**responsible** *a.* مسؤول masuool
reside *v.* يقيم yoqeem	**rest** *v.* يرتاح yartaah
residence *n.* إقامة eqaamah	**rest** *n.* بقية baqiyyah
resident *a.* مقيم moqeem	**restaurant** *n.* مطعم mat'am
resident *n.* مقيم moqeem	**restive** *a.* مضطرب modtarrib
residual *a.* متبقّي motabaqqi	**restoration** *n.* 1 استصلاح estislaah
residue *n.* بقايا baqaaya	**restoration** *n.* 2 استعادة esti'aadah
resign *v.* يستقيل yastaqeel	**restore** *v.* 1 يستصلح yastaslih
resignation *n.* استقالة estiqaalah	**restore** *v.* 2 يستعيد yasta'eed
resist *v.* يقاوم yoqaawim	**restrain** *v.* يكبح yakbah
resistance *n.* مقاومة moqaawamah	**restrict** *v.* يقيّد yoqayyid
	restriction *n.* تقييد taqyeed

restrictive *a.* مقيّد moqayyid

result *v.* ينتج yantoj

result *n.* نتيجة nateejah

resume *v.* يستأنف yastaunif

resume *n.* سيرة ذاتية seeraton dhaatiyyah

resumption *n.* استئناف estiunaaf

resurgence *n.* تَجْديد tajdeed

resurgent *a.* متجدّد motajaddid

retail *v.* يبيعبالمُفَرَق yabee'o bilmofarraq

retail *n.* بَيْعبالمُفَرَق bay'on bilmofarraq

retail *adv.* بِسِعْرالمُفَرَق bisi'ril mofarraq

retail *adj.* بِسِعْرالمُفَرَق bisi'ril mofarraq

retailer *n.* تاجِرالمُفَرَق taajirol mofarraq

retain *v.* يتحفّظ yatahaffadd

retaliate *v.* ينتقم yantaqim

retaliation *n.* انتقام entiqaam

retard *v.* يتخلّف yatakhallaf

retardation *n.* تخلف takhallof

retention *n.* إحْتِجاز ehtijaaz

retentive *a.* مُحْتَجِز mohtajiz

reticence *n.* تحفّظ tahaffodd

reticent *a.* متحفّظ motahaffidd

retina *n.* شبكيةالعين shabakatol 'ayn

retinue *n.* حاشيةالملك haashiyatol malik

retire *v.* يتقاعد yataqaa'ad

retirement *n.* تقاعد taqaa'od

retort *v.* يحسم yahsim

retort *n.* رادّحاسم radon haasim

retouch *v.* ينمّق yonammiq

retrace *v.* يعودعلىعقبيه aada 'ala 'oqbayh

retread *v.* يغيّرسطحالإطار yoghayyiro sathal etaar

retread *n.* تغيير سطح الاطار taghyeero sathil etaar

retreat *v.* يتراجع yataraaja'

retrench *v.* يلغي yalghi

retrenchment *n.* تخفيض takhfeed

retrieve *v.* يسترد yastarrid

retrospect *n.* أثر رجعي uatharon raj'iy

retrospection *n.* تأثررجعي tautheeron raj'iy

retrospective *a.* بأثررجعي biuatharin raj'iy

return *v.* يعود ya'ood

return *n.* عودة awdah

revel *v.* يستمتع yastamti'

revel *n.* استمتاع estimtaa'

revelation *n.* وحي wahy

reveller *n.* محتفل mohtafil

revelry *n.* احتفال ehtifaal

revenge *v.* ينتقم yantaqim

revenge *n.* انتقام entiqaam

revengeful *a.* حقود haqood

revenue *n.* دخل dakhl

revere *v.* يبجّل yobajjil

reverence *n.* تبجيل tabjeel

reverend *a.* موقر mowaqqar

reverent *a.* مُبَجّل mobajjil

reverential *a.* تبجيلي tabjeeliy

reverie *n.* فكرةخيالية fikraton

khayaaliyyah

reversal *n.* انعكاس en'ikaas
reverse *a.* عكسي aksiy
reverse *n.* عكس aks
reverse *v.* يعكس ya'kis
reversible *a.* معكوس ma'koos
revert *v.* يعيد yo'eed
review *v.* يستعرض yasta'rid
review *n.* استعراض esti'raad
revise *v.* 1 يراجع yoraaji'
revise *v.* 2 ينقّح yonaqqih
revision *n.* 1 مراجعة moraaja'ah
revision *n.* 2 تنقيح tanqeeh
revival *n.* إحياء ehyaau
revive *v.* يحي yohyi
revocable *a.* لاغي laaghi
revocation *n.* إلغاء elghaau
revoke *v.* يُبطل yobtil
revolt *v.* يتمرّد yatamarrad
revolt *n.* تمرد tamarrod
revolution *n.* ثورة thawrah
revolutionary *a.* ثوري thawriy
revolutionary *n.* ثوري thawriy
revolve *v.* يدور yadoor
revolver *n.* مسدس mosaddas
reward *n.* مكافأة mokaafauah
reward *v.* يكافئ yokaafiu
rhetoric *n.* بلاغة balaaghah
rhetorical *a.* بلاغي balaaghiy
rheumatic *a.* روماتيزمي romatizmiy
rheumatism *n.* روماتيزم romatizm
rhinoceros *n.* وحيدالقرن waheedol qarn
rhyme *n.* قافية qaafiyah
rhyme *v.* يَتَقَفّى yataqaffa

rhymester *n.* شاعردييء shaa'iron radeeu
rhythm *b.* إيقاع ueeqaa'
rhythmic *adj.* إيقاعي ueeqaa'iy
rib *n.* ضلع dil'
ribbon *n.* وشاح wishaah
rice *n.* أرز uaroz
rich *a.* غني ghanniy
riches *n.* غنى ghina
richness *a.* غنى ghina
rick *n.* إلتواء eltiwaau
rickets *n.* كساح kosaah
rickety *a.* متداع motadaa'i
rickshaw *n.* مَرْكَبَةٌبِعَجَلَتَين markabaton bi'ajalatayn
rid *v.* يتخلّص yatakhallas
riddle *n.* احجية uohjiyah
riddle *v.* يحيّر yohayyir
ride *v.* يركب yarkab
ride *n.* ركوب rokoob
rider *n.* راكب raakib
ridge *n.* جبل قمة qimmato jabal
ridicule *v.* يسخر yaskhar
ridicule *n.* سخرية sokhriyah
ridiculous *a.* سخيف sakheef
rifle *v.* يُفَتِش yofattish
rifle *n.* بندقية bondoqiyyah
rift *n.* صدع sada'
right *a.* يَمين yameen
right *adv* تماما tamaaman
right *n.* حق haq
right *v.* يُصَحِح yosahhih
righteous *a.* صالح saalih
rigid *a.* جامد jaamid
rigorous *a.* صارم saarim
rigour *n.* صرامة saraamah

rim *n.* حافة haafah

ring *n.* خاتم khaatam

ring *v.* يَقْرَع yaqra'

ringlet *n.* حليقة holayqah

ringworm *n.* القوباءالحلقية ualqawbaauol halaqiyyah

rinse *v.* يشطف yashtif

riot *n.* شغب shaghab

riot *v.* يشاغب yoshaaghib

rip *v.* يمزّق yomazziq

ripe *adj.* ناضج naadij

ripen *v.* ينضج yandoj

ripple *n.* تموج tamawwoj

ripple *v.* يتموّج yatamawwaj

rise *v.* يرتفع yartafi'

rise *n.* ارتفاع ertifaa'

risk *v.* يخاطر yokhaatir

risk *n.* خطر khatar

risky *a.* محفوف بالمخاطر mahfoofon bilmakhaatir

rite *n.* طقس taqs

ritual *n.* طقس taqs

ritual *a.* طقسي taqsiy

rival *n.* منافس monaafis

rival *v.* ينافس yonaafis

rivalry *n.* تنافس tanaafos

river *n.* نهر nahr

rivet *n.* برشام birshaam

rivet *v.* يُبَرشِم yobarshim

rivulet *n.* غدير ghadeer

road *n.* طريق tareeq

roam *v.* يتجوّل yatajawwal

roar *n.* هدير hadeer

roar *v.* يهدر yahdir

roast *v.* يشو yashwi

roast *adj.* مشوي mashwi

roast *n.* شواء shiwaau

rob *v.* يسلب yaslib

robber *n.* لص lis

robbery *n.* سرقة sariqah

robe *n.* رداء ridaau

robe *v.* يرتدي عَباءَه yartadi 'abaauah

robot *n.* رجل آلي rajolon uaaliy

robust *a.* قوي qawiy

rock *v.* يَهُز yahiz

rock *n.* صخرة sakhrah

rocket *n.* صاروخ saarookh

rod *n.* قضيب qadeeb

rodent *n.* قارض qaarid

roe *n.* يحمور yahmoor

rogue *n.* وَغد waghd

roguery *n.* احتيال ehtiyaal

roguish *a.* غيرشريف ghayro shareef

role *n.* دور dawr

roll *n.* لفة laffah

roll *v.* يدحرج yodahrij

roll-call *n.* تَفَقُّدالحضور tafaqqodol hodoor

roller *n.* بكرة bakarah

romance *n.* قصةحب qissato hob

romantic *a.* رومانسي romaansiy

romp *v.* يَلعَب بِصَخَب yal'abo bisakhab

romp *n.* لَعِب صاخِب la'ibon saakhib

rood *n.* صليب saleeb

roof *n.* سقف saqf

roof *v.* يغَطّي بِسَقْف yoghatti bisaqf

rook *n.* 1 مخادع mokhaadi'

rook *n.* 2 غُراب القَيظ ghoraabol qaydd

rook *v.* يغش yaghish	**row** *n.* 1 صف saf
room *n.* غرفة ghorfah	**row** *v.* 1 يصفف yosaffif
roomy *a.* فسيح faseeh	**row** *n.* 2 نيئ nayyiu
roost *n.* مَجثَم majtham	**row** *v.* 2 يُجذِّف yojaddif
roost *v.* يَجثُم yajthim	**row** *n.* 3 خصام khisaam
root *n.* جذر jidhr	**rowdy** *a.* مشاكس moshaakis
root *v.* يَتأصّل yatauassal	**royal** *a.* 1 ملكي malakiy
rope *n.* حبل habl	**royal** *a.* 2 مخلص mokhlis
rope *v.* يَربط yarbit	**royalist** *n.* 1 ملكي malakiy
rosary *n.* مسبحة masbahah	**royalist** *n.* 2 مخلص mokhlis
rose *n.* وردة wardah	**royalty** *n.* 1 ملكية malakiyyah
roseate *a.* وردي wardiy	**royalty** *n.* 2 إخلاص ekhlaas
rostrum *n.* منبر minbar	**rub** *v.* يدعك yad'ak
rosy *a.* وردي wardiy	**rubber** *n.* مطاط mattaat
rot *n.* عفن afan	**rubbish** *n.* قمامة qomaamah
rot *v.* يتعفّن yata'affan	**rubble** *n.* أنقاض uanqaad
rotary *a.* دوار dawwaar	**ruby** *n.* ياقوت yaaqoot
rotate *v.* يتناوب yatanaawab	**rude** *a.* فظ fadd
rotation *n.* تناوب tanaawob	**rudiment** *n.* أوَّلي uawwaliy
rote *n.* روتين rooteen	**rudimentary** *a.* بدائي bidaauiy
rouble *n.* روبل roobil	**rue** *v.* يندم yandam
rough *a.* عنيف aneef	**rueful** *a.* محزن mohzin
round *a.* دائري daauiriy	**ruffian** *n.* خسيس khasees
round *adv.* حول hawl	**ruffle** *n.* يناصيب yanaaseeb
round *n.* جولة jawlah	**ruffle** *v.* يُكَدِّر yokaddir
round *v.* يَدورُحَوّلَ yadooro hawl	**rug** *n.* سجادة sijjaadah
rouse *v.* يحرّض yoharrid	**rugged** *a.* وعر wa'r
rout *v.* يهزم yahzim	**ruin** *n.* خراب kharaab
rout *n.* هزيمة hazeemah	**ruin** *v.* يخرّب yoKharrib
route *n.* مسار masaar	**rule** *n.* حكم hokm
routine *n.* روتين rooteen	**rule** *v.* يحكم yahkom
routine *adj.* روتيني rooteeniy	**ruler** *n.* حاكم haakim
rove *v.* يطوف yatoof	**ruling** *n.* حكم hikm
rover *n.* 1 رحّالة rahhaalah	**rum** *n.* الروم uarrom
rover *n.* 2 قرصان qorsaan	**rum** *adj.* غريب ghareeb

rumble *v.* يَدَوِّي yodawwi	**rut** *n.* أُخدود uokhdood
rumble *n.* دَوِي dawiy	**ruthless** *a.* قاس qaasi
ruminant *a.* مجتر mojtar	**rye** *n.* جاودار jaawdaar
ruminant *n.* مجتر mojtar	
ruminate *v.* يجتر yajtar	
rumination *n.* اجترار ejtiraar	
rummage *v.* يبعثر yoba'thir	

S

rummage *n.* بعثرة ba'tharah	
rummy *n.* سكير sakeer	
rumour *n.* إشاعة eshaa'ah	**sabbath** *n.* السبت uassabt
rumour *v.* يشيع yoshee'	**sabotage** *n.* تخريب takhreeb
run *v.* 1 يدير yodeer	**sabotage** *v.* يخرب yokharrib
run *n.* 1 شَوط shawt	**sabre** *n.* سيف المبارزة sayfol mobaarazah
run *v.* 2 يركض yarkod	**sabre** *v.* يجرح بالسيف yajraho bissayf
run *n.* 2 ركض rakd	**saccharin** *n.* سكرين sokkareen
rung *n.* درجة darajah	**saccharine** *a.* سكري sokkariy
runner *n.* عداء addaau	**sack** *n.* كيس kees
rupee *n.* روبية roobyah	**sack** *v.* يطرد yatrid
rupture *n.* تمزّق tamazzoq	**sacrament** *n.* سر مقدّس sirron moqaddas
rupture *v.* يمزّق yomazziq	**sacred** *a.* مقدس moqaddas
rural *a.* ريفي reefiy	**sacrifice** *n.* تضحية tad hiyah
ruse *n.* حيلة heelah	**sacrifice** *v.* يضحّي yodahhi
rush *n.* 1 اندفاع endifaa'	**sacrificial** *a.* ذبيحة dhabeehah
rush *v.* 1 يندفع yandafi'	**sacrilege** *n.* تدنيس tadnees
rush *n.* 2 حشائش hashaauish	**sacrilegious** *a.* مدنّس modannis
rust *n.* صدأ sadau	**sacrosanct** *a.* مقدّس moqaddas
rust *v.* يصدأ yasdau	**sad** *a.* حزين hazeen
rustic *a.* ريفي reefiy	**sadden** *v.* يحزن yahzan
rustic *n.* قَروي qarawiy	**saddle** *n.* سرج sarj
rusticate *v.* يعيش في الريف ya'eesho fi rreef	**saddle** *v.* يسرّج yosarrij
rustication *n.* تريف tarayyof	**sadism** *n.* سادية saadiyyah
rusticity *n.* سذاجة sadhaajah	**sadist** *n.* سادي saadiy
rusty *a.* صدئ sadiu	**safe** *a.* آمن uaamin
rut *adj.* شبق shabiq	

safe *n.* خزنة khaznah	salvage *n.* إنقاذ enqaadh
safeguard *n.* حماية himaayah	salvage *v.* ينقذ yonqidh
safeguard *v.* يحرس yahros	salvation *n.* خلاص khalaas
safety *n.* سلامة salaamah	same *a.* نفس nafs
saffron *n.* زعفران za'faraan	sample *n.* عيّنة ayyinah
saffron *adj.* زعفراني za'faraaniy	sample *v.* يأخذعيّنة yaukhodho 'ayyinah
sagacious *a.* فطن fatin	sanatorium *n.* مصحة masahhah
sagacity *n.* حصافة hafaasah	sanctification *n.* تقديس taqdees
sage *n.* مريمية miryamiyyah	sanctify *v.* يقدّس yoqaddis
sage *a.* حكيم hakeem	sanction *n.* جزاء jazaau
sail *n.* شراع shiraa'	sanction *v.* يجاز yojaazi
sail *v.* يبحر yobhir	sanctity *n.* قداسة qadaasah
sailor *n.* بحّار bahhaar	sanctuary *n.* ملاذ malaadh
saint *n.* قدّيس qiddees	sand *n.* رمل raml
saintly *a.* طاهر taahir	sandal *n.* صندل sandal
sake *n.* أجل jl	sandalwood *n.* خشب الصندل khashabo ssandal
salable *a.* رائج raauij	sandwich *n.* شطيرة shateerah
salad *n.* سلطة salatah	sandwich *v.* يحشر yahshor
salary *n.* راتب raatib	sandy *a.* رملي ramliy
sale *n.* يبيع yabee'	sane *a.* عاقل aaqil
salesman *n.* بائع baaui'	sanguine *a.* متفائل motafaauil
salient *a.* بارز baariz	sanitary *a.* صحّي sihhiy
saline *a.* ملحي milhiy	sanity *n.* عقلانية aqlaaniyyah
salinity *n.* ملوحة moloohah	sap *n.* 1 عُصارة osaarah
saliva *n.* لعاب lo'aab	sap *v.* 1 يُنهِك yonhik
sally *n.* تهجّم tahajjom	sap *n.* 2 خندق khandaq
sally *v.* يتهجّم yatahajjam	sap *v.* 2 يحفرخندقا yahfiro khandaqan
saloon *n.* صالون saaloon	sapling *n.* شجيرة shojayrah
salt *n.* ملح milh	sapphire *n.* ياقوت أزرق yaaqooton uzraq
salt *v.* يملّح yomallih	
salty *a.* مالح maalih	sarcasm *n.* سخرية sokhriyah
salutary *a.* مفيد mofeed	sarcastic *a.* ساخر saakhir
salutation *n.* تحية tahiyyah	sardonic *a.* تهكمي tahakkomiy
salute *v.* يحيّي yohayyi	
salute *n.* تحية tahiyyah	

satan *n.* إبليس eblees

satanic *adj.* شيطاني shaitaaniy

satanically *adv.* بشيطانية bishaitaaniyyah

satchel *n.* حقيبةمدرسية haqeebah madrasiyyah

satellite *n.* قمرصناعي qamaron sinaa'iy

satiable *a.* مشبع moshabba'

satiate *v.* يشبع yoshabbi'

satiety *n.* تخمة tokhmah

satin *n.* حرير hareer

satin *adj.* حريري hareeriy

satire *n.* سخرية sokhriyah

satirical *a.* ساخر saakhir

satirist *n.* هاجي haajiu

satirize *v.* يهجو yahjo

satisfaction *n.* رضا rida

satisfactory *a.* مرض marad

satisfy *v.* يرض yordi

saturate *v.* يتشبّع yatashabba'

saturation *n.* تشبّع tashabbo'

Saturday *n.* السبت uassabt

sauce *n.* صلصة salsah

saucer *n.* صحن sahn

saunter *v.* يَمْشيالهُوَينا yamshil howayna

savage *a.* متوحش motawahhish

savage *n.* متوحش motawahhish

savagery *n.* وحشية wahshiy

save *v.* 1 يحفظ yahfadd

save *v.* 2 ينقذ yonqidh

save *prep.* عدا ما maa 'ada

saviour *n.* منقذ monqidh

savour *n.* 1 لذة ladhdhah

savour *v.* 1 يتلذّذ yataladhdhadh

savour *n.* 2 ذوق dhawq

savour *v.* 2 يتذوّق yatadhawwaq

savour *v.* 3 يفوح yafooh

saw *n.* 1 منشار minshaar

saw *v.* 1 ينشر yanshor

saw *n.* 2 مثل mathal

say *v.* 1 يقول yaqool

say *n.* 1 فرصة forsah

say *v.* 2 يفترض yaftarid

say *n.* 2 حق haq

say *adv.* مثلاً mathalan

scabbard *n.* قراب qiraab

scabies *n.* جرب jarab

scaffold *n.* سقالة saqqaalah

scale *n.* 1 جدول jadwal

scale *v.* 1 يقيس yaqees

scale *n.* 2 مستوى mostawa

scale *v.* 2 يتدرّج yatadarraj

scale *n.* 3 حرشف harshaf

scale *v.* 3 يقشر yaqshor

scalp *n.* فروةالرأس farwato rraus

scamper *v.* يعدو ya'do

scamper *n.* عدو adw

scan *v.* يتفحّص yatafahhas

scan *n.* فحص fahs

scandal *n.* فضيحة fadeehah

scandalize *v.* يغيظ yogheedd

scant *a.* ضئيل daueel

scanty *a.* ضئيل daueel

scapegoat *n.* كبشفداء kabsho fidaau

scar *n.* ندب nodb

scar *v.* يشوّه yoshawwih

scarce *a.* نادر naadir

scarcely *adv.* نادراً nadiran

scarcity n. ندر nodr

scare n. فزع faza'

scare v. يفزع yofzi'

scarf n. وشاح wishaah

scatter v. يبعثر yobauthir

scavenger n. زبال zabbaal

scene n. مشهد mashhad

scenery n. منظر manddar

scenic a. مشهدي mashhadiy

scent n. رائحة raauihah

scent v. 1 يعطّر yo'attir

scent v. 2 يتقفّى أثر yataqaffa uathar

sceptic n. شكّاك shakkaak

sceptical a. مشكّك moshakkik

scepticism n. شك shak

sceptre n. صولجان sawlajaan

schedule n. جدول jadwal

schedule v. يجدول yojadwil

scheme n. مخطط mokhattat

scheme v. يخطّط yokhattit

schism n. شقاق shiqaaq

scholar n. باحث baahith

scholarly a. متعلّم mota'allim

scholarship n. 1 منحة دراسية minhaton draasiyyah

scholarship n. 2 تحصيل علمي tahseelon 'ilmiy

scholastic a. دراسي draasiy

school n. مدرسة madrasah

science n. علم ilm

scientific a. علمي ilmiy

scientist n. عالم alim

scintillate v. يتألّق yatauallaq

scintillation n. تألّق taualloq

scissors n. مقص miqas

scoff n. هزأ haziua

scoff v. يهزأ yahzau

scold v. يؤنّب youannib

scooter n. سكوتر skootir

scope n. مدى mada

scorch v. يشيط yasheet

scorch n. شيط sheet

score n. علامة alaamah

score v. يسجّل yosajjil

scorer n. هداف haddaaf

scorn n. احتقار ehtiqaar

scorn v. يحتقر yahtaqir

scorpion n. عقرب aqrab

Scot n. 1 اسكتلاندي eskotlaandi

scot n. 2 ضريبة dareebah

scotch a. اسكتلاندي eskotlaandi

scotch n. إسفين esfeen

scot-free a. بلا ضريبة bila dareebah

scoundrel n. وغد waghd

scourge n. عذاب adhaab

scourge v. يعذّب yo'adhdhib

scourge n. سوط sawt

scourge v. يجلد yajlid

scout n. كشاف kashshaaf

scout v. يستكشف yastakshif

scowl v. يعبس ya'bis

scowl n. عبوس oboos

scramble v. يخفق yakhfiq

scramble n. إندفاع endifaa'

scrap n. خردة khordah

scratch n. خدش khadsh

scratch v. يخدش yakhdish

scrawl v. يخربش yokharbish

scrawl n. خربشة kharbashah

scream v. يصرخ yasrokh

scream n. صرخة sarkhah

screen *n.* شاشة shaashah	**seat** *v.* يقعد yoq'id
screen *v.* يعرض ya'rid	**secede** *v.* ينفصل yanfasil
screw *n.* برغي borghi	**secession** *n.* انفصال enfisaal
screw *v.* يلف yalif	**secessionist** *n.* انفصالي enfisaaliy
scribble *v.* يخربش yokharbish	**seclude** *v.* يعزل ya'zil
scribble *n.* خربشة kharbashah	**secluded** *a.* منعزل mon'azil
script *n.* نَص nas	**seclusion** *n.* عزلة ozlah
scripture *n.* كتاب مقدّس kitaabon moqaddas	**second** *a.* ثاني thaani
	second *n.* ثانية thaaniyah
scroll *n.* مخطوطة makhtootah	**second** *v.* يثنّي yothanni
scrutinize *v.* يدقّق yodaqqiq	**secondary** *a.* ثانوي thaanawiy
scrutiny *n.* تدقيق tadqeeq	**seconder** *n.* مُعاوِن mo'aawin
scuffle *n.* عراك iraak	**secrecy** *n.* سرية sirriyyah
scuffle *v.* يعارك yo'aarik	**secret** *a.* سري sirriy
sculpt *v.* ينحت yanhat	**secret** *n.* سر sir
sculptor *n.* نحات nahhaat	**secretariat** (e) *n.* أمانة uamaanah
sculptural *a.* نحتي nahtiy	**secretary** *n.* أمين uameen
sculpture *n.* 1 نحت naht	**secrete** *v.* يفرز yafriz
sculpture *n.* 2 تمثال timthaal	**secretion** *n.* إفراز efraaz
scythe *n.* منجل minjal	**secretive** *a.* متحفّظ motahaffidd
scythe *v.* يَحِش yahish	**sect** *n.* طائفة taauifah
sea *n.* بحر bahr	**sectarian** *a.* طائفي taauifiy
seal *n.* ختم khitm	**section** *n.* مقطع maqta'
seal *n.* فقمة faqamah	**sector** *n.* قطاع qitaa'
seal *v.* يختم yakhtim	**secure** *a.* آمن uaamin
seam *n.* درز darz	**secure** *v.* يؤمّن youmin
seam *v.* يَدرِز dadroz	**security** *n.* أمن uamn
seamy *a.* عابس aabis	**sedan** *n.* سيارة sayyaarah
search *n.* بحث bahth	**sedate** *a.* رزين razeen
search *v.* يبحث yabhath	**sedate** *v.* يهدئ yohaddiu
season *n.* موسم mawsim	**sedative** *a.* مهدئ mohaddiu
season *v.* يبهّر yobahhir	**sedative** *n.* مهدى mohaddiu
seasonable *a.* ملائم molaauim	**sedentary** *a.* مستقر mostaqir
seasonal *a.* موسمي mawsimiy	**sediment** *n.* راسب raasib
seat *n.* مقعد miq'ad	**sedition** *n.* فتنة fitnah

seditious *a.* محرّض moharrid

seduce *v.* يغوي yaghwi

seduction *n.* إغواء eghwaau

seductive *adj.* مغر moghri

see *v.* ينظر yanddor

seed *n.* بذرة bidhrah

seed *v.* يزرع yazra'

seek *v.* يبحث yabhath

seem *v.* يبدو yabdo

seemly *a.* لائق laauiq

seep *v.* يتسرّب yatasarrab

seer *n.* عَرّاف arraaf

seethe *v.* يهتاج yahtaaj

segment *n.* قطعة qit'ah

segment *v.* يقطّع yaqta'

segregate *v.* يفصل yafsil

segregation *n.* فصل fasl

seismic *a.* زلزالي zilzaaliy

seize *v.* يستحوذ yastahwidh

seizure *n.* مصادرة mosaadarah

seldom *adv.* نادراً naadiran

select *v.* يختار yakhtaar

select *adj.* مُنتَخَب montakhab

selection *n.* اختيار ekhtiyaar

selective *a.* انتقائي entiqaauiy

self *n.* نفس nafs

selfish *a.* أناني uanaaniy

selfless *a.* ناكرالذات naakiro dhdhaat

sell *v.* يبيع yabee'

seller *n.* بائع baaui'

semblance *n.* مظهر maddhar

semen *n.* مني maniy

semester *n.* فصل fasl

seminal *a.* منوي manawiy

seminar *n.* حلقةدراسية halqaton diraasiyyah

senate *n.* مجلسالشيوخ majliso shshoyookh

senator *n.* سناتور sinator

senatorial *a.* مشيخي mashyakhiy

send *v.* يرسل yorsil

senile *a.* خرف kharif

senility *n.* شيخوخة shaikhookhah

senior *a.* الكَبير ualkabeer

senior *n.* الأعلىمقاماً ualua'la maqaaman

seniority *n.* أقدمية uaqdamiyyah

sensation *n.* شعور sho'oor

sensational *a.* مثير motheer

sense *n.* إحساس ehsaas

sense *v.* يحس yahis

senseless *a.* عديمالاحساس adeemol ehsaas

sensibility *n.* عقلانية aqlaaniyyah

sensible *a.* معقول ma'qool

sensitive *a.* حساس hassaas

sensitivity *n.* حساسية hasaasiyah

sensual *a.* حسي hissiy

sensualist *n.* شهواني shahwaaniy

sensuality *n.* شهوانية shahwaaniyyah

sensuous *a.* حسي hissiy

sentence *n.* 1 جملة jomlah

sentence *n.* 2 حكم hokm

sentence *v.* يحكم yahkim

sentience *n.* إحساس ehsaas

sentient *a.* واع waa'i

sentiment *n.* عاطفة aatifah

sentimental *a.* 1 وجداني wojdaaniy

sentimental *a.* 2 عاطفي aatifiy

sentinel *n.* حارس haaris

sentry *n.* خفير khafeer

separable *a.* ممكنفصله momkin fasloh

separate *v.* يفصل yafsil

separate *a.* منفصل monfasil

separation *n.* فصل fasl

sepsis *n.* تعفنالدم ta'affono ddam

September *n.* أيلول uaylool

septic *a.* عفن afin

sepulchre *n.* ضَريح dareeh

sepulture *n.* ضَريح dareeh

sequel *n.* تتمة tatimmah

sequence *n.* تسلسل tasalsol

sequester *v.* يعزل ya'zil

serene *a.* هادئ haadiu

serenity *n.* صفاء safaau

serf *n.* تابع taabi'

serge *n.* قماش qimaash

sergeant *n.* رقيب raqeeb

serial *a.* متسلسل motasalsil

serial *n.* مسلسل mosalsal

series *n.* سلسلة silsilah

serious *adj.* جذّي jaddiy

sermon *n.* خطبة khidbah

sermonize *v.* يوعظ yoo'idd

serpent *n.* أفعى uaf'a

serpentine *n.* اعوج ua'waj

servant *n.* خادم khaadim

serve *v.* يخدم yakhdim

serve *n.* ضَربَةًمَبدَئِيَه darbaton mabdauiyyah

service *n.* خدمة khidmah

service *v.* يَفحَصالآلة yafhasol uaalah

serviceable *a.* نافع naafi'

servile *a.* ذليل dhaleel

servility *n.* خنوع khonoo'

session *n.* جلسة jalsah

set *v.* يضع yadha'

set *adj.* مُصَمَّم mosammim

set *n.* مجموعة majmoo'a

settle *v.* 1 يحل yahil

settle *v.* 2 يستقر yastaqir

settlement *n.* 1 تسوية taswiyah

settlement *n.* 2 إستقرار estiqraar

settler *n.* مستوطن mostawtin

seven *n.* سبعة sab'ah

seven *adj.* سبعة sab'ah

seventeen *n., a* سبعةعشر sab'ato 'ashar

seventeenth *a.* السابععشر uassaabi'o 'ashar

seventh *a.* سابع saabi'

seventieth *a.* السبعون uassab'oon

seventy *n., a* سبعون sab'oon

sever *v.* يقطع yaqta'

several *adj.* عدة iddah

severance *n.* قطع qat'

severe *a.* حاد haad

severity *n.* حدَة hiddah

sew *v.* يخيط yakheet

sewage *n.* مجاري majaari

sewer *n.* 1 خيّاط khayyaat

sewer *n.* 2 صرفصحّي sarfon sihhiy

sewerage *n.* مجاري majaari

sex *v.* يجنّس yojannis

sex *n.* جنس jins

sexily *adv.* بإغراء biuighraau

sexual *a.* جنسي jinsiy

sexuality *n.* حياةجنسية hayaaton jinsiyyah

sexy *adj.* مغر moghri

shabby *a.* رث rath

shackle *n.* قيد qayd

shackle *v.* يقيد yoqayyid

shade *n.* ظل ddil

shade *v.* يظلّل yoddallil

shadow *n.* خيال khayaal

shadow *v.* يخفي yokhfi

shadowy *a.* غامضة ghaamid

shaft *n.* رمح romh

shake *v.* يهتز yahtaz

shake *n.* هزة hazzah

shaky *a.* مهتز mohtaz

shallow *a.* ضحل dahl

sham *v.* يدّعي yad'i

sham *n.* 1 مزيّف mozayyaf

sham *n.* 2 دجّال dajjaal

sham *adj.* مزيّف mozayyaf

shame *n.* عار aar

shame *v.* يخجل yakhjal

shameful *a.* مخجل mokhjil

shameless *a.* وقح waqih

shampoo *n.* شامبو shaambo

shampoo *v.* يغسل بالشامبو yaghsilo bishshaambo

shanty *adj.* كوخ kookh

shape *n.* شكل shakl

shape *v.* يشكّل yoshakkil

shapely *a.* جميل jameel

share *v.* 1 يشارك yoshaarik

share *v.* 2 يتقاسم yataqaasam

share *n.* 1 حصة hossah

share *n.* 2 سهم sahm

shark *n.* سمك القرش samakol qirsh

sharp *a.* 1 حاد haad

sharp *a.* 2 نبيه nabeeh

sharp *a.* 3 مفاجئ mofaajiu

sharp *adv.* 1 حاد haad

sharp *adv.* 2 بالتحديد bittahdeed

sharpen *v.* يشحذ yashhadh

sharpener *n.* مبراة mibraah

sharper *n.* أدق uadaq

shatter *v.* يتحطم yatahattam

shave *v.* يحلق yohalliq

shave *n.* قصة qassah

shawl *n.* شال shaal

she *pron.* هي hiyah

sheaf *n.* حزمة hozmah

shear *v.* يجز yajiz

shears *n. pl.* مجزات mojizzaat

shed *v.* يخسر yakhsar

shed *n.* سقيفة saqeefah

sheep *n.* خروف kharoof

sheepish *a.* خجول khajool

sheer *a.* محض mahd

sheet *n.* 1 ورقة waraqah

sheet *n.* 2 غطاء ghidaau

sheet *v.* يغطّي yoghatti

shelf *n.* رف raf

shell *n.* 1 قذيفة qadheefah

shell *n.* 2 صدفة sadafah

shell *v.* يقصف yaqsif

shelter *n.* مأوى mauwa

shelter *v.* يأوي yauwi

shelve *v.* يضع على الرف yadha'o 'ala rraf

shepherd *n.* راعي raa'i

shield *n.* درع dir'

shield *v.* يتدرّع yatadarra'

shift *v.* ينقل yanqil

shift *n.* نقلة naqlah

shifty *a.* داهية daahiyah

shilling *n.* شلن shilin

shilly-shally *v.* يَتَلَكَّأ yatalakkau

shilly-shally *n.* تلكُّؤ talakkou

shin *n.* قصبة qasabah

shine *v.* يتألق yatauallaq

shine *n.* لمعة lam'a

shiny *a.* لامع laami'

ship *n.* سفينة safeenah

ship *v.* يشحن yashhan

shipment *n.* شحنة shahnah

shire *n.* مقاطعة moqaata'ah

shirk *v.* يَتَمَلَّص yatamallas

shirker *n.* متملّص motamallis

shirt *n.* قميص qamees

shiver *v.* يرتجف yartajif

shoal *n.* 1 فَوْج من الأسماك fawjon minal uasmaak

shoal *n.* 2 مياه ضحلة miyaahon dahlah

shock *n.* صدمة sadmah

shock *v.* يصدم yasdim

shoe *n.* حذاء hidhaau

shoe *v.* يصرف yasrif

shoot *v.* 1 يصيب yoseeb

shoot *v.* 2 يتبرعم yatabarra'

shoot *v.* 3 يتحرك بسرعة yataharrako bisor'ah

shoot *v.* 4 يسجّل yosajjil

shoot *n.* 1 طلقة talqah

shoot *n.* 2 برعم bor'om

shop *n.* متجر matjar

shop *v.* يشتري yashtari

shore *n.* شاطئ shaatiu

short *n.* فلم قصير filmon qaseer

short *a.* قصير qaseer

short *adv.* باختصار bikhtisaar

shortage *n.* نقص naqs

shortcoming *n.* عيب ayb

shorten *v.* يقصّر yoqassir

shortly *adv.* قريباً qareeban

shorts *n. pl.* سروال قصير sirwaalon qaseer

shot *n.* طلقة talqah

shoulder *n.* كتف katif

shoulder *v.* يواجه yowaajih

shout *n.* صيحة sayhah

shout *v.* يصيح yaseeh

shove *v.* يحشر yahshor

shove *n.* دفعة daf'ah

shovel *n.* مجرفة mijrafah

shovel *v.* يجرف yajrof

show *v.* يعرض ya'rid

show *n.* عرض ard

shower *n.* دش dosh

shower *v.* يستحم yastahim

shrew *n.* 1 زبابه zabbaabah

shrew *n.* 2 امرأة سليطة emrauaton saleetah

shrewd *a.* داهية daahiyah

shriek *n.* زعقة za'qah

shriek *v.* يزعق yaz'aq

shrill *a.* شديد shadeed

shrine *n.* مزار mazaar

shrink *v.* ينكمش yankamish

shrinkage *n.* انكماش enkimaash

shroud *n.* كفن kafan

shroud *v.* يكفن yakfin

shrub *n.* شجيرة shojayrah

shrug *v.* يهزّ الكتفين yahizol katifayn

shrug *n.* هزّ الكتفين hazzol katifayn	**sign** *v.* يوقّع yowaqi'
shudder *v.* يرتج yartajj	**signal** *n.* إشارة eshaarah
shudder *n.* ارتجاج ertijaaj	**signal** *a.* مرموق marmooq
shuffle *v.* 1 يخلط yakhlit	**signal** *v.* يشير yosheer
shuffle *v.* 2 يتخبّط yatakhabbat	**signatory** *n.* موقّع mowaqi'
shuffle *n.* 1 خلط ورق اللعب khalto waraqi lla'ib	**signature** *n.* توقيع tawqee'
shuffle *n.* 2 تخبّط takhabbat	**significance** *n.* أهميّة uahammiyah
shun *v.* يتجنب yatajannab	**significant** *a.* مهم mohim
shunt *v.* يناور yonaawir	**signification** *n.* مغزى maghza
shut *v.* يغلق yoghliq	**signify** *v.* يدلّل yodallil
shutter *n.* مصراع misraa'	**silence** *n.* صمت samt
shuttle *n.* مكوك makkook	**silence** *v.* يسكت yoskit
shuttle *v.* يسافر باستمرار yosaafiro bistimraar	**silencer** *n.* كاتم kaatim
shuttlecock *n.* ريشة اللعب reeshato lla'ib	**silent** *a.* صامت saamit
shy *n.* خجول khajool	**silhouette** *n.* خيال khayaal
shy *v.* يبتعد yabta'id	**silk** *n.* حرير hareer
sick *a.* مريض mareed	**silken** *a.* حريري hareeriy
sickle *n.* منجل minjal	**silky** *a.* حريري hareeriy
sickly *a.* واهن waahin	**silly** *a.* سخيف sakheef
sickness *n.* مرض marad	**silt** *n.* طمي tami
side *n.* جانب jaanib	**silt** *v.* يسد yasid
side *v.* يتحيّز yatahayyaz	**silver** *n.* فضة fiddah
siege *n.* حصار hisaar	**silver** *adj.* فضي fiddiy
siesta *n.* قيلولة qayloolah	**silver** *v.* فضّض faddada
sieve *n.* غربال ghirbaal	**similar** *a.* مشابه moshaabih
sieve *v.* يغربل yogharbil	**similarity** *n.* تشابه tashaaboh
sift *v.* ينخل yankhal	**simile** *n.* تشبيه tashbeeh
sigh *n.* تنهّد tanahhod	**similitude** *n.* شبه shabah
sigh *v.* يتنهّد yatanahhad	**simmer** *v.* 1 يطهو yatho
sight *n.* مشهد mashhad	**simmer** *v.* 2 يضطرب yadtarib
sight *v.* يراقب yoraaqib	**simple** *a.* بسيط baseet
sightly *a.* ممتع momti'	**simpleton** *n.* مغفل moghaffal
sign *n.* علامة alaamah	**simplicity** *n.* بساطة basaatah
	simplification *n.* تبسيط tabseet

simplify v. يبسّط yobassit

simultaneous a. متزامن motazaamin

sin n. خطيئة khateeuah

sin v. يخطئ yokhtiu

since prep. مندأن mondho uan

since conj. بماأن bimaa uanna

since adv. منذ mondho

sincere a. صادق saadiq

sincerity n. صدق sidq

sinful a. مذنب modhnib

sing v. يغنّي yoghanni

singe v. يحرق yahriq

singe n. حرق harq

singer n. مطرب motrib

single a. 1 وحيد waheed

single a. 2 موحّد mowahhad

single a. 3 أعزب ua'zab

single n. 1 غرفةلواحد ghorfaton liwaahid

single n. 2 تذكرةذهاب tadhkarato dhihaab

single n. 3 أغنية uoghniyah

single v. يختار yakhtaar

singular a. مفرد mofrad

singularity n. تفرد tafarrod

singularly adv. متفرد motafarrid

sinister a. شرير shirreer

sink v. يغرق yaghraq

sink n. مغسلة mighsalah

sinner n. آثم aathim

sinuous a. متعرج mota'arrij

sip v. يرشف yarshof

sip n. رشفة rashfah

sir n. سيّد sayyid

siren n. صفارةإنذار saffaarato endhaar

sister n. أخت uokht

sisterhood n. أختيّة uokhtiyyah

sisterly a. أختي uokhtiy

sit v. يجلس yajlis

site n. موقع mawqi'

situation n. حالة haalah

six n., a ستة sittah

sixteen n., a. ستعشرة sitto 'ashrah

sixteenth a. سادسعشر saadiso 'ashar

sixth a. سادس saadis

sixtieth a. الستون uassittoon

sixty n., a. ستون sittoon

sizable a. كبير kabeer

size n. حجم hajm

size v. يرتّبحسبالحجم yorattibo hasabal hajm

sizzle v. يسلق yasliq

sizzle n. أزيز uazeez

skate n. حذاءالتزلّج hidhaauo ttazalloj

skate v. يتزلّج yatazallaj

skein n. خصلةخيوط khislato khoyoot

skeleton n. هيكلعظمي haykalon 'addmiy

sketch n. رسم rasm

sketch v. يرسم yarsom

sketchy a. ضئيل dhaueel

skid v. ينزلق yanzaliq

skid n. انزلاق enzilaaq

skilful a. ماهر maahir

skill n. مهارة mahaarah

skin n. جلد jild

skin v. يسلخ yaslakh

skip *v.* 1 يقفز yaqfiz

skip *v.* 2 يتجاهل yatajaahal

skip *n.* 1 قفزة qafzah

skip *n.* 2 تجاهل tajaahol

skipper *n.* ربان robbaan

skirmish *n.* مناوشة monaawashah

skirmish *v.* يناوش yonaawish

skirt *n.* تنورة tannoorah

skirt *v.* يتجنبموضوع yatajannabo mawdoo'an

skit *n.* مسرحيةهزلية masrahiyyaton hazaliyyah

skull *n.* جمجمة jomjomah

sky *n.* سماء samaau

sky *v.* يقذف yaqdhif

slab *n.* لوح lawh

slack *a.* ركود rokood

slacken *v.* يتراخ yataraakha

slacks *n.* بنطال bintaal

slake *v.* يخمد yakhmid

slam *v.* يعنف yo'annif

slam *n.* ضربة darbah

slander *n.* افتراء eftiraau

slander *v.* يفتري yaftari

slanderous *a.* افترائي eftiraauiy

slang *n.* عامية aammiyyah

slant *v.* يميل yameel

slant *n.* مائل mauil

slap *n.* صفعة saf'ah

slap *v.* يصفع yasfa'

slash *v.* يجرح yajrah

slash *n.* جرح jorh

slate *n.* أردواز uardiwaaz

slattern *n.* وسخ wasakh

slatternly *adj.* بقذارة biqazaarah

slaughter *n.* ذبيحة dhabeehah

slaughter *v.* يذبح yadhbah

slave *n.* عبد abd

slave *v.* يستعبد yasta'bid

slavery *n.* عبودية oboodiyyah

slavish *a.* عَبدي abdiy

slay *v.* يذبح yadhbah

sleek *a.* أملس uamlas

sleep *v.* ينام yanaam

sleep *n.* نوم nawm

sleeper *n.* نائم naauim

sleepy *a.* نعسام na'saan

sleeve *n.* كم kam

sleight *n.* خدعة Khid'ah

slender *n.* مرهف morhaf

slice *n.* شريحة shareehah

slice *v.* يشرّح yosharrih

slick *adj.* ماكِر maakir

slide *v.* يتزحلق yatazahlaq

slide *n.* شريحة shareehah

slight *a.* طفيف tafeef

slight *n.* إنتهار entihaar

slight *v.* يَنتَهِر yantahir

slim *a.* نحيل naheel

slim *v.* ينحل yanhal

slime *n.* لعاب lo'aab

slimy *a.* غروي gharawiy

sling *n.* 1 مِقلاع miqlaa'

sling *n.* 2 حَمَالة hammaalah

slip *v.* ينزلق yanzaliq

slip *n.* زَلَه zallah

slipper *n.* شبشب shibshib

slippery *a.* زلق zaliq

slipshod i. مبتذل mobtadhal

slit *n.* شق shaq

slit *v.* يشق yashoq	smallpox *n.* جدري jadariy
slogan *n.* شعار shi'aar	smart *a.* 1 أنيق uaneeq
slope *n.* منحدر monhadir	smart *a.* 2 ذكي dhakiy
slope *v.* ينحدر yanhadir	smart *v.* يتألَم yatauallam
sloth *n.* كسل kasil	smart *n.* وَخزَه wakhzah
slothful *n.* كسول kasool	smash *v.* يسحق yashaq
slough *n.* 1 مستنقع mostanqa'	smash *n.* تَحَطُم tahattom
slough *n.* 2 جلدالثعبان jildol uaf'a	smear *v.* يلطّخ yolattikh
slough *v.* يَذرِف yadhrif	smear *n.* لطخة latkhah
slovenly *adj.* قذر qadhir	smell *n.* رائحة raauihah
slow *adj.* بطيء bateeu	smell *v.* يشم yashom
slow *v.* يبطئ yobtiu	smelt *v.* يَصهَرالمَعادِن yasharol ma'aadin
slowly *adv.* ببطء bibotu	smile *n.* ابتسامة ebtisaamah
slowness *n.* بطء botu	smile *v.* يبتسم yabtasim
sluggard *n.* كسلان kaslaan	smith *n.* حَدّاد haddaad
sluggish *a.* راكد raakid	smock *n.* مَريول maryool
sluice *n.* قَناةتَضريفالماء qanaato tasreefil maau	smog *n.* ضَبْخَن dabkhan
slum *n.* حيالفقراء hayol foqaraau	smoke *n.* دخان dokhaan
slumber *v.* يَهْجَع yahja'	smoke *v.* يدخّن yodakhkhin
slumber *n.* هجوع hojoo'	smoky *a.* مدخن modakhkhin
slump *n.* ركود rokood	smooth *a.* سلس salis
slump *v.* يركد yarkod	smooth *v.* يملّس yomallis
slur *n.* افتراء eftiraau	smother *v.* يخنق yakhniq
slush *n.* ثَلْجذائِب thaljon dhaauib	smoulder *v.* يدخّن yodakhkhin
slushy *a.* ذائب dhaauib	smug *a.* معتدبنفسه mo'taddon binafsih
slut *n.* فاسقة faasiqah	smuggle *v.* يهرّب yoharrib
sly *a.* خبيث khabeeth	smuggler *n.* مهرّب moharrib
smack *n.* 1 صفعة saf'ah	snack *n.* وجبةخفيفة wajbah khafeefah
smack *v.* 1 يَصفَع yasfa'	snag *n.* عقبة aqabah
smack *n.* 2 إيحاء ueehaau	snail *n.* حلزون halazoon
smack *v.* 2 يوحي بِ yowhi bi-	snake *n.* ثعبان tho'baan
small *a.* صغير sagheer	snake *v.* يتلوّى yatalawwa
small *n.* صغير sagheer	snap *v.* يَعُض ya'od
smallness *adv.* صغر sighar	

snap *n.* لَقْطَة laqtah

snap *adj.* مُتَسَرِّع motasarri'

snare *n.* كمين kameen

snare *v.* يَصيدُبالفخ yaseedo bilfakh

snarl *n.* زمجرة zamjarah

snarl *v.* يزمجر yozamjer

snatch *v.* ينتزع yantazi'

snatch *n.* خطف khatf

sneak *v.* يتسلَل yatasallal

sneak *n.* خائن khaauin

sneer *v.* يسخر yaskhar

sneer *n.* سخرية sokhriyah

sneeze *v.* يعطس ya'tis

sneeze *n.* عطسة atsah

sniff *v.* يشم yashim

sniff *n.* نَشْق nashq

snob *n.* متكبر motakabbir

snobbery *n.* خيلاء khaylaau

snobbish *v.* مُتَكَبِّر motakabbir

snore *v.* يشخر yashkhar

snore *n.* شخير shakheer

snort *v.* يَنْخُر yankhor

snort *n.* نَخْر nakhr

snout *n.* خطم khatm

snow *n.* ثلج thalj

snow *v.* تثلج tothlij

snowy *a.* ثلجي thaljiy

snub *v.* يَنْتَهِر yantahir

snub *n.* إنْتِهار entihaar

snub *adj.* أفطس uaftas

snuff *n.* سَعوط sa'oot

snug *n.* دافئ daafiu

so *adv.* جدا jiddan

so *conj.* هكذا haakadha

soak *v.* ينقع yanqa'

soak *n.* نقع naq'

soap *n.* صابون saaboon

soap *v.* يَفْركبالصَابون yafriko bissaaboon

soapy *a.* صابوني saabooniy

soar *v.* يحوم yahoom

sob *v.* يَنْشِج yanshoj

sob *n.* نَشيج nasheej

sober *a.* رزين razeen

sobriety *n.* رزانة razaanah

sociability *n.* مؤانسة mouaanasah

sociable *a.* إجْتِماعي ejtimaa'iy

social *n.* اجتماعي ejtimaa'iy

socialism *n.* اشتراكية eshtiraakiyyah

socialist *n,a* اشتراكي eshtiraakiy

society *n.* مجتمع mojtama'

sociology *n.* علمالإجتماع ilmol ejtimaa'

sock *n.* جورب jawrab

socket *n.* مقبس maqbas

sod *n.* مَخْضَرَه makhdarah

sodomite *n.* لوطي lootiy

sodomy *n.* لواط lowaat

sofa *n.* أريكة uareekah

soft *n.* ناعم naa'im

soften *v.* يلَين yolawwin

soil *n.* تربة torbah

soil *v.* يوسخ yowassikh

sojourn *v.* يقيممؤَقتاً yoqeemo mouaqqatan

sojourn *n.* إقامةمؤَقتة eqaamaton mouaqqatah

solace *v.* يعزَي yo'azzi

solace *n.* عزاء azaau

solar *a.* شمسي shamsiy

solder *n.* لحام lihaam

solder *v.* يلحم yalhim

soldier *n.* جندي jondiy

soldier *v.* يتجنّد yatajannad

sole *n.* 1 نَعل na'l

sole *n.* 2 سَمَك موسى samako moosa

sole *v.* ينعَل yan'al

sole *adj.* وحيد waheed

solemn *a.* رصين raseen

solemnity *n.* إجلال ejlaal

solemnize *v.* يحتفل بتجلّي yahtafil bitajallin

solicit *v.* يلتمس yaltamis

solicitation *n.* التماس eltimaas

solicitor *n.* محامي mohaami

solicitous *a.* التماسي eltimaasiy

solicitude *n.* اهتمام ehtimaam

solid *a.* متين mateen

solid *n.* صلب salb

solidarity *n.* تضامن tadaamon

soliloquy *n.* مونولوج monolooj

solitary *a.* انفرادي enfiraadiy

solitude *n.* عزلة ozlah

solo *n.* فردي fardiy

solo *adj.* منفرد monfarid

solo *adv.* بانفراد binfiraad

soloist *n.* عازف منفرد aazifon monfarid

solubility *n.* ذوبانية dhawabaaniyyah

soluble *a.* ذائب dhaauib

solution *n.* 1 حل hal

solution *n.* 2 محلول mahlool

solve *v.* يحل yahil

solvency *n.* 1 ملاءة مالية milaauaton maaliyyah

solvency *n.* 2 قابلية الذوبان qaabiliyyato dhdhawabaan

solvent *a.* مذاب modhaab

solvent *n.* مذيب modheeb

sombre *a.* كئيب kaueeb

some *a.* ما maa

some *pron.* بعض ba'd

somebody *pron.* ما شخص shakhson maa

somebody *n.* ما شخص shakhson maa

somehow *adv.* ما بطريقة bitareeqatin ma

someone *pron.* ما شخص shakhson maa

somersault *n.* شَقْلَبَه shaqlabah

somersault *v.* يتشقلب yatashaqlab

something *pron.* شيء shayu

something *adv.* شيءا shayuan

sometime *adv.* ما وقت في fi waqtin ma

sometimes *adv.* أحياناً uahyaanan

somewhat *adv.* قليلاً qaleelan

somewhere *adv.* في مكان ما fi mkaanin ma

somnambulism *n.* سرنمة sarnamah

somnambulist *n.* مسرنم mosarnim

somnolence *n.* نعاس no'aas

somnolent *n.* نعسان na'saan

son *n.* إبن ebn

song *n.* أغنية uoghniyah

songster *n.* مغنّي moghanni

sonic *a.* صوتي sawtiy

sonnet *n.* قصيدة qaseedah	souvenir *n.* تذكار tidhkaar
sonority *n.* مصوتي maswatiyyah	sovereign *n.* مالك maalik
soon *adv.* قريباً qareeban	sovereign *adj.* ذوسيادةdho siyaadah
soot *n.* سخام sokhaam	sovereignty *n.* سيادة siyaadah
soot *v.* يسخّم yosakhkhim	sow *v.* يزرع yazra'
soothe *v.* يُهَدِّى yohaddiu	sow *n.* خنزيره khanzeerah
sophism *n.* مغالطة moghaalatah	space *n.* فضاء fadaau
sophist *n.* سوفي soofiy	space *v.* يباعِد yobaa'id
sophisticate *v.* يعقّد yo'aqqid	spacious *a.* واسع waasi'
sophisticated *a.* محنّك mohannak	spade *n.* مجرفة mijrafah
sophistication *n.* تطوّر tatawwor	spade *v.* يجرف yajrif
sorcerer *n.* ساحِر saahir	span *n.* امتداد emtidaad
sorcery *n.* سحر sihr	span *v.* يَمتَدَّفوقَ yamtaddo fawqa
sordid *a.* دنيء daneeu	Spaniard *n.* إسباني esbaaniy
sore *a.* متورّم motawarrim	spaniel *n.* كلب السبنيلي kalbol sbanyili
sore *n.* قرحة qorhah	Spanish *a.* إسباني esbaaniy
sorrow *n.* حزن hozn	Spanish *n.* اللغةالإسبانية ualloghatol esbaaniyyah
sorrow *v.* يحزن yahzan	spanner *n.* مفتاح miftaah
sorry *a.* آسِف uaasif	spare *v.* يُجَنِب yojannib
sort *n.* نوع naw'	spare *adj.* إحتياطي ehtiyaatiy
sort *v.* يفرز yafriz	spare *n.* قطَع غَيار qita'o ghayaar
soul *n.* روح rooh	spark *n.* شرارة sharaarah
sound *a.* عاقل aaqil	spark *v.* يشعل yosh'il
sound *v.* يَرِنُ yarin	sparkle *v.* يتلألأ yatalaulau
sound *n.* صوت sawt	sparkle *n.* تلألؤ talaulou
soup *n.* حساء hasaau	sparrow *n.* سنونو sanono
sour *a.* حامض haamid	sparse *a.* متناثر motanaathir
sour *v.* يحمض yohammid	spasm *n.* تشنج tashannoj
source *n.* مصدر masdar	spasmodic *a.* تشنجي tashannojiy
south *n.* جنوب janoob	spate *n.* فيض fayd
south *adj.* جنوبي janoobiy	spatial *a.* مكاني makaaniy
south *adv.* نحوالجنوب nahwal janoob	spawn *n.* فرخ farkh
southerly *a.* جنوبي janoobiy	spawn *v.* يفرخ yofarrikh
southern *a.* جنوبي janoobiy	

speak v. يتحدّث yatahaddath

speaker n. متحدّث motahaddith

spear n. رمح romh

spear v. يضرب بالرمح yadribo birromh

spearhead n. رأس الحربة rausol hirbah

spearhead v. يقود yaqood

special a. خاص khaas

specialist n. متخصص motakhassis

speciality n. تخصص takhassos

specialization n. تخصص takhassos

specialize v. يتخصَص yatakhassas

species n. نوع naw'

specific a. معيّن mo'ayyan

specification n. مواصفة mowaasafah

specify v. يحدّد yohaddid

specimen n. عينة ayyinah

speck n. بقعة boq'ah

spectacle n. مشهد mashhad

spectacular a. مذهل modhhil

spectator n. مشاهد moshaahid

spectre n. شبح shabah

speculate v. يتكهّن yatakahhan

speculation n. تكهّن takahhon

speech n. خطاب khitaab

speed n. سرعة sor'ah

speed v. يسرع yosri'

speedily adv. بسرعة bisor'ah

speedy a. عاجل aajil

spell n. 1 لعنة la'nah

spell v. يسحر yashar

spell n. 2 فترة fatrah

spend v. 1 يصرف yasrif

spend v. 2 يقضي yaqdi

spendthrift n. تبذير tabdheer

sperm n. مني maniy

sphere n. كرة korah

spherical a. كروي korawiy

spice n. تابل taabil

spice v. يتبّل yotabbil

spicy a. متبّل motabbal

spider n. عنكب ankab

spike n. شوكة shawkah

spike v. يمسمر yomasmir

spill v. يسكب yaskob

spill n. انسكاب ensikaab

spin v. يدور yadoor

spin n. دوران dawaraan

spinach n. سبانخ sabaanikh

spinal a. فقريّ fiqariy

spindle n. مغزل maghzal

spine n. عمود فقري amoodon fiqariy

spinner n. غزّال ghazzaal

spinster n. عانس aanis

spiral n. دوّامة dawwaamah

spiral a. حلزوني halazooniy

spirit n. روح rooh

spirited a. حيويّ hayawiy

spiritual a. روحاني roohaaniy

spiritualism n. روحانية roohaaniyyah

spiritualist n. روحاني roohaaniy

spirituality n. روحانية roohaaniyyah

spit v. يبصق yabsoq

spit n. بصاق bosaaq

spite n. رغم raghm

spittle *n.* لعاب lo'aab

spittoon *n.* مبصقة mibsaqah

splash *v.* يَرشُق yarshoq

splash *n.* رشْق rashq

spleen *n.* طحال tohaal

splendid *a.* رائع raaui'

splendour *n.* روعة raw'ah

splinter *n.* شظية shaddiyyah

splinter *v.* يكسرإلىشظايا yaksiro ela shaddaaya

split *v.* ينقسم yanqasim

split *n.* انقسام enqisaam

spoil *v.* 1 يدلّل yodallil

spoil *v.* 2 يُتلِف yotlif

spoil *n.* غنيمة ghaneemah

spoke *n.* شُعاع الدَولاب sho'aa'o ddoolaab

spokesman *n.* متحدّثبإسم motahaddithon biuism

sponge *n.* إسفنج essfanj

sponge *v.* يمسحبالإسفنج yamsaho biluisfanj

sponsor *n.* راعي raa'i

sponsor *v.* يرعى yar'a

spontaneity *n.* عفوية afawiyyah

spontaneous *a.* عفوي afawiy

spoon *n.* ملعقة mil'aqah

spoon *v.* يجرف yajrif

spoonful *n.* ملءملعقة miluo mil'aqah

sporadic *a.* متقطع motaqatti'

sport *n.* رياضة riyaadah

sport *v.* يَرتَدي yartadi

sportive *a.* رياضي riyaadiy

sportsman *n.* رياضي riyaadiy

spot *n.* بقعة boq'ah

spot *v.* يتنبّهإلى yatanabbaho ela

spotless *a.* بلاعيب bila 'ayb

spousal *n.* زوجي zawjiy

spouse *n.* زوج zawj

spout *n.* صنبور sonboor

spout *v.* يَنبَجِس yanbajis

sprain *n.* التواء eltiwaau

sprain *v.* يلوي yalwi

spray *n.* رذاذ radhaadh

spray *v.* يرش yarosh

spread *v.* 1 يدهن yadhan

spread *v.* 2 ينتشر yantashir

spread *n.* 1 معجونالدهن ma'joono ddahn

spread *n.* 2 انتشار entishaar

spree *n.* انغماس enghimaas

sprig *n.* غُصلوج oslooj

sprightly *a.* مرح marih

spring *v.* يبزغ yabzogh

spring *n.* ربيع rabee'

sprinkle *v.* يرش yarosh

sprint *v.* يعدو ya'do

sprint *n.* عدو adw

sprout *v.* يبرعم yobar'im

sprout *n.* برعم bor'om

spur *n.* مِهماز mihmaaz

spur *v.* يحفّز yohaffiz

spurious *a.* زائف zaauif

spurn *v.* يزدري yazdari

spurt *v.* يَتَدَفَّق yatadaffaq

spurt *n.* تفجر tafajjor

sputnik *n.* قمرصناعي qamaron sinaa'iy

sputum *n.* بصاق bosaaq

spy *n.* جاسوس jaasoos

spy *v.* يتجسّس yatajassas

squad n. فرقة firqah

squadron n. سَريَه sariyyah

squalid a. قذر qadhir

squalor n. قذارة qadhaarah

squander v. يبدد yobaddid

square n. 1 مَيدان maydaan

square n. 2 مربع morabba'

square adj. مربع morabba'

square v. يُسَوّيحساب yosawwi hisaab

squash v. يسحق yashaq

squash n. يَقطين yaqteen

squat v. يجلس القرفصاء yajlisol qorfosaau

squeak v. يصرصر yosarsir

squeak n. صرير sareer

squeeze v. يضغط yadhghat

squint v. يَحُول yahwil

squint n. حول hawal

squire n. قاضيالصلح qaadi ssolh

squirrel n. سنجاب sinjaab

stab v. يطعن yat'an

stab n. طعنة ta'nah

stability n. استقرار estiqraar

stabilization n. استقرار estiqraar

stabilize v. يستقر yastaqir

stable a. مستقر mostaqir

stable n. إسطبل establ

stable v. يضعفيالاسطبل yada'o fil establ

stadium n. استاد estaad

staff n. 1 موظفون mowaddddafoon

staff n. 2 عصا asa

staff v. يُزَوِّدبالمُوَظَّفين yozawwido bilmowaddddafeen

stag n. ظبي ddabi

stage n. مرحلة marhalah

stage v. يمثّل yomathil

stagger v. يترنّح yatarannah

stagger n. ترنح tarannoh

stagnant a. راكد raakid

stagnate v. يركد yarkod

stagnation n. ركود rokood

staid a. رزين razeen

stain n. وصمة wasmah

stain v. يلطّخ yolattikh

stainless a. مضادللصدأ modaadon lissadau

stair n. سلَم sollam

stake n. 1 حصة hossah

stake n. 2 وَتَد watad

stake v. يُراهن yoraahin

stale a. غَيرطازج ghayro taazaj

stale v. يتبوّل yatabawwal

stalemate n. طريقمسدود tareeqon masdood

stalk n. ساق saaq

stalk v. يلاحق yolaahiq

stall n. 1 مربط rarbat

stall n. 2 كُشك koshk

stall v. يُعَطِّل yo'attil

stallion n. فحل fahl

stalwart a. قويالبنية qawiyol bonyah

stalwart n. قويالبنية qawiyol bonyah

stamina n. تحمّل tahammol

stammer v. يَتَلَعثَم yatala'tham

stammer n. تَلَعثُم tala'thom

stamp n. ختم khitm

stamp v. يختم yakhtim

stampede *n.* فرارجماعي faraaron jamaa'iy

stampede *v.* يحث على فرارجماعي yahitho 'ala faraarin jamma'iy

stand *v.* يقف yaqif

stand *n.* موقف maqif

standard *n.* معيار mi'yaar

standard *adj.* إعتيادي e'tiyaadiy

standardization *n.* توحيد tawheed

standardize *v.* يوحّد yowahhid

standing *n.* مكانة makaanah

standpoint *n.* وجهةنظر wojhato naddar

standstill *n.* توقفتام tawaqqof taam

stanza *n.* مقطعشعري maqta'on shi'riy

staple *n.* 1 قوت qoot

staple *n.* 2 دَبّوس dabboos

staple *adj.* أساسي uasaasiy

staple *v.* يُدَبِّس yodabbis

star *n.* نجمة najmah

star *v.* يَقومُ بِدَوُرِ البُطولَه yaqoomo bidawril botoolah

starch *n.* نشاء nashau

starch *v.* يُنَشّي yonshi

stare *v.* يحدّق yohaddiq

stare *n.* جَريء jareeu

stark *adv.* تماما tamaaman

stark *adj.* صَريح sareeh

starry *a.* نجمي najmiy

start *v.* يبدأ yabdau

start *n.* بداية bidaayah

startle *v.* يجفل yajfal

starvation *n.* التضورجوعاً uattadawworo joo'an

starve *v.* يجوع yajoo'

state *n.* دولة dawlah

state *v.* يصرّح yosarrih

stateliness *n.* مجد majd

stately *a.* فخم fakhm

statement *n.* بيان bayaan

statesman *n.* رجلدولة rajolo dawlah

static *n.* كهرباءساكِنه kahrobaauon saakinah

static *adj.* ساكِن saakin

statics *n.* علمالسكون ilmo ssokoon

station *n.* محطة mahattah

station *v.* يُرَكِّز yorakkiz

stationary *a.* ثابت thaabit

stationer *n.* قرطاسي qirtaasiy

stationery *n.* قرطاسية qirtaasiyyah

statistical *a.* إحصائي ehsaauiy

statistician *n.* إحصائي ehsaauiy

statistics *n.* إحصائيات ehsaauiyyat

statue *n.* تمثال timthaal

stature *n.* قامة qaamah

status *n.* حالة haalah

statute *n.* قانون qaanoon

statutory *a.* قانوني qaanooniy

staunch *a.* قوي qawiy

stay *v.* يبقى yabqa

stay *n.* إقامة eqaamah

steadfast *a.* ثابت thaabit

steadiness *n.* ثبات thabaat

steady *a.* ثابت thaabit

steady *v.* يثبت yathbot

steal *v.* يسرق yasriq

stealthily *adv.* خلسة khilsah

steam *n.* بخار bokhaar

steam *v.* يبخّر yabakhir

steamer *n.* سفينةبخارية safeenaton bokhaariyyah

steed *n.* فرس faras

steel *n.* فولاذ foolaadh

steep *a.* حاد haad

steep *v.* يَنْتَقِع yantaqi'

steeple *n.* برجالكنيسة borjol kaneesah

steer *v.* يقود yaqood

stellar *a.* ممتاز momtaaz

stem *n.* جذع jidh'

stem *v.* ينبثق yanbathiq

stench *n.* نتانة nataanah

stencil *n.* مرسام mirsaam

stencil *v.* يطبعبالمرسام yatba'o bilmirsaam

stenographer *n.* مختزل mokhtazil

stenography n. اختزال ekhtizaal

step *n.* خطوة khotwah

step *v.* يخطو yakhto

steppe *n.* سَهب sahb

stereotype *n.* شكلنمطي shaklon namatiy

stereotype *v.* ينمّط yonammit

stereotyped *a.* نمطي namatiy

sterile *a.* معقّم mo'aqqam

sterility *n.* عقم oqm

sterilization *n.* تعقيم ta'qeem

sterilize *v.* يعقّم yo'aqqim

sterling *a.* خالِص khaalis

sterling *n.* استرليني estirleeni

stern *a.* صارم saarim

stern *n.* مؤَخَّرُالسَّفِينَه mouakhkhiro ssafeenah

stethoscope *n.* سماعةالطبيب samma'ato ttabeeb

stew *n.* يخنة yakhnah

stew *v.* يطهو yatho

steward *n.* مضيف modeef

stick *n.* عصا asa

stick *v.* يلصق yolsiq

sticker *n.* لاصقة laasiqah

stickler *n.* مدقق modaqqiq

sticky *n.* لزج lazij

stiff *n.* تيبس tayabbos

stiffen *v.* يتيبّس yatayabbas

stifle *v.* يخنق yakhniq

stigma *n.* وصمةعار wasmato 'aar

still *a.* ساكِن saakin

still *adv.* لايزال laa yazaal

still *v.* يسكّن yosakkin

still *n.* لَقْطَة laqtah

stillness *n.* سكون sokoon

stilt *n.* ركيزة rakeezah

stimulant *n.* منبه monabbih

stimulate *v.* يحفّز yohaffiz

stimulus *n.* حافز haafiz

sting *v.* يلدغ yaldagh

sting *n.* لدغة ladghah

stingy *a.* بخيل bakheel

stink *v.* ينتن yanton

stink *n.* نتن natin

stipend *n.* راتب raatib

stipulate *v.* يشترط yashtarit

stipulation *n.* شرط shart

stir *v.* ضجة dajjah

stirrup *n.* ركاب السرج rokaabo ssarj

stitch *n.* غرزة ghorzah

stitch *v.* يخيط yakheet

stock *n.* 1 بَضائع badaaui'

stock *n.* 2 قرض تجاري qardon tijaariy

stock *v.* يخزن yakhzin

stock *a.* شائع shaaui'

stocking *n.* جورب jawrab

stoic *n.* رواقي rawaaqiy

stoke *v.* يُزَوِّد بالوَقود yozawwido bilwaqood

stoker *n.* وَقّاد waqqaad

stomach *n.* معدة mi'dah

stomach *v.* يتحمّل yatahammal

stone *n.* حجر hajar

stone *v.* يَرجُم yarjim

stony *a.* حجري hajarriy

stool *n.* براز boraaz

stoop *v.* ينحدر yanhadir

stoop *n.* محدودب mohdawdab

stop *v.* يتوقَّف yatawaqqaf

stop *n.* موقف mawqif

stoppage *n.* توقف tawaqqof

storage *n.* تخزين takhzeen

store *n.* مخزن makhzan

store *v.* يخزِّن yokhazzin

storey *n.* طابق taabiq

stork *n.* لقلق laqlaq

storm *n.* عاصفة aasifah

storm *v.* يعصف ya'saf

stormy *a.* عاصف aasif

story *n.* قصة qissah

stout *a.* شجاع shojaa'

stove *n.* موقد mawqid

stow *v.* يخَبِّئ yokhabbiu

straggle *v.* يَتَخَلَّف عن الرَّكب yatakhallafo 'ani rrakb

straggler *n.* مُتَخَلِّف عن الرَّكب motakhallifon 'ani rrakb

straight *a.* مستقيم mostaqeem

straight *adv.* رأسا rausan

straighten *v.* يسوِّ yosawwi

straightforward *a.* صريح sareeh

straightway *adv.* حالا haalan

strain *v.* يَلوي yalwi

strain *n.* 1 إلتِواء eltiwaau

strain *n.* 2 سلالة solaalah

strait *n.* مضيق madeeq

straiten *v.* يضيق yadeeq

strand *v.* يعلق yo'laq

strand *n.* ساحل saahil

strange *a.* غريب ghareeb

stranger *n.* غريب ghareeb

strangle *v.* يخنق yakhniq

strangulation *n.* خنق khanq

strap *n.* حزام hizaam

strap *v.* يحزِم yohazzim

stratagem *n.* حَرِبَيَّه خُدعَه khid'aton harbiyyah

strategic *a.* إستراتيجي estraatijiy

strategist *n.* إستراتيجي estraatijiy

strategy *n.* إستراتيجيّة estraatijiyyah

stratum *n.* طبقة tabaqah

straw *n.* قش qash

strawberry *n.* فراولة farawlah

stray *v.* يشرَد yashrod

stray *adj.* متشرِّد motasharrid

stray *n.* حيوان شارد hayawaanon shaarid

stream *n.* جدول jadwal

stream *v.* يتدفَّق yatadaffaq

streamer n. قُصاصَهطَويلَه qosaasaton taweelah

streamlet n. نهير nohayr

street n. شارع shaari'

strength n. قوة qowwah

strengthen v. يعزّز yo'azziz

strenuous a. مضني modniy

stress n. 1 ضَغط daght

stress n. 2 إجهاد ejhaad

stress v. 1 يُؤكِّد youakkid

stress v. 2 يجهد yojhid

stretch v. يمتد yamtad

stretch n. امتداد emtidaad

stretcher n. نقالة naqqaalah

strew v. ينثر yanthor

strict a. صارم saarim

stricture n. تضيق tadyeeq

stride v. يَخطو yakhto

stride n. خطوة khatwah

strident a. حاد haad

strife n. صراع siraa'

strike v. يضرب Yadrib

strike n. إضراب edraab

striker n. مهاجم mohaajim

string n. سلسلة silsilah

string v. يربط yarbit

stringency n. صرامة saraamah

stringent a. صارم saarim

strip n. شريط shareet

strip v. يعزّي yo'arri

stripe n. خطوط khotoot

stripe v. يقلّم yoqallim

strive v. يسعى yas'a

stroke n. سكتة saktah

stroke v. يربّت yorabbit

stroke n. ضَربَه darbah

stroke n. نَوبَةمَرَضِيَّه nawbaton maradiyyah

stroll v. يتجوّل yatajawwal

stroll n. تجول tajawwol

strong a. قوي qawiy

stronghold n. معقل mi'qal

structural a. هيكلي haykaliy

structure n. هيكل haykal

struggle v. يناضل yonaadil

struggle n. نضال nidaal

strumpet n. عاهر aahir

strut v. يتبختر yatabartakh

strut n. تبختر tabartokh

stub n. عقبالسيجارة oqbo seejaarah

stubble n. قصبة qasabah

stubborn a. عنيد aneed

stud n. مِسمار mismaar

stud v. يغَطّيبالمَسامير yoghatti bilmasaameer

student n. طالب taalib

studio n. ستوديو stoodio

studious a. مواظب mowaaddib

study v. يدرس yadros

study n. 1 دِراسَه diraasah

study n. 2 مكتب maktab

stuff n. مادة maaddah

stuff v. يحشش yahshi

stuffy a. خانق khaaniq

stumble v. يتعثر yata'athar

stumble n. تعثر ta'athor

stump n. عقب oqb

stump v. يطفئ yotfiu

stun v. يصدم yasdim

stunt v. يُعيق yo'eeq

stunt *n.* عملمثير analon motheer

stupefy *v.* يخدّر yokhaddir

stupendous *a.* مذهل modhhil

stupid *adj.* غبي ghabiy

stupidity *n.* غباء ghabaau

sturdy *a.* متين mateen

sty *n.* 1 زَريبة zareebah

sty *n.* 2 وَذَقه wadqah

stye *n.* وَذَقه wadqah

style *n.* نمط namat

subdue *v.* يقهر yaqhar

subject *n.* موضوع mawqoo'

subject *adj.* خاضع khaadi'

subject *v.* يتعرّض yata'arrad

subjection *n.* إخضاع ekhdaa'

subjective *a.* ذاتي dhaatiy

subjudice *adj.* محتقر mohtaqir

subjugate *v.* يخضع yakhda'

subjugation *n.* استعباد esti'baad

sublet *v.* يؤجّر youajjir

sublimate *v.* يتسامى yatasaama

sublime *a.* سامي saami

sublime *n.* سمو somow

sublimity *n.* مهابة mahaabah

submarine *n.* غواصة ghawwasah

submarine *adj.* مائي maauiy

submerge *v.* يغمر Yaghmir

submission *n.* تقديم taqdeem

submissive *a.* منقاد monqaad

submit *v.* يقدّم yoqaddim

subordinate *adj.* مرؤوس maruoos

subordinate *n.* تابع taabi'

subordinate *v.* يُخضِع yokhdi'

subordination *n.* تبعية taba'iyyah

subscribe *v.* يشترك yashtarik

subscription *n.* اشتراك eshtiraak

subsequent *a.* لاحق laahiq

subservience *n.* خنوع khonoo'

subservient *a.* خنوع khonoo'

subside *v.* يهدئ yahdau

subsidiary *a.* فرعي fir'iy

subsidize *v.* يعين yo'een

subsidy *n.* إعانة e'aanah

subsist *v.* يحيى yahya

subsistence *n.* عيش aysh

substance *n.* جوهر jawhar

substantial *a.* جوهري jawhariy

substantially *adv.* جوهرياً jawhariyyan

substantiate *v.* يثبت yathbot

substantiation *n.* إثبات ethbaat

substitute *n.* بديل badeel

substitute *v.* يستبدل yastabdil

substitution *n.* استبدال estibdaal

subterranean *a.* جوفي jawfiy

subtle *n.* خفي khafiy

subtlety *n.* حدةالذهن hiddato dhihn

subtract *v.* يطرح yatrah

subtraction *n.* طرح tarh

suburb *n.* ضاحية daahiyah

suburban *a.* ضاحيي daahiyiy

subversion *n.* تخريب takhreeb

subversive *a.* مخرّب mokharrib

subvert *v.* يخرّب yokharrib

succeed *v.* ينجح yanjah

success *n.* نجاح najaah

successful *a* ناجح naajih

succession *n.* خلافة khilaafah

successive *a.* متعاقب mota'aaqib

successor *n.* خليفة khaleefah
succour *n.* عون awn
succour *v.* يعاون yo'aawin
succumb *v.* يستسلم yastaslim
such *a.* كهذا kahaadha
such *pron.* هكذا haakadha
suck *v.* يمتص yamtas
suck *n.* مص mas
suckle *v.* يرضع yarda'
suckling *n.* رضيع radee'
sudden *n.* مفاجئ mofaajiu
suddenly *adv.* فجأة fajuah
sue *v.* يقاضي yoqaadi
suffer *v.* يعاني yo'aayin
suffice *v.* يكفي yakfi
sufficiency *n.* كفاية kifaayah
sufficient *a.* كاف kaafi
suffix *n.* لاحق laahiq
suffix *v.* يلحق yolhiq
suffocate *v.* يختنق yakhtaniq
suffocation *n.* اختناق ekhtinaaq
suffrage *n.* حق الاقتراع haqqo eqtiraa'
sugar *n.* سكّر sokkar
sugar *v.* يحلّي yohalli
suggest *v.* يقترح yaqtarih
suggestion *n.* اقتراح eqtiraah
suggestive *a.* موح mowhi
suicidal *a.* انتحاري entihaariy
suicide *n.* انتحار entihaar
suit *n.* بدلة badlah
suit *v.* يناسب yonaasib
suitability *n.* ملاءمة molaauamah
suitable *a.* مناسب monaasib
suite *n.* جناح janaah

suitor *n.* عاشق aashiq
sullen *a.* نكد nakad
sulphur *n.* كبريت kibreet
sulphuric *a.* كبريتي kibreetiy
sultry *a.* قائظ qaauidd
sum *n.* مجموع majmoo'
sum *v.* يجمع yajma'
summarily *adv.* بشكل ملخص bishaklin molakhas
summarize *v.* يلخص yolakhkhis
summary *n.* ملخص molakhkhas
summary *adj.* ملخص molakhkhas
summer *n.* صيف sayf
summit *n.* قمة qimmah
summon *v.* يستجمع yastajmi'
summons *n.* استدعاءات estid'aauaat
sumptuous *a.* باذخ baadhikh
sun *n.* شمس shams
sun *v.* يَتَشَمَّس yatashammas
Sunday *n.* الأحد ualuahad
sunder *v.* ينفصل yanfasil
sundary *a.* انفصال enfisaal
sunny *a.* مشمس moshmis
sup *v.* يتعشّى yata'ashsha
sup *n.* رشفة rashfah
superabundance *n.* غزارة ghazaarah
superabundant *a.* غزير ghazeer
superb *a.* رائع raaui'
superficial *a.* سطحي sat hiy
superficiality *n.* سطحية sat hiyyah
superfine *a.* رقيق raqeeq
superfluity *n.* فضالة fadaalah

superfluous *a.* غير ضروري ghayro darooriy

superhuman *a.* خارق khaariq

superintend *v.* يشرف yoshrif

superintendence *n.* إشراف eshraaf

superintendent *n.* مشرف moshrif

superior *a.* متفوق motafawwiq

superiority *n.* تفوّق tafawwoq

superlative *a.* مفضّل mofaddal

superlative *n.* صيغةالتفضيل seeghato ttafdeel

superman *n.* سوبرمان soobirmaan

supernatural *a.* خارق khaariq

supersede *v.* ينسخ yansakh

supersonic *a.* فوقصوتي fawqo sawtiy

superstition *n.* خرافة khoraafah

superstitious *a.* خرافي khoraafiy

supertax *n.* ضريبةإضافية dareebaton edaafiyyah

supervise *v.* يشرف yoshrif

supervision *n.* إشراف eshraaf

supervisor *n.* مشرف moshrif

supper *n.* عشاء ashaau

supple *a.* مطواع mitwaa'

supplement *n.* تكملة takmilah

supplement *v.* يكمّل yokammil

supplementary *a.* تكميلي takmeeliy

supplier *n.* مزوّد mozawwid

supply *v.* يزوّد yozawwid

supply *n.* مؤن mouan

support *v.* يدعم yad'am

support *n.* دعم da'm

suppose *v.* يفترض yaftarid

supposition *n.* افتراض eftiraad

suppress *v.* يقمع yaqma'

suppression *n.* قمع qam'

supremacy *n.* سيادة siyaadah

supreme *a.* أعلى ua'la

surcharge *n.* ضريبةإضافية dareebaton edaafiyyah

surcharge *v.* يطلبضريبةإضافية yatlobo dareebatan edaafiyyah

sure *a.* 1 متأكّد motauakkid

sure *a.* 2 موثوق mawthooq

surely *adv.* بالتأكيد bittaukeed

surety *n.* ضمانة damaanah

surf *n.* أمواج uamwaaj

surf *v.* يَتَزَلَّجعلىالمَوج yatazallajo 'alal mawj

surface *n.* سطح sath

surface *v.* ينبثق yanbathiq

surfeit *n.* تخمة tokhmah

surge *n.* 1 موجة mawja

surge *n.* 2 تيار tayyaar

surge *v.* يَموج yamooj

surgeon *n.* جرّاح jarraah

surgery *n.* عمليةجراحية amaliyyaton jiraahiyyah

surmise *n.* حدس hads

surmise *v.* يتكهّن yatakahhan

surmount *v.* يتجاوز yatajaawaz

surname *n.* لقب laqab

surpass *v.* يفوق yafooq

surplus *n.* فائض faauid

surprise *n.* مفاجأة mofaajauah

surprise *v.* يفاجئ yofaajiu

surrender *v.* يستسلم yastaslim

surrender n. استسلام estislaam
surround v. يحيط yoheet
surroundings n. محيط moheet
surtax n. ضريبةإضافية dareebaton edaafiyyah
surveillance n. مراقبة moraaqabah
survey n. مسح mash
survey v. يَستَعْوِض yasta'rid
survival n. بقاء baqaau
survive v. يحيى yahya
suspect v. يشك yashok
suspect a. مشكوك mashkook
suspect n. مشتبهفيه moshtabahon feeh
suspend v. يعلّق yo'alliq
suspense n. تشويق tashweeq
suspension n. تعليق ta'leeq
suspicion n. اشتباه eshtibaah
suspicious a. مشبوه moshtabah
sustain v. يتحمّل yatahammal
sustenance n. رزق rizq
swagger v. يختال yakhtaal
swagger n. اختيال ekhtiyaal
swallow v. يبتلع yabtali'
swallow n. 1 ابتلاع ebtilaa'
swallow n. 2 سنونو sanono
swamp n. مستنقع mostanqa'
swamp v. يُغْرِق yoghriq
swan n. بجعة baja'ah
swarm n. سرب sarb
swarm v. يَعِجّ ya'ij
swarthy a. داكن daakin
sway v. 1 يتأثّر yatauaththar
sway v. 2 يتأرجح yatauarjah
sway n. 1 سَيطَره saytarah

sway n. 2 تمايل tamaayol
swear v. يقسم yaqsim
sweat n. عرق araq
sweat v. يعرق ya'raq
sweater n. سترة sotrah
sweep v. يكنس yaknos
sweep n. تكنيس taknees
sweeper n. كناس kannas
sweet a. حلو hilw
sweet n. حلوى halwa
sweeten v. يحلّي yohalli
sweetmeat n. حلوى halwa
sweetness n. حلاوة halaawah
swell v. يتضخّم yatadakhkham
swell n. تضخم tadakhom
swift a. سريع saree'
swim v. يسبح yasbah
swim n. سباحة sibaahah
swimmer n. سبّاح sabbaah
swindle v. يخدع yakhda'
swindle n. خداع khidaa'
swindler n. مخادع mokhaadi'
swine n. خنزير khanzeer
swing v. يتأرجح yatauarjah
swing n. أرجوحة uorjoohah
Swiss n. اللغةالسويسرية ualloghatol ssweesriyyah
Swiss adj. سويسري sweesriy
switch n. مقبس maqbas
switch v. يحوّل yohawwil
swoon n. إغماء eghmaau
swoon v. يفقدالوعي yafqidol wa'y
swoop v. ينقض yanqad
swoop n. انقضاض enqidaad
sword n. سيف sayf

sycamore *n.* جميز jommayz

sycophancy *n.* تملّقبإذلال
tamalloqon biuidhlaal

sycophant *n.* ذليل متملّق
motamalliqon dhaleel

syllabic *n.* مقطعي maqta'iy

syllable *n.* مقطع maqta'

syllabus *n.* منهج manhaj

sylph *n.* فتاةرشيقةfataaton
rasheeqah

sylvan *a.* غابي ghaabiy

symbol *n.* رمز ramz

symbolic *a.* رمزي ramziy

symbolism *n.* رمزية ramziyyah

symbolize *v.* يرمز yarmiz

symmetrical *a.* متماثل
motamaathil

symmetry *n.* تناظر tanaaddor

sympathetic *a.* متعاطف
mota'aatif

sympathize *v.* يتعاطف yata'aataf

sympathy *n.* تعاطف ta'aatof

symphony *n.* سمفونية
simfooniyyah

symposium *n.* ندوة nadwah

symptom *n.* عارض aarid

symptomatic *a.* عَرَضي aradiy

synonym *n.* مرادف moraadif

synonymous *a.* مترادف
motaraadif

synopsis *n.* ملخص molakhkhas

syntax *n.* عِلمالنّحوilmo nnahw

synthesis *n.* تركيب tarkeeb

synthetic *a.* اصطناعي estinaa'i

synthetic *n.* مصطنع mostana'

syringe *n.* حقنة hoqnah

syringe *v.* يحقن yahqin

syrup *n.* شراب sharaab

system *n.* نظام niddaam

systematic *a.* منهجي manhajiy

systematize *v.* يمنهج yomanhij

T

table *n.* طاولة taawilah

table *n.* جدول jadwal

table *v.* يضععلىالطاولةyada'o 'ala
ttaawilah

table *v.* يجدول yojadwil

tablet *n.* لوح lawh

tablet *n.* قرصدواء qors dawaau

tablet *v.* يكتب yaktob

taboo *n.* محرم moharram

taboo *adj.* محرم moharram

taboo *v.* يحرّم yoharrim

tabular *a.* مجدول mojadwal

tabulate *v.* يصنَف yosannif

tabulation *n.* تبويب tabweeb

tabulator *n.* منظمالجداول
monaddddimol jadaawil

tacit *a.* ضمني dimniy

taciturn *a.* قليلالكلامqaleelol
kalaam

tackle *n.* معالجة mo'aalajah

tackle *v.* يعالج yo'aalij

tact *n.* براعة baraa'ah

tactful *a.* لبق labiq

tactician *n.* مخطّط mokhattit

tactics *n.* مخطّطات mokhattataat

tactile *a.* حسي hissiy

tag *n.* بطاقة bitaaqah

tag *v.* يعلم yo'allim

tail *n.* ذيل dhayl

tailor *n.* خياط khayyat

tailor *v.* يخيط yakheet

taint *n.* لَطْخَه latkhah

taint *v.* يُلَطِّخ yolatikh

take *v.* يأخذ yaukhodh

tale *n.* حكاية hikaayah

talent *n.* موهبة mawhibah

talisman *n.* طلسم talsam

talk *v.* يحدَث yohaddith

talk *n.* حديث hadeeth

talkative *a.* ثرثار tharthaar

tall *a.* طويل taweel

tallow *n.* شحم shahm

tally *n.* سِجِل sijil

tally *v.* يَتلائم yatalaauam

tamarind *n.* تمرهندي tamron hindiy

tame *a.* مروَض morawwad

tame *v.* يروَض yorawwid

tamper *v.* يتلاعب yatalaa'ab

tan *v.* 1 يَدْبغ yadbogh

tan *v.* 2 يسمر yasmar

tan *n., a.* مَدبوغ madboogh

tangent *n.* مماس mamaas

tangible *a.* ملموس malmoos

tangle *n.* تشابك tashaabok

tangle *v.* يتشابك yatashaabak

tank *n.* 1 دبابة dabbaabah

tank *n.* 2 صِهُريج sihreej

tanker *n.* ناقلة naaqilah

tanner *n.* دباغ dabbaagh

tannery *n.* مدبغة madbaghah

tantalize *v.* يعذّب yo'adhdhib

tantamount *a.* مُعادِل-لِ mo'aadilon li-

tap *n.* 1 صنبور sonboor

tap *n.* 2 نَقْرَه naqrah

tap *v.* 1 يتنصت yatanassat

tap *v.* 2 يَنْقُر yanqor

tape *n.* شريط shareet

tape *v.* يسجّل yosajjil

taper *v.* يَسْتَدِق yastadiq

taper *n.* شَمْعَةٌرَفِيعَه sham'aton rafee'ah

tapestry *n.* نسيج naseej

tar *n.* قطران qatraan

tar *v.* يزفَت yozaffit

target *n.* هدف hadaf

tariff *n.* تعريف ta'reef

tarnish *v.* يَفْقِدالبَريق yafqidol bareeq

task *n.* مهمة mohimmah

task *v.* يعطي مهمة yo'ti mohimmah

taste *n.* ذوق dhawq

taste *v.* يتذوَق yatadhawwaq

tasteful *a.* حَسَن الذَوق hasano dhdhawq

tasty *a.* لذيذ ladheedh

tatter *n.* خِرقَه khirqah

tatter *v.* يصبح كالخرقة yosbiho kalkhirqah

tattoo *n.* وشم washm

tattoo *v.* يوشِم yawshim

taunt *v.* يتهكم yatahakkam

taunt *n.* تهكم tahakkom

tavern *n.* حانة haanah

tax *n.* ضريبة dareebah

tax *v.* يفرض ضريبة yafrido dareebah

taxable *a.* خاضع للضريبة khaadi'on liddareebah

taxation *n.* فرض الضرائب fardo ddaraauib

taxi *n.* سيارة أجرة sayyarato uojrah

taxi *v.* يدرج yadroj

tea *n.* شاي shaay

teach *v.* يعلَم yo'allim

teacher *n.* معلم mo'allim

teak *n.* خشب الساج khashabo ssaaj

team *n.* فريق fareeq

tear *v.* يمزق yomazziq

tear *n.* 1 دمعة dam'ah

tear *n.* 2 تمزق tamazzoq

tearful *a.* دامع daami'

tease *v.* يُضايق yodaayiq

teat *n.* حلمة halamah

technical *n.* تقني tiqaniy

technicality *n.* تقنية tiqaniyyah

technician *n.* فني faniy

technique *n.* تقنية tiqaniyyah

technological *a.* تقني tiqaniy

technologist *n.* تقني tiqaniy

technology *n.* تقنية tiqaniyyah

tedious *a.* ممل momil

tedium *n.* ملل malal

teem *v.* يزخَر yozakhkhir

teenager *n.* مراهق moraahiq

teens *n. pl.* مراهقون moraahiqoon

teethe *v.* ينبت سنه yanboto sinnoh

teetotal *a.* ممتنع عن المسكرات momtani'on 'anil mosakkiraat

teetotaller *n.* ممتنع عن المسكرات momtani'on 'anil mosakkiraat

telecast *n.* بث bath

telecast *v.* يبث yabith

telecommunications *n.* إتصالات برقية ettisaalaaton barqiyyah

telegram *n.* برقية barqiyyah

telegraph *n.* مبرقه mibraqah

telegraph *v.* يبرق yobriq

telegraphic *a.* برقي barqiy

telegraphist *n.* عامل البرقية aamilol barqiyyah

telegraphy *n.* إبراق ebraaq

telepathic *a.* خواطري khawaatiriy

telepathist *n.* عالم خواطر aalimol khawaatir

telepathy *n.* توارد خواطر tawaarodol khawaatir

telephone *n.* هاتف haatif

telephone *v.* يتصل yattasil

telescope *n.* مزقاب mirqaab

telescopic *a.* مزقبي mirqabiy

televise *v.* يتلفز yotalfiz

television *n.* تلفاز talfazah

tell *v.* يخبر yokhbir

teller *n.* راوي raawi

temper *n.* مزاج mazaaj

temper *v.* يُسكِن yosakkin

temperament *n.* مزاج mizaaj

temperamental *a.* مزاجي mizaajiy

temperance *n.* زهد zohd

temperate *a.* معتدل mo'tadil

temperature *n.* درجة حرارة darajato haraarah

tempest *n.* زوبعة zawba'a

tempestuous *a.* عاصف aasif

temple *n.* 1 هيكل haykal

temple *n.* 2 صَدغ sadgh

temporal *a.* زمني zamani

temporary *a.* مؤقت mouaqqat

tempt *v.* يغري yoghri

temptation *n.* إغراء eghraau

tempter *n.* مغري moghri

ten *n., a* عشرة asharah

tenable *a.* مدافع عنه modaafa'on 'anh

tenacious *a.* عنيد aneed

tenacity *n.* عناد inaad

tenancy *n.* إيجار ueejaar

tenant *n.* مستأجر mostaujir

tend *v.* يميل yameel

tendency *n.* ميل mayl

tender *n.* 1 مُغتَني mo'tani

tender *v.* يعرض رسمياً ya'rido rasmiyyan

tender *n.* 2 عطاء ataau

tender *adj.* لين layyin

tenet *n.* عقيدة aqeedah

tennis *n.* كرة المضرب koratol madrib

tense *adj.* 1 متوتر motawattir

tense *adj.* 2 مَشدود mashdood

tense *n.* صيغة الفعل seeghatol fi'l

tense *v.* يُوَتِّر yowattir

tension *n.* توتر tawattor

tent *n.* خيمة khaymah

tentative *a.* تَجريبي tajreebiy

tenure *n.* حيازة hiyaazah

term *n.* مصطلح mostalah

term *n.* مُدَّة moddah

term *n.* فصل fasl

term *v.* يُدعى yod'a

terminable *a.* منتهي montahi

terminal *a.* نهائي nihaauiy

terminal *n.* محطة mahattah

terminate *v.* ينهي yonhi

termination *n.* إنهاء enaau

terminological *a.* مصطلحي mostalahiy

terminology *n.* علم المصطلحات ilmol mostalahaat

terminus *n.* محطة أخيرة mahattah uakheerah

terrace *n.* شرفة shorfah

terrible *a.* رهيب raheeb

terrier *n.* وجار wajjaar

terrific *a.* رائع raaui'

terrify *v.* يروّع yorawwi'

territorial *a.* إقليمي eqleemiy

territory *n.* إقليم eqleem

terror *n.* إرهاب erhaab

terrorism *n.* إرهاب erhaab

terrorist *n.* إرهابي erhaabiy

terrorize *v.* يرهب yorhib

terse *a.* مقتضب moqtadab

test *v.* يختبر yakhtabir

test *n.* اختبار ekhtibaar

testament *n.* عهد ahd

testicle *n.* خصية khisyah

testify *v.* يشهد yashhad

testimonial *n.* شهادة shahaadah

testimony *n.* شهادة shahaadah

tete-a-tete *n.* لقاء وجهاً لوجه liqaauon wajhan liwajh

tether *n.* حبل الدابّه hablo ddaabbah

tether *v.* يربط الدابّه yarbito ddaabbah

text *n.* نص nas

textile *a.* نسيجي naseejiy

textile *n.* نسيج naseej

textual *n.* نصي nassiy

texture *n.* نسيج naseej

thank *v.* يشكر yashkor

thanks *n.* شكراً shokran

thankful *a.* شاكر shaakir

thankless *a.* ناكرللجميل naakiron lijjameel

that *adj.* ذلَك dhaalika

that *dem. pron.* ذلَك dhaalika

that *rel. pron.* الذي ualladhi

that *adv.* إلى هذاالحَد elaa haadhal had

that *conj.* أن uanna

thatch *n.* قش qash

thatch *v.* بالقش يغطّي yoghatti bilqash

thaw *v.* يذوب yathoob

thaw *n.* ذَوَبان dhawabaan

theatre *n.* مسرح masrah

theatrical *a.* مسرحي masrahiy

theft *n.* سرقة sariqah

their *a.* هم ـ hom

theirs *pron.* لهم lahom

theism *n.* الايمان بالخالق ualueemano bilkhaaliq

theist *n.* مؤمن moumin

them *pron.* هم - hom

thematic *a.* مواضيعي mawaadee'iy

theme *n.* موضوع mawdoo'

then *adv.* 1 عِندَئِذ indauidh

then *adv.* 2 ثم thomma

then *adj.* آنذاك uaanadhaak

thence *adv.* ثم من min thammah

theocracy *n.* حكومةدينية hokoomaton deeniyyah

theologian *n.* لاهوتي laahootiy

theological *a.* لاهوتي laahootiy

theology *n.* لاهوت laahoot

theorem *n.* مبرهمات mobarhimaat

theoretical *a.* نظري naddariy

theorist *n.* واضع النظرية waadi'o nnaddariyyah

theorize *v.* يضع نظرية yada'o naddariyyah

theory *n.* نظرية naddariyyah

therapy *n.* علاج ilaaj

there *adv.* هناك honaak

thereabouts *adv.* في مكان ما fi mkaanin ma

thereafter *adv.* بعد ذلك ba'da dhaalik

thereby *adv.* بالتالي bittaali

therefore *adv.* لذلك lidhaalik

thermal *a.* حراري haraariy

thermometer *n.* ميزان الحرارة mizaanol haraarah

thermos (flask) *n.* ترمس tirmos

thesis *n.* أطروحة utroohah

thick *a.* سميك sameek

thick *n.* ثِخَن thikhan

thick *adv.* بسمك bisomk

thicken *v.* يغلظ yoghlidd

thicket *n.* دغل daghl

thief *n.* لص lis

thigh *n.* فخذ fakhdh

thimble *n.* كشتبان koshtbaan

thin *a.* 1 رقيق raqeeq

thin *a.* 2 رفيع rafee'

thin *v.* يَخِف yakhif

thing *n.* شيء shayu

think v. يعتقد ya'taqid	**thread** n. خيط khayd
thinker n. مفكر mofakkir	**thread** v. يدخل الخيط yodkhilol khayt
third a. ثالث thaalith	**threadbare** a. رث rath
third n. ثالث thaalith	**threat** n. تهديد tahdeed
thirdly adv. ثالثاً thaalithan	**threaten** v. يهدّد yohaddid
thirst n. عطش atash	**three** n. ثلاثة thalaathah
thirst v. يتعطّش yata'attash	**three** adj. ثلاثة thalaathah
thirsty a. 1 متعطش mota'atish	**thresh** v. يدرس yadros
thirsty a. 2 ظمآن ddamuaan	**thresher** n. درّاسة darraasah
thirteen n. ثلاثة عشر thalaathato 'ashar	**threshold** n. عتبة atabah
thirteen adj. ثلاثة عشر thalaathato 'ashar	**thrice** adv. ثلاث مرّات thalaatho marrat
thirteenth a. ثالث عشر thaalith 'ashar	**thrift** n. إدخار eddikhaar
thirtieth a. الثلاثون uaththalaathoon	**thrifty** a. مقتصد moqtasid
thirtieth n. الثلاثون uaththalaathoon	**thrill** n. رعشة ra'shah
thirty n. ثلاثون thalaathoon	**thrill** v. يشوّق yoshawwiq
thirty adj. ثلاثون thalaathoon	**thrive** v. يزدهر yazdahir
thistle n. شوك shawk	**throat** n. حنجرة honjarah
thither adv. هناك honaak	**throaty** a. مبحوح mabhooh
thorn n. شوكة shawkah	**throb** v. ينبض yanbid
thorny a. شائك shaauik	**throb** n. نبض nabd
thorough adj. شامل shaamil	**throe** n. ألم نوبة nawbato ualam
thoroughfare n. شارع shaari'	**throne** n. عرش arsh
though conj. رغم أن raghma anna	**throne** v. يتوّج yotawwij
though adv. مع ذلك ma'a dhaalik	**throng** n. حشد hashd
thought n. فكرة fikrah	**throng** v. يحتشد yahtashid
thoughtful a. مدروس madroos	**throttle** n. صمام خانق sammaamon khaaniq
thousand n. ألف alf	**throttle** v. يخنق yakhniq
thousand adj. ألف alf	**through** prep. خلال khilaal
thrall n. مستعبد mosta'bid	**through** adv. خلال khilaal
thralldom n. عبودية oboodiyyah	**through** adj. منتهي montahi
thrash v. يجلد yajlid	**throughout** adv. في كل الارجاء fi kollil uarjaau
	throughout prep. طوال tawaal

throw v. يرمي yarmi
throw n. رمية ramyah
thrust v. يدفع yadfa'
thrust n. دفعة daf'ah
thud n. جلجلة jaljalah
thud v. يجلجل yojaljil
thug n. سفاح saffaah
thumb n. إبهام ebhaam
thumb v. يستعملالابهام yasta'milol ebhaam
thump n. رطم ratm
thump v. يرطم yartim
thunder n. رعد ra'd
thunder v. يرعد yar'id
thunderous a. مدو modwi
Thursday n. الخميس ualkhamees
thus adv. بالتالي bittaali
thwart v. يحبط yohbit
tiara n. عِمامَهمرصعةبالمجوهرات amaamaton morassa'aton bilmojawharaat
tick n. 1 تكتكة taktakah
tick n. 2 علامة alaamah
tick n. 3 قرادة qaraadah
tick v. 1 يَتِك yatik
tick v. 2 يعلّم yo'allim
ticket n. تذكرة tadhkarah
tickle v. يدغدغ yodaghdigh
ticklish a. حساسللدغدغة hassaason liddaghdaghah
tidal a. مدّي maddiy
tide n. مد madd
tidings n. pl. بشرى boshra
tidiness n. ترتيب tarteeb
tidy a. مرتّب morattab

tidy v. يرتّب yorattib
tie v. يربط yarbit
tie n. عنق ربطة rabtato 'onoq
tier n. طبقة tabaqah
tiger n. نمر namir
tight a. ضيق dayyeq
tighten v. يضيّق yadeeq
tigress n. نمرة namirah
tile n. قرميد qarmeed
tile v. يضعالقرميد yada'ol qarmeed
till prep. حتى hatta
till conj. حتى hatta
till v. يَفلَح yaflah
till n. دُرجالنُقود dorjo nnoqood
tilt v. يميل yameel
tilt n. ميلان mayalaan
timber n. خشب khashab
time n. وقت waqt
time n. إيقاع ueeqaa'
time n. مَرَّه marrah
time v. يوقّت yowaqqit
timely a. متزامن motazaamin
timid a. خجول khajool
timidity n. خجل khajal
timorous a. هيّاب hayyaab
tin n. 1 قصدير qasdeer
tin n. 2 علبة olbah
tin v. يعلّب yo'allib
tincture n. صبغة sabghah
tincture v. يصبغ yasbigh
tinge n. مسحة mashah
tinge v. يمسح yamsah
tinker n. سَمْكَري samkariy
tinsel n. أشرطةللزينة uashritaton lizzeenah

tint n. خَفيف اللَون lawnon khafeef

tint v. يلوِّن yolawwin

tiny a. صغير sagheer

tip n. 1 حافَة haafah

tip v. 1 يَقَلِّم yoqallim

tip n. 2 بَقْشيش baqsheesh

tip v. 2 يُعْطي بَقْشيشاً yo'ti baqsheeshan

tip n. 3 معلومة ma'loomah

tip (off) v. 3 يعلم yo'lim

tip n. 4 مَكان رَمي القُمامَه mkaano ramyil qomaamah

tip v. 4 يميل yameel

tipsy a. سكران sakraan

tirade n. تعنيف ta'neef

tire v. يتعب yot'ib

tire n. إطار etaar

tiresome a. متعب mot'ib

tissue n. نسيج naseej

titanic a. جبّار jabbaar

tithe n. ضريبةالعشر dareebatol 'oshr

title n. 1 عنوان onwaan

title n. 2 لقب laqab

title v. يلقّب yolaqqib

titular a. ملقَّب molaqqab

toad n. دفضع difda'

toast n. خبز محمّص khobzon mohammas

toast v. يحمّص yohammis

tobacco n. تبغ tibgh

today adv. اليوم ualyawm

today n. اليوم ualyawm

toe n. اصبع القدم esba'ol qadam

toe v. يمشي قدماً yamshi qodoman

toffee n. حلوى halwa

toga n. سترة sotrah

together adv. معاً ma'an

toil n. كدح kadh

toil v. يكدح yakdah

toilet n. مرحاض mirhaad

toils n. pl. شراك shiraak

token n. رمز ramz

tolerable a. مقبول maqbool

tolerance n. تسامح tasaamoh

tolerant a. متسامح motasaamih

tolerate v. يتحمَّل yatahammal

toleration n. تحمّل tahammol

toll n. مِقدار الضَرَر miqdaaro ddarar

toll n. رسوم rosoom

toll v. يَدق yadoq

tomato n. طماطم tamaatim

tomb n. قبر qabr

tomboy n. فتاةمسترجلة fataaton mostarjilah

tomcat n. قط qit

tome n. مجلد mojallad

tomorrow n. غد ghad

tomorrow adv. غداً ghadan

ton n. طن ton

tone n. نغمة naghmah

tone n. صَلابه salaabah

tone v. يَنْسَجِم yansajim

tongs n. pl. ملقط milqat

tongue n. لسان lisaan

tonic a. منشِّط monashshit

tonic n. 1 منشط monashshit

tonic n. 2 مياه غازِيَّه miyaahon ghaaziyyah

tonight n. الليلة uallaylah

tonight adv. الليلة uallaylah

tonne *n.* طن ton

tonsil *n.* اللوزةالحلق lawzatol halq

tonsure *n.* لُوزِي lowaziy

too *adv.* أيضاً uaydan

tool *n.* أداة uadaah

tooth *n.* سن sin

toothache *n.* وجعأسنان waja'o uasnaan

toothsome *a.* لذيذ ladheedh

top *n.* 1 أعلى ua'la

top *v.* يضيف yadeef

top *n.* 2 قمة qimmah

topaz *n.* توباز toobaaz

topic *n.* موضوع mawdoo'

topical *a.* موضعي mawdoo'iy

topographer *n.* عالمالتضاريس alamo ttadaarees

topographical *a.* تضاريسي tadaareesiy

topography *n.* تضاريس tadaarees

topple *v.* يقلب yoqallib

topsy *turvy* a. رأسأعلىعقب rausan 'ala 'aqib

topsy turvy *adv.* رأسأعلىعقب rausan 'ala 'aqib

torch *n.* شعلة sho'lah

torment *n.* عذاب adhaab

torment *v.* يعذّب yo'adhdhib

tornado *n.* زوبعة zawba'ah

torpedo *n.* قظيفة qaddeefah

torpedo *v.* ينسف yansif

torrent *n.* سيل sayl

torrential *a.* متدفق motadaffiq

torrid *a.* حار haar

tortoise *n.* سلحفاة solhofaah

tortuous *a.* متعرج mota'arrij

torture *n.* تعذيب ta'dheeb

torture *v.* يعذّب yo'adhdhib

toss *v.* يتقلّب yataqallab

toss *n.* رمية ramyah

total *a.* كلي kolliy

total *n.* مجموع majmoo'

total *v.* يجمع yajma'

totality *n.* كلية kolliyyah

totalitarian *adj.* دكتاتوري dictaatooriy

touch *v.* يلمس yalmis

touch *n.* لمس lams

touchy *a.* حتّاس hassaas

tough *a.* صارم saarim

toughen *v.* يقوّي yoqawwi

tour *n.* جولة jawlah

tour *v.* يتجوّل yatajawwal

tourism *n.* سياحة siyaahah

tourist *n.* سائح saauih

tournament *n.* مباراة mobaaraah

towards *prep.* نحو nahwa

towel *n.* منشفة minshafah

towel *v.* ينشف yonashshif

tower *n.* برج borj

tower *v.* يَرتَفِع yartafi'

town *n.* بلدة baldah

township *a.* بلدي baladiy

toy *n.* لعبة lo'bah

toy *v.* يعبث ya'bath

trace *n.* أثر uathar

trace *v.* يتعقب yata'aqqab

traceable *a.* متعقّب mota'aqqib

track *n.* مسار masaar

track *v.* أَثَر يَقْتَفى yataqaffa uathar

tract *n.* مسلك maslak

tract *n.* منطقه mantiqah

traction *n.* جر jar

tractor *n.* جرّار jarraar

trade *n.* تجارة tijaarah

trade *v.* يتاجر yotaajir

trader *n.* تاجر taajir

tradesman *n.* تاجر taajir

tradition *n.* تقليد taqleed

traditional *a.* تقليدي taqleediy

traffic *n.* مرور moroor

traffic *v.* يتاجِر yotaajir

tragedian *n.* كاتب تراجيديا kaatibo traajeedia

tragedy *n.* مأساة mausaah

tragic *a.* مأساوي mausaawiy

trail *n.* 1 أثر uathar

trail *n.* 2 مسار masaar

trail *v.* يتعقّب yata'aqab

trailer *n.* مقطورة maqtoorah

train *n.* قطار qitaar

train *v.* يدرّب yodarrib

trainee *n.* متدرب motadarrib

training *n.* تدريب tadreeb

trait *n.* سمة simah

traitor *n.* خائن khaauin

tram *n.* حافلة كهربائية haafilaton kahrabaauiyyah

trample *v.* يسحق yashaq

trance *n.* نشوة nashwah

tranquil *a.* هادئ haadiu

tranquility *n.* هدوء hodoou

tranquillize *v.* يهدئ yohaddiu

tranquillizer *n.* مهدئ mohaddiu

transact *v.* يتعامل yata'aamal

transaction *n.* تداول tadaawol

transcend *v.* يتجاوز yatajaawaz

transcendent *a.* متعال mota'aali

transcribe *v.* ينسخ yansakh

transcriber *n.* ناسخ naasikh

transcription *n.* نسخ naskh

transfer *n.* حوالة howaalah

transfer *v.* ينقل yanqil

transferable *a.* محوّل mohawwil

transfiguration *n.* التجلّي uattajalli

transfigure *v.* يتجلّى yatajalla

transform *v.* يحوّل yohawwil

transformation *n.* تحول tahawwol

transgress *v.* يتجاوز yatajaawaz

transgression *n.* مخالفة mokhaalafah

transit *n.* عبور oboor

transition *n.* انتقال entiqaal

transitive *n.* متعد mota'addi

transitory *adj.* عابر qaseerol uamad

translate *v.* يترجم yotarjim

translation *n.* ترجمة tarjamah

transmigration *n.* هجرة hijrah

transmission *n.* 1 نقل naql

transmission *n.* 2 بث bath

transmit *v.* 1 ينقل yanqil

transmit *v.* 2 يبث yaboth

transmitter *n.* مرسل morsil

transparent *a.* شفاف shaffaaf

transplant *v.* يزرع yazra'

transplant *n.* زراعة ziraa'ah

transport *v.* ينقل yanqil

transport *n.* وسيلة نقل waseelato naql

transportation *n.* وسائل النقل wasaauilo nnaql

trap *n.* فخ fakh	**trial** *n.* محاكمة mohaakamah
trap *v.* يحصر yahsor	**triangle** *n.* مثلث mothallath
trash *n.* قمامة qomaamah	**triangular** *a.* ثلاثي tholaathiy
travel *v.* يسافر yosaafir	**tribal** *a.* قبلي qabaliy
travel *n.* سفر safar	**tribe** *n.* قبيلة qabeelah
traveller *n.* مسافر mosaafir	**tribulation** *n.* محنة mihnah
tray *n.* صينية seeniyyah	**tribunal** *n.* محكمة mahkamah
treacherous *a.* غادر ghadir	**tributary** *n.* رافد raafid
treachery *n.* غدر ghadr	**tributary** *a.* تقديري taqdeeriy
tread *v.* يدوس yadoos	**tribute** *n.* تقدير taqdeer
tread *n.* وَقْعُ الأقْدام waq'ol uaqdaam	**trick** *n.* خدعة khid'ah
treason *n.* خيانة khiyaanah	**trick** *v.* يخدع yakhda'
treasure *n.* كنز kanz	**trickery** *n.* تحايل tahaayol
treasure *v.* يُثَمِّن yothammin	**trickle** *v.* ينقط yanqot
treasurer *n.* أمين صندوق meeno sondooq	**trickle** *n.* سيلان sayalaan
	trickster *n.* محتال mohtaal
treasury *n.* خزينة khazeenah	**tricky** *a.* صعب sa'b
treat *v.* 1 يعالج yo'aalij	**tricolour** *a.* ثلاثي الألوان tholaathiyol ualwaan
treat *v.* 2 يُعامِل yo'aamil	
treat *n.* وَليمَه waleemah	**tricolour** *n.* الألوان الثلاثة ualualwaano ththalaathah
treatise *n.* مقالة maqaalah	
treatment *n.* 1 علاج ilaaj	**tricycle** *n.* دراجة بثلاث عجلات darraajaton bithalaathi 'ajalaat
treatment *n.* 2 مُعامَلَه mo'aamalah	
treaty *n.* معاهدة mo'aahadah	**trifle** *n.* 1 تافه taafih
tree *n.* شجرة shajarah	**trifle** *n.* 2 كعكة المربى ka'katol morabba
trek *v.* يرحل yarhal	
trek *n.* رحلة rihlah	**trifle** *v.* يتلاعب yatalaa'ab
tremble *v.* يرتجف yartajif	**trigger** *n.* زناد zinaad
tremendous *a.* هائل haauil	**trigger** *v.* يُشْعِل yosh'il
tremor *n.* زلزال zilzaal	**trim** *a.* مقلَّم moqallam
trench *n.* خندق khandaq	**trim** *n.* تقليم taqleem
trench *v.* يخندق yokhandiq	**trim** *v.* يقلّم yoqallem
trend *n.* اتجاه ettijaah	**trinity** *n.* ثالوث thaalooth
trespass *v.* يتخطى yatakhatta	**trio** *n.* ثلاثي tholaathiy
trespass *n.* تجاوز tajaawoz	**trip** *v.* يتعرقل yata'arqal
	trip *n.* رحلة rihlah

tripartite *a.* ثلاثي tholaathiy

triple *a.* ثلاثي tholaathiy

triple *v.t.,* يضاعف ثلاث مرّات yodaa'ifo thalaatha marraat

triplicate *a.* ثلاثي tholaathiy

triplicate *n.* توائم ثلاث tawaauimo thalaath

triplicate *v.* يضاعف ثلاث مرّات yodaa'ifo thalaatha marraat

triplication *n.* المضاعفة ثلاث مرّات ualmodaa'fato thalaatha marraat

tripod *n.* ثلاثي القوائم tholaathiyol qawaauim

triumph *n.* انتصار entisaam

triumph *v.* ينتصر yantasir

triumphal *a.* انتصاري entisaariy

triumphant *a.* منتصر montasir

trivial *a.* تافه taafih

troop *n.* قوات qwwaat

troop *v.* يَحْتَشِد yahtashid

trooper *n.* فارس faaris

trophy *n.* نُصُب تِذكاري nasbon tidhkaariy

tropic *n.* مدار madaar

tropical *a.* استوائي estiwaauiy

trot *v.* يُهَرْوِل yoharwil

trot *n.* خبب khabab

trouble *n.* مشكلة moshkilah

trouble *v.* يُقْلِق yoqliq

troublesome *a.* مزعج mozuij

troupe *n.* فرقة firqah

trousers *n. pl* بنطال bintaal

trowel *n.* مجرفة mijrafah

truce *n.* هدنة hodnah

truck *n.* شاحنة shaahinah

true *a.* صحيح saheeh

trump *n.* ورقة رابحة waraqaton raabihah

trump *v.* يستعمل ورقة رابحة yasta'milo waraqatan raabihah

trumpet *n.* بوق booq

trumpet *v.* يُبَوِّق yobawwiq

trunk *n.* جذع jidh'

trust *n.* ثقة thiqah

trust *v.* يثق yathiq

trustee *n.* وصي wasiy

trustful *a.* واثق waathiq

trustworthy *a.* موثوق mawthooq

trusty *n.* موثوق mawthooq

truth *n.* حقيقة yaqeeqah

truthful *a.* صادق saadiq

try *v.* يحاول yohaawil

try *n.* محاولة mohaawalh

trying *a.* شاق shaaq

tryst *n.* موعد غرامي maw'idon gharaamiy

tub *n.* حوض hawd

tube *n.* أنبوب uonboob

tuberculosis *n.* السل uassol

tubular *a.* أنبوبي uonboobiy

tug *v.* يَجُر yajor

tuition *n.* 1 تَعْليم ta'leem

tuition *n.* 2 رسوم التَّعْليم rosoomo tta'leem

tumble *v.* يتعثر yata'aththar

tumble *n.* تَعَثُر ta'aththor

tumbler *n.* 1 قَدَح كبير qadahon kabeer

tumbler *n.* 2 بهلوان bahlawaan

tumour *n.* ورم waram

tumult *n.* شغب shaghab

tumultuous *a.* صاخب saakhib

tune *n.* لحن lahn

tune *v.* يظبط yaddbit

tunnel *n.* نفق nafaq

tunnel *v.* يحفرنفق yahfiro nafaq

turban *n.* عمامة maamah

turbine *n.* مُحَرِّكمائي moharrikon maauiy

turbulence *n.* اضطراب edtiraab

turbulent *a.* مضطرب modtarib

turf *n.* حلبةسباقالخيل halabato sibaaqil khayl

turkey *n.* ديكحبشي deekon habashiy

turmeric *n.* كركم korkom

turmoil *n.* اضطراب edtiraab

turn *v.* 1 يدير yodeer

turn *v.* 2 يحوّل yohawwil

turn *n.* 1 دور dawr

turn *n.* 2 إنعطاف en'itaaf

turner *n.* خرّاط kharraat

turnip *n.* لفت lift

turpentine *n.* زيتالتربنتين zayto ttirbinteen

turtle *n.* سلحفاة solhofaah

tusk *n.* ناب naab

tussle *n.* صراع siraa'

tussle *v.* يصارع yosaari'

tutor *n.* مدرس modarris

tutorial *a.* تدريسي tadrees

tutorial *n.* برنامجتعليمي barnaamajon ta'leemiy

twelfth *a.* الثانيعشر uathaani 'ashar

twelfth *n.* الثانيعشر uathaani 'ashar

twelve *n.* اثناعشر ethna 'ashar

twentieth *a.* العشرون ual'ishroon

twentieth *n.* العشرون ual'ishroon

twenty *a.* عشرون ishroon

twenty *n.* عشرون ishroon

twice *adv.* مرّتين marratayn

twig *n.* غصين ghosayn

twilight *n.* شفق shafaq

twin *n.* توأم tawuam

twin *adj.* توأم tawuam

twinkle *v.* يَتَلألأ yatalaulau

twinkle *n.* تلألُؤ talaulou

twist *v.* يَفْتِل yaftil

twist *n.* 1 حيلة heelah

twist *n.* 2 إلتواء eltiwaau

twitter *n.* تغريد taghreed

twitter *v.* يغرّد yogharrid

two *n.* اثنان ethnaan

two *a.* اثنان ethnaan

twofold *a.* مضاعف modaa'af

type *n.* نوع naw'

type *v.* يطبع yatba'

typhoid *n.* التيفوئيد uatteefooueed

typhoon *n.* إعصار e'saar

typhus *n.* التيفوس uatteefos

typical *a.* نموذجي namoodhajiy

typify *v.* يجسدالخصائص yojassidol khasaauis

typist *n.* طابع taabi'

tyranny *n.* طغيان toghyaan

tyrant *n.* طاغية taaghiyah

tyre *n.* إطار etaar

U

udder n. ضرع dar'
uglify v. يقبح yoqabbih
ugliness n. قبح qobh
ugly a. قبيح qabeeh
ulcer n. قرحة qorhah
ulcerous a. متقرّح motaqarrih
ulterior a. خفي khafiy
ultimate a. نهائي nihaauiy
ultimately adv.في النهاية fi nnihaaya
ultimatum n. إنذار endhaar
umbrella n. مظلة middallah
umpire n. حكم hakam
umpire v.t., يحكم yohakkim
unable a. غير قادر ghayr qaadir
unanimity n. إجماع ejmaa'
unanimous a. بالإجماع bil ejmaa'
unaware a.غيرمدرك ghayr modrik
unawares adv. على حين غرة ala heeni ghirrah
unburden v. يرفّعنه yoraffiho 'anh
uncanny a. غريب ghareeb
uncertain a.غيرمؤكد ghayr mouakkad
uncle n. عم am
uncouth a. غيرمألوف ghayr mauloof
under prep. تحت taht
under adv. تحت taht
under adj. أدنى uadna
undercurrent n. تيارتحتي tayyaaron tahtiy

underdog n. المهضوم حقه ualmahdoomo haqqoh
undergo v. يخضع yakhda'
undergraduate n. جامعي jaami'iy
underhand a. مخادع mokhaadi'
underline v. يبرز yobriz
undermine v. يستخف yastakhif
underneath adv. تحت taht
underneath prep. تحت taht
underneath adj. سفلي sofliy
understand v. يفهم yafham
undertake v. يباشر yobaashir
undertone n. لون خافت lawnon khaafit
underwear n. ملابس داخلية mlaabiwon daakhiliyyah
underworld n. الجحيم ualjaheem
undo v. 1 يحَل yahill
undo v. 2 يتراجع yataraaja'
undue a. غيرضروري ghayr darooriy
undulate v. 1 يتموج yatamawwaj
undulate v. 2 يكبر yakbor
undulation n. تموج tamawwoj
unearth v. يكشف yakshif
uneasy a.غيرمستقر ghayr mostaqir
unfair adj. غيرمنصف ghayr monsif
unfold v. يتكشف yatakashshaf
unfortunate a. مؤسف mousif
ungainly a. صعب المراس sa'bol miraas
unhappy a. تعيس ta'ees
unification n. توحيد tawheed

union *n.* إتحاد ettihaad	**up** *prep.* فوق fawq
unionist *n.* إتحادي ettihaadiy	**upbraid** *v.* يلوم yaloom
unique *a.* فريد fareed	**upheaval** *n.* جيشان jayshaan
unison *n.* انسجام ensijaam	**uphold** *v.* يدعم yad'am
unit *n.* وحدة wihdah	**upkeep** *n.* صيانة siyaanah
unite *v.* يوحِد yowahhid	**uplift** *v.* يرفع yarfa'
unity *n.* وحدة wihdah	**uplift** *n.* رفع raf'
universal *a.* عالمي aalamiy	**upon** *prep.* على ala
universality *n.* عالميّة aalamiyyah	**upper** *a.* أعلى ua'la
universe *n.* كون kawn	**upright** *a.* مستقيم mostaqeem
university *n.* جامعة jaami'ah	**uprising** *n.* ثورة thawrah
unjust *a.* ظالم ddaalim	**uproar** *n.* صخب sakhab
unless *conj.* إذا إلا ella edha	**uproarious** *a.* هائج haauij
unlike *adj.* مختلف mokhtalif	**uproot** *v.* يقتلع yaqtali'
unlike *prep.* علىعكس ala 'aks	**upset** *v.* 1 يقلق yoqliq
unlikely *a.* مِنغيرالأرجح min ghayril uarjah	**upset** *v.* 2 يحزن yohzin
unmanned *a.* غيرمراقب ghayr moraaqab	**upshot** *n.* نتيجة nateejah
	upstart *n.* مغرور maghroor
unmannerly *adj.* فظ fadd	**up-to-date** *a.* محدّث mohaddath
unprincipled *a.* بلامبادئ bila mabaadiu	**upward** *a.* تصاعدي tasaa'odiy
	upwards *adv.* صعودًا so'oodan
unreliable *a.* غيرجديربالثقة ghayr jadeerin biththiqah	**urban** *a.* حضري hadariy
	urbane *a.* لطيف lateef
unrest *n.* اضطراب edtraab	**urbanity** *n.* تحضّر tahaddor
unruly *a.* جامح jaamih	**urchin** *n.* 1 ولَدشَقي waladon shaqiy
unsettle *v.* يشوّش yoshawwish	
unsheathe *v.* يستل yastall	**urchin** *n.* 2 قنفذ qonfodh
until *prep.* حتى hatta	**urge** *v.* يحث yahith
until *conj.* حتى hatta	**urge** *n.* رغبةملحّة raghbah molihhah
untoward *a.* غيرمؤات ghayro mouaatin	
	urgency *n.* طارئ taariu
unwell *a.* مريض mareed	**urgent** *a.* عاجل aajil
unwittingly *adv.* عنغيرقصد an ghayri qasd	**urinal** *n.* مبولة mibwalah
	urinary *a.* بولي bawliy
up *adv.* انتهى entaha	**urinate** *v.* يتبوّل yatabawwal

urination *n.* تبول tabawwol

urine *n.* بول bawl

urn *n.* جرة jarrah

usage *n.* استعمال esti'maal

use *n.* استخدام estikhdaam

use *v.* يستخدم yastakhdim

useful *a.* مفيد mofeed

usher *n.* مُرشِد morshid

usher *v.* يُرشِد yorshid

usual *a.* معتاد mo'taad

usually *adv.* عادةً aadah

usurer *n.* مراب moraabi

usurp *v.* يغتصب yaghtasib

usurpation *n.* اغتصاب eghtisaab

usury *n.* ربا riba

utensil *n.* أداة uadaah

uterus *n.* رحم rahm

utilitarian *a.* منفعي manfa'iy

utility *n.* فائدة faauidah

utilization *n.* استخدام estikhdaam

utilize *v.* يستخدم yastakhdim

utmost *a.* أقصى uaqsa

utmost *n.* قصارى qosaara

utopia *n* . المدينةالفاضلة ualmadeenatol faadilah

utopian *a.* فاضل faadil

utter *v.* يلفظ yalfidd

utter *adj.* مطلق motlaq

utterance *n.* كلام kalaam

utterly *adv.* تماماً tamaaman

vacancy *n.* شاغروظيفي shaagher waddeefi

vacant *a.* شاغر shaagher

vacate *v.* يخلي yakhli

vacation *n.* عطلة otlah

vaccinate *v.* يلقح yolaqqih

vaccination *n.* تلقيح talqeeh

vaccinator *n.* ملقح molaqih

vaccine *n.* لقاح loqaah

vacillate *v.* يتأرجح yatauarjah

vacuum *n.* فراغ faraagh

vacuum *v.* يكنس yaknis

vagabond *n.* تشرد tasharrod

vagabond *adj.* متشرد motasharrid

vagary *n.* نَزوَه nazwah

vagina *n.* مهبل mihbal

vague *a.* غامض ghaamid

vagueness *n.* غموض ghomood

vain *a.* دونجدوى doona jadwa

vainglorious *a.* مختال mokhtaal

vainglory *n.* تيه teeh

vainly *adv.* عبثًا abathan

vale *n.* واد waad

valiant *a.* شجاع shojaa'

valid *a.* صالح saalih

validate *v.* يتحققمنصحة yatahaqqaqo min sihhat

validity *n.* صحة sihhah

valley *n.* واد waad

valour *n.* بسالة basaalah

valuable *a.* قيم qayyim

valuation *n.* تقييم taqweem

value *n.* قيمة qeemah

value *v.* يقيّم yoqayyim

valve *n.* صمام sammaam

van *n.* عربة arabah

vanish *v.* يتلاش yatalaasha

vanity n. خيلاء khaylaau

vanquish v. يقهر yaqhar

vaporize v. يتبخّر yatabakhkhar

vaporous a. ضبابي dabaabiy

vapour n. بخار bokhaar

variable a. متغير motaghayyir

variance n. فرق farq

variation n. تنوّع tanawwo'

varied a. متنوّع motanawwi'

variety n. تشكيلة tashkeelah

various a. مُتَنَوّع motanawwi'

varnish n. طلاءالورنيش tilaauol warneesh

varnish v. يطليبالورنيش yatli bil warneesh

vary v. يختلف yakhtalif

vasectomy n. قطعالقناةالدافقة qat'ol qanaati ddafiqah

vaseline n. فازلين faazleen

vast a. رحب rahib

vault n. 1 قبو qabo

vault n. 2 وَثبَه wathbah

vault v. يَثِب yathib

vegetable n. خضار khodaar

vegetable a. خضاري khodaariy

vegetarian n. نباتي nabaatiy

vegetarian adj. نباتي nabaatiy

vegetation n. حياةنباتية hayaaton nabaatiyyah

vehemence n. عنف onf

vehement a. عنيف aneef

vehicle n. مركبة markabah

vehicular a. مركبي markabiy

veil n. حجاب hijaab

veil v. يحجب yahjib

vein n. 1 عرق irq

vein n. 2 وَريد wareed

vein v. يعزّق yo'arriq

velocity n. تسارع tasaaro'

velvet n. مخمل mokhmal

velvety a. مخملي mokhmaliy

venal a. قابلللرشوة qaabilon lirrashwah

venality n. فساد fasaad

vendor n. بائع baaui'

venerable a. جَليل jaleel

venerate v. يُبَجِّل yobajjil

veneration n. تبجيل tabjeel

vengeance n. انتقام entiqaam

venial a. عرضي aradiy

venom n. سم som

venomous a. سام saam

vent n. منفس manfas

ventilate v. ينفّس yonaffis

ventilation n. تهوية tahwiyah

ventilator n. مروحة marwahah

venture n. مُجازَفَه mojaazafah

venture v. يُجازِف yojaazif

venturesome a. مغامر moghaamir

venturous a. مغامر moghaamir

venue n. موقع mawqi'

veracity n. صحة sihhah

verendah n. شرفة shorfah

verb n. فعل fi'l

verbal a. 1 فعلي fi'liy

verbal a. 2 شفوي shafawiy

verbally adv. شفويًا shafawiyyan

verbatim a. حرفي harfiy

verbatim adv. حرفيا harfiyan

verbose a. مطنب motnib

verbosity n. إسهاب eshaab

verdant *a.* أخضر uakhdar	**veteran** *a.* مُحَنّك mohannak
verdict *n.* حكم hokm	**veterinary** *a.* بيطري baytariy
verge *n.* حافة haafah	**veto** *n.* حق النقض haqqo nnaqd
verification *n.* تحقق tahaqqoq	**veto** *v.* يَنقُض yanqod
verify *v.* يتحقق من yatahaqqaq	**vex** *v.* يغيظ yogheedd
verisimilitude *n.* واقعيّه waaqi'iyyah	**vexation** *n.* إغاظة eghaaddah
veritable *a.* حقيقي haqeeqiy	**via** *prep.* بواسطة biwaasitat
vermillion *n.* أحمر برتقالي uahmaron bortoqaaliy	**viable** *a.* حيوي hayawiy
vermillion *a.* أحمر برتقالي uahmaron bortoqaaliy	**vial** *n.* قارورة qaaroorah
vernacular *n.* عامية aamiyyah	**vibrate** *v.* يهتز yahtaz
vernacular *a.* دارج daarij	**vibration** *n.* اهتزاز ehtizaaz
vernal *a.* ربيعي rabee'iy	**vicar** *n.* كاهن kaahin
versatile *a.* متعدد الجوانب mota'addidol jawaanib	**vicarious** *a.* مناب monaab
versatility *n.* تَعَدُّد الجوانب ta'addodol jawaanib	**vice** *n.* 1 رَذيلَه radheelah
	vice *n.* 2 مِلزَمَه milzamah
verse *n.* آية uaayah	**viceroy** *n.* نائب الملك naauibol malik
versed *a.* متمكن motamakkin	**vice-versa** *adv.* والعكس صحيح wal'akso saheeh
versification *n.* نظم الشعر naddmo shshi'r	**vicinity** *n.* جوار jiwaar
versify *v.* ينظم الشِّعرَ yonadddimo shshi'r	**vicious** *a.* أثيم uatheem
version *n.* إصدار esdaar	**vicissitude** *n.* انقلاب enqilaab
versus *prep.* مقابل moqaabil	**victim** *n.* ضحية dahiyyah
vertical *a.* عمودي amoodiy	**victimize** *v.* يجعل منه ضحية yaj'alo minho dahiyyah
verve *n.* نشاط nashaat	**victor** *n.* منتصر montasir
very *a.* جدًا jiddan	**victorious** *a.* منتصر montasir
vessel *n.* سفينة safeenah	**victory** *n.* إنتصار entisaar
vest *n.* سترة sotrah	**victuals** *n. pl* مؤن mouan
vest *v.* يعهد ya'had	**vie** *v.* يَتَنافَس yatanaafas
vestige *n.* بقايا baqaaya	**view** *n.* 1 رأي rauy
vestment *n.* رداء ridaau	**view** *n.* 2 مشهد mashhad
veteran *n.* محارب قديم mohaaribon qadeem	**view** *v.* نظرة يلقي yolqi naddrah
	vigil *n.* يقظة yaqadhah
	vigilance *n.* يقظة yaqadhah
	vigilant *a.* حذر hadhir

vigorous *a.* مُنْتَفِحِل mostafhil	**visionary** *a.* حالم haalim
vile *a.* خَسِيس khasees	**visionary** *n.* ذوبصيرة dho baseerah
vilify *v.* يضم yadhom	**visit** *n.* زيارة ziyaarah
villa *n.* فيلا filla	**visit** *v.* يزور yazoor
village *n.* قرية qaryah	**visitor** *n.* زائر zaauir
villager *n.* قروي qarawiy	**vista** *n.* أفق uofoq
villain *n.* وغد waghd	**visual** *a.* بصري basariy
vindicate *v.* يبرر yobarrir	**visualize** *v.* يتصوّر yatasawwar
vindication *n.* تبرئة tabriuah	**vital** *a.* حيوي hayawiy
vine *n.* كرمة karmah	**vitality** *n.* حيوية hayawiyyah
vinegar *n.* خل khal	**vitalize** *v.* يحي yohyi
vintage *n.* خمر khamr	**vitamin** *n.* فيتامين feetaameen
violate *v.* ينتهك yantahik	**vitiate** *v.* يعطب yo'tib
violation *n.* انتهاك entihaak	**vivacious** *a.* مرح marih
violence *n.* عنف onf	**vivacity** *n.* حيوية hayawiyyah
violent *a.* عنيف aneef	**viva** *voce* adv. شفهيا shafawiyyan
violet *n.* بنفسجي banafsajiy	**viva voce** adj. شفهي shafawiy
violin *n.* كمان kamaan	**viva voce** *n.* إمتحان شفوي emtihaanon shafawiy
violinist *n.* عازف كمان aazifo kamaan	**vivid** *a.* حيوي hayawiy
virgin *n.* عذراء adhraau	**vixen** *n.* ثَعْلَبَه tha'labah
virgin adj. بكر bikr	**vocabulary** *n.* مفردات mofradaat
virginity *n.* عذرية odhriyyah	**vocal** *a.* صوتي sawtiy
virile *a.* فحل fahl	**vocalist** *n.* مغني moghanni
virility *n.* فحولة fohoolah	**vocation** *n.* مهنة mihnah
virtual adj. ظاهري ddaahiriy	**vogue** *n.* موضة moodah
virtue *n.* فضيلة fadeelah	**voice** *n.* صوت sawt
virtuous *a.* فاضل faadil	**voice** *v.* يُعَبِر عن yo'abbir 'an
virulence *n.* خبث khobth	**void** *a.* باطل baatil
virulent *a.* خبيث khabeeth	**void** *v.* يبطل yobtil
virus *n.* فيروس fayroos	**void** *n.* فراغ faraagh
visage *n.* محيا mohayya	**volcanic** *a.* بركاني borkaaniy
visibility *n.* وضوح wodooh	**volcano** *n.* بركان borkaan
visible *a.* مرئي maruiy	**volition** *n.* إرادة eraadah
vision *n.* رؤية rouyah	

volley *n.* وابل waabil

volley *v.* يُطلِقُوابل yotliqo waabil

volt *n.* فولت folt

voltage *n.* جهد johd

volume *n.* حجم hajm

voluminous *a.* ضخم dakhm

voluntarily *adv.* طوعًا taw'an

voluntary *a.* طوعي taw'iy

volunteer *n.* متطوع motatawwi'

volunteer *v.* يتطوع yatatawwa'

voluptuary *n.* شهواني shahwaaniy

voluptuous *a.* شهواني shahwaaniy

vomit *v.* يتقيأ yataqayyau

vomit *n.* قيء qayu

voracious *a.* شره sharih

votary *n.* منذور mandhoor

vote *n.* 1 تصويت tasweet

vote *n.* 2 صوت sawt

vote *v.* يصوّت yosawwit

voter *n.* ناخب naakhib

vouch *v.* يجزم yajzim

voucher *n.* قسيمة qaseemah

vouchsafe *v.* يتعطف yata'attaf

vow *n.* نذر nadhr

vow *v.* ينذر yandhor

vowel *n.* صائت saauit

voyage *n.* رحلة rihlah

voyage *v.* يرحل yarhal

voyager *n.* رحالة rahhaalah

vulgar *a.* سوقي sooqiy

vulgarity *n.* سوقيّه sooqiyyah

vulnerable *a.* 1 معرّض mo'arrad

vulnerable *a.* 2 ضعيف da'eef

vulture *n.* نسر nisr

W

wade *v.* يَخوض yakhood

waddle *v.* يتهاد yatahaada

waft *v.* يهب yahob

waft *n.* نسيم naseem

wag *v.* يهز yahoz

wag *n.* هزة hazzah

wage *v.* يَشِن yashin

wage *n.* أجر uajr

wager *n.* رهان rihaan

wager *v.* يراهن yoraahin

wagon *n.* عربة arabah

wail *v.* يولول yowalwil

wail *n.* عويل aweel

wain *n.* نَقل عَرَبَة arabato naql

waist *n.* وسط wist

waistband *n.* حزام hizaam

waistcoat *n.* معطف mi'taf

wait *v.* ينتظر yantaddir

wait *n.* انتظار entiddaar

waiter *n.* نادل naadil

waitress *n.* نادلة naadilah

waive *v.* يتنازل yatanaazal

waiver *n.* معاهدةتنازل mo'ahadato tanaazol

wake *v.* يوقظ yooqidd

wake *n.* 1 أعقاب ua'qaab

wake *n.* 2 يقظة yaqaddah

wakeful *a.* أرق uariq

walk *v.* يمشي yamshi

walk *n.* مشي mashy

wall *n.* جدار jidaar

wall *v.* يحيطبجدار yoheeto bijidaar

wallet *n.* محفظة mihfaddah	**warrantee** *n.* مضمون madmoon
wallop *v.* يخبط yakhbit	**warrantor** *n.* ضامن daamin
wallow *v.* يتخبط yatakhabbat	**warranty** *n.* ضمان damaan
walnut *n.* جوز jawz	**warren** *n.* وجار wijaar
walrus *n.* حصان البحر hisaanol bahr	**warrior** *n.* محارب mohaarib
wan *a.* شاحب shaahib	**wart** *n.* ثؤلول thoulool
wand *n.* صولجان sawlajaan	**wary** *a.* حذر hadhir
wander *v.* يتجوّل yatajawwal	**wash** *v.* يغسل yaghsil
wane *v.* يتضاءل yatadaaual	**wash** *n.* غسيل ghaseel
wane *n.* تضاؤل tadaauol	**washable** *a.* قابل للغسل qaabilon lil ghasl
want *v.* يريد yoreed	**washer** *n.* غسّالة ghassaalah
want *n.* رغبة raghdah	**wasp** *n.* دبور dabboor
wanton *a.* لَعوب la'oob	**waspish** *a.* لاذع laadhi'
war *n.* حرب harb	**wassail** *n.* نَخب nakhb
war *v.* يحارب yohaarib	**wastage** *n.* 1 اتلاف etlaaf
warble *v.* يغرّد yogharrid	**wastage** *n.* 2 اسراف esraaf
warble *n.* تغريد taghreed	**waste** *a.* عديم الفائدة adeemol faauidah
warbler *n.* مطرب motrib	**waste** *n.* نفايات nifaayaat
ward *n.* جناح jannah	**waste** *v.* 1 يتلف yotlif
ward *v.* يحرس yahris	**waste** *v.* 2 يسرف yosrif
warden *n.* حارس haaris	**wasteful** *a.* مسرف mosrif
warder *n.* سجّان sajjaan	**watch** *v.* يشاهد yoshaahid
wardrobe *n.* خزانة khizaanah	**watch** *n.* يد ساعة saa'atol yad
wardship *n.* وصاية wisaayah	**watchful** *a.* ساهر saahir
ware *n.* سلعة sil'ah	**watchword** *n.* كلمة السر kalimato ssir
warehouse *v.* مستودع mostawda'	**water** *n.* ماء maau
warfare *n.* حرب harb	**water** *v.* يسقي yasqi
warlike *a.* حربي harbiy	**waterfall** *n.* شلال shallaal
warm *a.* دافئ daafiu	**water-melon** *n.* بطيخ batteekh
warm *v.* يدفّئ yodaffiu	**waterproof** *a.* محمي ضد الماء mahmiyyon didal maau
warmth *n.* دفء difu	**waterproof** *n.* محمي ضد الماء mahmiyyon didal maau
warn *v.* يحذّر yohadhir	
warning *n.* تحذير tahdheer	
warrant *n.* مذكرة modhakkarah	
warrant *v.* يضمن yadman	

waterproof v. يحمي ضدالماء yahmi didal maau	**wedge** n. إسفين esfeen
watertight a. مانع للماء maani'on lil maau	**wedge** v. يحشر yahshor
watery a. مائي maauiy	**wedlock** n. زواج zawaaj
watt n. واط waat	**Wednesday** n. الأربعاء ual uarbi'aau
wave n. موجة mawjah	**weed** n. عشبةضارة oshbaton daarrah
wave v. يلوّح yolawwih	**weed** v. يزيل yozeel
waver v. يترَدَد yataraddad	**week** n. أسبوع uosboo'
wax n. شمع sham'	**weekly** a. أسبوعي uosboo'iy
wax v. يشمَع yoshammi'	**weekly** adv. أسبوعِيا uosboo'iyan
way n. طريق tareeq	**weekly** n. أسبوعي uosboo'iy
wayfarer n. رحّالة rahhaalah	**weep** v. يبكي yabki
waylay v. يَتَرَبَّص yatarabbas	**weevil** n. سوسة soosah
wayward a. عاص asi	**weigh** v. يوزن yozin
weak a. ضعيف da'eef	**weight** n. وزن wazn
weaken v.t. & i يضعف yad'of	**weightage** n. ترجيح tarjeeh
weakling n. طفل ضعيف tiflon da'eef	**weighty** a. ثقيل thaqeel
weakness n. ضعف do'f	**weir** n. سياج siyaaj
weal n. سراء sarraau	**weird** a. غريب ghareeb
wealth n. ثروة tharwah	**welcome** a. مرحَب morahhib
wealthy a. ثري thariy	**welcome** n. ترحيب tarheeb
wean v. يفطم yaftim	**welcome** v. يرحَب yorahhib
weapon n. سلاح silaah	**weld** v. يلحم yolhim
wear v. يرتدي yartadi	**weld** n. لحام lahhaam
weary a. مُرهَق morhaq	**welfare** n. رفاهِيّه rafaahiyah
weary v. يرهق yorhiq	**well** a. جيد jayyid
weather n. جو jaw	**well** adv. جيداً jayyidan
weather v. يهترئ yahtariu	**well** n. بئر biur
weave v. يحيك yaheek	**well** v. يَتَدَفَق yatadaffaq
weaver n. حائك haauik	**wellington** n. جزمة jazmah
web n. شبكة shabakah	**well-known** a. معروف ma'roof
webby a. شبكي shabakiy	**well-read** a. واسع الاطلاع waasi'ol uittilaa'
wed v. يتزوج yatazawwaj	**well-timed** a. حسن التوقيت hasano ttawqeet
wedding n. زفاف zifaaf	

well-to-do *a.* ثري thariy

welt *n.* حاشِيَه haashiyah

welter *n.* فوضى fawda

wen *n.* كيس حميد keeson hameed

wench *n.* فتاة fataah

west *n.* غرب gharb

west *a.* غَربي gharbiy

west *adv.* نَحوالغَرب nahwal gharb

westerly *a.* غربي gharbiy

westerly *adv.* غربي gharbiy

western *a.* غربي gharbiy

wet *a.* رطب ratib

wet *v.* يرطب yorattib

wetness *n.* رطوبة rotoobah

whack *v.* يَضربِبشِدَه yadribo bishiddah

whale *n.* حوت hoot

wharfage *n.* مرفأللقوارب marfauon lilqawaarib

what *a.* أي uay

what *pron.* ما ma

what *interj.* ماذا maadha

whatever *pron.* أياكان uayyan kaan

wheat *n.* قمح qamh

wheedle *v.* يتملَق yatamallaq

wheel *n.* عجلة ajalah

wheel *v.* ينقل yanqil

whelm *v.* يغطي yoghati

whelp *n.* جرو jarw

when *adv.* مَتى mata

when *conj.* عندما indama

whence *adv.* من أين min uayn

whenever *conj.* كلما kollama

whenever *adv.* عندما indama

where *adv.* أين uayn

where *conj.* حيث hayth

whereabout *adv.* أين uayn

whereabout *n.* مكان makaan

whereas *conj.* حين في fee heen

whereat *conj.* عند ind

wherein *adv.* حيث hayth

whereupon *conj.* عندئذ indauidh

wherever *adv.* أينما uaynama

whet *v.* يشحذ yashhadh

whether *conj.* سواء sawaau

which *pron.* الذي ualadhi

which *adj.* أي uay

whichever *pron* أيهم uayyohom

whiff *n.* نفحة nafhah

while *n.* آونة aawinah

while *conj.* بينما baynama

while *v.* يقضيوقته yaqdi waqtah

whim *n.* نزوة nazwah

whimper *v.* يتذمر yatadhammar

whimsical *a.* غريبالأطوار ghareebol uatwaar

whine *v.* يئن yauin

whine *n.* أنين uaneen

whip *v.* يجلد yajlid

whip *n.* سوط sawt

whipcord *n.* حبلمتين hablon mateen

whir *n.* أزيز uazeez

whirl *v.* يَدَوِم yodawwim

whirl *n.* دوامة dawwaamah

whirligig *n.* لعبةالدوامة lo'bato ddawwaamah

whirlpool *n.* دوامة dawwaamah

whirlwind *n.* زوبعة zawba'ah

whisk *v.* يخفق yakhfiq

whisk *n.* خفَاقة khaffaaqah

whisker *n.* شارب shaarib	wick *n.* فَتيلَه fateelah
whisky *n.* ويسكي wiski	wicked *a.* شِرّير shirreer
whisper *v.* يهمس yahmis	wicker *n.* خَيزَران khayzaraan
whisper *n.* همس hams	wicket *n.* بوابةصغيرة bawwaabaton sagheerah
whistle *v.* يصفر yasfir	
whistle *n.* صفارة saffaarah	wide *a.* واسع waasi'
white *a.* أبيض uabyad	wide *adv.* واسع waasi'
white *n.* أبيض uabyad	widen *v.* يوسّع yowassi'
whiten *v.* يبيّض yobayyid	widespread *a.* واسعالنطاق waasi'o nnitaaq
whitewash *n.* 1 تبرئة tabriuah	
whitewash *n.* 2 تبييض tabyeed	widow *n.* أرمل uarmal
whitewash *v.* 1 يبرئ yobarriu	widow *v.* يترمَل yatarammal
whitewash *v.* 2 يبيّض yobayyid	widower *n.* أرمل uarmal
whither *adv.* أين الى ela uayn	width *n.* عرض ard
whitish *a.* مبيض mobayyid	wield *v.* يمارس yomaaris
whittle *v.* يبري yabri	wife *n.* زوجة zawjah
whiz *v.* ياز yauiz	wig *n.* شعرمستعار sha'ron mosta'aar
who *pron.* من man	
whoever *pron.* أياكان uayyan kaan	wigwam *n.* خَيمَةالهنودالخُمر khaymatol honoodil homr
whole *a.* كامل kaamil	wild *a.* وحشي wahshiy
whole *n.* وَحْدَهكامِلَه wihdaton kaamilah	wilderness *n.* قفر qafr
whole-hearted *a.* عطوف atoof	wile *n.* حيلة heelah
wholesale *n.* تجارةالجملة tijaaratol jomlah	will *n.* 1 إرادَه eraadah
	will *n.* 2 رغبة raghbah
wholesale *adj.* بالجملة biljomlah	will *n.* 3 وَصِيَه wasiyyah
wholesale *adv.* بالجملة biljomlah	will *v.* سوف sawfa
wholesaler *n.* تاجرجملة tajirol jomlah	willing *a.* مستعد mosta'id
wholesome *a.* مفيد mofeed	willingness *n.* استعداد esti'daad
wholly *adv.* كلّيًا kolliyan	willow *n.* صفصاف safsaaf
whom *pron.* من man	wily *a.* مراوغ moraawigh
whore *n.* عاهر ahir	wimble *n.* مثقاب mithqaab
whose *pron.* لمن liman	wimple *n.* خمار khimaar
why *adv.* لماذا limaadha	win *v.* يكسب yaksab
	win *n.* كسب kasb
	wince *v.* يجفل yajfal

winch *n.* ونش winsh

wind *n.* رياح riyaah

wind *v.* 1 يلف yalof

wind *v.* 2 يَتَعَرَّج yata'arraj

windbag *n.* ثرثار tharthaar

winder *n.* لَفَّاف laffaf

windlass *v.* مرفاع mirfaa'

windmill *n.* طاحونةهوائية
taahoonaton hawaauiyyah

window *n.* نافذة naafidhah

windy *a.* عاصف aasif

wine *n.* نبيذ nabeedh

wing *n.* جناح janaah

wink *v.* يغمز yaghmiz

wink *n.* غمزة ghamzah

winner *n.* فائز faauiz

winnow *v.* يُغَرْبِل yogharbil

winsome *a.* فاتن faatin

winter *n.* شتاء shitaau

winter *v.* يمضي الشتاء yomdhi
shshitaau

wintry *a.* شتوي shatawiy

wipe *v.* يمسح yamsah

wipe *n.* مسح mash

wire *n.* سلك silk

wire *v.* يُرسِلُ بَرقِيَّةً yorsilobarqiyyah

wireless *a.* لاسلكي laasilkiy

wireless *n.* لايلكي laasilkiy

wiring *n.* تشابك tashaabok

wisdom *n.* حكمة hikmah

wisdom-tooth *n.* ضرس العقل dirsol
'aql

wise *a.* حكيم hakeem

wish *n.* أمنية uomniyah

wish *v.* يتمنى yatamanna

wishful *a.* مرغوب marghoob

wisp *n.* خصلةشعر khislatosha'ar

wistful *a.* حزين hazeen

wit *n.* دم خفة khiffato dam

witch *n.* ساحرة saahirah

witchcraft *n.* سحر sihr

witchery *n.* شعوذة sha'wadhah

with *prep.* مع ma'

withal *adv.* كذلك kadhaalik

withdraw *v.* ينسحب yansahib

withdrawal *n.* انسحاب ensihaab

withe *n.* مربطمن الأغصان marbaton
minal uaghsaan

wither *v.* يذبل yadhbal

withhold *v.* يمنع yamna'

within *prep.* ضمن dimn

within *adv.* في الدّاخل fi ddaakhil

within *n.* الدّاخِل uaddaakhil

without *prep.* بدون bidoon

without *adv.* من الخارج minal
khaarij

without *n.* الخارج ualkhaarij

withstand *v.* يتحمّل yatahammal

witless *a.* أحمق uahmaq

witness *n.* شاهد shaahid

witness *v.* يشهد yashhad

witticism *n.* مُلْحَه molhah

witty *a.* بارع baari'

wizard *n.* مشعوذ mosha'widh

wobble *v.* يتمايل yatamaayal

woe *n.* ويل yayl

woebegone *a.* مكتئب moktauib

woeful *n.* محزن mohzin

wolf *n.* ذئب dhiub

woman *n.* امرأة emraua

womanhood *n.* أنوثة uonoothah

womanish *n.* أنثوي uonthawiy

womanise v.	يؤنّث	youannith
womaniser n.	زير نساء	zeer nisaau
womb n.	رحم	rahm
wonder n.	عجب	ajab
wonder v.	يتعجّب	yata'ajjab
wonderful a.	رائع	raaui'
wondrous a.	عجيب	ajeeb
wont a.	متعود	mota'awwid
wont n.	عادة	aadah
wonted a.	معتاد	mo'taad
woo v.	يَتَوَدَّد	yatawaddad
wood n.	خشب	khashab
woods n.	غابة	ghaabah
wooden a.	خشبي	khashabiy
woodland n.	غابة	ghaabah
woof n.	لحمة	lohmah
wool n.	صوف	soof
woollen a.	صوفي	soofiy
woollen n.	صوفي	soofiy
word n.	كلمة	kalimah
word v.	يُعَبِّر	yo'abbir
wordy a.	مطنب	motnib
work n.	عمل	amal
work v.	يعمل	ya'mal
workable a.	عملي	amali
workaday a.	مبتذل	mobtadhal
worker n.	عامل	aamil
workman n.	عامل	aamil
workmanship n.	صنعة	san'ah
workshop n.	ورشة	warshah
world n.	عالم	aalam
worldling n.	أرضي	uardiy
worldly a.	دنيوي	donyawiy
worm n.	دودة	doodah
wormwood n.	مرارة	marraarah

worn a.	بالي	baali
worry n.	قلق	qalaq
worry v.	يقلق	yaqlaq
worsen v.	يفاقم	yofaaqim
worship n.	عبادة	ibaadah
worship v.	يعبد	ya'bid
worshipper n.	عابد	aabid
worst n.	أسوأ	uaswau
worst adj.	أسوأ	uaswau
worst v.	يَتَغَلَّب	yataghallab
worsted n.	خيط صوفي	khayton soofiy
worth n.	قيمة	qeemah
worth adj.	قيم	qayyim
worthless a.	عديم القيمة	adeemol qeemah
worthy a.	مستحق	mostahiq
would-be a.	ليكون	liyakoon
wound n.	جرح	jorh
wound v.	يجرح	yajrah
wrack n.	سفينة غارقة	safeenaton ghaariqah
wraith n.	طيف	tayf
wrangle v.	يشاحن	yoshaahin
wrangle n.	مشاحنة	moshaahanah
wrap v.	يلف	yalif
wrap n.	وشاح	wishaah
wrapper n.	غلاف	ghilaaf
wrath n.	غضب	ghadab
wreath n.	إكليل	ekleel
wreathe v.	يطوي	yatwi
wreck n.	حطام	hotaam
wreck v.	يحطّم	yohattim
wreckage n.	حطام	hotaam
wrecker n.	مدمّر	modammir
wren n.	صعو	sa'w

wrench *n.* خَلع khal'

wrench *v.* يَفتِل yaftil

wrest *v.* ينتزع yantazi'

wrestle *v.* يصارع yosaari'

wrestler *n.* مصارع mosaari'

wretch *n.* بائس baauis

wretched *a.* بائس baauis

wrick *n.* التواء eltiwaau

wriggle *v.* يتملص yatamallas

wriggle *n.* تَلَوٍّ talawwi

wring *v.* يقحم yoqhim

wrinkle *n.* تجعد taja"od

wrinkle *v.* يجعّد yoja"id

wrist *n.* معصم mi'sam

writ *n.* أمر uamr

write *v.* يكتب yaktob

writer *n.* كاتب kaatib

writhe *v.* يطوي yatwi

wrong *a.* خاطئ khaatiu

wrong *adv.* خاطئ khaatiu

wrong *v.* يَظلُم yaddlim

wrongful *a.* غير مشروع ghayr mashroou

wry *a.* ساخر saakhir

xerox *n.* 1 آلة نسخ aalat naskh

xerox *n.* 2 نسخة noskhah

xerox *v.* ينسخ yansakh

Xmas *n.* عيد الميلاد eed almeelaad

x-ray *n.* أشعة سينية uashi"a seeniyyah

x-ray *v.* يفحص yafhas

xylophagous *a.* آكل الخشب aakil alkhashab

xylophilous *a.* يعيش على الخشب ya'eesh 'alal khashab

xylophone *n.* الزيلوفون azzaylofoon

yacht *n.* مركب شراعي (يخت) markib shiraa'iy (yakht)

yacht *v.* أبحر بيخت abhara biyakht

yak *n.* 1 ثور التبت thawr altibit

yak *n.* 2 ثرثرة thartharah

yak *v.* يثرثر yotharthir

yap *v.* يثرثر yotharthir

yap *n.* نبحة nabhah

yard *n.* ساحة saahah

yarn *n.* 1 خيط الغزل khayt alghazl

yarn *n.* 2 قصة qissah

yawn *v.* تثاءب tathaauab

yawn n. تثاءب tathaauob

year *n.* سنة sanah

yearly *a.* سنوي sanawiy

yearly *adv.* سنوي sanawiy

yearn *v.* يتوق yatooq

yearning *n.* توق tawq

yeast *n.* خميرة khameerah

yell *v.* يصرخ yasrokh

yell *n.* صرخة sarkha

yellow *a.* 1 جبان jabaan

yellow *a.* 2 أصفر asfar

yellow *n.* أصفر asfar

yellow v. يصفر yasfar
yellowish a. مصفر mosfir
Yen n. الين alyin
yen n. اشتياق eshtiyaaq
yen v. يشتاق yashtaaq
yes adv. نعم na'am
yesterday n. أمس ams
yesterday adv. بالأمس bil ams
yet adv. بعد ba'd
yet conj. معذلك ma' dhaalikah
yield v. ينتج yantoj
yield n. محصول mahsool
yoke n. نير nayr
yoke v. 1 يربطبالنير yarbit binnayr
yoke v. 2 يسرق yasriq
yolk n. صفارالبيض safaar al bayd
yonder a. هذا haadha
yonder adv. هناك honaak
yonder n. مسافةبعيدة masaafah ba'eedah
young a. شاب shaab
young n. 1 صغير sagheer
young n. 2 صغيرالحيوان sagheer al hayawaan
youngster n. شاب shaab
youth n. شباب shabaab
youthful a. فتي fatiy

Z

zany n. مهرج moharrij
zany a. ممتع momti'
zeal n. حماس hamaas
zealot n. متعصب mota'assib

zealous a. متحمس motahammis
zebra n. حمارالوحش himaar alwahsh
zenith n. ذروة thorwah
zephyr n. نسيمعليل naseem 'aleel
zero n. صفر sifr
zest n. حماس hamaas
zigzag n. خطمتعرج khat mota'arrij
zigzag adj. متعرج mota'arrij
zigzag adv. بتعرج bita'arroj
zigzag v. يتعرج yata'arraj
zinc n. زنك zink
zip n. 1 سحاب sahhaab
zip n. 2 رمزبريدي ramz bareediy
zip v. يغلق yoghliq
zipper n. سحاب sahhaab
zodiac n. دولاب الأبراج doolaab aluabraaj
zonal a. منطقي mantiqiy
zone n. منطقة mantiqah
zoo n. حديقةالحيوانات hadeeqat alhayawaanaat
zoological a. حيواني hayawaaniy
zoologist n. عالمالحيوان aalim alhayawaan
zoology n. علمالحيوان ilm alhayawaan
zoom n. تقريب taqreeb
zoom v. يقرب yoqarrib

Arabic to English

A

'aabid *n.* عابد worshipper

'aabir *adj.* عابر transitory

'aabis *adj.* عابس morose

'aadah *n.* عادة habit

'aadah *adv.* عادة ordinarily

'aadatan *adv.* عادةً usually

'aadil *adj.* عادل fair

'aadiy *adj.* عادي normal

'aahil *n.* عاهل monarch

'aahir *n.* عاهر prostitute

'aaj *n.* عاج ivory

'aajil *adj.* عاجل urgent

'aajiz *adj.* عاجز disabled

'aakis *n.* عاكس reflector

'aakis *adj.* عاكس reflective

'aalam *n.* عالم world

'aalamiy *adj.* عالمي universal

'aalamiyyah *n.* عالمية universality

'aali *adj.* عال loud

'aaliyan *adv.* عاليا aloft

'aam *n.* عام year

'aam *adj.* 1 عام general

'aam *adj.* 2 عام public

'aamil *n.* 1 عامل factor

'aamil *n.* 2 عامل labourer

'aamil *n.* 3 عامل operator

'aammiyyah *n.* عامية slang

'aamoodo ssoor *n.* عامودالسور pale

'aanah *n.* عانة loin

'aanis *n.* عانس spinster

'aaqil *adj.* عاقل sane

'aar *n.* عار dishonour

'aari *adj.* عار naked

'aari *adj.* عاري nude

'aari *n.* عاري nude

'aarid *n.* عارض symptom

'aaridah *n.* عارضة girder

'aashiq *n.* عاشق lover

'aasif *adj.* عاصف stormy

'aasifah *n.* عاصفة storm

'aasimah *n.* عاصمة capital

'aasimiy *adj.* عاصمي capital

'aatifah *n.* عاطفة passion

'aatifiy *adj.* عاطفي sentimental

'aauid *n.* عائد repatriate

'aauidaat *n.* عائدات proceeds

'aauilah *n.* عائلة family

'aauim *adv.* عائم afloat

'aauiq *n.* عائق hindrance

'aazif *n.* عازف instrumentalist

'aazil *n.* عازل insulator

'abaauah *n.* عباءة cloak

'abaq *adj.* عبق fragrant

'abath *n.* عبث futility

'abathan *adv.* عبثًا vainly

'abbaarah *n.* عبّارة ferry

'abd *n.* عبد slave

'abdiy *adj.* عَبدي slavish

'abqariy *n.* عبقري genius

'abr *prep.* عبر across

'ad *n.* عد count

'adaalah *n.* عدالة justice

'adaawah *n.* عداوة enmity

'adad *n.* عدد number

'adadiy *adj.* عددي numerical

'adalah *n.* عضلة muscle

'adaliy *adj.* عضلي muscular
'adamiyyah *n.* عدمية nihilism
'adas *n.* عدس lentil
'adasah *n.* عدسة lens
'addaad *n.* عداد counter
'addaau *n.* عداء runner
'addah *n.* عضة bite
'addamah *n.* عظمة grandeur
'addamah *n.* عظمة majesty
'addeem *adj.* عظيم great
'addeem *adj.* عظيم mighty
'addm *n.* عظم bone
'adeed *adj.* عديد numerous
'adhaab *n.* عذاب agony
'adhaab *n.* عذاب scourge
'adhaab *n.* عذاب torment
'adhraau *n.* عذراء maiden
'adow *n.* عدو enemy
'adw *n.* عدو sprint
'adwa *n.* عدوى infection
'afan *n.* عفن mould
'afan *adj.* عفن musty
'afan *n.* 1 عفن rot
'afan *n.* 2 عفن fungus
'afawiy *adj.* عفوي spontaneous
'afawiyyah *n.* عفوية spontaneity
'afeef *adj.* عفيف chaste
'afin *adj.* عفن septic
'afw *n.* عفو pardon
'ahd *n.* عهد covenant
'ajab *n.* عجب wonder
'ajal *n.* عجل hurry
'ajalah *n.* عجلة wheel
'ajeeb *adj.* عجيب wondrous
'ajeen *n.* عجين dough

'ajeenatah *n.* عجينة paste
'ajooz *adj.* عجوز elderly
'ajz *n.* 1 عجز deficit
'ajz *n.* 2 عجز disability
'aks *adj.* عكس contrary
'aks *n.* عكس reverse
'aksiy *adj.* عكسي reverse
'ala *prep.* على on
'alaamah *n.* 1 علامة mark
'alaamah *n.* 2 علامة sign
'alaaqah *n.* 1 علاقة affair
'alaaqah *n.* 2 علاقة relevance
'alaawah *n.* علاوة bonus
'alaawah *n.* علاوة premium
'alaf *n.* علف feed
'alam *n.* علم flag
'alanan *adv.* علناً openly
'alaniy *adj.* علني overt
'alaqah *n.* علقة leech
'alim *n.* عالم scientist
'am *n.* عم uncle
'ama *n.* عمى blindness
'amal *n.* 1 عمل business
'amal *n.* 2 عمل deed
'amal *n.* 3 عمل occupation
'amaliy *adj.* عملي practical
'amaliy *n.* 1 عملية operation
'amaliyyah *n.* 2 عملية practicability
'amaliyyah *n.* 3 عملية process
'amaliyyan *adv.* عملياً practically
'amdan *adv.* عمداً purposely
'ameed *n.* 1 عميد brigadier
'ameed *n.* 2 عميد dean
'ameel *n.* عميل client

'ameeq *adj.* 1 عميق deep

'ameeq *adj.* 2 عميق profound

'amma *n.* عمة aunt

'amood *n.* عمود column

'amoodiy *adj.* عمودي vertical

'an *prep.* عن about

'anaadah *n.* عنادة adamant

'anbar *n.* عنبر hold

'andaleeb *n.* عندليب nightingale

'aneed *adj.* عنيد adamant

'aneef *adj.* 1 عنيف fierce

'aneef *adj.* 2 عنيف rough

'ankab *n.* عنكب spider

'ankaboot *n.* عنكبوت spider

'aqaauidiy *adj.* عقائدي dogmatic

-ha *n.* عقبة obstacle

'aqd *n.* 1 عقد contract

'aqd *n.* 2 عقد decade

'aqeedah *n.* عقيدة creed

'aqeem *adj.* عقيم futile

'aql *n.* عقل mind

'aqlaaniy *adj.* عقلاني rational

'aqlaaniyyah *n.* عقلانية rationality

'aqliy *adj.* عقلي mental

'aqliyyah *n.* عقلية mentality

'aqrab *n.* عقرب scorpion

'arabah *n.* عربة cart

'arabiy *n.* عربي Arab

'arabiy *adj.* عربي Arabic

'aradiy *adj.* عرضي accidental

'araq *n.* عرق sweat

'ard *n.* 1 عرض display

'ard *n.* 2 عرض offer

'ard *n.* 3 عرض width

'ard *n.* 4 عرض exhibition

'areedah *n.* عريضة petition

'areen *n.* عرين den

'arees *n.* عريس groom

'aroos *n.* عروس bride

'arqalah *n.* عرقلة obstruction

'arraaf *n.* عَرّاف seer

'arsh *n.* عرش throne

'asa *n.* عصا stick

'asab *n.* عصب nerve

'asal *n.* عسل honey

'aseedah *n.* عصيدة porridge

'aseer *adj.* عسير indigestible

'aseer *n.* عصير juice

'ashaau *n.* عشاء dinner

'asharah *n.*, a عشرة ten

'asheeq *n.* عشيق paramour

'asheeqah *n.* عشيقة mistress

'ashriy *adj.* عشري decimal

'ashwaauiy *adj.* عشوائي ndiscriminate

'ashwaauiy *adj.* عشوائي random

'asi *adj.* عاص wayward

'askar *n.* عسكر military

'askarriy *adj.* عسكري martial

'asr *n.* عصر era

'ataalah *n.* عطالة inertia

'ataau *n.* عطاء tender

'atash *n.* عطش thirst

'athah *n.* عثّة moth

'atir *adj.* عطر odorous

'atiyyah *n.* عطية gratuity

'atoof *adj.* عطوف whole-hearted

'atsah *n.* عطسة sneeze

'atshaan *adj.* عطشان athirst

'attaar *n.* عطار druggist	'inaad *n.* عناد tenacity
'awdah *n.* عودة return	'inab *n.* عنب grape
'aweel *n.* عويل wail	'ind *conj.* عند whereat
'awn *n.* عون succour	'indama *pron.* عندما as
'awwaamah *n.* عوامة buoy	'indama *conj.* عندما when
'ayb *n.* 1 عيب flaw	'indama *adv.* عندما whenever
'ayb *n.* 2 عيب shortcoming	'indauidh *adv.* عِندَئِذ then
'ayn *n.* عين eye	'indauidh *conj.* عندئذ whereupon
'aysh *n.* عيش subsistence	'iqaab *n.* عقاب punishment
'ayyinah *n.* عينة specimen	'iqaabiy *adj.* عقابي punitive
'azaau *n.* عزاء consolation	'iqaar *n.* عقار estate
'azbaau *adj.* عزباء maiden	'iraak *n.* عراك fight
'azeez *adj.* عزيز dear	'irdah *adj.* عرضة liable
'azl *n.* عزل insulation	'irq *n.* عرق vein
'azm *n.* عزم bent	'irqiy *adj.* عرقي racial
'feef *n.* عفيف agnus	'irqiyyah *n.* عرقية racialism
'ibaadah *n.* عبادة worship	'irs *n.* عرس rat
'ibaarah *n.* عبارة phrase	'isaabah *n.* عصابة gang
'ibrah *n.* عِبْرَه moral	'ishq *n.* عشق adoration
'ibu *n.* عبء burden	'ishroon *adj.* عشرون twenty
'idaau *n.* عداء animosity	'ishroon *n.* عشرون twenty
'iddah *adj.* عدة several	'isyaan *n.* عصيان defiance
'iffa *n.* عفة chastity	'itaab *n.* عتاب reproach
'ijjah *n.* عجّة omelette	'iwaau *n.* عواء howl
'ijl *n.* عجل calf	'iwad *n.* عوض offset
'ilaaj *n.* علاج remedy	'iyaadah *n.* عيادة clinic
'ilaajiy *adj.* علاجي remedial	'izbah *n.* عزبة manor
'ilkah *n.* علكة gum	'izbawiy *adj.* عزبوي manorial
'illiyyah *n.* علية loft	'maamah *n.* عمامة turban
'ilm *n.* علم science	'oboodiyyah *n.* عبودية slavery
'ilmaaniy *n.* علماني layman	'oboor *n.* عبور transit
'ilmiy *adj.* علمي scientific	'oboos *n.* عبوس frown
'imaad *n.* عماد mainstay	'odaal *adj.* عضال incurable
'imlaaq *n.* عملاق giant	'oddah *n.* عدة kit
'imlah *n.* عملة currency	'odhr *n.* عذر excuse

'odhriyyah *n.* عذرية virginity
'odw *n.* 1 عضو member
'odw *n.* 2 عضو organ
'odwaan *n.* عدوان aggression
'odwaaniy *adj.* عدواني aggressive
'odwiy *adj.* عضوي organic
'odwiyyah *n.* عضوية membership
'okkaaz *n.* عكاز crutch
'olaybah *n.* عليبة canister
'olbah *n.* علبة carton
'omdah *n.* عمدة mayor
'ommaad *n.* عماد baptism
'omoolah *n.* عمولة commission
'omooman *adv.* عموما generally
'omq *n.* 1 عمق depth
'omq *n.* 2 عمق profundity
'omr *n.* عمر age
'onf *n.* عنف violence
'onoq *n.* عنق neck
'onsor *n.* عنصر element
'onsoriyyah *n.* عنصرية racism
'onsorriy *adj.* عنصري racist
'onwaan *n.* 1 عنوان address
'onwaan *n.* 2 عنوان heading
'onwaan *n.* 3 عنوان title
'ood *n.* 1 عود lute
'ood *n.* 2 عود stick
'oq'oq *n.* عقعق magpie
'oqaar *n.* عقار drug
'oqb *n.* عقب stump
'oqd *n.* عقد necklace
'oqdah *n.* عقدة knot
'oqm *n.* عقم sterility
'oqoobah *n.* عقوبة penalty
'ordah *adj.* عرضة apt

'orf *n.* 1 عرف custom
'orf *n.* 2 عرف mane
'orfiy *adj.* عرفي customary
'oriy *n.* عري nudity
'orsi *adj.* عرسي nuptial
'osaabah *n.* عصابة blindfold
'osaarah *n.* عصارة sap
'osh *n.* عش nest
'oshb *n.* عشب grass
'oshbah *n.* عشبة herb
'oslooj *n.* عسلوج sprig
'othmaaniy *n.* عثماني ottoman
'otlah *n.* عطلة vacation
'otr *n.* عطر perfume
'oyaynah *n.* عيينة eyelet
'ozlah *n.* عزلة isolation
'ozoobah *n.* عذوبة celibacy
mi'maariy *n.* معماري architect
hom *adj.* ـهم their
a'laa *adv.* أعلى above
aathim *n.* آثم sinner
aawinah *n.* آونة while
abhara *v.* أبحر sail
akaadeemiy *adj.* أكاديمي academic
akaadeemiyah *n.* أكاديمية academy
alf *n.* ألف thousand
alf *adj.* ألف thousand
ams *n.* أمس yesterday
areekah *n.* 1 أريكة couch
asfar *adj.* أصفر yellow
asfar *n.* أصفر yellow
asliy *adj.* أصلي aboriginal

B

ba'd *prep.* بعد after

ba'd *adv.* بعد yet

ba'd *pron.* بعض some

ba'eed *adv.* بعيد afar

ba'eed *adj.* بعيد far

ba'eedan *adv.* بعيدا away

ba'ood *n.* بعوض mosquito

ba'tharah *n.* بعثرة rummage

baab *n.* باب door

baabawiy *adj.* بابوي papal

baabawiyyah *n.* بابوية papacy

baabil *n.* بابل Babel

baadhikh *adj.* باذخ sumptuous

baadhinjaan *n.* باذنجان brinjal

baadi *adj.* بادئ conspicuous

baadiuah *n.* بادئة initial

baadiuah *n.* بادئة prefix

baahit *adj.* باهت lacklustre

baahith *n.* باحث scholar

baakhirah *n.* باخرة cruiser

baaki *adj.* باكي lachrymose

baali *adj.* بال outmoded

baali *adj.* بالي worn

baaligh *adj.* بالغ adult

baaloo'ah *n.* بالوعة cesspool

baaloon *n.* بالون balloon

baanooraama *n.* بانوراما panorama

baaqah *n.* باقة bunch

baaqi *n.* باقي remainder

baari' *adj.* بارع witty

baarid *adj.* بارد cold

baariz *adj.* بارز 1 notable

baariz *adj.* بارز 2 outstanding

baaroomitr *n.* بارومتر barometer

baasil *adj.* باسل intrepid

baastil *n.* باستِل pastel

baatil *adj.* باطل invalid

baatiniy *adj.* باطِني inward

baaui' *n.* بائع salesman

baauis *adj.* بائس 1 miserable

baauis *adj.* بائس 2 piteous

baazillaau *n.* بازيلاء pea

babaghaau *n.* ببغاء parrot

badaanah *n.* بدانة obesity

badaaui' *n.* بَضائع stock

badal *n.* بدل lieu

badaniy *adj.* بدني corporal

badawiy *n.* بدوي nomad

badawiy *adj.* بدوي nomadic

badee' *adj.* بديع adorable

badeel *adj.* بديل alternative

badeel *n.* بديل substitute

badeen *adj.* بدين fat

badhaauah *n.* بذاءة immodesty

badlah *n.* بدلة suit

baghaau *n.* بغاء prostitution

bagheed *adj.* بغيض abominable

baghl *n.* بغل mule

baheej *adj.* بهيج jolly

baheemah *n.* بهيمة beast

bahhaar *n.* بحّار sailor

bahjah *n.* بهجة joy

bahlaqah *adv.* بحلقة agaze

bahlawaan *n.* بهلوان acrobat

bahr *n.* بحر sea

bahriy *adj.* بحري marine

bahth *n.* 1 بحث research
bahth *n.* 2 بحث search
baja'ah *n.* بجعة swan
bakarah *n.* بكرة pulley
bakheel *n.* بخيل miser
bakheel *adj.* بخيل stingy
bakhkhoor *n.* بخور incense
bakteerya *a n.* بكتيريا bacteria
balaaghah *n.* بلاغة eloquence
balaaghiy *adj.* بلاغي rhetorical
balaahah *n.* بلاهَه idiocy
balad *n.* بلد country
baladiy *adj.* بلدي municipal
baladiyyah *n.* بلدية municipality
balah *n.* بلح date
baldah *n.* بلدة town
baleed *adj.* بليد obtuse
baleegh *adj.* بليغ eloquent
balloor *n.* بلور crystal
balloot *n.* بلوط acorn
balsam *n.* بلسم balsam
banafsaj *n.* بنفسج Wild Viola
banafsajiy *adj.* بنفسجي purple
band *n.* بند item
banjar *n.* بنجر beet
bannaatiy *adj.* بناتي girlish
bannaau *n.* بناء mason
baqaau *n.* بقاء survival
baqaaya *n.* بقايا residue
baqarah *n.* بقرة cow
baqiyyah *n.* بقية rest
baqqaal *n.* بقّال grocer
baqqaalah *n.* بقالة grocery
baqsheesh *n.* بَقْشيش tip
baraa'ah *n.* براعة mastery

baraauah *n.* براءة innocence
barad *n.* برد hail
barakah *n.* بركة blessing
bard *n.* برد cold
bareed *n.* بريد post
bareediy *adj.* بريدي postal
bareeq *n.* بريق lustre
bareetaaniy *adj.* بريطاني British
bareeu *adj.* بريء innocent
barghooth *n.* برغوث flea
barlamaan *n.* برلمان parliament
barlamaaniy *n.* برلماني parliamentarian
barlamaaniy *adj.* برلماني parliamentary
barmaauiy *adj.* برمائي amphibious
barmeel n. برميل barrel
barnaamaj *n.* برنامج programme
barq *n.* برق lightening
barqiy *adj.* برقي telegraphic
barqiyyah *n.* برقية telegram
barqooq *n.* برقوق plum
barraad *n.* بزاد cooler
basaalah *n.* بسالة valour
basaatah *n.* بساطة simplicity
basal *n.* بصل onion
basariy *adj.* بصري optic
baseerah *n.* بصيرة foresight
baseet *adj.* بسيط simple
basharah *n.* بشرة complexion
bashi' *adj.* بشع hideous
basmah *n.* بصمة imprint
bastanah *n.* بستنة horticulture
bat *n.* بط duck

bataaniyyah *n.* بطانية blanket
bataatis *n.* بطاطس potato
batal *n.* بطل hero
batalah *n.* بتلة petal
batalah *n.* بطلة heroine
bateeu *adj.* بطيء slow
bath *n.* بث broadcast
batn *n.* بطن abdomen
batniy *adj.* بطني abdominal
batr *n.* بتر mutilation
battaariyyah *n.* بطارية battery
batteekh *n.* بطيخ watermelon
bawaabah *n.* بوابة gate
bawaaseer *n.* بواسير piles
bawl *n.* بول urine
bawliy *adj.* بولي urinary
bay'on bilmofarraq *n.* بَيع بالمُفَرَق retail
bayaan *n.* بيان statement
bayaaniy *adj.* بياني graphic
baydah *n.* بيضة egg
baydawiy *adj.* بيضوي oval
baydawiy *n.* بيضوي oval
bayn *prep.* بين between
baynama *conj.* بينما while
bayt *n.* بيت house
baytariy *adj.* بيطري veterinary
beerah *n.* بيرة beer
beeroqraatiy *n.* بيروقراطي bureaucrat
beeroqraatiyyah *n.* بيروقراطية bureaucracy
beeuah *n.* بيئة environment
bi'thah *n.* بعثة expedition
bibalaash *adv.* ببلاش gratis

bibokhl *adj.* ببخل miserly
bibotu *adv.* ببطء slowly
bid'ah *n.* بدعة fad
bidaa'ah *n.* بضاعة merchandise
bidaauiy *adj.* بدائي primitive
bidaayah *n.* بداية beginning
bidhrah *n.* بذرة seed
bidiqqah *adv.* بدقة minutely
bidoon *prep.* بدون without
bidu *n.* بدء commencement
biesti'daad *adv.* باستعداد readily
bihimd *adv.* بحمد benignly
bihtiyaaj *adv.* باهتياج amuck
bijaanib adj. بجانب against
bijaanib *prep.* بجانب beside
bijaanib *adv.* بجانب by
bikhtisaar *adv.* باختصار short
bikr *adj.* بكر virgin
bil'ard *prep.* بالعرض athwart
bil ams *adv.* بالأمس yesterday
bil ejmaa' *adj.* بالإجماع unanimous
bil fi'l *adv.* بالفعل actually
bil kaamil *adv.* بالكامل all
bil uakmal *adv.* بالأكمل altogether
bil'adl *adv.* بالعدل justly
bil'ard *adv.* بالعرض across
biljomlah *adj.* بالجملة wholesale
biljomlah *adv.* بالجملة wholesale
bilkaad *adv.* بالكاد barely
bilotf *adv.* بلطف nicely
biluahrah *adv.* بالأحرى rather
biluakhas *adv.* بالأخص particularly

bima'zal *adv.* بمعزل aloof

bimoraa'aat *adj.* بمراعاة considerate

binaau *n.* بناء masonry

binabaalah *adv.* بنبالة nobly

binfiraad *adv.* بانفراد solo

bintaal *n.* بنطال trousers

biqazaarah *adj.* بقذارة slatternly

biqorb *adv.* بقرب along

birifq *adv.* برفق lightly

birkah *n.* بركة pond

birraghm *conj.* بالرغم although

birshaam *n.* برشام rivet

bisaraahah *adv.* بصراحة downright

bishaitaaniyyah *adv.* بشيطانية satanically

bishiddah *adv.* بشدّة hard

biskweet *n.* بسكويت biscuit

bisomk *adv.* بسمك thick

bisor'ah *adv.* بسرعة speedily

bit *n.* بت bit

bita'arroj *adv.* بتعرّج zigzag

bitaanah *n.* بطانة lining

bitaaqah *n.* بطاقة card

bitahawwir *adv.* بتهور headlong

bitama' *adv.* بطمع avidly

bitamahhol *adv.* بتمهّل leisurely

bittab' *adv.* بالطبع naturally

bittahdeed *adv.* بالتحديد specifically

bittali *adv.* بالتالي hence

bittaukeed *adv.* بالتأكيد certainly

biuighraau *adv.* بإغراء sexily

biuikhlaas *adv.* بإخلاص heartily

biuikhlaas *adv.* بخلاص bonafide

biuinsaaf *adv.* بإنصاف fairly

biuism *n.* باسم behalf

biur *n.* بئر well

biwaasitat *prep.* بواسطة via

biwodooh *adv.* بوضوح clearly

biyaano *n.* بيانو piano

bo'd *n.* بعد dimension

bohayrah *n.* بحيرة lake

bokhaar *n.* بخار steam

bondoq *n.* بندق nut

bondoqiyyah *n.* بندقية rifle

bonniy *adj.* بني brown

bonya *n.* بنية physique

boolo *n.* بولو polo

boom *n.* بوم owl

booq *n.* بوق trumpet

boosah *n.* بوصة inch

boosalah *n.* بوصلة compass

bootaas *n.* بوتاس potash

bootaasyom *n.* بوتاسيوم potassium

boq'ah *n.* بقعة spot

bor'om *n.* برعم bud

boraaz *n.* براز stool

borghi *n.* برغي screw

borj *n.* برج tower

borkaan *n.* بركان volcano

borkaaniy *adj.* بركاني volcanic

borooz *n.* بروز prominence

bortoqaal *n.* برتقال orange

bortoqaaliy *adj.* برتقالي orange

bosaaq *n.* بصاق spit

bosaylah *n.* بصيلة bulb

boshra *n.* بشرى tidings
bostaan *n.* بستان orchard
bostaaniy *n.* بستاني gardener
bothrah *n.* بثرة pimple
botoolah *n.* بطولة heroism
botooliy *adj.* بطولي heroic
botu *n.* بطء slowness
bous *n.* بؤس misery
bous *n.* بؤس wretch
breel *n.* بريل Braille
bronz *n.* برونز bronze
bronziy *adj.* برونزي bronze
brooteen *n.* بروتين protein

da''aamah *n.* دعامة ancon
da'eef *adj.* ضعيف feeble
da'm *n.* دعم support
da'wa *n.* دعوى litigation
da'wah *n.* 1 دعوة convocation
da'wah *n.* 2 دعوة invitation
daa'i *n.* داع propagandist
daa'iyah *n.* داعية advocate
daabit *n.* 1 ضابط controller
daabit *n.* 2 ضابط officer
daafi' *n.* دافع motive
daafiu *adj.* دافئ warm
daahiyah *adj.* داهية resourceful
daahiyah *n.* ضاحية suburb
daahiyiy *adj.* ضاحيي suburban
daakhil *prep.* داخل inside
daakhil *n.* داخل interior

daakhiliy *adj.* داخلي internal
daakhiliyyan *adv.* داخلياً inland
daakin *adj.* داكن dark
daal *adv.*, ضال astray
daami' *adj.* دامع tearful
daamin *n.* ضامن warrantor
daamir *adj.* ضامر lank
daar *n.* دار parlour
daar *adj.* ضار noxious
daarij *adj.* دارج vernacular
daau *n.* داء disease
daauikh *adj.* دائخ giddy
daauim *adj.* دائم durable
daauiman *adv.* دائماً always
daauin *n.* دائن creditor
daauirah *n.* دائرة circle
daauiriy *adj.* دائري round
dab' *n.* ضبع hyena
dabaab *n.* ضباب fog
dabaabiy *adj.* ضبابي mist
dabbaagh *n.* دباغ tanner
dabboor *n.* دبور wasp
dabboos *n.* دَبوس staple
dabkhan *n.* ضَبخَن smog
daboos *n.* دبوس pin
dadroz *v.* يَدرز seam
daf' *n.* دفع payment
daf'ah *n.* 1 دفعة impulse
daf'ah *n.* 2 دفعة shove
daffah *n.* دفة helm
dafn *n.* دفن burial
daftar *n.* دفتر notebook
dagheenah *n.* ضغينة grudge
daghl *n.* دغل thicket
daght *n.* ضغط pressure

dahaau *n.* دهاء guile
dahd *n.* دحض refutation
dahik *n.* ضحك laughter
dahikah *n.* ضحكة laugh
dahiyyah *n.* ضحية victim
dahl *adj.* ضحل shallow
daj *n.* ضج din
dajaajah *n.* دجاجة chicken
dajal *n.* دجل imposture
dajeej *n.* ضجيج noise
dajjaal *n.* دجّال sham
dajjah *n.* ضجة ado
dakhaamah *n.* ضخامة immensity
dakhl *n.* دخل income
dakhm *adj.* ضخم gigantic
daleel *n.* 1 دليل clue
daleel *n.* 2 دليل directory
daleel *n.* 3 دليل evidence
dalw *n.* دلو bucket
dam *n.* دم blood
dam'ah *n.* دمعة tear
damaan *n.* ضمان guarantee
damaanah *n.* ضمانة surety
damawiy *adj.* دموي bloody
damdamah *n.* دمدمة growl
dameer *n.* 1 ضمير conscience
dameer *n.* 2 ضمير pronoun
damghah *n.* دمغة cachet
damj *n.* دمج incorporation
dammaadah *n.* ضمادة bandage
danas *n.* دنس defile
daneeu *adj.* دنيء sordid
daqeeq *adj.* 1 دقيق accurate
daqeeq *adj.* 2 دقيق delicate
daqeeq *adj.* 3 دقيق minute

daqeeqah *n.* دقيقة minute
daqeeqiy *adj.* دقيقي mealy
dar' *n.* ضرع udder
daraawah *n.* ضراوة fury
darajah *n.* 1 درجة degree
darajah *n.* 2 درجة grade
darar *n.* ضرر damage
darb *n.* 1 ضرب multiplication
darb *n.* 2 ضرب type
darb *n.* 3 ضرب hitting
darbah *n.* ضربة blow
darbah *n.* ضَربَه stroke
dardashah *n.* دردشة chat
dareebah *n.* ضريبة tax
dareeh *n.* 1 ضَريح sepulchre
dareeh *n.* 2 ضريح tomb
daroorah *n.* ضرورة necessity
darooriy *n.* ضروري necessary
darooriy *adj.* ضروري necessary
darraaj *n.* دراج cyclist
darraajah *n.* دراجة bicycle
darraasah *n.* درّاسة thresher
dars *n.* درس lesson
darz *n.* درز seam
daseesah *n.* دسيسة intrigue
daueel *adj.* ضئيل scant
dawaahi *n.pl.* ضواحي outskirts
dawaajin *n.* دواجن poultry
dawaam *n.* دوام permanence
dawaau *n.* دواء medicine
dawaauiy *adj.* دوائي medicinal
dawaraan *n.* دوران spin
dawdaau *v.* ضوضاء clutter
dawiy *n.* دَوي rumble
dawlah *n.* دولة nation

dawlah *n.* دولة state

dawliy *adj.* دولي international

dawr *n.* 1 دور turn

dawr *n.* 2 دور role

dawrah *n.* دورة cycle

dawriy *n.* دوري league

dawriy *adj.* دوري periodical

dawriyyah *n.* 1 دورية patrol

dawriyyah *n.* 2 دورية periodical

dawu *n.* ضوء light

dawwaamah *n.* دوّامة spiral

dawwaar *adj.* دوّار rotary

dawwaasah *n.* دوّاسة pedal

dayf *n.* ضيف guest

dayn *n.* دين debt

dayr *n.* دير monastery

dayyiq *adj.* ضيق narrow

dazzeenah *n.* دزينة dozen

ddaahirah *n.* ظاهرة phenomenon

ddaahiriy *adj.* ظاهري virtual

ddaahiriyyan *adv.* ظاهريا outwardly

ddaalim *adj.* ظالم unjust

ddabi *n.* ظبي stag

ddabyah *n.* ظبية doe

ddalaam *n.* ظلام dark

ddalaam *n.* ظلم injustice

ddamuaan *adj.* ظمآن thirsty

ddaraafah *n.* ظرافة amiability

ddareef *adj.* ظريف amiable

ddarf *n.* 1 ظرف adverb

ddarf *n.* 2 ظرف circumstance

ddarf *n.* 3 ظرف envelope

ddarfiy *adj.* ظرفي adverbial

ddhr *n.* ظهر back

ddil *n.* ظل shade

deek *n.* ديك cock

deemoqraatiy *adj.* ديمقراطي democratic

deemoqraatiyyah n. ديمقراطية democracy

deenaameet *n.* ديناميت dynamite

deeniy *adj.* ديني religious

dha *art.* ذا an

dhaakirah *n.* ذاكرة memory

dhaalika *dem. pron.* ذلَك that

dhaatiy *adj.* ذاتي subjective

dhaauib *adj.* ذائب soluble

dhabdhabah *n.* ذبذبة oscillation

dhabeehah *adj.* ذبيحة sacrificial

dhabeehah *n.* ذبيحة slaughter

dhahab *n.* ذهب gold

dhahabiy *adj.* ذهبي golden

dhakaau *n.* ذكاء intelligence

dhakar *adj.* ذكر male

dhakar *n.* ذكر male

dhakheerah *n.* ذخيرة ammunition

dhakiy *adj.* ذكي clever

dhaleel *adj.* ذليل servile

dham *n.* ذم invective

dhameem *adj.* ذميم obnoxious

dhanab *n.* ذنب tail

dhanb *n.* ذنب guilt

dhaqn *n.* ذقن chin

dharee'ah *n.* ذريعة pretext

dharrah *n.* ذرة atom

dharriy *adj.* ذري atomic

dhawabaan *n.* ذوَبان thaw

dhawabaaniyyah *n.* ذوبانية solubility

dhawq *n.* ذوق 1 decorum
dhawq *n.* ذوق 2 taste
dhayl *n.* ذيل tail
dhikr *n.* ذكر mention
dhikra *n.* ذكرى anniversary
dhimniy *adj.* ضمني implicit
dhiraa' *n.* ذراع arm
dhiub *n.* ذئب wolf
dho'r *n.* ذعر panic
dhobaabah *n.* ذبابة fly
dhohool *n.* ذهول amazement
dhorah *n.* ذرة corn
dhoriyyah *n.* ذرية progeny
dhorwah *n.* ذروة climax
di'aayah *n.* دعاية publicity
dibaaghah *n.* دباغة tanning
diblomaasiy *n.* دبلوماسي diplomat
diblomaasiy *adj.* دبلوماسي diplomatic
diblomaasiyyah *n.* دبلوماسية diplomacy
dibloom *n.* دبلوم diploma
dictaatooriy *adj.* دكتاتوري totalitarian
did *prep.* ضد against
difaa' *n.* دفاع defence
difaa'iy *adv.* دفاعي defensive
difda' *n.* دفضع toad
difda' *n.* ضفدع frog
diffah *n.* ضفّة bank
difu *n.* دفء warmth
diktaatoor *n.* دكتاتور dictator
dil' *n.* ضلع rib
dil'iy *adj.* ضلعي costal
dilta *n.* دلتا delta

dimaagh *n.* دماغ brain
dimaaghiy *adj.* دماغي cerebral
dimn *prep.* ضمن within
dinim *n.* دنيم jean
diqqah *n.* دقّة accuracy
dir' *n.* درع armour
diraasah *n.* دراسة study
dirham *n.* درهم dram
dirs *n.* ضرس molar
dirsiy *adj.* ضرسي molar
diyaafah *n.* ضيافة hospitality
diyaanah *n.* ديانة religion
diyaanah *n.* دين religion
do'f *n.* ضعف weakness
dob *n.* دب bear
dof'ah *n.* دفعة 1 advance
dof'ah *n.* دفعة 2 batch
dohn *n.* دهن fat
dohniy *adj.* دهني greasy
dokhaan *n.* دخان smoke
dokhn *n.* دخن millet
dokhool *n.* دخول entry
doktooraah *n.* دكتوراه doctorate
domyah *n.* دمية doll
donyawiy *adj.* دنيوي worldly
doodah *n.* دودة worm
doolaar *n.* دولار dollar
dooq *n.* دوق duke
dosh *n.* دش shower
dostoor *n.* دستور constitution
draabzeen *n.* درابزين railing
draama *n.* دراما drama
draamiy *adj.* درامي dramatic
draasiy *adj.* دراسي scholastic

E

e'aadah *n.* إعادة reinstatement

e'aanah *n.* إعانة subsidy

e'daad *n.* إعداد preparation

e'daam *n.* إعدام execution

e'faau *n.* إعفاء discharge

e'jaab *n.* إعجاب admiration

e'laam *n.* إعلام intimation

e'laam *n.* إعلام notification

e'laamiy *adj.* إعلامي informative

e'laan *n.* إعلان advertisement

e'laan *n.* إعلان announcement

e'laan *n.* إعلان declaration

e'laan *n.* إعلان proclamation

e'saar *n.* إعسار insolvency

e'saar *n.* إعصار cyclone

e'saar *n.* إعصار hurricane

e'saar *n.* إعصار typhoon

e'tibaar *n.* إعتبار consideration

e'tidaau *n.* إعتداء abuse

e'tidaau *n.* اعتداء assault

e'tidhaar *n.* اعتذار apology

e'tilaal *n.* اعتلال morbidity

e'timaad *n.* إعتماد appropriation

e'timaad *n.* اعتماد dependence

e'tiqaad *n.* إعتقاد belief

e'tiqaal *n.* اعتقال arrest

e'tiraad *n.* اعتراض 1 interception

e'tiraad *n.* اعتراض 2 objection

e'tiraaf *n.* إعتراف admittance

e'tiraaf *n.* اعتراف 1
acknowledgement

e'tiraaf *n.* اعتراف 2 confession

e'tiyaadiy *adj.* إعتيادي standard

e'tizaal *n.* إعتزال abdication

ebaadah *n.* إبادة annihilation

ebhaam *n.* إبهام thumb

eblees *n.* إبليس Satan

ebn *n.* إبن son

ebnah *n.* ابنة daughter

ebnato uakh *n.* ابنةأخ niece

ebno uaawa *n.* ابن آوى jackal

ebno uakh *n.* ابن أخ nephew

ebraaq *n.* إبراق telegraphy

ebrah *n.* إبرة needle

ebreeq *n.* إبريق jug

ebreeq *n.* إبريق kettle

ebtaal *n.* إبطال nullification

ebtidaauiy *adj.* إبتدائي elementary

ebtihaaj *n.* إبتهاج mirth

ebtihaaj *n.* ابتهاج cheer

ebtihaaj *n.* ابتهاج jubilation

ebtikaar *n.* ابتكار innovation

ebtilaa' *n.* إبتلاع gulp

ebtilaa' *n.* ابتلاع swallow

ebtilaau *n.* إبتلاء affliction

ebtisaamah *n.* ابتسامة smile

ebtizaaz *n.* إبتزاز graft

ebtizaaz *n.* ابتزاز blackmail

ebzeem *n.* إبزيم buckle

edtiraab *n.* إضطراب psychosis

edaafah *n.* إضافة addition

edaafiy *adj.* إضافي additional

edaafiy *adj.* إضافي extra

edaafiy *adv.* إضافي overtime

edaafiy *n.* إضافي overtime

edaafiy *adj.* اضافي adscititious

edaanah *n.* إدانة condemnation

edaanah *n.* إدانة conviction
edaarah *n.* إدارة administration
edaarah *n.* إدارة management
edaariy *adj.* إداري managerial
edaariy *adj.* إداريِ administrative
edaauah *n.* إضاءة illumination
eddfar *n.* إظفر nail
eddi'aau *n.* ادعاء pretension
eddi'au *n.* ادعاء allegation
eddikhaar *n.* إدخار thrift
edh'aan *n.* إذعان deference
edha *conj.* إذا if
edhlaal *n.* إذلال humiliation
edhniy *adj.* إذني promissory
edkhaal *n.* إدخال insertion
edkhaal *n.* ادخال admission
edmaan *n.* إدمان addiction
edmihlaal *n.* إضمحلال decay
edraab *n.* إضراب strike
edraak *n.* إدراك cognizance
edraak *n.* إدراك perception
edraak *n.* إدراك realization
edtihaad *n.* اضطهاد persecution
edtiraab *n.* اضطراب disorder
edtiraab *n.* اضطراب turbulence
edtiraab *n.* اضطراب turmoil
edtraab *n.* اضطراب unrest
eflaas *n.* إفلاس bankruptcy
efraaz *n.* إفراز secretion
efraazaat *n.* إفرازات discharge
eftaar *n.* إفطار breakfast
eftiraad *n.* إفتراض presumption
eftiraad *n.* افتراض assumption
eftiraadhiy *n.* إفتراضي default
eftiraadiy *adj.* افتراضي
hypothetical

eftiraau *n.* افتراء slander
eftiraauiy *adj.* افترائي slanderous
eftitaah *n.* افتتاح opening
eftitaahiy *adj.* إفتتاحي inaugural
eftitaahiyyah *n.* إفتتاحية editorial
eghaaddah *n.* إغاظة vexation
eghaathah *n.* إغاثة relief
eghdaab *n.* إغضاب aggravation
eghfaal *n.* إغفال omission
eghlaaq *n.* إغلاق closure
eghmaau *n.* إغُماء swoon
eghraau *n.* إغراء allurement
eghraau *n.* إغراء lure
eghraau *n.* إغراء temptation
eghtisaab *n.* اغتصاب rape
eghtiyaal *n.* اغتيال assassination
eghwaau *n.* إغواء seduction
ehaanah *n.* إهانة insult
ehbaat *n.* إحباط frustration
ehmaal *n.* إهمال negligence
ehraaq *n.* إحراق burning
ehsaan *n.* إحسان benevolence
ehsaas *n.* 1 إحساس feeling
ehsaas *n.* 2 إحساس hunch
ehsaas *n.* 3 إحساس sense
ehsaauiy *adj.* إحصائي statistical
ehsaauiy *n.* إحصائي statistician
ehsaauiyyat *n.* إحصائيات
statistics
ehtidaan *n.* احتضان embrace
ehtifaal *n.* إحتفال festivity
ehtifaal *n.* احتفال celebration
ehtifaal *n.* احتفال revelry
ehtifaaliy *adj.* إحتفاليِ ceremonial

ehtifaaliy *adj.* احتفالي festive
ehtijaaj *n.* احتجاج invocation
ehtijaaj *adj.* احتجاج outcry
ehtijaaj *n.* احتجاج protest
ehtijaaj *n.* احتجاج protestation
ehtijaaz *n.* إحتِجاز retention
ehtikaak *n.* احتكاك friction
ehtikaar *n.* إحتكار monopoly
ehtilaal *n.* إحتلال occupation
ehtimaal *n.* احتمال endurance
ehtimaal *n.* احتمال likelihood
ehtimaal *n.* احتمال probability
ehtimaal *n.* احتمال prospect
ehtimaaliyyah *n.* إحتمالية potentiality
ehtimaam *n.* اهتمام attention
ehtimaam *n.* اهتمام solicitude
ehtiqaar *n.* إحتقار abasement
ehtiqaar *n.* احتقار contempt
ehtiqaar *n.* احتقار scorn
ehtiraam *n.* إحترام decency
ehtiraam *n.* احترام esteem
ehtiraam *n.* احترام respect
ehtiraas *n.* إحتراس caution
ehtiyaajaat *adv.* احتياجات needs
ehtiyaajiy *adj.* احتياجي needful
ehtiyaal *n.* احتيال fraud
ehtiyaal *n.* احتيال knavery
ehtiyaal *n.* احتيال roguery
ehtiyaaliy *adj.* إحتيالي fraudulent
ehtiyaataat *n.* إحتياطات precaution
ehtiyaatiy *adj.* إحتياطي spare
ehtizaaz *n.* اهتزاز vibration
ehyaau *n.* إحياء revival

ejaazah *n.* إجازة leave
ejhaad *n.* إجهاد stress
ejhaad *n.* إجهاض abortion
ejhaad *n.* إجهاض miscarriage
ejlaal *n.* إجلال homage
ejlaal *n.* إجلال solemnity
ejmaa' *n.* إجماع consensus
ejmaa' *n.* إجماع unanimity
ejmaaliy *adj.* إجمالي gross
ejraau *n.* إجراء proceeding
ejraau *n.* إجراء procedure
ejtihaad *n.* اجتهاد diligence
ejtimaa' *n.* 1 إجتماع convener
ejtimaa' *n.* 2 اجتماع meeting
ejtimaa'iy *adj.* إجتماعي sociable
ejtimaa'iy *n.* اجتماعي social
ejtiraar *n.* اجترار rumination
ejtiyaah *n.* اجتياح invasion
ekbaar *n.* إكبار obeisance
ekhdaa' *n.* إخضاع subjection
ekhfaau *n.* إخفاء hiding
ekhlaas *n.* إخلاص devotion
ekhlaas *n.* إخلاص fidelity
ekhlaas *n.* إخلاص royalty
ekhlaau *n.* إخلاء evacuation
ekhtibaar *n.* اختبار test
ekhtifaau *n.* اختفاء disappearance
ekhtilaas *n.* اختلاس misappropriation
ekhtinaaq *n.* اختناق suffocation
ekhtiraa' *n.* اختراع invention
ekhtiraaq *n.* اختراق penetration
ekhtisaar *n.* إختصار abridgement
ekhtisaar *n.* اختصار abbreviation
ekhtisaas *n.* إختصاص jurisdiction

ekhtisaas *n.* اختصاص competence	eltiwaau *n.* التواء wrick
ekhtitaaf *n.* اختطاف abduction	eltiwaau *n.* التواء sprain
ekhtiyaal *n.* اختيال swagger	eltizaam *adj.* إلتزام abiding
ekhtiyaar *n.* اختيار selection	eltizaam *n.* إلتزام commitment
ekhtiyaariy *adj.* اختياري optional	eltizaam *n.* التزام obligation
ekhtizaal *n.* اختزال stenography	elzaamiy *adj.* إلزامي compulsory
ekleel *n.* إكليل wreath	elzaamiy *adj.* إلزامي mandatory
ekraah *n.* إكراه compulsion	embiryaaliy *adj.* إمبريالي imperial
ektisaab *n.* إكتساب acquirement	embraatoor *n.* إمبراطور emperor
ektisaab *n.* إكتساب acquisition	embraatoorah *n.* إمبراطورة empress
ektishaaf *n.* اكتشاف discovery	embraatootiyyah *n.* إمبراطورية empire
ektiuaab *n.* إكتآب depression	
ela *prep.* إلا except	emkaaniyyah *n.* إمكانية potential
ela *prep.* إلى for	emkaaniyyah *n.* إمكانية possibility
ela *prep.* إلى into	emlaau *n.* إملاء dictation
elaah *n.* إله deity	emma *a.,* إما either
elaah *n.* إله god	emraua *n.* امرأة woman
elaahah *n.* إلهة goddess	emsaak *n.* إمساك constipation
elaahiy *adj.* إلهي divine	emtidaad *n.* امتداد span
elaahiy *adj.* إلهي godly	emtihaan *n.* إمتحان quiz
elghaau *v.* إلغاء abolition	emtihaan *n.* امتحان probation
elghaau *n.* إلغاء cancellation	emtilaau *n.* إمتلاء fullness
elghaau *n.* إلغاء repeal	emtinaa' *n.* إمتناع refrain
elghaau *n.* إلغاء revocation	emtinaan *n.* إمتنان gratitude
elhaad *n.* إلحاد atheism	emtithaal *n.* إمتثال compliance
elhaam *n.* إلهام inspiration	emtiyaaz *n.* 1 امتياز excellence
ella *prep.* إلى but	emtiyaaz *n.* 2 امتياز privilege
ella edha *conj.* إذا إلا unless	en'ikaas *n.* 1 انعكاس reflection
elsaaq *n.* إلصاق adhesion	en'ikaas *n.* 2 انعكاس reversal
eltihaab *n.* التهاب inflammation	en'ikaasiy *adj.* انعكاسي reflexive
eltimaas *n.* التماس solicitation	en'itaaf *n.* إنعطاف turn
eltimaasiy *adj.* التماسي solicitous	enaau *n.* إنهاء termination
eltiwaau *n.* إلتواء rick	endhaar *n.* إنذار caution
eltiwaau *n.* إلتواء strain	
eltiwaau *n.* إلتواء twist	

endhaar *n.* إنذار ultimatum
endibaat *n.* انضباط discipline
endifaa' *n.* إندفاع lunge
endifaa' *n.* إندفاع scramble
endifaa' *n.* اندفاع rush
enfaaq *n.* إنفاق expenditure
enfijaar *n.* انفجار explosion
enfiraadiy *adj.* انفرادي solitary
enfisaal *n.* انفصال detachment
enfisaal *n.* انفصال separation
enfisaaliy *n.* انفصالي secessionist
enghimaas *n.* انغماس spree
enhimaak *n.* انهماك preoccupation
enhinaau *n.* انحناء bend
enhiraaf *n.* إنحراف aberrance
enhiraaf *n.* إنحراف deviation
enhiraaf *n.* إنحراف perversion
enhiyaar *n.* انهيار breakdown
enhiyaaz *n.* انحياز bias
enjaab *n.* انجاب reproduction
enjaabiy *adj.* إنجابي natal
enjaabiy *adj.* إنجابي reproductive
enjaaz *n.* إنجاز accomplishment
enjaaz *n.* إنجاز achievement
enjeel *n.* إنجيل gospel
enkaar *n.* إنكار denial
enkhifaad *n.* إنخفاض depression
enkimaash *n.* إنكماش deflation
enkimaash *n.* انكماش shrinkage
enqaadh *n.* إنقاذ rescue
enqaas *n.* إنقاص decrement
enqibaad *n.* انقباض contraction
enqidaad *n.* إنقضاض pounce
enqidaad *n.* انقضاض swoop

enqidaau *n.* انقضاء expiry
enqilaab *n.* انقلاب coup
enqisaam *n.* انقسام split
enqitaa' *n.* انقطاع interruption
ensaan *adj.* إنسان human
ensaaniy *adj.* إنساني humane
ensaaniy *adj.* إنساني humanitarian
ensaaniyyah *n.* إنسانية humanity
ensihaab *n.* انسحاب withdrawal
ensihaar *n.* انصهار fusion
ensijaam *n.* إنسجام harmony
ensijaam *n.* انسجام unison
ensikaab *n.* انسكاب spill
entaaj *n.* إنتاج output
entaaj *n.* إنتاج production
entaaj *n.* انتاج reproduction
entaajiyyah *n.* إنتاجية productivity
entaha *adv.* انتهى up
entibaa' *n.* إنطباع impression
entibaah *n.* انتباه heed
entidaab *n.* انتداب deputation
entiddaam *n.* إنتظام regularity
entiddaar *n.* انتظار wait
entihaak *n.* انتهاك infringement
entihaak *n.* انتهاك violation
entihaal *n.* إنتحال impersonation
entihaar *n.* إنتهار slight
entihaar *n.* إنتهار snub
entihaar *n.* انتحار suicide
entihaariy *adj.* انتحاري suicidal
entihaaziy *n.* انتهازي profiteer
entihaaziyyah *n.* انتهازية opportunism
entikaas *n.* انتكاس relapse

entikhaab *n.* انتخاب election	**eraadah** *n.* إرادة volition
entimaau *n.* انتماء affiliation	**eraadah** *n.* إرادَه will
entiqaal *n.* انتقال transition	**eraban** *adv.* إرباً asunder
entiqaam *n.* انتقام retaliation	**erfaaq** *n.* إرفاق annexation
entiqaam *n.* انتقام revenge	**erhaab** *n.* إرهاب terror
entiqaam *n.* انتقام vengeanc	**erhaab** *n.* إرهاب terrorism
entiqaauiy *adj.* انتقائي selective	**erhaabiy** *n.* إرهابي terrorist
entisaab *n.* انتصاب erection	**erhaaq** *n.* إرهاق overwork
entisaam *n.* انتصار triumph	**ershaadiy** *adj.* إرشادي indicative
entisaar *n.* إنتصار victory	**erth** *n.* إرث patrimony
entisaariy *adj.* انتصاري triumphal	**ertibaak** *n.* ارتباك confusion
entishaar *n.* إنْتِشار prevalence	**ertiBaat** *n.* ارتباط correlation
entishaar *n.* انتشار spread	**ertidaad** *n.* ارتداد rebound
enzilaaq *n.* انزلاق skid	**ertifaa'** *n.* إرتفاع altitude
eqaalah *n.* إقالة dismissal	**ertifaa'** *n.* ارتفاع 1 elevation
eqaamah *n.* إقامة accommodation	**ertifaa'** *n.* ارتفاع 2 height
eqaamah *n.* إقامة residence	**ertijaaf** *n.* ارتجاف quiver
eqaamah *n.* إقامة stay	**ertijaaj** *n.* ارتجاج shudder
eqdaam *n.* إقدام pluck	**ertitaam** *n.* ارتطام collision
eqhaam *n.* إقحام interjection	**es'aaf** *n.* إسعاف ambulance
eqleem *n.* إقليم canton	**esaabah** *n.* إصابة injury
eqleem *n.* إقليم territory	**esaauah** *n.* إساءة misuse
eqleemiy *adj.* إقليمي provincial	**esba'** *n.* إصبع finger
eqleemiy *adj.* إقليمي territorial	**esba'ol qadam** *n.* اصبع القدم toe
eqleemiy *adj.* إقليمي regional	**esbaaniy** *adj.* إسباني Spanish
eqnaa' *n.* إقناع persuasion	**esdaar** *n.* إصدار issue
eqtaa' *n.* إقطاع benefice	**esdaar** *n.* إصدار version
eqtaa'iy *adj.* إقطاعي feudal	**esfeen** *n.* إسفين scotch
eqtibaas *n.* اقتباس quotation	**esfeen** *n.* إسفين wedge
eqtiraa' *n.* اقتراع ballot	**esh'aa'** *n.* إشعاع radiance
eqtiraah *n.* إقتراح proposition	**esh'aa'** *n.* إشعاع radiation
eqtiraah *n.* اقتراح suggestion	**esh'aar** *n.* إشعار notice
eqtiraaniy *adj.* إقتراني conjunct	**eshaa'ah** *n.* إشاعة hearsay
eqtisaad *n.* اقتصاد economy	**eshaa'ah** *n.* إشاعة rumour
eqtisaadiy *adj.* اقتصادي economical	**eshaab** *n.* إسهاب verbosity

eshaal *n.* إسهال diarrhoea

eshaarah *n.* إشارة indication

eshaarah *n.* إشارة signal

eshghaal *n.* إشغال occupancy

eshkaaliyah *adj.* إشكالية problematic

eshmiuzaaz *n.* اشمئزاز repugnance

eshraaf *n.* إشراف superintendence

eshraaf *n.* إشراف supervision

eshtibaah *n.* اشتباه suspicion

eshtibaak *n.* اشتباك clash

eshtibaak *n.* اشتباك engagement

eshtiraak *n.* اشتراك subscription

eshtiraakiy *adj.* اشتراكي communal

eshtiraakiy *n.* اشتراكي socialist

eshtiraakiyyah *n.* اشتراكية socialism

eshtiyaaq *n.* اشتياق yen

eskaafiy *n.* إسكافي cobbler

eskotlaandi *n.* اسكتلاندي Scot

eskotlaandi *adj.* اسكتلاندي scotch

eslaah *n.* إصلاح redress

eslaah *n.* إصلاح reform

eslaah *n.* إصلاح reformation

eslaah *n.* إصلاح repair

eslaahiy *adj.* إصلاحي reformatory

eslaahiyyah *n.* إصلاحية reformatory

esm *n.* اسم name

esm *n.* اسم noun

esmant *n.* أسمنت cement

esmant *n.* إسمنت concrete

esmiy *adj.* اسمي nominal

esqaat *n.* إسقاط projection

esraaf *n.* إسراف extravagance

esraaf *n.* إسراف prodigality

esraaf *n.* إسراف profligacy

esraaf *n.* إسراف profusion

esraaf *n.* اسراف wastage

esraar *n.* إصرار determination

esraar *n.* إصرار insistence

esraar *n.* إصرار persistence

essfanj *n.* إسفنج sponge

estaad *n.* استاد stadium

establ *n.* إسطبل barn

establ *n.* إسطبل stable

estakaan *v.* استكان nuzzle

estee'aab *n.* استيعاب assimilation

esteeraad *n.* استيراد import

esti'aadah *n.* إستعادة recovery

esti'aadah *n.* استعادة reclamation

esti'aadah *n.* استعادة restoration

esti'aarah *n.* استعارة allegory

esti'aarah *n.* استعارة metaphor

esti'aariy *adj.* استعاري allegorical

esti'baad *n.* استعباد subjugation

esti'daad *n.* استعداد readiness

esti'daad *n.* استعداد willingness

esti'laam *n.* استعلام query

esti'maal *n.* استعمال usage

esti'maariy *adj.* استعماري colonial

esti'raad *n.* استعراض review

estibdaad *n.* استبداد autocracy

estibdaadiy *adj.* استبدادي autocratic

estibdaal *n.* استبدال substitution

estibtaan *n.* استبطان introspection

estibyaan *n.* استبيان questionnaire

estid'aau *n.* استدعاء calling

estid'aauaat *n.* استدعاءات summons

estidaam *n.* اصطدام clash

estidlaal *n.* استدلال inference

estifhaamiy *adj.* استفهامي interrogative

estifsaar *n.* إستفسار inquiry

estiftaau *n.* استفتاء plebiscite

estiftaau *n.* استفتاء referendum

estifzaaz *n.* إستفزاز provocation

estifzaaziy *adj.* استفزازي provocative

estighlaal *n.* إستغلال taking advantage

estighlaal *n.* استغلال exploit

estihaalah *n.* استحالة impossibility

estihlaaf *n.* استحلاف adjuration

estihlaak *n.* استهلاك consumption

estihlaaliy *adj.* استهلالي introductory

estihqaaq *n.* استحقاق due

estihsaan *n.* إستحسان approbation

estihwaau *n.* استهواء fascination

estihzaau *n.* استهزاء mockery

estijaabah *n.* استجابة response

estijmaam *n.* استجمام recreation

estijwaab *n.* استجواب interrogation

estikhbaaraat *n.* استخبارات intelligence

estikhdaam *n.* استخدام use

estikhdaam *n.* استخدام utilization

estikhlaas *n.* إستخلاص abstraction

estikshaaf *n.* استكشاف exploration

estilaahiy *adj.* اصطلاحي idiomatic

estimraar *n.* استمرار continuation

estimraariyyah *n.* إستمرارية continuity

estimtaa' *n.* استمتاع relish

estimtaa' *n.* استمتاع revel

estinaa'i *adj.* اصطناعي synthetic

estinaa'iy *adj.* اصطناعي artificial

estinkaar *n.* استنكار denunciation

estinkaar *n.* استنكار disapproval

estintaaj *n.* استنتاج conclusion

estinzaaf *n.* استنزاف drain

estiqaalah *n.* استقالة resignation

estiqbaal *n.* استقبال reception

estiqlaal *n.* استقلال independence

estiqraar *n.* إستقرار settlement

estiqraar *n.* استقرار stability

estiqraar *n.* استقرار stabilization

estiqraau *n.* إستقراء induction

estiraahah *n.* استراحة break

estiraahah *n.* استراحة lounge

estirkhaau *n.* استرخاء relaxation

estirleeni *n.* استرليني sterling

estish'aariy *adj.* إستشعاري detective

estishhaadiy *n.* استشهاد martyrdom

estislaah *n.* استصلاح 1 reclamation

estislaah *n.* استصلاح 2 restoration

estislaam *n.* استسلام surrender

estithmaar *n.* استثمار investment

estithnaau *n.* استثناء exception

estithnaauiy *adj.* استثنائي extraordinary

estitlaa' *n.* استطلاع poll

estiunaaf *n.* استئناف appeal

estiunaaf *n.* استئناف resumption

estiwaauiy *adj.* استوائي tropical

estiyaau *n.* استياء discontent

estiyaau *n.* استياء displeasure

estiyaau *n.* استياء dissatisfaction

estiyaau *n.* استياء resentment

estraatijiy *adj.* إستراتيجي strategic

estraatijiy *n.* إستراتيجي strategist

estraatijiyyah *n.* إستراتيجية strategy

etaalah *n.* إطالة prolongation

etaar *n.* إطار frame

etaar *n.* إطار tire

etaar *n.* إطار tyre

ethbaat *n.* إثبات substantiation

ethm *n.* إثم misdeed

ethna 'ashar *n.* اثنا عشر twelve

ethnaan *n.* اثنان two

ethnaan *adj.* اثنان two

etlaaf *n.* اتلاف wastage

etlaaq *n.* إطلاق launch

etlaaq *n.* إطلاق release

etlaaqan *adv.* إطلاقاً absolutely

etmaam *n.* إتمام completion

etmiunaan *n.* اطمئنان contentment

etnaab *n.* إطناب redundancy

etqaan *n.* إتقان proficiency

etraau *n.* إطراء compliment

etraau *n.* إطراء flattery

ettifaaq *n.* إتفاقية agreement

ettifaaq *n.* اتفاق deal

ettifaaq *n.* اتفاق pact

ettifaaqiyyah *n.* اتفاقية convention

ettihaad *n.* إتحاد union

ettihaad *n.* اتحاد federation

ettihaadiy *n.* إتحادي unionist

ettihaadiy *adj.* اتحادي federal

ettihaam *n.* إتهام accusation

ettihaam *n.* اتهام indictment

ettijaah *n.* اتجاه direction

ettijaah *n.* اتجاه trend

ettisaa' *n.* اتساع breadth

ettisaal *n.* اتصال liaison

ettisaal *n.* اتصال dial

ettizaan *n.* اتزان poise

eutimaan *n.* ائتمان credit

ewazzah *n.* إوزة goose

ez'aaj *n.* إزعاج agitation

ez'aaj *n.* إزعاج annoyance

ez'aaj *n.* إزعاج botheration

ez'aaj *n.* إزعاج irritation

ez'aaj *n.* إزعاج nuisance

ez'aaz *n.* إزعاج discomfort

ezaalah *n.* إزالة removal

ezdihaar *n.* إزدهار bloom

ezdihaar *n.* ازدهار prosperity

ezdiraau *n.* ازدراء disdain

ezdiraau *n.* ازدراء disrespect

ezmeel *n.* إزميل chisel

F

fa''aal *adj.* فعال effective

fa'aaliyyah *n.* فعالية efficacy

faa'iliyyah *n.* فاعلية potency
faadih *adj.* فاضح flagrant
faadil *n.* فاضل moralist
faadil *adj.* فاضل virtuous
faahish *adj.* فاحش obscene
faajir *adj.* فاجر licentious
faakhir adj. فاخر luxurious
faakihah *n.* فاكهة fruit
faaks *n.* فاكس fax
faani *adj.* فانٍ mortal
faanillah *n.* فانلة flannel
faanoos *n.* فانوس lantern
faarid *adj.* فارض imposing
faarigh *adj.* فارغ empty
faarigh *n.* فراغ blank
faariq *n.* فارق difference
faaris *n.* فارس knight
faashil *adv.* فاشل abortive
faasid *adj.* 1 فاسد corrupt
faasid *adj.* 2 فاسد foul
faasil *adj.* فاصل separator
faasil *n.* فاصل interval
faasilah *n.* فاصلة comma
faasiq *adj.* فاسق lascivious
faasiqah *n.* فاسقة slut
faasoolyaau *n.* فاصوليا bean
faatih *adj.* فاتح light
faatih *n.* فاتح conqueror
faatin *adj.* فاتن winsome
faatir *adj.* 1 فاتر frigid
faatir *adj.* 2 فاتر lukewarm
faatoorah *n.* فاتورة invoice
faauid *adj.* فائض abundant
faauid *n.* فائض surplus
faauidah *n.* 1 فائدة advantage

faauidah *n.* 2 فائدة interest
faauiz *n.* فائز winner
faazleen *n.* فازلين vaseline
fadaalah *n.* فضالة superfluity
fadaau *n.* فضاء space
fadd *adj.* فظ rude
faddaa'ah *n.* فظاعة atrocity
faddaan *n.* فدان acre
faddee' *adj.* فظيع atrocious
fadeehah *n.* فضيحة scandal
fadeelah *n.* فضيلة virtue
fadfaad *adj.* فضفاض loose
fahd *n.* فهد leopard
fahl *n.* فحل stallion
fahl *adj.* فحل virile
fahm *n.* فحم coal
fahm *n.* فهم comprehension
fahras *n.* فهرس catalogue
fahs *n.* فحص examination
fahsh *n.* فحش obscenity
fajr *n.* فجر dawn
fajuah *adv.* فجأة suddenly
fajwah *n.* فجوة gap
fak *n.* فك jaw
fakh *n.* فخ trap
fakhdh *n.* فخذ thigh
fakhkhaar *n.* فخار pottery
fakhm *adj.* فخم palatial
fakhoor *adj.* فخور proud
fakhriy *adj.* فخري honorary
falak *n.* فلك orb
fallaah *n.* فلاح peasant
fallaaheen *n.* فلاحين peasantry
falleen *n.* فلين cork
falsafah *n.* فلسفة philosophy

falsafiy *adj.* فلسفي philosophical
fam *n.* فم mouth
fan *n.* فن art
fanaau *n.* 1 فناء courtyard
fanaau *n.* 2 فَناء mortality
faniy *n.* فني technician
fadaau *n.* فنان artist
fanniy *adj.* فني artistic
faqamah *n.* فقمة seal
faqarah *n.* فقرة paragraph
faqat *adv.* فقط only
faqd *n.* فقد loss
faqeer *n.* فقير pauper
faqeer *adj.* فقير poor
faqr *n.* فقر poverty
faraamil *n.* فرامل brake
faraashah *n.* فراشة butterfly
faradiyyah *n.* فرضية hypothesis
farah *n.* فرح joy
faransiy *adj.* فرنسي French
faras *n.* فرس mare
farawlah *n.* فراولة strawberry
fard *n.* فرد individual
fard *n.* فرض imposition
fardiy *adj.* فردي odd
fardiy *n.* فردي solo
fardiyyah *n.* فردية individualism
fareed *adj.* فريد unique
fareeq *n.* فريق team
fareesah *n.* فريسة prey
farkh *n.* فرخ spawn
farq *n.* فرق difference
farqa'ah *n.* فرقعة bang
farw *n.* فرو fur
fasaa'idan *adv.* فصاعدا onwards

fasaad *n.* فساد corruption
faseeh *adj.* فسيح capacious
faseel *n.* فصيل faction
faseelah *n.* فصيلة platoon
fasfasah *n.* فصفصة lucerne
fashal *n.* فشل failure
fasl *n.* 1 فصل chapter
fasl *n.* 2 فصل term
fasl *n.* 3 فصل segregation
fasliy *adj.* فصلي quarterly
fata *n.* فتى lad
fataah *n.* فتاة girl
fateel *n.* فتيل fuse
fateelah *n.* فَتيلَه wick
fath *n.* فتح conquest
fath *adj.* فتح open
fathah *n.* فتحة opening
fatin *adj.* فطن sagacious
fatiy *adj.* فتيّ youthful
fatm *n.* فطم ablactation
fatq *n.* فتق hernia
fatrah *n.* فترة period
faul *n.* فأل omen
faur *n.* فأر mouse
faus *n.* فأس axe
fawda *n.* فوضى chaos
fawdaawiy *adv.* فوضوي chaotic
fawdawiy *n.* فوضوي anarchist
fawdawiyyah *n.* فوضوية anarchism
fawj *n.* فوج regiment
fawq *prep.* فوق above
fawq *adv.* فوق over
fawq *adv.* فَوقَ on
fawrah *n.* فورة outburst

fawran *adv.* فوراً instantly	**film** *n.* فيلم film
fawriy *adv.* فوري forthwith	**finjaan** *n.* فنجان beaker
fawriy *a* فوري immediate	**fiqariy** *adj.* فقري spinal
fayadaan *n.* فيضان flood	**fiqh** *n.* فقه jurisprudence
fayd *n.* فيض spate	**fiqhiy** *n.* فقيه jurist
faylaq *n.* فيلق legion	**fir'** *n.* فرع branch
faylaqiy *n.* فيلقي legionary	**fir'iy** *adj.* فرعي subsidiary
faylasoof *n.* فيلسوف philosopher	**firaakh** *n.* فراخ brood
fayroos *n.* فيروس virus	**firaar** *n.* فرار escape
fayyaal *n.* فيال mahout	**firaash** *n.* فراش bedding
faza' *n.* فزع scare	**firqah** *n.* 1 فرقة band
fazzaa'ah *n.* فزّاعة bogle	**firqah** *n.* 2 فرقة squad
feel *n.* فيل elephant	**fitnah** *n.* فتنة sedition
feema ba'd *adv.* فيمابعد after	**fitnah** *n.* فطنة acumen
feetaameen *n.* فيتامين vitamin	**fitr** *n.* فطر mushroom
feezyaau *n.* فيزياء physics	**fitriy** *adj.* فطري innate
feezyaauiy *n.* فيزيائي physicist	**fiuah** *n.* فئة category
fi *prep.* 1 في at	**fodool** *n.* فضول curiosity
fi *prep.* 2 في in	**fodooliy** *adj.* فضولي curious
fi'l *n.* فعل verb	**fohoolah** *n.* فحولة virility
fi'lan *adv.* فعلاً indeed	**fojoor** *n.* فجور immorality
fi'liy *adj.* 1 فعلي verbal	**fokaahah** *n.* فكاهة humour
fi'liy *adj.* 2 فعلي actual	**fokaahiy** *adj.* فكاهي comic
fidaau *n.* فداء redemption	**fokaahiy** *n.* فكاهي humorist
fidaauiy *n.* فدائي guerrilla	**folt** *n.* فولت volt
fiddah *n.* فضة silver	**fondoq** *n.* فندق hotel
fiddiy *adj.* فضي silver	**foolaadh** *n.* فولاذ steel
fidyah *n.* فدية ransom	**foqaa'ah** *n.* فقاعة bubble
fijil *n.* فجل radish	**foqdaan** *n.* فقدان loss
fikrah *n.* 1 فكرة idea	**forn** *n.* فرن oven
fikrah *n.* 2 فكرة notion	**forsah** *n.* فرصة opportunity
fikriy *adj.* فكري intellectual	**forshaah** *n.* فرشاة brush
filfil *n.* فلفل pepper	**fosayfisaau** *n.* فسيفساء mosaic
filim *n.* فلم film	**fosfaat** *n.* فوسفات phosphate
filla *n.* فيلا villa	**fosfoor** *n.* فوسفور phosphorus

fosooq *n.* فسوق debauchery
fosq *n.* فسق debauch
fostaan *n.* فستان dress
fostaan *n.* فستان frock
fowaaq *n.* فواق hiccup
fowwaha *n.* فوهة nozzle

G

ghaabah *n.* غابة forest
ghaabiy *adj.* غابي sylvan
ghaadib *adj.* غاضب angry
ghaafil *adj.* غافل inattentive
ghaali *adj.* غالي expensive
ghaaliban *adv.* غالباً often
ghaalon *n.* غالون gallon
ghaamid *adj.* 1 غامض ambiguous
ghaamid *adj.* 2 غامض mysterious
ghaamiq *adj.* غامق dark
ghaar *n.* غار laurel
ghaarah *n.* غارة raid
ghaauib *adj.* غائب absent
ghaauim *adj.* غائم cloudy
ghaaz *n.* غاز gas
ghaaziy *adj.* 1 غازي aeriform
ghaaziy *adj.* 2 غازي gassy
ghabaau *n.* غباء stupidity
ghabiy *v.* غابي burk
ghabiy *adj.* غبي stupid
ghad *n.* غد tomorrow
ghadaau *n.* غداء lunch
ghadab *n.* غضب rage
ghadan *adv.* غداً tomorrow

ghadeer *n.* غدير rivulet
ghadir *adj.* غادر treacherous
ghadr *n.* غدر treachery
ghafwah *n.* غفوة doze
ghaleedd *n.* غليظ boor
ghalyoon *n.* غليون pipe
ghamr *n.* غمر immersion
ghamz *n.* غمز ogle
ghamzah *n.* غمزة wink
ghaneemah *n.* غنيمة booty
ghanniy *adj.* غني rich
gharaam *n.* 1 غرام amour
gharaamah *n.* غرامة fine
gharaamiy *adj.* غرامي amorous
gharad *n.* غرض purpose
gharawiy *adj.* غروي slimy
gharb *n.* غرب west
gharbiy *adv.* غربي westerly
gharbiy *adj.* غربي western
ghareeb *adj.* 1 غريب alien
ghareeb *adj.* 2 غريب strange
ghareeb *n.* غريب stranger
ghareezah *n.* غريزة instinct
ghareeziy *adj.* غريزي instinctive
ghasaq *n.* غسق dusk
ghaseel *n.* 1 غسيل laundry
ghaseel *n.* 2 غسيل wash
ghashshaash *n.* غشاش cheat
ghassaalah *n.* غسالة washer
ghathayaan *n.* غثيان nausea
ghatrasah *n.* غطرسة arrogance
ghats *n.* غطس dive
ghawghaau *n.* غوغاء mob
ghawr *n.* غور depression
ghawwasah *n.* غواصة submarine

ghaybiy *adj.* غيبي metaphysical
ghayboobah *n.* غيبوبة coma
ghaydd *n.* غيظ fret
ghayoor *adj.* غيور jealous
ghayrah *n.* غيرة jealousy
ghazaal *n.* غزال deer
ghazaarah *n.* غزارة superabundance
ghazeer *adj.* غزير superabundant
ghazzaal *n.* غزال spinner
ghidhaau *n.* غذاء food
ghilaaf *n.* 1 غلاف casing
ghilaaf *n.* 2 غلاف wrapper
ghina *n.* غنى richness
ghiraau *n.* غراء glue
ghirbaal *n.* غربال sieve
ghishaau *n.* غشاء membrane
ghitaau *n.* 1 غطاء cover
ghitaau *n.* 2 غطاء lid
ghiyaab *n.* غياب absence
ghleesireen *n.* غليسيرين glycerine
ghobaar *n.* غبار dust
ghoddah *n.* غدة gland
ghofraan *n.* 1 غفران indulgence
ghofraan *n.* 2 غفران remission
ghol *n.* غل fetter
ghomood *n.* غموض mystery
ghoolf *n.* غولف golf
ghoorillaa *n.* غوريلا gorilla
ghoraab *n.* غراب crow
ghorayr *n.* غرير badger
ghorfah *n.* غرفة room
ghoroor *n.* غرور egotism
ghorzah *n.* غرزة stitch
ghosayn *n.* غصين twig

ghosh *n.* غش cheating
ghosn *n.* غصن branch
ghraam *n.* 2 غرام gramme

H

-hom *pron.* هم them
-ha *pron.* ها her
-ha *adj.* ها her
-ha *pron.* 1 ه him
-ha *pron.* 2 ه his
haabit *adj.* هابط downward
haad *adj.* 1 حاد acute
haad *adj.* 2 حاد sharp
haad *adj.* 3 حاد steep
haadha *adj.* هذا yonder
haadinah *n.* حاضنة nursery
haadir *n.* 1 حاضر attendant
haadir *n.* 2 حاضر present
haadith *n.* 1 حادث accident
haadith *n.* 2 حادث incident
haadiu *adj.* 1 هادئ pacific
haadiu *adj.* 2 هادئ tranquil
haafah *n.* حافة edge
haaffah *n.* حافلة bus
haafidd *adj.* حافظ preservative
haafir *n.* حافر hoof
haafiz *n.* حافز incentive
haaj *n.* حاج pilgrim
haajah *n.* حاجة need
haajib *n.* 1 حاجب chamberlain
haajib *n.* 2 حاجب eyebrow
haajis *n.* 1 هاجس obsession

haajis *n.* هاجس 2 premonition	**haawi** *n.* هاوي amateur
haajiu *n.* هاجي satirist	**haawin** *v.* هاون mortar
haajiz *n.* حاجز barrier	**haawiyah** *n.* هاوية abyss
haakadha *pron.* هكذا such	**haazim** *adj.* حازم resolute
haakadha *conj.* هكذا so	**habeeb** *n.* حبيب darling
haakim *n.* حاكم ruler	**habl** *n.* حبل rope
haakimah *n.* حاكمة governess	**habriyyah** *n.* هبرية dandruff
haal *n.* هال cardamom	**habs** *n.* حبس confinement
haalah *n.* حالة 1 case	**had** *n.* حد 1 border
haalah *n.* حالة 2 situation	**had** *n.* حد 2 limit
haalan *adv.* حالا straightway	**hadaad** *n.* حداد mourning
haalim *adj.* حالم visionary	**hadaarah** *n.* حضارة civilization
haaliy *adj.* حالي current	**hadaathah** *n.* حداثة modernity
haami *n.* حامي protector	**hadabah** *n.* هضبة plateau
haamid *n.* حامض 1 acid	**hadaf** *n.* هدف target
haamid *n.* حامض 2 citrus	**hadariy** *adj.* حضري urban
haamid *adj.* حامض sour	**hadath** *n.* حدث event
haamidiy *adj.* حامضي citric	**hadd** *n.* حظ luck
haamil *n.* حامل carrier	**haddaad** *n.* حدّاد blacksmith
haamil *adj.* حامل pregnant	**haddaaf** *n.* هداف scorer
haamish *n.* هامش margin	**haddeer** *n.* حظير pen
haamishiy *adj.* هامشي marginal	**haddr** *n.* حظر prohibition
haanah *n.* حانة bar	**hadeed** *n.* حديد iron
haar *adj.* حار hot	**hadeel** *n.* هديل coo
haarib *adj.* هارب fugitive	**hadeeqah** *n.* حديقة garden
haaris *n.* حارس guard	**hadeer** *n.* هدير roar
haashiyah *n.* حاشية postscript	**hadeeth** *adj.* حديث modern
haashiyah *n.* حاشية retinue	**hadeeth** *n.* حديث talk
haasil *n.* حاصل quotient	**hadhf** *n.* حذف omission
haasim *adj.* حاسم decisive	**hadhir** *adj.* حذر cautious
haatif *n.* هاتف phone	**hadhlaqah** *n.* حذلقة pedantry
haauij *adj.* هائج rampant	**hadiyyah** *n.* هدية gift
haauik *n.* حائك weaver	**hadm** *n.* هضم digestion
haauil *adj.* هائل 1 enormous	**hads** *n.* حدس intuition
haauil *adj.* هائل 2 tremendous	**hadsiy** *adj.* حدسي intuitive

hafaasah *n.* حصافة sagacity

haffaar *n.* حفّار drill

hafnah *v.* حفنة pinch

hafwah *n.* هفوة lapse

hai *adj.* حي alive

hai *n.* حي neighbourhood

haj *n.* حج pilgrimage

hajar *n.* حجر stone

hajarriy *adj.* حجري stony

hajeen n. هجين hybrid

hajeen adj. هجين mongrel

hajm *n.* حجم magnitude

hajz *n.* حجز reservation

hakam *n.* حكم referee

hakeem *adj.* 1 حكيم judicious

hakeem *adj.* 2 حكيم wise

hakkah *n.* حكة itch

hal *n.* حل solution

halaawah *n.* حلاوة sweetness

halabah *n.* حلبة arena

halamah *n.* حلمة nipple

halaqah *n.* حلقة loop

halawaaniy *n.* حلواني confectioner

halazoon *n.* حلزون snail

halazooniy *adj.* حلزوني spiral

haleeb *n.* حليب milk

haleeb *adj.* حليبي milky

haleef *n.* حليف ally

haliyyan *adv.* حالياً presently

hallaaq *n.* حلاق barber

haloob *adj.* حلوب milch

halqiy *adj.* حلقي guttural

halwa *n.* حلوى candy

hamaamah *n.* حمامة pigeon

hamaaqah *n.* حماقة blunder

hamaas *n.* حماس enthusiasm

hamaasah *n.* حماسة fervour

hamajiy *n.* همجي barbarian

hamajiy *adj.* همجي barbarous

hamajiyyah *n.* همجية barbarism

hamal *n.* حمل lamb

hameed *adj.* حميد benign

hameem *adj.* حميم intimate

hamhamah *n.* همهمة hum

haml *n.* 1 حمل load

haml *n.* 2 حمل pregnancy

hamlah *n.* حملة campaign

hamma *n.* حمى fever

hammaal *n.* حمّال porter

hammaalah *n.* حَمَالَة sling

hammaam *n.* حمام bath

hamoolah *n.* حمولة cargo

hams *n.* همس whisper

hamsah *n.* همسة hiss

hanak *n.* حنك palate

hanakiy *adj.* حنكي palatal

handasah *n.* هندسة geometry

handasiy *adj.* هندسي geometrical

haneen *n.* حنين nostalgia

hanoon *adj.* حنون affectionate

haq *n.* حق right

haqeebah *n.* حقيبة bag

haqeeqah *n.* حقيقة truth

haqeeqiy *adj.* حقيقي real

haqeer *adj.* حقير despicable

haql *n.* حقل field

haqn *n.* حقن injection

haqood *adj.* حقود revengeful

haqqan *adv.* حقاً really

haraarah *n.* حرارة heat	**hash** *adj.* 2 هش fragile
haraariy *adj.* حراري thermal	**hasharah** *n.* حشرة insect
haraj *n.* هرج pandemonium	**hashd** *n.* حشد crowd
harakah *n.* حركة motion	**hasheesh** *n.* حشيش weeds
haram *n.* هرم pyramid	**hashrajah** *n.* حشرجة rattle
haraqah *n.* حرقة blister	**hashwah** *n.* حشوة padding
harb *n.* حرب war	**hasm** *n.* حَسم rebate
harbiy *adj.* حربي warlike	**hasnaau** *n.* حسناء belle
hareeq *n.* حريق fire	**hasood** *adj.* حسود envious
hareer *n.* حرير silk	**hasriy** *adj.* حصري exclusive
hareeriy *adj.* حريري satin	**hassaas** *adj.* حساس sensitive
harees *adj.* حريص careful	**hath** *n.* حث inducement
harees *n.* هَريس mash	**hatmiy** *adj.* حتمي imperative
hareesh *n.* حريش centipede	**hatta** *adv.* حتى even
harf *n.* حرف letter	**hatta** *conj.* حتى till
harfiy *adj.* حرفي literal	**hatta** *prep.* حتى until
harfiyan *adv.* حرفيا literally	**hawaau** *n.* هواء air
harfo jar *n.* جر حرف preposition	**hawaauiy** *adj.* 1 هوائي aerial
harq *n.* حرق burn	**hawaauiy** *adj.* 2 هوائي airy
harraath *n.* حزاث ploughman	**hawaauiyyaat** *n.* هوائيات antennae
harshaf *n.* حرشف scale	
hasaad *n.* حاصد harvester	**hawal** *n.* حول squint
hasaad *n.* حصاد harvest	**hawas** *n.* هوس mania
hasaah *n.* حصاة pebble	**hawd** *n.* حوض tub
hasaanah *n.* حسنة impunity	**hawl** *prep.* حول about
hasaanah *n.* حصانة immunity	**hawl** *adv.* حول round
hasaasiyah *n.* 2 حساسية sensitivity	**hawliy** *n.* حولي annalist
hasaasiyyah *n.* 1 حساسية allergy	**hayaah** *n.* حياة life
hasaau *n.* حساء soup	**hayaaj** *n.* هياج commotion
hasad *v.* حسد envy	**hayawaan** *n.* حيوان animal
hasan *adj.* حسن fine	**hayawaaniy** *adj.* حيواني zoological
hasbah *n.* حصبة measles	**hayawiy** *adj.* 1 حيوي dynamic
haseen *adj.* حصين immune	**hayawiy** *adj.* 2 حيوي viable
haseerah *n.* حصيرة mat	**hayawiyyah** *n.* حيوية vitality
hash *adj.* 1 هش brittle	

haybah *n.* هيبة prestige
haydh *n.* حيض menstruation
haydhiy *adj.* حيضي menstrual
haydroojeen *n.* هيدروجين hydrogen
haykal *n.* 1 هيكل structure
haykal *n.* 2 هيكل temple
haykaliy *adj.* هيكلي structural
haymanah *n.* هيمنة domination
haytah *adj.* حيطة prudential
hayth *conj.* حيث where
hayth *adv.* حيث wherein
hayuah *n.* هيئة body
hayyaab *adj.* هياب timorous
haz *n.* حز notch
hazal *n.* هزل pleasantry
hazaliy *adj.* هزلي comical
hazau *n.* هزء gibe
hazeel *n.* هزيل lean
hazeel *adj.* هزيل meagre
hazeemah *n.* هزيمة defeat
hazeen *n.* حزين mournful
hazeen *adj.* حزين sad
haziua *n.* هزأ scoff
hazm *n.* 1 حزم packing
hazm *n.* 2 حزم determination
hazzah *n.* هزة shake
hboob *n.* حبوب grain
heelah *n.* حيلة trick
heerah *n.* حيرة perplexity
hibah *n.* هبة offering
hibr *n.* حبر ink
hiddah *n.* حدة intensity
hidhaau *n.* حذاء shoe
hifdd *n.* حفظ preservation

hijaab *n.* حجاب veil
hijjah *n.* حجة argument
hijrah *n.* هجرة immigration
hikaayah *n.* حكاية tale
hikmah *n.* حكمة wisdom
hilw *adj.* حلو sweet
himaar *n.* حمار donkey
himaayah *n.* حماية protection
himam *n.* حمم lava
himdiy *adj.* حمضي acid
himyah *n.* حمية diet
hindibaau *n.* هندباء dandelion
hindiy *adj.* هندي Indian
hir *n.* هر cat
hiraajah *n.* حراجة forestry
hiraajiy *n.* حراجي forester
hiraawah *n.* هراوة maul
hirafiy *n.* حرفي artisan
hiraqliy *adj.* هرقلي herculean
hirbah *n.* حربة spear
hirfah n. حرفة craft
hirmaan *n.* 1 حرمان bereavement
hirmaan *n.* 2 حرمان deprivation
hisaab *n.* 1 حساب account
hisaab *n.* 2 حساب calculation
hisaabiy *n.* حسابي arithmetic
hisaabiy *adj.* حسابي arithmetical
hisaan *n.* حصان horse
hisaar *n.* حصار siege
hisn *n.* حصن fortress
hissiy *adj.* حسي sensuous
histeeriy *adj.* هستيري hysterical
histeerya *n.* هستيريا hysteria
hiwaar *n.* حوار dialogue
hiwaayah *n.* هواية hobby

hiyaadiy *adj.* حيادي neutral	**hoqnah** *n.* حقنة syringe
hiyaazah *n.* حيازة possession	**hor** *adj.* حر free
hiyah *pron.* هي she	**horaau** *n.* هراء nonsense
hizaam *n.* حزام belt	**horayr** *n.* هرير kitten
hizb *n.* حزب party	**horj** *n.* حرج forest
hizbiyyah *n.* حزبية partisan	**horq** *n.* حرق burn
hob *n.* حب love	**horriyyah** *n.* حرية freedom
hobaybiy *adj.* حبيبي cereal	**hory** *n.* هُري granary
hoboot *n.* هبوط decline	**hosn** *n.* حسن prettiness
hobootan *adv.* هبوطاً downward	**hossah** *n.* حصة share
hodb *n.* هدب frill	**hotaam** *n.* حطام wreckage
hodn *n.* حضن lap	**hotool** *n.* هطول downpour
hodnah *n.* هدنة truce	**howa** *pron.* 2 هو it
hodood *n.* 1 حدود frontier	**howaalah** *n.* حوالة transfer
hodood *n.* 2 حدود borders	**howah** *pron.* 1 هو he
hodoor *n.* حضور attendance	**howiyyah** *n.* هوية identity
hodoou *n.* هدوء tranquillity	**howwar** *n.* حور poplar
hofrah *n.* حفرة pit	**hozmah** *n.* حزمة bundle
hojoo' *n.* هجوع slumber	**hozn** *n.* حزن grief
hojoom *n.* هجوم attack	
hojoomiy *adj.* هجومي offensive	
hojrah *n.* حجرة room	
hokm *n.* 1 حكم governance	
hokm *n.* 2 حكم judgement	
hokoomah *n.* حكومة government	**ibno 'am** *n.* ابن عم cousin
holaam *n.* هلام jelly	**-i** *adj.* ـي my
holayqah *n.* حليقة ringlet	
holm *n.* حلم dream	
hona *adv.* هنا here	
honaak *adv.* هناك there	
honjarah *n.* حنجرة throat	
hoodhiy *n.* حوذي coachman	**jaad** *adj.* جاد earnest
hooriy *n.* حوري merman	**jaadhibiyyah** *n.* 1 جاذبية attraction
hooriyyah *n.* حورية mermaid	**jaadhibiyyah** *n.* 2 جاذبية gravity
hoot *n.* حوت whale	**jaaf** *adj.* جاف dry

jaahid *adj.* جاهد laboured	**jadhdhaab** *adj.* جذاب attractive
jaahil *adj.* جاهل ignorant	**jadhriy** *adj.* جذري drastic
jaahiz *adv.* جاهز pat	**jadwal** *n.* 1 جدول stream
jaami' *n.* جامع collector	**jadwal** *n.* 2 جدول table
jaami'ah *n.* جامعة university	**jadwal** *n.* 3 جدول schedule
jaami'iy *n.* جامعي undergraduate	**jafaaf** *n.* جفاف drought
jaamid *adj.* جامد rigid	**jahannamiy** *adj.* جهنمي infernal
jaamih *adj.* جامح unruly	**jaheem** *adj.* جحيم hell
jaamoos *n.* جاموس buffalo	**jahl** *n.* جهل ignorance
jaani *n.* جاني reaper	**jahoor** *n.* جهور loud
jaanib *n.* 1 جانب aspect	**jalabah** *n.* جلبة fuss
jaanib *n.* 2 جانب side	**jalad** *n.* جلد fortitude
jaaniban *adv.* جانباً aside	**jaldah** *adj.* جلدة lash
jaar *n.* جار neighbour	**jaleed** *n.* جليد ice
jaarih *n.* جارح accipitridae	**jaleediy** *adj.* جليدي icy
jaarih *adj.* جارح injurious	**jaleel** *adj.* جَليل venerable
jaasoos *n.* جاسوس spy	**jaljalah** *n.* جلجلة jingle
jaaui' *adj.* جائع hungry	**jallaad** *n.* جلّاد executioner
jaauiz *adj.* جائز permissible	**jalmood** *n.* جلمود boulder
jaauizah *n.* جائزة award	**jalsah** *n.* جلسة session
jaawdaar *n.* جاودار rye	**jaltah** *n.* جلطة clot
jabaan *n.* جبان coward	**jam'iyyah** *n.* جمعية assembly
jabaan *n.* جبين forehead	**jamaa'iy** *adj.* جماعي collective
jabal *n.* جبل mountain	**jamaaheeriy** *n.* جماهير populace
jabaliy *adj.* جبلي mountainous	**jamaal** *n.* جمال beauty
jabbaar *adj.* جبّار titanic	**jamal** *n.* جمل camel
jabhah *n.* جبهة front	**jameel** *adj.* جميل beautiful
jad *n.* جد forefather	**janaah** *n.* 2 جناح wing
jadaarah *n.* جدارة merit	**janaazah** *n.* جنازة funeral
jadaarah *n.* جدارية mural	**janeen** *n.* جنين embryo
jadariy *n.* جدري smallpox	**jannah** *n.* 1 جناح ward
jaddiy *adj.* جدّي serious	**jannah** *n.* جنة paradise
jadeed *adj.* جديد new	**janoob** *n.* جنوب south
jadeelah *n.* جديلة cue	**janoobiy** *adj.* جنوبي southern
jadeer *adj.* جدير meritorious	**jar** *n.* جر traction

jaraad *n.* جراد locust	**jawz** *n.* جوز walnut
jarab *n.* جرب scabies	**jawzatol hind** *n.* جوزةالهند coconut
jaras *n.* جرس bell	
jareedah *n.* جريدة gazette	**jayashaan** *n.* جيشان upheaval
jareemah *n.* جريمة crime	**jayb** *n.* جيب pocket
jareeu *adj.* جريء bold	**jaysh** *n.* جيش army
jarraah *n.* جزاح surgeon	**jayyaash** *adj.* جياش maudlin
jarraar *n.* 1 جزار drawer	**jayyid** *adj.* جيد good
jarraar *n.* 2 جزار tractor	**jayyidan** *adv.* جيداً well
jarrah n. جرة jar	**jazaau** *n.* جزاء recompense
jarw *n.* جرو puppy	**jazaauiy** *adj.* جزائي penal
jarzah *n.* جرزة jersey	**jazarah** *n.* جزرة carrot
jasad *n.* جسد body	**jazeerah** *n.* جزيرة island
jasadiy *adv.* جسدي bodily	**jazr** *n.* جزر ebb
jasadiy *adj.* جسدي physical	**jazzaar** *n.* جزار butcher
jaseem *adj.* جسيم momentous	**jeel** *n.* جيل generation
jasha' *n.* جشع greed	**ji'ah** *n.* جعة malt
jashi' *adj.* جشع greedy	**jibn** *n.* جبن cheese
jasoor *adj.* جسور hardy	**jidaal** *n.* جدال argument
jathm *n.* جثم perch	**jidaar** *n.* جدار wall
jaw *n.* 1 جو atmosphere	**jidaariy** *adj.* جداري mural
jaw *n.* 2 جو weather	**jidan** *adv.* جداً highly
jawaab *n.* جواب answer	**jiddan** *adj.* جدًا very
jawaafah *n.* جوافة guava	**jidh'** *n.* جذع trunk
jawaaz *n.* جواز passport	**jidhr** *n.* جذر root
jawfiy *adj.* جوفي subterranean	**jihaaz** *n.* جهاز device
jawhar *n.* جوهر essence	**jild** *n.* 1 جلد leather
jawharah *n.* جوهرة jewel	**jild** *n.* 2 جلد skin
jawhariy *adj.* جوهري substantial	**jimaa'** *n.* جماع intercourse
jawhariyyan *adv.* جوهرياً substantially	**jinaas** *n.* جناس alliteration
	jinaauiy *adj.* جنائي criminal
jawlah *n.* جولة tour	**jineeh** *n.* جنيه pound
jawqah *n.* جوقة choir	**jinniyyah** *n.* جنّية fairy
jawrab *n.* جورب sock	**jins** *n.* جنس sex
jawwaal *n.* جوّال ranger	**jinsiy** *adj.* جنسي sexual

jis *n.* جص plaster
jisr *n.* جسر bridge
jiwaar *n.* جوار vicinity
jiwaariy *adj.* جواري neighbourly
jiyooloogiy *adj.* جيولوجي geological
jiyooloogiy *n.* جيولوجي geologist
jiyooloogya *n.* جيولوجيا geology
jizmah *n.* جزمة boot
jlookooz *n.* جلوكوز glucose
jobn *n.* جبن cowardice
jodhaam *n.* جذام leprosy
joghraafiy *n.* جغرافي geographer
joghraafiy *adj.* جغرافي geographical
joghraafya *n.* جغرافيا geography
johd n. جحد odium
johd *n.* 1 جهد effort
johd *n.* 2 جهد voltage
johr *n.* جحر burrow
jomhoor *n.* جمهور audience
jomhoor *n.* جمهور public
jomhooriy *adj.* جمهوري republican
jomhooriy *n.* جمهوري republican
jomhooriyyah *n.* جمهورية republic
jomjomah *n.* جمجمة skull
jomlah *n.* جملة sentence
jommayz *n.* جميز sycamore
jondiy *n.* جندي soldier
jonhah *n.* جنحة misdemeanour
jonoon *n.* جنون insanity
jonooniy *adj.* جنوني lunatic
joo' *n.* جوع hunger

joodah *n.* جودة quality
jor'ah *n.* جرعة dose
joraab *n.* جراب pouch
joraabiy *n.* جرابي marsupial
jorf *n.* جرف cliff
jorh *n.* جرح wound
jorm *n.* 1 جرم crime
jorm *n.* 2 جرم luminary
jorthoomah *n.* جرثومة germ
jurrah *n.* جرأة boldness
josaym *adj.* جسيم particle
joththah *n.* جثة corpse
jozayu *n.* جزيء molecule
jozayuiy *adj.* جزيئي molecular
jozu *n.* جزء part
jozuiy *adj.* جزئي partial

K

ka- *pron.* كـ as
ka'b *n.* كعب heel
ka'kah *n.* كعكة cake
kaabih *n.* كابح curb
kaabil *n.* كابل cable
kaaboos *n.* كابوس nightmare
kaadih *adj.* كادح industrious
kaadih *n.* كادح peon
kaafi *adj.* كاف sufficient
kaafi *adj.* كافي adequate
kaafoor *n.* كافور camphor
kaahil *n.* كاحل ankle
kaahin *adj.* كاهن ministrant
kaahin *n.* كاهن priest

kaahinah *n.* كاهنة priestess
kaamil *adj.* 1 كامل complete
kaamil *adj.* 2 كامل full
kaamin *adj.* كامن latent
kaanoon uaththaani *n.* كانون الثاني January
kaanoonol uawwal *n.* الأول كانون December
kaardinaal *n.* كاردينال cardinal
kaardinaaliy *adj.* كاردينالي cardinal
kaarithah *n.* كارثة disaster
kaarithiy *adj.* كارثي disastrous
kaastard *n.* كاسترد custard
kaathooleeki *adj.* كاثوليكي catholic
kaatib *n.* 1 كاتب author
kaatib *n.* 2 كاتب clerk
kaatib *n.* 3 كاتب writer
kaatidraauiyyah *n.* كاتدرائية cathedral
kaatim *n.* كاتم silencer
kaauin *n.* كائن being
kaauin *adj.* كائن existing
kaawi *adj.* كاوي caustic
kabeer *adj.* كبير big
kabh *n.* كبح rein
kabid *n.* كبد liver
kabsh *n.* كبش ram
kabsoolah *n.* كبسولة capsule
kabsooliy *adj.* كبسولي capsular
kabt *n.* كبت inhibition
kadh *n.* كدح toil
kadhaab *n.* كذاب liar
kadhaalikah *adv.* كذلك likewise
kadhoob *adj.* كذوب mendacious

kadmah *n.* كدمة bruise
kaf *n.* كف palm
kafaalah *n.* كفالة bail
kafaauah *n.* كفاءة efficiency
kafan *n.* كفن shroud
kafou *adj.* كفؤ efficient
kahaadha *adj.* كهذا such
kahanoot *n.* كهنوت priesthood
kahf *n.* كهف cave
kahrobaau *n.* كهرباء electricity
kahrobaauiy *adj.* كهربائي electric
kal qird *adj.* كالقرد apish
kalaam *n.* كلام speech
kalabshah *n.* كلبشة handcuff
kalb *n.* كلب dog
kalbah *n.* كلبة bitch
kalimah *n.* كلمة word
kallaab *n.* كلاب hook
kalmotawaqa' *adv.* كالمتوقع as expected
kam *n.* 1 كم quantum
kam *n.* 2 كم sleeve
kama *adv.* كما as
kamaal *n.* كمال perfection
kamaan *n.* كمان violin
kameen *n.* كمين ambush
kammaamah *n.* كمامة muzzle
kammi *adj.* كمي quantitative
kammiyyah *n.* كمية quantity
kammiyyah *n.* كميه lot
kaneesah *n.* كنيسة church
kannas *n.* كناس sweeper
kanz *n.* كنز treasure
kanzah *n.* كنزة sweeter
karaahiyah *n.* كراهية hate

karaaj *n.* كراج garage
karaamah *n.* كرامة dignity
karam *n.* كرم generosity
karam *n.* كرم kindness
karb *n.* كرب anguish
karbeed *n.* كربيد carbide
karboon *n.* كربون carbon
kareeh *adj.* كريه loathsome
kareem *adj.* كريم kind
karkarah *n.* كركرة gobble
karmah *n.* كرمة vine
kasal *n.* كسل laziness
kasb *n.* كسب gain
kashshaaf *n.* كشاف scout
kaslaan *adj.* كسلان indolent
kaslaan *n.* كسلان sluggard
kasool *n.* كسول lazy
kasool *adj.* كسول lethargic
kasr *n.* كسر fracture
kassaarah *n.* كسّارة cracker
kastanaau *n.* كستناء chestnut
kastanaauiy *adj.* كستنائي maroon
katabah *adj.* كتبة clerical
kateebah *n.* كتيبة battalion
kathaafah *n.* 1 كثافة consistency
kathaafah *n.* 2 كثافة density
katheef *adj.* كثيف dense
katheer *adj.* كثير much
katheer *n.* كثير plenty
katheeran *adv.* كثيرا much
katif *n.* كتف shoulder
kauaabah *n.* كآبة melancholy
kaueeb *adj.* كئيب melancholic
kaus *n.* كأس goblet
kawaykab *adj.* كويكب asteroid

kawkab *n.* كوكب planet
kawkabah *n.* كوكبة constellation
kawkabiy *adj.* كوكبي planetary
kawmah *n.* كومة pile
kawn *n.* كون universe
kawniy *adj.* كوني cosmic
kayaan *n.* كيان entity
kayf *adv.* كيف how
kayfama *adv.* كيفما however
keemyaau *n.* كيمياء chemistry
keeneen *n.* كينين quinine
kees *n.* كيس sack
khaadi' *adj.* خاضع subject
khaadif *adj.* خاطف cursory
khaadim *n.* خادم servant
khaadimah *n.* خادمة maid
khaafit *adj.* خافت dim
khaal *n.* خال uncle
khaalah *n.* خالة aunt
khaali *adj.* خال devoid
khaalid *adj.* خالد immortal
khaalis *adj.* خالص pure
khaam *adj.* خام raw
khaamil *adj.* خامل inert
khaan *n.* خان inn
khaanah *n.* خانة cell
khaaniq *adj.* خانق stuffy
khaarij *adv.* خارج out
khaarij *n.* خارج outside
khaarij *prep.* خارج outside
khaarijan *adj.* خارجا outdoor
khaarijan *adv.* خارجا outside
khaarijiy *adj.* خارجي external
khaariq *adj.* خارق supernatural
khaaroof *n.* خاروف lamb

khaas *adj.* 1 خاص private
khaas *adj.* 2 خاص special
khaassah *n.* خاصة particular
khaatam *n.* خاتم ring
khaatibah *n.* خاطبة matchmaker
khaatimah *n.* خاتمة epilogue
khaatiu *adj.* خاطئ incorrect
khaatiu *adv.* خاطئ wrong
khaauif *adj.* خائف afraid
khaauin *adj.* خائن disloyal
khaauin *n.* خائن traitor
khabab *n.* خبب trot
khabbaaz *n.* خباز baker
khabeer *n.* خبير expert
khabeeth *adj.* خبيث malignant
khad *n.* خد cheek
khadaar *n.* خضار green
khadsh *n.* خدش scratch
khafaqaan *n.* خفقان palpitation
khafeef *adj.* خفيف light
khafeer *n.* خفير sentry
khaffaaqah *n.* خفاقة whisk
khaffaash *n.* خفاش bat
khafiy *adj.* خفي invisible
khafiy *n.* خفي subtle
khajal *n.* خجل shyness
khajool *n.* خجول shy
khajool *adj.* خجول timid
khal *n.* خل vinegar
khal' *n.* خَلع wrench
khalaas *n.* خلاص salvation
khalal *n.* خلل defect
khalawiy *adj.* خلوي cellular
khalee' *adj.* خليع lewd
khaleefah *n.* خليفة successor

khaleej *n.* خليج gulf
khaleelah *n.* خليلة concubine
khaleet *n.* خليط mixture
khalf *prep.* خلف after
khalf *adv.* خلف behind
khalfiy *adj.* خلفي back
khalfiyyah *n.* 1 خلفية background
khalfiyyah *n.* 2 خلفية rear
khaliyyah *n.* خلية cell
khallaq *adj.* خلّاق creative
khalq *n.* خلق creation
khaltah *n.* خلطة concoction
khameerah *n.* خميرة yeast
khamr *n.* خمر vintage
khamsah *n.* خمسة five
khamsato 'ashar *n.* خمسة عشر fifteen
khamsoon *n.* خمسون fifty
khandaq *n.* خندق ditch
khanoo' *adj.* خنوع subservient
khanq *n.* خنق strangulation
khanzeer *n.* خنزير swine
khanzeerah *n.* خنزيره sow
kharaab *n.* خراب ruin
kharazah *n.* خرزة bead
kharbashah *n.* خربشة scribble
khardal *n.* خردل mustard
khareef *n.* خريف autumn
khareetah *n.* خريطة map
kharif *adj.* خرف senile
kharkharah *n.* خرخرة purr
kharoof *n.* خروف sheep
kharq *n.* خرق breach
kharraat *n.* خراط lather
khartoosh *n.* خرطوش blank

khartooshah *n.* خرطوشة cartridge
kharwa' *n.* خروع castor oil
khasaarah *n.* خسارة loss
khasees *adj.* خسيس ignoble
khasees *n.* خسيس ruffian
khashab *n.* خشب wood
khashabah *n.* خشبة log
khashabiy *adj.* خشبي wooden
khashin *adj.* خشن coarse
khasm *n.* 1 خصم adversary
khasm *n.* 2 خصم discount
khat *n.* خط line
khatar *n.* خطر danger
khatau *n.* خطأ error
khateeb *n.* خطيب orator
khateer *adj.* خطير dangerous
khateeuah *n.* خطيئة sin
khatf *n.* خطف snatch
khatm *n.* خطم snout
khawaatiriy *adj.* خواطري telepathic
khawf *n.* خوف fear
khawkh *n.* خوخ peach
khayaal *n.* 1 خيال fiction
khayaal *n.* 2 خيال shadow
khayaaliy *adj.* خيالي imaginary
khayaar *n.* خيار choice
khayd *n.* خيط thread
khaylaau *n.* خيلاء vanity
khaymah *n.* خيمة tent
khayr *n.* خير good
khayriy *adj.* خيري charitable
khayyat *n.* خياط tailor
khayzoraan *n.* خيزران bamboo
khazaf *n.* خزف ceramics

khazeenah *n.* خزينة treasury
khaznah *n.* خزنة safe
khazzaaf *n.* خزاف potter
khazzaan *n.* خزّان reservoir
khid'ah *n.* خدعة trick
khidaa' *n.* خداع deceit
khidbah *n.* خطبة sermon
khidmah *n.* خدمة service
khiffah *n.* خفة levity
khilaaf *n.* خلاف disagreement
khilaafah *n.* خلافة succession
khilaal *prep.* خلال during
khilaal *adv.* خلال through
khilsah *adv.* خلسة stealthily
khimaar *n.* خمار wimple
khinjar *n.* خنجر dagger
khirqah *n.* خرقة rag
khirreej *n.* خريج graduate
khisaam *n.* خصام antagonism
khisaamiy *adj.* خصامي quarrelsome
khisb *adj.* خصب fertile
khisyah *n.* خصية testicle
khitaab *n.* خطاب speech
khitaabiy *adj.* خطابي oratorical
khitm *n.* ختم seal
khittah *n.* خطة plan
khiyaanah *n.* خيانة treason
khiyaar *n.* خيار cucumber
khizaanah *n.* خزانة cabinet
khobth *n.* خبث malignancy
khobz *n.* خبز bread
khodaar *n.* خضار vegetable
khodaariy *adj.* خضاري vegetable
khodbah *n.* خطبة engagement

khodrah *n.* خضرة greenery

khold *n.* خلد mole

kholkhaal *n.* خلخال anklet

kholood *n.* خلود immortality

khonfosaau *n.* خنفساء beetle

khonoo' *n.* خنوع subservience

khoodhah *n.* خوذة helmet

khoraafah *n.* خرافة superstition

khoraafiy *adj.* خرافي superstitious

khordah *n.* خردة junk

khortoom *n.* خرطوم hose

khosoobah *n.* خصوبة fertility

khosoof *n.* خسوف eclipse

khosoosiyyah *n.* 1 خصوصية peculiarity

khosoosiyyah *n.* 2 خصوصية privacy

khota *n.* خطى pace

khotoorah *n.* خطورة gravity

khotwah *n.* خطوة step

khowaytim *n.* خويتم annulet

khozaami *n.* خزامي lavender

kibreet *n.* 1 كبريت sulphur

kibreet *n.* 2 كبريت matches

kibreetiy *adj.* كبريتي sulphuric

kibriyaau *n.* كبرياء pride

kidhbah *n.* كذبة lie

kifaayah *adv.* كفاية enough

kifaayah *n.* كفاية sufficiency

kila *adj.* كلا both

kila *pron* كلا both

kila *conj.* كلا both

kils *n.* كلس lime

kilya *n.* كلية kidney

kimbyaalah *n.* كمبيالة draft

kimyaauiy *adj.* كيميائي chemical

kinyah *n.* كنية nickname

kisrah *n.* كسرة crumb

kiswah *n.* كسوة livery

kitaab *n.* كتاب book

kitaabiy *n.* كتابي bookish

kittaan *n.* 1 كتان linen

kittaan *n.* 2 كتان nettle

Klaaseekiy *adj.* كلاسيكي classic

Klaaseekiy *n.* كلاسيكي classic

kloor *n.* كلور chlorine

kofr *n.* كفر atonement

kohool *n.* كحول alcohol

kol *pron* 1 كل all

kol *pron.* 2 كل each

kol *adj.* كل every

kolira *n.* كوليرا cholera

kollama *conj.* كلما whenever

kolliy *adj.* كلي total

kolliyan *adv.* كليًا wholly

kolliyyah *n.* 1 كلية college

kolliyyah *n.* 2 كلية totality

koloneel *n.* كولونيل colonel

kommathra *n.* كمثرى pear

koo' *n.* كوع elbow

koob *n.* كوب cup

kookh *n.* كوخ cottage

kookh *adj.* كوخ shanty

korah *n.* 1 كرة ball

korah *n.* 2 كرة sphere

korawiy *adj.* كروي spherical

korh *n.* كره dislike

korkom *n.* كركم turmeric

korraasah *n.* كراسة brochure

korraath *n.* كرّاث leek
korsiy *n.* كرسي chair
kosaah *n.* كساح rickets
koshk *n.* كشك booth
koshk *n.* كُشك stall
koshtbaan *n.* كشتبان thimble
kosoof *n.* كسوف eclipse
kotayyib *n.* كتيّب pamphlet
kotlah *n.* 1 كتلة block
kotlah *n.* 2 كتلة mass
kozbarah *n.* كزبرة coriander
krikit *n.* كريكيت cricket
kroom *n.* كروم chrome

L

la'ib *n.* لعب play
la'n *n.* لعن damnation
la'nah *n.* لعنة curse
la'oob *adj.* لَعوب wanton
la'qah *n.* لعقة lick
laa *adj.* لا no
laa uinsaaniy *adj.* لاإنساني inhuman
laa'ib *n.* لاعب player
laadhi' *adj.* لاذع pungent
laaghi *adj.* لا غ null
laahiq *n.* لاحق suffix
laahiq *adj.* لاحق subsequent
laahiqan *adv.* لاحقاً next
laahoot *n.* لاهوت theology
laahootiy *n.* لاهوتي theologian
laahootiy *adj.* لاهوتي theological

laajiu *n.* لاجئ refugee
laakin *conj.* لكن however
laama *n.* لاما lama
laami' *adj.* لامع shiny
laamobaalaah *n.* لامبالاة apathy
laaqit *n.* لاقط collector
laasilkiy *adj.* لاسلكي wireless
laasilkiy *n.* لايلكي wireless
laasiq *n.* لاصق adhesive
laasiq *adj.* لاصق adhesive
laasiqah *n.* لاصقة sticker
laauiq *adj.* لائق decent
labiq *adj.* لبق tactful
labouah *n.* لبؤة lioness
ladghah *n.* لدغة sting
ladh' *n.* لذع pungency
ladhdhah *n.* لذة savour
ladheedh *n.* لذيذ dainty
ladheedh *adj.* لذيذ delicious
lafdd *n.* لفظ pronunciation
laffaf *n.* لَفّاف winder
laffah *n.* لفة roll
laghawiy *n.* لغوي linguist
laghawiy *adj.* لغوي linguistic
lahab *n.* لهب flame
lahddah *adv.* لحظة awhile
lahddah *n.* لحظة moment
lahddiy *adj.* لحظي momentary
lahhaam *n.* لحام weld
lahjah *n.* لهجة dialect
lahm *n.* لحم meat
lahn *n.* لحن melody
lahom *pron.* لهم theirs
lajnah *n.* لجنة committee
lakmah *n.* لكمة punch

lam'a *n.* لمعة shine

lama'aan *n.* لمعان gloss

lamhah *n.* لمحة glance

lams *n.* لمس touch

lana *pron.* لنا our

laqab *n.* لقب title

laqeet *n.* لقيط bantling

laqlaq *n.* لقلق crane

laqtah *n.* لَقْطَةً snap

lateef *adj.* لطيف pleasant

lathgha *n.* لثغة lisp

latkhah *n.* لطخة smear

laueem *a.* لئيم mean

lawh *n.* لوح board

lawhah *n.* 1 لوحة painting

lawhah *n.* 2 لوحة panel

lawm *n.* لوم blame

lawn *n.* لون colour

lawz *n.* لوز almond

layaaqah *n.* لياقة decorum

layaaqah *n.* لياقة propriety

layl *n.* ليل night

layliy *adj.* ليلي nocturnal

laymoon *n.* ليمون lemon

lays *adv.* ليس not

laysa *adv.* ليس no

layyin *adj.* لين tender

lazij *n.* لزج sticky

lbaan *n.* ألبان dairy

lee *pron.* لي mine

liberal *n. adj.* ليبرالي liberal

leef *n.* ليف fibre

leen *n.* لين laxity

libaas *n.* لباس outfit

lidhaalik *adv.* لذلك therefore

lift *n.* لفت turnip

lihaaf *n.* لحاف quilt

lihyah *n.* لحية beard

lijaam *n.* لجام bridle

lijaam *n.* لجام harness

likol *adv.* لكل each

likol *prep.* لكل per

lil uasaf *interj.* للأسف alas

limaadha *adv.* لماذا why

liman *pron.* لمن whose

liqaau *n.* لقاء encounter

lis *n.* لص thief

lisaan *n.* لسان tongue

litir *n.* لتر litre

liuannah *conj.* لأن because

liwaau *n.* لواء brigade

liyakoon *adj.* ليكون would-be

lo'aab *n.* لعاب saliva

lo'bah *n.* لعبة game

lob *n.* لب pulp

lobbiy *adj.* لُبي pulpy

loblaab *n.* لبلاب ivy

loghah *n.* لغة language

loghz *n.* لغز puzzle

lohaath *n.* لهاث pant

lohmah *n.* لحمة woof

lojoou *n.* لجوء asylum

lojoou *n.* لجوء recourse

lolaakamah *n.* ملاكمة boxing

lootas *n.* لوتس lotus

lootiy *n.* لوطي sodomite

loqaah *n.* 1 لقاح pollen

loqaah *n.* 2 لقاح vaccine

loqmah *n.* لقمة morsel

lotf *n.* لطف complaisance

loulah *n.* لؤلؤة pearl
loum *n.* لؤم meanness
lowaat *n.* لواط sodomy
lowaatiy *adj.* لواطي gay
lowaatiy *n.* لواطي gay
lowaziy *n.* لُوزي tonsure

M

ma *pron.* ما what
ma ba'd *prep.* بعد ما beyond
ma ba'd *adv.* بعد ما beyond
ma' *prep.* مع with
ma' dhaalikah *adv.* معذلك nonetheless
ma' dhaalikah *conj.* معذلك yet
ma'aash *n.* معاش pension
ma'an *adv.* معاً together
ma'awiy *adj.* معوي intestinal
ma'bad *n.* معبد pagoda
ma'bar *n.* معبر passage
ma'bood *n.* معبود idol
ma'dan *n.* معدن metal
ma'daniy *adj.* معدني metallic
ma'had *n.* معهد institute
ma'hoodon *adj.* معهود promised
ma'idiy *adj.* معدي gastric
ma'iy *n.* معي bowel
ma'joon *n.* 1 معجون cream
ma'joon *n.* 2 معجون tooth-paste
ma'koos *adj.* معكوس reversible
ma'loomah *n.* معلومة information
ma'moodiyyah *n.* معمودية baptism

ma'nah *n.* معنى meaning
ma'nawiyyaat *n.* معنويات morale
ma'qool *adj.* 1 معقول reasonable
ma'qool *adj.* 2 معقول sensible
ma'rad *n.* معرض gallery
ma'rakah *n.* معركة battle
ma'rifah *n.* معرفة knowledge
ma'roof *n.* مَعروف favour
ma'roof *adj.* معروف well-known
ma'shooqah *n.* معشوقة lass
ma'soom *adj.* معصوم infallible
ma'tooh *adj.* معتوه daft
maa *adj.* ما some
maa 'ada *prep.* عدا ما save
maa'iz *n.* ماعز goat
maaddah *n.* مادة matter
maaddiyyah *n.* مادية materialism
maadha *interj.* ماذا what
maadi *adj.* ماضي past
maadi *n.* ماضي past
maadiy *adj.* 2 مادي physical
maahir *n.* ماهر adept
maahir *adj.* ماهر skilful
maajisteer *n.* ماجستير master
maakir *adj.* ماكر cunning
maal *n.* مال money
maalih *adj.* مالح salty
maalik *n.* مالك owner
maaliy *adj.* مالي financial
maama *n.* ماما mum
maani' *adj.* مانع prohibitory
maanih *n.* مانح donor
maanjo *n.* مانجو mango
maarshal *n.* مارشال marshal
maau *n.* ماء water

maauah *n.* مائة hundred
maaui' *adj.* مائع fluid
maauil *adj.* مائل italic
maauil *n.* مائل slant
mab'ooth *n.* مبعوث emissary
mabdau *n.* مبدأ precept
mabdau *n.* مبدأ principle
mabhooh *adj.* مبحوح throaty
mabkhara *n.* مبخرة censer
mablagh *n.* مبلغ amount
mabna *n.* مبنى construction
mada *n.* مدى extent
madaar *n.* 1 مدار orbit
madaar *n.* 2 مدار tropic
madakhkhah *n.* مضخة pump
madaniy *adj.* مدني civic
madaniy *n.* مدني civilian
madbaghah *n.* مدبغة tannery
madboogh *n., a.* مَدبوغ tan
madd *n.* مد tide
maddah *n.* مَدّة lay
maddhar *n.* مظهر appearance
maddiy *adj.* 1 مادي material
maddiy *adj.* مَدّي tidal
madeeh *n.* مديح praise
madeen *n.* مدين debtor
madeenah *n.* مدينة city
madeeq *n.* مضيق strait
madfa' *n.* مدفع cannon
madfa'iyyah *n.* مدفعية artillery
madfoo' *adj.* مدفوع payable
madh'oor *adj.* مذعور aghast
madhbah *n.* مذبح altar
madhhab *n.* مذهب doctrine
madhhab *adj.* مذهَب gilt

madhmoom *n.* مذموم disrepute
madkhal *n.* مدخل access
madkhal *n.* مدخل entrance
madkhanah *n.* مدخنة chimney
madmoon *adj.* مضمون guaranteed
madmoon *n.* مضمون purport
madrasah *n.* مدرسة school
madroob *n.* 1 مضروب multiplicand
madroob *n.* 2 مضروب battered
madroos *n.* مدروس forethought
madroos *adj.* مدروس thoughtful
madyah *n.* مَطِيّه mount
mafhoom *adj.* مفهوم apprehensive
mafhoom *n.* مفهوم concept
mafsal *n.* مَفصَل joint
maftooh *adv.* مفتوح open
maghfoor *adj.* مغفور pardonable
maghroor *n.* مغرور upstart
maghza *n.* مغزى signification
maghzal *n.* مغزل spindle
mahaabah *n.* مهابة sublimity
mahaar *n.* محار oyster
mahaarah *n.* مهارة skill
mahal *n.* 1 محل place
mahal *n.* 2 محل shop
mahalli *n.* محل sweetener
mahalliy *adj.* محلي local
mahattah *n.* محطة station
mahboob *n.* محبوب beloved
mahboob *adj.* محبوب lovable
mahd *adj.* محض sheer
mahd *n.* مهد cradle
mahddoodd *adj.* محظوظ fortunate

mahddoor *adj.* محظور prohibitive
mahdood *adj.* محدود limited
mahfoof *adj.* محفوف fraught
mahjaah *n.* مَشجاه melodrama
mahjar *n.* مَخجَر quarry
mahkamah *n.* محكمة court
mahlool *n.* محلول solution
mahmiy *adj.* محمي protected
mahmool *adj.* محمول portable
mahr *n.* مهر dowry
mahsood *adj.* محسود enviable
mahsool *n.* محصول crop
mahw *n.* محو obliteration
mahwoos *n.* مهووس maniac
mahzalah *n.* مهزلة farce
majaari *n.* مجاري sewage
majaauah *n.* مجاعة famine
majallah *n.* مجلّة magazine
majarrah *n.* مجرة galaxy
majd *n.* مجد glory
majdhoom *n.* مجذوم leper
majdhoom *adj.* مجذوم leprous
majeed *adj.* مجيد glorious
majhool *adj.* مجهول anonymous
majlis *n.* مجلس council
majmoo' *n.* مجموع sum
majmoo'ah *n.* 1 مجموعة collection
majmoo'ah *n.* 2 مجموعة group
majnoon *adj.* مجنون insane
majnoon *n.* مجنون lunatic
majtham *n.* مَجثَم roost
majzarah *n.* مجزرة massacre
makaan *n.* 1 مكان whereabout
makaan *n.* 2 مكان place
makaanah *n.* مكانة standing

makaaniy *adj.* مكاني spatial
makbas *n.* مكبس piston
makhaad *n.* مخاض labour
makhbau *n.* مخبأ hide
makhbaz *n.* مخبز bakery
makhdarah *n.* مَخضَره lawn
makhdoo' *n.* مخدوع gull
makheed *n.* مخيض buttermilk
makhlooq *n.* مخلوق creature
makhloot *n.* مخروط cone
makhraj *n.* مخرج exit
makhratah *n.* مخرطة lathe
makhsiy *n.* مخصي eunuch
makhtootah *n.* مخطوطة scroll
makhzan *n.* مخزن store
makkook *n.* مكوك shuttle
makr *n.* مكر cunning
maktab *n.* 1 مكتب bureau
maktab *n.* 2 مكتب desk
maktab *n.* 3 مكتب office
maktabah *n.* مكتبة library
mal'oon *adj.* ملعون accursed
malaabis *n.* ملابس clothes
malaadh *n.* ملاذ haven
malaadh *n.* ملاذ sanctuary
malaak *n.* ملاك angel
malaarya *n.* ملاريا malaria
malaf *n.* ملف file
malakiy *n.* ملكي royalist
malakiy *adj.* 1 ملكي royal
malakiyyah *n.* 2 ملكية monarchy
malakiyyah *n.* 3 ملكية royalty
malal *n.* ملل tedium
malbas *n.* ملبس clothing
malfoof *n.* ملفوف cabbage

malha *n.* ملهى cabaret
malhamiy *n.* ملحمي epic
malik *n.* ملك king
malikah *n.* ملكة queen
maljau *n.* ملجأ refuge
mallaah *n.* ملاح navigator
malmoos *adj.* ملموس tangible
malyoon *n.* مليون million
malyooneer *n.* مليونير millionaire
mamaas *n.* مماس tangent
mamar *n.* ممر lane
mamdood *adj.* ممدود lay
mamlakah *n.* مملكة kingdom
mamsahah *n.* ممسحة mop
man *pron.* 1 من who
man *pron.* 2 من whom
man' *n.* منع prevention
manaa'iy *adj.* مناعي immune
manaakh *n.* مناخ climate
manaarah *n.* منارة beacon
manawiy *adj.* منوي seminal
manboodh *adj.* منبوذ outcast
manboodh *n.* مَنبوذ outsider
manddar *n.* منظر landscape
manddoor *n.* منظور perspective
mandhoor *n.* مندور votary
mandoob *n.* مندوب delegate
manee' *adj.* منيع impenetrable
manfa *n.* منفى exile
manfa'iy *adj.* منفعي utilitarian
manfadh *n.* 1 منفذ loop-hole
manfadh *n.* 2 منفذ port
manfas *n.* منفس vent
manghaneez *n.* منغنيز manganese
manhaj *n.* منهج syllabus

manhajiy *adj.* منهجي methodical
manhal *n.* منحل apiary
manhoos *adj.* منحوس luckless
maniy *n.* مني sperm
manjam *n.* منجم mine
manqoolaat *n.* منقولات movables
manshau *n.* منشئ originator
manshoor *n.* منشور leaflet
mantiq *n.* منطق logic
mantiq *n.* منطق rationale
mantiqah *n.* منطقة region
mantiqiy *adj.* 1 منطقي logical
mantiqiy *n.* منطقي logician
mantiqiy *adj.* 2 منطقي zonal
manwiy *adj.* منوي intent
manzil *n.* 1 منزل domicile
manzil *n.* 2 منزل home
maq'ad *n.* مقعد bench
maqaal *n.* مقال essay
maqaalah *n.* مقالة article
maqbad *n.* مقبض handle
maqbarah *n.* مقبرة cemetery
maqbas *n.* مقبس socket
maqbas *n.* مقبس switch
maqbool *adj.* 1 مقبول admissible
maqbool *adj.* 2 مقبول tolerable
maqdhoof *adj.* مقذوف projectile
maqdirah *n.* مقدرة ability
maqha *n.* مقهى cafe
maqif *n.* 3 موقف stand
maqroou *adj.* مقروء legible
maqroou *adv.* مقروء legibly
maqsaf *n.* مقصف canteen
maqsood *adj.* مقصود intentional

maqsoorah *n.* مقصورة compartment

maqt *n.* مقت abhorrence

maqta' *n.* 1 مقطع syllable

maqta' *n.* 2 مقطع section

maqta'iy *n.* مقطعي syllabic

maqtarah *n.* مقطرة distillery

maqtoorah *n.* مقطورة trailer

mar'a *n.* مرعى pasture

maraasimo *n.* مراسم ceremonies

marad *adj.* مرض satisfactory

marad *n.* مرض sickness

marah *n.* مرح merriment

maraq *n.* مرق broth

marzi *adj.* مرضي complacent

mareed *n.* مريض patient

mareed *adj.* مريض unwell

mareer *adj.* مرير bitter

marfau *n.* مرفأ port

marghoob *adj.* مرغوب desirable

marha *interj.* مرحى hurrah

marhalah *n.* مرحلة phase

marih *adj.* 1 مرح jolly

marih *adj.* 2 مرح vivacious

marin *adj.* مرن flexible

marj *n.* مرج meadow

marjah *n.* مرجة lea

marji' *n.* مرجع reference

markabah *n.* مركبة vehicle

markabiy *adj.* مركبي vehicular

markaziy *adj.* مركزي central

markiz *n.* مركز centre

marmooq *adj.* مرموق prestigious

marraarah *n.* مرارة wormwood

marrah *adv.* مرة once

marrah *n.* مَرَّه time

marratayn *adv.* مرتين twice

marsa *n.* مرسى anchorage

marshah *n.* مرشح filter

marsoom *n.* مرسوم decree

martabaan *n.* مرطبان jar

martabah *n.* مرتبة rank

marthi *adj.* مرثي deplorable

maruiy *adj.* مرئي visible

maruoos *adj.* مرؤوس subordinate

marwahah *n.* 2 مروحة ventilator

maryool *n.* مَريول smock

mas *n.* مص suck

mas'a *n.* مسعى endeavour

mas'ad *n.* مصعد lift

mas'oor *adj.* مسعور frantic

masaafah *n.* مسافة distance

masaahah *n.* مساحة area

masaar *n.* مسار track

masaau *n.* مساء evening

masahhah *n.* مصحة sanatorium

masarrah *n.* مسرة gaiety

masarrah *n.* مسرة gratification

masbahah *n.* مسبحة rosary

masbak *n.* مسبك foundry

masdar *n.* مصدر source

maseeh *n.* مسيح messiah

maseehiy *n.* مسيحي Christian

maseehiy *adj.* مسيحي Christian

maseer *n.* مصير destiny

maseerah *n.* مسيرة march

masfoofah *n.* مصفوفة matrix

mash *n.* 1 مسح survey

mash *n.* 2 مسح wipe

mashah *n.* مسحة tinge

mashbak *n.* مشبك clasp

mashdhoob *n.* مشذوب lop

mashdood *adj.* مَشْدُود tense

mashghool *adj.* مشغول busy

mashhad *n.* 1 مشهد act

mashhad *n.* 2 مشهد scene

mashhadiy *adj.* مشهدي scenic

mashhoon *adj.* مشحون fraught

mashhoor *adj.* مشهور famous

mashiyah *n.* ماشية cattle

mashkook *adj.* مشكوك suspect

mashlool *n.* مشلول cripple

mashlool *adj.* مشلول paralytic

mashooq *n.* مسحوق powder

mashoor *adj.* مصهور molten

mashoorah *n.* مشورة counsel

mashrahah *n.* مشرحة morgue

mashriq *n.* مشرق orient

mashroo' *n.* مشروع project

mashroot *adj.* مشروط conditional

mashtal *n.* مشتل nursery

mashuoom *adj.* مشؤوم ominous

mashwi *adj.* مشوي roast

mashy *n.* مشي walk

mashyah *n.* مشية gait

mashyakhiy *adj.* مشيخي senatorial

masjid *n.* مسجد mosque

maskan *n.* مسكن abode

maskh *n.* مسخ metamorphosis

maskoon *adj.* مسكون inhabitable

maslahah *n.* مصلحة benefit

maslak *n.* مسلك tract

masmoo' *adj.* مسموع audible

masna' *n.* مصنع factory

masnad *n.* مسند predicate

masrad *n.* مسرد glossary

masrah *n.* مسرح theatre

masrahiy *adj.* مسرحي theatrical

masrahiyya *n.* مسرحية play

masrif *n.* مصرف bank

masrifiy *n.* مصرفي banker

masrooqaat *n.* مسروقات loot

masroor *adj.* مسرور content

massaasah *n.* مصاصة lollipop

masualah *n.* مسألة matter

masuool *adj.* مسؤول responsible

masuooliyyah *n.* مسؤولية responsibility

maswatiyyah *n.* مصوتي sonority

masyaf *n.* مصيف bower

mat'am *n.* مطعم restaurant

mata *adv.* متى when

mataahah *n.* متاهة labyrinth

matar *n.* مطر rain

matbakh *n.* مطبخ kitchen

mateen *adj.* متين sturdy

mathaanah *n.* مثانة bladder

mathaf *n.* متحف museum

mathal *n.* 1 مثل instance

mathal *n.* 2 مثل proverb

mathalan *adv.* مثلاً say

mathaliy *adj.* مثلي proverbial

mathar *n.* مطهر purgatory

matheel *n.* مثيل double

matjar *n.* متجر shop

matlab *n.* مطلب requirement

matraan *n.* مطران archbishop

matrook *adj.* متروك left

mattaat *n.* مطاط rubber

mattaatiy *adj.* مطاطي elastic

matyar *n.* مطير aviary

maudobah *n.* مأدبة banquet

mauiy *adj.* مائي aquatic

maukool *n.* مأكول eatable

maukool *adj.* مأكول edible

mauloof *adj.* مألوف familiar

maumooriyyah *n.* مأمورية errand

mausaah *n.* مأساة tragedy

mausaawiy *adj.* مأساوي tragic

mausoor *adj.* مأسور captive

mauwa *n.* مأوى shelter

mauziq *n.* مأزق predicament

maw'id *n.* 1 موعد appointment

maw'id *n.* 2 موعد date

mawaadee'iy *adj.* مواضيعي thematic

mawaddah *n.* مودّة affection

mawdoo'iy *adj.* موضعي topical

mawdoo'iy *adj.* مَوضوعي objective

mawhibah *n.* موهبة talent

mawhoob *adj.* موهوب gifted

mawjah *n.* 1 موجة surge

mawjah *n.* 2 موجة wave

mawjood *adv.* موجود about

mawkib *n.* موكب procession

mawlid *n.* مولد birth

mawqi' *n.* موقع site

mawqid *n.* موقد stove

mawqif *n.* 1 موقف attitude

mawqif *n.* 2 موقف stop

mawqoo' *n.* موضوع subject

mawrid *n.* مورد resource

mawrooth *adj.* موروث heritable

mawsim *n.* موسم season

mawsimiy *adj.* موسمي seasonal

mawsoo'ah *n.* موسوعة encyclopaedia

mawt *n.* موت death

mawt *n.* ميت decease

mawthooq *adj.* موثوق trustworthy

mawthooq *n.* موثوق trusty

mawthooq *adj.* مَوثوق sure

mawthooq *adj.* موثوق trustful

mawtin *n.* موطن habitat

mawzah *n.* موزة banana

mayalaan *n.* ميلان tilt

maydaan *n.* مَيدان square

maykrofoon *n.* ميكروفون microphone

mayl *n.* 1 ميل bent

mayl *n.* 2 ميل liking

mayl *n.* 3 ميل tendency

maymoon *adj.* ميمون auspicious

maysam *n.* ميسم chalice

mayyit *adj.* ميت dead

mayyizah *n.* ميزة feature

mazaad *n.* مزاد auction

mazaajiy *adj.* مزاجي moody

mazaar *n.* مزار shrine

mazeed *adj.* مزيد further

mazeej *n.* مزيج blend

mazmoor *n.* مزمور psalm

mazooh *adj.* مزروح jocular

mazra'ah *n.* مزرعة farm

meedaaliyah *n.* ميدالية medal

meekaaneeka *n.* ميكانيكا mechanics

meekaaneeki *n.* ميكانيكي mechanic

meekaaneeki *adj.* ميكانيكي mechanical

meel *n.* ميل mile

meena *n.* مينا enamel

meenaau *n.* ميناء harbour

meethaaq *n.* ميثاق charter

meezaaniyyah *n.* ميزانية budget

mi'dah *n.* معدة stomach

mi'qal *n.* معقل stronghold

mi'sam *n.* معصم wrist

mi'taf *n.* معطف coat

mi'wal *n.* معول mattock

mi'yaar *n.* معيار norm

mi'yaariy *adj.* معياري standard

mibraah *n.* مبراة sharpener

mibrad *n.* مِبْرَد file

mibraqah *n.* مِبْرَقَه telegraph

mibsaqah *n.* مبصقة spittoon

mibsharah *n.* مبشرة grater

mibwalah *n.* مبولة urinal

middallah *n.* 1 مظلَّة canopy

middallah *n.* 3 مظلة umbrella

middalliy *n.* مظلي parachutist

midhwad *n.* مذود manger

midhyaa' *n.* مذياع radio

midlaah *n.* مدلاة locket

midrab *n.* مضرب racket

midyaaf *adj.* مضياف hospitable

miftaah *n.* مفتاح key

miftaah *n.* مفتاح spanner

mighnaatees *n.* مغناطيس magnet

mighnaateesiy *adj.* مغناطيسي magnetic

mighnaateesiyyah *n.* مغناطيسية magnetism

mighrafah *n.* مغرفة ladle

mighsalah *n.* مغسلة sink

mihbal *n.* مهبل vagina

mihbat *n.* مهبط landing

mihfaddah *n.* 1 محفظة portfolio

mihfaddah *n.* 2 محفظة wallet

mihmaaz *n.* مهماز spur

mihnah *n.* محنة plight

mihnah *n.* مهنة profession

mihnah *n.* مِهْنَه post

mihraath *n.* محراث plough

mihrajaan *n.* مهرجان festival

mihraqah *n.* 1 محرقة holocaust

mihraqah *n.* 2 محرقة incinerator

mihwar *n.* محور axis

mijdaaf *n.* مجداف paddle

mijdaaf *n.* مجذاف oar

mijhar *n.* 1 مجهر binocular

mijhar *n.* 2 مجهر microscope

mijhariy *adj.* مجهري microscopic

mijrafah *n.* مجرفة shovel

mikhlab *adj.* مخبل idiotic

mikhlab *n.* مخلب claw

miknasah *n.* مكنسة broom

mil'aqah *n.* ملعقة spoon

milaahah *n.* ملاحة navigation

milh *n.* ملح salt

milhiy *adj.* ملحي saline

milqat *n. pl.* ملقط tongs

miluo ffam *n.* مِلْءالفَم mouthful

milzamah *n.* مِلْزَمَه vice

mimkhadah *n.* ممخضة churn

min *prep.* من from

minassah *n.* منصة platform

minbar *n.* منبر rostrum

mindeel *n.* منديل handkerchief
minfaakh *n.* منفاخ bellows
minfadah *n.* منفضة duster
minhaaj *n.* منهاج curriculum
minhah *n.* منحة grant
minjal *n.* منجل sickle
minkhas *n.* منخس goad
minqaar *n.* منقار beak
minshaar *n.* منشار saw
minshafah *n.* منشفة towel
miq'ad *n.* مقعد seat
miqas *n.* مقص scissors
miqlaa' *n.* مقلاع sling
miqlah *n.* مقلاة fry
miqyaas *n.* مقياس measure
mirfaa' *n.* مرفاع crane
mirhaad *n.* مرحاض toilet
mirham *n.* مرهم ointment
mirjal *n.* مرجل boiler
mirqaab *n.* مرقاب telescope
mirqabiy *adj.* مرقبي telescopic
mirqahah *n.* مروحة 1 fan
mirsaah *n.* مرساة anchor
mirsaam *n.* مرسام stencil
mirsad *n.* مرصد observatory
miruaah *n.* مرآة mirror
miryamiyyah *n.* مريمية sage
misbaah *n.* مصباح lamp
misbaar *n.* مسبار probe
misfaah *n.* مصفاة refinery
mishkaah *n.* مشكاه niche
mishmish *n.* مشمش apricot
mishnaqah *n.* مشنقة gallows
mishrat *adj.* مشرط lancet
misht *n.* مشط comb

misk *n.* مسك musk
mislaat *n.* مسلاط projector
mismaar *n.* مسمار nail
mismaariyyah *n.* مسمرية mesmerism
misraa' *n.* مصراع shutter
miswaddah *n.* مسودة draft
mithaal *n.* مثال example
mithaaliy *adj.* مثالي ideal
mithaaliy *n.* مثالي idealist
mithaaliyyah *n.* مثالية idealism
mithl *adj.* مثل like
mithqaab *n.* مثقاب wimble
mithqab *n.* مثقب auger
mitr *n.* متر meter
mitraas *n.* متراس barricade
mitraqah *n.* مطرقة hammer
mitriy *adj.* متري metric
mitwaa' *adj.* مطواع supple
miuawiy *n.* مئوي centenarian
miudhanah *n.* مئذنة minaret
miuzar *n.* مئزر apron
mizaaj *n.* مزاج temperament
mizlaaj *n.* مزلاج latch
mizmaar *n.* مزمار pipe
mizraab *n.* مزراب gutter
mo'aad *adj.* معاد inimical
mo'aadalah *n.* معادلة equation
mo'aadi *adj.* معاد bellicose
mo'aadil *adj.* معادل equivalent
mo'aafa *adj.* معافى hale
mo'aahadah *n.* معاهدة treaty
mo'aakis *adj.* معاكس opposite
mo'aalaj *adj.* معالج curable

mo'aalajah n. معالجة 1 homeopathy

mo'aalajah n. معالجة 2 tackle

mo'aalij n. معالج homeopath

mo'aamalah n. مُعامَلَه treatment

mo'aanaah n. معاناة hardship

mo'aaradah n. معارضة opposition

mo'aasir adj. معاصر contemporary

mo'aatabah n. معاتبة admonition

mo'aawin n. مُعاوِن seconder

mo'abbir adj. معبر expressive

mo'addal n. معدل rate

mo'adi adj. معاد hostile

mo'affin adj. مُعَفِّن rank

mo'allaq adj. معلَّق abeyant

mo'allaq n. معلَّق commentator

mo'allib n. معلَّب bottler

mo'allim n. معلم teacher

mo'ammir adj. معمَّر aged

mo'ammir n. معمَّر perennial

mo'aqqad adj. معقَّد complex

mo'aqqam adj. معقم sterile

mo'arrad adj. معرَّض vulnerable

mo'assar adj. معسر insolvent

mo'awwiq adj. معوَّق obstructive

mo'ayyan adj. معيَّن certain

mo'ddam adj. معظم most

mo'di adj. معد contagious

mo'dilah n. معضلة dilemma

mo'fah adj. معفى exempt

mo'iddaat n. معدات gear

mo'jab n. معجب fan

mo'jaziy adj. معجزي miraculous

mo'jizah n. معجزة miracle

mo'taad adj. معتاد usual

mo'tabar adj. معتبر considerable

mo'tadi n. معتدي aggressor

mo'tadil adj. معتدل moderate

mo'tal adj. معتل morbid

mo'tamid n. معتمد dependant

mo'tamid adj. معتمد dependent

mo'tani n. مُعتَني tender

mo'tim adj. معتم overcast

mobaadarah n. مبادرة initiative

mobaalaghah n. مبالغة exaggeration

mobaaraah n. مباراة match

mobaarazah n. مبارزة duel

mobaashir adj. مباشر direct

mobaashir adv. مباشر live

mobadhdhir adj. مبذر prodigal

mobadhdhir adj. مبذر profligate

mobahraj adj. مُبَهرَج pretentious

mobajjil adj. مُبَجِّل reverent

mobakkir adj. مبكر early

mobakkiran adv. مبكراً early

mobarhimaat n. مبرهمات theorem

mobarrar adj. مبرَّر justifiable

mobarrir n. مبرر justification

mobashshir n. مبشر missionary

mobayyed n. مبيض ovary

mobayyid adj. مبيض whitish

mobdi' n. مبدع creator

mobeed n. مبيد exterminator

mobhir n. مبهر dazzle

mobtadhal adj. مبتذل workaday

mobtadiu n. مبتدئ apprentice

mobtadiu *adj.* مبتدئ junior
mobtadiu *n.* مبتدع innovator
mobtahij *adj.* مبتهج mirthful
mobtakar *adj.* مبتكر inventive
mod hik *adv.* مضحك funny
mod hik *adj.* مضحك humorous
modaa'af *adj.* مضاعف twofold
modaad *n.* مضاد antonym
modaad *pref.* مضاد contra
modaan *n.* مدان convict
modaar *adj.* مدار manageable
modaarrah *n.* مضارة bigamy
modaayaqah *n.* مضايقة
harassment
modakhkhim *n.* مضخم amplifier
modakhkhin *adj.* مدخن smoky
modallik *n.* مدلك masseur
modammir *n.* مدمّر wrecker
modannas *adj.* مدنس profane
modannis *adj.* مدنّس sacrilegious
modaqqiq *n.* مدقق stickler
modarraj *n.* مدرج amphitheatre
modarrib *n.* مدرب coach
modarris *n.* مدرس tutor
modawwin *n.* مدوّن book-keeper
modda'i *n.* مدعي plaintiff
moddaaharah *n.* مظاهرة
demonstration
moddah *n.* مدة duration
moddah *n.* مُدَة term
moddallah *n.* مظلّة 2 parachute
modeef *n.* مضيف 1 host
modeef *n.* مضيف 2 steward
modeer *n.* مدير director
modeeu *adj.* مضيء lucent

modhaab *adj.* مذاب solvent
modhakkar *adj.* مذكر masculine
modhakkarah *n.* مذكرة 1 agenda
modhakkarah *n.* مذكّرة 2 diary
modhakkarah *n.* مذكرة 3
warrant
modhakkir *adj.* مذكّر reminiscent
modhannab *n.* مذنب comet
modheeb *n.* مذيب solvent
modhhil *adj.* مذهل spectacular
modhish *n.* مدهش dandy
modhnib *n.* مذنب culprit
modhnib *adj.* مذنب guilty
modjir *adj.* مضجر irksome
modmaj *adj.* مدمج compact
modmaj *n.* مدمج merger
modmin *n.* مدمن addict
modniy *adj.* مضني strenuous
modraj *adj.* مدرج incorporate
modrik *adj.* مدرك perceptive
modtahad *n.* مضطهد oppressor
modtarib *n.* مضطرب psychopath
modtarib *adj.* مضطرب turbulent
modwi *adj.* مدو thunderous
mof'am *adj.* مفعم replete
mofaajauah *n.* مفاجأة surprise
mofaajiu *adj.* مفاجئ abrupt
mofaajiu *n.* مفاجئ sudden
mofaaraqah *n.* مفارقة paradox
mofaatahah *n.* مفاتحة overture
mofaawadaat *n.* مفاوضات parley
mofaawid *n.* مفاوض negotiator
mofaddal *n.* مفضل favourite
mofaddal *adj.* مفضّل superlative
mofajjir *n.* مفجّر bomber

mofakkir *n.* مفكّر intellect
mofakkiroon *n.* مفكّرون intelligentsia
mofarqa'ah *n.* مفرقعة cracker
mofarrikh *adj.* مفرّخ brood
mofassal *adj.* مفصل detailed
mofattish *n.* مفتش inspector
mofawwad *n.* مفوّض commissioner
mofawwadiyyah *n.* مفوضيّة commission
mofeed *adj.* مفيد useful
moflis *n.* مفلس bankrupt
moflis *adj.* مفلس penniless
mofrad *adj.* مفرد singular
mofradaat *n.* مفردات vocabulary
mofzi' *adj.* مفزع dreadful
moghaalatah *n.* مغالطة fallacy
moghaamarah *n.* مغامرة adventure
moghaamir *adj.* مغامر adventurous
moghaazalah *n.* مغازلة flirt
moghadhi *adj.* مغذ nutritious
moghaffal *n.* مغفّل fool
moghallaf *n.* مغلف envelope
moghallaf *adj.* مغلف enveloped
moghanna *adj.* مغنّى lyrical
moghanni *n.* مغنّي vocalist
moghatta *adj.* مغطّى covered
moghlaq *adj.* مغلق close
moghram *adj.* مغرم fond
moghri *adj.* مغر seductive
moghri *n.* مغري tempter
moghtaal *n.* مغتال assassinated
mohaabbaah *n.* محاباة favouritism

mohaadarah *n.* محاضرة lecture
mohaadathah *n.* محادثة conversation
mohaadhaah *n.* محاذاة alignment
mohaadi *adj.* محايد neuter
mohaadi *n.* محايد neuter
mohaadir *n.* محاضر lecturer
mohaafidd *adj.* محافظ conservative
mohaafidd *n.* محافظ governor
mohaajim *n.* مهاجم striker
mohaajir *n.* مهاجر immigrant
mohaakaah *n.* مُحاكاة simulation
mohaakamah *n.* محاكمة trial
mohaamaah *n.* محاماة advocacy
mohaami *n.* محام lawyer
mohaarib *adj.* محارب belligerent
mohaarib *n.* محارب warrior
mohaasabah *n.* محاسبة accountancy
mohaasib *n.* محاسب accountant
mohaawalah *n.* محاولة attempt
mohaddad *adj.* محدد particular
mohaddad *adj.* محدّد specific
mohaddath *adj.* محدّث up-to-date
mohaddiu *n.* مهدئ tranquilizer
mohaddiu *adj.* مهدى sedative
mohadhdhab *adj.* مهذب courteous
mohajjan *adj.* مهجّن hybrid
mohakkim *n.* محكّم arbitrator
mohalhal *adj.* مهلهل flimsy
mohallaf *n.* محلف juror
mohallil *n.* محلّل analyst
mohammas *adj.* محمّص toasted

mohandis *n.* مهندس engineer	mohsin *adj.* محسن benevolent
mohannak *adj.* مُحَنَّك veteran	mohtaaj *adj.* محتاج needy
moharram *adj.* محرّم inviolable	mohtaal *adj.* محتال crook
moharram *n.* محرم taboo	mohtaal *n.* محتال impostor
moharrib *n.* مهرّب smuggler	mohtadir *adj.* محتضر moribund
moharrid *adj.* محرّض seditious	mohtafil *n.* محتفل reveller
moharrij *n.* مهرّج clown	mohtajiz *adj.* مُحتَجِز retentive
moharrik *n.* 1 محرّك engine	mohtakir *n.* محتكر monopolist
moharrik *n.* 2 محرّك mover	mohtal *n.* 1 محتل occupant
moharrir *n.* 1 محرّر editor	mohtal *n.* 2 محتل occupier
moharrir *n.* 2 محرّر liberator	mohtam *adj.* مهتم interested
mohattam *adj.* محتّم inevitable	mohtamal *adj.* محتمل probable
mohawwil *n.* محوّل convert	mohtaqir *adj.* محتقر subjudice
mohawwil *adj.* محوّل transferable	mohtaram *adj.* محترم respectful
mohaymin *adj.* مهيمن dominant	mohtarif *n.* محترف ace
mohayya *n.* محيا visage	mohtarif *adj.* محترف professional
mohayyij *adj.* مهيج irritant	
mohayyij *n.* مهيّج irritant	mohtashim *n.* متحشّم prude
mohdawdab *n.* محدودب stoop	mohtashim *adj.* محتشم bashful
moheeb *adj.* مهيب majestic	mohtawa *n.* محتوى content
moheet *adj.* محيط ambient	mohtaz *adj.* مهتز shaky
moheet *n.* 1 محيط circumference	mohzin *adj.* محزن rueful
moheet *n.* 2 محيط ocean	mohzin *n.* محزن woeful
moheet *n.* 3 محيط surroundings	moja"ad *adj.* مجعّد curly
moheetiy *adj.* محيطي oceanic	mojaadil *adj.* مجادل argute
mohib *adj.* محب loving	mojaamalah *n.* مجاملة courtesy
mohim *adj.* مهم important	mojaazafah *n.* مُجازَفَه venture
mohimmah *n.* مهمة task	mojaddadan *adv.* مجدّداً again
mohkam *adj.* محكم fast	mojaddif *n.* مجدّف oarsman
mohmal *n.* مهمل idler	mojadwal *adj.* مجدول tabular
mohmal *adj.* مهمل negligible	mojallad *n.* مجلد tome
mohmar *adv.* محمر ablush	mojamma' *n.* مجمّع compound
mohmil *adj.* مهمل careless	mojannah *adj.* مجنّح winged
mohqir *adj.* محقر contemptuous	mojarrad *adj.* مجرد abstract
mohsim *n.* محسن philanthropist	mojarrad *adv.* مجرد mere

mojassam *n.* مجسّم figure

mojawharaat *n.* مجوهرات jewellery

mojaz *adj.* 1 موجز brief

mojdi *adj.* مجدي meaningful

mojizzaat *n. pl.* مجزات shears

mojmal *n.* مجمل gross

mojrim *n.* مجرم criminal

mojtahid *adj.* مجتهد diligent

mojtama' *n.* مجتمع community

mojtar *adj.* مجتر ruminant

mojtar *n.* مجتر ruminant

mojzi *adj.* مجزي remunerative

moka''ab *n.* مكعب cube

moka''ab *adj.* مكعب cubiform

mokaafauah *n.* مكافأة reward

mokammil *adj.* مكمل complementary

mokarrar *adj.* مكرر duplicate

mokaththaf *adj.* مكثف intensive

mokawwam *adv.* مكوم aheap

mokawwin *adj.* مكون component

mokhaadi' *adj.* مخادع crafty

mokhaadi' *n.* مخادع swindler

mokhaalafah *n.* مخالفة transgression

mokhaalafah *n.* مخلفات foul

mokhaat *n.* مخاط mucus

mokhaatab *n.* مخاطب addressee

mokhaatib *n.* مخاطب addresser

mokhaatiy *adj.* مخاطي mucous

mokhaddar *adj.* مخدّر numb

mokhaddir *n.* 1 مخدر narcotic

mokhaddir *n.* 2 مخدّر anaesthetic

mokhallal *n.* مخلل pickle

mokhammas *n.* مخمّس pentagon

mokhannath *adj.* مخنث effeminate

mokharrib *adj.* مخرّب subversive

mokhassas *n.* مخصص allotment

mokhattat *n.* مخطط scheme

mokhattataat *n.* مخططات tactics

mokhattit *n.* مخطط tactician

mokhayyam *n.* مخيم camp

mokhayyilah *n.* مخيلة imagination

mokhbir *n.* 1 مخبر detective

mokhbir *n.* 2 مخبر informer

mokheef *adj.* مخيف fearful

mokhjal *adj.* مخجل ashamed

mokhjil *adj.* مخجل shameful

mokhlis *n.* مخلص devotee

mokhlis *adj.* مخلص loyal

mokhlis *n.* مخلص royalist

mokhmal *n.* مخمل velvet

mokhmaliy *adj.* مخملي velvety

mokhmarah *n.* مخمرة brewery

mokhtaal *adj.* مختال vainglorious

mokhtabar *n.* مختبر laboratory

mokhtalif *adj.* مختلف different

mokhtari' *n.* مخترع inventor

mokhtas *adj.* مختص respective

mokhtazil *n.* مختزل stenographer

moklif *adj.* مكلف costly

mokrah *adj.* مكره averse

moktauib *adj.* مكتئب woebegone

molaahadda *n.* ملاحظة note

molaam *adj.* ملام culpable

molaauamah *n.* 1 ملاءمة convenience

molaauamah *n.* 2 ملاءمة suitability

molaauim *adj.* 1 ملائم convenient

molaauim *adj.* 2 ملائم seasonable

molaazim *n.* ملازم lieutenant

molaffaq *n.* ملفق figment

molakhas *n.* 1 ملخص abstract

molakhkhas *adj.* ملخص summary

molakhkhas *n.* 2 ملخص synopsis

molammih *adj.* ملمّح allusive

molaqih *n.* ملقح vaccinator

molaqqab *adj.* ملقّب titular

molaqqin *n.* ملقّن prompter

molattikh *adj.* ملطّخ blotted

molayyin *adj.* ملين laxative

molhah *n.* مُلحَه witticism

molhaq *n.* 1 ملحق appendix

molhaq *n.* 2 ملحق attachment

molhid *n.* ملحد atheist

molhiq *adj.* ملحق annectent

molih *n.* ملح persist

molih *adj.* ملح persistent

molim *adj.* ملم conversant

molkiy *adj.* 2 ملكيّ proprietary

molkiyyah *n.* 1 ملكية ownership

mollaa *n.* ملّا mullah

moloohah *n.* ملوحة salinity

molsaq *n.* 1 ملصق label

molsaq *n.* 2 ملصق poster

moltahib *n.* ملتهب abscess

moltahib *adv.* ملتهب aflame

moltahib *adj.* ملتهب inflammatory

moltamis *n.* ملتمس petitioner

moltawi *adj.* ملتوي bent

molzam *n.* ملزم bound

molzim *adj.* ملزم obligatory

momaarasah *n.* ممارسة practice

momaatalah *n.* مماطلة procrastination

momaathil *adj.* مماثل analogous

momaathil *n.* مماثل equal

momarrid *n.* ممرّض nurse

momaththil *n.* 1 ممثّل actor

momaththil *n.* 2 ممثل representative

momaththil *adj.* ممثل representative

momaththilah *n.* ممثّلة actress

momawwil *n.* ممول financier

momayyi' *adj.* مميّع dilute

momeet *adj.* مميت mortal

momil *adj.* ممل dull

momkin *adj.* ممكن possible

momtaaz *adj.* ممتاز excellent

momtahan *n.* ممتحَن examinee

momtahin *n.* ممتحِن examiner

momtalak *n.* ممتلك asset

momtalakaat *n.* ممتلكات property

momtan *adj.* ممتن grateful

momti' *adj.* ممتع enjoyable

momtir *adj.* ممطر rainy

mon'azil *n.* منعزل recluse

mon'azil *adj.* منعزل secluded

mon'ish *adj.* منعش brisk

monaab *adj.* مناب vicarious

monaafasah *n.* منافسة competition

monaafiq *n.* منافق hypocrite
monaafiq *adj.* منافق hypocritical
monaafis *n.* منافس rival
monaaqashah *n.* مناقشة debate
monaasabah *n.* مناسبة occasion
monaasib *n.* مناسب fit
monaasib *adj.* مناسب suitable
monaawarah *n.* مناورة manoeuvre
monaawashah *n.* مناوشة skirmish
monabbih *n.* 1 منبه alarm
monabbih *n.* 2 منبه stimulant
monaddddam *adj.* منظم orderly
monaddddamah *n.* منظمة organization
monaddddif *n.* منظف cleaner
monaddim *n.* منظم regulator
monaffir *adj.* منفر repulsive
monajjim *n.* منجم astrologer
monammaq *adj.* منمق flowery
monashshit *adj.* منشط tonic
monashshit *n.* منشط tonic
monassaq *adj.* منسق co-ordinate
monawwauaat *n.* منوعات miscellany
mondafi' *adj.* مندفع impulsive
mondho *adv.* منذ ago
mondho uan *prep.* منذ أن since
monfajir *n.* منفجر ordnance
monfarid *adj.* منفرد solo
monfasil *adj.* منفصل separate
monghamis *n.* منغمس debauchee
monhadar *n.* منحدر grade
monhadir *n.* منحدر slope

monhak *adj.* منهك haggard
monhana *n.* منحنى curve
monharif *adj.* 1 منحرف oblique
monharif *adj.* 2 منحرف perverse
monharif *v.* منحرف pervert
monhat *adj.* منحط decadent
monjaz *adj.* منجز accomplished
monkhafad *n.* منخفض low
monkhafid *adj.* منخفض low
monkhafidan *adv.* منخفضاً low
monolooj *n.* مونولوج soliloquy
monqaad *adj.* منقاد submissive
monqarid *adj.* منقرض extinct
monqidh *n.* منقذ saviour
monsaal *adj.* منصاع docile
monsif *adj.* منصف equitable
montabih *adj.* منتبه attentive
montabiq *adj.* منطبق applicable
montada *n.* منتدى forum
montaddar *adj.* منتظر pending
montaddim *adj.* منتظم regular
montahi *adj.* منتهي terminable
montaj *n.* منتج produce
montaja' *n.* منتجع resort
montakhab *adj.* مُنتَخَب select
montasaf *adj.* مُنتَصَف middle
montasaf *adj.* منتصف mid
montashi *adj.* مُنتَشٍ rapt
montasib *adj.* منتصب erect
montasir *n.* منتصر victor
montasir *adj.* منتصر victorious
monza'ij *adj.* منزعج irritable
moodah *n.* موضة fashion
moojaz *adj.* 2 موجز concise
moojaz *n.* 1 موجز conspectus

moojaz n. موجز 2 precis
mooji' adj. موجع grievous
moomis n. مومس courtesan
moomyaau n. مومياء mummy
mooseeqa n. موسيقى music
mooseeqiy adj. موسيقي musical
mooseeqiy n. موسيقي musician
moq'ad n. مُقعَد handicapped
moqa''ar adj. مقعر concave
moqaabalah n. مقابلة interview
moqaabil prep. مقابل versus
moqaadaah n. مقاضاة prosecution
moqaamir n. مقامر gambler
moqaaranah n. مقارنة comparison
moqaarin adj. مقارن comparative
moqaas adj. مقاس measurable
moqaata'ah n. مقاطعة 1 boycott
moqaata'ah n. مقاطعة 2 province
moqaatil n. مقاتل combatant
moqaawamah n. مقاومة resistance
moqaawil n. مقاول contractor
moqaawim adj. مقاوم resistant
moqaayadah n. مقايدة barter
moqabbilaat n. مقبلات appetizer
moqaddar adj. مقدَّر appreciable
moqaddar n. مقدَّر estimate
moqaddas adj. مقدس sacred
moqaddimah n. مقدمة introduction
moqallad adj. مقلَّد mimic
moqallad n. مقلَّد mimic
moqallam adj. مقلَّم trim
moqallid n. مقلد imitator

moqawwas adj. مقوَّس bent
moqawwim n. مقوِّم constituent
moqayyid adj. مقيَّد restrictive
moqeem adj. مقيم resident
moqeem n. مقيم resident
moqlah n. مقلة eyeball
moqni' adj. مقنع cogent
moqtadab adj. مقتضب terse
moqtarah n. مقترح proposal
moqtasid adj. مقتصد thrifty
moqtataf n. مقتطف extract
moraa'aah n. مراعاة observance
moraabi n. مراب usurer
moraadif n. مرادف synonym
moraafaqah n. مرافقة accompaniment
moraafiq n. مرافق escort
moraahaqah n. مراهقة adolescence
moraahiq adj. مراهق adolescent
moraahiq n. مراهق teenager
moraaja'ah n. مراجعة revision
moraaqab adj. مراقب monitored
moraaqabah n. مراقبة surveillance
moraaqib n. مراقب invigilator
moraasalah n. مراسلة correspondence
moraasil n. مراسل correspondent
moraawaghah n. مراوغة elusion
moraawigh adj. مراوغ elusive
morabba n. مربى jam
morabba' n. مربع square
morabba' adj. مربع square
morabi n. مرب pedagogue

morahhib *adj.* مرحّب welcome
morakkab *adj.* مركّب compound
morakkib *n.* مركّب compounder
morashshah *n.* مرشّح candidate
morattab *adj.* مرتّب tidy
morattibaat *n.* مرطبات refreshment
morawwad *adj.* مروّض tame
morawwi' *adj.* مروّع ghastly
morbih *adj.* مربح profitable
moreeb *adj.* مريب equivocal
moreeh *adj.* مريح comfortable
morhaf *n.* مرهف slender
morhaq *adj.* مزهق weary
morjaan *n.* مرجان coral
moroor *n.* 1 مرور passage
moroor *n.* 2 مرور traffic
morshid *n.* مرشد usher
morsil *n.* مرسل transmitter
mortafi' *adv.* مرتفع aloud
mortafi' *adj.* مرتفع high
mortazaqa *adj.* مرتزق mercenary
morthaah *n.* مرثاة elegy
mos'if *n.* مسعف medic
mosaa'adah *n.* مساعدة assistance
mosaa'id *n.* مساعد assistant
mosaa'id *adj.* مساعد auxiliary
mosaab *n.* مصاب casualty
mosaabaqah *n.* مسابقة contest
mosaadafah *n.* مصادفة coincidence
mosaadarah *n.* مصادرة confiscation
mosaadif *adj.* 1 مصادف accidental
mosaadif *adj.* 2 مصادف equivalent

mosaafir *n.* مسافر traveller
mosaahamah *n.* مساهمة contribution
mosaalahah *n.* مصالحة reconciliation
mosaalim *adj.* مسالم peaceable
mosaari' *n.* مصارع wrestler
mosaawaah *n.* مساواة equality
mosaddas *n.* مسدس revolver
mosaffi *n.* مصفٍ purist
mosaghghar *n.* مصغر miniature
mosaghghar *adj.* مصغر miniature
mosajjil *n.* 1 مسجّل registrar
mosajjil *n.* 2 مسجّل recorder
mosallah *adj.* مسلّح armed
mosallah *n.* مسلّح militant
mosalsal *n.* مسلسل serial
mosamma *n.* مسمّى namesake
mosammim *adj.* مصمّم set
mosarnim *n.* مسرنم somnambulist
mosatah *adj.* مسطّح flat
mosawwaq *adj.* مسوّق marketable
mosawwir *n.* مصوّر photographer
mosbaq *adj.* مسبق prior
mosbaqan *adv.* مسبق ahead
moseebah *n.* مصيبة calamity
moseeu *adj.* مسيء abusive
moseeu *n.* مسيء offender
mosfir *adj.* مصفر yellowish
mosha'widh *n.* مشعوذ wizard
mosha'widhah *n.* مشعوذة hag
moshaabih *adj.* مشابه similar
moshaabih *prep.* مُشابه like
moshaadaah *n.* مشادة altercation

moshaah *n.* مشاة infantry
moshaah *n.* مشاة pedestrian
moshaahanah *n.* مشاحنة wrangle
moshaahid *n.* مشاهد spectator
moshaakis *adj.* مشاكس rowdy
moshaarakah *n.* مشاركة participation
moshaarik *n.* مشارك participant
moshabba' *adj.* مشبع satiable
moshajjar *adj.* مشجّر leafy
moshakkal *adj.* مشكل motley
moshakkik *adj.* مشكّك sceptical
mosharrad *n.* مشرّد fugitive
moshra' *n.* مشرع legislator
mosharrif *adj.* مشرّف honourable
mosharrif *n.* مشرّف overseer
moshawwash *adj.* مشوّش addle
moshawwiq *adj.* مشوّق agog
moshi' *adj.* مشع radiant
moshil *n.* مسهل purgative
moshil *adj.* مسهل purgative
moshkil *adj.* مشكل troublesome
moshkilah *n.* مشكلة problem
moshmauiz *adj.* مشمئز loath
moshmis *adj.* مشمس sunny
moshrif *adj.* مشرف overlooking
moshrif *n.* مشرف supervisor
moshriq *adj.* مشرق bright
moshshi' *adj.* مشع eminent
moshta'il *adj.* مشتعل inflammable
moshta'il *adv.* مشتعل ablaze
moshtabah *adj.* مشبوه suspicious
moshtahi *n.* مشتهي appetent
moshtarak *adj.* مشترك joint

moshtarayaat *n.* مشتريات procurement
moshtari *n.* مشتر buyer
moskir *n.* مسكر intoxicant
moslih *n.* مصلح reformer
moslim *adj.* مسلم Muslim
moslim *n.* مسلم Muslim
mosrif *adj.* مسرف extravagant
mosta'aar *n.* مستعار pseudonym
mosta'bid *n.* مستعبد thrall
mosta'id *adj.* مستعد ready
mosta'marah *n.* مستعمرة colony
mosta'mir *n.* مستعمر colonialist
mostabid *n.* مستبد autocrat
mostad'i *n.* مستدعي caller
mostafeed *n.* مستفيد payee
mostafham *n.* مستفحم interrogative
mostafhil *adj.* مُستفحِل vigorous
mostahaq *adj.* مستحق due
mostahdar *n.* مستحضر product
mostaheel *adj.* مستحيل impossible
mostahiq *adj.* مستحق worthy
mostalah *n.* مصطلح term
mostalahiy *adj.* مصطلحي terminological
mostalim *n.* مستلم recipient
mostami' *n.* مستمع listener
mostamir *n.* مستمر persist
mostamir *adj.* مستمر persistent
mostana' *n.* مصطنع synthetic
mostanqa' *n.* مستنقع swamp
mostanqa'iy *adj.* مستنقعي marshy
mostaqbal *n.* مستقبل future

mostaqbaliy *adj.* مستقبلي future	**mota'allim** *n.* متعلم learner
mostaqeem *adj.* مستقيم straight	**mota'allim** *adj.* متعلم literate
mostaqil *adj.* مستقل independent	**mota'alliq** *adj.* متعلّق relevant
mostaqir *adj.* مستقر stable	**mota'ammid** *adj.* متعمّد deliberate
mostash'ir *adj.* مستشعر antenuptial	**mota'aqqib** *adj.* متعقّب traceable
mostashaar *n.* مستشار counsellor	**mota'aqqil** *adj.* متعقّل prudent
mostashfa *n.* مستشفى hospital	**mota'arrij** *adj.* متعرّج sinuous
mostaslah *adj.* مستصلح repairable	**mota'arrij** *adj.* متعرّج zigzag
mostateel *adj.* مستطيل oblong	**mota'assib** *n.* متعصّب fanatic
mostateel *n.* مستطيل rectangle	**mota'assib** *adj.* متعصّب intolerant
mostateeliy *adj.* مستطيلي rectangular	**mota'atish** *adj.* متعطش thirsty
mostaujar *adj.* مستأجر let	**mota'awwid** *adj.* متعوّد accustomed
mostaujir *n.* مستأجر tenant	**mota'awwid** *adj.* متعود wont
mostaunaf *n.* مستأنف appellant	**motaaba'ah** *n.* متابعة pursuance
mostawa *n.* مستوى scale	**motaabaqah** *n.* مطابقة conformity
mostawda' *n.* مستودع warehouse	**motaabiq** *adj.* مطابق identical
mostawi *adj.* 1 مستوي level	**motaah** *adj.* متاح available
mostawi *adj.* 2 مستوي plane	**motaakhim** *adj.* متاخم adjacent
mostawsaf *n.* مستوصف dispensary	**motaala'ah** *n.* مطالعة perusal
mostawtin *n.* مستوطن settler	**motaalabah** *n.* مطالبة claim
mostayqidd *adj.* مستيقظ awake	**motaalib** *n.* مطالب claimant
mot'ah *n.* متعة enjoyment	**motaaradah** *n.* مطاردة pursuit
mot'ib *adj.* متعب tiresome	**motabaadal** *adj.* متبادل mutual
mota'aali *adj.* متعال transcendent	**motabaadal** *adj.* متبادل reciprocal
mota'aaqib *adj.* متعاقب successive	**motabaahi** *n.* متباه pomp
mota'aatif *adj.* متعاطف sympathetic	**motabaahi** *adj.* متباه pompous
mota'addi *n.* متعد transitive	**motabaari** *n.* متباري agonist
mota'addid *adj.* متعدد multiple	**motabaayin** *adj.* متباين dissimilar
mota'affin *adj.* متعفن mouldy	**motabajjih** *n.* متبجح brag
mota'allam *adj.* متعلم learned	**motabaqqi** *adj.* متبقّي residual
	motabbal *adj.* متبّل spicy
	motadaa'i *adj.* متداع rickety

motadaffiq *n.* متدفق consonant
motadaffiq *adj.* متدفق torrential
motadarrib *n.* متدرّب intern
motadhammir *n.* متذمر nag
motafaa'il *adj.* متفاعل reactionary
motafaauil *n.* متفائل optimist
motafaauil *adj.* متفائل optimistic
motafajji' *n.* متفجع mourner
motafajjir *n.* متفجر explosive
motafajjir *adj.* متفجر explosive
motafarrid *adv.* متفرد singularly
motafarrij *n.* مُتَفَرِّج on-looker
motafarriqaat *adj.* متفرقات miscellaneous
motafashshi *adj.* متفشّي rampant
motafawwiq *adj.* متفوق superior
motaghatris *adj.* متغطرس arrogant
motaghatris *n.* متغطرس bully
motaghayyir *adj.* متغير variable
motahaarib *adj.* متحارب belligerent
motahaddith *n.* متحدّث speaker
motahadhliq *n.* متحذلق pedantic
motahaffidd *adj.* متحفّظ secretive
motahalhil *adj.* متهلل jubilant
motahammis *adj.* متحمس enthusiastic
motaharrik *adj.* متحرك animate
motahawwil *adj.* متحول mutative
motahawwir *adj.* متهور reckless
motahayyiz *adv.* متحيز ex-parte
motahayyiz *adj.* متحيز partial
motahhir *n.* مطهّر antiseptic
motahhir *adj.* مطهّر antiseptic
motajaanis *adj.* متجانس homogeneous

motajaanisah *adj.* متجانسة congenial
motajaddid *adv.* متجدّد anew
motajaddid *adj.* متجدّد resurgent
motajassid *adj.* متجسد incarnate
motakaafiu *adj.* متكافئ morganatic
motakaamil *adj.* متكامل integral
motakabbir *n.* متكبر snob
motakabbir *v.* مُتَكَبِّر snobbish
motakarrir *n.* متكرر frequent
motakarrir *adj.* متكرر recurrent
motakhallif *n.* مُتَخَلِّف backward
motakhallif *adj.* مُتَخَلِّف underdeveloped
motakhassis *n.* متخصص specialist
motallaq *n.* مطلق divorced
motamaathil *adj.* متماثل symmetrical
motamakkin *adj.* متمكن versed
motamalliq *adj* متملق slimy
motamallis *n.* متملّص shirker
motamarrid *n.* متمرد rebel
motamarrid *adj.* متمرد rebellious
motamarrin *n.* متمرن probationer
motamarris *n.* متمرّس practitioner
motamayyiz *adj.* متميز distinct
motanaaghim *adj.* متناغم harmonious
motanaaqid *adj.* متناقض paradoxical
motanaasib *adj.* متناسب proportional

motanaasib *n.* متناسب
proportionate

motanaathir *adj.* متناثر sparse

motanaawib *adj.* متناوب alternate

motanabbih *adj.* متنبه alert

motanaqqil *adj.* متنقل ambulant

motanawwi' *adj.* متنوع varied

motanazzah *n.* متنزه park

motaqaa'is *n.* متقاعس laggard

motaqaati' *adj.* متقاطع cross

motaqaauid *n.* متقاعد pensioner

motaqaddim *adj.* متقدم forward

motaqallib *adj.* متقبل receptive

motaqallib *adj.* متقلب astatic

motaqarrih *adj.* متقرح ulcerous

motaqashshif *adj.* متقشف austere

motaqatti' *adj.* متقطع sporadic

motaqawwis *adj.* متقوس arch

motaraabit *adj.* مترابط
interdependent

motaraadif *adj.* مترادف
synonymous

motaraaji' *adj.* متراجع declining

motaraakhi *adj.* متراخي lax

motaraddad *n.* متردد haunt

motaraddid *adj.* متردد reluctant

motarahhil *adj.* مترهل flabby

motarjim *n.* مترجم interpreter

motasaahil *adj.* متساهل lenient

motasaamih *adj.* 1 متسامح
indulgent

motasaamih *adj.* 2 متسامح
tolerant

motasaawi *adj.* 1 متساو equal

motasaawi *adj.* 2 متساو even

motasalliq *n.* متسلق mountaineer

motasalsil *n.* متسلسل
chronological

motasalsil *adj.* متسلسل serial

motasarri' *adj.* متسرع hasty

motasawwil *n.* متسول beggar

motashaa'ir *n.* متشاعر poetaster

motashaabih *adj.* متشابه alike

motashaauim *n.* متشائم
pessimist

motashaauim *adj.* متشائم
pessimistic

motashannij *adj.* متشنج jerky

motasharrid *adj.* متشرد stray

motashawwiq *adj.* متشوق keen

motatallab *adj.* مُتَطَلَّب requisite

motatarrif *n.* متطرف extremist

motatawwi' *n.* متطوع volunteer

motauaamir *n.* متآمر conspirator

motauakhkhir *adv.* متأخر late

motauakhkhir *adj.* متأخر overdue

motauakhkhiraat *n.pl.* متأخرات
arrears

motauakkad *adj.* متأكد certain

motaualliq *adj.* متألق resplendent

motauammil *adj.* متأمل pensive

motauasil *adj.* متأصل inherent

motawa'ik *adj.* متوعك indisposed

motawaadi' *adj.* متواضع modest

motawaafiq *adj.* متوافق compliant

motawaali *adj.* متوالي consecutive

motawaasil *adj.* متواصل
continuous

motawaddid *n.* متودد courtier

motawahhij *adv.* متوهج aglow

motawahhish *adj.* متوحش savage

motawahhish *n.* متوحش savage

motawajjib *adj.* متوجب incumbent

motawarrim *adj.* متورّم sore

motawassit *adj.* 1 متوسط average

motawassit *adj.* 2 متوسط intermediate

motawassit *n.* متوسط mean

motawassit *adj.* 3 متوسط median

motawattir *adj.* متوتر tense

motawwal *adj.* مطول lengthy

motazaamin *adj.* متزامن simultaneous

motazammit *n.* متزمّت puritan

motazammit *adj.* متزمّت puritanical

motee' *adj.* مطيع obedient

mothaabarah *n.* مثابرة perseverance

mothallath *n.* مثلث triangle

mothamman *n.* مثمن octagon

mothaqqaf *adj.* مثقف intellectual

mothbat *adj.* مثبت corroborative

motheer *adj.* مثير sensational

mothmir *adj.* مثمر productive

mothqal *adj.* مثقل indebted

mothqil *adj.* مثقل burdensome

motlaq adj. مطلق absolute

motmaasik *adj.* متماسك cohesive

motnib *adj.* مطنب verbose

motqan *adj.* متقن proficient

motraf *adj.* مترف luxuriant

motrib *n.* مطرب singer

mottaham *n.* متّهم accused

mottasiq *adj.* متسق consistent

mouaamarah *n.* مؤامرة conspiracy

mouaanasah *n.* مؤانسة sociability

mouaati *adj.* مؤات favourable

mouaddab *adj.* مؤدب polite

mouaddab *n.* مؤدب preceptor

mouaddi *n.* مؤد performer

mouahhal *adj.* مؤهل eligible

mouahhal *n.* مؤهّل qualification

mouakhkhar *adj.* مؤخر recent

mouakhkharan *adv.* مؤخّراً recently

mouakhkhirah *n.* مؤخرة bottom

mouakkad *adj.* مؤكّد affirmative

mouan *n.* مؤن supply

mouannath *adj.* مؤنّث feminine

mouaqqat *n.* مؤقت interim

mouaqqat *adj.* مؤقّت temporary

mouarrakh *n.* مؤرخ antedate

mouarrikh *n.* مؤرخ historian

mouashshir *n.* 1 مؤشر indicator

mouashshir *n.* 2 مؤشّر marker

mouassasah *n.* مؤسسة institution

mouassis *n.* مؤسس founder

mouaththir *adj.* 1 مؤثر impressive

mouaththir *adj.* 2 مؤثر influential

mouayyid *n.* مؤيَد exponent

moudhi *adj.* مؤذ mischievous

moulim *adj.* مؤلم painful

moumin *n.* مؤمن theist

mousif *adj.* مؤسف unfortunate

moutaman *n.* مؤتمن confidant

moutamar *n.* مؤتمر conference

mowaaddib *adj.* مواظب studious

mowaafaqah *n.* موافقة approval

mowaafiq *n.* موافق assent

mowaajahah *n.* مواجهة confrontation

mowaali *n.* موالي loyalist

mowaarabah *n.* مواربة quibble

mowaasafah *n.* مواصفة specification

mowaatanah *n.* مواطنة citizenship

mowaatin *n.* مواطن citizen

mowaau *n.* مواء mew

mowaazi *adj.* مواز parallel

mowaddah *adj.* موضح articulate

mowaddddaf *n.* موظَف employee

mowaddddafoon *n.* موظفون staff

mowaddddif *n.* موظِف employer

mowahhad *adj.* موحَد single

mowallid *n.* مولد generator

mowaqi' *n.* موقَع signatory

mowaqqar *adj.* موقر reverend

mowasil *n.* موصل conductor

mowhi *adj.* موح suggestive

mozaah *n.* مزاح banter

mozaal *adj.* مزال removable

mozaari' *n.* مزارع farmer

mozaawadah *n.* مزاودة bid

mozaawid *n.* مزاود bidder

mozawwaj *adj.* مزوَج marriageable

mozawwar *adj.* مزوَر counterfeit

mozawwid *n.* مزوَد supplier

mozawwir *n.* مزور counterfeiter

mozayyaf *adj.* مزيَف forged

mozayyif *n.* مزيَف forger

mozdahir *adj.* مزدهر prosperous

mozdawaj *n.* مزدوج double

mozdawaj *adj.* مزدوج dual

mozhah *n.* مزحة gag

mozmin *adj.* مزمن chronic

mozuij *adj.* مزعج troublesome

mutaraaji' *adv.* متراجع aback

N

na''aanah *n.* نعامة ostrich

na'am *adv.* نعم yes

na'eeq *n.* نعيق caw

na'i *adj.* نعي obituary

na'jah *n.* نعجة ewe

na'l *n.* نَعل sole

na'naa' *n.* نعناع mint

na'saan *adj.* نعسان sleepy

na'saan *n.* نعسان somnolent

na'sh *n.* 1 نعش casket

na'sh *n.* 2 نعش coffin

na't *n.* نعت adjective

naa'im *n.* ناعم soft

naab *n.* ناب tusk

naadij *adj.* ناضج mature

naadil *n.* نادل waiter

naadilah *n.* نادلة waitress

naadir *adj.* نادر rare

naadiran *adv.* نادراً seldom

naafi' *adj.* نافع serviceable

naafidhah *n.* نافذة window

naafoorah *n.* نافورة fountain

naajih *a* ناجح successful

naakhib *n.* ناخب voter

naakhiboon *n.* ناخبون electorate

naaqid *adj.* ناقد censorious

naaqid *n.* ناقد critic

naaqil *n.* ناقل carrier

naaqilah *n.* ناقلة tanker

naaqis *adj.* ناقص imperfect

naaqis *prep.* ناقص minus

naaqis *n.* ناقص minus

naariy *adj.* ناري fiery

naashir *n.* ناشر publisher

naashiu *adj.* ناشئ nascent

naasik *n.* ناسك hermit

naasikh *n.* ناسخ transcriber

naasiyah *n.* ناصية forelock

naasoor *n.* ناسور fistula

naatij *n.* ناتج product

naauim *n.* نائم sleeper

naay *n.* ناي flute

naayloon *n.* نايلون nylon

nabaat *n.* نبات flora

nabaatiy *n.* نباتي vegetarian

nabaatiy *adj.* نباتي vegetarian

nabawiy *adj.* نبوي prophetic

nabd *n.* نبض pulse

nabeedh *n.* نبيذ wine

nabeeh *adj.* نبيه sharp

nabeel *adj.* نبيل noble

nabeel *n.* نبيل nobleman

nabhah *n.* نبحة yap

nabiy *n.* نبي prophet

naboouah *n.* نبوءة prophecy

naboouiy *adj.* نبوئي oracular

nabtah *n.* نبتة plant

nada *n.* ندى dew

nadam *n.* ندم remorse

nadb *n.* ندب lament

naddaafah *n.* نظافة cleanliness

naddariy *adj.* نظري theoretical

naddariyyah *n.* نظرية theory

naddddaaraat *n.* نظارات barnacles

nadddaarah *n.* نظارة glasses

naddeef *adv.* نظيف clean

naddeef *adj.* نظيف clean

naddeer *n.* نظير counterpart

naddrah *n.* نظرة gaze

nadheer *n.* نذير precursor

nadhl *n.* نذل cad

nadhr *n.* نذر vow

nadi *n.* ناد club

nadij *n.* ناضج adult

nadwah *n.* ندوة symposium

nafaq *n.* نفق tunnel

nafaqah *n.* نفقة expense

nafas *n.* نفس breath

nafkhah *n.* نفخة puff

nafs *n.* 1 نفس psyche

nafs *adj.* نفس same

nafs *n.* 2 نفس self

nafsaaniy *adj.* نفساني psychological

nafsi *pron.* نفسي myself

nafsiy *adj.* نفسي psychic

nafy *n.* 1 نفي banishment

nafy *n.* 2 نفي negation

naghmah *n.* نغمة tone

nahaalah *n.* نحالة apiculture

nahm *n.* نهم gluttony

nahawiy *n.* نحوي grammarian

nahb *n.* نهب ravage

nahdah *n.* نهضة renaissance

naheel *adj.* نحيل slim

naheeq *n.* نهيق bray	**namoodhajiy** *adj.* نموذجي typical
nahhaab *n.* نهاب marauder	**naq'** *n.* نقع soak
nahhaas *n.* نحاس brass	**naqaabah** *n.* نقابة guild
nahhaat *n.* نحات sculptor	**naqaau** *n.* نقاء purity
nahim *adj.* نهم insatiable	**naqd** *n.* 1 نقد cash
nahj *n.* نهج approach	**naqd** *n.* 2 نقد criticism
nahlah *n.* نحلة bee	**naqdiy** *adj.* نقدي monetary
nahr *n.* نهر river	**naqeed** *n.* نقيض antithesis
naht *n.* نحت sculpture	**naqeesah** *n.* نقيصة demerit
nahtiy *adj.* نحتي sculptural	**naqiy** *a* نقي pure
nahw *n.* نحو grammar	**naql** *n.* 1 نقل carriage
nahwa *prep.* نحو towards	**naql** *n.* 2 نقل transmission
najaah *n.* نجاح success	**naqlah** *n.* نقلة shift
najaasah *n.* نجاسة impurity	**naqqaal** *adj.* نقّال mobile
najis *adj.* نجس impure	**naqqaalah** *n.* نقالة stretcher
najjaar *n.* نجّار carpenter	**naqrah** *n.* نقرة click
najmah *n.* نجمة star	**naqs** *n.* نقص shortage
najmiy *adj.* نجمي starry	**naqsh** *n.* نقش inscription
nakad *n.* نكد petulance	**nard** *n.* نرد dice
nakad *adj.* نكد sullen	**narjis** *n.* نرجس daffodil
nakhah n. نكهة flavour	**nas** *n.* نَص script
nakhb *n.* نَخُب wassail	**nasab** *n.* نسب lineage
nakheel *n.* نخيل palm	**naseeb** *n.* نصيب quota
nakhr *adj.* نخر carious	**naseehah** *n.* نصيحة advice
nakhr *n.* نَخُر snort	**naseej** *n.* 1 نسيج tissue
nakhz *n.* نخز poke	**naseej** *n.* 2 نسيج textile
nakirah *pron.* نكره nobody	**naseejiy** *adj.* نسيجي textile
naks *adv.* نكص recoil	**naseem** *n.* نسيم breeze
namat *n.* نمط pattern	**naseer** *n.* نصير henchman
namatiy *adj.* نمطي stereotyped	**naseer** *adj.* نَصير partisan
nameemah *n.* نميمة gossip	**nashaat** *n.* نشاط verve
namir *n.* نمر tiger	**nashau** *n.* نشاء starch
namirah *n.* نمرة tigress	**nasheed** *n.* نشيد anthem
namlah *n.* نملة ant	**nasheej** *n.* نَشيج sob
namoodhaj *n.* نموذج model	**nasheet** *n.* نشيط alacrity

nasheet *adj.* نشيط energetic
nashq *n.* نَشْق sniff
nashr *n.* نشر propagation
nashrah *n.* نشرة brochure
nashwah *n.* نشوة rapture
naskh *n.* نسخ transcription
nasl *n.* نسل offspring
nassiy *n.* نصي textual
nataanah *n.* نتانة stench
nateejah *n.* نتيجة result
nathr *n.* نثر prose
natin *n.* نتن stink
nauib *n.* نائب deputy
nauim *adv.* نائم asleep
naw' *n.* 1 نوع breed
naw' *n.* 2 نوع sort
naw'iy *adj.* نوعي qualitative
nawawiy *adj.* نووي nuclear
nawbaat *n.* نوبات innings
nawbah *n.* 1 نوبة fit
nawbah *n.* 2 نوبة frenzy
nawm *n.* نوم sleep
nawras *n.* نورس gull
nayl *n.* نيل attainment
nayr *n.* نير yoke
nayyiu *n.* نيئ row
nayzak *n.* نيزك meteor
nayzakiy *adj.* نيزكي meteoric
naz' *n.* نزع disarmament
nazaahah *n.* نزاهة impartiality
nazeeh *adj.* نزيه impartial
naziq *adj.* نَزِق quixotic
nazwah *n.* نزوة caprice
nazwah *n.* نَزْوَه vagary
nazwah *adj.* نزوي capricious

neeliy *n.* نيلي indigo
neesaan *n.* نيسان April
ni'mah *n.* نعمة grace
nibtoon *n.* نبتون Neptune
nidaal *n.* نضال struggle
niddaam *n.* 1 نظام order
niddaam *n.* 2 نظام system
nifaaq *n.* نفاق hypocrisy
nifaayaat *n.* نفايات litter
nift *n.* نفط oil
nihaauiy *adj.* 1 نهائي terminal
nihaauiy *adj.* 2 نهائي ultimate
nihaayah *n.* نهاية finish
nijaarah *n.* نجارة carpentry
nims *n.* نمس mongoose
nisbah *n.* نسبة ratio
nisbiy *adj.* نسبي relative
nisf *n.* نصف half
nisf *adj.* نصف half
nisr *n.* نسر eagle
nisyaan *n.* نسيان oblivion
nitaaq *n.* نطاق domain
nitroojeen *n.* نتروجين nitrogen
niyon *n.* نيون neon
niyyah *n.* نية intent
nizaa' *n.* نزاع dispute
no'aas *n.* نعاس somnolence
nobaah *n.* نباح bark
nobl *n.* نبل nobility
nodb *n.* ندب scar
nodj *n.* نضج maturity
nodr *n.* ندر scarcity
nodrah *n.* ندرة paucity
nofoodh *n.* نفوذ influence
nofoor *n.* نفور aversion

nohaas *n.* نحاس copper

nohayr *n.* نهير streamlet

nokaaf *n.* نكاف mumps

nokhaa' *n.* نخاع marrow

nokraan *n.* نكران denial

noktah *n.* نكتة joke

nomow *n.* نمو growth

noqros *n.* نقرس gout

noqsaan *n.* نقصان decrease

noqtah *n.* 1 نقطة dot

noqtah *n.* 2 نقطة point

nosh *n.* نصح advisability

noskhah *n.* نسخة copy

notoou *n.* نتوء lump

nowaah *n.* 1 نواة kernel

nowaah *n.* 2 نواة nucleus

nowl *n.* نول loom

nozhah *n.* نزهة picnic

nozol *n.* نزل hostel

nozoolan *adv.* نزولا downwards

nyootroon *n.* نيوترون neutron

Q

qaa'ah قاعة hall

qaa'idah *n.* قاعدة base

qaa'idiy *adj.* قاعدي basal

qaabid *n.* قابض clutch

qaabilah *n.* قابلة midwife

qaabiliyyah *n.* قابلية capability

qaadi *n.* قاضي judge

qaadir *adj.* قادر able

qaafilah *n.* قافلة caravan

qaafiyah *n.* قافية rhyme

qaahil *n.* قاحل barren

qaalib *n.* قالب cast

qaamah *n.* قامة stature

qaamoos *n.* قاموس dictionary

qaanoon *n.* قانون law

qaanooniy *adj.* قانوني legal

qaarah *n.* قارة continent

qaarib *n.* قارب boat

qaarid *n.* قارض rodent

qaariu *n.* قارئ reader

qaariy *adj.* قاري continental

qaaroorah *n.* قارورة vial

qaasi *adj.* قاس harsh

qaasir *n.* قاصر minor

qaati' *adj.* قاطع conclusive

qaati' *n.* قاطع partition

qaatil *adj.* قاتل deadly

qaatil *n.* قاتل murderer

qaatirah *n.* قاطرة locomotive

qaauid *n.* قائد commander

qaauidd *adj.* قائظ sultry

qaauim *n.* قائم perpendicular

qaauim *adj* قائم on

qaauim *adv.* قائم afoot

qaauimah *n.* قائمة list

qabaliy *adj.* قبلي tribal

qabdah *n.* 2 قبضة grip

qabdhah *n.* 1 قبضة fist

qabeeh *adj.* قبيح ugly

qabeelah *n.* قبيلة tribe

qabil *adj.* قابل amenable

qabl *adv.* قبل ago

qabl *conj.* قبل before

qabl *prep.* قبل before

qabo *n.* قبو vault
qabr *n.* قبر grave
qabtanah *n.* قبطنة captaincy
qadaasah *n.* قداسة sanctity
qadaau *n.* 1 قضاء elimination
qadaau *n.* 2 قضاء judicature
qadaauiy *adj.* قضائي judicial
qadah *n.* قَدَح mug
qadam *n.* قدم foot
qaddaa'ah *n.* قضاعة otter
qaddeefah *n.* قظيفة torpedo
qadeeb *n.* 1 قضيب bar
qadeeb *n.* 2 قضيب penis
qadeem *adj.* قديم old
qadhaarah *n.* قذارة filth
qadheefah *n.* قذيفة projectile
qadhf *n.* 1 قذف defamation
qadhf *n.* 2 قذف throwing
qadhir *adj.* قذر filthy
qadiyyah *n.* 1 قضية issue
qadiyyah *n.* 2 قضية case
qadm *n.* قضم nibble
qafas *n.* قفص cage
qafr *n.* قفر wilderness
qafzah *n.* قفزة jump
qahqarah *v.* قهقرة cackle
qahwah *n.* قهوة coffee
qal'ah *n.* قلعة castle
qalam *n.* 1 قلم pen
qalam *n.* 2 قلم pencil
qalaq *n.* قلق anxiety
qalawiy *n.* قلوي alkali
qalb *n.* 1 قلب heart
qalb *n.* 2 قلب overthrowing
qalbiy *adj.* قلبي cardiac

qaleel *adj.* قليل few
qaleel *n.* قليل modicum
qaleelan *adv.* قليلاً little
qaliq *adj.* قلق anxious
qalliyyah *n.* أقلية minority
qam' *n.* قمع oppression
qam'iy *adj.* قمعي oppressive
qamar *n.* 1 قمر moon
qamar *n.* 2 قمر satellite
qamariy *adj.* قمري lunar
qamees *n.* قميص shirt
qamh *n.* قمح oat
qamlah *n.* قملة louse
qanaah *n.* 2 قناة channel
qanah *n.* 1 قناة canal
qannaas *n.* قناص assassin
qar' *n.* قرع gourd
qaraabah *n.* قرابة kinship
qaraadah *n.* قرادة tick
qaraar *n.* 1 قرار decision
qaraar *n.* 2 قرار determination
qarawiy *adj.* قَروي rustic
qarawiy *n.* قروي villager
qard *n.* قرض loan
qareeb *adj.* 1 قريب akin
qareeb *n.* 1 قريب close
qareeb *n.* 2 قريب kin
qareeb *adj.* 2 قريب near
qareeb *adv.* قريب nigh
qareeb *prep.* قريب nigh
qareeb *n.* قريب relative
qareeb *adj.* 3 قريب proximate
qareeban *adv.* قريباً soon
qarmeed *n.* قرميد brick
qarn *n.* 1 قرن century

qarn *n.* 2 قرن horn	qawl *n.* قول saying
qarnabeet *n.* قرنبيط broccoli	qawmiy *n.* قومي nationalist
qarniyyah *n.* قرنية cornea	qawniyyah *n.* قومية nationality
qarsanah *n.* قرصنة piracy	qaws *n.* 1 قوس arch
qaryah *n.* قرية village	qaws *n.* 2 قوس bow
qas *n.* 1 قص narration	qaws *n.* 3 قوس parenthesis
qas *n.* 2 قص cutting	qayd *n.* قيد shackle
qasab *n.* قصب cane	qayloolah *n.* قيلولة nap
qasabah *n.* 1 قصبة shin	qayu *n.* قيء vomit
qasabah *n.* 2 قصبة stubble	qayyim *adj.* قيم valuable
qasam *n.* 1 قسم department	qazam *n.* قزم dwarf
qasam *n.* قسم oath	qeemah *n.* قيمة value
qasd *n.* قصد intention	qeeraat *n.* قيراط carat
qasdeer *n.* قصدير tin	qeethaar *n.* قيثار harp
qaseedah *n.* قصيدة poem	qeethaarah *n.* قيثارة guitar
qaseemah *n.* قسيمة voucher	qidam *n.* قدم antiquity
qaseer *adj.* قصير short	qiddees *n.* قديس saint
qasf *n.* قصف bombardment	qilaadah *n.* قلادة necklace
qash *n.* قش straw	qillah *n.* قلة dearth
qash'areerah *n.* قشعريرة chill	qimaar *n.* قمار gambling
qasht *n.* كشط graze	qimaash *n.* قماش fabric
qasr *n.* قصر palace	qimmah *n.* 1 قمة peak
qasriy *adj.* قسري forcible	qimmah *n.* 2 قمة summit
qassah *n.* قصة shave	qinaa' *n.* قناع mask
qast *n.* قسط instalment	qinnab *n.* قنب hemp
qaswah *n.* قسوة cruelty	qiraab *n.* قراب scabbard
qat' *n.* قطع severance	qiraauah *n.* قراءة reading
qat'iy *adj.* قطعي conclusive	qird *n.* قرد monkey
qatee' *n.* قطيع herd	qirfah *n.* قرفة cinnamon
qatl *n.* قتل murder	qirsh *n.* قرش penny
qatraan *n.* قطران tar	qirtaas *n.* قرطاس ply
qatrah *n.* قطرة drop	qirtaasiy *n.* قرطاسي stationer
qattaarah *n.* قطّارة drip	qirtaasiyyah *n.* قرطاسية stationery
qawiy *adj.* 1 قوي potent	
qawiy *adj.* 2 قوي strong	qishr *n.* قشر peel

qishrah *n.* قشرة crust	qorbaan *n.* قربان oblation
qism *n.* 2 قسم partition	qorhah *n.* قرحة ulcer
qismah *n.* قسمة division	qormoziy *n.* قرمزي crimson
qissah *n.* قصة narrative	qors *n.* قرص disc
qit *n.* قط cat	qorsaan *n.* قرصان pirate
qit'ah *n.* قطعة segment	qosaara n. قصارى utmost
qitaa' *n.* قطاع sector	qoswa *n.* قصوى utmost
qitaal *n.* قتال fight	qotb *n.* قطب pole
qitaaliy *adj.* قتالي combatant	qotbiy *n.* قطبي polar
qitaaliy *n.* قطار train	qotn *n.* قطن cotton
qiyaadah *n.* قيادة leadership	qotr *n.* قطر diameter
qiyaas *n.* قياس measurement	qowwah *n.* قوة force
qobaalah *adj.* قبالة against	qronfol *n.* قرنفل clove
qobba'aatiy *n.* قبعاتي milliner	qwwaat *n.* قوات troop
qobba'ah *n.* قبعة hat	
qobbah *n.* قبة dome	
qobbarah *n.* قبرة lark	
qobbah *n.* قبح ugliness	
qoblah *n.* قبلة kiss	
qobool *n.* قبول acceptance	

R

qobtaan *n.* قبطان captain	ra'awiy *adj.* رعوي pastoral
qodoman *adv.* قدماً forth	ra'd *n.* رعد thunder
qodrah *n.* قدرة capability	ra'shah *n.* رعشة jerk
qoffaaz *n.* قفاز glove	raa'i *n.* 1 راعي shepherd
qofl *n.* قفل lock	raa'i *n.* 2 راعي sponsor
qolonsowah *n.* قلنسوة hood	raabit *n.* رابط link
qomaamah *n.* قمامة garbage	raabitah *n.* رابطة association
qomrah *n.* قمرة cabin	raadium *n.* راديوم radium
qonbolah *n.* قنبلة bomb	raafi'ah *n.* رافعة lever
qonfodh *n.* قنفذ urchin	raafid *adj.* رافد confluent
qonsol *n.* قنصل ambassador	raafid *n.* رافد tributary
qoot *n.* قوت staple	raahah *n.* راحة comfort
qorb *prep.* قرب by	raahib *n.* راهب monk
qorb *n.* 1 قرب proximity	raahibah *n.* راهبة nun
qorb *n.* 2 قرب closeness	raakib *n.* 1 راكب passenger
	raakib *n.* 2 راكب rider

raakid *adj.* راكد idle
raami *n.* رامٍ pitcher
raasib *n.* راسب sediment
raatib *n.* راتب salary
raaui' *adj.* رائع fabulous
raauid *n.* 1 رائد major
raauid *n.* 2 رائد pioneer
raauihah *n.* رائحة fragrance
raauij *adj.* رائج salable
raawi *n.* راوي narrator
raayah *n.* راية banner
rabee' *n.* ربيع spring
rabee'iy *adj.* ربيعي vernal
rad *n.* رد reply
radee' *n.* رضيع infant
radeeu *adj.* رَديء nasty
radhaadh *n.* رذاذ drizzle
radheelah *n.* رَذيلَه vice
raf *n.* رف shelf
raf' *n.* رفع uplift
rafaahiyah *n.* رفاهِيَه welfare
rafd *n.* رفض refusal
rafee' *adj.* رفيع thin
rafeeq *n.* رفيق companion
rafrafah *n.* رفرفة flutter
raghbah *n.* رغبة desire
ragheef *n.* رغيف loaf
raghm *n.* رغم spite
raghwah *n.* رغوة foam
rahaan *n.* رهان bet
rahbanah *n.* رهبنة monasticism
raheeb *adj.* رهيب terrible
raheel *n.* رحيل departure
raheem *adj.* رحيم merciful
raheenah *n.* رهينة hostage

raheeq *n.* رحيق nectar
rahhaalah *n.* رحالة voyager
rahib *adj.* رحب vast
rahm *n.* رحم womb
rahmah *n.* رحمة mercy
raj'iy *adj.* رجعي backward
rajol *n.* رجل man
rakd *n.* ركض run
rakeek *adj.* ركيك prosaic
rakeezah *n.* ركيزة stilt
rakhees *adj.* رخيص cheap
raklah *n.* ركلة kick
ramaad *n.* رماد ash
ramaadiy *adj.* رمادي grey
raml *n.* رمل sand
ramliy *adj.* رملي sandy
rammah *n.* رماح lancer
ramshah *n.* رمشة flicker
ramyah *n.* رمية throw
ramz *n.* رمز symbol
ramziy *adj.* رمزي symbolic
ramziyyah *n.* رمزية symbolism
rannan *adj.* رنّان resonant
raqaabah *n.* رقابة censorship
raqam *n.* رقم digit
raqamiy *adj.* رقمي numeral
raqeeb *n.* 1 رقيب censor
raqeeb *n.* 2 رقيب sergeant
raqeeq *adj.* رقيق thin
raqsah *n.* رقصة dance
rarbat *n.* مربط stall
rasaas *n.* رصاص lead
rasaasah *n.* رصاصة bullet
rasaasiy *adj.* رصاصي leaden
raseef *n.* رصيف pavement

raseen adj. رصين solemn
rashaaqah n. رشاقة agility
rasheeq adj. رشيق agile
rashfah n. رشفة sip
rashq n. رشُق splash
rashq n. رقش mottle
rashwah n. رشوة bribe
rasm n. 1 رسم fee
rasm n. 2 رسم painting
rasmah n. رسمة drawing
rasmiy adj. رسمي formal
rasmiyyan adv. رسمياً officially
rasool n. رسول messenger
rassaam n. رسام painter
rataabah n. رتابة monotony
rataanah n. رطانة jargon
rateeb adj. رتيب monotonous
rath adj. رث shabby
ratib adj. رطب damp
ratm n. رطم thump
rauees adj. رئيس chief
rauees n. رئيس master
raueesiy adj. رئيسي main
rauoof adj. رؤوف gracious
rauoom adj. رؤوم motherly
raus n. 1 رأس cape
raus n. 2 رأس head
rausan adv. رأسا straight
rausomaaliy n. رأسمالي capitalist
rauy n. رأي opinion
raw'ah n. روعة splendour
rawaaqiy n. رواقي stoic
rawath n. روث dung
ray n. ري irrigation
raythama prep. ريثما while

razaanah n. رزانة sobriety
razeen adj. رزين sedate
rdiy adj. أرضي earthly
reefiy adj. ريفي rural
reehaan n. ريحان basil
reeshah n. ريشة feather
ri'aayah n. رعاية care
riba n. ربا usury
ribaat n. رباط bond
ribh n. 1 ربح profit
ribh n. 2 ربح win
rida n. رضى content
rida n. رداء robe
rihaan n. رهان wager
rihlah n. رحلة journey
rimaahah n. رماحة gallop
risaalah n. رسالة letter
rithaau n. رثاء lamentation
riuaasiy adj. رئاسي presidential
riuah n. رئة lung
riwaaq n. رواق arcade
riwaauiy n. روائي novelist
riwaayah n. رواية novel
riyaadah n. رياضة sport
riyaadiy n. رياضي athlete
riyaadiy adj. 1 رياضي athletic
riyaadiy adj. 2 رياضي mathematical
riyaadiy n. رياضي mathematician
riyaah n. رياح wind
rizq n. رزق livelihood
rizq n. رزق sustenance
ro'b n. رعب horror
rob' n. ربع quarter
robbaan n. ربان skipper

robbama *adv.* ربما perhaps
rodf *n.* ردف buttock
rodhah *n.* ردهة lobby
roghma *conj.* رغم albeit
rojhaan *n.* رجحان
preponderance
rojoolah *n.* رجولة manhood
rojooliy *adj.* رجولي manly
rokaaz *n.* ركاز ore
rokbah *n.* ركبة knee
rokhaam *n.* رخام marble
rokn *n.* ركن corner
rokoob *n.* ركوب ride
rokood *adj.* ركود slack
rokood *n.* ركود recession
romaansiy *adj.* رومانسي romantic
romatizm *n.* روماتيزم rheumatism
romatizmiy *adj.* روماتيزمي
rheumatic
romh *n.* رمح spear
romsh *n.* رمش eyelash
roobil *n.* روبل rouble
roobyah *n.* روبية rupee
rooh *n.* روح soul
rooh *n.* روح spirit
roohaaniy *adj.* روحاني spiritual
roohaaniy *n.* روحاني spiritualist
roohaaniyyah *n.* روحانية
spirituality
rooteen *n.* روتين rote
rooteen *n.* روتين routine
rooteeniy *adj.* روتيني routine
roq'ah *n.* رقعة patch
roqiy *n.* رقي apotheosis
rosgh *n.* رسغ wrist

rosghiy *adj.* رسغي carpal
rosoom *n.* رسوم toll
rotoobah *n.* رطوبة humidity
rouyah *n.* رؤية vision

S

sa'aadah *n.* 1 سعادة Excellency
sa'aadah *n.* 2 سعادة happiness
sa'b *adj.* صعب difficult
sa'eed *adj.* سعيد happy
sa'oot *n.* سعوط snuff
sa'w *n.* صغو wren
saa'ah *n.* 1 ساعة clock
saa'ah *n.* 2 ساعة hour
saa'i *n.* ساعي courier
saa'id *n.* ساعد forearm
saabi' *adj.* سابع seventh
saabiq *n.* سابق antecedent
saabiq *adj.* سابق previous
saabiqah *n.* سابقة precedent
saabiqan *adv.* سابقاً formerly
saaboon *n.* صابون soap
saabooniy *adj.* صابوني soapy
saadhaj *adj.* ساذج naive
saadiq *adj.* صادق honest
saadis *adj.* سادس sixth
saadiso 'ashar *adj.* سادس عشر
sixteenth
saadiy *n.* سادي sadist
saadiyyah *n.* سادية sadism
saafi *n.* صاف net
saafi *adj.* صاف net

saahah *n.* ساحة yard
saahil *n.* ساحل coast
saahiliy *adj.* ساحلي littoral
saahir *n.* ساحر magician
saahir *adj.* ساهر watchful
saahirah *n.* ساحرة witch
saajid *adj.* ساجد prostrate
saakhib *adj.* صاخب noisy
saakhir *n.* ساخر cynic
saakhir *adj.* ساخر sarcastic
saakhit *adj.* ساخط indignant
saakin *adj.* ساكِن static
saakin *n.* ساكِن occupant
saalib *adj.* سالب minus
saalif *prep.* سالف afore
saalih *n.* صالح favour
saalih *adj.* 1 صالح righteous
saalih *adj.* 2 صالح valid
saaloon *n.* صالون saloon
saam *adj.* سام poisonous
saami *adj.* سامي sublime
saamit *adj.* صامت mute
saani' *n.* صانع manufacturer
saaq *n.* 1 ساق leg
saaq *n.* 2 ساق stalk
saarim *adj.* صارم stern
saariyah *n.* سارية mast
saarookh *n.* صاروخ rocket
saauid *adj.* سائد prevalent
saauigh *adj.* سائغ palatable
saauigh *n.* صائغ goldsmith
saauih *n.* سائح tourist
saauil *n.* سائل fluid
saauil *adj.* سائل liquid
saauiq *n.* سائق driver

saauit *n.* صائت vowel
sab *n.* صب casting
sab'ah *n.* 1 سبعة seven
sab'ah *n.* 2 سبعة lioness
sab'ah *adj.* سبعة seven
sab'ato 'ashar *n.,* a سبعةعشر seventeen
sab'oon *n.,* a سبعون seventy
sabaah *n.* صباح morning
sabaanikh *n.* سبانخ spinach
sabab *n.* سبب cause
sababiy *adj.* سببي causal
sababiyyah *n.* سببية causality
sabbaabah *n.* سبابة forefinger
sabbaah *n.* سبّاح swimmer
sabbaar *n.* صبّار cactus
sabeel *n.* سبيل avenue
sabghah *n.* صبغة dye
sabiy *n.* صبي boy
saboor *adj.* صبور patient
sabr *n.* صبر patience
sad *n.* سد dam
sad *n.* صد repulse
sada *n.* صدى echo
sada' *n.* صدع rift
sadaad *n.* سداد repayment
sadad *n.* صدد regard
sadafah *n.* صدفة shell
sadaqah *n.* صدقة charity
sadau *n.* صدأ rust
saddaadah *n.* سدّادة cork
sadeed *n.* صديد pus
sadeem *n.* سديم nebula
sadeeq *n.* صديق friend
sadeeqah *n.* صديقة girl-friend

sadgh n. صَدْغ temple
sadhaajah n. سذاجة naivety
sadiu adj. صدئ rusty
sadmah n. صدمة shock
sadr n. صدر chest
saf n. 1 صف class
saf n. 2 صف row
saf'ah n. صفعة slap
safaarah n. سفارة embassy
safaau n. صفاء serenity
safar n. سفر travel
safeef n. صفيف array
safeehah n. 1 صَفيحَة plate
safeehah n. 2 صفيحة tin
safeenah n. سفينة ship
saffaah n. سفاح thug
saffaarah n. صفارة whistle
safhah n. صفحة page
safqah n. صفقة bargain
safsaaf n. صفصاف willow
sagheer n. صغير little
sagheer adj. صغير small
sahaabah n. سحابة cloud
sahaabah n. صحابة kith
sahaafah n. صحافة journalism
sahafiy n. صحافي journalist
sahb n. 1 سحب draw
sahb n. 2 سحب pull
sahb n. سَهْب steppe
saheefah n. صحيفة journal
saheeh adv. صحيح aright
saheeh adj. صحيح correct
saheel n. صهيل neigh
saheeq adj. سحيق immemorial
sahhaab n. سَحّاب zipper

sahl adj. سهل easy
sahl n. سهل plain
sahm n. 1 سهم arrow
sahm n. 2 سهم share
sahn n. صحن plate
sahraau n. صحراء desert
sajeen n. سجين prisoner
sajjaan n. سجان jailer
sak n. صك cheque
sakan n. سكن dwelling
sakeer n. سكري diabetes
sakeer n. سكير drunkard
sakhaau n. سخاء largesse
sakhab n. صخب uproar
sakheef adj. سخيف ridiculous
sakhiy adj. سخي generous
sakhrah n. صخرة rock
sakht n. سخط indignation
sakraan adj. سكران tipsy
saktah n. سكتة stroke
salaabah n. صَلابة tone
salaah n. صلاة prayer
salaah n. صلاح goodness
salaam n. سلام peace
salaamah n. 1 سلامة integrity
salaamah n. 2 سلامة safety
salaf n. سلف ancestor
salafan adv. سلفاً beforehand
salafiy adj. سلفي ancestral
salatah n. سلطة salad
salb adj. 1 صلب cast-iron
salb adj. 2 صلب hard
salb n. صلب solid
salbiy n. سلبي negative
salbiy adj. سلبي passive

salbiyyah *adj.* سلبية adverse
saleeb *n.* صليب cross
saleel *n.* سليل descendant
saleem *adj.* سليم intact
salis *adj.* سلس smooth
sallah *n.* سلة basket
salq *n.* سلق boil
salsah *n.* صلصة sauce
salsalah *n.* صلصلة clink
saltaa'oon *n.* سلطعون crab
sama'iyyah *adj.* سمعية auditive
samaad *n.* سماد compost
samaah *n.* سماح allowance
samaau *n.* سماء sky
samaawiy *adj.* سماوي celestial
samak *n.* سمك fish
sameek *adj.* سميك thick
samkariy *n.* سمكري plumber
sammaam *n.* صمام valve
sammaan *n.* سمّان quail
sammoor *n.* سمور beaver
samn *n.* سمن margarine
samt *n.* صمت silence
san'ah *n.* صنعة workmanship
sanah *n.* سنة year
sanawbar *n.* صنوبر pine
sanawiy *adj.* سنوي annual
sandal *n.* صندل sandal
sandooq *n.* صندوق box
sanono *n.* سنونو sparrow
saqee' *n.* صقيع frost
saqeefah *n.* سقيفة shed
saqeem *adj.* سقيم puny
saqf *n.* سقف ceiling
saqqaalah *n.* سقالة scaffold

saqr *n.* صقر hawk
sara' *n.* صرع epilepsy
saraab *n.* سراب mirage
saraahah *n.* صراحة frankness
saraamah *n.* صرامة rigour
sarataan *n.* سرطان cancer
sarb *n.* سرب swarm
sardiy *adj.* سردي narrative
saree' *adv.* سريع fast
saree' *adj.* سريع quick
sareeh *adj.* صريح blunt
sareeh *adv.* صريح outright
sareer *n.* سرير bed
sareer *n.* صرير creak
sarf *n.* صرف drainage
sarh *n.* صرح edifice
sariqah *n.* سرقة theft
sariyyah *n.* سريّه squadron
sarj *n.* سرج saddle
sarkhah *n.* صرخة scream
sarnamah *n.* سرنمة somnambulism
sarraau *n.* سراء weal
sarsoor *n.* صرصور cockroach
sarw *n.* سرو cypress
sat hiy *adj.* 1 سطحي superficial
sat hiy *adj.* 2 سطحي facile
sat hiyyah *n.* سطحية superficiality
sath *n.* 1 سطح surface
sath *n.* 2 سطح ceiling
satw *n.* سطو burglary
sawaad *n.* سواد melancholia
sawaau *adv.* سواء alike
sawaau *conj.* سواء whether

sawfa v. سوف will	sha'eer n. شعير barley
sawlajaan n. صولجان wand	sha'riyyah n. شعرية lattice
sawma'ah n. صومعة hermitage	sha'wadhah n. شعوذة witchery
sawt n. سوط whip	shaa'ir n. شاعر poet
sawt n. 1 صوت sound	shaa'irah n. شاعرة poetess
sawt n. 2 صوت voice	shaa'iriy adj. شاعري poetic
sawt n. 3 صوت vote	shaa'iriyyah n. شاعرية poesy
sawtiy adj. 1 صوتي acoustic	shaab adj. شاب young
sawtiy adj. 2 صوتي phonetic	shaab n. شاب youngster
sawtiyyaat n. صوتيات acoustics	shaadh adj. شاذ anomalous
sayalaan n. سيلان trickle	shaagher adj. شاغر vacant
sayd n. صيد game	shaagher n. شاغر vacancy
saydaliyyah n. صيدلي chemist	shaahib adj. شاحب pale
saydaliyyah n. صيدلية pharmacy	shaahid n. شاهد witness
sayf n. سيف sword	shaahinah n. شاحنة truck
sayf n. صيف summer	shaakir adj. شاكر thankful
sayfiy adj. صيفي aestival	shaal n. شال shawl
sayhah n. صيحة shout	shaambo n. شامبو shampoo
sayl n. سيل torrent	shaamil adj. شامل inclusive
saymaau n. سيماء countenance	shaaq adj. شاق laborious
saytarah n. سيطره control	shaarah n. شارة badge
sayyaad n. صياد hunter	shaari' n. شارع street
sayyarah n. سيارة car	shaarib n. شارب moustache
sayyid n. سيد mister	shaashah n. شاشة monitor
sayyidah n. سيدة lady	shaatiu n. شاطئ beach
sayyiu adj. سيئ bad	shaaui' adj. شائع stock
sayyiuah n. سيئة disadvantage	shaauik adj. شائك barbed
seeghah n. صيغة formula	shaauin adj. شائن nefarious
seejaar n. سيجار cigar	shaay n. شاي tea
seejaarah n. سيجارة cigarette	shabaab n. شباب youth
seeniyyah n. صينية tray	shabah n. شبح ghost
seerah n. سيرة biography	shabah n. شبه likeness
sha'ar n. شعر hair	shabaka n. 1 شبكة network
sha'biy adj. شعبي popular	shabakah n. 2 شبكة web
sha'biyyah n. شعبية popularity	shabakiy adj. شبكي webby

shabakiyyah *n.* شبكية retina
shabeeh *n.* شَبيه like
shabiq *adj.* شبق lustful
shaddiyyah *n.* شظية splinter
shadeed *adj.* شديد intense
shafaq *n.* شفق twilight
shafaqah *n.* شفقة pity
shafawiy *adj.* 1 شفوي oral
shafawiy *adj.* 2 شفوي verbal
shafawiyyan *adv.* 1 شفوياً orally
shafawiyyan *adv.* 2 شفويًا verbally
shaffaaf *adj.* شفاف transparent
shafrah *n.* شفرة blade
shaghab *n.* شغب riot
shahaadah *n.* 1 شهادة certificate
shahaadah *n.* 2 شهادة testimony
shahaamah *n.* شهامة chivalry
shaheed *n.* شهيد martyr
shaheeh *adj.* شحيح scarce
shahiyyah *n.* شهية appetite
shahm *n.* شحم grease
shahm *adj.* شهم chivalrous
shahmah *n.* شحمة lobe
shahn *n.* شحن freight
shahnah *n.* شحنة shipment
shahr *n.* شهر month
shahriyyan *adv.* شهريا monthly
shahriyyan *adj.* شهرياً monthly
shahwaaniy *n.* شهواني sensualist
shahwaaniy *adj.* شهواني voluptuous
shahwaaniyyah *n.* شهوانية sensuality
shahwah *n.* شهوة lust

shaikhookhah *n.* شيخوخة senility
shaitaaniy *adj.* شيطاني satanic
shajaa'ah *n.* شجاعة bravery
shajarah *n.* شجرة tree
shajiy *adj.* شجي melodious
shak *n.* شك scepticism
shakheer *n.* شخير snore
shakhs *n.* شخص person
shakhsiy *adj.* شخصي personal
shakhsiyyah *n.* 1 شخصية character
shakhsiyyah *n.* 2 شخصية personality
shakis *adj.* شكس petulant
shakkaak *n.* شكّاك sceptic
shakl *n.* شكل shape
shakwa *n.* شكوى complaint
shalal *n.* شلل paralysis
shallaal *n.* شلال waterfall
sham' *n.* شمع wax
sham'ah *n.* شمعة candle
shamaal *n.* شمال north
shamaalan *adv.* شَمالا northerly
shamaaliy *adj.* شمالي northern
shammaam *n.* شمام melon
shammaas *n.* شمّاس deacon
shams *n.* شمس sun
shamsiy *adj.* شمسي solar
shanee' *adj.* شنيع heinous
shaq *n.* شق slit
shaqeeq *n.* شقيق brother
shaqeeqah *n.* 1 شقيقة sister
shaqeeqah *n.* 2 شقيقة migraine
shaqlabah *n.* شَقْلَبَه somersault
shaqqah *n.* شقة apartment

shar *n.* شر evil

shar'iy *adj.* شرعي legitimate

shar'iyyah *n.* شرعية legitimacy

sharaab *n.* شراب beverage

sharaakah *n.* شراكة partnership

sharaakiy *adj.* شراكي corporate

sharaarah *n.* شرارة spark

sharaf *n.* شرف honour

sharah *n.* شره glutton

sharee'ah *n.* شريعة canon

shareehah·*n.* 1 شريحة slide

shareehah *n.* 2 شريحة slice

shareek *n.* شريك partner

shareet *n.* 1 شريط strip

shareet *n.* 2 شريط tape

shareetiy *adj.* شريطي lacy

sharih *adj.* شره voracious

sharikah *n.* شركة company

sharis *adj.* شرس ferocious

sharj *n.* شرج anus

sharjiy *adj.* شرجي anal

shark *n.* شرك pitfall

sharq *n.* شرق east

sharqan *adv.* شرقاً east

sharqiy *adj.* 1 شرقي eastern

sharqiy *adj.* 2 شرقي oriental

shart *n.* شرط condition

shartiy *n.* شرطي prerequisite

sharwah *n.* شروة buy

shatawiy *adj.* شتوي wintry

shateerah *n.* شطيرة sandwich

shawk *n.* شوك thistle

shawkah *n.* شوكة thorn

shawq *n.* شوق longing

shawt *n.* شَوط run

shaykh *n.* شيخ sheikh

shaytaan *n.* شيطان devil

shayu *pron.* شيء something

shayu *n.* شيء thing

shayuan *adv.* شيءا something

shbaat *n.* شباط February

sheefrah *n.* شيفرة cipher

sheek *n.* شيك gallant

sheet *n.* شيط scorch

shi'aar *n.* شعار emblem

shi'r *n.* شعر poetry

shibl *n.* شبل cub

shibshib *n.* شبشب slipper

shifaau *n.* شفاء recovery

shiffah *n.* شفة lip

shijaar *n.* شجار quarrel

shilin *n.* شلن shilling

shiqaaq *n.* شقاق schism

shiraa' *n.* شراع sail

shiraak *n. pl.* شراك toils

shiraau *n.* شراء purchase

shirreer *adj.* شرير evil

shiryaan *n.* شريان artery

shitaau *n.* شتاء winter

shitaranj *n.* شطرنج chess

shiwaau *n.* شواء roast

sho'aa' *n.* شعاع beam

sho'lah *n.* شعلة torch

sho'oor *n.* شعور sensation

shodhoodh *n.* شذوذ anomaly

shohrah *n.* شهرة fame

shojaa' *adj.* شجاع brave

shojayrah *n.* شجيرة sapling

shokran *n.* شكراً thanks

shorb *n.* شرب drink

shorfah *n.* شرفة terrace
shortah *n.* شرطة police
shortiy *n.* شرطي policeman
shoum *n.* شؤم nemesis
shoyoo'iy *n.* شيوعي communist
shoyoo'iyyah *n.* شيوعية communism
si'r *n.* سعر price
sibaahah *n.* سباحة swim
sibaaq *n.* سباق race
sibyaaniy *adj.* صِبياني juvenile
sidq *n.* صدق sincerity
sifah *n.* صفة facet
sifr *n.* صفر zero
sighar *adv.* صغر smallness
sihhah *n.* 1 صحة health
sihhah *n.* 2 صحة validity
sihhiy *adj.* 1 صحي healthy
sihhiy *adj.* 2 صحي hygienic
sihliyyah *n.* سحلية lizard
sihr *n.* سحر charm
sihr *n.* سحر sorcery
sihreej *n.* صِهريج tank
sihriy *adj.* سحري magical
sijil *n.* سجل record
sijjaadah *n.* سجادة carpet
sijn *n.* سجن jail
sikkeen *n.* سكين knife
sil'ah *n.* سلعة commodity
silaah *n.* سلاح weapon
silah *n.* صلة connection
silk *n.* سلك wire
silmiy *adj.* سلمي peaceful
silsaal *n.* صلصال clay
silsilah *n.* 1 سلسلة chain

silsilah *n.* 2 سلسلة series
simaagh *n.* صملاخ cerumen
simah *n.* سمة attribute
simfooniyyah *n.* سمفونية symphony
simsaar *n.* سمسار jobber
sin *n.* سن tooth
sinaa'ah *n.* صناعة industry
sinaa'iy *adj.* صناعي industrial
sinator *n.* سناتور senator
sindaan *n.* سندان anvil
sindiyaan *n.* سنديان oak
sinjaab *n.* سنجاب squirrel
sinnar *n.* صِنّار plane
sint *n.* سنت cent
sir *n.* سر secret
siraa' *n.* صراع conflict
sirk *n.* سيرك circus
sirriy *adj.* سري confidential
sirriyyah *n.* سرية secrecy
sitaarah *n.* ستارة curtain
sittah *n., a.* ستة six
sitto 'ashrah *n., a.* ستعشرة sixteen
sittoon *n., a.* ستّون sixty
siwaar *n.* سوار bracelet
siyaadah *n.* سيادة supremacy
siyaah *n.* صياح hoot
siyaahah *n.* سياحة tourism
siyaaj *n.* سياج fence
siyaam *n.* صيام fast
siyaanah *n.* صيانة maintenance
siyaaq *n.* سياق context
siyaasah *n.* سياسة policy
siyaasiy *adj.* سياسي political

siyaasiy *n.* سياسي politician
skootir *n.* سكوتر scooter
smaau *n.* سماء sky
smaawiy *adj.* سماوي heavenly
so'aal *n.* سعال cough
so'oobah *n.* صعوبة difficulty
so'ood *n.* صعود ascent
so'oodan *adv.* صعودًا upwards
sobaat *n.* سبات hibernation
sodaa' *n.* صداع headache
sodhj *n.* سذج provincialism
sofliy *adj.* سفلي underneath
sohoolah *n.* سهولة ease
sojood *n.* سجود prostration
sokhaam *n.* سخام soot
sokhf *n.* سخف absurdity
sokhriyah *n.* 1 سخرية irony
sokhriyah *n.* 2 سخرية sarcasm
sokkaan *n.* سكان population
sokkar *n.* سكّر sugar
sokkareen *n.* سكرين saccharin
sokkariy *adj.* 1 سكري sugary
sokkariy *adj.* 2 سكري saccharine
sokoon *n.* سكون stillness
solaalah *n.* 1 سلالة dynasty
solaalah *n.* 2 سلالة strain
solhofaah *n.* سلحفاة tortoise
sollam *n.* سلم ladder
solook *n.* سلوك behaviour
soltaan *n.* سلطان dominion
soltah *n.* سلطة authority
som *n.* سم poison
som'ah *n.* سمعة reputation
somow *n.* 1 سمو eminence
somow *n.* 2 سمو Highness

son' *n.* صنع make
sonboor *n.* صنبور tap
sonnaarah *n.* صنّارة fishhook
soobirmaan *n.* سوبرمان superman
soof *n.* صوف wool
soofiy *n.* صوفي sophist
soofiy *adj.* 1 صوفي mystic
soofiy *n.* 1 صوفي mystic
soofiy *adj.* 2 صوفي woollen
soofiy *n.* 2 صوفي woollen
sooq *n.* سوق market
sooqiy *adj.* سوقي vulgar
sooqiyyah *n.* سوقيّه vulgarity
soorah *n.* صورة photograph
soosah *n.* سوسة weevil
soou *adv.* سوء ill
soqoot *n.* سقوط downfall
sor'ah *n.* سرعة speed
sorwaal n. سروال pantaloon
sotrah n. سترة sweater
souaal *n.* سؤال question
sowariy *adj.* 1 صوري photographic
sowariy *adj.* 2 ضُوَري mock
stoodio *n.* ستوديو studio
sweesriy *adj.* سويسري Swiss

T

ta'aadol *n.* تعادل draw
ta'aamol *n.* تعامل dealing
ta'aatof *n.* تعاطف sympathy
ta'aawon *n.* تعاون co-operation
ta'aawoniy *adj.* تعاوني co-operative

ta'aayosh *n.* تعايش co-existence	taa'ah *n.* طاعة obedience
ta'ab *n.* تعب fatigue	taa'oon *adj.* طاعون plague
ta'addod *n.* تعدد multitude	taabi' *n.* تابع subordinate
ta'addodiyyah *n.* تعددية multiplicity	taabi' *n.* 1 طابع stamp
ta'ahhod *n.* تعهد pledge	taabi' *n.* 2 طابع typist
ta'ajjob *n.* تعجّب exclamation	taabi'ah *n.* طابعة printer
ta'allom *n.* تعلم learning	taabil *n.* تابل spice
ta'aqqol *n.* تعقّل prudence	taabiq *n.* طابق floor
ta'arrof *n.* تعرف identification	taaboor *n.* طابور queue
ta'arroq *n.* تعرّق perspiration	taaboot *n.* تابوت cist
ta'assob *n.* تعصب intolerance	taafih *adj.* تافه insignificant
ta'assofiy *adj.* تعسفي arbitrary	taaghiyah *n.* طاغية tyrant
ta'athor *n.* تعثر stumble	taahir *adj.* طاهر saintly
ta'aththor *n.* تعثّر tumble	taahoonah *n.* 1 طاحونة grinder
ta'beer *n.* تعبير expression	taahoonah *n.* 2 طاحونة mill
ta'deel *n.* تعديل adjustment	taaj *n.* تاج crown
ta'deel *n.* تعديل modification	taajir *n.* تاجر merchant
ta'dheeb *n.* تعذيب torture	taalib *n.* طالب student
ta'ees *adj.* تعيس unhappy	taam *adj.* تام crass
ta'leem *n.* تعليم education	taaqah *n.* طاقة energy
ta'leemaat *n.* تعليمات instruction	taaqam *n.* طاقم crew
ta'leemiy *adj.* تعليمي educational	taareekh *n.* 1 تاريخ date
ta'leeq *n.* 1 تعليق commentary	taareekh *n.* 2 تاريخ history
ta'leeq *n.* 2 تعليق suspension	taareekhiy *adj.* تاريخي historical
ta'meem *n.* تعميم circulation	taarid *adj.* طارد repellent
ta'nah *n.* طعنة stab	taariu *n.* طارئ emergency
ta'neef *n.* تعنيف tirade	taauib *adj.* تائب repentant
ta'qeed *n.* تعقيد sophistication	taauifah *n.* طائفة sect
ta'qeed *n.* تعقيد complication	taauifiy *adj.* طائفي sectarian
ta'qeem *n.* تعقيم sterilization	taauirah *n.* طائرة plane
ta'reef *n.* تعريف definition	taauish *adj.* طائش mindless
ta'weed *n.* تعويض compensation	taawilah *n.* طاولة table
ta'zeez *n.* تعزيز reinforcement	taawoos *n.* طاووس peacock
ta'ziyah *n.* تعزية condolence	taazaj *adj.* طازج fresh
	tab' *n.* طبع reprint

tab'ah *n.* طبعة edition

taba'iyyah *n.* تبعية subordination

tabaahi *n.* تباه pomposity

tabaayon *n.* تباين contrast

tabanni *n.* تبنّي adoption

tabaq *n.* طبق dish

tabaqah *n.* 1 طبقة caste

tabaqah *n.* 2 طبقة layer

tabar'om *n.* تبرعم germination

tabartokh *n.* تبختر strut

tabassor *n.* تبصر insight

tabattol *n.* تبتل celibacy

tabawwol *n.* تبول urination

tabbaakh *n.* طبّاخ cook

tabdeel *n.* تَبديل permutation

tabdheer *n.* تبذير spendthrift

tabee'ah *n.* طبيعة nature

tabee'iy *adj.* طبيعي natural

tabee'iy *n.* طبيعي naturalist

tabeeb *n.* 1 طبيب doctor

tabeeb *n.* 2 طبيب physician

tabjeel *n.* تبجيل reverence

tabjeeliy *adj.* تبجيلي reverential

tabl *n.* طبل drum

tabreed *n.* تبريد refrigeration

tabriuah *n.* تبرئة vindication

tabseet *n.* تبسيط simplification

tabweeb *n.* تبويب tabulation

tabyeed *n.* تبييض whitewash

tad hiyah *n.* تضحية sacrifice

tadaakhol *n.* تداخل overlap

tadaamon *n.* تضامن solidarity

tadaarees *n.* تضاريس topography

tadaareesiy *adj.* تضاريسي topographical

tadaauol *n.* تضاؤل wane

tadaawol *n.* 1 تداول deliberation

tadaawol *n.* 2 تداول transaction

tadaffoq *n.* تدفق flow

tadakhkhol *n.* تدخل interference

tadakhkhom *n.* تضخم inflation

tadanni *n.* تدنّي inferiority

tadarroj *n.* تدرج gradation

tadhakkor *n.* تذكّر reminiscence

tadhammor *n.* تذمر murmur

tadhkarah *n.* تذكرة ticket

tadhkeer *n.* تذكير reminder

tadkheem *n.* تضخيم amplification

tadleek *n.* تدليك massage

tadmeen *n.* تضمين inclusion

tadmeer *n.* تدمير destruction

tadnees *n.* تدنيس sacrilege

tadqeeq *n.* تدقيق scrutiny

tadreeb *n.* تدريب training

tadreejiy *adj.* تدريجي gradual

tadrees *adj.* تدريسي tutorial

tadween *n.* تدوين notation

tadyeeq *n.* تضيق stricture

tafaa'ol *n.* تفاعل reaction

tafaahah *n.* تفاهة insignificance

tafaahom *n.* تفاهم amity

tafaani *n.* تفان dedication

tafaauol *n.* تفاؤل optimism

tafaawod *n.* تفاوض negotiation

tafaawot *n.* تفاوت disparity

tafah *adj.* طفح rash

tafahhos *n.* تفحّص check

tafajjor *n.* تفجر spurt

tafarrod *n.* تفرد singularity

tafawwoq *n.* تفوّق superiority

tafdeel *n.* تفضيل preference
tafdeeliy *adj.* تفضيلي preferential
tafeef *adj.* طفيف slight
tafrah *n.* 1 طفرة leap
tafrah *n.* 2 طفرة mutation
tafseel *n.* تفصيل detail
tafseeliy *adj.* تفصيلي elaborate
tafseer *n.* تفسير explanation
tafteesh *n.* تفتيش inspection
tafw *n.* طفو buoyancy
tafweed *n.* تفويض mandate
taghayyob *n.* تغيب absence
taghdhiyah *n.* تغذية nutrition
taghreed *n.* تغريد twitter
taghyeer *n.* تغيير change
tahaalof *n.* تحالف coalition
tahaarah *n.* طهارة purgation
tahaayol *n.* تحايل trickery
tahabbob *n.* تحبب endearment
tahaddi *n.* تحد challenge
tahaddor *n.* تحضّر urbanity
tahaffodd *n.* تحفظ reticence
tahajjom *n.* تهجّم sally
tahakkom *n.* تحكّم control
tahakkom *n.* تهكم taunt
tahakkomiy *adj.* تهكمي sardonic
tahallol *n.* تحلل decomposition
tahammol *n.* تحمّل toleration
tahaqqoq *n.* تحقق verification
taharrob *n.* تهرّب evasion
tahasson *n.* تحسن improvement
tahattom *n.* تحطم crash
tahawwol *n.* تحول transformation
tahawwor *n.* تهور imprudence

tahayyoj *n.* تهيج irritation
tahayyoz *n.* تحيز partiality
tahayyoz *n.* تحيز prejudice
tahdeed *n.* تهديد threat
tahdeeq *n.* تحديق glare
tahdeeriy *adj.* تحضيري preparatory
tahdeeth *n.* تحديث modernization
tahdheer *n.* تحذير warning
taheen *n.* طحين flour
tahhaan *n.* طحان miller
tahiyyah *n.* تحية salute
tahkeem *n.* تحكيم arbitration
tahleel *n.* تحليل analysis
tahleeliy *adj.* تحليلي analytical
tahmil *v.* تحمل conceive
tahniuah *n.* تهنئة congratulation
tahqeeq *n.* 1 تحقيق fulfilment
tahqeeq *n.* 2 تحقيق investigation
tahreed *n.* تحريض instigation
tahreer *n.* 1 تحرير liberation
tahreer *n.* 2 تحرير release
tahreeriy *adj.* تحريري editorial
tahseen *n.* تحسين refinement
taht *adv.* تحت below
taht *prep.* تحت under
taht *adv.* تحت underneath
tahweedah *n.* تهويدة lullaby
tahweel *n.* تحويل conversion
tahwiyah *n.* تهوية ventilation
taj'eed *n.* تجعيد crimp
taja"od *n.* تجعد wrinkle
tajaahol *n.* تجاهل disregard
tajaawoz *n.* 1 تجاوز excess
tajaawoz *n.* 2 تجاوز trespass

tajaddod *n.* تجدّد regeneration	**takhreeb** *n.* تخريب sabotage
tajammo' *n.* تجمع rally	**takhreem** *n.* تخريم lace
tajannob *n.* تجنب avoidance	**takhsees** *n.* تخصيص allocation
tajashshou *n.* تجشّؤ belch	**takhteet** *n.* تخطيط calligraphy
tajassod *n.* تجسد incarnation	**takhweef** *n.* تخويف intimidation
tajawwol *n.* تجول stroll	**takhweel** *n.* تخويل approbation
tajdeed *n.* تجديد renewal	**takhzeen** *n.* تخزين storage
tajfeef *n.* تجفيف arefaction	**taklifah** *n.* تكلفة cost
tajmeeliy *adj.* تجميلي cosmetic	**takmeeliy** *adj.* تكميلي supplementary
tajneed *n.* تجنيد draft	
tajreebiy *adj.* تَجْريبي experimental	**takmilah** *n.* تكملة supplement
	taknees *n.* تكنيس sweep
tajreed *n.* تجريد abstraction	**taktakah** *n.* تكتكة tick
tajreediy *adj.* تجريدي abstract	**tal** *n.* تل hill
tajribah *n.* 1 تجربة experience	**tala'thom** *n.* تَلَعْثُم stammer
tajribah *n.* 2 تجربة experiment	**talaa'ob** *n.* تلاعب manipulation
tajseed *n.* تجسيد embodiment	**talaamos** *n.* تلامس contact
tajweef *n.* تجويف cavity	**talaaq** *n.* طلاق divorce
tak'eebi *adj.* تكعيبي cubical	**talab** *n.* 1 طلب application
takaafou *n.* تكافؤ parity	**talab** *n.* 2 طلب request
takaathor *n.* تكاثر proliferation	**talakkou** *n.* تلكّؤ shilly-shally
takahhon *n.* تكهّن speculation	**talaulou** *n.* تلألؤ sparkle
takallof *n.* تكلّف affectation	**talawwi** *n.* تَلَوٍّ wriggle
takhabbat *n.* تخبّط shuffle	**talawwoth** *n.* تلوّث pollution
takhabbob *n.* تخبّب canter	**taleeq** *adj.* 1 طليق fluent
takhallof *n.* تخلف retardation	**taleeq** *adj.* 2 طليق free
takhassos *n.* تخصص specialization	**talfazah** *n.* تلفاز television
	talfeeq *n.* تلفيق fabrication
takhaththor *n.* تخثر curd	**talmeeh** *n.* تلميح insinuation
takhdeer *n.* تخدير anaesthesia	**talqah** *n.* طلقة shot
takhfeed *n.* تخفيض reduction	**talqeeh** *n.* تلقيح vaccination
takhfeef *n.* تخفيف mitigation	**talsam** *n.* طلسم talisman
takhlees *n.* تخليص clearance	**tama'** *adv.* طمع avidity
takhmeen *n.* تخمين guess	**tamaaman** *adv.* تماما entirely
takhmeer *n.* تخمير fermentation	**tamaathol** *n.* تماثل analogy

tamaatim *n.* طماطم tomato

tamaayol *n.* تمايل sway

tamalloq *n.* تملّق adulation

tamarrod *n.* تمرد rebellion

tamawwoj *n.* تموج ripple

tamayyoz *n.* تميز distinction

tamazzoq *n.* تمزق rupture

tameemah *n.* تميمة amulet

tamheed *n.* تمهيد prelude

tamheediy *adj.* تمهيدي preliminary

tami *n.* طمي silt

tamjeed *n.* تمجيد glorification

tammaa' *adj.* طماع avid

tamooh *n.* طموح aspirant

tamooh *adj.* طموح ambitious

tamron hindiy *n.* تمرهندي tamarind

tamtheel *n.* 1 تمثيل acting

tamtheel *n.* 2 تمثيل representation

tamweeh *n.* تمويه disguise

tamweel *n.* تمويل finance

tamyeel *n.* تمييل italics

tamyeez *n.* تمييز discrimination

tanaaddor *n.* تناظر symmetry

tanaafor *n.* تنافر repulsion

tanaafos *n.* تنافس rivalry

tanaafosiy *adj.* تنافسي competitive

tanaaqod *n.* تناقض contradiction

tanaasoq *n.* تناسق consistency

tanaawob *n.* تناوب rotation

tanaazol *n.* تنازل renunciation

tanabboh n. تنبه alertness

tanabbou *n.* تنبؤ prediction

tanaffos *n.* تنفس respiration

tanahhod *n.* تنهد sigh

tanakkor *n.* تنكر disguise

tanaqqol *n.* تنقّل mobility

tanawwo' *n.* تنوّع variation

tanddeem *n.* تنظيم polity

taneen *n.* طنين buzz

tanhiyah *n.* تنحية disqualification

tanmiyah *n.* تنمية development

tannoorah *n.* تنورة skirt

tanqeeb *n.* تنقيب excavation

tanqeeh *n.* تنقيح revision

tanqeet *n.* تنقيط punctuation

tanqiyah *n.* تنقية purification

tanseeq *n.* تنسيق co-ordination

tanweem *n.* تنويم anaesthesia

taqaa'od *n.* تقاعد retirement

taqaa'os *n.* تقاعس inaction

taqaaleed *n.* تقاليد traditions

taqaato' *n.* تقاطع junction

taqabbol *n.* تقبّل acquiescence

taqawwos *v.* تقوّس arch

taqdeem *adj.* تقدمي progressive

taqdeem *n.* تقديم submission

taqdeer *n.* 1 تقدير appreciation

taqdeer *n.* 2 تقدير estimation

taqdeeriy *adj.* تقديري tributary

taqdees *n.* تقديس sanctification

taqiy *adj.* تقي pious

taqleed *n.* 1 تقليد imitation

taqleed *n.* 2 تقليد tradition

taqleediy *adj.* تقليدي traditional

taqleem *n.* تقليم trim

taqreeb *n.* تقريب zoom

taqreeban *adv.* تقريبا nearly

taqreebiy *adj.* تقريبي approximate
taqreer *n.* تقرير report
taqs *n.* طقس rite
taqseem *n.* تقسيم division
taqsiy *adj.* 1 طقسي liturgical
taqsiy *adj.* 2 طقسي ritual
taqwa *n.* تقوى piety
taqweem *n.* تقويم calendar
taqyeed *n.* تقييد restriction
taqyeem *n.* تقييم assessment
taraabot *n.* ترابط interdependence
taraajo' *n.* تراجع abatement
taraakom *n.* تراكم accumulation
tarab *n.* طرب glee
taraddod *n.* 1 تردد frequency
taraddod *n.* 2 تردد hesitation
taraf *n.* ترف luxury
taraf *n.* طرف limb
tarahhol *n.* ترهل cutis
tarannoh *n.* ترنح stagger
tarayyof *n.* تريّف rustication
tarbeet *n.* تربيت pat
tard *n.* 1 طرد eviction
tard *n.* 2 طرد parcel
tareedah *n.* طريدَه quarry
tareeq *n.* طريق road
tareeqah *n.* طريقة way
tarh *n.* طرح subtraction
tarheeb *n.* ترحيب welcome
tarjamah *n.* ترجمة translation
tarjeeh *n.* ترجيح weightage
tarkeeb *n.* 2 تركيب installation
tarkeebah *n.* 1 تركيب composition

tarkeez *n.* 1 تركيز concentration
tarkeez *n.* 2 تركيز focus
tarkhees *n.* ترخيص licence
tarneemah *n.* ترنيمة hymn
tarqiyah *n.* تَرقِيه promotion
tarsheeh *n.* ترشيح nomination
tarteeb *n.* 1 ترتيب arrangement
tarteeb *n.* 2 ترتيب tidiness
tarweej *n.* ترويج promotion
tasaa'odiy *adj.* تصاعدي upward
tasaadom *n.* تصادم collision
tasaahol *n.* تساهل lenience
tasaahomiy *adj.* تساهمي associate
tasaamoh *n.* تسامح tolerance
tasaaro' *n.* تسارع acceleration
tasaddo' *n.* تصدّع crack
tasaffoh *n.* تصفح browse
tasalloh *n.* تسلح armament
tasalloq *n.* تسلّق climb
tasalsol *n.* 1 تسلسل hierarchy
tasalsol *n.* 2 تسلسل sequence
tasammom *n.* تسمم intoxication
tasarro' *n.* تسرع haste
tasarrob *n.* تسرب leakage
tasarrof *n.* تصرّف mannerism
tasawwof *n.* تصوف mysticism
tasawwor *n.* تصور conception
tasdeed *n.* تسديد reimbursement
tasdeeq *v.* تصديق certify
tasdeer *n.* تصدير export
tasfeeq *n.* تصفيق applause
tasfiyah *n.* تصفية liquidation
tashaaboh *n.* تشابه resemblance
tashaabok *n.* تشابك tangle
tashaauom *n.* تشاؤم pessimism

tashaawor *n.* تشاور consultation
tashabbo' *n.* تشبع saturation
tashannoj *n.* تشنج spasm
tashannojiy *adj.* تشنجي spasmodic
tasharrod *n.* تشرّد vagabond
tashawwoq *n.* تشوّق keenness
tashawwosh *n.* تشوش muddle
tashbeeh *n.* تشبيه simile
tashdeed *n.* تشديد emphasis
tasheeh *n.* تصحيح correction
tasheel *n.* تسهيل facility
tashheem *n.* تشحيم lubrication
tashheer *n.* تشهير libel
tashkeel *n.* تشكيل formation
tashkeelah *n.* تشكيلة variety
tashkhees *n.* 1 تشخيص personification
tashkhees *n.* 2 تشخيص diagnoses
tashkhees *n.* تشخيص diagnosis
tashree' *n.* تشريع legislation
tashree'iy *adj.* تشريعي legislative
tashreeh *n.* تشريح anatomy
tashreehiy *adj.* تشريحي anatomical
tashweeq *n.* تشويق suspense
tashweesh *n.* تشويش blur
tasjeel *n.* تسجيل registration
tasleeh *n.* تصليح renovation
tasleem *n.* تسليم delivery
tasliyah *n.* تسلية entertainment
tasmeem *n.* تصميم design
tasmiyah *n.* تسمية nomenclature
tasneef *n.* تصنيف classification
tasreef *n.* تصريف disposal

tasreeh *n.* تصريح permit
tasreehah *n.* تسريحة hair style
tasweer *n.* 1 تصوير photography
tasweer *n.* 2 تصوير portrayal
tasweeriy *adj.* تَصُويري pictorial
tasweet *n.* تصويت vote
taswiyah *n.* تسوية settlement
tataabo' *n.* تتابع relay
tataali *n.* تتالي cascade
tataffol *n.* تطفل intrusion
tatawwor *n.* تطور evolution
tatbee' *n.* تطبيع normalization
tatbeeq *n.* تطبيق application
tathaauob *n.* تثاءب yawn
tatimmah *n.* تتمة sequel
tatreez *n.* تطريز embroidery
tatweej *n.* تتويج coronation
tauaakol *adj.* تآكل corrosive
tauaakol *n.* تآكل erosion
taualloq *n.* تألق brilliance
tauammol *n.* تأمّل meditation
tauammoliy *adj.* تأملي meditative
tauaqlom *n.* تأقلم adaptation
tauawwoh *n.* تأوه groan
tauir *n.* طائر bird
taujeel *n.* تأجيل postponement
taukeed *n.* تأكيد confirmation
tauleeh *n.* تأليه apotheosis
taumeem *n.* تأميم nationalization
taumeen *n.* تأمين insurance
tauneeb *n.* تأنيب reprimand
tauneeb *n.* تأنيب reproof
tausees *n.* تأسيس establishment
tauseesiy *adj.* تأسيسي constituent
tautheer *n.* تأثير impact

taw'an *adv.* طوعًا voluntarily

taw'iy *adj.* طوعي voluntary

tawa'ok *n.* توعك malaise

tawaado' *n.* تواضع modesty

tawaafoq *n.* توافق concord

tawaal *prep.* طوال throughout

tawaariu *n.* طوارئ contingency

tawaasol *n.* تواصل communication

tawaatou *n.* تواطؤ collusion

tawaazi *n.* تواز parallelism

tawaazon *n.* توازن balance

tawaddod *n.* تودد courtship

tawahhoj *n.* توهج glow

tawaqqo' *n.* توقع expectation

tawaqqof *n.* توقف halt

tawarrod *n.* تورد flush

tawasso' *n.* توسع expansion

tawassol *n.* توسل entreaty

tawassot *n.* توسط mediocrity

tawattor *n.* توتر tension

tawbah *n.* توبة repentance

tawbeekh *n.* توبيخ rebuke

tawddeef *n.* توظيف recruit

tawdeeh *n.* توضيح clarification

taweel *adj.* 1 طويل long

taweel *adj.* 2 طويل tall

tawfeer *n.* توفير provision

tawheed *n.* توحيد consolidation

tawheed *n.* توحيد standardization

tawheed *n.* توحيد unification

tawjeeh *n.* توجيه guidance

tawleefah *n.* توليفة conjuncture

tawq *n.* توق yearning

tawqee' *n.* توقيع signature

tawreet *n.* توريط implication

tawriyah *n.* تَورِيه pun

tawsiyah *n.* توصية recommendation

tawuam *n.* توأم twin

tawuam *adj.* توأم twin

tawzee' *n.* توزيع distribution

tayabbos *n.* تيبس stiffness

tayaraan *n.* طيران flight

tayf *n.* طيف wraith

tayr *n.* طير fowl

taysh *n.* طيش indiscretion

tayyaar *n.* تيار current

tayyah *n.* طية fold

tayyib *adj.* طيِّب good

tazahzoh *n.* تزحزح budge

tazakhrof *n.* تزخرف luxuriance

tazkiyah *n.* تزكية acclamation

tazweer *n.* تزوير forgery

tbaadol *n.* تبادل exchange

teeh *n.* تيه vainglory

teen *n.* تين fig

teen *n.* طين mud

tha'lab *n.* ثعلب fox

tha'labah *n.* ثَعلَبه vixen

thaabit *adj.* 1 ثابت constant

thaabit *adj.* 2 ثابت steadfast

thaalith *adj.* ثالث third

thaalith *n.* ثالث third

thaalith 'ashar *adj.* ثالثعشر thirteenth

thaalithan *adv.* ثالثًا thirdly

thaalooth *n.* ثالوث trinity

thaanawiy *adj.* ثانوي secondary

thaani *adj.* ثاني second

thaaniyah *n.* ثانية second

thabaat *n.* ثبات steadiness

thadiy *adj.* ثدي mammary

thadiyyaat *n.* ثدييات mammal

thady *n.* ثدي breast

thaghrah *n.* ثغرة lacuna

thakl *n.* ثكل bereavement

thaknah *n.* ثكنة barrack

thalaathah *n.* ثلاثة three

thalaathah *adj.* ثلاثة three

thalaathato 'ashar *n.* ثلاثةعشر thirteen

thalaathato 'ashar *adj.* ثلاثةعشر thirteen

thalaathoon *n.* ثلاثون thirty

thalaathoon *adj.* ثلاثون thirty

thalj *n.* ثلج snow

thaljiy *adj.* ثلجي snowy

thaljon dhaauib *n.* ثَلجذائِب slush

thallaajah *n.* ثلاجة refrigerator

thalm *n.* ثلم furrow

thamaaniyah *n.* ثمانية eight

thamaaniyato 'ashar *adj.* ثمانية عشر eighteen

thamaanoon *n.* ثمانون eighty

thameen *adj.* ثمين precious

thanaau *n.* ثناء commendation

thaqaafah *n.* ثقافة culture

thaqaafiy *adj.* ثقافي cultural

thaqeel *adj.* ثقيل heavy

thariy *adj.* ثري wealthy

tharthaar *adj.* ثرثار talkative

thartharah *n.* ثرثرة babble

tharwah *n.* ثروة wealth

thawaraan *n.* ثوران eruption

thawb *n.* ثوب gown

thawm *n.* ثوم garlic

thawr *n.* ثور ox

thawrah *n.* ثورة revolution

thawriy *adj.* ثوري revolutionary

thawriy *n.* ثوري revolutionary

thikhan *n.* ثِخَن thick

thiqah *n.* ثقة confidence

tho'baan *n.* ثعبان snake

thoghaau *n.* ثغاء bleat

tholaathiy *adj.* ثلاثي triangular

tholaathiy *n.* ثلاثي trio

thomaaniy *adj.* ثماني octangular

thomaaniy *n.* ثماني octave

thomma *adv.* ثم then

thonaauiy *pref* ثنائي bi

thonaauiy *adj.* ثنائي binary

thoqb *n.* ثقب piercing

thoulool *n.* ثؤلول wart

tibaa'ah *n.* طباعة print

tibbiy *adj.* طبي medical

tibgh *n.* تبغ tobacco

tibn *n.* تبن hay

tidhkaar *n.* تذكار souvenir

tidhkaariy *adj.* تذكاري memorial

tifl *n.* طفل child

tijaarah *n.* تجارة commerce

tijaariy *adj.* تجاري commercial

tikraar *n.* تكرار repetition

tilaau *n.* طلاء paint

tilaawah *n.* تلاوة recitation

tilmeedh *n.* تلميذ pupil

timsaah *n.* تمساح crocodile

timthaal *n.* تمثال sculpture

timthaal *n.* تمثال statue

tinneen *n.* تنين dragon

tiqaniy *n.* تقني technologist

tiqaniy *adj.* تقني technical

tiqaniyyah *n.* تقنية technology

tirmos *n.* ترمس thermos

tiryaaq *n.* ترياق antidote

tis'ah *n.* تسعة nine

tis'ato 'ashar *n.* تسعةعشر nineteen

tis'oon *n.* تسعون ninety

tishreeno ththaani *n.* تشرينالثاني November

tishreenol uawwal *n.* تشرينالأول October

to'm *n.* طعم bait

tofayliy *n.* طفيلي parasite

toffaahah *n.* تفاحة apple

tofoolah *n.* طفولة childhood

tofooliy *adj.* طفولي childish

toghyaan *n.* طغيان tyranny

tohaal *n.* طحال spleen

tohfah *n.* تحفة masterpiece

tohlob *n.* طحلب moss

tohmah *n.* تهمة charge

tojhid *v.* تجهض miscarry

tokhmah *n.* تخمة glut

tomooh *n.* طُموح ambition

tomtir *v.* تمطر rain

ton *n.* طن ton

toobaaz *n.* توباز topaz

tool *n.* طول length

toot *n.* توت mulberry

toqaddom *n.* تقدم progress

toraab *n.* تراب soil

toraabiy *adj.* ترابي earthen

toraath *n.* تراث heritage

torbah *n.* تربة soil

toshriq *v.* تشرق rise

tothlij *v.* تثلج snow

tyyaar *n.* طيار pilot

U

u'tidaal *n.* إعتدال moderation

ua'la *adj.* أعلى supreme

ua'la *n.* أعلى top

ua'la *adj.* أعلى upper

ua'ma *adj.* أعمى blind

ua'maq *adj.* أعمق inmost

ua'qaab *n.* أعقاب wake

ua'raj *adj.* أعرج lame

ua'waj *adj.* اعوج serpentine

ua'zab *n.* أعزب bachelor

ua'zab *adj.* أعزب single

uaab *n.* آب August

uaadhaar *n.* آذار March

uaadhriyoon *n.* آذريون marigold

uaafah *n.* 1 آفة blight

uaafah *n.* 2 آفة pest

uaakhar *adj.* آخر another

uaakhar *adv.* آخر else

uaakhar *pron.* آخر other

uaakhir *adv.* آخر last

uaakhirah *adv.* آخرة hereafter

uaalaatiy *adj.* آلاتي instrumental

uaalah *n.* آلة machine

uaalah *n.* ألة instrument

uaaliy *adj.* آليّ automatic

uaaliyyah *n.* آلية mechanism

uaameen *interj.* آمين amen

uaamin *adj.* 1 آمن safe

uaamin *adj.* 2 آمن secure

uaanadhaak *adj.* آنذاك then

uaanisah *n.* آنسة miss

uaaniyah *n.* آنية vase

uaasif *adj.* آسف sorry

uaatoon *n.* أتون forge

uaayah *n.* آية verse

uab *n.* 1 أب dad

uab *n.* 2 أب father

uab jadiy *adj.* أبجدي alphabetical

uabadan *adv.* 1 أبدا ever

uabadan *adv.* 2 أبدًا never

uabadan *adv.* 3 أبداً none

uabadiy *adj.* 1 أبدي eternal

uabadiy *adj.* 2 أبدي everlasting

uabadiyyah *n.* أبدية eternity

uabawiy *adj.* 1 أبوي parental

uabawiy *adj.* 2 أبوي paternal

uabkam *adj.* 1 أبكم dumb

uabkam *n.* 2 أبكم mute

uablah *adj.* أبله asinine

uablah *n.* أبله idiot

uabnoos *n.* أبنوس ebony

uabo zorraq *n.* أبو زرزق jay

uabrashiyyah *n.* أبرشية parish

uabyad *adj.* أبيض white

uabyad *n.* أبيض white

uadaah *n.* 1 أداة implement

uadaah *n.* 2 أداة utensil

uadaah *n.* 3 أداة tool

uadaau *n.* أداء performance

uadab *n.* 1 أدب literature

uadab *n.* 2 أدب politeness

uadabiy *adj.* أدبي literary

uadaq *n.* أدق sharper

uadawaat *n. pl* أدوات paraphernalia

uaddaakhil *n.* الدّاخل within

uaddalw *n.* الدلو Aquarius

uaddddohr *n.* الظهر noon

uaddibq *n.* الدبق mistletoe

uaddolq *n.* الدلق marten

uadeeb *n.* أديب litterateur

uadghaal *n.* أدغال jungle

uadha *n.* آذى hurt

uadhiyyah *n.* أذية mischief

uadna *adj.* 1 أدنى inferior

uadna *adj.* 2 أدنى minimal

uadna *adj.* 3 أدنى minimum

uadramah *v.* أضرم kindle

uaf'a *n.* أفعى serpent

uafdal *adj.* أفضل better

uafdal *adv.* أفضل better

uaflaatooniy *adj.* أفلاطوني platonic

uaftas *adj.* أفطس snub

uafyoon *n.* أفيون opium

uaghlabiyyah *n.* أغلبية majority

uahad *n.* أحَد someone

uahada 'ashar *n.* أحدعشر eleven

uahammiyah *n.* أهمية significance

uahammiyyah *n.* أهمية importance

uahmaq *adj.* أحمق foolish

uahmar *adj.* أحمر red

uahmar *n.* أحمر red

uahshaau *n.* أحشاء entrails

uahwan *adj.* أهون lesser

uahyaanan *adv.* 1 أحياناً sometimes

uahyaanan *adv.* 2 أحيانا occasionally

uahyaauiy *n.* أحيائي biologist

uajash *adj.* أجش hoarse

uajl *n.* أجل sake

uajnabiy *adj.* أجنبي foreign

uajnabiy *n.* أجنبي foreigner

uajr *n.* أجر wage

uajwaf *adj.* أجوف hollow

uajyaal *n.* أجيال generations

uakbar *adj.* أكبر elder

uakbar *adv.* أكبر bigger

uakhawiy *adj.* أخوي fraternal

uakhawiyyah *n.* أخوية fraternity

uakhbaar *n.* أخبار news

uakhdar *n.* أخضر green

uakhdar *adj.* أخضر green

uakhdh *n.* أخذ taking

uakheer *adj.* أخير last

uakheer *n.* أخير last

uakheeran *adv.* 1 أخيرا eventually

uakheeran *adv.* 2 أخيراً lastly

uakhlaaq *n.* أخلاق ethics

uakhlaaqiy *adj.* 1 أخلاقي ethical

uakhraq *adj.* أخرق clumsy

uakimmah *n.* أكمة hillock

uakmal *adj.* أكمل entire

uakoon أكون am

uakthar *adv.* أكثر further

uakthar *adj.* أكثر more

ual banjo *n.* البانجو banjo

ual hawaauiy *n.* الهوائي aerial

ual hawliyyaat *n.pl.* الحوليات annals

ual jabr *n.* الجبر algebra

ual kheemyaau *n.* الخيمياء alchemy

ual kol *n.* الكل all

ual mo'ayyan *n.* المعين assignee

ual uabjadiyyah *n.* الأبجدية alphabet

ual ualif *n.* الألف alpha

ual ualominyom *n.* الألومنيوم aluminium

ual uantaarktik *adj.* الأنتاركتيك Antarctic

ual uarbi'aau *n.* الأربعاء Wednesday

ual uaroroot *n.* الأروروت arrowroot

ual uasbaq *adj.* الأسبق antecedent

ual yaansoon *n.* اليانسون aniseed

ual'aab *n.* ألعاب games

ual'adhraau *n.* العذراء Virgo

ual'afo *n.* العفو amnesty

ual'aqrab *n.* العقرب Scorpio

ual'arabiyyah *n.* العربية Arabic

ual'ishroon *adj.* العشرون twentieth

ual'ishroon *n.* العشرون twentieth

ualadhi *pron.* الذي which

ualam *n.* ألم ache

ualam *n.* ألم ailment

ualam *n.* ألم pain

ualbaaba *n.* البابا pope

ualbaaraafeen *n.* البارافين paraffin

ualbatoola *n.* البتولا birch

ualbitrool *n.* البترول petrol

ualbiyaano *n.* البيانو piano

ualboom *n.* ألبوم album

ualbraaghraatiyyah *n.* البراغماتية pragmatism

ualbraandi *n.* البراندي brandy

ualeef *n.* أليف domestic

ualenjleeziyyah *n.* الإنجليزية English

ualesbaaniyyah *n.* الإسبانية Spanish

ualfaransiyyah *n.* الفرنسية French

ualfish *n.* الفصح Easter

ualfiyyah *n.* ألفية millennium

ualgharb *n.* الغرب occident

ualhaaki *n.* الحاكي gramophone

ualhamal *n.* الحمل Aries

ualhamo *n.* الحمو in-laws

ualhodoor *n.* الحضور advent

ualhokee *n.* الهكي hockey

ualimmbiryaaliyyah *n.* الإمبريالية imperialism

ualjadi *n.* الجدي Capricorn

ualjaheem *n.* الجحيم underworld

ualjinsol bashariy *n.* البشر mankind

ualjomo'ah *n.* الجمعة Friday

ualkaalsyom *n.* الكلسيوم calcium

ualkaathooleekiyyah *n.* الكاثوليكية Catholicism

ualkabeer *adj.* الكبير senior

ualkadmiyom *n.* الكادميوم cadmium

ualkamaan *n.* الكمان violin

ualkhaarij *n.* الخارج without

ualkhamees *n.* الخميس Thursday

ualkomonwilth *n.* الكومنولث commonwealth

ualkoobalt *n.* الكوبالت cobalt

ualkoomeedyah *n.* الكوميديا comedy

ualkoont *n.* الكونت count

uallaamaadiyyah *adj.* اللامادية immaterial

uallaatatbeeqiyyah *n.* اللاتطبيقية impracticability

uallaauindibaat *n.* اللاانضباط indiscipline

uallaawojood *n.* اللاوجود nonentity

ualladhi *rel. pron.* الذي that

uallaktooz *n.* اللاكتوز lactose

uallaylah *n.* الليلة tonight

uallaylah *adv.* الليلة tonight

uallibraaliyyah *n.* الليبرالية liberalism

uallogharithmaat *n.* اللوغارثمات logarithm

ualmaamooth *n.* الماموث mammoth

ualmaaraathoon *n.* الماراثون marathon

ualmaas *n.* الماس diamond

ualman *n.* المن manna

ualmaraasi *n.* المراسي moorings

ualmarrikh *n.* المريخ Mars

ualmaseeh *n.* المسيح Christ

ualmaseehiyyah *n.* المسيحية Christianity

ualmileesha *n.* الميليشا militia

ualmink *n.* المنك mink

ualmoltahimah *n.* الملتحمة conjunctiva

ualmor *n.* المر myrrh

ualmoshtari *n.* المشتري Jupiter

ualmostaqeem *n.* المستقيم rectum

ualoomeenaat *n.* ألومينات aluminate

ualqaadir *adj.* القادر almighty

ualqabw *n.* القبو bunker

ualqooloon *n.* القولون colon

ualuaan *adv.* الآن now

ualuaan *conj.* الآن now

ualuaas *n.* الآس myrtle

ualuahad *n.* الأحد Sunday

ualuahyaau *n.* الأحياء living

ualuakheer *adj.* الأخير latter

ualuaqal *adj.* الأقل least

ualuaqal *adv.* الأقل least

ualuaqtaab *n.* الأقطاب antipodes

ualuasad *n.* الأسد Leo

ualueerlaandiyyah *n.* الايرلندية Irish

ualueetaaliyyah *n.* الإيطالية Italian

ualuithnayn n. الإثنين Monday

ualuoksoojeen *n.* الأوكسجين oxygen

ualuolombyaad *n.* الأولمبياد Olympiad

ualwaahid *pron.* الواحَد one

ualwihdaaniyyah *n.* الوحدانية oneness

ualwihdiwojoodi *n.* الوحديوجودي pantheist

ualyaasameen *n.* الياسمين jasmine

ualyaraqaan *n.* اليرقان jaundice

ualyawm *adv.* اليوم today

ualyawm *n.* اليوم today

ualyin *n.* الين Yen

ualyoonaaniyyah *n.* اليونانية Greek

uam'aam *n.* أمعاء intestine

uamaam *adj.* أمام front

uamaanah *n.* 1 أمانة honesty

uamaanah *n.* 2 أمانة secretariat (e)

uamal *n.* أمل hope

uambeer *n.* أمبير ampere

uameen *n.* أمين secretary

uameen *adj.* أمين honest

uameer *n.* أمير prince

uameeraal *n.* أميرال admiral

uameerah *n.* أميرة princess

uameeriy *adj.* أميري princely

uamlas *adj.* أملس sleek

uamn *n.* أمن security

uamr *n.* 1 أمر command

uamr *n.* 2 أمر demand

uamthal *n.* أمثل optimum

uamthal *adj.* أمثل optimum

uamti'ah *n.* أمتعة baggage

uamti'ah *n.* أمتعة luggage

uamwaaj *n.* أمواج surf

uan *pref.* أن be

uana *pron.* أنا I

uana *pron.* أنا me

uanaaniy *adj.* أناني selfish

uanaaqah *n.* أناقة elegance

uanaddeer *n.* النظير nadir

uananaas *n.* أناناس pineapple

uaneen *n.* أنين moan
uaneen *n.* أنين whine
uaneeq *adj.* أنيق dainty
uaneeq *adj.* أنيق elegant
uaneeq *adj.* أنيق neat
uaneeq *adj.* أنيق smart
uanf *n.* أنف nose
uanfiy *adj.* أنفي nasal
uanfiy *n.* أنفي nasal
uanna *conj.* أن that
uannarjisiyyah *n.* النرجسية narcissism
uannikoteen *n.* النيكوتين nicotine
uanqaad *n.* أنقاض rubble
uaqal *prep.* أقل below
uaqal *adj.* أقل less
uaqal *n.* أقل less
uaqal *adv.* أقل less
uaqal *prep.* أقل less
uaqdamiyyah *n.* أقدمية seniority
uaqsa *adj.* أقصى extreme
uaqsa *adj.* أقصى maximum
uaqsa *adj.* أقصى utmost
uaqsa *adv.* أقصى most
uarba'ah *n.* أربعة four
uarba'ato 'ashrah *n.* أربعةعشرة fourteen
uarba'oon *n.* أربعون forty
uard *n.* 1 أرض earth
uard *n.* 2 أرض ground
uard *n.* 3 أرض land
uardi shawki *n.* أرضيشوكي artichoke
uardiwaaz *n.* أردواز slate
uardiy *n.* أرضي worldling

uardiyyah *n.* أرضيّة floor
uareekah *n.* 2 أريكة sofa
uariq *adj.* أرق wakeful
uaristoqraatiy *n.* أرستقراطي aristocrat
uaristoqraatiyyah *n.* أرستقراطية aristocracy
uarmal *n.* أرمل widow
uarnab *n.* 1 أرنب hare
uarnab *n.* 2 أرنب rabbit
uaroz *n.* أرز rice
uarrabo *n.* الربو asthma
uarriyaadiyyat *n.* الرياضيات mathematics
uarroboobiy *n.* الربوبي deist
uarroboobiyyah *n.* الربوبية deism
uarrom *n.* الروم rum
uarsheef *n.pl.* أرشيف archives
uarwaah *n.* أرواح manes
uarz *n.* أرز cedar
uasaalah *n.* أصالة originality
uasaas *n.* 1 أساس basis
uasaas *n.* 2 أساس ground
uasaasiy *n.* 2 أساسي main
uasaasiy *adj.* 3 أساسي major
uasaasiy *adj.* 4 أساسي primary
uasaasiy *adj.* 5 أساسي staple
uasad *n.* أسد lion
uasadiy *adj.* أسدي leonine
uasaf *n.* أسف regret
uasam *adj.* أصم deaf
uasbaq *adj.* أسبق premier
uasbistos *n.* أسبستوس asbestos
uaseer *n.* أسير captive
uasfal *adv.* أسفل below

uasfal *prep.* أسفل beneath

uasfal *n.* أسفل bottom

uashimbaanziy *n.* الشمبانزي chimpanzee

uaskafah *n.* أسكفة lintel

uasl *n.* أصل ancestry

uasl *n.* أصل descent

uasl *n.* أصل origin

uasla' *adj.* أصلع bald

uasliy *adj.* أصلي indigenous

uasliy *adj.* أصلي native

uasliy *n.* أصلي native

uasliy *adj.* أصلي original

uasliy *n.* أصلي original

uasr *n.* أسر captivity

uassaabi'o 'ashar *adj.* السابع عشر seventeenth

uassaabiq *pron* السابق former

uassaadah *n.* السادة Messrs

uassaaj *n.* الساج teak

uassab'oon *adj.* السبعون seventieth

uassabt *n.* السبت Sabbath

uassabt *n.* السبت Saturday

uassandal *n.* الصندل sandalwood

uasseen *n.* الصين China

uassiba *n.* الصبا boyhood

uassittoon *adj.* الستون sixtieth

uassol *n.* السل tuberculosis

uassowariyyah *n.* الصورية imagery

uassweesriyyah *n.* السويسرية Swiss

uaswau *n.* أسوأ worst

uaswau *adj.* أسوأ worst

uat'aab *n.* أتعاب honorarium

uathaani 'ashar *a.* الثاني عشر twelfth

uathaani 'ashar *n.* الثاني عشر twelfth

uathaath *n.* أثاث furniture

uathar *n.* 1 أثر effect

uathar *n.* 2 أثر trail

uathar *n.* 3 أثر trace

uathariy *adj.* أثري antique

uathariy *n.* أثير ether

uatheem *adj.* أثيم vicious

uaththalaathoon *adj.* الثلاثون thirtieth

uaththalaathoon *n.* الثلاثون thirtieth

uaththawr *n.* الثور bull

uatlas *n.* أطلس atlas

uattaali *adj.* التالي next

uattaasi'ah *adj.* التاسعة ninth

uattaba'iyyah *n.* التبعية appurtenance

uattajalli *n.* التجلّي transfiguration

uattanbool *n.* التنبول betel

uattannoob *n.* التنوب fir

uattarsaanah *n.* الترسانة arsenal

uattasi'o 'ashar *adj.* التاسع عشر nineteenth

uatteefoouŗeed *n.* التيفوئيد typhoid

uatteefos *n.* التيفوس typhus

uattis'oon *adj.* التسعون ninetieth

uawlawiyyah *n.* أولوية priority

uawsat *n.* أوسط alto

uawwal *adj.* أول first

uawwal *n.* أول first

uawwalan *adv.* أولاً first

uawwaliy *adj.* أولي initial
uawwaliy *n.* أُوَّلي rudiment
uay *adj.* أي any
uay *adv.* أي any
uay *adv.* أي namely
uay *adj.* أي what
uay *adj.* أي which
uayd *n.* أيض metabolism
uaydan *adv.* أيضاً also
uaydan *adv.* أيضاً either
uaydan *adv.* أيضاً moreover
uaydan *adv.* أيضاً too
uayl *n.* أيل deer
uaylool *n.* أيلول September
uayn *adv.* أين where
uayn *adv.* أين whereabout
uaynama *adv.* أينما wherever
uayyaar *n.* أيّار May
uayyohom *pron* أيهم whichever
uazaliy *adj.* أزلي infinite
uazaliyyah *n.* أزلية infinity
uazeez *n.* 1 أزيز sizzle
uazeez *n.* 2 أزيز whir
uazmah *n.* أزمة crisis
uazraq *n.* أزرق blue
uazzaan *n.* الزان beech
uazzanjafr *n.* الزنجفر cinnabar
uazzauidah *n.* الزائدة appendix
uazzaylofoon *n.* الزيلوفون xylophone
udwaau *n.* أضواء limelight
ueehaam *n.t.* إيهام delude
ueehaau *n.* إيحاء smack
ueejaabiy *adj.* إيجابي positive
ueejaar *n.* إيجار lease

ueejaar *n.* إيجار tenancy
ueejaar *n.* إيجار rent
ueejaaz *n.* إيجاز brevity
ueeman *n.* إيمان faith
ueemau *n.* إيماء pantomime
ueemauah *n.* إيماءة gesture
ueeqaa' *n.* 1 إيقاع beat
ueeqaa' *n.* 2 إيقاع rhythm
ueeqaa'iy *adj.* إيقاعي rhythmic
ueerlaandiy *adj.* ايرلندي Irish
ueetaaliy *adj.* إيطالي Italian
uflaam *n.* أفلام movies
ufsha *v.* أفشى blurt
uhaadiy *adj.* أحادي monocular
ui'taaq *n.* إعتاق manumission
uidhn *n.* إذن permission
uiltihaabo ssahaaya *n.* سحايا meningitis
ukhlaaqiy *adj.* 2 أخلاقي moral
ukhlaaqiyyah *n.* أخلاقية morality
ul'oshr *n.* العشر tithe
uloohiyyah *n.* ألوهية divinity
umaam *prep.* أمام before
umoomah *n.* أمومة motherhood
uo'joobah *n.* أعجوبة marvel
uobbahah *n.* أبهة pageantry
uobra *n.* أوبرا opera
uodhon *n.* أذن ear
uodhoniy *adj.* أذني auriform
uofoq *n.* أفق horizon
uofoq *n.* أفق vista
uoghniyah *n.* أغنية single
uoghniyah *n.* أغنية song
uohfoorah *n.* أحفورة fossil
uohjiyah *n.* احجية riddle

uohliyyah *n.* أهلية aptitude

uojrah *n.* 1 أجرة fare

uojrah *n.* 2 أجرة pay

uokhdood *n.* 1 أخدود groove

uokhdood *n.* 2 أخدود rut

uokhowwah *n.* 1 أخوة brotherhood

uokht *n.* أخت sister

uokhtiy *adj.* أختي sisterly

uokhtiyyah *n.* أختية sisterhood

uokhwah *n.* 2 أخوة confraternity

uolfah *n.* ألفة affinity

uolfah *n.* ألفة intimacy

uoloohiyyah *n.* الوهية godhead

uomigha *n.* أوميغا omega

uommiy *adj.* أمي illiterate

uommiyyah *n.* أمية illiteracy

uomniyah *n.* أمنية wish

uomo uarba'atin wa uarba'oon *n.* ام وأربعين وأربعة millipede

uomoomah *n.* أمومة maternity

uomoomiy *adj.* أمومي maternal

uomoomiy *adj.* أمومي motherlike

uonaas *n.* أناس people

uonboob *n.* أنبوب pipe

uonboob *n.* أنبوب tube

uonboobiy *adj.* أنبوبي tubular

uonoothah *n.* أنوثة womanhood

uonshootah *n.* أنشوطة noose

uontha *adj.* أنثى female

uontha *n.* أنثى female

uonthawiy *n.* أنثوي womanish

uoofirhool *n.* أوفرهول overall

uoola *adj.* أولى maiden

uorjoohah *n.* أرجوحة swing

uorjowaaniy *n.* أرجواني lilac

uorkistra *n.* أوركسترا orchestra

uorkistriy *adj.* أوركستري orchestral

uorthoodhoksiy *adj.* ارثوذكسي orthodox

uorthoodhoksiyyah *n.* أرثوذكسية orthodoxy

uosboo' *n.* أسبوع week

uosboo'ayn *n.* أسبوعين fort-night

uosboo'iy *adj.* أسبوعي weekly

uosboo'iy *n.* أسبوعي weekly

uosboo'iyan *adv.* أسبوعيا weekly

uosloob *n.* 1 أسلوب diction

uosloob *n.* 2 أسلوب manner

uosood *adj.* أسود black

uosqof *n.* أسقف bishop

uostaadh *n.* أستاذ professor

uostool *n.* أسطول fleet

uostoorah *n.* 2 أسطورة legend

uostoorah *n.* 3 أسطورة myth

uostooriy *adj.* 1 أسطوري legendary

uostooriy *adj.* 2 أسطوري mythical

uostooriy *adj.* 3 أسطوري mythological

uostowaanah *n.* أسطوانة cylinder

usaasiy *adj.* 1 أساسي fundamental

usbaqiyyah *n.* أسبقية precedence

usloob *n.* 3 أسلوب method

ustoorah *n.* 1 أسطورة fable

utroohah *n.* أطروحة thesis

uwqiyyah *n.* أوقية ounce

W

wa *conj.* و and
wa ellah *conj.* وإلا otherwise
wa'd *n.* وعد promise
wa'i *adj.* واع conscious
wa'ir *adj.* وعر bumpy
wa'y *n.* وعي awareness
waa'id *adj.* واعد promising
waa'idd *n.* واعظ preacher
waabil *n.* وابل volley
waad *n.* واد valley
waadih *adj.* 1 واضح apparent
waadih *adj.* 2 واضح obvious
waafir *adj.* وافر bountiful
waafir *adv.* وافر galore
waahah *n.* واحة oasis
waahid *adj.* واحد one
waahin *adj.* واهن sickly
waajib *n.* 1 واجب duty
waajib *n.* 2 واجب must
waajihah *n.* واجهة facade
waalidah *n.* والدة mother
Waaqi *adj.* واقي protective
waaqi' *n.* واقع reality
waaqi'iy *n.* واقعي realist
waaqi'iy *adj.* واقعي realistic
waaqi'iyyah *n.* واقعية realism
waasi' *adj.* واسع broad
waasi' *adv.* واسع wide
waat *n.* واط watt
waathiq *adj.* واثق confident
wabaau *n.* وباء epidemic
wad' *n.* 1 وضع case

wad' *n.* 2 وضع condition
wad' *n.* 3 وضع posture
wad'iyyah *n.* وضعيَه pose
wadaa' *n.* وداع farewell
wadaa'an *interj.* وداعاً farewell
waddeefah *n.* 1 وظيفة function
waddeefah *n.* 2 وظيفة job
wadee' *adj.* وديع meek
wadee' *adj.* وضيع menial
wadee'ah *n.* وديعة deposit
wadqah *n.* وَدْقَه stye
wafd *n.* وفد delegation
wafra *n.* وفرة abundance
waghd *n.* وغد villain
wahd *n.* وهد ravine
waheed *adj.* 1 وحيد alone
waheed *adj.* 2 وحيد lonesome
waheed *adj.* 3 وحيد single
wahm *n.* وهم delusion
wahsh *n.* وحش monster
wahshiy *adj.* وحشي monstrous
wahshiy *n.* وحشية savagery
wahy *n.* وحي revelation
wajbah *n.* وجبة meal
wajh *n.* وجه face
wajhiy *adj.* وجهي facial
wajjaar *n.* وجار terrier
wakaalah *n.* وكالة agency
wakeel *n.* وكيل agent
wakhz *n.* وخز throb
wakhzah *n.* وخزة prick
wala *conj.* ولا nor
walaau *n.* ولاء loyalty
walad *n.* ولد boy
walah *n.* وله infatuation

waleemah *n.* وليمة feast

waliy *n.* ولي custodian

walla'ah *n.* ولاعة lighter

wameed *n.* وميض flash

waqaahah *n.* وقاحة insolence

waqaaui' *n.* وقائع chronicle

waqfah *n.* وقفة pause

waqih *adj.* وقح shameless

waqood *n.* وقود fuel

waqoor *adj.* وقور magisterial

waqqaad *n.* وَقّاد stoker

waqt *n.* وقت time

waraau *prep.* وراء behind

waram *n.* ورم tumour

waraqah *n.* 1 ورقة leaf

waraqah *n.* 2 ورقة paper

waraqah *n.* 3 ورقة sheet

wardah *n.* وردة rose

wardiy *adj.* وردي roseate

wardiy *adj.* وردي rosy

wareed *n.* وَريد vein

wareeth *n.* وريث heir

warshah *n.* ورشة workshop

wasaatah *n.* وساطة mediation

wasakh *n.* وسخ slattern

wasat *prep.* وسط amid

wasat *n.* وسط middle

waseelah *adj.* وسيلة expedient

waseelah *n.* وسيلة means

waseem *adj.* وسيم handsome

waseet *n.* 1 وسيط intermediary

waseet *n.* 2 وسيط medium

wasf *n.* وصف description

wasfah *n.* 1 وصفة recipe

wasfah *n.* 2 وصفة prescription

wasfiy *adj.* وصفي descriptive

washeek *adj.* وشيك imminent

washm *n.* وشم tattoo

washwashah *n.* وشوشة bruit

wasikh *adj.* وسخ dirty

wasiy *n.* وصي guardian

wasiyyah *n.* 1 وصيّة commandment

wasiyyah *n.* 2 وصيّة will

waslah *n.* وصلة circuit

wasmah *n.* وصمة stain

watad *n.* وتد peg

wataniy *adj.* 1 وطني national

wataniy *n.* وطني patriot

wataniy *adj.* 2 وطني patriotic

wataniyyah *n.* وطنية patriotism

watar *n.* وتر chord

wathaniy *n.* وثني idolater

wathbah *n.* وَثْبه vault

watheeqah *n.* وثيقة document

waud *n.* وأد infanticide

wazeer *n.* وزير minister

wazn *n.* وزن weight

wi'aau *n.* وعاء pot

wihdah *n.* 1 وحدة module

wihdah *n.* 2 وحدة unit

wihdah *n.* 3 وحدة unity

wijaar *n.* وجار warren

wijhah *n.* وجهة destination

wilaadah *n.* ولادة birth

winsh *n.* ونش winch

wiqaauiy *adj.* وقائي preventive

wiraathah *n.* 1 وراثة heredity

wiraathah *n.* 2 وراثة inheritance

wiraathiy *n.* وراثي hereditary

wiraathiy *adj.* وراثي inborn

wirk *n.* ورك hip

wisaadah *n.* وسادة cushion

wisaam *n.* وسام garter

wisaayah *n.* وصاية custody

wishaah *n.* وشاح scarf

wiski *n.* ويسكي whisky

wist *n.* وسط waist

wizaarah *n.* وزارة ministry

woddiy *adj.* ودي cordial

wodooh *n.* 1 وضوح clarity

wodooh *n.* 2 وضوح visibility

wodoou *n.* وضوء ablution

wojayh *n.* وجيه facet

wojdaaniy *adj.* وجداني sentimental

wojood *n.* 1 وجود existence

wojood *n.* 2 وجود presence

wosool *n.* وصول arrival

ya'bath *v.* يعبث fiddle

ya'bid *v.* يعبد worship

ya'bis *v.* يعبس frown

ya'bor *v.* يعبر cross

ya'dhor *v.* يعذر excuse

ya'dim *v.* يعدم lynch

ya'do *v.* يعدو sprint

ya'dol *v.* يعدل revoke

ya'eesh *v.* يعيش live

ya'fi *v.* يعفي exempt

ya'fo *v.* يعفو pardon

ya'had *v.* يعهد entrust

ya'har *v.* يعهر prostitute

ya'id *v.* يعد promise

ya'idd *v.* يعظ preach

ya'ij *v.* يعجّ swarm

ya'im *v.* 1 يعم engulf

ya'im *v.* 2 يعم pervade

ya'jin *v.* يعجن masticate

ya'kis *v.* 1 يعكس counter

ya'kis *v.* 2 يعكس reflect

ya'kis *v.* 3 يعكس reverse

ya'laq *v.* يعلق strand

ya'mad *v.* يعمد intend

ya'mal *v.* 1 يعمل function

ya'mal *v.* 2 يعمل work

ya'ni *v.* يعني imply

ya'od *v.* يعد count

ya'od *v.* يعض bite

ya'ood *v.* يعود return

ya'oom *v.* يعوم float

ya'qid *v.* 1 يعقد hold

ya'qid *v.* 2 يعقد knot

ya'qil *v.* يعقل rationalize

ya'raq *v.* يعرق sweat

ya'rib *v.* يعرب construe

ya'rid *v.* 1 يعرض offer

ya'rid *v.* 2 يعرض show

ya'rif *v.* يعرف know

ya'roj *v.* يعرج limp

ya'saf *v.* يعصف storm

ya'shaq *v.* يعشق adore

ya'si *v.* يعصي disobey

ya'sor *v.* 1 يعصر juice

ya'sor *v.* 2 يعصر squeeze

ya'tabir *v.* 1 يعتبر consider

ya'tabir v. 2 يعتبر regard	yabhath v. 2 يبحث seek
ya'tadhir v. يعتذر apologize	yabiod v. يبعد away
ya'tadi v. يعتدي assault	yabith v. يبث broadcast
ya'tamid v. يعتمد depend	yabki v. يبكي weep
ya'tamid v. يعتمد adopt	yabla' v. يبلع gulp
ya'taqid v. يعتقد believe	yablogh v. 1 يبلغ reach
ya'taqil v. يعتقل apprehend	yablogh v. 2 يبلغ grow-up
ya'tarid v. 1 يعترض intercept	yabni v. يبني construct
ya'tarid v. 2 يعترض object	yabqa v. 1 يبقى last
ya'tarif v. 1 يعترف acknowledge	yabqa v. 2 يبقى remain
ya'tarif v. 2 يعترف confess	yabri v. يبري whittle
ya'taz v. يعتز cherish	yabrod v. يبرد file
ya'tazil v. يعتزل abdicate	yabroz v. يبرز outline
ya'tazim v. يعتزم intend	yabshor v. يبشر grate
ya'thor v. يعثر find	yabsim v. يبصم imprint
ya'tis v. يعطس sneeze	yabsoq v. يبصق spit
ya'wi v. يعوي howl	yabta'id v. يبتعد shy
ya'zif v. يعزف play	yabtahij v. يبتهج rejoice
ya'zil v. 1 يعزل insulate	yabtakir v. يبتكر innovate
ya'zil v. 2 يعزل isolate	yabtali v. يبتلي afflict
ya'zo v. يعزو ascribe	yabtali' v. يبتلع swallow
yaanaseeb n. يانصيب lottery	yabtasim v. يبتسم smile
yaani' adj. يانع mellow	yabtaz v. يبتز blackmail
yaaqoot n. ياقوت ruby	yabtor v. يبتر mutilate
yaauis adj. يائس desperate	yabzogh v. 1 يبزغ dawn
yabakhir v. 2 يبخر steam	yabzogh v. 2 يبزغ spring
yabdau v. يبدأ begin	yad n. يد hand
yabdau v. يبدأ initial	yad hak v. يضحك laugh
yabdau v. يبدأ initiate	yad'ak v. يدعك rub
yabdau v. يبدأ start	yad'am v. 1 يدعم prop
yabdhor v. يبذر seed	yad'am v. 2 يدعم support
yabdo v. يبدو seem	yad'i v. يدَّعي sham
yabee' v. يبيع sell	yad'o v. 1 يدعو call
yabeed v. يبيد annihilate	yad'o v. 2 يدعو invite
yabhath v. 1 يبحث research	yad'of v. يضعف weaken

yada' *v.* 1 يضع lay
yada' *v.* 2 يضع put
yadawiy *adj.* يدوي manual
yadbigh *v.* يدبغ tincture
yadbit *v.* يضبط adjust
yadbogh *v.* يَدبُغ tan
yaddbit *v.* يظبط tune
yaddhar *v.* يظهر appear
yaddlim *v.* يَظلُم wrong
yaddmau *v.* يظمأ thirst
yadeen *v.* يدين owe
yadeeq *v.* يضيق tighten
yadfa' *v.* 1 يدفع pay
yadfa' *v.* 2 يدفع push
yadfin *v.* يدفن bury
yadghat *v.* 1 يضغط compress
yadghat *v.* 2 يضغط press
yadh'ar *v.* يذعر panic
yadhad *v.* يدحض disprove
yadhan *v.* يدهن spread
yadhbah *v.* يذبح slay
yadhbal *v.* يذبل wither
yadhghat *v.* 3 يضغط squeeze
yadhhab *v.* يذهب go
yadhil *v.* يذل humiliate
yadhim *v.* يذم asperse
yadhkor *v.* يذكر mention
yadhom *v.* يضم encompass
yadhoob *v.* يذوب dissolve
yadhrif *v.* يَذرِف slough
yadil *v.* يدل direct
yadkhol *v.* يدخل enter
yadman *v.* 1 يضمن enclose
yadman *v.* 2 يضمن guarantee
yadmij *v.* يدمج merge

yadoj *v.* يضج fuss
yadokh *v.* يضخ pump
yadol *v.* يضل get lost
yadol *v.* يطل overlook
yadookh *v.* يدوخ daze
yadoor *v.* 1 يدور revolve
yadoor *v.* 2 يدور spin
yadoos *v.* 1 يدوس pedal
yadoos *v.* 2 يدوس tread
yadoq *v.* يَدق knock
yadrib *v.* 1 يضرب multiply
yadrib *v.* 2 يضرب strike
yadrib *v.* 3 يضرب beat
yadroj *v.* يدرج taxi
yadros *v.* 1 يدرس study
yadros *v.* 2 يدرس thresh
yadtahid *v.* يضطهد persecute
yadtarib *v.* يضطرب simmer
yadthor *v.* يدثر muffle
yaf'al *v.* يفعل do
yafdah *v.* يفضح expose
yafeed *v.* يفيض flood
yafham *v.* يفهم understand
yafhas *v.* يفحص examine
yafi *v.* يفي fulfil
yaflah *v.* يَفلَح till
yafod *v.* يفض dissolve
yafooh *v.* يفوح savour
yafooq *v.* 1 يفوق excel
yafooq *v.* 2 يفوق surpass
yafor *v.* يفر decamp
yafqid *v.* يفقد lose
yafqid *v.* يفقد miss
yafqis *v.* يفقص hatch
yafrid *v.* يفرض impose

yafrik v. يفرك brush

yafriz v. 1 يفرز secrete

yafriz v. 2 يفرز sort

yafrom v. يفرم mince

yafsakh v. يفسخ annul

yafshal v. يفشل fail

yafsid v. يفسد botch

yafsil v. يفصل separate

yafsoq v. يفسق debauch

yaftah v. يفتح open

yaftakhir v. يفتخر pride

yaftari v. يفتري slander

yaftarid v. يفترض assume

yaftaris v. يفترس devour

yaftil v. يَفْتِل twist

yaftim v. يفطم wean

yaftin v. يفتن fascinate

yaghatti v. يغطّي cover

yaghfal v. يغفل overlook

yaghfo v. يغفو doze

yaghfor v. يغفر forgive

yaghish v. يغش cheat

yaghmir v. يغمر submerge

yaghmis v. يغمس dip

yaghmiz v. يغمز wink

yaghosh v. يغش adulterate

yaghot v. 1 يغطّ bestrew

yaghot v. 2 يغطّ be asleep

yaghraq v. يغرق drown

yaghrif v. يغرف ladle

yaghris v. 1 يغرس instil

yaghris v. 2 يغرس plant

yaghshi v. يغشي blear

yaghsho v. يغشو faint

yaghsil v. 1 يغسل launder

yaghsil v. 2 يغسل wash

yaghtaadd v. يغتاظ fret

yaghtaal v. يغتال assassinate

yaghtanim v. يغتنم deject

yaghtasib v. يغتصب rape

yaghtos v. يغطس dive

yaghwi v. يغوي seduce

yaghzo v. يغزو invade

yahaasir v. يحاصر besiege

yahbik v. يحبك knit

yahbit v. 1 يهبط descend

yahbit v. 2 يهبط land

yahdau v. يهدأ calm

yahdau v. يهدّئ subside

yahdhi v. يهذي rave

yahdhif v. يحذف delete

yahdhor v. يهذر gabble

yahdi v. يهدي dedicate

yahdif v. يهدف aim

yahdim v. يهدم demolish

yahdim v. يهضم digest

yahdir v. يهدر roar

yahdol v. يهدل coo

yahdor v. يحضر attend

yahdor v. يهدر rush

yahdoth v. يحدث occur

yaheej v. يهيّج *commove*

yaheek v. يحيك weave

yahfadd v. 1 يحفظ memorise

yahfadd v. 2 يحفظ preserve

yahfir v. يحفر dig

yahfo v. يهفو lapse

yahib v. يهب flame

yahid v. 1 يحد border

yahid v. 2 يحد limit

yahik v. يحك itch
yahil v. 1 يحل settle
yahil v. 2 يحل solve
yahill v. 3 يخَل undo
yahin v. يحن crave
yahis v. يحس sense
yahish v. يَحِشُ scythe
yahith v. يحث urge
yahja' v. يَهْجَع slumber
yahjib v. يحجب veil
yahjim v. يهجم attack
yahjis v. يهجس obsess
yahjiz v. يحجز reserve
yahjo v. يهجو satirize
yahjob v. يحجب overshadow
yahjor v. يهجر forsake
yahkim v. 1 يحكم sentence
yahkom v. 2 يحكم govern
yahlak v. يهلك perish
yahlam v. يحلم dream
yahlib v. يحلب milk
yahmi v. يحمي protect
yahmil v. يحمل carry
yahmis v. يهمس whisper
yahmiyyah n. مَحْمِيَّة preserve
yahmoor n. يحمور roe
yahnith v. يحنث break (a promise)
yahob v. يهب waft
yahom v. يهم matter
yahoodiy n. يهودي Jew
yahoom v. يَحوم soar
yahooz v. يحوز have
yahos v. يحس detect
yahot v. يحط alight

yahoz v. يهز wag
yahqid v. يحقد grudge
yahqin v. يحقن inject
yahrim v. يحرم deprive
yahriq v. يحرق burn
yahrob v. يهرب escape
yahros v. يحرس guard
yahros v. يَهْرس mash
yahroth v. يحرث plough
yahsab v. 3 يحسب reckon
yahshi v. يحشى stuff
yahshid v. يحشد mobilize
yahsho v. يحشو stuff
yahshor v. يحشر wedge
yahsib v. 1 يحسب account
yahsib v. 2 يحسب calculate
yahsid v. يحسد envy
yahsid v. يحصد harvest
yahsim v. يحسم retort
yahsol v. يحصل get
yahsor v. يحصر confine
yahtaaj v. يحتاج need
yahtaaj v. يهتاج seethe
yahtaal v. يحتال bilk
yahtadin v. 1 يحتضن embrace
yahtadin v. 2 يحتضن incubate
yahtafidd v. يحتفظ keep
yahtafil v. يحتفل celebrate
yahtaj v. يحتج protest
yahtakir v. يحتكر monopolize
yahtal v. يحتل occupy
yahtam v. يهتم care
yahtaqir v. يحتقر despise
yahtarim v. يحترم respect
yahtariq v. يحترق blaze

yahtaris *v.* يحترس beware	**yajuor** *v.* يجؤر bellow
yahtariu *v.* يهترئ weather	**yajzi** *v.* يجزي recompense
yahtashid *v.* يَحْتَشِد troop	**yajzim** *v.* يجزم vouch
yahtaz *v.* يهتز vibrate	**yajzor** *v.* يجزر massacre
yahwi *v.* يحوي contain	**yakbah** *v.* يكبح restrain
yahwil *v.* يَحْوِل squint	**yakbor** *v.* يكبر undulate
yahya *v.* يحيى survive	**yakdah** *v.* يكدح toil
yahzan *v.* يحزن mourn	**yakdhib** *v.* يكذب lie
yahzau *v.* يهزأ gibe	**yakdim** *v.* يكدم contuse
yahzim *v.* يحزم pack	**yakfal** *v.* يكفل bail
yahzim *v.* يهزم defeat	**yakfi** *v.* يكفي suffice
yaj'al *v.* يجعل make	**yakfin** *v.* يكفن shroud
yajbir *v.* يجبر compel	**yakfor** *v.* يكفر atone
yajdhib *v.* 1 يجذب attract	**yakhaaf** *v.* يخاف fear
yajdhib *v.* 2 يجذب draw	**yakhajjil** *v.* يخجّل embarrass
yajfal *v.* يجفل startle	**yakhbit** *v.* يخبط wallop
yajib *v.* يجب must	**yakhbiz** *v.* يخبز bake
yajiz *v.* يجز mow	**yakhda'** *v.* يخدع trick
yajlib *v.* يجلب bring	**yakhda'** *v.* 1 يخضع subjugate
yajlid *v.* يجلد whip	**yakhda'** *v.* 2 يخضع undergo
yajlis *v.* يجلس sit	**yakhdim** *v.* يخدم serve
yajma' *v.* 1 يجمع compile	**yakhdish** *v.* يخدش scratch
yajma' *v.* 2 يجمع gather	**yakheet** *v.* يخيط sew
yajma' *v.* 3 يجمع group	**yakhfiq** *v.* 1 يخفق pulsate
yajma' *v.* 4 يجمع sum	**yakhfiq** *v.* 2 يخفق whisk
yajni *v.* يجني reap	**yakhfit** *v.* يخفت diminish
yajoo' *v.* يجوع starve	**yakhif** *v.* يَخِف thin
yajor *v.* يجر drag	**yakhiz** *v.* يخز prick
yajra' *v.* يجرع drench	**yakhjal** *v.* يخجل blush
yajrah *v.* يجرح wound	**yakhla'** *v.* يخلع dethrone
yajrof *v.* يجرف shovel	**yakhliq** *v.* يخلق create
yajrou *v.* يجرؤ dare	**yakhlit** *v.* 1 يخلط confuse
yajshou *v.* يجشأ belch	**yakhlit** *v.* 2 يخلط shuffle
yajtar *v.* يجتر ruminate	**yakhlo** *v.* يخلو empty
yajthim *v.* يجثم perch	**yakhmid** *v.* يخمد slake

yakhnah *n.* يخنة stew	**yakhto** *v.* يَخطو stride
yakhniq *v.* يخنق strangle	**yakhzin** *v.* يخزن stock
yakhod *v.* يخض churn	**yaknis** *v.* يكنس vacuum
yakhood *v.* يَخوض wade	**yaknos** *v.* يكنس sweep
yakhoon *v.* يخون betray	**yakoon** *v.* يكون be
yakhor *v.* يخور moo	**yakrah** *v.* يكره hate
yakhriq *v.* يخرق breach	**yaksab** *v.* يكسب gain
yakhroj *v.* 1 يخرج emerge	**yakshif** *v.* يكشف disclose
yakhroj *v.* 2 يخرج exit	**yaksi** *v.* يكسي clothe
yakhrom *v.* يخرم perforate	**yaksir** *v.* يكسر break
yakhsar *v.* يخسر lose	**yakso** *v.* يكسو encase
yakhsom *v.* يخصم deduct	**yaksol** *v.* يكسل laze
yakht *n.* يخت yacht	**yaktashif** *v.* يكتشف discover
yakhtaal *v.* يختال swagger	**yaktasib** *v.* يكتسب acquire
yakhtaar *v.* يختار select	**yaktauib** *v.* يكتئب mope
yakhtabir *v.* يختبر test	**yaktob** *v.* يكتب write
yakhtabiu *v.* يختبئ hide	**yakwi** *v.* يكوي iron
yakhtafi *v.* يختفي disappear	**yal'ab** *v.* يلعب play
yakhtalif *v.* 1 يختلف differ	**yal'an** *v.* يلعن curse
yakhtalif *v.* 2 يختلف vary	**yal'aq** *v.* يلعق lick
yakhtaliq *v.* يختلق feign	**yalbis** *v.* يلبس dress
yakhtalis *v.* يختلس misappropriate	**yaldagh** *v.* يلدغ sting
yakhtalit *v.* يختلط mingle	**yaleen** *v.* يلين relent
yakhtaniq *v.* يختنق choke	**yalfidd** *v.* يلفظ utter
yakhtari' *v.* يخترع invent	**yalghi** *v.* يلغي cancel
yakhtariq *v.* يخترق penetrate	**yalhaq** *v.* يلحق follow
yakhtasir *v.* 1 يختصر abbreviate	**yalhath** *v.* يلهث gasp
yakhtasir *v.* 2 يختصر abridge	**yalkom** *v.* يلكم punch
yakhtatif *v.* 1 يختطف abduct	**yalma'** *v.* يلمع glitter
yakhtatif *v.* 2 يختطف snap-shoot	**yalmah** *v.* يلمح glance
yakhtib *v.* يخطب betroth	**yalmis** *v.* يلمس touch
yakhtif *v.* يخطف kidnap	**yalof** *v.* 1 يلف wind
yakhtim *v.* 1 يختم seal	**yalof** *v.* 2 يلف wrap
yakhtim *v.* 2 يختم stamp	**yaloom** *v.* يلوم blame
	yalsa' *v.* يلسع nettle

yaltamis *v.* يلتمس petition	**yan'al** *v.* ينعَل sole
yaltaqi *v.* يلتقي meet	**yan'am** *v.* ينعم grace
yaltazim *v.* يلتزم abide	**yan'aq** *v.* ينعق caw
yalthogh *v.* يلثغ lisp	**yanaam** *v.* ينام sleep
yalwi *v.* يلوي sprain	**yanaaseeb** *n.* يناصيب ruffle
yamdah *v.* يمدح acclaim	**yanassif** *v.* ينصّف halve
yamdogh *v.* يمضغ chew	**yanba'ith** *v.* ينبعث emit
yameel *v.* يميل 1 tend	**yanbah** *v.* ينبح bark
yameel *v.* يميل 2 tilt	**yanbahir** *v.* ينبهر dazzle
yameel *v.* يميل tip	**yanbajis** *v.* يَنْبَجِس spout
yameen *adj.* يَمين right	**yanbathiq** *v.* ينبثق stem
yamho *v.* يمحو erase	**yanbatih** *v.* ينبطح duck
yamid *v.* يمد extend	**yanbid** *v.* ينبض throb
yamlau *v.* يملأ fill	**yanbish** *v.* ينبش paw
yamlik *v.* يملك own	**yanbodh** *v.* ينبذ renounce
yamna' *v.* يمنع forbid	**yandafi'** *v.* يندفع rush
yamnah *v.* يمنح award	**yandali'** *v.* يندلع erupt
yamooj *v.* يَموج surge	**yandam** *v.* يندم rue
yamoot *v.* يموت die	**yandam** *v.* ينضم join
yamor *v.* يمر pass	**yandamij** *v.* يندمج commune
yamqot *v.* يمقت loathe	**yanddor** *v.* ينظر look
yamrah *v.* يمرح frolic	**yandhor** *v.* ينذر vow
yamsah *v.* يمسح wipe	**yandob** *v.* يندب lament
yamshi *v.* يمشي walk	**yandoj** *v.* ينضج 1 mature
yamtad *v.* يمتد stretch	**yandoj** *v.* ينضج 2 ripen
yamtahin *v.* يمتحن quiz	**yanfajir** *v.* ينفجر explode
yamtalik *v.* يمتلك possess	**yanfasil** *v.* ينفصل secede
yamtani' *v.* يمتنع refrain	**yanfi** *v.* ينفي exile
yamtas *v.* يمتص absorb	**yanfokh** *v.* ينفخ puff
yamtathil *v.* يمتثل comply	**yanghamis** *v.* ينغمس indulge
yamtati *v.* يَمْتَطي mount	**yanhaar** *v.* ينهار collapse
yamwi *v.* يموي mew	**yanhaaz** *v.* ينحاز bias
yamzah *v.* يمزح gag	**yanhab** *v.* ينهب ransack
yamzah *v.* يمزح joke	**yanhadir** *v.* ينحدر 1 slope
yamzij *v.* يمزج mix	**yanhadir** *v.* ينحدر 2 stoop

yanhaj v. ينهج approach	**yanqosh** v. ينقش carve
yanhal v. ينحل slim	**yanqosh** v. ينقش engrave
yanhamik v. ينهمك preoccupy	**yanqot** v. ينقط trickle
yanhani v. ينحي disqualify	**yansa** v. ينسى forget
yanhany v. ينحني bow	**yansah** v. ينصح advise
yanhaq v. ينهق bray	**yansahib** v. ينسحب withdraw
yanhash v. يَنهَش maul	**yansajim** v. يَنسَجِم tone
yanhassir v. ينحصر ebb	**yansakh** v. ينسخ copy
yanhat v. ينحت sculpt	**yansakh** v. 1 نسخ copy
yanjadhib v. ينجذب gravitate	**yansakh** v. 2 نسخ reproduce
yanjah v. ينجح succeed	**yanshat** v. ينشط bustle
yanjarif v. ينجرف drift	**yanshau** v. ينشأ originate
yanjo v. ينجو outlive	**yanshoj** v. يَنشِج sob
yankamish v. ينكمش shrink	**yanshor** v. 1 ينشر publish
yankhal v. ينخل sift	**yanshor** v. 2 ينشر saw
yankhar v. ينخر grunt	**yansib** v. ينصب erect
yankhaz v. ينخز poke	**yansif** v. ينسف torpedo
yankor v. ينكر abnegate	**yantabih** v. ينتبه notice
yankos v. ينكص recoil	**yantaddir** v. ينتظر wait
yanmo v. ينمو grow	**yantadib** v. ينتدب depute
yanooh v. ينوح bewail	**yantafikh** v. ينتفخ billow
yanoq v. ينق nag	**yantahik** v. ينتهك infringe
yanqa' v. ينقع soak	**yantahil** v. ينتحل impersonate
yanqad v. يَنقَضّ pounce	**yantahir** v. يَنتَهِر slight
yanqadi v. ينقضي elapse	**yantahiz** v. ينتهز profiteer
yanqalib v. ينقلب capsize	**yantakhib** v. ينتخب elect
yanqasim v. ينقسم split	**yantami** v. ينتمي belong
yanqil v. 1 ينقل deliver	**yantaqi'** v. يَنتَقِع steep
yanqil v. 2 ينقل transfer	**yantaqim** v. ينتقم retaliate
yanqod v. ينقد criticize	**yantashir** v. ينتشر spread
yanqod v. يَنقُض veto	**yantasir** v. ينتصر triumph
yanqor v. ينقر click	**yantawi** v. ينطوي involve
yanqor v. يَنقُر tap	**yantazi'** v. ينتزع snatch
yanqos v. ينقص decrease	**yanthor** v. 1 ينثر sow
yanqos v. ينقص lack	**yanthor** v. 2 ينثر strew

yantif v. ينتف pluck

yanton v. ينتن stink

yantoq v. ينطق pronounce

yanza' v. ينزع disarm

yanzaliq v. ينزلق slip

yanzif v. ينزف bleed

yaqa' v. 1 يقع fall

yaqa' v. 2 يقع lie

yaqaddah n. 1 يقظة awakening

yaqaddah n. 2 يقظة wake

yaqadhah n. 3 يقظة vigil

yaqbal v. يقبل accept

yaqbid v. 1 يقبض catch

yaqbid v. 2 يقبض grip

yaqdhif v. يقذف fling

yaqdi v. 1 يقضي eradicate

yaqdi v. 2 يقضي spend

yaqdim v. يقضم munch

yaqeen n. يقين certainty

yaqees v. يقيس measure

yaqfiz v. يقفز jump

yaqhar v. 1 يقهر conquer

yaqhar v. 2 يقهر vanquish

yaqidd adj. 1 يقظ observant

yaqidd adj. 2 يقظ awake

yaqif v. 1 يقف pause

yaqif v. 2 يقف stand

yaqlaq v. يقلق worry

yaqli v. يقلي fry

yaqlib v. 1 يقلب invert

yaqlib v. 2 يقلب overthrow

yaqma' v. يقمع oppress

yaqood v. يقود conduct

yaqood v. 1 يقود drive

yaqood v. 2 يقود lead

yaqool v. يقول say

yaqoom v. 1 يقوم stand up

yaqoom v. 2 يقوم do

yaqos v. 1 يقص narrate

yaqos v. 2 يقص cut

yaqra' v. يقرع ring

yaqrau v. يقرأ read

yaqrid v. يقرض lend

yaqros v. يقرص pinch

yaqshor v. يقشر scale

yaqshot v. يقشط raze

yaqshot v. يكشُط graze

yaqsid v. 1 يقصد mean

yaqsid v. 2 يقصد aim

yaqsif v. يقصف bombard

yaqsim v. 1 يقسم divide

yaqsim v. 2 يقسم swear

yaqta' v. 1 يقطع disconnect

yaqta' v. 2 يقطع cross

yaqtabis v. يقتبس quote

yaqtali' v. يقتلع uproot

yaqtari' v. يقترع ballot

yaqtaribo v. يقترب near

yaqtarid v. يقترض borrow

yaqtarih v. يقترح suggest

yaqteen n. يقطين pumpkin

yaqtol v. يقتل kill

yaqtor v. يقطر drip

yar'a v. 1 يرعى nurse

yar'a v. 2 يرعى nurture

yar'a v. 3 يرعى sponsor

yar'a v. 4 يرعى graze

yar'id v. يرعد thunder

yara v. يرى see

yaraqah n. يرقة caterpillar

yarbid v. يربض crouch	**yarshoq** v. يَرشُق splash
yarbit v. 1 يربط attribute	**yarso** v. يرسو dock
yarbit v. 2 يربط tie	**yarsod** v. يرصد observe
yarda v. يرضى be content	**yarsom** v. يرسم draw
yarda' v. يرضع suckle	**yartaah** v. يرتاح rest
yarfa' v. 1 يرفع lift	**yartabit** v. 1 يرتبط engage
yarfa' v. 2 يرفع boost	**yartabit** v. 2 يرتبط be associated with
yarfod v. 1 يرفض refuse	
yarfod v. 2 يرفض reject	**yartad** v. يرتد rebound
yarghab v. يرغب fancy	**yartadi** v. يرتدي wear
yarhal v. يرحل voyage	**yartafi'** v. يرتفع rise
yarhin v. يرهن let	**yartajif** v. يرتجف tremble
yarin v. يَرِنّ ring	**yartajj** v. يرتج shudder
yarji' v. 1 يرجع refer	**yartakib** v. يرتكب commit
yarji' v. 2 يرجع return	**yartashif** v. يرتشف nip
yarjim v. يَرجُم stone	**yartatim** v. يرتطم bump
yarka' v. يركع kneel	**yartaui** v. يرتئي opine
yarkab v. يركب ride	**yarthi** v. يرثي commiserate
yarkhi v. يرخي loosen	**yartim** v. يرطم thump
yarkil v. يركل kick	**yaruad** v. يرئد pioneer
yarkod v. يركد stagnate	**yarwi** v. يروي irrigate
yarkod v. يركض run	**yarzah** v. يرزح languish
yarmah v. يرمح lance	**yas'a** v. يسعى strive
yarmi v. يرمي throw	**yas'ad** v. يصعد ascend
yarmiz v. يرمز symbolize	**yas'ol** v. يسعل cough
yarmoh v. يرمح gallop	**yasaar** n. يسار left
yarmosh v. 1 يرمش blink	**yasaariy** n. يساري leftist
yarmosh v. 2 يرمش flicker	**yasbah** v. يسبح swim
yarod v. 1 يرد reply	**yasbigh** v. يصبغ dye
yarod v. 2 يرد repay	**yasbiq** v. يسبق precede
yarosh v. يرش spray	**yasbor** v. يَسبُر probe
yarqos v. يرقص dance	**yasdau** v. يصدأ rust
yarshah v. يرشح ooze	**yasdim** v. 1 يصدم shock
yarshi v. يرشي bribe	**yasdim** v. 2 يصدم hit
yarshof v. يرشف sip	**yaseedo** v. يَصيد hunt

yaseegh v. يصيغ formulate	**yashol** v. يصهل neigh
yaseeh v. 1 يصيح crow	**yashom** v. يشم smell
yaseeh v. 2 يصيح shout	**yashra'** v. يشرع embark
yaseer v. يسير walk	**yashrab** v. يشرب drink
yasfa v. يصفى leach	**yashrah** v. 1 يشرح elucidate
yasfa' v. يصفع slap	**yashrah** v. 2 يشرح explain
yasfar v. يصفر yellow	**yashrod** v. يشرد stray
yasfir v. يصفر whistle	**yashta'il** v. يشتعل sparkle
yash'or v. يشعر feel	**yashtaaq** v. يَشتاق pine
yashab v. 1 يسحب draw	**yashtabik** v. يشتبك engage
yashab v. 2 يسحب pull	**yashtaghil** v. يشتغل work
yashaq v. يسحق crush	**yashtahi** v. يشتهي covet
yashar v. يسحر enchant	**yashtari** v. يشتري purchase
yashar v. يصهر forge	**yashtarik** v. 1 يشترك participate
yashba' v. يشبع become full	**yashtarik** v. 2 يشترك join
yashbik v. يشبك entangle	**yashtarit** v. يشترط stipulate
yasheet v. يشيط scorch	**yashtif** v. يشطف rinse
yashfa v. يشفى recover	**yashtir** v. يشطر bisect
yashfaq v. يشفق pity	**yashwi** v. يشو roast
yashhad v. 1 يشهد testify	**yasid** v. يسد plug
yashhad v. 2 يشهد witness	**yasif** v. 1 يصف prescribe
yashhadh v. يشحذ sharpen	**yasif** v. 2 يصف describe
yashhan v. يشحن ship	**yasil** v. يصل reach
yashhob v. يشحب pale	**yasin** v. يسن enact
yashid v. يَشد lace	**yasir** v. يصر insist
yashil v. يشل paralyse	**yasjin** v. يسجن imprison
yashin v. يَشن wage	**yasjod** v. يسجد prostrate
yashiq v. يشق crack	**yaskhab** v. يصخب clamour
yashjob v. يشجب denounce	**yaskhar** v. يسخر ridicule
yashkhar v. يشخر snore	**yaskob** v. يسكب spill
yashko v. يشكو complain	**yaskon** v. يسكن inhabit
yashkor v. يشكر thank	**yaskot** v. يسكت go silent
yashm n. يشم jade	**yaslakh** v. يسلخ skin
yashmal v. يشمل include	**yaslib** v. يسلب rob
yashok v. يشك doubt	**yasliq** v. يسلق boil

yasma' *v.* يسمع hear	**yastad'i** *v.* 1 يستدعي invoke
yasmah *v.* يسمح allow	**yastad'i** *v.* 2 يستدعي call
yasmar *v.* يسمر tan	**yastadim** *v.* يصطدم collide
yasna' *v.* يصنع make	**yastadiq** *v.* يستدق taper
yasnid *v.* يسند support	**yastadrik** *v.* يستدرك rectify
yasob *v.* يصب pour	**yastafeed** *v.* يستفيد benefit
yasod *v.* يصد fend	**yastafiz** *v.* يستفز provoke
yasom *v.* يسم poison	**yastafsir** *v.* يستفسر inquire
yasood *v.* 1 يسود blacken	**yastagheeb** *v.* يستغيب absent
yasood *v.* 2 يسود prevail	**yastaghil** *v.* يستغل exploit
yasoogh *v.* يصوغ mould	**yastaghriq** *v.* يستغرق engross
yasoom *v.* يصوم fast	**yastahdir** *v.* يستحضر evoke
yasooq *v.* يَسوق drive	**yastahim** *v.* يستحم bathe
yasqi *v.* يسقي water	**yastahiq** *v.* يستحق deserve
yasqol *v.* يصقل refine	**yastahith** *v.* يستحث goad
yasqot *v.* يسقط plunge	**yastahlif** *v.* يستحلف adjure
yasra' *v.* يصرع floor	**yastahlik** *v.* يستهلك consume
yasrif *v.* 1 يصرف dismiss	**yastahwidh** *v.* يستحوذ seize
yasrif *v.* 2 يصرف spend	**yastahziu** *v.* يستهزئ mock
yasriq *v.* يسرق steal	**yastajmi'** *v.* يستجمع summon
yasrod *v.* يسرد recount	**yastajwib** *v.* يستجوب interrogate
yasrokh *v.* يصرخ scream	**yastakhdim** *v.* يستخدم utilize
yasta'bid *v.* يستعبد enslave	**yastakhif** *v.* يستخف undermine
yasta'eed *v.* 1 يستعيد reclaim	**yastakhlis** *v.* 1 يستخلص conclude
yasta'eed *v.* 2 يستعيد restore	**yastakhlis** *v.* 2 يستخلص extract
yasta'lim *v.* يستعلم query	**yastakshif** *v.* يستكشف explore
yasta'mil *v.* يستعمل use	**yastalim** *v.* يستلم receive
yasta'rid *v.* 1 يستعرض parade	**yastall** *v.* يستل unsheathe
yasta'rid *v.* 2 يستعرض review	**yastalzim** *v.* يستلزم necessitate
yastaad *v.* 1 يصطاد fish	**yastami'** *v.* يستمع listen
yastaad *v.* 2 يصطاد hunt	**yastamid** *v.* يستمد derive
yastaau *v.* يستاء resent	**yastamir** *v.* يستمر ply
yastab'id *v.* يستبعد exclude	**yastamni** *v.* يستمني masturbate
yastabdil *v.* يستبدل replace	**yastamti'** *v.* يستمتع enjoy
yastabtin *v.* يستبطن introspect	**yastanbit** *v.* يستنبط devise

yastanfiz v. يستنفز drain
yastanid v. يستند base
yastanshiq v. يستنشق inhale
yastansikh v. يستنسخ clone
yastantij v. يستنتج conclude
yastanzif v. يستنزف drain
yastaqeel v. يستقيل resign
yastaqir v. 1 يستقر settle
yastaqir v. 2 يستقر stabilize
yastardi v. يسترضي appease
yastareeh v. يستريح rest
yastarkhi v. يسترخي relax
yastarrid v. يسترد retrieve
yastash'ir v. يستشعر conjecture
yastashhid v. يستشهد cite
yastaslih v. 1 يستصلح restore
yastaslih v. 2 يستصلح reclaim
yastaslim v. يستسلم surrender
yastatee' v. يستطيع can
yastathmir v. يستثمر invest
yastathni v. يستثني except
yastatir v. يستتر lurk
yastatli' v. يستطلع canvass
yastaunif v. 1 يستأنف appeal
yastaunif v. 2 يستأنف resume
yastaw'ib v. 1 يستوعب understand
yastaw'ib v. 2 يستوعب hold
yastawrid v. يستورد import
yasual v. يسأل ask
yat han v. يطحن grind
yat'aawan v. يتعاون co-operate
yat'ab v. يتعب exhaust
yat'an v. يطعن stab
yata'aadal v. يتعادل draw
yata'aamal v. 1 يتعامل handle

yata'aamal v. 2 يتعامل transact
yata'aataf v. يتعاطف sympathize
yata'aayash v. يتعايش cohabit
yata'affan v. يتعفّن rot
yata'ahhad v. يتعهّد pledge
yata'ajjab v. يتعجّب marvel
yata'allam v. يتعلّم learn
yata'allaq v. يتعلّق pertain
yata'ammad v. 1 يتعمّد deliberate
yata'ammad v. 2 يتعمّد be baptised
yata'aqqab v. يتعقّب trace
yata'arqal v. يتعرقل trip
yata'arrad v. يتعرّض subject
yata'arraf v. 1 يتعرّف meet
yata'arraf v. 2 يتعرّف recognize
yata'arraj v. يَتَعَرَّج wind
yata'ashsha v. يتعشّى dine
yata'athar v. يتعثر stumble
yata'attaf v. يتعطف vouchsafe
yata'attash v. يتعطّش thirst
yata'awwad v. يتعود habituate
yatabaadal v. يتبادل exchange
yatabaaha v. يتباهى boast
yatabajjah v. يتبجّح brag
yatabakhkhar v. يتبخّر evaporate
yatabanna v. يتبنّى adopt
yatabar'am v. يتبرعم germinate
yatabarra' v. يتبرع donate
yatabarraj v. يتبرّج powder
yatabartakh v. يتبختر strut
yatabawwal v. يتبوّل urinate
yatadaa'a v. يتداعى falter
yatadaakhal v. يتداخل overlap
yatadaarab v. يتضارب conflict

yatadaaual v. يتضاءل wane
yatadaffaq v. يتدفق flow
yatadakhkhal v. يتدخل intervene
yatadakhkham v. يتضخم swell
yatadarra' v. يتدرع shield
yatadarrab v. يتدرّب rehearse
yatadarraj v. يتدرج scale
yataddaahar v. يتظاهر pretend
yatadhakkar v. يتذكّر remember
yatadhammar v. يتذمّر grumble
yatadhawwaq v. يتذوّق taste
yatafaa'al v. يتفاعل react
yatafaawad v. يتفاوض negotiate
yatafahhas v. 1 يتفحّص check
yatafahhas v. 2 يتفحّص scan
yatafakkar v. يتفكر mull
yatafawwaq v. 1 يتفوّق surpass
yatafawwaq v. 2 يتفوّق excel
yataghadda v. يتغدّى lunch
yataghallab v. 1 يتغلّب outdo
yataghallab v. 2 يتغلّب overcome
yatagharghar v. يتغرغر gargle
yataghatras v. يتغطرس bully
yatahaada v. يتهادى plod
yatahaalaf v. يتحالف ally
yatahaawar v. يتحاور confer
yatahadda v. يتحدّى challenge
yatahaddar v. يتحضر get ready
yatahaddath v. يتحدّث speak
yatahaffadd v. يتحفظ retain
yatahajjam v. يتهجّم sally
yatahajjar v. يتحجر ossify
yatahakkam v. يتحكّم control
yatahakkam v. يتهكم taunt
yatahallal v. يتحلّل decompose

yatahammal v. يتحمّل tolerate
yatahaqqaq v. 1 يتحقق materialize
yatahaqqaq v. 2 يتحقق check
yataharrak v. يتحرك move
yataharrash v. يَتَحَرّش molest
yatahassan v. يتحسّن ameliorate
yatahassas v. يَتَحَسّس grope
yatahattam v. يتحطم crash
yatahayyad v. يتحيد deviate
yatahayyaz v. يتحيز side
yatajaahal v. يتجاهل ignore
yatajaawaz v. 1 يتجاوز exceed
yatajaawaz v. 2 يتجاوز surmount
yatajaddad v. يتجدّد regenerate
yatajalla v. يتجلّى transfigure
yatajallat v. يتجلط clot
yatajamhar v. يتجمهر mob
yatajannab v. 1 يتجنب avoid
yatajannab v. 2 يتجنب shun
yatajannad v. يتجنّد soldier
yatajassad v. يَتَجَسّد materialize
yatajassas v. يتجسّس spy
yatajawwal v. يتجوّل wander
yatakaathar v. يتكاثر breed
yatakahhan v. يتكهّن speculate
yatakarrar v. يتكرّر recur
yatakashshaf v. يتكشف unfold
yatakattal v. يتكتل cluster
yatakayyaf v. يتكيّف adapt
yatakhaalat v. يتخالط intermingle
yatakhabbat v. يتخبّط blunder
yatakhabbat v. يتخبط wallow
yatakhalla v. يتخلّى abandon
yatakhallaf v. يتخلّف fall behind
yatakhallas v. يتخلّص dispose

yatakhammar *v.* يتخمّر ferment
yatakharraj *v.* يتخرج graduate
yatakhassas *v.* يتخصّص specialize
yatakhatta *v.* يتخطّى trespass
yatakhayyal *v.* يتخيّل imagine
yatala'tham *v.* يتلعثم stammer
yatalaa'ab *v.* 1 يتلاعب manipulate
yatalaa'ab *v.* 2 يتلاعب tamper
yatalaasha *v.* يتلاش fade
yatalaauam *v.* يَتلائم tally
yataladhdhadh *v.* يتلذّذ savour
yatalakkau *v.* يتلكأ loiter
yatalaulau *v.* يتلألأ sparkle
yatalawwa *v.* يتلوّى snake
yatamaayal *v.* يتمايل wobble
yatamaddad *v.* يتمدّد lie
yatamallaq *v.* يتملّق wheedle
yatamallas *v.* يتملص wriggle
yatamallas *v.* يتملّص elude
yatamanna *v.* يتمنّى wish
yatamarkaz *v.* 1 يتمركز rank
yatamarkaz *v.* 2 يتمركز be based
yatamarrad *v.* يتمرّد rebel
yatamawwaj *v.* يتموّج ripple
yatamtim *v.* يُتَمْتِم mumble
yatanaafas *v.* يتنافس compete
yatanaawab *v.* يتناوب rotate
yatanaawal *v.* يتناول commune
yatanaazal *v.* يتنازل concede
yatanabbah *v.* يتنبه be alert
yatanabbau *v.* يتنبأ predict
yatanaffas *v.* يتنفّس breathe
yatanahhad *v.* يتنهّد sigh
yatanaqqal *v.* يتنقل move
yatanashshat *v.* يتنشّط limber
yatanassat *v.* يتنصت tap
yatanazzah *v.* يتنزّه picnic
yataqaa'ad *v.* يتقاعد retire
yataqaasam *v.* يتقاسم share
yataqaata' *v.* يتقاطع intersect
yataqabbal *v.* يتقبّل acquiesce
yataqaddam *v.* يتقدم advance
yataqaffa *v.* 1 يَتَقَفّى rhyme
yataqaffa *v.* 2 يتقفّى follow suit
yataqallab *v.* يتقلّب toss
yataqallas *v.* يتقلّص contract
yataqanna' *v.* يتقنّع mask
yataqayyau *v.* يتقيأ vomit
yataraaja' *v.* 1 يتراجع retreat
yataraaja' *v.* 2 يتراجع undo
yataraakam *v.* يتراكم accumulate
yataraakha *v.* يتراخ slacken
yataraawah *v.* يَتراوَح range
yatarabbas *v.* يَتَربَّص waylay
yataraddad *v.* 1 يتردّد haunt
yataraddad *v.* 2 يتردّد hesitate
yatarammal *v.* يترمّل widow
yatarannah *v.* يترنّح stagger
yatarattab *v.* يترتب ensue
yatarauuas *v.* يترأس preside
yatasaadam *v.* يتصادم collide
yatasaama *v.* يتسامى sublimate
yatasaara' *v.* يتسارع accelerate
yatasaara' *v.* يتصارع grapple
yatasaffah *v.* يتصفّح browse
yatasakka' *v.* يتسكّع fool
yatasallal *v.* يتسلّل sneak
yatasallaq *v.* يتسلّق climb
yatasarrab *v.* يتسرب leak

yatasarraf *v.* يتصرّف behave	**yatawaafad** *v.* يتوفّق flock
yatasawwaq *v.* يتسوّق shop	**yatawaanah** *v.* يتوان dawdle
yatasawwar *v.* 1 يتصوّر conceive	**yatawaasal** *v.* يتواصل communicate
yatasawwar *v.* 2 يتصوّر picture	**yatawaasat** *v.* يتواسط mediate
yatashaabak *v.* يتشابك interlock	**yatawaddad** *v.* يتودّد court
yatashaahan *v.* يتشاحن bicker	**yatawahhaj** *v.* يتوهّج glow
yatashaawar *v.* يتشاور consult	**yatawalla** *v.* يتولّى assume
yatashabba' *v.* يتشبّع saturate	**yatawaqqa'** *v.* 1 يتوقّع anticipate
yatashabbath *v.* يتشبّث cling	**yatawaqqa'** *v.* 2 يتوقّع expect
yatashammas *v.* يتشمّس bask	**yatawaqqaf** *v.* يتوقّف stop
yatashaqlab *v.* يتشقلب somersault	**yatawarrad** *v.* يتورّد flush
yatataaba' *v.* يتتابع relay	**yatawassal** *v.* يتوسّل beg
yatataabaq *v.* يتطابق correspond	**yatawassat** *v.* 1 يتوسّط average
yatataffal *v.* يتطفّل intrude	**yatawassat** *v.* 2 يتوسّط mediate
yatatallab *v.* يتطلّب require	**yatawassat** *v.* 3 يتوسّط centre
yatatarraf *v.* يتطرّف overdo	**yatayabbas** *v.* يتيبّس stiffen
yatatawwa' *v.* يتطوّع volunteer	**yatazaaman** *v.* يتزامن coincide
yatatawwar *v.* يتطوّر evolve	**yatazaawaj** *v.* يتزاوج mate
yatathaauab *v.* يتثاءب yawn	**yatazahlaq** *v.* يتزحلق slide
yatauaamar *v.* يتآمر conspire	**yatazahzah** *v.* يتزحزح budge
yatauaamar *v.* يتآمر plot	**yatazallaj** *v.* يتزلّج skate
yatauakhkhar *v.* يتأخّر be late	**yatba'** *v.* يتبع follow
yatauakkad *v.* يتأكّد ascertain	**yatba'** *v.* 1 يطبع print
yatauallaf *v.* يتألّف consist	**yatba'** *v.* 2 يطبع type
yatauallam *v.* يتألّم suffer	**yatbokh** *v.* يطبخ cook
yatauallaq *v.* يتألّق outshine	**yateem** *n.* يتيم orphan
yatauammal *v.* 1 يتأمّل contemplate	**yateer** *v.* يطير fly
yatauammal *v.* 2 يتأمّل meditate	**yathbot** *v.* يثبت substantiate
yatauaqlam *v.* يتأقلم acclimatise	**yathbot** *v.* يثبّت steady
yatauarjah *v.* يتأرجح sway	**yathghi** *v.* يثغي bleat
yatauassal *v.* يتأصّل root	**yathib** *v.* يثب vault
yatauaththar *v.* يتأثّر sway	**yathiq** *v.* يثق trust
yatauawwah *v.* يتأوّه groan	**yathkol** *v.* يثكل bereave
	yathni *v.* 1 يثني dissuade

yathni v. 2 يثني fold	yausaf v. يأسف regret
yatho v. يطهو cook	yausor v. 1 يأسر begird
yathoor v. يثور rampage	yausor v. 2 يأسر capture
yathqob v. يثقب pierce	yauti v. يأتي come
yathuar v. يثأر avenge	yauwi v. يأو accommodate
yatin v. يطن buzz	yawm n. يوم day
yatli v. يطلي paint	yawmiy adv. يومي adays
yatlo v. يتلو recite	yawmiy adj. يومي daily
yatlob v. يطلب request	yawmiy n. يومي daily
yatmah v. يطمح aspire	yawmiyyan adv. يوميا daily
yatmauin v. يطمئن reassure	yawrith v. يورث bequeath
yatmis v. يطمس obliterate	yawshim v. يوشم tattoo
yatoob v. يتوب repent	yawsim v. يوسم knight
yatoof v. يطوف rove	yayl n. ويل woe
yatooq v. يتوق yearn	yayuas v. ييأس despair
yatooq v. يطوق long	yaz'am v. يزعم allege
yatrah v. 1 يطرح subtract	yaz'aq v. يزعق shriek
yatrah v. 2 يطرح knock down	yazdahir v. يزدهر flourish
yatrah v. 3 يطرح place	yazdari v. يزدري disdain
yatrod v. يطرد expel	yazeed v. يزيد increase
yatrok v. يترك leave	yazhaf v. 1 يزحف crawl
yatroq v. يطرق knock	yazhaf v. 2 يزحف creep
yattahim v. يتهم accuse	yazim v. يزم tighten
yattasil v. يتصل call	yazoor v. يزور visit
yattazin v. يتزن poise	yazra' v. يزرع plant
yatwi v. يطوي fold	yo'aadi v. يعادي antagonize
yaudhan v. يأذن authorize	yo'aadil v. 1 يعادل equal
yauhol v. يأهل house	yo'aadil v. 2 يعادل equalize
yauin v. يئن moan	yo'aalij v. 1 يعالج tackle
yauiz v. يايز whiz	yo'aalij v. 2 يعالج treat
yaukhodh v. يأخذ take	yo'aamil v. يعامل treat
yaukol v. يأكل eat	yo'aaniq v. يعانق caress
yaumal v. يأمل hope	yo'aaqib v. يعاقب punish
yaumor v. يأمر command	yo'aarid v. يعارض oppose
yaus n. يأس despair	yo'aarik v. يعارك battle

yo'aatib v. يعاتب reproach

yo'aawin v. يعاون assist

yo'aayin v. يعاني suffer

yo'abbir v. يعبّر express

yo'abbiu v. يعبّئ fill

yo'ad v. يُعدّ be considered

yo'addddim v. 1 يعظم glorify

yo'addddim v. 2 يعظّم maximize

yo'addil v. يعدّل modify

yo'adhdhib v. يعذّب torture

yo'ajjil v. يعجّل hurry

yo'allib v. يعلّب can

yo'allim v. 1 يعلّم tag

yo'allim v. 2 يعلّم teach

yo'alliq v. 1 يعلّق comment

yo'alliq v. 2 يعلّق hang

yo'alliq v. 3 يعلّق suspend

yo'ammid v. يعمّد baptize

yo'ammim v. يعمّم circulate

yo'ammir v. 1 يُعمّر fix

yo'ammir v. 2 يُعمّر age

yo'annif v. يعنّف slam

yo'anwin v. يعنون label

yo'aqqid v. يعقّد complicate

yo'aqqim v. يعقّم sterilize

yo'arqil v. يعرقل obstruct

yo'arri v. يعرّ denude

yo'arri v. يعرّي strip

yo'arrid v. يعرّض expose

yo'arrif v. 1 يعرّف acquaint

yo'arrif v. 2 يعرّف define

yo'arriq v. يعرّق vein

yo'ashshish v. يعشّش nest

yo'attil v. يعطّل disrupt

yo'attir v. يعطّر perfume

yo'attir v. يعطّر scent

yo'awwid v. يعوّض compensate

yo'awwiq v. يعوّق hinder

yo'ayyin v. يعيّن appoint

yo'azzi v. يعزّي condole

yo'azziz v. 1 يعزّز promote

yo'azziz v. 2 يعزّز strengthen

yo'di v. يعدي infect

yo'eeb v. يعيب blemish

yo'eed v. 1 يعيد repeat

yo'eed v. 2 يعيد revert

yo'een v. يعين assist

yo'eeq v. يعيق handicap

yo'id v. يعد prepare

yo'jab v. يعجب admire

yo'jib v. يعجب impress

yo'lim v. يعلم inform

yo'lin v. 1 يعلن advertise

yo'lin v. 2 يعلن declare

yo'rib v. يعرب express

yo'ti v. يعطي give

yo'tib v. يعطب vitiate

yo'tiq v. يعتق enfranchise

yo'tiq v. يعتق manumit

yob'id v. يبعد banish

yobaa'id v. يباعد space

yobaahith v. يباحث discuss

yobaaligh v. يبالغ exaggerate

yobaarik v. يبارك bless

yobaariz v. يبارز duel

yobaashir v. يباشر commence

yobaddid v. يبدد squander

yobaddil v. يبدّل alternate

yobahhir v. يبهّر season

yobajjil v. يبجّل revere

yobakhkhir v. يبخر cense

yobar'im v. يرعم sprout

yobarmij v. يرمج programme

yobarrid v. يبرد cool

yobarrir v. يبرر justify

yobarriu v. يبرئ whitewash

yobarshim v. يُبَرشِم rivet

yobassit v. يبسط simplify

yobatbit v. يُبَطبِط quack

yobauthir v. يبعثر scatter

yobawwiq v. يُبَوِق trumpet

yobayyid v. 1 يبيض bleach

yobayyid v. 2 يبيض whiten

yobhij v. يبهج delight

yobhir v. يبحر sail

yobligh v. يبلغ tell

yobriq v. يبرق telegraph

yobriz v. يبرز underline

yobtil v. 1 يبطل invalidate

yobtil v. 2 يبطل revoke

yobtiu v. يبطئ slow

yod'a v. يُدعى term

yodaa'ib v. يداعب banter

yodaa'if v. يضاعف double

yodaafi' v. يدافع defend

yodaahi v. يضاه emulate

yodaawi v. يداوي heal

yodaayiq v. يُضايِق tease

yodabbis v. يُدَبِس staple

yodaffiu v. يدفئ warm

yodaghdigh v. يدغدغ tickle

yodahhi v. يضحي sacrifice

yodahrij v. يدحرج roll

yodakhkhim v. يضخم amplify

yodakhkhin v. 1 يدخن smoke

yodakhkhin v. 2 يدخن smoulder

yodalli v. يدل dangle

yodallik v. يدلك massage

yodallil v. يدلل spoil

yodallil v. يضلل misguide

yodammid v. يضمد bandage

yodanni v. يدني lower

yodannis v. يدنس profane

yodaqqiq v. يدقق scrutinize

yodardish v. يدردش chat

yodarrib v. يدرب train

yodarrij v. يدرج grade

yodawwi v. يدوي echo

yodawwim v. يُدَوِم whirl

yodawwin v. يُدَوِن note down

yodayyiq v. يضيق strict

yoddallil v. يظلل shade

yoddhir v. يظهر manifest

yoddlim v. يَظلُم darken

yodeef v. يضيف add

yodeem v. يديم perpetuate

yodeen v. يدين condemn

yodeer v. 1 يدير manage

yodeer v. 2 يدير turn

yodeeu v. يضيء light

yodhabdhib v. يذبذب oscillate

yodhakkir v. يذكر remind

yodhhil v. يذهل astonish

yodkhil v. يدخل insert

yodmin v. يدمن addict

yodrij v. يدرج incorporate

yodrik v. يدرك realize

yofaajiu v. يفاجئ surprise

yofaaqim v. يفاقم worsen

yofaawid v. يفاوض parley

yofaddil v. يفضّل prefer	**yoghliq** v. يغلق close
yofajjir v. يفجّر blast	**yoghni** v. 1 يغني substitute
yofakkir v. يفكر think	**yoghni** v. 2 يغني enrich
yofannid v. يفنّد confute	**yoghri** v. يغري tempt
yofarqi' v. يفرقع crackle	**yoghriq** v. يُغرِق swamp
yofarrigh v. يفرّغ empty	**yohaadhi** v. يحاذي align
yofarrikh v. يفرّخ spawn	**yohaadir** v. يحاضر lecture
yofarriq v. 1 يفرّق contrast	**yohaadith** v. يحادث converse
yofarriq v. 2 يفرّق disperse	**yohaafidd** v. يحافظ maintain
yofassil v. 1 يفصّل tailor	**yohaajir** v. يهاجر immigrate
yofassil v. 2 يفصّل detail	**yohaaki** v. يُحاكي emulate
yofassir v. يفسّر interpret	**yohaami** v. يحام champion
yofattih v. يفتّح brighten	**yohaarib** v. يحارب fight
yofattish v. يُفتِّش rifle	**yohaawil** v. يحاول try
yofattit v. يفتّت crumble	**yohaawir** v. يحاور debate
yofawwid v. يفوّض delegate	**yohabbidh** v. يحبّذ favour
yofeed v. يفيد avail	**yohaddid** v. 1 يحدّد determine
yofqir v. يفقر impoverish	**yohaddid** v. 2 يحدّد specify
yofsid v. يفسد corrupt	**yohaddid** v. يهدّد threaten
yofzi' v. يفزع scare	**yohaddiq** v. يحدّق stare
yoghaadir v. يغادر depart	**yohaddir** v. يحضّر civilize
yoghaazil v. يغازل flirt	**yohaddith** v. 1 يحدّث modernize
yoghadhdhi v. يغذّي nourish	**yohaddith** v. 2 يحدّث refresh
yoghallif v. يغلّف envelop	**yohaddith** v. 3 يحدّث talk
yoghanni v. يغنّي sing	**yohaddiu** v. يُهَدِّئ soothe
yogharbil v. يغربل sieve	**yohadhdhib** v. يهذّب geld
yogharrib v. 1 يغرّب alienate	**yohadhir** v. يحذّر warn
yogharrib v. 2 يغرّب westernise	**yohaffiz** v. يحفّز stimulate
yogharrid v. يغرّد twitter	**yohajjir** v. يهجّر displace
yogharrim v. يغرّم fine	**yohalli** v. يحلّي sweeten
yoghayyir v. يغيّر change	**yohallil** v. يحلّل analyse
yoghdib v. يغضب infuriate	**yohallil** v. يهلّل exult
yogheedd v. يغيظ enrage	**yohalliq** v. يحلق shave
yogheer v. يغير raid	**yohamhim** v. يهمهم hum
yoghlidd v. يغلظ thicken	**yohammid** v. يحمض sour

yohammil v. يحمَل load	yoheel v. يُحيل transmit
yohammis v. يحمَص toast	yoheen v. يهين insult
yohannit v. يحنّط embalm	yoheet v. يحيط surround
yohanniu v. يهنئ congratulate	yohib v. يحب love
yohaqiq v. 1 يحقق attain	yohmil v. يهمل neglect
yohaqqiq v. 2 يحقّق investigate	yohrij v. يحرج embarrass
yoharrib v. يهزب smuggle	yohriz v. يحرز win
yoharrid v. يحرّض instigate	yohyi v. يحي revive
yoharrif v. يحرّف misrepresent	yohyi v. يحيي enliven
yoharrik v. 1 يحرّك activate	yohzin v. يحزن grieve
yoharrik v. 2 يحرّك animate	yoja"id v. يجعّد wrinkle
yoharrim v. يحرّم taboo	yojaadil v. يجادل argue
yoharrir v. 1 يحرّر free	yojaanis v. يجانس assort
yoharrir v. 2 يحرّر edit	yojaawib v. يجاوب answer
yoharwil v. يهرول jog	yojaawir v. يجاور adjoin
yohashrij v. يحشرج rattle	yojaazi v. يجاز sanction
yohassin v. يحسّن improve	yojaazi v. يجازي remunerate
yohassin v. 1 يحصّن fortify	yojaazif v. يُجازف venture
yohassin v. 2 يحصّن immunize	yojad v. يوجد exist
yohattib v. يحطّب hew	yojaddid v. يجدّد renew
yohattim v. يحطّم wreck	yojaddif v. 1 يجدّف row
yohawwil v. 1 يحوّل divert	yojaddif v. 2 يجدّف blaspheme
yohawwil v. 2 يحوّل switch	yojadwil v. يجدول schedule
yohawwil v. 3 يحوّل transform	yojaffif v. يجفّف dry
yohawwit v. يحوّط surround	yojahhiz v. 1 يجهّز equip
yohaymin v. يهيمن dominate	yojahhiz v. 2 يجهّز prepare
yohayyi v. يحيّي greet	yojaljil v. يجلجل jingle
yohayyid v. يحيّد neutralize	yojammid v. يجمّد freeze
yohayyir v. يحيّر baffle	yojammil v. يجمّل beautify
yohazzim v. يحزّم strap	yojannib v. يُجنّب spare
yohbit v. 1 يحبط abort	yojannid v. يجنّد enlist
yohbit v. 2 يحبط frustrate	yojannin v. يجنّن dement
yohddir v. يحظر prohibit	yojannis v. يجنّس sex
yohdir v. يهدر waste	yojarrib v. يجرّب experience
yohdith v. يحدث cause	yojarrid v. يجرّد bare

yojarrim v. يجرم incriminate	**yokhandiq** v. يخندق trench
yojarriu v. يجرئ embolden	**yokharbish** v. يخربش scribble
yojassid v. 1 يجسد embody	**yokharkhir** v. يخرخر purr
yojassid v. 2 يجسد personify	**yokharrib** v. 1 يخرب damage
yojassir v. يجسر bridge	**yokharrib** v. 2 يخرب sabotage
yojawwif v. يجوف hollow	**yokhassis** v. يخصص allocate
yojazziu v. يجزئ portion	**yokhattit** v. يخطط plan
yojeeb v. يجيب answer	**yokhawwil** v. يخول entitle
yojhid v. يجهد stress	**yokhayyib** v. يخيب disappoint
yokaafiu v. يكافئ reward	**yokhayyim** v. يخيم camp
yokabbil v. يكبل handcuff	**yokhazzin** v. يخزن store
yokabbir v. يكبر magnify	**yokhbir** v. يخبر tell
yokaddir v. يكدر ruffle	**yokhdi'** v. يخضع subordinate
yokahrib v. يكهرب electrify	**yokheef** v. يخيف frighten
yokallif v. يكلف cost	**yokhfi** v. يخفي hide
yokammil v. يكمل supplement	**yokhfid** v. يخفض lower
yokammim v. يكمم muzzle	**yokhfiq** v. يخفق fail
yokanni v. يكني nickname	**yokhfit** v. يخفت dim
yokarrir v. يكرر repeat	**yokhjil** v. يخجل shame
yokarris v. يكرس devote	**yokhli** v. يخلي evacuate
yokaththif v. يكثف intensify	**yokhsib** v. يخصب fertilize
yokawwim v. يكوم pile	**yokhtir** v. يخطر notify
yokhaalif v. يخالف disagree	**yokhtiu** v. 1 يخطئ mistake
yokhaatib v. يخاطب address	**yokhtiu** v. 2 يخطئ sin
yokhaatir v. يخاطر risk	**yokhzi** v. يخزي dishonour
yokhabbiu v. يخبئ hide	**yokmil** v. يكمل complete
yokhaddir v. يخدر stupefy	**yokuib** v. يكأب depress
yokhaffid v. يخفض lessen	**yolaahidd** v. يلاحظ note
yokhaffif v. 1 يخفف lighten	**yolaahiq** v. يلاحق stalk
yokhaffif v. 2 يخفف relieve	**yolaaqi** v. يلاقي encounter
yokhallid v. يخلد immortalize	**yolabbi** v. يلبي cater
yokhallil v. يخلل pickle	**yolablib** v. يلبب pulp
yokhallis v. يخلص redeem	**yolakhkhis** v. يلخص summarize
yokhammin v. يخمن guess	**yolammi'** v. يلمع polish
yokhammir v. يخمر brew	**yolammih** v. يلمح insinuate

yolaqqib *v.* يلقّب title
yolaqqih *v.* يلقّح vaccinate
yolattikh *v.* يلطّخ stain
yolawwih *v.* يلوّح wave
yolawwin *v.* يلوّن colour
yolawwin *v.* يليّن soften
yolawwith *v.* يلوّث pollute
yolhim *v.* يلحم weld
yolhim *v.* يلهم inspire
yolhiq *v.* 1 يلحق append
yolhiq *v.* 2 يلحق attach
yolih *v.* يلح persist
yolqi *v.* يلقي cast
yolsiq *v.* يلصق stick
yolzim *v.* يلزم oblige
yomaaris *v.* يمارس exercise
yomaatil *v.* يماطل procrastinate
yomahhid *v.* يمهّد pave
yomajjid *v.* يمجّد glorify
yomakkin *v.* يمكّن empower
yomallih *v.* يملّح salt
yomallis *v.* يملّس smooth
yomanhij *v.* يمنهج systematize
yomarkiz *v.* يمركز centralise
yomarrir *v.* يمرر embitter
yomasmir *v.* 1 يمسمر mesmerize
yomasmir *v.* 2 يمسمر spike
yomaththil *v.* 1 يمثّل act
yomaththil *v.* 2 يمثّل represent
yomawwel *v.* يموّل finance
yomawwih *v.* يموّه disguise
yomayyi' *v.* يميّع liquefy
yomayyiz *v.* 1 يميّز discriminate
yomayyiz *v.* 2 يميّز distinguish
yomazziq *v.* يمزّق rip

yomeet *v.* يميت doom
yomiu *v.* يومئ nod
yomkin *v.* يمكن may
yomli *v.* يملي dictate
yonaadi *v.* ينادي page
yonaadil *v.* يناضل struggle
yonaafis *v.* ينافس contest
yonaaqish *v.* يناقش dispute
yonaashid *v.* يناشد implore
yonaasib *v.* 1 يناسب become related
yonaasib *v.* 2 يناسب fit
yonaasib *v.* 3 يناسب proportion
yonaawir *v.* يناور manoeuvre
yonaawish *v.* يناوش skirmish
yonabbih *v.* ينبه alarm
yonaddddif *v.* ينظّف clean
yonaddddim *v.* 1 ينظّم organize
yonaddddim *v.* 2 ينظّم regiment
yonaffidh *v.* ينفّذ implement
yonaffis *v.* ينفّس ventilate
yonammiq *v.* ينمّق retouch
yonammit *v.* ينمّط stereotype
yonaqqi *v.* ينقّ purify
yonaqqib *v.* ينقّب excavate
yonaqqih *v.* ينقّح revise
yonaqqit *v.* ينقّط punctuate
yonashshif *v.* ينشّف towel
yonassiq *v.* ينسّق co-ordinate
yonawwir *v.* ينوّر enlighten
yonfiq *v.* ينفق expend
yonhi *v.* ينهي end
yonhik *v.* ينهك sap
yonjib *v.* ينجب beget
yonjiz *v.* ينجز achieve

yonkir v. ينكر deny

yonqidh v. ينقذ rescue

yonshi v. يُنَشّي starch

yonshiu v. ينشئ establish

yontakis v. ينتكس relapse

yontij v. ينتج produce

yoo'idd v. يوعظ sermonize

yoobeel n. يوبيل jubilee

yoodi' v. يودع deposit

yoofi v. يوف fulfil

yoolad v. يولد born

yoolih v. يوله infatuate

yoomid v. يومض flash

yoonaaniy adj. يوناني Greek

yooqidd v. يوقظ wake

yoorith v. يورث inherit

yoosi v. يوصي recommend

yoosi' v. يوسع expand

yoosif v. يوصف describe

yoosif v. يوصف portray

yoq'id v. يقعد seat

yoqaabil v. يقابل interview

yoqaadi v. يقاضي prosecute

yoqaamir v. يقامر gamble

yoqaarin v. يقارن compare

yoqaati' v. 1 يقاطع boycott

yoqaati' v. 2 يقاطع interrupt

yoqaatil v. يقاتل fight

yoqaawim v. يقاوم resist

yoqaayid v. يقايض barter

yoqabbih v. يقبّح uglify

yoqabbil v. يقبّل kiss

yoqaddim v. 1 يقدّم introduce

yoqaddim v. 2 يقدّم provide

yoqaddim v. 3 يقدّم submit

yoqaddir v. 1 يقدّر appreciate

yoqaddir v. 2 يقدّر estimate

yoqaddis v. يقدّس sanctify

yoqallib v. يقلب topple

yoqallid v. يقلّد imitate

yoqallil v. يقلّل reduce

yoqallim v. يقلّم prune

yoqallis v. يقلّص constrict

yoqarrib v. يقرّب zoom

yoqarrir v. يقرّر decide

yoqashir v. يقشّر peel

yoqassim v. يقسّم partition

yoqassir v. يقصّر shorten

yoqatti' v. يقطّع put in pieces

yoqattib v. يقطّب stitch

yoqattir v. يقطّر distil

yoqawwi v. يقوّي toughen

yoqayyid v. 1 يقيّد restrict

yoqayyid v. 2 يقيّد shackle

yonaasib v. 1 يقيّم assess

yoqayyim v. 2 يُقَيّم rate

yoqdim v. يقدم intend

yoqeel v. يقيل dismiss

yoqeem v. يقيم reside

yoqfil v. يقفل lock

yoqhim v. يقحم wring

yoqif v. يوقف cease

yoqliq v. يُقلِق trouble

yoqni' v. يقنع convince

yoqta' v. يقطّع be chopped

yor'ib v. يرعب frighten

yoraafi' v. يرافع plead

yoraafiq v. يرافق accompany

yoraahin v. يراهن bet

yoraaji' v. يراجع revise

yoraaqib *v.* 1 يراقب censor	**yorhiq** *v.* يرهق overwork
yoraaqib *v.* 2 يراقب invigilate	**yorja** *adv.* يرجى kindly
yoraaqib *v.* 3 يراقب monitor	**yorjiu** *v.* يرجئ postpone
yoraawigh *v.* يراوغ dodge	**yorshid** *v.* يُرشِد usher
yorabbi *v.* يُرَبّي rear	**yorshid** *v.* يُرشد pilot
yorabbit *v.* يربّت stroke	**yorshih** *v.* يرشح filter
yoraffih *v.* يرفّه unburden	**yorsil** *v.* يرسل send
yorafrif *v.* يرفرف flutter	**yos'id** *v.* يسعد please
yorahhib *v.* يرحّب welcome	**yosa''ir** *v.* يسعّر price
yorahhil *v.* يرحّل deport	**yosaa'id** *v.* يساعد help
yorajjih *v.* يرجّح out-balance	**yosaabiq** *v.* يسابق race
yorakhkhis *v.* 1 يرخّص cheapen	**yosaadir** *v.* يصادر confiscate
yorakhkhis *v.* 2 يرخّص license	**yosaafir** *v.* يسافر travel
yorakkib *v.* 1 يركّب compound	**yosaahib** *v.* يصاحب befriend
yorakkib *v.* 2 يركّب install	**yosaahim** *v.* يساهم contribute
yorakkiz *v.* 1 يركّز concentrate	**yosaalih** *v.* يصالح reconcile
yorakkiz *v.* 2 يُرَكِّز station	**yosaari'** *v.* يصارع wrestle
yorannim *v.* يرنّم chant	**yosaawi** *v.* يساو equal
yoraqqi' *v.* يرقع patch	**yosaawim** *v.* يساوم haggle
yoraqqim *v.* يُرَقِّم number	**yosabbib** *v.* 1 يسبّب cause
yorashih *v.* يرشح nominate	**yosabbib** *v.* 2 يسبّب occasion
yorassi' *v.* يرضّع stud	**yosabbik** *v.* يسبك cast
yorattib *v.* 1 يرتّب arrange	**yosaddid** *v.* يسدّد repay
yorattib *v.* 2 يرتّب tidy	**yosaddiq** *v.* 1 يصدّق believe
yorattib *v.* يرطّب moisten	**yosaddiq** *v.* 2 يصدّق ratify
yorawwi' *v.* يروّع terrify	**yosaddir** *v.* يصدّر export
yorawwid *v.* يروّض tame	**yosaffi** *v.* 1 يصفّي filter
yorawwij *v.* يروّج promote	**yosaffi** *v.* 2 يصفّي settle (the accounts)
yorbih *v.* يربح profit	
yorbik *v.* يربك confuse	**yosaffif** *v.* يصفّف line
yordi *v.* يرضي satisfy	**yosaffih** *v.* يصفّح laminate
yoreed *v.* يريد want	**yosaffiq** *v.* يصفّق clap
yoreeh *v.* يريح comfort	**yosaffir** *v.* يصفّر assibilate
yorfiq *v.* يرفق annex	**yosahhih** *v.* يصحّح correct
yorhib *v.* يرهب terrorize	**yosahhil** *v.* يسهّل ease

yosajjil *v.* 1 يسجّل enrol	**yosawwir** *v.* 3 يصوّر photograph
yosajjil *v.* 2 يسجّل register	**yosawwit** *v.* يصوّت vote
yosajjil *v.* 3 يسجّل score	**yosaytir** *v.* يُسيطر control
yosajjil *v.* 4 يسجّل tape	**yosayyij** *v.* يسيّج fence
yosakhkhim *v.* يسخّم soot	**yosbih** *v.* يصبح become
yosakhkhin *v.* يسخّن heat	**yosdir** *v.* يصدر issue
yosakhkhir *v.* يسخّر harness	**yoseeb** *v.* 1 يصيب injure
yosakkin *v.* 1 يسكن populate	**yoseeb** *v.* 2 يصيب hit
yosakkin *v.* 2 يُسَكِّن temper	**yoseeb** *v.* 3 يصيب shoot
yosalli *v.* يسلّي entertain	**yoseeu** *v.* يسيء offend
yosalli *v.* يصلّي pray	**yosh'il** *v.* 1 يشعل inflame
yosallih *v.* يسلّح arm	**yosh'il** *v.* 2 يُشعِل trigger
yosallim *v.* يسلّم hand	**yoshaabih** *v.* يشابه resemble
yosallit *v.* يسلّط project	**yoshaaghib** *v.* يشاغب riot
yosammi *v.* يسمّ name	**yoshaahid** *v.* يشاهد watch
yosammid *v.* يسمّد manure	**yoshaahin** *v.* يشاحن wrangle
yosammim *v.* يسمّم intoxicate	**yoshaajir** *v.* يشاجر quarrel
yosammim *v.* 1 يصمّم design	**yoshaarik** *v.* 1 يشارك participate
yosammim *v.* 2 يصمّم premeditate	**yoshaarik** *v.* 2 يشارك share
yosannif *v.* يصنّف classify	**yoshabbi'** *v.* يشبع satiate
yosarri *v.* يصرّ creak	**yoshabbih** *v.* يشبّه liken
yosarri' *v.* يسرع speed	**yoshaddid** *v.* يشدّد emphasize
yosarrif *v.* يصرّف conjugate	**yoshadhdhib** *v.* يشذب lop
yosarrih *v.* يسرّح discharge	**yoshahhir** *v.* يشهّر libel
yosarrih *v.* 1 يصرّح permit	**yoshajji'** *v.* يشجّع encourage
yosarrih *v.* 2 يصرّح state	**yoshajjir** *v.* يشجّر afforest
yosarrij *v.* يسرّج saddle	**yoshakhis** *v.* يشخّص diagnose
yosarsir *v.* يصرصر squeak	**yoshakkil** *v.* 1 يشكّل constitute
yosawwi *v.* يسوّ straighten	**yoshakkil** *v.* 2 يشكّل shape
yosawwi *v.* 1 يسوّي level	**yoshammi'** *v.* يشمّع wax
yosawwi *v.* 2 يُسَوِّي settle	**yosharri'** *v.* يشرّع legislate
yosawwid *v.* يسوّد draft	**yosharrif** *v.* يشرّف honour
yosawwiq *v.* يسوّق market	**yosharrih** *v.* 1 يشرّح dissect
yosawwir *v.* 1 يصوّر depict	**yosharrih** *v.* 2 يشرّح slice
yosawwir *v.* 2 يصوّر film	**yoshawwih** *v.* 1 يشوّه distort

yoshawwih v. يشوّه 2 scar

yoshawwiq v. يشوّق thrill

yoshawwish v. يشوّش 1 blur

yoshawwish v. يشوّش 2 unsettle

yoshee' v. يشيع rumour

yosheer v. يشير 1 point

yosheer v. يشير 2 signal

yoshfi v. يشفي cure

yoshi' v. يشع radiate

yoshrif v. يشرف supervise

yoshriq v. يشرق irradiate

yoskit v. يسكت silence

yoslih v. يصلح 1 reform

yoslih v. يصلح 2 repair

yosqit v. يسقط drop

yosri' v. يسرع hurry

yosrif v. يسرف lavish

yot'ib v. يتعب tire

yotaabi' v. يتابع pursue

yotaabiq v. يطابق match

yotaajir v. يتاجر trade

yotaalib v. يطالب claim

yotaaq adj. يطاق endurable

yotaarid v. يطارد chase

yotabbi' v. يطبّع normalize

yotabbib v. يطبب heal

yotabbil v. يتبّل spice

yotabbil v. يطبل drum

yotabbiq v. يطبّق apply

yotahhir v. يطهّر 1 cleanse

yotahhir v. يطهّر 2 purge

yotajawwaj v. يتزوّج marry

yotalfiz v. يتلفز televise

yotalliq v. يطلّق divorce

yotammim v. يتمّم complete

yotamuin v. يطمئن comfort

yotaqtiq v. يطقطق brustle

yotarjim v. يترجم translate

yotarri v. يطري soften

yotarriz v. يطرّز embroider

yotawwaj v. يتوّج culminate

yotawwij v. يتوّج crown

yotawwiq v. يطوّق encircle

yotawwir v. يطوّر develop

yotee' v. يطيع obey

yoteel v. يطيل prolong

yotfiu v. يطفئ extinguish

yothaabir v. يثابر persevere

yothabbit v. يثبّت bolt

yothammin v. يُثَمِّن treasure

yothanni v. يثني second

yothaqqif v. يثقّف educate

yonaasib v. يثرثر babble

yothbit v. يثبت prove

yothbit v. يثبط discourage

yotheer v. يثير 1 arouse

yotheer v. يثير 2 excite

yothqil v. يثقل burden

yothri v. يثري enrich

yotkhim v. يتخم glut

yotli' v. يطلع apprise

yotlif v. يُتْلِف spoil

yotliq v. يطلق 1 launch

yotliq v. يطلق 2 release

yotri v. يطري flatter

youaddi v. يأد 1 perform

youaddi v. يأد 2 result

youaddi v. يؤدّ perform

youahhil v. يأهل qualify

youahhil v. يؤهّل qualify

youajjil *v.* يأجَل adjourn	**yowaddi'** *v.* يودَع consign
youajjil *v.* يؤَجَل postpone	**yowaddih** *v.* يوضَح clarify
youajjir *v.* يؤَجَر rent	**yowaffiq** *v.* يوفَق conciliate
youakhkhir *v.* يؤَخَر delay	**yowahhid** *v.* 1 يوحَد standardize
youakkid *v.* يأكد assert	**yowahhid** *v.* 2 يوحَد unite
youakkid *v.* 1 يؤَكد confirm	**yowahhil** *v.* يوحَل puddle
youakkid *v.* 2 يؤَكِّد stress	**yowajjih** *v.* يوجَه guide
youallif *v.* يؤَلَف compose	**yowallid** *v.* يولَد generate
youammim *v.* يأمَم nationalize	**yowalwil** *v.* يولول wail
youammin *v.* يأمَن insure	**yowaqqi'** *v.* يوقَع sign
youammin *v.* يؤمَن secure	**yowaqqit** *v.* يوقَت time
youannib *v.* يؤَنَب reprimand	**yowarrit** *v.* يورَط implicate
youannis *v.* يؤَنس humanize	**yowasil** *v.* يوصَل conduct
youannith *v.* يؤَنث womanise	**yowassid** *v.* يوسَد cushion
youaqlim *v.* يؤَقلم naturalize	**yowassikh** *v.* يوسَخ soil
youarrikh *v.* يؤَرَخ date	**yowattin** *v.* يوطَن localize
youashshir *v.* يؤَشر indicate	**yowattir** *v.* يؤَتِّر tense
youassis *v.* يؤَسَس found	**yowazzi'** *v.* يوزَع distribute
youaththir *v.* يؤَثر influence	**yowhi** *v.* يوحي muse
youaththith *v.* يؤَثث furnish	**yoyabbis** *v.* ييبس harden
youattir *v.* يؤَطِر frame	**yoyassir** *v.* ييسَر facilitate
youayyid *v.* يؤَيَد endorse	**yoyattim** *v.* ييتم orphan
youdhi *v.* يؤذي harm	**yoz'ij** *v.* يزعج disturb
youkil *v.* يؤَكل feed	**yoz'il** *v.* يزعل upset
youlim *v.* يؤَلم pain	**yozaawid** *v.* يزاود auction
youmin *v.* يؤمن believe	**yozaawij** *v.* يزاوج pair
yowaafiq *v.* 1 يوافق agree	**yozaddid** *v.* يزبد foam
yowaafiq *v.* 2 يوافق approve	**yozaffit** *v.* يزفَت tar
yowaajih *v.* يواجه face	**yozajjij** *v.* يزجَج glaze
yowaarib *v.* يوارب quibble	**yozakhkhir** *v.* يزخَر teem
yowaasil *v.* يواصل continue	**yozakhrif** *v.* يزخرف ornament
yowaazi *v.* يوازي parallel	**yozalzil** *v.* يزلزل quake
yowaazin *v.* يوازن balance	**yozamjir** *v.* يزمجر growl
yowabbikh *v.* يوبَخ rebuke	**yozaqziq** *v.* يزقزق cheep
yowaddddif *v.* يوظَف recruit	**yozarrir** *v.* يزرر button

yozawwid v. يزوّد supply
yozawwij v. يزوّج wed
yozawwir v. يزوّر forge
yozayyin v. يزيّن decorate
yozayyit v. يزيّت oil
yozeel v. يزيل remove
yozhir v. يزهر blossom
yozin v. يوزن weigh

Z

za'eem n. زعيم leader
za'faraan n. زعفران saffron
za'faraaniy adj. زعفراني saffron
za'm n. زعم pretence
za'q n.i. زعق bawl
za'qah n. زعقة shriek
za'roor n. زعرور hawthorn
zaahid n. زاهد ascetic
zaahid adj. زاهد ascetic
zaahif n. 1 زاحف creeper
zaahif n. 2 زاحف reptile
zaauid adj. زائد plus
zaauid n. زائد plus
zaauif adj. زائف false
zaauir n. زائر visitor
zaawiy adj. زاوي angular
zaawiyah n. زاوية angle
zabbaabah n. زبابه shrew
zabbaal n. زبال scavenger
zabeeb n. زبيب raisin
zaboon n. زبون customer
zahf n. زحف crawl

zahr n. زهر cauliflower
zahrah n. زهرة blossom
zahriy n. زهيي pink
zahriy adj. زهيي pink
zakham n. زخم momentum
zakhrafah n. زخرفة decoration
zaliq adj. زلق slippery
zallah n. زَلَّه slip
zamani adj. زمني temporal
zameel n. زميل colleague
zamjarah n. زمجرة snarl
zanbaq n. زنبق lily
zangabeel n. زنجبيل ginger
zaqzaqah n. زقزقة peep
zaraafah n. زرافة giraffe
zareebah n. زريبة cote
zarneekh n. زرنيخ arsenic
zawaaj n. زواج marriage
zawba'a n. زوبعة tempest
zawj n. 1 زوج couple
zawj n. 2 زوج husband
zawjah n. زوجة wife
zawjiy adj. 1 زوجي even
zawjiy adj. 2 زوجي spousal
zawjiyyah adj. زوجية conjugal
zayt n. زيت oil
zaytiy adj. زيتي oily
zaytoon n. زيتون olive
zeenah n. زينة garland
zibdiyyah n. زبدية bowl
zifaaf n. زفاف wedding
zift n. زِفت pitch
zilzaal n. زلزال earthquake
zilzaaliy adj. زلزالي seismic
zinaa n. زنا adultery

zinaad *n.* زناد trigger
zindeeq *n.* زنديق libertine
zink *n.* زنك zinc
zinzaanah *n.* زنزانة cell
zir *n.* زر button
ziraa'ah *n.* 1 زراعة agriculture
ziraa'ah *n.* 2 زراعة transplant
ziraa'iy *adj.* زراعي agricultural
ziraa'iy *n.* زراعي agriculturist
ziubaq *n.* زئبق mercury
ziubaqiy *adj.* زئبقي mercurial
ziy *n.* زي costume
ziyaadah *n.* زيادة increase
ziyaarah *n.* زيارة visit
zo'nofah *n.* زعنفة fin

zobdah *n.* زبدة butter
zohaar *n.* زحار dysentery
zohd *n.* زهد temperance
zojaaj *n.* زجاج glass
zojaajah *n.* زجاجة bottle
zokaam *n.* زكام cold
zokhrofiy *adj.* زخرفي ornamental
zolaal *n.* زلال albumen
zomorrod *n.* زمرد emerald
zonboor *n.* زنبور hornet
zonjiy *n.* زنجي negro
zonjiyyah *n.* زنجية negress
zoqaaq *n.* زقاق alley
zorraq *n.* زرق glaucoma